ISBN 978-1-330-04949-5
PIBN 10013099

1 MONTH OF
FREE
READING

at

www.ForgottenBooks.com

By purchasing this book you are eligible for one month membership to ForgottenBooks.com, giving you unlimited access to our entire collection of over 700,000 titles via our web site and mobile apps.

To claim your free month visit:

www.forgottenbooks.com/free13099

English
Français
Deutsche
Italiano
Español
Português

www.forgottenbooks.com

Mythology Photography **Fiction**
Fishing Christianity **Art** Cooking
Essays Buddhism Freemasonry
Medicine **Biology** Music **Ancient**
Egypt Evolution Carpentry Physics
Dance Geology **Mathematics** Fitness
Shakespeare **Folklore** Yoga Marketing
Confidence Immortality Biographies
Poetry **Psychology** Witchcraft
Electronics Chemistry History **Law**
Accounting **Philosophy** Anthropology
Alchemy Drama Quantum Mechanics
Atheism Sexual Health **Ancient History**
Entrepreneurship Languages Sport
Paleontology Needlework Islam
Metaphysics Investment Archaeology
Parenting Statistics Criminology
Motivational

DEACON & PETERSON, PRINTERS,
66 SOUTH THIRD STREET.

TABLE OF CONTENTS.

BOOK IV.—OF REMEDIES.

TABLE OF CONTENTS.

INSTITUTES

OF

AMERICAN LAW.

BOOK IV.—OF REMEDIES.

2414. In the preceding books, the rights of persons, and the rights which they have over property, have been discussed, it now remains for us to inquire what are the remedies which the law has provided to recompense those whose rights have been violated, and what protection it affords to prevent the violation of those rights.

2415. *Remedy* is a figurative expression, which signifies the means employed, which the law has provided, to enforce a right or to redress an injury. It is a maxim of law that there is no wrong without a remedy : *ubi jus ibi remedium.*(a) If a man has a right, he must have the means to vindicate and maintain it ; and it is said there is no right without a remedy ; for, want of a right and want of a remedy are reciprocal : *lex semper dabit remedium.*(b) Remedies are very numerous and may be variously classified. It is sometimes difficult to make a selection which shall the best secure a right or redress a wrong. The mistake in

---

(a) Johnstone *v.* Sutton, 1 T. R. 512 ; Co. Litt. 197, b. See Bac. Ab. Actions in general, B ; 1 Chit. Gen. Pr. part 1, c. 1.

(b) Ashby *v.* White, 2 Ld. Raym. 953 ; Winsmore *v.* Greenbank, Willes, 577. It is said it is owing to this maxim, that the action of trespass on the case owes its origin.

selecting a remedy may cause unnecessary litigation, or the total loss of a just claim.

There are many remedies which the law has put in the hands of the parties themselves, as will be fully explained hereafter; if, instead of adopting one of these, resort is had to litigation, it is evident that the expense and danger of such a course are unnecessarily incurred.

The importance of selecting a proper remedy is made manifest by the following statement, copied from a celebrated text writer :(a) "Recently, a *common law barrister*, very eminent for his legal attainments, sound opinions, and great practice, advised that there was *no remedy whatever* against a married woman, who, having a considerable separate estate, had joined with her husband in a promissory note for 2500*l.*, for a debt of her husband, because he was of opinion that the contract of a married woman is absolutely void, and referred to a decision to that effect, viz. Marshal *v.* Rutton,(b) he not knowing, or forgetting, that in *equity*, under such circumstances, payment might have been enforced out of the separate estate. And afterward, a very eminent *equity counsel*, equally erroneously advised, in the same case, that the remedy was *only in equity*, although it appeared upon the face of the case, *as then stated*, that, after the death of her husband, the wife had *promised* to pay, in consideration of forbearance, and upon which promise she might have been *arrested and sued at law*. If the common law counsel had pro. perly advised proceedings in equity, or if the equity counsel had advised proceedings by arrest *at law*, upon the promise, after the death of the husband, the whole debt would have been paid. But, upon this latter opinion, a bill in chancery was filed, and so much time elapsed before decree, that a great part of the property was dissipated, and the wife escaped, with the residue, into France, and the creditor thus wholly *lost his debt*,

---

(a) 2 Chit. Pr. 303, note.   (b) 8 T. R. 545.

which would have been recovered, if the proper proceedings had been adopted in the first or even second instance. This is one of the *very numerous* cases almost daily occurring, illustrative of the consequences of the want of, at least, a *general* knowledge of *every* branch of law."

This book will be divided into nine titles : 1, of the precautions to be adopted before the commencement of an action ; 2, of remedies without legal assistance ; 3, of courts in general ; 4, of the courts of the United States ; 5, of the state courts ; 6, of actions in general ; 7, of parties to an action ; 8, of proceedings in an action ; 9, of the different forms of actions.

TITLE I.—OF PRECAUTIONS TO BE ADOPTED BEFORE THE COMMENCEMENT OF AN ACTION.

2416. When a party has been aggrieved, and is desirous of obtaining redress for the violation of his rights, he should adopt the best means to put himself completely in the right, and to secure the evidence requisite to support his case. As most persons are ignorant of the means to be adopted to gain that end, the party should immediately apply to some professional man to aid him. This title will be divided into three chapters, which shall relate to, 1, the choice of a professional man ; 2, the brief of the case ; 3, the means of securing evidence.

CHAPTER I.—THE CHOICE OF A PROFESSIONAL MAN.

2417. Although a party may himself conduct a suit brought by or against him, yet experience proves that it is very dangerous for him to manage his own case, whatever may be his learning or qualities. He labors generally under such an excitement, that it would be difficult to behave with that temperance and discretion so necessary in the proper management of a cause; besides it is proper that he should not come in personal collision with the opponent, for ,this would produce many indiscreet acts which would be prejudicial to his cause.

The principal law agents in this country are, 1, officers known in the courts of common law, by the name of *attorneys;* in courts of equity, as *solicitors;* and in courts of admiralty, as *proctors;* 2, *counsellors;* 3, *notaries;* 4, *conveyancers.*

SECTION 1.—OF ATTORNEYS, SOLICITORS, AND PROCTORS.

2418. An *attorney at law,* is an officer in a court of common law jurisdiction, who has been admitted in such court to the practice of the law, after an examination as to his qualification, and is duly authorized to manage the cause of any client who may confide in him, as his advocate.

Attorneys are not admitted to practice unless they have qualified themselves by previous study, and have undergone an examination, according to the rules of the court; they are also required to be men of good moral character. In general, persons applying to be received as attorneys, have had the benefit of a liberal education, but although this is a great advantage, yet it is not indispensably necessary, and many attorneys, in this country, have become highly distinguished, who are self-made men. In modern times, a knowledge of the Latin and French languages, however imperfect, is sufficient, and the Greek may, in great measure, be dispensed with.

2419. The duties of an attorney, where the offices of attorney and counsellor are not separated, is to con_ duct the suit of his client through the courts, and to take all proper and lawful measures to represent his case fully and fairly before the court and jury. It is not less his duty to advise him, in the preliminary stages of the cause, as to the best mode of a just settlement of it, either by compromise or otherwise when it can be done, and, if not, to direct him as to the best mode of securing his evidence, and putting himself in the right, when that depends upon himself.

SECTION 2.—OF COUNSELLORS AT LAW.

2420. In some courts, as in the supreme court of the United States, advocates are divided into *counsellors at law* and *attorneys at law;* these two classes are kept separate, and no person is permitted to practice both.(*a*)

In those courts it is the duty of the attorney to examine the case, collect all the facts, and make a clear brief of them, and of the points of law on which the case can be supported. This brief is submitted to counsel, and on it he relies for the true statement of the facts.

2421. It is the duty of the counsel to draft or review and correct the pleadings, to manage the cause in court on the trial, and, during the whole course of the suit, to apply the established principles of law to the exigencies of the case. He is not bound, as is sometimes vulgarly supposed, to take any unjust or unfair advantage for the purpose of overthrowing justice, on the contrary he should always remember he is one of her ministers. In giving their advice to their clients, and in the management of their causes, professional men have duties to perform to their clients, to the public, and to themselves. In such cases they have thrown upon them something which they owe to the fair administration of justice, as well as to the private interests of their employers. The interest propounded

---

(*a*) 2 Dall. 399.

for them ought in their own apprehension to be just, or at least fairly disputable; and when such interests are propounded they ought not to be pursued *per fas et nefas.*(a) Still, however, counsel ought not to undertake, in a doubtful case, to be at once judge, jury, and arbitrator, and decide against a client who may have a just cause.

2422. In the selection of an attorney, solicitor, or proctor, it is essentially important to select not a mere lawyer, but a man of known high character as to honor and honesty, as well as for his knowledge of all his professional duties, and also of adequate knowledge of the world, and a good negotiator; one who is disposed to avoid litigation, and above all, one who has not any connection with the expected adversary.

2423. There are men in the profession whose long established character for honor, honesty and learning, is so well known, that it is not difficult to select from among them; but there are others who, though not so well known, are still deserving of patronage on account of their personal merit and learning. In the selection of these the following rules should be observed:

1. A purchaser should never employ, on his behalf, an attorney or solicitor who is concerned for the vendor of the estate; in such a case, the attorney would be placed in a position unpleasant to himself, of deciding between the conflicting interests of the parties, and it might become impracticable for him to act with honor toward both of his employers.

2. A *cestui que trust* should not select the trustee to act for him, in a case relating to the trust property, though the trustee may be an attorney, for their interest might conflict with each other; and again, the interest of the attorney might be opposed to that of the trustee. Indeed, the attorney himself, feeling a

---

(a) 1 Hagg. R. 222.

just sense of delicacy, would not consent to act as attorney, and, as such, perform those acts which he was bound to do as trustee.

3. No attorney, solicitor or counsel should be employed, who has been concerned for the opposite party in any other suit or business, by which he would be enabled to take advantage of facts previously communicated to him confidentially, or incidentally, and which would be injurious to the latter. Nor can an attorney, who has been employed by one of the parties, give up his client and become concerned for the other; for, having obtained his client's secrets, he cannot lawfully make any use of them to his disadvantage; and, if he attempts to do so, he will be restrained.(a)

2424. The selection and employment of an attorney or other professional man is called a *retainer*. Although it is not indispensably necessary that the retainer should be in writing, unless required by the other side, it is still very expedient.(b) It is, therefore, highly proper, particularly when the client is a stranger, to require from him a written retainer, signed by himself; and, in order to avoid the insinuation that it was obtained by contrivance, it should be witnessed by one or more respectable persons. When there are several plaintiffs, it should be signed by all, and not by one for himself and others, especially if they are trustees or assignees of a bankrupt or insolvent. The retainer should also state whether it be given for a general or qualified authority.

The practice of obtaining a written retainer, is for

(a) Chalmondeley v. Clinton, 19 Ves. 261, 273.

(b) In Maryland and in Maine the attorney need not have a warrant of attorney to appear. Henck v. Todhunter, 7 Har. & John. 275; Penobscot Boom Corporation v. Lamson, 4 Shepl. 224; Bridgton v. Bennett, 10 Shepl. 420. In some states, as Pennsylvania and Illinois, a warrant of attorney to appear is not required, unless demanded by the other side. Lynch v. Commonwealth, 16 S. & R. 368; Campbell v. Galbraith, 5 Watts, 423.

the advantage of both the attorney and the client. It is better for the attorney, because he gets rid of all difficulty about proving his retainer; and it is better for many clients, as it puts them on their guard, and prevents them from being drawn into law suits, without their own express direction.(a)

At the time of giving the retainer, it is usual for the client to pay a sum of money to the attorney, for the purpose of insuring his services; this is called a *retaining fee*. When an attorney is thus employed, there is an implied contract, on his part, that he will use due diligence in the course of legal proceedings, but it is not an undertaking to obtain a judgment.(b) He is bound to act with the most scrupulous honor, and to attend to the interest of his client only.(c)

SECTION 3.—OF NOTARIES PUBLIC.

2425. A notary or *notary public* is an officer appointed in the several states under their respective constitutions and laws. These officers are common all over the continent of Europe, where they exercise much more power than they do in England.(d) Their

(a) Owen v. Ord, 3 Car. & P. 349.
(b) Gallaher v. Thompson, Wright, R. 446. See Cox v. Livingston, 2 W. & S. 103 ; Hogg v. Martin, Riley, 156 ; Wilson v. Russ, 7 Shepl. 421 ; Mardis v. Shackleford, 4 Ala. 493 ; Wilcox v. Plummer, 4 Pet. 172.
(c) Galbraith v. Elder, 8 Watts, 81 ; Cleavinger v. Reimer, 3 W. & S. 486.
(d) These officers were known among the Romans, but in Rome they were not at first invested with a public character. Originally slaves, but afterward freemen, had *tables* in the *forum*, or public place, whose profes_ sion was to receive, *excipere*, the agreements of citizens who applied to them to reduce their contracts to writing. They were then called *tabel_ lions*, from *tabula* or *tabella*, which in this sense meant those tables or plates covered with wax, which were then used instead of paper. Tabel_ lions differed from notaries in many respects : they had judicial jurisdiction in some cases, and from their judgments there were no appeals. Notaries were then the clerks or aiders of the tabellions, they received the agree_ ments of parties which they reduced to short *notes*, and, on this account, they were called *notaries*. These contracts were not binding until they were written *in extenso*, which was done by the tabellions. In after times, the notaries themselves wrote out at length these contracts, which was

acts have long, by common consent, of merchants and courts of all nations, had peculiar weight and respect attached to them.

SECTION 4.—OF CONVEYANCERS.

2426. A *conveyancer* is one who makes it his business to draw deeds of conveyance of lands for others. These are not officers appointed by law, any one having the right to exercise that profession. It is usual for conveyancers to act as brokers for the seller. In these cases, the conveyancer should examine with scrupulous exactness the title to the lands which are conveyed by his agency, and, if this be found good, that the estate is altogether unincumbered. In cases of doubt, he should always suggest to his employer to take the advice of counsel.

Conveyancers also act as brokers for the loan of money on real estate, secured by mortgage. In these cases, the same care should be observed, that the title is good, and the property is clear of incumbrances.

For this purpose the conveyancer should make a *brief of title*, that is, an abridgment of all the patents, deeds, indentures, agreements, records, and papers relating to the estate.

In making a brief of title, the practitioner should be careful to place every deed and other paper in chronological order. The date of each deed; the names of the parties; the description of the property, and all covenants affecting the estate, should be particularly inserted.

A vendor of an interest in realty ought to have his

---

called *engrossing*. When thus engrossed, the contract was signed by the parties, when they could sign, if not, mention was made of that fact. As these contracts required to be proved in court in case of dispute. it became usual, and afterward it was required, that they should be recorded on the public registers, in order to give them complete authenticity. Merl. Répert. verbo Notaire, § 1 ; Encyclopédie de D'Alembert, verbo Tabellion ; 6 Toull. n. 211, note.

title investigated, abstracted, and evidence in proof of it, ready to be produced and established before he sells, for if he sells with a confused title, or without being ready to produce deeds and vouchers, he must be at the expense of clearing it.(*a*)　He is bound, at his own expense, to furnish the purchaser with an abstract of his muniments, and deduce a clear title to the estate.(*b*)

CHAPTER II.—OF THE BRIEF OF THE CASE.

2427. A prudent practitioner and professional adviser, will, as soon as he has been employed in a case, obtain a correct statement of the facts; for this purpose he ought to put in writing all questions in the slightest degree connected with the case, not forgetting such as, if answered in the affirmative, would be most against his client; this is requisite, because many clients tell only the side of the case most favorable to themselves. These questions should all be answered fully in writing. Not satisfied with this examination, the attorney should read all papers connected with the case, and examine all the witnesses within his reach, and make memoranda of what they say.

2428. Being thus possessed of the facts, the attorney should make a *brief of the case*, that is, a detailed statement of the facts; and by that means ascertain what is wanting to support the plaintiff's case, when he acts for the plaintiff. When he is the attorney of the defendant, his brief should extend to all the pleadings, and also to the points of law or questions raised by the issue. Such a full brief should contain :

(*a*) 1 Chit. Pr. 304; Wilson *v.* Allen, 1 Jac. & Walk. 623, 624; Sugd. on Vend. 294.

(*b*) Sugd. on Vend. 294.

1. A statement of the names of the parties, and their residences ` and occupations, the character in which they sue and are sued, and wherefore they prosecute or resist the action.

2. The name of the court where the action is brought, the number and term of the action, and the names of the respective attorneys.

3. An extract of the docket entries.

4. A clear and distinct abridgment of all the pleadings.

5. A regular, chronological, and methodical statement of the facts, in plain common language.

6. A summary of the points or questions in issue, and of the proof which is to support the issues, mentioning specially the names of the witnesses by which the facts are to be proved, or if there be written evidence, an abstract of such evidence.

7. The personal character of the witnesses should be mentioned; whether their moral character is good, bad or doubtful, whether they are naturally timid or over zealous, whether firm or wavering.

8. When known, the evidence of the opposite party, and such facts as are calculated to oppose, confute or repel it.

Perspicuity and conciseness are the most desirable qualities of a brief, but when the facts are material they cannot be too numerous; when the argument is convincing and weighty, it cannot be too extended.

———

CHAPTER III.—OF THE MEANS OF SECURING EVIDENCE.

2429. After having made a brief, it is easy to perceive what is requisite to enable the plaintiff to make out his case; and what the defendant needs to complete his defence. Before suit is brought, both parties may do many acts which will enable them, the one to maintain his action, and the other to establish his defence. •

SECTION 1.—ACTS TO BE DONE BY PLAINTIFF BEFORE ACTION BROUGHT, TO SECURE EVIDENCE.

2430. It may be premised that even before a cause of action arises, many acts may be done to entitle the plaintiff to recover, after it has arisen, or which may defeat the plaintiff. A purchaser of personal goods should take possession of them, or, if they are in the hands of a third person, he should give notice to him that he has become the purchaser of them, and, after such notice, the possessor will part with them at his peril: for the same reason, an assignee of a chose in action should give notice of the assignment to the debtor, and all securities for such a debt or chose in action should be required to be delivered to the assignee. The want of this precaution may subject the assignee to a loss, for, until notice, the assignor would be entitled to receive payment, or, if he assigned to another person who had no notice, he would be entitled to the chose in action, if he gave the first notice, in preference to the first assignee, and acquire a *better equity.*

2431. The purchaser of real estate should see that his title is clear and free from incumbrances, and place his deed upon record, within the time prescribed by law. The deeds should also be delivered to the purchaser; for if the vendor should retain them, and afterward sell to a third person, who had no notice of the first sale, and the deed was not recorded, the latter would be entitled to the property if his deed was first recorded.

2432. When a party is bound to fulfil a condition precedent to entitle himself to the performance of a contract, he must be cautious to perform such condition.

2433. In some cases, in order to make a party responsible, notice must be given to him and a request that he should fulfil his engagement; for example, notice of non-payment of a bill of exchange must be given to an indorser to hold him responsible. As a general rule, whenever the defendant's liability to perform an act depends on another occurrence which is best known to the plaintiff, and of which the defendant is not bound to take notice, the plaintiff must prove that due notice was in fact given.(a)

2434. It is advisable, if not necessary, in many cases to give notice, make demands, and require explanations, before action brought. Not unfrequently, in such cases, litigation may be avoided, but if it has to be resorted to, the party may so place himself in the right, that, on this account alone, he will have the favorable ear of the court and jury, and, in some cases in equity, he may throw the costs on the opposite party. When a man's wife, child, or apprentice is unlawfully detained by another, a demand for the restoration of them should be made.(b) If goods have been illegally taken away, or wrongfully detained, it is proper to make a demand of them, before action brought, unless they have been taken and held in such a manner as to amount to a conversion. Notice must be given to a sheriff not to sell the goods he has levied upon, when they belong to another than the defendant.(c) Before making an entry on the land of another to carry away your goods, a request should be made to him to deliver them to you.(d) And before entering upon the land of another to abate a private nuisance, a request to remove it should first be made.(e)

(a) Lundie v. Robertson, 7 East, 231.
(b) Fawcett v. Beaver, 2 Lev. 63; Winsmore v. Greenbank, Willes, 582.
(c) Dean v. Whittaker, 1 Car. & P. 347.
(d) Anthony v. Hany, 8 Bing. 191.
(e) Lonsdale v. Nelson, 2 Bar. & Cr. 302, 311; Willes, 583.

SECTION 2.—ACTS TO BE DONE BY DEFENDANT BEFORE
ACTION. BROUGHT.

2435. In anticipation of difficulties which may arise, it frequently becomes highly proper, if not indispensable, that notice should be given, and the want of it may render the party liable to an action, which could not have been sustained against him, if such notice had been given. The following are a few of the numerous cases of this class :

2436.—1. When a wife has, by her unlawful conduct, induced her husband to withdraw from her the general authority with which the laws presumed he had invested her to purchase goods as his agent, he is bound, in good faith, to inform those who would be likely to trust her on his account, that she has no longer any authority to buy on his credit. He should therefore give a public notice prohibiting third persons from trusting her on his credit ; and it is advisable to give a private notice to such persons as have before sold to her on credit. Though, when the wife has committed adultery, such notice is not indispensable, yet it is always prudent to give it. This notice, whether general or special, will be of no avail, if the husband has causelessly turned his wife away, and refused her necessaries, if the wife buy nothing but necessaries.

2437.—2. But a son or a daughter have not the same authority to buy on the father's credit, that the wife has to buy on that of her husband; if, therefore, the parent desires to withdraw the authority of his child, he should give private notice to such persons as may have before trusted him ; a public notice is not requisite.

2438.—3. When an agent or servant has been authorized, expressly or by implication, to buy goods on credit of the principal, and the authority is withdrawn, notice of that fact should be given.

2439.—4. Upon the same principle, when two

persons have been in partnership, the presumption of its continuance is sufficient to authorize a person to trust one of the partners, in the name of the firm; and when it has been dissolved, notice should be given specially to all persons who have before dealt with the partnership, and generally by public advertisement in the newspapers to all other persons.

2440.—5. In cases of an expected suit on a contract, when the proposed defendant admits something to be due, care should be taken to make a lawful tender of it. A *tender* is an offer to perform an act which the party offering is bound to perform to the party to whom the offer is made. A tender may be made of money, or of specific articles, and, as the manner of making it is different, the two modes will be separately considered.

First. To make a valid tender of money, the following requisites are necessary :

1st. It must be made by a person *capable of paying;* for if it be made by a stranger, without the consent of the debtor, it will be insufficient.(*a*)

2dly. It must be made to the creditor *having capacity to receive* it, or to his authorized agent.

3dly. The *whole sum due must be offered;* an offer of a greater sum, demanding change, is not a good tender, as if a half eagle be tendered in payment of four dollars, demanding change of one dollar. But an offer of twenty eagles, when only fifteen were due, with a request to return the difference, has been held to be a good tender of fifteen eagles.(*b*)

4thly. An offer of the money must be made by *producing it,* and counting it in the presence of the

---

(*a*) Contrary to this general rule, it has been decided in Pennsylvania, that a tender of money for an infant, by his uncle, is good, though not appointed guardian at the time of the tender.   Brown *v.* Dysinger, 1 Rawle, 408.

(*b*) Bettershee *v.* Davis, 3 Campb. 70 ; Spigbey *v.* Hide, 1 Camph. 181. See Hubbard *v.* Chenango Bank, 8 Cowen, 88.

creditor,(a) unless the creditor states he will not receive it, because more is due to him, in which case its production may be dispensed with ;(b) but a mere dispute respecting the amount of the debt, without expressly dispensing with its production, will not excuse the omission.(c)

5thly. The money tendered must be the *lawful coin* of the United States, or such foreign coin as is made current by law. A note for so many dollars, "in gold and silver," must therefore be paid in money, and it cannot be satisfied by a tender of bullion, gold and silver bars, old spoons and rings, or indeed any thing but lawful coin.(d) But a tender in bank notes, if not objected to on that account, will be good.(e) And a tender was held good when made by a check contained in a letter, requesting a receipt in return, which the plaintiff sent back, demanding a larger sum, without objecting to the nature of the tender.(f)

6thly. The tender should be made *at the time agreed upon* for the performance of the contract; if made afterward, it only goes in mitigation of damages, provided it be made before suit brought.(g) It must be made in day time, before the light is entirely gone.(h)

7thly. The tender must be made to a person *capable of receiving the money;* when there are several joint obligees, the tender to one is a tender to all.(i)

8thly. The tender must be made *at the place agreed upon* for the payment, or, if there be no place ap-

---

(a) Fuller v. Little, 7 N. Hamp. 535.
(b) Thomas v. Evans, 10 East, 101. But see Behaly v. Hatch, Walker, 369.
(c) Dickinson v. Shee, 4 Esp. 68.
(d) Hart v Flynn, 8 Dana, 190.
(e) Williams v. Rorr, 7 Mis. 556 ; Noe v. Hodges, 3 Humph. 162 ; Sea. well v. Henry, 6 Ala. 226 ; Ball v. Stanley, 5 Yerg. 199.
(f) 8 D. P. C. 442.
(g) 7 Taunt. 787.
(h) 7 Greenl. 31 : Bac. Ab. Tender, D.
(i) Warder v. Arell, 2 Wash. 297.

pointed for that purpose, a tender to the person is good.(*a*)

9thly. The tender must be an unconditional and unqualified offer to pay the money, because if the creditor were to accept it, the claim for the residue might be thereby prejudiced; therefore a tender of a certain sum accompanied by a request of a receipt in full, or upon condition that it shall be received for the whole balance due, or that a particular document shall be given up or cancelled, is insufficient.(*b*)

The effect of a tender, when properly made, is to defeat the plaintiff in a suit which he may afterward bring; when the plaintiff has a direct cause of action, the only effect of the tender and refusal is to expose the plaintiff to the loss of interest and costs, if the defendant pleads the tender and brings the money into court.(*c*)

The benefit of the tender *will be lost*, however, if at any time afterward a demand is made of the debtor to pay the debt, and he fails to pay, because the money tendered belongs, to a certain extent, though not in every particular, to the creditor,(*d*) and if the debtor has made use of it, he cannot plead that he tendered the money and has always been ready since, *en tout temps pris*, to pay it. But in order to effect this destructive quality as to the tender, the demand must be made at some reasonable time, for if it be made at an unreasonable hour, it will not avoid the effect of a tender.(*e*)

(*a*) Slingerland *v*. Morse, 8 John. 476 ; Litt. Sel. Cas. 132. See Hunter *v*. Le Conte, 6 Cowen, 728.

(*b*) Haxham *v*. Smith, 2 Camph. 21 ; Holton *v*. Brown, 18 Verm. (3 Washb) 224 ; Glasscott *v*. Day, 5 Esp. R. 48.

(*c*) Cornell *v*. Green, 10 S. & R. 14 ; Law *v*. Jackson, 9 Cowen, 641 ; S. C. 5 Cowen, 248 ; Raymond *v*. Bearnard, 12 John. 274.

(*d*) The money so far belongs to the creditor that the debtor has no right to use it, and such use of it as deprives him of the opportunity of paying the creditor when he demands it, defeats the tender ; yet it does not belong to the creditor so as to entitle him to the identical money, nor would it be his loss if it should be lost.

(*e*) Tucker *v*. Buffum, 16 Pick. 46.

Secondly. With regard to the tender of *specific arti-cles*, it is a rule that they are to be tendered at some particular place, and not, as in the case of money, to the person of the creditor wherever found. When no place is expressly designated in the contract, the place of delivery is to be ascertained by the intent of the parties, to be collected from the nature of the case and its circumstances. If, for example, the contract is for the delivery of goods from the seller to the buyer on demand, the former being a manufacturer of such goods, or a dealer in them, no place being particularly named, the manufactory or store of the seller will be considered as the place intended, and a tender there will be sufficient. The intent of the parties here, is the guide. For the same reason, when the goods are at another place at the time of sale, the intention must be presumed to be, that the goods should be delivered there.

When the articles are cumbrous, and the place of delivery is not designated, nor to be inferred from circumstances, the presumed intention is that they shall be delivered at such reasonable place as the creditor shall appoint; and if, upon being requested, if within the state, to appoint a place, he refuses, or neglects, or appoints an unreasonable place, the right of appointment passes to the debtor, who is bound to give notice to the creditor of such appointment, if practicable, and a proper tender of the goods will pass the title to the creditor, and the creditor will be absolved from the obligation.(*a*)

With regard to the *manner* of tendering the goods, it may be observed that when specific articles are tendered, if they are part of a larger quantity, they should be so designated and set apart, that the creditor

---

(*a*) Co. Litt. 210, b; Aldrich *v*. Albee, 1 Greenl. 120. See Bixby *v*. Whitney, 5 Greenl. 192; Slingerland *v*. Morse, 8 John. 474. Vide ante, n. 941 to 952.

may see and know what is offered to be his own.(a) And when an offer of packages is made, those packages must be tendered under such circumstances, that the person who is to pay for the goods shall have an opportunity afforded him, before he can be called upon to part with his money, of seeing that the goods presented for his acceptance, are in reality those for which he has contracted.(b)

We have seen that a tender of money must be made on the day it becomes due, and that when made afterward, it goes only in mitigation of damages. The rule with regard to the *time* when a tender of specific articles must be made is different; if it be not made at the day, it cannot be made afterward.(c)

When stock is to be tendered, every thing must be done by the debtor to enable him to transfer it, but it is not absolutely requisite that it should be transferred,(d)

2441.—6. For the purpose of defending himself from an expected action on a contract, the defendant may, in many cases, before the commencement of the action, purchase or obtain a negotiable bill or note upon which the expected plaintiff is indebted, and, if sued afterward, he may avail himself of a set off.

TITLE II.—OF REMEDIES WITHOUT LEGAL ASSISTANCE.

2442. These remedies are of various kinds: 1, by the act of the party aggrieved; 2, by the act of both parties; 3, by operation of law.

(a) Veazy v. Harmony, 7 Greenl. 91.
(b) Isherwood v. Whitmore, 11 M. & W. 347.
(c) Day v. Lafferty, 4 Pike, 450.
(d) Str. 504, 533, 579.

CHAPTER I.—OF REMEDIES BY THE ACT OF THE PARTY AGGRIEVED.

2443. If there are two things diametrically opposed to each other, they are violence and law: *in societate civili aut lex aut vis valet.* The law rules every fact and every human action, it is present every where, and so exerts its salutary influence, as to prevent force from intruding itself any where to do justice. Force can seldom be used except by the magistrate to attain the ends of the law. The rule *ne privatus sibi ipsi jus dicat* is, in the social state, not only a law, but a condition of existence.

There are some situations, however, where a party has not the time or opportunity to invoke the aid of the magistrate: *non habui capium·magistratus adeundi.* In those rare exceptions, which prove the existence of the rule, the law has put a limited remedy in the hands of the party injured. He acts, not in opposition, but under the sanction, and in accordance, with the law. There can be no law against the law.

The party aggrieved may remove or redress an injury, 1, by self-defence, and the defence of those related to him; 2, by recaption and entry; 3, by the removal of nuisances and other injuries; 4, by distress.

SECTION 1.—OF SELF-DEFENCE.

2444. The subject of self-defence, and of the defence of relations and of property, real and personal, has been fully considered elsewhere, so that here it is only necessary to refer to the subject.(*a*)

SECTION 2.—OF RECAPTION AND RE-ENTRY.

2445. Recaption is the act of a person who has been deprived of the custody of another, to whom he is legally entitled, by which he regains the peaceable

---

(*a*) Ante, n. 203.

custody of such person ; or of the owner of personal or real property who has been deprived of his possession, by which he retakes the possession peaceably. It may be made of a person, of personal property, or of real estate. In every case it must be done peaceably, without occasioning a breach of the peace, or doing an injury to a third person, who has not been guilty of the wrong.(a)

2446.—1. Recaption of a *person* is the act by which one has been unlawfully deprived of the custody of another, to which he is lawfully entitled, by which he regains the peaceable custody of such person.

The right of recaption of a person is *confined* to a husband in taking his wife ; a parent, his child, when he has the lawful custody of such child ; a guardian of the person, his ward ; and, according to Blackstone, a master, his servant; but this must be only when the servant assents to the recaption, unless he is an apprentice bound to render services, and stay with his master. The owner of a slave has also a right to recapture him, even in those states where slavery is not tolerated, if the slave has escaped and gone there without his master's consent.(b) In these cases the party injured may enter the house of the wrong doer, without a demand being first made, the outer door being open, and take and carry away the person wrongfully detained. He may also, for that purpose, enter the house of the person harboring, who was not concerned in the abduction, if he can do so peaceably, but a demand should be first made.(c)

But if the person attempting to make the recaption be resisted with force, his remedy is by an application to a court, or a judge, who will grant a writ of *habeas*

(a) 2 Rolle's R. 55, 56, 208 ; 2 Roll. Ab, 565.
(b) Const. of U. S.
(c) See Anthony *v.* Haney, 8 Bing. 186.

corpus on behalf of the person having a right to the custody.

2447.—2. By recaption of *personal property* is understood the act of the owner of chattels who has been deprived of his possession, by which he retakes possession peaceably. For this purpose, when he has been dispossessed, he may in general justify the retaking them from the house and custody of the wrong doer, even without a previous request to redeliver them.(*a*) But in this kind of recaption too much care cannot be observed to avoid any personal injury or breach of the peace.

When, on the contrary, the chattels have not been originally illegally seized, but are merely wrongfully detained, the owner must request a redelivery; nor can the owner without leave, enter the house or land of a third person, not privy to the wrongful retainer, to take his goods out of it.(*b*)

If the property taken has been altered in its form, or improved, without altering it into a different species, the owner may retake the whole.(*c*)

When goods are obtained of a purchaser by false and fraudulent pretences, no property passes, and the vendor may lawfully rescue and retake them, even by stratagem, wherever he can find them.(*d*)

In some cases the party injured has no remedy by action at law, and the right of recaption is the only one which avails him; as where one of several joint tenants, or tenants in common, of a chattel, takes the exclusive possession of the property.(*e*) But though the injured party has no remedy at law, yet, in some

---

(*a*) Anon. 3 Salk. 169; Weaver *v.* Bush, 8 T. R. 78.
(*b*) Roll. Ab. 565; Bac. Ab. Trespass, E; 8 Bing. 186.
(*c*) Ante, n. 505.
(*d*) Earl of Bristol *v.* Willsmore, 1 Barn. & Cr. 514; S. C. 2 D. & R. 755.
(*e*) Cubitt *v.* Porter, 8 Barn. & Cr. 269.

cases, equity will regulate the enjoyment of such joint property.

As to the *extent* of force which the owner of real property may use, it is a rule that to justify an entry into the house or land of another to retake personal property, it must be shown that it was improperly taken away, or received, or detained, and placed by the wrong doer in his house or land; in this case an entry may be made without previous request.(*a*)   In all other cases, to entitle the owner to retake such property, the owner can only justify *moliter manus*, nor can he without leave, as before observed, enter the house of a third person, not privy to the wrongful detainer, to take his goods, if they get there through his own default.(*b*)

Goods which have been *obtained fraudulently*, under color of a contract, may be retaken by the seller, because no title passed to the pretended purchaser. The seller may, in like manner, retake goods which he has sold without fraud, if they are *in transitu*, that is, if they have not arrived at their place of destination, and the purchaser has become insolvent, and for this purpose he may use any means short of force.(*c*)

The owner of a chattel has a right to take it into his possession, although he never possessed it before, as where a man purchases a specific chattel, for example, the horse Napoleon; and he pays for him or tenders the price to the seller, if the seller refuses to deliver him, he may take him, if he can do so peaceably; but if the sale be not of a specific chattel, as if a man sell one hundred bushels of wheat, to be taken out of a certain heap, the purchaser cannot justify taking it, because no property in the wheat passed to

---

(*a*) Crawford *v.* Hunter, 8 T. R. 18.
(*b*) 8 Bing. 186.
(*c*) Lickbarrow *v.* Mason, 2 T. R. 75; In re Constantia, 6 Rob. R. 324.

the buyer until the wheat was measured and separated from the mass.

2448.—3. By *entry* or *reëntry* of lands, which is a kind of recaption, is meant the resumption or retaking possession of land which the party lately had. A celebrated writer(*a*) says, that the owner of such land, after being disseised, if he cannot reënter by fair means, may legally regain the possession thereof by force, unless he were put to the necessity of bringing his action by having neglected to reënter in due time, that is, twenty years. But this dictum, unsupported by any authority, may well be questioned,(*b*) for it is a universal principle, that whenever a man has an opportunity to apply to the law, for the redress of an injury, he is bound to invoke its aid, and not take the remedy in his own hands, which might lead to a breach of the peace. If the owner enters by force, he may be indicted for a breach of the peace; but he will retain the lawful possession of his estate, and the original wrong doer cannot maintain a civil action for such regaining possession, as far as regards any alleged injury to the house or land, or the expulsion, though he may perhaps maintain an action for any unnecessary personal injury which he may have sustained, or for any damage to his furniture which could have been avoided.

SECTION 3.—OF THE ABATEMENT OF NUISANCES.

2449. When discussing the remedy for a nuisance in a preceding title,(*c*) we considered the right, which any one who was annoyed by it, had to remove it, and the remedy afforded by courts of equity will be considered under the head of equity.(*d*)

(*a*) Hawk. B. 1, c. 28, n. 3, s. 1.
(*b*) See Rex *v.* Scott, 3 Burr, 1698 ; King *v.* Wilson, 8 T. R. 357.
(*c*) Ante, n. 2387.
(*d*) Post, B. 5, part 1, tit. 3, c. 1, s. 2, § 1, art. 3, n. 3.

SECTION 4.—OF THE REMEDY BY DISTRESS.

2450. A *distress* is defined to be the taking of a personal chattel, without legal process, from the possession of the wrong doer, into the hands of the party grieved, as a pledge for the redress of an injury, the performance of a duty, or the satisfaction of a demand.(*a*) The thing seized is also called a distress.

This remedy is coëval with the common law, and its origin appears to be concealed in the night of time. It probably was not fully established till some period during what are called the feudal times. When the feudal system prevailed in its fullest vigor, the reasons for which a distress can now be made, were sufficient to cause a forfeiture of the feud. In the course of time, this system of forfeiture was changed, and the law was mitigated so far, that the lord was entitled to seize the distress, and afterward to sell it. Though the law has been changed in this particular, still it is important to remember the origin of this remedy ; for if it would be known, in any given case, whether at common law recourse may be had to a distress, to enforce the duties connected with a tenure, we have only to ascertain, whether, if the ancient law had continued unchanged, the tenement would have been forfeited by their non-observance. Although this rule is simple and easy of application, it may be well to illustrate it by one or two examples : if the landlord has aliened the seigniory or reversion, he is no longer a party to the tenure, and, therefore, as no forfeiture of the land can accrue to him, he cannot distrain ; so that the distrainor must be entitled to the reversion when the distress is made ; for the same reason if he has accepted a new tenant, no distress can be taken for the arrears of rent due from the ancient one. It

---

(*a*) 3 Bl. Com. 6.

has however been held that if the tenant holds over, a distress may be made while he continues in possession.

2451. It is the opinion of a learned writer,(a) that this notion of distraining was derived from the civil law, which gave "the creditor the faculty of selling out of several pledges which were pledged to him, that which he chose to pay the obligation or discharge the claim which was due to him;" the words of the Pandects, which he cites, are *creditoris arbitrio permittitur, ex pignoris sibi obligatis quibus velit distractis, ad suum commodum pervinere.(b)* A considerable difference will easily be perceived between the Roman and our law on this subject. In the former the pignus and hypotheca were pledges delivered by the debtor, or taken by the creditor under particular stipulations; whereas the remedy of distress by the English law, which has been adopted, with some ameliorations, in many parts of the United States, of taking a pledge or security out of the hands of another, for the satisfaction of a demand, exists without his consent.

2452. In some of the states of the Union, the essential parts of the statute and common law of England, have been adopted in relation to distresses; this is the case in Pennsylvania, New York, New Jersey, Delaware, Indiana, Illinois, Maryland, and Virginia.(c) In Kentucky, Florida, Texas and Georgia, and perhaps some other states, the right of distress exists, but it is placed under some wise restrictions; the landlord must make application to a judge or other officer designated by the law, make oath that the rent is due, and obtain a warrant from him, by virtue of

(a) Gilb. on Distresses, 2.
(b) Dig. 20, 5, 8. The creditor has the faculty of selling, of several things which have been pledged to him, that which he may choose to satisfy his claim.
(c) 3 Kent, Com. 472, 4th ed.

which a distress is made by a sheriff or constable. In Massachusetts,(a) Alabama, Mississippi, North Carolina, and Ohio, the right of distress does not seem to exist. And in North Carolina, it has been judicially declared to be of no force in the state.(b) The remedy in Louisiana is not the same, but the law gives a lien, in certain cases, on the goods of the tenant.(c) In the New England states, where they attach property on original or mesne process, the law of distress for rent, as practiced in England, does not exist.(d)

2453. A distress may be made for several purposes, but always to enforce an obligation either conventional or legal, or to prevent a wrong.

1. Cattle may be distrained damage feasant, but frequently the action of trespass is a preferable remedy. They cannot be so distrained by a person who has a mere possession and not a legal title to the land. They must be taken while doing damage, and not after it is done, or while they are off the land. After they have been distrained, the cattle must not be beaten, nor worked, nor used.(e)

2. By virtue of sundry legislative acts which give that remedy, a distress may be made of goods for the purpose of enforcing a duty, as to pay taxes.

3. The principal use of the remedy by distress is to enforce the payment of rent. In the discussion of the subject, it will be convenient to consider, 1, the kinds of rent for which a distress may be made; 2, the persons who may make it; 3, the goods which may be distrained; 4, the time when the distress may be made; 5, where it may be made; 6, the manner of making it, and of disposing of the goods distrained; and 7, the effect of a distress. But it must

(a) 4 Dane's Ab. c. 110, art. 3, p. 126.
(b) Dalyleish v. Grandy, C. & Norw. 22; Deaver v. Rice, 3 Batt. 431.
(c) Civil Code of Lo. art. 2675—2679.
(d) Kent, Com. 473, 4th ed.
(e) 1 Chit. Pr. 656—659.

28   OF REMEDIES.

No 2454   Book 4, tit. 2, chap. 1, sec. 4, § 1, art. 1.   No 2454.

be remembered that this is the remedy at common
law, and as it has been altered by the English statutes,
varied in some points in perhaps most of the states of
the Union.

§ 1.—Of the rent for which a distress may be made. .

Art. 1.—*Of the nature of the rent.*

2454. A distress may, in general, be taken for any
kind of rent in arrear, the detention of which, beyond
the day of payment, is an injury to him who is entitled to receive it.(a)

The rent must be reserved out of a corporeal hereditament, and must be certain in its quantity, extent
and time of payment, or at least be capable of being
reduced to a certainty.(b)   When the rent is a *certain*
quantity of grain, the landlord may distrain for so
many bushels in arrears and name the value, in order
that if the goods should not be replevied, or the arrears tendered, the officer may know what amount of
money is to be raised by the sale, and in such case the
tenant may tender the arrears in grain.(c)   And so
where the rent may be reduced to a certainty, as when
on the demise of a grist-mill, the lessee was to render
one-third of the toll, it was held the lessor might distrain for the rent.(d)

But when the rent is not certain, and it cannot be
reduced to a certainty, no distress can be made; as
where by the agreement the lessee was to pay no rent,
and in lieu of it, he was to make repairs;(e) or where
the tenant agreed instead of rent to render " one half

(a) 3 Bl. Com. 6.
(b) Co. Litt. 96, a; Diller v. Roberts, 13 S. & R. 64; Wells v. Hornish, 3
Penna. R. 30.
(c) 13 S. & R. 52.   See Jones v. Grundrim, 3 W. & S. 531; Helvor v.
Pott, 3 Penn. St. R. 179.
(d) Fry v. Jones, 2 Rawle, 11.
(e) Grier v. Cowan, Addis. R. 347.

part of all the grain of every kind, and of all the hemp, flax, potatoes, apples, fruit, and other produce of whatever kind that should be planted, raised, sown, or produced, on or out of the demised premises;" the landlord cannot perhaps distrain at all, on account of the uncertainty.(a)

Art. 2.—Of the amount of the rent for which a distress may be made.

2455. With respect to the amount of the rent for which the lessor may make a distress, it may be laid down, as a general rule, that whatever can properly be considered as a part of the rent, may be distrained for, without considering the particular mode in which it is agreed to be paid; so that where a person entered into possession of certain premises, subject to the approbation of the landlord, which was afterward obtained, by agreeing to pay rent in advance, from the time he came into possession, it was determined, in England, that the landlord might distrain for the whole sum accrued before and after the agreement.(b)

No distress can be made for interest for rent;(c) but it may be recovered from the tenant by action, unless under particular circumstances (d)

Nor can a distress be taken for a *nomine pœnæ*, unless a special power to distrain be annexed to it by deed.(e)

By *nomine pœnæ* is meant the name of a penalty

(a) Warren v. Forney, 13 S. & R. 52. But see Reinhart v. Olwine, 5 W. & S. 157.

(b) Cowp. 784. In New York it was determined that an agreement that the rent should be paid in advance, is a personal covenant on which an action lies, but not distress. 1 John. 384. The supreme court of Pennsylvania declined to decide this point, as it was not necessarily before them. Diller v. Roberts, 13 S. & R. 60. See Martin's Appeal, 5 W. & S. 221.

(c) Bantleon v. Smith, 2 Binn. 146.

(d) Obermyer v. Nichols, 6 Binn. 159.

(e) Vide Popham, 92.

30 OF REMEDIES.

No 2456   *Book* 4, tit. 2, chap 1, sec 4, § 2, art 1, 2, 3   No. 2458.

incurred by the lessee to the lessor, for the non-payment of rent on the day appointed by the lease or agreement for its payment;(*a*) it is usually a gross sum of money, though it may be any thing else, appointed to be paid by the tenant to the reversioner, if the duties are in arrear, in addition to the duties themselves.(*b*)

§ 2.—Of the persons entitled to make a distress.

Art. 1.—*By tenant in severalty.*

2456. When the landlord is sole owner of the estate, out of which the rent is payable to him, he may of course distrain in his own right. He must then have the right of reversion, for if he has parted with that, he has no title.(*c*)

Art. 2.—*By joint tenants.*

2457. Joint tenants, when convenient, should all join in making the distress, and this is the better way, as it removes difficulties which may afterward arise. Still, however, as they have, each of them, an estate in every part of the rent, each may distrain alone for the whole, although he must afterward account with his companions for their respective shares of the rent.(*d*)

Art. 3.—*By tenants in common.*

2458. Tenants in common do not, like joint tenants, hold by one title and by one right, but by different titles, and have several estates : one cannot, therefore, distrain for the whole of the rent, for if he did, he would distrain for that to which he has no title ; each should, therefore, distrain separately for his share.(*e*) But when from necessity this cannot be done, as where

---

(*a*) 2 Litt. Ab. 221.   (*d*) 3 Salk. 204.
(*b*) Ham. N. P. 411, 412.   (*e*) Litt. s. 317.
(*c*) Ante, n. 2450.

OF REMEDIES WITHOUT LEGAL ASSISTANCE. 31

No 2459   Book 4, tit. 2, chap 1, sec. 4, § 2, art. 4.   No 2459.

the thing due is a horse, which is incapable of division, all the tenants in common must join in the distress.(a)   Each tenant in common is entitled to receive from the lessee his proportion of the rent; and, therefore, when a person holding under two tenants in common, paid the whole rent to one of them, after having received a notice to the contrary from the other, it was held the party who gave the notice might afterward distrain.(b)

As tenants in common have no original privity of estate between them, as to their respective shares, one may lease his part of the land to the other, rendering rent, for which a distress may be made, as if the land had been demised to a stranger.(c)

Art. 4.—By husband and wife.

2459. At common law, in cases of distrainable rents, the distress was incident to the reversion, except in the case of a rent charge.   And as in all cases, where the wife has an estate of freehold only, or of freehold of inheritance, the immediate freehold of such lands in leases is not in the husband alone, but in the husband and wife, in right of the wife; when distress is made in respect of such reversion, it ought to be joint, as following the nature of their estate, whether the rent accrued before or after the coverture.(d)

But where the reversion is a chattel real, as if a woman be possessed of a term of twenty years, and before coverture makes a lease for ten years, the husband has a right during the coverture to vest this chattel in himself, by reducing it into possession, and in that case, as the wife would have no right, he must alone distrain for the rent.

(a) Co. Litt. 197, a.
(b) Harrison v. Barnby, 5 T. R. 246.
(c) Bro. Ab. Distress, pl. 65.
(d) Bro. Avowry, pl. 70.

Art. 5.—*By tenant by the curtesy.*

2460. A tenant by the curtesy, has an estate of freehold in the lands of his wife, and in contemplation of law, a reversion on all lands of the wife leased for years or lives, and may distrain at common law for rents reserved thereon. The chattels real of the wife on her death vest absolutely in the husband, and if out of such chattel real a rent is payable, he alone is entitled to distrain.

Art. 6.—*By tenant in dower.*

2461. A woman may be endowed of rent as well as of land; if, therefore, a husband, tenant in fee, make a lease for years, reserving rent, and die, his widow shall be endowed of one-third part of the reversion by metes and bounds, together with a third part of the rent.(*a*) The rent in this case is apportioned by the act of law, and therefore if the widow be endowed of a third part of a rent in fee, she may distrain for that third part, and the heir shall have the right to distrain for the other part of the rent.(*b*)

Art. 7.—*By tenant for life.*

2462. A tenant for life, whether for his own life or that of another, has an estate of freehold, and when he makes a lease for years, reserving rent, he is entitled to distrain upon the lessee. It may here be remarked, that, at common law, if a tenant for life made a lease for years, if he should so long live, at a certain rent, payable quarterly, and died before the quarter-day, the tenant was discharged of that fraction of a quarter's rent by the act of God,(*c*) for no one

---

(*a*) Co. Litt. 32, a.
(*b*) Bro. Ab. Avowry, pl. 139.
(*c*) Clunn's case, 10 Co. 128.

OF REMEDIES WITHOUT LEGAL ASSISTANCE. 33

No. 2463.   Book 4, tit. 2, chap 1, sec. 4, § 2, art. 8, 9.   No. 2466.

was entitled to recover it; but this was remedied by statute of 11 Geo. II., c. 19, s. 15, which gives an action to the executors or administrators of the tenant for life; and this equitable provision has been adopted in perhaps all the states of the Union.

Art. 8.—By the heir or devisee.

2463.—1. The heir when entitled to the reversion may distrain for rent arrear which becomes due after the ancestor's death; and in order to ascertain whether the rent became due before or after the death of the ancestor, we must recollect that the rent does not become due, for this purpose, until the last minute of the natural day, and if the ancestor die between sunset and midnight, the heir and not the executor shall have the rent.(*a*)   And if the rent be payable at one of two periods, at the choice of the lessee, and the lessor die between them, the rent being unpaid, it will go to the heir.(*b*)

2464.—2. Devisees, like heirs, may distrain in respect of their reversionary estate; for by a devise of the reversion, the rent will pass with its incidents.(*c*)

Art. 9.—By trustees and guardians.

2465.—1. Trustees in whom the legal estate is vested, as trustees of a married woman, or assignees of an insolvent, may of course distrain in respect of their legal estates, in the same manner as if they were beneficially interested therein.

2466.—2. Guardians may make leases of their ward's lands in their own names, which will be good

---

(*a*) 1 Saund. 287. For the purpose of making a reëntry, the rent is considered due at sunset. Com. Dig. Rent, D 7; Bac. Ab. Rent, I; Jackson *v.* Harrison, 17 John. 66.
(*b*) Clun's case, 10 Co. 128, b.
(*c*) Sacheverell *v.* Frogate, 1 Ventr. 161.

34   OF REMEDIES.

No. 2467.   Book 4, tit 2, chap 1, sec. 4, § 3, art. 1   No. 2468.

during the minority of the ward, and consequently in respect of such leases, they possess the same powers of making distress as other persons granting leases in their own rights.(a)

§ 3.—Of the things which may or may not be distrained.

2467. In general, goods found upon the premises demised to a tenant, are liable to be distrained by a landlord for rent, whether such goods belong in fact to the tenant or to other persons.(b)   But such goods are sometimes privileged from distress, first, absolutely; secondly, conditionally.

Art. 1.—Of the goods absolutely exempt from distress.

2468. Goods are absolutely privileged from distress for various reasons :

1. Because they are protected on account of the *rights of their owners.*   Of this kind are the goods of a person who has some interest in the land, jointly with the distrainor, as those of a joint tenant, which, although found upon the land, are not subject to distress. The goods of a former tenant, rightfully on the land, cannot be distrained for another's rent; for example, a tenant at will, if quitting upon a notice from his landlord, is entitled to the emblements or growing crops ; and, therefore, even after they are reaped, if they remain on the land, for the purpose of husbandry, they cannot be distrained for rent due by the second tenant, and they are equally protected in the hands of his vendee.(c)   The goods of an ambassador or other foreign minister, who is protected

---

(a) Shopland v. Rydler, Cro. Jac. 55, 98.
(b) In some states this right is limited. In Texas a distress can be made only on the crop which grew upon the land, and even that is restricted as to time.   Dallam's Dig. of Laws of Texas, 199, 200.
(c) Eaton v. Southby, Willes, 131.

by act of congress from all actions, cannot be distrained.

2. Because no one can have *property in them*. As every thing which is distrained is presumed to be the property of the wrong doer, it follows that such things in which no man can have an absolute and valuable property, as cats and dogs, and animals *feræ naturæ*, cannot be distrained; because in animals *feræ naturæ* there can be no property without possession, and as the property in them is lost with the loss of possession, they are incapable of being held as a pledge.(*a*)   Yet if deer, which are of a wild nature, are kept in a private inclosure, for the purpose of sale or profit, this so far changes their nature, by reducing them to a kind of stock or merchandise, that they may be distrained for rent.(*b*)

3. Because they cannot be *restored to the owner* in the same plight in which they were taken, such as milk, fruit, and the like, which would be spoiled.(*c*)

4. Because they are *fixed to the freehold* and make a part of it, or are constructively annexed to it.   Things affixed or annexed to the freehold, as furnaces, windows, doors, and the like, cannot be distrained, because they are not personal chattels, but belong to the realty.(*d*)   And this rule extends to such things as are essentially a part of the freehold, although for a time separated from it, as a millstone removed to be picked; for this is a matter of necessity, and it remains in contemplation of law a part of the freehold.(*e*)   Deeds, which relate to the realty, would probably be also exempted from distress.   Upon the same principle of annexation, grass, corn growing in the ground, and the like, could not be distrained, but the English statute of 11 Geo. II., c. 19, s. 8, the

(*a*) Ham. N. P. 375.
(*b*) 3 Bl. Com. 7.
(*c*) 3 Bl. Com. 9.
(*d*) Co. Litt. 47, b.
(*e*) Bro. Ab. Distress, pl. 23 ; Gorton *v.* Faulkner, 4 T. R. 567.

36 OF REMEDIES.

No. 2468.   Book 4, tit. 2, chap. 1, sec 4, § 3, art. 1.   No. 2468.

principles of which have been adopted, perhaps, in most of the states of the Union, enables the landlord or lessor to seize all sorts of grass, hops, fruits, roots, pulse, or other product whatsoever, which shall be growing on any part of the premises demised, as a distress for rent. It has, however, been held, that the word *product* is confined to the products of a similar nature with those specified in the statute, to all of which the process of becoming ripe, and of being cut, gathered, made and laid up, when ripe, is incidental; and therefore does not extend to trees, shrubs and plants growing in a nursery ground.(*a*)

5. Because it is against the *policy of law* that they should be distrained. Goods are privileged in cases where the proprietor is either compelled from *necessity* to place his goods-upon the land, or where he does so for *commercial purposes.* Natural justice would require that the goods of the defaulter only should be distrained to pay his rent. It is for this reason, that goods placed upon the land, as a matter of necessity, are not liable to be distrained; such as the goods of a traveller at an inn, or goods placed upon the land of a neighbor to save them from fire, or in case of goods put on shore, to save them from shipwreck. Again, the interests of the community require that commerce should be encouraged; for adventurers would not engage in speculations, if the property embarked were to be made liable for debts which they never contracted. Hence goods landed at a wharf, or deposited in a warehouse on storage, cannot be distrained.(*b*) On the same principle, it has been decided that the goods of a boarder are not liable to be distrained for

(*a*) Clark *v.* Gaskarth, 8 Taunt. 431.
(*b*) Brown *v.* Simms, 17 S. & R. 138; Himely *v.* Wyatt, 1 Bay, 102; Walker *v.* Johnson. 4 McCord, 552; Thompson *v.* Masheter, 1 Bing. 283; Francis *v.* Wyatt, Burr. 1498, 1502; Owen *v.* Boyle, 9 Shepl. 47, where the meaning of *warehouse* is explained. See Bevan *v.* Crooks, 7 Watts & Serg. 452; Elford *v.* Clark, 2 Brevard, 88.

rent due by the keeper of the boarding bouse;(*a*) unless used by the tenant with the boarder's consent.(*b*) Valuable things in the way of trade, are not liable to distress; as a horse standing in a smith's shop to be shod, or, as above stated, in a common inn; or cloth at a tailor's house to be made into a coat; or corn sent to a mill to be ground; for these are protected for the benefit of trade.(*c*)

6. Because they are in the *custody of the law;* for the distrainor cannot then lawfully take them into possession. Goods taken in execution cannot therefore be distrained; but the goods which have been distrained and replevied are no longer in legal custody, and they may be distrained by another landlord for subsequent rent.(*d*)

7. Because they are protected *by some legislative enactment.* In some states goods are protected from distress or execution to a certain amount; in others, certain tools, furniture, school books, and such other things as are deemed necessary to a poor family, are exempted from distress, execution or sale.

Art. 2.—Of the goods conditionally exempt from distress.

2469. Having considered in the preceding article what goods are absolutely exempt from distress, it remains to be ascertained what goods are conditionally privileged. These may be distrained, but only under certain circumstances. They are:

1. Beasts of the plough, which are exempt if there be a sufficient distress besides, on the land whence the rent issues.(*e*)

2. Implements of trade, as a loom in actual use, and there is a sufficient distress besides.(*f*)

(*a*) Riddle *v.* Welden, 5 Whart. 9.
(*b*) Mathews *v.* Stone, 1 Hill, 565. See 5 Blackf. 489.
(*c*) 3 Bl. Com. 8; Youngblood *v.* Lowry, 2 McCord, 39. See Hoskins *v.* Paul, 4 Halst. 110.
(*d*) Woglam *v.* Cowperthwaite, 2 Dall. 68.
(*e*) Co. Litt. 47, a; Bac. Ab. Distress, B.
(*f*) Simpson *v.* Hartopp, Willes, 517.

3. Other things in actual use, as a horse on which a man is riding, an axe in the hands of a person cutting wood, and the like.(a)

§ 4.—Of the time when a distress ought to be made.

2470.—1. At common law, the distress must be made *during the continuance of the lease*, as the relation of lessor and lessee must exist; but it has been decided, contrary to this general rule, that a lessor may seize and distrain the goods of a tenant holding over.(b) The distress cannot be made till the rent is due by the terms of the lease; as rent is not due, 'for this purpose, until the last minute of the natural day on which it is reserved, it follows that a distress for rent cannot be made on that day.(c) As a general rule, a previous demand is not necessary, although there is a clause in the lease that the lessor may distrain for rent, " being lawfully demanded,"(d) the making of the distress, like the commencement of an action, being a demand in such case. It is however advisable to make a demand. But where a lease provides for a special demand, as if the clause were that if- the rent should happen to be behind, it should be demanded at a particular place, *not on the land*, or be demanded *of the person of the tenant*, then such a special demand is requisite to support the distress.(e)

2471.—2. A distress for rent cannot be made during the night, but must be made in day time;(f) though a distress damage feasant may be made during the night.(g)

        (a) Co. Litt. 47, a.
        (b) Keilw. 96.   Vide ante, n. 2450.
        (c) 1 Saund. 287; Co. Litt. 476, n. 6.
        (d) Bac. Ab. Rent, I; Bradb. on Dist. 124.
        (e) Bac. Ab. Rent, I; Plowd. 69.
        (f) Co. Litt. 142, a.
        (g) Heyden v. Godsale, Palm. 280.

§ 5.—Of the place where a distress may be made.

2472. A distress may be taken either on the land or off the land.

Art. 1.—On the land.

2473. When a distress is taken for the arrears of a duty arising out of a tenure, or charge upon land, it may be seized upon any part of the land out of which such duty issues, or on which it is chargeable, and the entire rent is chargeable on every part of the land; where, therefore, there is a lease of a tract of land, which is afterward held by several tenants, the lessor or landlord may distrain for the whole rent upon the land of any of them.(*a*) But the thing seized must be upon the land, and not merely attached to it by a rope; as a barge floating in a river, attached to the leased premises by a rope, is not liable to distress.(*b*)

It follows, from the principle already laid down, that if two separate pieces of land are let by two separate demises, although both are contained in one lease, a joint distress cannot be made for them, for this would be to make the rent of one issue out of the other.(*c*) But when lands lying in different counties are let together by one demise, at one entire rent, and it does not appear that the lands are *not* separate from each other, one distress may be made for the whole rent.(*d*)

When there is a house upon the leased premises, the distress may be made in the house; an outer door or other inlet cannot be broken to make a distress, but if either be open, an inner door may be broken for the purpose, taking care, in all cases, first to make a demand, and also not unnecessarily to do more damage than is requisite.(*e*)

(*a*) Roll. Ab 617.
(*b*) 6 Bingh. 150; S. C. 19 E. C. L. R. 36.
(*c*) Rep. temp. Hardw. 245.
(*d*) Ld. Raym. 55 S. C.; 12 Mod 76.
(*e*) Comb. 47; Cas. temp. Hard. 168.

40　　　　OF REMEDIES.

No. 2474.　　　Book 4, tit. 2, chap. 1, sec. 4, § 5, art. 2.　　　No. 2474.

Art. 2.—Off the land.

2474. At common law, when the duty arises out of a tenure, and the lord, coming to distrain, sees the beasts upon the land, and before he can seize them, the tenant drives them off, the lord may follow the cattle *freshly* into any place, even a public highway, to which they are driven, and there distrain them. This is on account of the fraud of the tenant, for, if the cattle go away of their own accord, he cannot pursue and take them.(*a*)

The English statutes of Ann. and George,(*b*) the principles of which have been incorporated in the laws of several states, provide that if any lessee shall fraudulently or clandestinely carry off his goods from the premises demised, in order to prevent the landlord's distress, the landlord may, within thirty days afterward, distrain them as if they had continued on the premises, provided they be not sold, within that time, for a valuable consideration and without notice.

To bring a case within the act, the removal must take place *after* the rent becomes due; it must be *secret* and not made in open day; for a removal made openly cannot be said to be clandestine within the meaning of the act.(*c*) It has, however, been made a question whether goods are protected that were fraudulently removed the night before the rent became due.(*d*)

Though the landlord may distrain upon the goods of a stranger on the demised premises, unless they are exempted for some of the causes above mentioned; because he is not required to make any discrimination between such goods and those of his tenant, when the

---

(*a*) 11 Hen. VII., M. 11, p. 4.
(*b*) 8 Ann. c. 14, s. 2; 11 Geo. II., c. 19, s. 1 and 2.
(*c*) Watson *v.* Maine, 3 Esp. N. P. C. 15; Grace *v.* Shively, 12 S. & R. 217.
(*d*) Furneaux *v.* Fotherby, 4 Camp. 135.

OF REMEDIES WITHOUT LEGAL ASSISTANCE. 41

No. 2475.   Book 4, tit. 2, chap 1, sec. 4, § 6, art. 1, 2.   No. 2477.

latter appears to be the owner,(a) yet the goods of a stranger are liable only while they are on the premises.(b)

§ 6.—Of the manner of making a distress.

2475. Under this head will be considered, 1, by whom the distress is to be made; 2, the form of seizing; 3, of the quantity of goods to be taken; 4, of the proceedings after the seizure.

Art. 1.—By whom the distress is to be made.

2476. At common law a distress for rent may be made either by the person to whom it is due, or, which is the preferable mode, by a constable or other officer, properly authorized by him as his bailiff. But in some of the states, the laws require that the distress should be made by a public officer, by virtue of a warrant issued by a magistrate.

If the distress be made without any authority from an officer, the lessor should properly authorize the bailiff to make the distress for him; for this purpose he should give him a written authority, or as it is usually called a *warrant of distress;* but a subsequent authority and recognition, given by the party for whose use the distress is made, is sufficient.(c)

Art. 2.—The form of seizing a distress.

2477. When the bailiff is provided with the requisite authority to make a distress, he should take the things subject to the distress, but he need not lay hands upon every individual chattel; upon entering the house, he may take hold of a chair, or any other thing, and declare that he seizes it in the name of all the goods within the dwelling.(d) He should declare

(a) Spencer v. McGowen, 13 Wend. 256; Hionely v. Wyatt, 1 Bay, 102; Reeves v. McKenzie, 1 Bailey, 497.
(b) Adams v. La Combe, 1 Dall. 440.
(c) Ham. N. P. 382.
(d) Dod v. Monger, 6 Mod. 215.

42   OF REMEDIES.

No 2478.   Book 4, tit 2, chap. 1, sec. 4, § 6, art. 3, 4   No 2479.

that he takes them as a distress, for the sum expressed in the warrant to be due by the tenant to the landlord, and that he takes them by virtue of such warrant, which warrant, if required, he ought to show ;(a) but although he does not declare the cause for which he takes the distress, yet it is not unlawful.(b)

Art. 3.—Of the quantity of goods to be taken.

2478. A distress should be made for the *whole demand* at one time, and the landlord should not harass the debtor with repeated distresses. By the whole demand is meant that which has accrued due at a day of payment, and not the gross amount of several sums, which have each become due at distinct days. For example, if rent is reserved quarterly, and remains unpaid for a whole year, the arrears of each quarter are distinct demands, and separate distresses may be made for each.(c) But the lessor is not bound to make separate distresses, as for rent due on different demises.(d)

When he distrains for the whole demand, but mistakes the value of the chattel taken, supposing it to be equal in value to the duty owing, when in fact it is not, he may distrain anew. In like manner he may make a new distress when he could not find a sufficiency of goods at the time of making the first.(e)

Art. 4.—Of proceedings after the seizure.

2479. After the goods are seized the distrainor has several duties to perform, among these are:

1. To make an inventory of the goods distrained

(a) 1 Leon. 50.
(b) 45 Edw. III., E. 13, p. 19.
(c) 2 Edw. III.. M. 10, p. 32; Gilb. on Distr. 65.
(d) See Legg v. Strudwick, 2 Salk. 414; Birch v. Wright, 1 T. R. 380.
(e) Bradb. on Distr. ; Gilb. on Distr. 64.

upon, a copy of which should be delivered to the lessee, together with a notice of taking of such distress, with a statement of the cause of taking the same.

2. The distrainor may leave or impound the distress on the premises for the time allowed by statute, but he becomes a trespasser afterward. As in many cases it is desirable for the sake of the tenant that the goods should not be sold as soon as the law permits, it is usual for him to sign an agreement or consent to their remaining on the premises for a longer time, in the custody of the distrainor or of a person appointed by him for that purpose.

3. While in his possession the distrainor has no right to use or work the cattle distrained, unless it be for the owner's benefit, as to milk a cow, or the like.(a)

4. Before the goods are sold they must be appraised by such persons as the statute of the state directs, in the manner pointed out by the act.

5. The next requisite is to give a lawful notice of the time and place of sale of the things distrained; after which, if they have not been replevied, they may be sold by the proper officer, who may apply the proceeds to the payment and satisfaction of the rent, and the expenses of the distress, appraisement and sale. The overplus, if any, is to be returned to the tenant.

§ 7.—Of the effects of a distress.

2480. When a distress is made the rent is satisfied to the value of the goods, unless they are returned to the lessee by mutual consent. And in case there has been a forfeiture of a lease, and rent has accrued since, a distress for such rent will be a waiver of the forfeiture.

(a) 5 Dane's Ab. 34.

CHAPTER II.—OF REMEDIES WITHOUT LEGAL ASSISTANCE
BY THE ACT OF BOTH PARTIES.

2481. There are two modes by which the parties can put an end to a dispute and settle it by their own joint act, namely, 1, accord; and 2, arbitration.

SECTION 1.—OF ACCORD AND SATISFACTION.(a)

2482. *Accord* is the settlement of a dispute or the satisfaction of a claim by an executed agreement between the party injuring and the party injured.

§ 1.—Of the parties to an accord.

2483. When there is but one party on each side, each must either by himself or his agent act and take a part in the agreement for an accord and satisfaction. When there are several joint obligors or joint trespassers, and the accord and satisfaction is made by one of them, it is good and available as to all.(b)   If, on the contrary, there are several joint claimants, and one of them, in the name of the whole, agrees to the accord and receives satisfaction, it will bind the rest, though no authority appears from them.(c)

§ 2.—Of the requisites to a good accord and satisfaction.

2484. The requisites of an accord are the following:

1. The accord must be *legal*. An agreement to drop a criminal prosecution, as a satisfaction for a larceny, the thief returning the goods and paying the owner damages, is void, and will be no bar to a future prosecution.

(a) See generally, Bac. Ab. h. t. ; Com. Dig. h. t. ; Com. Dig. Pleader, 2 V. 8 ; 3 Chit. Com. Law, 687 to 698 ; 2 Greenl. Ev. § 28.

(b) Strang v. Holmes, 7 Cowen, 224 ; Ruble v. Turner, 2 H. & M. 38 ; Dafresne v. Hutchinson, 3 Taunt. 117.

(c) Wallace v. Kelsall, 7 M. & W. 264.

2. It must be *advantageous* to the party claiming the performance of a contract or damages for an injury; hence, restoring to the plaintiff his chattels, or his land, of which the defendant has wrongfully dispossessed him, will not be a consideration to support a promise by the plaintiff not to sue him for those injuries.(*a*) In contracts for the payment of a sum of money, the mere payment of a less sum will not be a good accord and satisfaction; but if the money was paid before it became due, or at a different place appointed for the payment, or, in case of a simple contract for a larger sum, a negotiable security given for a less sum, may be a good satisfaction. The acceptance of a collateral thing of value, whenever and wherever delivered, is a good satisfaction; or a mutual agreement to discontinue two cross actions, acted on accordingly, will be a good accord.(*b*)

3. It must be *certain;* hence an agreement that the defendant shall relinquish the possession of a house in satisfaction of a claim is not valid, unless it be also agreed at what time it shall be relinquished.(*c*)

4. The defendant must be *privy* to the contract. If therefore the consideration for the promise not to sue proceeds from another, the defendant is a stranger to the agreement, and the circumstance that the promise was made to him will render the agreement of no avail. But if the accord has been made by authority of the defendant, it will be good, although the subject matter did not proceed from him, as when the obligation or security of a third person, who is *sui juris*, is accepted in lieu of the claim, it is sufficient.(*d*)

5. The accord must be *executed*, for, till then, it is no satisfaction. Whether an accord, with a tender of

(*a*) Bac. Ab. Accord, A; Perk. § 749; Keeler *v.* Neal, 2 Watts, 424.
(*b*) Foster *v.* Trull, 12 John. 456.
(*c*) Samford *v.* Cutliffe, Yelv. 125
(*d*) Booth *v.* Smith, 3 Wend. 66; Kearslake *v* Morgan, 5 T. R. 513; Gullen *v.* McGillicuddy, 2 Dana, 90; Wentworth *v.* Wentworth, 5 N. Hamp. 410.

satisfaction, without acceptance, is sufficient, is a point upon which the authorities are not entirely agreed, as may be seen by a reference to the cases mentioned in the note.(a)

§ 3.—Of the effect of an accord and satisfaction.

2485. An accord with a satisfaction lawfully made, is a *complete bar to a future action;* it is a kind of payment of the debt. It is a species of sale by the debtor to the creditor, but it differs from it in this, that it is not valid until the delivery of the article by the debtor to the creditor, and there is no warranty in the thing given, except perhaps the title, for, in regard to this, it cannot be doubted that if the debtor gave, on an accord and satisfaction, the goods of the creditor himself, through a mistake, or of another person, there would be no satisfaction.

SECTION 2.—OF ARBITRATION.

2486. The second mode of settling disputes by the acts of both parties without a suit is by arbitration, of which, however, there are several kinds, some of them being made under a rule of court, as will be more fully explained hereafter.

An *arbitration* is a submission and reference of a matter in dispute concerning property, or in relation to a personal wrong, to the decision of one or more persons, called *arbitrators*, who are to render a judgment thereupon, called an *award*.

§ 1.—Of the submission.

2487.—1. The submission is *an agreement* by which the parties name and appoint arbitrators to decide the

---

(a) Cumber v. Vane, 1 Str. 425; Heathcote v. Crookshanks, 2 T. R. 24; Lynn v. Bruce, 2 H. Bl. 317; Clark v. Diusmore, 5 N. Hamp. 136; James v. David. 5 T. R. 141; Coit v. Houston, 3 John. Cas. 249; Russell v. Lytle, 6 Wend. 390; 1 Smith's Lead. Cas. 146.

matter in dispute between them, and bind themselves reciprocally to perform the award, or what shall be arbitrated.

2488.—2. As to its *form* the submission may be by parol, with mutual promises to perform the award; it may be by deed, containing a similar agreement; or by a rule of court; or by any other mode pointed out by statute. It is usual in all cases to state within what time the arbitrators shall meet, and that their award shall be delivered before a particular day.

2489.—3. As to the *matters* referred, it is to be observed that the extent of the submission may be various, according to the pleasure of the parties; it may be of only one, or of all civil matters in dispute, but no criminal matter can be referred.

2490. A submission is somewhat similar to a compromise; by the former the parties select judges, who are to decide how the parties are to settle their disputes; by the latter, the parties themselves become their own judges, and arrange the mode of settlement. In both, the parties may bind themselves under a penalty, to fulfil the agreement.

§ 2.—Of the parties to the submission.

2491.—1. When there is but one party to the submission on each side, they both must agree, but this need not be done in person; and sometimes they will be presumed to have given their consent, when there is no evidence of it; for example, an attorney may refer a matter to arbitration, without any special authority of his client,(*a*) so may selectmen of a town, who are its general agents,(*b*) or the agents of a town specially appointed to prosecute or defend a suit.(*c*)

(*a*) Somers *v.* Balabrega, 1 Dall. 164; Holker *v.* Parker, 7 Cranch, 436; Talbot *v.* McGee, 4 Monr. 377; Buckland *v.* Conway, 16 Mass. 396. But see Alton *v.* Gilmanton, 2 N. Hamp. 488; Haynes *v.* Wright, 4 Hayw. 65.
(*b*) Boston *v.* Brazer, 11 Mass. 449. Sed vide 5 Conn. 367.
(*c*) Schoff *v.* Bloomfield, 8 Verm. 472.

2492.—2. One who is appointed by law to manage the affairs of another, may submit a matter in dispute between himself, in his character of guardian, or trustee, of another.(*a*)

2493.—3. In order to submit to an arbitration, the party must be *sui juris;* an infant cannot, therefore, make a valid submission to arbitration.(*b*)

2494.—4. When there are several persons, either as plaintiffs or defendants, for example, partners who are jointly entitled or jointly bound, the submission of one, for himself and his associates, is good.(*c*)

§ 3.—Of the arbitrators and umpire.

2495. As arbitrators are judges between the parties, they must be *sui juris;* they ought to have no interest in the matter in dispute, and be perfectly indifferent between the parties.

An infant cannot, in general, be appointed an arbitrator, nor can a married woman fill that office ; yet instances may be found where such a woman has been an arbitratrix.(*d*)

The fact that the arbitrator is interested, or closely connected with the opposite party, will, in general, disqualify him to act as such ; but if a person so situated should, either through inattention, or because of the high opinion entertained of his integrity and judgment, be appointed an arbitrator, the party will not be allowed afterward to impeach the award, on the ground of an improper appointment, unless such appointment was made under a mistake. For if the interest of the arbitrator in the subject of reference, or his relationship to the opposite party, being unknown at

---

(*a*) Weed *v.* Ellis, 3 Cuin. 253 ; Weston *v.* Stuart, 2 Fairf. 326 ; Hutchins *v.* Johnson, 12 Conn. 376.
(*b*) Baker *v.* Lovett, 6 Mass. 80 ; Britton *v.* Williams, 6 Munf. 458.
(*c*) Wilcox *v.* Singleton, Wright, 420 ; Southard *v.* Steele, 3 Monr. 435.
(*d*) Kyd on Awards, 71.

the time of the nomination, arose, or were discovered subsequently, the party aggrieved would probably be relieved.(*a*)

The award should be made also by a man who is not infamous; an award made by a man convicted of perjury was set aside.(*b*)

When there are several arbitrators, it is usual to authorize them in the submission, in case of disagreement, to appoint another arbitrator, who is called an *umpire.* When this power is delegated, it must be properly exercised, and not left to chance; as where the arbitrators, not being able to agree as to the person proper to be appointed, cast lots which of the arbitrators should have the nomination of the umpire; this was considered as an improper mode of nominating the umpire, and the court set aside the award.(*c*)

§ 4.—Of the award.(*d*)

2496. The judgment of the arbitrators is called an *award,* and the paper on which the judgment is written bears the same name. To make a good award, it must have the following qualities: 1, it must conform to the submission; 2, it must be certain; 3, it must be mutual; 4, possible to be performed; 5, final; 6, formal; 7, must have some effect.

Art. 1.—*The award must conform to the submission.*

2497. The arbitrators being judges selected for a particular purpose, and having no other jurisdiction than that given them by the submission, it is manifest that the award must be confined within the powers

---

(*a*) Vide Earle *v.* Stocker, 2 Vern. 251.
(*b*) Parker *v.* Burroughs, Colles' P. C. 257.
(*c*) Harris *v.* Mitchell, 2 Vern. 485; Wills *v.* Cooke, 2 B. & A. 218.
(*d*) Com. Dig. Arbitrament, E; Bac. Dig. Arbitrament, E; Kyd on Aw.
h. t.; Caldwell on Arb. h. t.; 3 Vin. Ab. 52, 372; Wats. on Arb. h. t.;
1 Saund. 326, n. 1, 2 and 3; Dane's Ab. c. 13.

50 OF REMEDIES.

No. 2498.   Book 4, tit. 2, chap. 2, sec. 2, § 4, art. 2.   No. 2498.

given to the arbitrators, because if their decision extends beyond such authority, this is an assumption of power not delegated, and which cannot, therefore, legally affect the parties.(a) But if the arbitrators transcend their authority, their award is not absolutely void, it is void only *pro tanto*, and if the void part does not affect the merit of the submission, the residue will be valid.(b)

When a time is prescribed within which the award must be made, it will not be valid if not made within that time.(c)

In those cases, when the submission is by verbal agreement, or by deed, the authority of the arbitrators may be revoked at any time before the making of the award; leaving the party who revokes liable to an action upon his agreement. The arbitrators then have no further authority, and an award made afterward is void, unless it has been provided otherwise in the submission.(d) And the death of either of the parties to a submission, before the award made, will, at common law, amount to a revocation.(e)

When the submission is made a rule of court, it cannot be revoked by the parties,(f) nor is the death of either of them a revocation.(g)

Art. 2.—The award must be certain.

2498. The award ought to be *certain*, and it must be so expressed that no reasonable doubt can arise on the face of it, as to the arbitrators' meaning, or the

---

(a) Solomons v. McKinstry, 13 John. 27; Bean v. Farnam, 6 Pick. 269.

(b) Taylor v. Nicholson, 1 H. & M. 67; S. P. 1 Rand. 449; McBride v. Hogan, 1 Wend. 326; Clement v. Durgin, 1 Greenl. 300; Skellings v. Coolidge, 14 Mass. 43; Peters v. Pierce, 8 Mass. 399; Martin v. Williams, 13 John. 264; Bacon v. Wilber, 1 Cowen, 117.

(c) Smith v. Spencer, 1 McCord, Ch. R. 93; Bac. Ab. Arbitrament, D; Mills v. Conner, 1 Blackf. 7; Hall v. Hall, 3 Conn. 308.

(d) McDougall v. Robertson, 2 Y. & J. 11; S. C. 4 Bing. 435.

(e) Edmunds v. Cox, 3 Dougl. 406; Cooper v. Johnson, 2 B. & Ald. 394.

(f) 12 Mass. 47.

(g) Bacon v. Crandon, 15 Pick. 79.

nature and extent of the duties imposed by it on the · parties.(*a*) An example of such uncertainty may be found in the following cases: an award directing one party to bind himself in an obligation for the quiet enjoyment of lands, without expressing in what sum the obligor should be bound.(*b*) Again, an award that one should give security to the other for the payment of a sum of money, or the performance of any particular act, when the kind of security is not specified.(*c*)

But an award is sufficiently certain, if its meaning can be ascertained and reduced to a certainty, as where it directed that one of the parties should pay the costs of a suit, without mentioning the amount, because the amount can be ascertained by taxation.(*d*)

Art. 3.—The award must be equal and mutual.

2499. An award must be *mutual*, that is, it must affect both parties; when it gives satisfaction to one, it must discharge the other, for otherwise it would be unjust. If, for example, the arbitrator should award to one of the parties fifty dollars, to be paid to him by the other, where a case of trespass had been submitted, without saying for what this money is to be paid, the award would be void, because, if the defendant paid it, he would still be liable for the trespass; but if, from the words of the award, it appeared that the trespass was discharged, it would be good.(*e*) Another example

---

(*a*) Grier *v.* Grier, 1 Dall. 173 ; Purdy *v.* Delavan, 1 Caines, 304 ; King *v.* Cook, Charlt. 288 ; Gonsales *v.* Deavens, 2 Yeates, 539 ; Hazeltine *v.* Smith, 3 Verm. 535 ; Barnet *v.* Gilson, 3 S. & R. 340 ; Jackson *v.* De Long, 9 John. 43.

(*b*) Roll. Ab. Arbitr. Q 4.

(*c*) Bac. Ab. Arbitr. E. See Thomas *v.* Moher, 3 Ohio, 267 ; Lawrence *v.* Hodgson, 1 Yo. & Jer. 16 ; Thornton *v.* Carson, 7 Cranch, 596.

(*d*) Macon *v.* Crump, 1 Call. 575 ; Cargey *v.* Aitcheson, 2 B. & Cr. 170 ; 2 Bing. 199.

(*e*) Bac. Ab. Arbitr. E 3 : Roll. Ab. 253 ; but the rule that the award must be mutual, is not so strictly applied now as formerly. Harrell *v.* McAlexander, 3 Rand. 94. See Weed *v.* Ellis, 3 Caines, 254 ; Gordon *v.* Tucker, 6 Greenl. 247 ; Gaylord *v.* Gaylord, 4 Day, 422 ; Kunckle *v.* Kunckle, 1 Dall. 364.

will fully explain this matter. Suppose that Peter and Paul submit all actions brought by Peter against Paul, and all actions by Paul against Peter, and the arbitrators find that Peter shall be discharged of all actions brought by Paul, without disposing of the other matters submitted to them, the award is void.(a)

Art. 4.—The award must be of a thing lawful and possible.

2500. The award must be of a thing *possible, lawful* and *reasonable*.

1. An award that could not by any *possibility* be performed, as if it directed that the party should deliver a deed which it was proved had been burned and totally destroyed, or to pay money at a day past, it would be clearly void; but if it directed a man to pay a certain sum of money, which the defendant was not then able to pay, it would be good, because the defendant might become able to do so, either by making the money, or it might be given to him. Again, an award that a stranger, over whom the defendant has no power or control, shall do an act, is void, because the defendant cannot compel him.

2. The thing ordered to be done must be *lawful*, for the law will not compel any one to perform an act which it forbids to be done; an award that a man shall commit a felony or a trespass, is, therefore, void; and it would be equally void, if it directed something contrary to the policy of law, as that Paul should marry Mary, because it is against public policy that marriages should be constrained.(b)

3. The award must also be *reasonable*, for if it be of things nugatory in themselves, and offering no advantage to either of the parties, it cannot be enforced.(c)

(a) Roll. Ab. 253, pl. 2; Schuyler v. Vandeveer, 2 Caines, 235.
(b) Roll. Ab. 252; 1 Swanst. 55.
(c) Kirby, 253.

Art. 5.—The award must be final.

2501. The award must be *final*, that is, it must conclusively adjudicate of the matters submitted, or, at least, of so much as is decided upon; for as an award may be good for part only, it must be final as to that part.(*a*) Thus, when the arbitrators award a thing not submitted, with a reservation to themselves of a future power of judging of the matter, and they award a thing within the submission; this is good as to the matter within the submission, for as to that it is final, and void as to the residue.(*b*)

Art. 6.—Form of the award.

2502. As to the *form*, the award may be by parol, that is, in writing, not by deed; and it may be by deed. But it ought to conform as to this to the requisitions of the submission; or, if it be under the provisions of a statute, it must be made according to its direction.

Art. 7.—Of the effect of the award.

1. *Of the remedy on the award.*

2503. When the submission was by parol, with mutual promises to perform the award, the remedy upon the award is by *an action of assumpsit;* and in such action the award is conclusive.(*c*)

When the submission was by deed, accompanied by an arbitration bond, which is a common bond, with a

---

(*a*) Bac. Ab. Arbitr. E 5; Young *v.* Shook, 4 Rawl. 304; Grier *v.* Grier, 1 Dall. 173; Sutton *v.* Horne, 7 S. & R. 228; Carnochan *v.* Christie, 11 Wheat. 446. See Com. Dig. Arbitr. E 15; King *v.* Cook, Charlt. 289; Archer *v.* Williamson, 2 Harr. & Gill. 67.

(*b*) Palm. 146; Cro. Jac. 315, 584; Cromwell *v.* Owings, 6 Har. & Joh. 10.

(*c*) See Tallis *v.* Sewell, 3 Ham. R. 513; Swicard *v.* Wilson, 2 Rep. Cons. Ct. 218.

54 OF REMEDIES.

No. 2504.   Book 4, tit 2, chap 2, sec 2, § 4, art. 7.   No. 2504.

condition that the parties will abide by the award, in this case the remedy is by an *action of debt*, for the penalty of the arbitration bond, or by an *action of covenant*, upon the deed of submission.

When the submission was made a rule of court, the remedy may be *by attachment* for contempt in not obeying the order of the court, or by execution upon the judgment entered up pursuant to the rule of court, or to the statute.

If the submission was made by authority of a particular statute, the remedy which it provides must be pursued.

The award is in general conclusive, but it may be impeached for any material defect apparent upon its face, such as excess of power by the arbitrators; defect of execution of power by omitting to consider a matter submitted, when such matter is important; or where a plain mistake of law has been made, as, where freight was allowed for a voyage, where the ship had never broken ground.

Fraud in obtaining the submission, or in procuring the award, by the successful party, or corruption in the arbitrators, will of course vitiate the award.

When the submission was lawfully revoked, it is clear the arbitrators had no longer any power to make the award. This revocation may be a fact, or in law, as by death.

2. *Effect of the award on the title of property.*

2504. An award does not so far affect property, real or personal, as to *transfer the title* to it by its mere force and operation. It is undisputed that when the award directs one to convey certain land to another, although an action will lie, or an attachment may be granted, in a proper case, for not conveying the land, or equity will decree a specific performance of the award,(a) yet the land does not pass by the mere force of the award.(b)

It has also been holden that a chattel does not pass by the award. All matters in difference between a landlord and tenant were submitted to arbitration; among other things it was awarded that the latter should deliver up to the former a stack of hay, then upon the premises, at a certain price to be paid for it by the landlord. The tenant refused to accept the money tendered, and would not deliver the hay, upon which the landlord brought an action of trover for it; the court held the action was not maintainable, because the title to the hay did not pass by the mere force of the award.(c)

But though the *title* to the property does not pass by the mere force of the award, yet the parties may submit to arbitration a dispute respecting the *right* to certain property, real or personal, and the award will be conclusive between them.(d)

CHAPTER III.—OF REMEDIES WITHOUT ACTION, BY THE OPERATION OF LAW.

2505. The remedies which are effected by operation of law are but few; they will be considered in separate sections.

SECTION 1.—OF THE RIGHT OF RETAINER.

2506. *Retainer* is the act of withholding what one has in one's hands by virtue of some right. The

---

(a) Philbrick *v.* Preble, 6 Shepl. 255; Pawling *v.* Johnson, 6 Litt. 1; Jones *v.* Boston Mill Corporation, 6 Pick. 148.

(b) Denn *v.* Allen, 1 Pen. 48; Imlay *v.* Wikoff, 1 South. 132.

(c) Hunter *v.* Rice, 15 East, 100.

(d) Doe *v.* Rosser. 3 East, 11; Blanchard *v.* Murray, 15 Verm. 548: Shelton *v.* Alcox, 11 Con. 240; Cox *v.* Jagger, 2 Cowen, 638; Whitney *v.* Holmes, 15 Mass. 153; Shepherd *v.* Ryers, 15 John. 497. See Tevis *v.* Tevis, 4 Monr. 47; Evans *v.* McKinsay, 6 Litt. 263.

56   OF REMEDIES.

No 2507.   Book 4, tit 2, chap. 3, sec 1, § 1, art. 1, 2.   No. 2509.

subject will be considered by inquiring, 1, who may retain; 2, against whom; 3, on what claims; 4, what amount may be retained.

§ 1.—Who may retain.

2507. An executor or administrator has a right to retain in certain cases, for a debt due to him by the estate of a testator or intestate. In inquiring into this right, it is natural to consider, 1, those cases where there is but one executor or administrator; 2, where there are several.

Art. 1.—Of the right of a sole executor to retain.

2508. A sole executor may retain in those cases where, if the debt instead of being due to him, had been due to a stranger, such stranger might have sued the executor and recovered judgment; or where the executor might, in the due administration of the estate, have lawfully paid the same.(*a*) He may, therefore, retain a debt due to himself,(*b*) or to himself in right of another,(*c*) or to another in trust for him;(*d*) the debt may also be retained when administration is committed to another, for the use of the creditor, who is a lunatic, or an infant.(*e*) An executor may retain before he has proved the will, and, when he dies, after having intermeddled with the goods of the testator, and before probate, his executor has the same power.(*f*)

Art. 2.—Of the right to retain when there are several executors.

2509. When there are several executors, and one has a claim against the estate of the deceased, he may retain with or without the consent of his coëxecu-

---

(*a*) Plumer *v.* Merchant, 3 Burr. 1380.
(*b*) 3 Bl. Com. 18.
(*c*) 3 Burr. 1380.
(*d*) Cockcroft *v.* Black, 2 P. Wms. 298.
(*e*) Franks *v.* Cooper, 4 Ves. 763.
(*f*) 3 P. Wms. 183; 11 Vin. Ab. 263.

tors ;(a) when there are several creditors among the executors, of equal degree, and the estate is insolvent, they are entitled to retain *pro rata.*(b)

§ 2.—Against whom an executor may retain.

2510. The right of retainer may be exercised, 1, where the deceased was bound alone; 2, where he was bound with others; 3, where the executor of the obligee is also executor of the obligor.

Art. 1.—*Where the deceased was bound alone.*

2511. Where the deceased was the sole obligor, and the executor was his creditor, the latter has a clear right to retain.

Art. 2.—*Where the testator was bound with others.*

2512. Where there are several debtors jointly and severally bound, and one of them appoints the obligee his executor,(c) or the obligee takes out letters of administration to his estate, the debt is immediately satisfied by way of retainer, when the executor or administrator has sufficient assets. But in such case the other debtors will be liable to the executor, *qua* executor, to contribute to the payment of the debt, unless the testator was the actual debtor, and the other obligors were his sureties.

Art. 3.—*When one person is executor of both obligor and obligee.*

2513. If the obligee make the executor or administrator of the obligor his own executor, it is a discharge of the debt, if as executor or administrator of the debtor he has assets sufficient; but if he has fully administered, or if no assets of the debtor's estate have

---

(a) Off. Ex. 33.
(b) Bac. Ab. Executors, A 9.
(c) Bac. Ab. Executors, A 9; Com. Dig. Administration, c. 1.

come to his hands, it is no discharge, for there is nothing for him to retain.

§ 3.—On what claims the executor may retain.

2514. Of the claims the executor may retain, we must consider, 1, their priority; 2, their nature.

1. Nearly all systems of law give some debts a *priority* over others in the case of an insolvent estate; funeral expenses, physician's bill for the last sickness of the deceased, and some others, have a preference over others in perhaps all the states of the Union. It would be difficult to make a table showing the order of paying the debts of an insolvent estate in each state, and it would lead to no practical result.

An executor having a claim of a particular class, cannot retain assets to pay himself to the injury of a creditor of a class having a preference over him; and the reason for this, independently of any statutory provision, is clear; he could not, by bringing a suit against himself, have obtained any advantage, or recovered in prejudice of such a creditor.(*a*) He may retain only where he has a superior claim or one of equal degree,(*b*) and in the latter case only *pro rata*.

In a case were two were jointly bound in a bond, one as principal and the other as surety, after which the principal died intestate and the surety took out administration to his estate, the bond being forfeited, the administrator paid the debt; it was held he could not retain as a specialty creditor, because being a party to the bond it became his own debt,(*c*) and, having paid it, he became a simple contract creditor and might retain as such.(*d*)

2. As to the *nature* of the claim for which an execu-

(*a*) Bac. Ab. Executors, A 9; Com. Dig. Administration, A 9.
(*b*) 3 Bl. Com. 18; 11 Vin. Ab. 261.
(*c*) 11 Vin. Ab. 265. But see Dorsheimer *v.* Bucher, 7 S. & R. 9.
(*d*) Com. Dig. Administration, c. 2, n.

tor may retain, it seems that damages which are in their nature arbitrary cannot be retained, because, till judgment, no man can foretell the amount; such as damages upon torts. But when the damages arise from a breach of a pecuniary contract, there is a certain measure for them, and such damages may well be retained.

As the executor is not bound to plead the act of limitations against a just debt, the act shall not operate against him.(*a*)

§ 4.—What amount may be retained.

2515. The *extent* of the right of retainer depends upon the fact whether the estate is solvent or insolvent.

1. When the estate of the testator is *solvent*, the executor may of course retain the whole of the debt due to him, together with interest.

2. When the estate is *insolvent*, his right to retain is then limited by the rights of other creditors, who are entitled to be paid as well as he. By the common law of England, a creditor could gain an advantage by bringing a suit against the executor and obtaining the first judgment, and, as the executor could not bring such a suit, he was allowed to retain the whole of his claim in preference to all other creditors, to compensate him for this want of capacity of suing himself.(*b*) In most of the states of this Union, a more equitable mode of making payment, in cases of insolvent estates, has been adopted, and no one is allowed to gain an advantage by bringing a suit against the executor; it follows, therefore, that the executor can lose nothing by his want of capacity of suing himself, and the law gives him the right to retain that to which he would have been entitled, if

(*a*) 1 Madd. Ch. 583.
(*b*) 3 Bl. Com. 18 ; 11 Vin. Ab. 261.

he had not been an executor, and no more. He may retain his debt *pro rata* with other creditors. Such is the case in Alabama, Connecticut, Illinois, Louisiana, Maine, Maryland, Massachusetts, Mississippi, Missouri, New Hampshire, Ohio, Pennsylvania, Rhode Island, South Carolina, and Vermont.(*a*) In some of the other states the common law right exists.

SECTION 2.—OF REMITTER.

2516. *Remitter* takes place when he who has the true property, or *jus proprietatis* in lands, is out of possession, and has no right to enter without recovering possession in an action, has afterward the freehold cast upon him, by some subsequent and of course defective title; in this case he is remitted or put back by operation of law, to his ancient and more certain title. This right of entry, which he has gained by a bad title, is, *ipso facto*, annexed to his own inherent good one, and the defeasible estate is utterly defeated and annulled by the instantaneous act of law, without his participation or consent. For example, if a tenant in tail discontinue the estate by a conveyance in fee, afterward disseise the discontinuee or grantee, and die seised; his heir shall hold as heir in tail under the original title, and not under the title acquired by the disseisin. By the operation of law he is instantaneously remitted to his better title. The reason assigned for this is, that being so remitted, the owner has no means of asserting his title, because being in possession, he cannot sue himself, and to prevent his loss the law places him in the same situation as if he had established his right by suit.

In order to enable the owner of the land to take advantage of this principle, the title must be cast upon him by the law, as by descent; for if he under-

---

takes to buy the subsequent estate or right of possession, he is considered as having waived his prior right,
and he is not therefore remitted.(a)

SECTION 3.—OF THE RIGHT OF LIEN.

2517. A third mode of acquiring a remedy by
operation of law is by *lien*. In its most extensive
signification, this term includes every case in which
real or personal property is charged with the payment
of any debt or duty; every such charge being denominated a lien on the property.(b) In a more limited
sense, and in that in which it is here used, it is the
right of detaining the property of another until some
claim is satisfied.

Besides the liens which arise by operation of law,
there are others created by the express contracts of
the parties.

Liens may be considered, 1, as to their kinds; 2, as
to the manner of acquiring them; 3, as to the claims
on which they attach; 4, as to the manner of losing
them; and 5, as to their effect.

§ 1.—Of the kind of liens.

2518.—1. When a person has a right to retain
property in respect of money or labor expended on
such particular property, this is a *particular lien*. For
example, where a tailor has made garments out of

(a) 3 Bl. Com. 20.
(b) In this general sense, a judgment obtained in a court of record is
generally a lien upon real estate; an execution when put in the sheriff's
hands, upon personal property. By statute many liens are created, as, for
example, recognizances and other obligations of record are sometimes made
liens; and persons furnishing materials, or doing work for the construction
of a building, have a lien upon it by statute in several of the states of the
Union. By the civil law this right existed; a person who furnished materials or performed work on a building had the privilege of hypothec. Dig.
20, 2, 1; Dig. 42, 6, 9, 1. The government has a lien for taxes, upon the
real estate on which they have been assessed. A landlord has a lien on
the goods of his tenant, while on the premises, for one year's rent, in
preference to an execution creditor.

cloth delivered to him for the purpose, he is not bound to part with the clothes until his employer has paid him for his services; nor the ship carpenter with a ship which he has repaired; nor can an engraver be compelled to deliver the seal which he has engraved for another, until his compensations have been paid.(a)

2519.—2. A *general lien* is one which binds all the property of the debtor in the hands of his creditor; as, where an agent has advanced moneys at different times for his principal, he has a general lien on all the goods of the principal in his hands, and he need not part with them till he is fully paid. But the debt which has this binding operation on the goods of the principal, must have been created in the course of the agency, and to this it will be strictly confined.(b) In the same way bankers, insurance brokers, and attorneys at law, have a lien on securities and papers which come into their hands respectively in the course of their business.(c)

2520.—3. Liens may also be divided into legal and equitable.

1. *Legal* liens are those which are recognized, and may be enforced in a court of law.

2. *Equitable* liens are valid only in a court of equity. The lien which the vendor of real estate has on the estate sold, for the purchase money remaining unpaid, is a familiar example of an equitable lien.(d)

§ 2.—How liens may be acquired.

2521. To create a lien, whether it be acquired by the agreement of the parties, either express or implied,

---

(a) 2 Roll. Ab. 92; Blake v. Nicholson, 3 M. & S. 167; Townsend v. Newell, 14 Pick. 332.

(b) Story on Ag. § 376; Liverm. on Ag. 38; Paley on Ag. by Lloyd, 140.

(c) Ex parte Nesbitt, 2 Sch. & Lef. 279; Ex parte Sterling, 16 Ves. 209; Olive v. Smith, 5 Taunt. 56; Spring v. So. Car. Ins. Co. 8 Wheat. 268; Story on Ag. § 381; Paley on Ag. by Lloyd, 81, 131.

(d) Matth. on Pres. 392.

or by act or operation of law, the following are essential requisites:

1. The party from whom it is acquired should have the absolute property or ownership in the thing which is the subject of the lien, or at least a right to vest it; for unless he has such right he can give no right to the creditor to hold it, the owner having the sole authority to bind or refuse to bind his property for the payment of a debt due by another.

2. The party claiming the lien must have an actual or constructive possession, with the assent, express or implied, of the party against whom the claim is made.(a)

3. The lien should arise upon an agreement, express or implied, and not for a specific purpose inconsistent with the express terms or the clear intent of the contract. Factors, for example, have a general lien for all claims arising from their agency, upon all goods belonging to their principal in their possession, which came to them as such. But should a horse, for example, be loaned by the principal to the agent for a particular purpose, the agent would have no lien upon it.(b)

2522. When a man acquires the possession of goods belonging to another, by finding, he has no lien against them for any expenses he has been put to in regard to them, except in one case; this is when goods are lost at sea. For the purpose of encouraging commerce, and to reward a man who runs considerable personal risks in saving such goods, the law allows the finder a compensation, known by the name of salvage,(c) and for this he has a lien. But when the finder of goods on land has been put to any expense

---

(a) 3 Chit. Com. Law, 547; Paley on Ag. by Lloyd, 137; Jordan v. James, 5 Ham. 88.

(b) Jarvis v. Rogers, 15 Mass. 389.

(c) Hartford v. Jones, 2 Salk. 654; S. C. 1 Ld. Raym. 393; Hamilton v. Davis, 5 Burr. 2732; Baring v. Day, 8 East, 57.

in relation to them, although he has no lien for such expenses, he is not left without a remedy. He may bring a suit against the owner and recover the value of such expenses. The reason assigned for this is, that if the rule were otherwise, ill disposed persons might turn boats and vessels adrift, or horses or cattle into the road, and then take them up, and refuse to give them up until they were paid their alleged expenses; and, therefore, the finder is required, and the law has put upon him the burden, to prove the quantum of his recompense to the satisfaction of the jury.(a)

2523. The lien cannot be acquired by obtaining possession of the goods tortiously; because, if for no other reason, no man can take advantage of his own wrong.(b)

§ 3.—Of the claims for which liens attach.

2524. The debts or claims for which liens properly attach, or which are to be secured by the lien, require several qualities, which will be separately considered.

1. In general, liens properly attach on liquidated demands, and not on those which sound only in damages, though, by express contract, they may attach even in such case; as, where the goods were to be held as an indemnity against a future contingent claim for damages.(c)

2. The claim for which the lien is asserted must be due or owing to the party claiming it in his own right, and not merely as agent for a third person. It must be a debt or demand due from the very person for whose benefit the party is acting, and not from a third person, although the goods may have been claimed through him.(d)

(a) Nicholson v. Chapman, 3 H. Bl. 354.
(b) Lempriere v. Pasley, 2 T. R. 485; Madden v. Kempster, 1 Camp. 12.
(c) 3 Chit. Com Law, 548.
(d) Paley, Ag. by Lloyd, 132.

3. The claim may be a particular debt, or a general balance due to the creditor by the owner of the goods. By the custom of the trade, an agent may have a lien upon the property of his employer, intrusted to him in the course of that trade, not only in respect of the management of that particular property, but for his general balance of accounts. To authorize a creditor to retain property under a claim of lien for a general balance, however, the usage of trade must be established to have been uniform and notorious, for although usages of trade enter into every contract, this is only where they are so notorious that they are presumed to be known to the party who is to be bound by them.

This general lien may also be created by the express or implied agreement of the parties; as when a merchant gives notice that he will not receive any property for the purpose of his trade or business, except on condition that he shall have a lien upon it, not only in respect to the charge arising upon the particular goods, but for the general balance of his account. In such case, all persons who, after a knowledge of such notice, deal with him, must be presumed to have acquiesced in it, and they will be bound as if they had expressly agreed to the provisions of the notice.(a)

But when it is the duty of the party to receive the goods, and he cannot refuse, without a violation of some rule of law, as in the case of a common carrier, it would perhaps be considered that he had no right to give such notice.(b)

§ 4.—How liens may be lost.

2525. A lien may be lost in several ways, the principal of which are the following:

1. It may be lost or waived by any act of the

(a) Kirkham v. Shallcross, 6 T. R. 14.
(b) 6 T. R. 14. See Wright v. Snell, 5 B. & Ald. 350; Oppenheim v. Russell, 3 Bos. & Pull. 42; Rushforth v. Hatfield, 7 East, 224.

parties, by which it may be surrendered or become inapplicable.

2. It may be lost by the payment of the debt which is a lien upon the goods, and the satisfaction of such debt by the creation of a new one may have that effect; as where a creditor holds the note of the owner of the goods, and he has a lien in consequence of it, if the parties afterward renew the debt by the creditor's taking a bond, and he gives up the note, with an agreement to cancel the old debt and create a new one, the lien on the goods will be lost.(a)

3. In general, possession is not only essential to the creation, but also to the continuance of the lien; it may, therefore, be lost by voluntarily parting with the possession of the goods. But to this rule there are some exceptions; for example, when a factor by lawful authority sells the goods of his principal, and parts with the possession under the sale, and such sale is made for the benefit of the factor, or the goods are assigned and delivered to a third person by way of pledge or security to the extent of the factor's lien, it is in effect a continuance of the factor's possession, and the lien is therefore retained.

§ 5.—Of the effect of liens.

2526. In general, the right of the holder of the lien is confined to the mere right of retainer. By the express agreement of the parties, the creditor may sell the goods on which he has a lien, but unless there is an express or implied contract, the holder has no right to sell them for the debt due him. In special cases there may be an implied power to sell, as where the goods are deposited to secure a loan of money, which is to be returned on a certain day, or where a factor makes advances or incurs liabilities on account of the

(a) Ante, n. 801, vol. i. p. 310.

consignment.(*a*) In some cases where the lien would not confer a power to sell, a court of equity would decree a sale.(*b*) Courts of admiralty will decree a sale to satisfy maritime liens.(*c*)

TITLE III.—OF COURTS IN GENERAL.

2527. A *court* is an incorporeal, political being, created for the purpose of administering justice judicially, and which requires for its existence, the presence of the judges, or a competent number of them, and a clerk or prothonotary, at the time during which, and at the place where, it is by law authorized to be held; and the performance of some public act indicative of a design to perform the functions of a court. According to Lord Coke, a court is a place where justice is judicially administered.(*d*) This definition has not been adopted, because it is conceived that the court is not a *place*, but the *judges and other officers*, properly organized, form the court.

In another sense, the judges, the clerk, or prothonotary, the attorneys, counsellors, solicitors, or proctors, and ministerial officers, are said to constitute the court.(*e*) And sometimes the judges alone are called the court.

In another place we have considered the organization of the courts under the constitution and laws of the United States, and of the state courts under the state constitutions. In this place it will be proper to take a view of their various kinds, and of their powers and jurisdictions. 1. When considered as to their powers,

---

(*a*) Pothonier *v.* Dawson, 1 Holt, R. 333; 3 Chit. Com. Law, 551; 1 Liverm. on Ag. 103.

(*b*) 1 Story, Eq. Jur. § 506; 2 Story, Eq. Jur. § 1216; Story, Ag. § 371.

(*c*) Abbott on Ship. part 3, c. 10, § 2; Story, Ag. § 371.

(*d*) Co. Litt. 58, a.

(*e*) When treating of the choice of a professional man, a short sketch of the powers and duties of attorney and counsel was given. Vide ante, n. 2418, 2420.

they are of record and not of record; 2, when compared to each other, they are supreme, superior and inferior; 3, when examined as to their original jurisdiction, they are civil or criminal; 4, when viewed as to their territorial jurisdiction, they are central or local; 5, when divided as to their objects, they are courts of law, courts of equity, admiralty courts, and courts martial.

CHAPTER I.—OF COURTS OF RECORD AND NOT OF RECORD.

2528.—1. By the common law, a *court of record* is one where the acts and judicial proceedings are enrolled in parchment for a perpetual memorial and testimony; which rolls are called the *records* of the courts. In the United States the acts and proceedings of such courts are written in books kept for that purpose, or in papers kept on file in the offices of the clerks or prothonotaries. The test of a court of record is whether it has or has not the power to fine and imprison; a court which possesses that power is a court of record, all other courts are not of record.(a) In this country a court which does not possess common law jurisdiction, and a seal, and a clerk or prothonotary, for the purpose of engrossing and keeping its proceedings, would not be considered a court of record.

The act of congress to establish an uniform rule of naturalization, etc., approved April 14, 1802, enacts that, for the purpose of admitting aliens to become citizens, that any court of record in any individual state, having common law jurisdiction and a seal, and a clerk or prothonotary, shall be considered a district court, within the meaning of that act.

2529.—2. All courts which do not come within the definition of a court of record, are courts not of record.

(a) Bac. Ab. Courts, D 2.

CHAPTER II.—OF SUPREME, SUPERIOR, AND INFERIOR COURTS.

2530. Courts of record are divided into supreme or superior courts, and inferior courts.

SECTION 1.—OF THE SUPREME OR SUPERIOR COURTS.

2531. A *supreme* court is one having jurisdiction over all other courts. Such a court possesses in general appellate jurisdiction, either by writ of error, or by appeal in other cases. The supreme or superior courts have their jurisdiction by the common law, and by the constitution of the United States, or of the state where located. And this common law jurisdiction cannot be taken away without the express negative words of a statute, unless by irresistible implication.(*a*)

2532. A supreme court, in general, has no original jurisdiction, except what may be given to it by the constitution. Its principal powers are to supervise the acts and proceedings of the inferior tribunals. This is done by writ of error and by appeal.

1. By *writ of error.* When, in course of the trial in an inferior court of law, it is alleged that the lower court has committed an error, the party aggrieved has a right to remove the cause, in civil actions, without the consent of the opposite party, into the supreme court;(*b*) for this purpose he sues out a writ of error from the supreme court, which writ commands the judges of the inferior court to send the record into the supreme court, there to be examined. The object of this writ is to correct an error of law committed in the course of the proceedings, which is not amendable or cured at common law, or by some statute of amendment, or jeofails.(*c*)

(*a*) Commonwealth *v.* McCloskey, 2 Rawle, 369 ; Buckinhoffen *v.* Martin, 3 Yeates, 479 ; Commonwealth *v.* White, 8 Pick, 435 ; Murfree *v.* Leiper, 1 Overt. 1 ; Overseers, &c. *v.* Smith, 2 S. & R. 363,

(*b*) Skipworth *v.* Hill, 2 Mass. 35 ; Drowne *v.* Stimpson, 2 Mass. 441.

(*c*) Wall *v.* Wall, 2 Harr. & Gill, 79 ; Chase *v.* Davis, 7 Verm. 476 ; Colley *v.* Latimer, 5 S. & R. 211.

The supreme court being thus possessed of the cause, does not try it again upon the merits, and it is immaterial what may be the state of the facts. This proceeding is less a suit between the parties than between the judgment rendered in the court below and the law; for the supreme court do not try the cause between the parties, but judge the judgment. If the court below have obeyed all the requisitions of the law, their judgment, however wrong as to the facts, cannot be impeached, and it will be *affirmed;* and if they have violated the law, however correct their judgment may be as to the facts, it will be *reversed.* The reason of this is, that the supreme court, in cases of error, do not try the facts.

2. By *appeal.* An appeal in a civil suit, is a proceeding unknown to the common law. It is authorized by statute in a variety of cases, and is regulated entirely by the provisions of the particular act; it cannot be extended beyond the plain and obvious import of the statute granting it.(*a*)

In cases of appeal the whole case is examined and tried, as if it had not been tried before.(*b*) But it is an essential criterion of appellate jurisdiction, that it revises and corrects the proceedings below, and does not create a new cause.(*c*)

SECTION 2.—OF INFERIOR COURTS.

2533. All other tribunals than the supreme court are *inferior courts.*(*d*) These courts have, in general, original jurisdiction in cases both at law and in equity. Unlike a supreme or superior court, an inferior tribunal is a court of limited jurisdiction, and it must appear on the face of its proceedings that it has jurisdiction, or its proceedings will be void.(*e*)

(*a*) Street *v.* Francis, 3 Ham. 277; 14 Mass. 420; 7 Pick. 321.
(*b*) Vide Dane's Ab. h. t.
(*c*) Marbury *v.* Madison, 1 Cranch, 137, 175; 3 Wheat. 600.
(*d*) Const. U. S. art. 3, s. 1.
(*e*) Kemp *v.* Kennedy, 5 Cranch, 172; S. C.; Pet. C. C. 36; Turner *v.* Bank of America, 4 Dall. 11.

CHAPTER III.—OF COURTS OF CIVIL AND CRIMINAL JURISDICTION.

SECTION 1.—OF COURTS OF CIVIL JURISDICTION.

2534. The courts of *civil jurisdiction* are those which are authorized by the common law, or by the constitution or statute, to decide upon all civil actions, and disputes between persons, in their private capacity; whether such matters relate to the persons of the parties, or to their personal or real property.

These courts may act with or without a jury. The inferior courts of common law cannot try any thing, unless specially invested with that power by statute, without the aid of a jury, the constitution of the United States having secured that mode of trial. " In suits at common law, where the value in controversy shall exceed twenty dollars," says the constitution,(a) " the right of trial by jury shall be preserved, and no fact, tried by a jury, shall be otherwise reëxamined in any court of the United States, than according to the rules of the common law." But courts of equity always act without a jury.

SECTION 2.—OF COURTS OF CRIMINAL JURISDICTION.

2535. A *criminal court* is one established for the repression of crimes and for their punishment. The constitution and laws have secured to the citizen a trial in these courts by a jury, which is the greatest bulwark which liberty has ever interposed between tyranny and its victim.

___

CHAPTER IV.—OF THE TERRITORIAL JURISDICTION OF COURTS.

2536. *Jurisdiction* is a power constitutionally conferred upon a court, a single judge, or a magistrate, to take cognizance and decide causes, according to law,

___

(a) Amendm. art. 9.

and to carry their sentence into execution. The tract of land or district within which a court, judge, or magistrate has jurisdiction, is called his *territory*, and his power in relation to his territory, is called his *territorial jurisdiction*.

Those courts which extend over the whole of the territory, which is governed by the same laws, may be called *central;* as the supreme court of the United States is a central court, because its jurisdiction extends over every part of the Union. In the same way the supreme court of each state is a central court within that state, because its powers extend over every part of the state.

The jurisdiction of some courts extends only over a part of the territory which is ruled by the same laws, these may be called *local;* such are the circuit and district courts of the United States, because their jurisdiction extends only over particular parts of the country, called *circuits* or *districts*. So the courts of common pleas, parish courts, city courts, and other similar tribunals which have only a local authority, may be called local courts.

CHAPTER V.—OF THE DIVISION OF COURTS AS TO THEIR OBJECTS.

2537. When considered as to the *object* of their jurisdiction, they are, 1, courts of common law; 2, courts of equity; 3, courts of admiralty; and, 4, courts martial.

SECTION 1.—OF COURTS OF COMMON LAW.

2538. Courts of *common law* are established to protect legal rights and to redress legal injuries. The remedies for the redress of wrongs and for the enforcement of rights, are distinguished into two classes; first, those which are administered in courts of common law; and, secondly, those which are administered in courts of equity. Rights which are recognized and protected, and wrongs which are redressed by the former courts, are called *legal rights* and *legal injuries*. Rights which are to be obtained, and wrongs from which the party can be relieved only by. courts of equity, are *equitable rights* and *equitable wrongs*. The former are said to be rights and wrongs at common law, and the remedies, therefore, are remedies at common law; the latter are said to be rights and wrongs in equity, and the remedies, therefore, are remedies in equity.

The courts of common law afford remedies by action, whenever the plaintiff has a legal right, whether the equitable right be in him or in another.

SECTION 2.—OF COURTS OF EQUITY.(*a*)

2539. *Courts of equity* are those which have jurisdiction in cases where the parties have only equitable rights. It is not easy to trace their history, and to determine how they originally obtained the jurisdiction they now exercise. Their authority and the extent of it have been subjects of much question, but time has firmly established them; and the limits of their jurisdiction seem to be in a great degree fixed and ascertained. In this country their authority is established by the constitution and statute law.(*b*)   .

(*a*) 1 Story on Eq. ch. 2; Mitf. Pl. Intr.; Cooper's Eq. Pl.
(*b*) The following just remarks, showing the origin of the jurisdiction of courts of equity, are taken from a report made by a committee appointed by the Society for Promoting the Amendment of the Law, in England, "to inquire whether the principles of Law and Equity can be administered in the same court, and by the same form of procedure; and in making such inquiry, to have regard to the provisions and operation of the New York Code." The committee say, "The Common Law of England is the work of a rude age, more anxious to protect the rights of the citizen from being overborne by the power of the barons, or undermined by the corruption of the judges, than to ascertain those rights clearly, or to enforce them completely. Hence the Common Law has ever looked with jealousy on the transfer, and indeed on the existence of rights not accompanied by possession; it has sought, by means of trial by jury, to place the administration of the law in the hands of the people themselves, and it has fettered judicial

§ 1.—Of the constitution of courts of equity.

2540. The judge of a court of equity, sometimes called a *court of chancery*, bears the title of *chancellor*. The equity jurisdiction, in some of the states, is, as in

---

discretion, by enforcing technical rules incapable of expansion, and by prescribing a strict and unvarying judgment. As society advanced, such a state of things naturally produced much injustice. Many rights arose which the courts of law either totally ignored, or only partially recognized ; and at length, toward the end of the fourteenth century, the evils arising from this illiberal system had reached such a pitch, that the clerical chancellors, after the example of the prætors at Rome, assumed a jurisdiction, in cases of peculiar hardship, to mitigate the severity, to supply the defects, and to extend the remedies of the common law. The principles upon which the chancellor proceeded were drawn in part from the civil law, and in part from abstract morality and justice ; and he asserted his jurisdiction, not by interfering directly with the proceedings or judgments of the courts of common law, which would have provoked a dangerous, and probably a successful resistance, but by personal influence exerted upon the litigants, whom he compelled, by the threat of punishment, to do whatever appeared to him upon the special circumstances of the individual case to be just, without reference to the maxims or the decisions of the courts of law. Thus did the ultimate power over property pass in a great measure from the courts of law, and thus was the duty of the legislature of adapting our jurisprudence to the emergencies of society as they arise, virtually transferred to a court of equity. So long as this state of things continued, a division of the courts of law and equity seems to have been absolutely necessary, for a fusion of them would have been nothing less than a complete abrogation of the law, and the substitution for it of the arbitrary discretion of a judge. And it is in this sense, and with reference to this system, that the committee understand and acquiesce in the justice of the celebrated opinion of Lord Bacon:—
' Omninò placet curiarum separatio ; neque enim servabitur distinctio casuum si fiat commixtio jurisdictionum, sed arbitrium legem trahet.'
 " At the present day this ' arbitrium' prevails no more in equity than at law. Precedent has superseded discretion—justice is no longer capable of being moulded in chancery with a view to relieving each individual wrong ; for it has long been considered, and rightly considered. that any system of law thus administered, varying, as it must do, with the opinions of each successive judge, is little better than absolute tyranny ; and the decrees of the chancellor, equally with the judgments of the common law judges, are now founded on general rules, the offspring of former decisions, and applicable alike to entire classes of cases. Indeed equity for more than a century past has become a system as fixed, as defined, and as incapable of further expansion, as the common law itself, against whose narrow principles it relieves. We have thus two systems of jurisprudence, of different origin, and employing different methods of procedure ; the principle of the one being to mitigate, correct, and assist the other, though it no longer possesses that flexibility and power of individualizing its relief, which such an office would seem to require."

England, vested in a high court of chancery, and such
courts are distinct from courts of law. But American
courts of equity are, in some instances, distinct from
those of law; in others, the same tribunals exercise
the jurisdiction both of courts of law and courts of
equity, though their forms of proceedings are different
in their two capacities. The supreme court of the
United States, and the circuit courts, are invested with
general equity powers, and act either as courts of law
or equity, according to the form of the process and the
subject of adjudication. In some of the states, as in
Virginia and South Carolina, the equity court is a distinct tribunal, having its appropriate judge or chancellor, and other officers. In most of the states, the two
jurisdictions centre in the same judicial officers, as in
the courts of the United States.

The extent of equity jurisdiction and proceedings
varies very much in different states; it is ample in
Connecticut, New Jersey, Maryland, Virginia, and
South Carolina; more restricted in Maine, Massachusetts, Rhode Island and Pennsylvania. And in some
states equity is administered entirely through the
forms of law. This is now the case in New York.

§ 2.—Of the jurisdiction of courts of equity.

2541. A court of equity has jurisdiction of equitable
rights only. Courts of law, acting according to the
strict principles of the common law, proceed according
to certain prescribed forms, render a general judgment
for or against the plaintiff. There are many cases in
which a simple judgment for either party, without
qualifications or conditions, will not do entire justice,
ex æquo et bono, to either party. Some modifications
of the rights of both parties are required in such cases;
some restraint on one side or the other; and some
peculiar arrangements, either present or future, temporary or perpetual.

In cases of this kind, where the courts of law cannot grant the proper remedy or relief, a remedy may be had, in those states where equity is administered, by applying to the courts of equity or chancery; for these tribunals are not limited or confined in their modes of relief, by such narrow regulations as govern courts of law, but grant relief to all parties, in cases where they have rights *ex æquo et bono*, and modify and fashion their relief according to circumstances.

2542. Courts of equity exercise jurisdiction in cases where a plain, adequate, and complete remedy cannot be had at law; that is, in common law courts.

The remedy at law must be *plain*, for, if it be doubtful and obscure at law, equity will assert a jurisdiction.

If the remedy be not *adequate* at law, and it fall short of what the party is entitled to, this will give jurisdiction to a court of equity.

And if it be not. *complete* at law, that is, reach the whole mischief and secure the rights of the parties, now and forever, it will be a sufficient ground for the interference of a court of equity, which will grant complete relief.

2543. The jurisdiction of a court of equity is either concurrent, exclusive or assistant.

1. Equity exercises *concurrent* jurisdiction with courts of law in cases where the rights are purely of a *legal* nature, but where other and more efficient aid is required than a court of law can afford, to meet the difficulties of the case, and insure full redress.

Formerly in some of these courts of law, all redress was refused, but now they grant it. In this manner jurisdiction having been once justly acquired, at a time when there was no such redress at law, it has been retained. The most common exercise of concurrent jurisdiction is in cases of account, accident, dower, fraud, mistake, partnership and partition. This remedy is often more complete in equity than it is at law. In many of these cases, and especially in some cases of fraud, mistake or accident, courts of law, not acting on equity principles, do not and cannot afford any redress; in others they do, but not always in so perfect a manner.(*a*)

2. Equity exercises an *exclusive* jurisdiction in all cases of mere *equitable rights*, that is, such rights as are not recognized in courts of law. Most of the cases of trust and confidence fall under this head. Its exclusive jurisdiction is also exercised in granting special relief beyond the reach of the common law. It will grant injunctions to prevent waste, or irreparable injury, or to secure a settled right, or to prevent vexatious litigations, or to compel the restitution of title deeds. It will appoint receivers of property, where it is in danger of misapplication; compel the surrender of securities improperly obtained; prohibit a party from leaving the country in order to avoid a suit; restrain the undue exercise of a legal right against conscience and equity; decree the specified performance of contracts respecting real estates; supply, in many cases, the imperfect execution of instruments, and reform and alter them according to the real intention of the parties; grant relief in the case of lost deeds or securities; and in all cases in which its interference is asked, its general rule is, that he who asks equity, must do equity.

3. Equity courts are also *assistant* to the jurisdiction of courts of law, in many cases, when the latter have no like authority.. A court of equity will remove legal impediments to the fair decision of a question depending at law. It will perpetuate the testimony of witnesses to rights and titles which are in danger of being lost before the matter can be tried; prevent a party from improperly setting up, at a trial, some title or claim, which would be inequitable; compel a party to discover, on his oath, facts which he knows, material

(*a*) This subject will be more fully considered in Book 5.

to the rights of the other party, but which a court of law cannot compel such party to discover; provide for the safety of property in dispute pending litigation; and counteract, control, or set aside fraudulent judgments.

2544. In the several states there are other courts, created under their respective constitutions or statutes, which, though not strictly courts of equity, possess many equitable powers; such as orphans' courts, surrogate courts, registers' courts. These, like regular courts of equity, administer justice without the aid of a jury.

SECTION 3.—OF COURTS OF ADMIRALTY.

2545. *Admiralty* is the name of a jurisdiction, which takes cognizance of suits and actions which arise in consequence of acts done upon or relating to the sea; or, in other words, of all transactions and proceedings relative to commerce and navigation, and to damages and injuries upon the sea.(a)

In the great nations of Europe, the term "admiralty jurisdiction," is uniformly applied to courts exercising jurisdiction over maritime contracts and concerns. It is familiarly known among the jurists of Scotland, England, France, Holland and Spain, as in the United States, and applied to their own courts, possessing substantially the same jurisdiction as did the English admiralty in the reign of Edward III.(b)

The constitution of the United States has delegated to the courts of the national government cognizance of "all causes of admiralty and maritime jurisdiction," and the act of September 24, 1789, c. 20, s. 9, has given the district court "cognizance of all civil causes

(a) De Lovio v. Boit, 2 Gallis, 398 ; The Jefferson, 10 Wheat. 428 ; Peyroux v. Howard, 7 Pet. 324 : Thackarey v. The Farmer, Gilp. 529.
(b) 2 Gall. 468.   See Bac. Ab. Courts of Admiralty ; Merl. Répert, h. t. ; Encyclopédie, h. t.

of admiralty and maritime jurisdiction," including all seizures under the laws of imposts, navigation, or trade of the United States, where the seizures are made, on waters navigable from the sea, by vessels of ten or more tons burden, within their respective districts, as upon the high seas ; saving to suitors, in all cases, the right of a common law remedy, when the common law is competent to give it.

Causes of this kind are to be tried by the district court, and not by a jury.(a)

The admiralty jurisdiction, expressly vested in the district court, embraces, also, captures made within the jurisdictional limits of the United States. By the act of April 20, 1818, s. 7, the district court shall take cognizance of complaints, by whomsoever instituted, in cases of captures made within the waters of the United States, or within a marine league of the coast or shore thereof.

SECTION 4.—OF COURTS MARTIAL.

2546. A *court martial* is one authorized by the articles of war, for the trial of all offences in the army or navy of the United States. The articles of war form a code for the government of the army.(b)

These courts are not permanent tribunals, but are appointed from time to time, as occasion requires. Article 64, directs that general courts martial may consist of any number of commissioned officers, from five to thirteen, inclusively ; but they shall not consist of less than thirteen, when the number can be convened without manifest injury to the service. The decision of the commanding officer who appoints the

---

(a) Croudson v. Leonard, 4 Cranch, 438 ; Yeaton v. United States, 5 Cranch, 281 ; Whelan v. United States, 7 Cranch, 112.
(b) Act of April 10, 1806.

court, as to the number that can be convened, without injury to the service, is conclusive.(a)

This is a court of limited authority, and to render its acts valid, the court must appear to have acted within its jurisdiction.(b)　Its powers extend over a person in the military service of the United States, but it has no jurisdiction over a citizen of the United States not employed in military service.(c)

If the court have not jurisdiction of the person, or subject matter, on which they pass, their judgment is null, and the members of the court, and the officers who execute their judgments, are trespassers.(d) And if, having jurisdiction, they pass sentence against an individual without notice, it is void.(e)

TITLE IV.—OF THE COURTS OF THE UNITED STATES.

2547. The judiciary of the United States was established, and exists, by virtue of the following provisions, contained in the third article of the constitution.

§ 1.—1. The judicial power of the United States shall be vested in one supreme court, and in such inferior courts as the congress may, from time to time, ordain and establish. The judges, both of the supreme and inferior courts, shall hold their offices during good behavior, and shall, at stated times, receive for their services a compensation which shall not be diminished during their continuance in office.

§ 2.—1. The judicial power shall extend to all cases in law and equity arising under this constitution, the

---

(a) 12 Wheat. 19.
(b) Duffield v. Smith, 3 S. & R. 590; Fox v. Wood, 1 Rawle, 143; Brooks v. Adams, 11 Pick. 442 ; 19 John. 7.
(c) Smith v. Shaw, 12 John. 257.
(d) Wise v. Withers, 3 Cranch, 331.
(e) Meade v. Deputy Marshal, 1 Brockenb. C. C. 324.

laws of the United States, and treaties made, or which shall be made, under their authority; to all cases affecting ambassadors, other public ministers and consuls; to all cases of admiralty and maritime jurisdiction; to controversies to which the United States shall be a party; to controversies between two or more states; between a state and citizens of another state; between citizens of different states; between citizens of the same state, claiming lands under grants of different states, and between a state, or a citizen thereof, and foreign states, citizens or subjects.

2. In all cases affecting ambassadors, other public ministers and consuls, and those in which a state shall be a party, the supreme court shall have original jurisdiction. In all other cases before mentioned, the supreme court shall have appellate jurisdiction, both as to law and fact, with such exceptions, and under such regulations, as the congress shall make.

3. The trial of all crimes, except in cases of impeachment, shall be by jury; and such trial shall be held in the state where the said crimes shall have been committed; but when not committed within any state, the trial shall be at such place or places as the congress may by law have directed.

By the amendments to the constitution, the following alterations have been made.

Art. 11. The judicial power of the United States shall not be construed to extend to any suit in law or equity, commenced or prosecuted against one of the United States by citizens of another state, or by citizens or subjects of any foreign state.

This title will be divided into two divisions. In the first a view of the central will be taken, and, in the second, of the local courts.

Division 1.—*Of the central courts of the United States.*

2548. The *central courts* are the senate, when organized to try impeachments, and the supreme court. The territorial jurisdiction of these courts extends over the whole country.

———

CHAPTER I.—OF THE SENATE OF THE UNITED STATES AS A COURT.

2549. The constitution of the United States(*a*) provides that the senate shall have the sole power of impeachments. When sitting for that purpose, the senators shall be on oath or affirmation. When the President of the United States is tried, the chief justice shall preside ; and no person shall be convicted without the concurrence of two-thirds of the members present.

It will be proper to consider, 1, the organization of this extraordinary tribunal; and, 2, its jurisdiction.

SECTION 1.—OF THE ORGANIZATION OF THE SENATE AS A COURT.

2550. Its organization differs, as it has, or has not for trial, the President of the United States. For the trial of an impeachment of the President of the United States, the presence of the chief justice is required, and he presides over the court; in this case there must also be a quorum of members present. For all

———

(*a*) Art. 1, s. 3.

other impeachments, it is sufficient if a quorum of senators be present.

SECTION 2.—OF THE JURISDICTION OF THE SENATE AS A COURT.

2551. The jurisdiction of the senate, as a court for the trial of impeachments, extends to the following officers, namely, the President and Vice-President, and all officers, civil or military, of the United States.(a)

2552. The offences for which they may be impeached are treason, bribery, and other high crimes and misdemeanors.(b)   The constitution defines treason as follows: "Treason against the United States shall consist only in levying war against them, or in adhering to their enemies, giving them aid and comfort."(c)   Not having defined bribery, recourse must be had to the common law for its definition.   The words "other high crimes and misdemeanors" not having been defined, recourse must be had to parliamentary practice and the common law, in order to ascertain what they are.(d)

———

CHAPTER II.—OF THE SUPREME COURT OF THE UNITED
STATES.

2553. The constitution vests the judicial power of the United States in one supreme court, and in such inferior courts as congress may, from time to time, ordain and establish.   This chapter will be divided into two sections: 1, of the organization of the supreme court; 2, of its jurisdiction.

(a) Const. art. 2, s. 4.   (c) Const. art. 3, s. 3.
(b) Const. art. 2, s. 4.   (d) Story on the Const. § 795.

84   OF REMEDIES.

No. 2554   Book 4, tit. 4, div 1, chap 2, sec 1, § 1, 2.   No. 2556.

SECTION 1.—OF THE ORGANIZATION OF THE SUPREME COURT.

2554. Under this section will be examined, 1, the appointment of the judges; 2, the number requisite to form a quorum; 3, the officers of the court; 4, the time when it is to be held; 5, the place where.

§ 1.—Of the appointment of the judges.

2555. The judges of the supreme court are appointed by the President of the United States, by and with the advice and consent of the senate.(a) They hold their offices during good behavior, and receive for their services a compensation which shall not be diminished during their continuance in office.(b) They consist of a chief justice and eight associate justices.(c)

§ 2.—The number requisite to form a quorum.

2556. Five judges are required to form a quorum;(d) but those attending on the day appointed for holding a session of the court, although less than five, have authority to adjourn the court from day to day, for twenty days, after the time appointed for the commencement of the session, unless five justices shall sooner attend; and the business shall not be continued over till the next session of the court until the expiration of the said twenty days. If, after the judges shall have assembled, on any day less than five shall assemble, the judge or judges so assembling shall have authority to adjourn the said court, from day to day, until a quorum shall attend, and, when expedient and proper, may adjourn the same without day.(e)

(a) Const. art. 2, s. 2.   (d) Act of March 3, 1837, s. 1.
(b) Const. art. 3, s. 1.   (e) Act of January 21, 1829.
(c) Act of March 3, 1837, s. 1.

OF COURTS OF THE UNITED STATES. 85

No 2557.   Book 4, tit 4, div. 1, chap 2, sec 1, § 3, 4.   No 2558.

§ 3.—Of the officers of the supreme court.

2557. The officers of this court are :

1. A *clerk*, who is appointed by the court. His duties are to keep a record of all the judicial acts of the court, and to keep and preserve all the records and papers confided to his care ; to make out writs and other process, to make exemplification of records and papers in his office, make out argument lists, and in general perform such other acts as the court may judicially direct to be done by him according to law.

2. *Attorneys* and *counsellors*, whose powers and duties have already been considered.(*a*) These are admitted to practice under certain rules and regulations established by the court.

3. A *marshal*, who is appointed by the president, by and with the consent of the senate ; his duties are to attend the supreme court, and to execute throughout his district all lawful precepts directed to him and issued under the authority of the United States ; and he shall have power to command all necessary assistance in the execution of his duty, and to appoint, as there shall be occasion, one or more deputies, who shall be removable from office by the judge of the district court, or the circuit court sitting within the district, at the pleasure of either.(*b*)

4. A *crier*, who is appointed by the court, and whose duty is to make proclamation of the opening and adjournment of the court, and perform sundry other services for the court, when required.

§ 4.—Of the time of holding the court.

2558. The session of the court commences on the second Monday of January, in each and every year.(*c*)

(*a*) Ante, n. 2418.
(*b*) Act of Sept. 24, 1789, sec. 27.
(*c*) Act of May 4, 1826.

The first Monday of August in each year is appointed as a return day.(*a*)

§ 5.—Of the place of holding the court.

2559. The supreme court is holden at the city of Washington ;(*b*) in case of a contagious sickness, the chief justice, or in his absence, his senior associates, may direct in what other place the court shall be held, and the court shall accordingly be adjourned to such place.(*c*)

SECTION 2.—OF THE JURISDICTION OF THE SUPREME COURT.

2560. Before we proceed to consider the jurisdiction of the supreme court, let us inquire into the nature and meaning of the term *jurisdiction*. Jurisdiction is the power constitutionally conferred upon a court, a judge, or a magistrate, to take cognizance of and decide causes according to law, and to carry their sentence, decree, or judgment into execution.(*d*) The tract of land over which such courts, judges or magistrates have jurisdiction, is called their *territory*, and the power in relation to this territory is called their *territorial jurisdiction*.

Jurisdiction is either *civil*, where the subject matter to be tried is not of a criminal nature ; or *criminal*, where the court is to punish crimes. It is *original*, when it is conferred on the court in the first instance; or *appellate*, which is when an appeal is given from the judgment of another court. It is *concurrent*, when it may be entertained by several courts ; in these cases of concurrent jurisdiction, it is a rule that the court which is first seized of the cause shall try it, to the exclusion of the other ; *exclusive*, when only one court has the right to determine or try the suit, action, or

(*a*) Act of April 29, 1802.
(*b*) Act of April 29, 1802.
(*c*) Act of February 25, 1799, s. 7.
(*d*) U. States *v.* Arredento, 6 Pet. 591; 9 John. 239.

matter in dispute. *Assistant* jurisdiction is that which is afforded by a court of chancery, in aid of a court of law; as, for example, by a bill of discovery. It is the law which gives jurisdiction; the consent of parties cannot confer it in a matter which the law excludes.(*a*)   But where the court has jurisdiction of the matter and of the person, and the defendant has some privilege which exempts him from the jurisdiction, he may waive the privilege.(*b*)   A case will illustrate this rule.   The circuit courts of the United States have no jurisdiction over ambassadors; if an ambassador should be tried in one of those courts, the whole proceeding may be avoided, although the defendant may have waived, expressly, or by implication, his right of not being sued there.   If, on the contrary, the defendant, who was subject to the jurisdiction, and was entitled to a privilege which exempted him for a time from being sued there, should waive the right, the jurisdiction would attach; as when a party attending court, voluntarily appeared to the action, and waived his privilege of exemption from being sued while attending court.

The jurisdiction of the supreme court is civil or criminal.

§ 1.—Of the civil jurisdiction.

2561. The civil jurisdiction is either original or appellate.

Art. 1.—*Of the original jurisdiction of the supreme court.*

2562. The *original* jurisdiction of the supreme court is given to that tribunal by the articles of the constitution already cited.(*c*)

By act of congress,(*d*) exclusive jurisdiction is vested

(*a*) Lindsey *v.* McClelland, 1 Bibb, 262; Parker *v.* Munday, Coxe, 70; Folby *v.* The People, Breeze, 31.
(*b*) Overstreet *v.* Brown, 4 McCord, 79.
(*c*) Const. art. 3.
(*d*) Act of September 24, 1789, s. 13.

in the supreme court of all controversies of a civil nature, where a state is a party, except between a state
and its citizens; and except, also, between a state and
citizens of other states or aliens, in which latter case it
shall have jurisdiction, but not exclusive jurisdiction.

In consequence of the decision of the case of Chis-
holm v. Georgia,(a) where it was held that assumpsit
might be maintained against a state, by a citizen of a
different state, the 11th article of the amendments of
the constitution was adopted, that " the judicial power
of the United States shall not be construed to extend
to any suit in law or equity, commenced or prosecuted
against one of the United States by citizens of another
state, or by citizens or subjects of a foreign state."

By the same act of congress,(b) the supreme court
shall have, exclusively, all such jurisdiction of suits or
proceedings *against* ambassadors, or other public ministers, or their domestics or domestic servants, as a court
of law can have or exercise consistently with the law
of nations; and original but not exclusive jurisdiction
of all suits brought *by* ambassadors or other public
ministers, or in which a consul or vice-consul shall be
a party.

The trial of issues in fact, in the supreme court, in
all actions at law against citizens of the United States,
shall be by jury.(c)

The constitution establishes the supreme court and
defines its jurisdiction. It enumerates the cases in
which its jurisdiction is original and exclusive, and
defines that which is appellate. Congress cannot,
therefore, vest in the supreme court original jurisdiction in a case in which the constitution has clearly not
given that court original jurisdiction; and affirmative
words in the constitution, declaring in what cases the

(a) 2 Dall. 419.
(b) Act of September 24, 1789, s. 13.
(c) Act of September 24, 1789, s. 13.

supreme court shall have original jurisdiction, must be construed negatively as to all other cases, or else the clause would be inoperative and useless.

In those cases where original jurisdiction is given to the supreme court, the judicial power of the United States cannot be exercised in its appellate form.(a) With the exception of those cases in which original jurisdiction is given to this court, there is none to which the judicial power extends, from which the original jurisdiction of the inferior courts is excluded by the constitution.

Art. 2.—Of the appellate jurisdiction of the supreme court.

2563. The appellate jurisdiction is vested in the supreme court by the constitution,(b) which provides that "in all other cases before mentioned, the supreme court shall have appellate jurisdiction, both as to law and fact, with such exceptions and under such regulations as the congress shall make." It exercises appellate jurisdiction in the following modes :

First Class.

2564. By writ of error from the final judgments of the circuit courts; of district courts, exercising the powers of circuit courts; and of the superior courts of the territories, exercising the powers of circuit courts in certain cases, where the matter in dispute, exclusive of costs, shall exceed the sum or value of two thousand dollars.(c) Of course no writ of error will lie when the sum or matter in controversy does not exceed two thousand dollars.(d)

It was decided that a writ of error did not lie to the

(a) Osborn v. Bank of U. S., 9 Wheat. 738.
(b) Art. 3, s. 2.
(c) Act of March 3, 1803, s. 2. See the San Pedro, 2 Wheat. 132.
(d) Durous Sean v. The United States, 6 Cranch, 307, 314. See 5 Cranch, 13 ; 4 Cranch, 216 ; 3 Dall. 401.

supreme court to reverse the judgment of a circuit court, in a civil action, by writ of error carried from the district court to the circuit court.(a) But this defect has since been remedied by act of congress,(b) by which it is enacted that writs of error shall lie to the supreme court from all judgments of a circuit court, in like manner, and under the same regulations, as are provided by law for writs of error for judgments upon suits originally brought in the circuit court.

Second Class.

2565. The supreme court has jurisdiction of appeals from the final decrees of the circuit courts; of the district courts exercising the powers of circuit courts; and of the superior courts of territories, exercising the powers of circuit courts in certain cases.

Third Class.

2566. The supreme court has also jurisdiction by writ of error from the final judgments and decrees of the highest courts of law and equity in a state, in the cases provided for by the judiciary act, which enacts(c) " That a final judgment or decree in any suit, in the highest court of law or equity of a state in which a decision in the suit could be had, where is drawn in question the validity of a treaty or statute of, or an authority exercised under, the United States, and the decision is against their validity; or where is drawn in question the validity of a statute of, or an authority exercised under, any state, on the ground of their being repugnant to the constitution, treaties, or laws, of the United States, and the decision is in favor of such their validity, or where is drawn in question the construction of any clause of the constitution, or of a

---

(a) The United States v. Goodwin, 7 Cranch, 108.
(b) Act of July 4, 1840, c. 20, s. 3.
(c) Act of September 24, 1789, s. 25.

treaty, or statute of, or commission held under, the United States, and the decision is against the title, right, privilege or exemption, specially set up or claimed by either party, under such clause of the said constitution, treaty, statute or commission, may be re-examined and reversed or affirmed in the supreme court of the United States, upon a writ of error, the citation being signed by the chief justice, or judge or chancellor, of the court, rendering or passing the judgment or decree complained of, or by a justice of the supreme court of the United States, in the same manner and under the same regulations, and the writ shall have the same effect as if the judgment or de-cree complained of, had been rendered or passed in a circuit court, and the proceeding upon the reversal shall also be the same, except that the supreme court, instead of remanding the cause for a final decision, as before provided, may, at their discretion, if the cause shall have been once remanded before, proceed to a final decision of the same, and award execution. But no other error shall be assigned or regarded as a ground of reversal, in any such case as aforesaid, than such as appears on the face of the record, and imme-diately respects the before mentioned questions of va-lidity of construction of the said constitution, treaties, statutes, commissions, or authorities, in dispute."

Fourth Class.

2567. The supreme court has also jurisdiction by certificate from the circuit court that the opinions of the judges are opposed on points stated, as provided for by the act of April 29, 1802, s. 6, in these words: " Whenever any question shall occur before a circuit court, upon which the opinions of the judges shall be opposed, the point upon which the disagreement shall happen, shall, during the same term, upon the request of either party, or their counsel, be stated under the

92 OF REMEDIES.

No 2568   Book 4, tit 4, div. 1, chap 2, sec 2, § 1, art 2.   No 2569.

direction of the judges, and certified under the seal of the court, to the supreme court at their next session to be held thereafter; and shall by the said court be finally decided. And the decision of the supreme court, and their order in the premises, shall be remitted to the circuit court, and be there entered of record, and shall have effect according to the nature of the said judgment and order: *Provided*, That nothing herein contained shall prevent the cause from proceeding, if, in the opinion of the court, further proceedings can be had without prejudice to the merits: *And provided also*, That imprisonment shall not be allowed, nor punishment in any case be inflicted, where the judges of the said court are divided in opinion upon the question touching the said imprisonment or punishment."

When the case comes before the supreme court, the judges will consider no other matter than the principle or points on which the judges were divided.(a)

Fifth Class.

2568. The judiciary act(b) authorizes the supreme court to admit to bail in criminal cases, and it was decided that the court had power to issue writs of *habeas corpus* in such cases, and that this jurisdiction was not original but appellate. It is the revision of the decision of an inferior court, by which a citizen has been committed to prison.(c)

Sixth Class.

2569. By the same act(d) the supreme court is authorized to issue writs of prohibition. A *writ of prohibition*

(a) Wayman v. Southard, 10 Wheat. 21 ; Devereaux v. Marr, 12 Wheat. 212.

(b) Act of September 24, 1789, s. 33.

(c) Ex parte Bollman, 4 Cranch, 75 ; See Ex parte Kearney, 7 Wheat. 38 ; 3 Pet. 193.

(d) Act of September 24, 1789, s. 13.

is one issued by a superior court, directed to the judges and parties of a suit in an inferior court, commanding them to cease from the prosecution of the same, upon a suggestion that the cause originally, or some collateral matter arising therein, does not belong to that jurisdiction, but to the cognizance of some other court.(a) The writ of prohibition may also be issued when, having jurisdiction, the inferior court has attempted to proceed by rules differing from those which ought to be observed;(b) or when, by the exercise of its jurisdiction, the inferior court would defeat a legal right.(c)

The act of congress gives power to the supreme court to issue writs of prohibition to the district courts, when proceeding as courts of admiralty and maritime jurisdiction; and such prohibition lies to the district court to stay proceedings *before sentence*, when that court entertains a jurisdiction not granted by the law of nations, or constitution or laws of the United States.(d)

Seventh Class.

2570. The judiciary act(e) gives further power to the supreme court to issue writs of *mandamus*. Mandamus is the name of a writ, the principal word of which, when the proceedings were in Latin, was *mandamus, we command*. It is a command issuing in the name of the sovereign authority from a superior court, having jurisdiction, and is directed to some person, corporation or court, within the jurisdiction of the superior court, requiring them to do some particular thing therein specified, which appertains to their

(a) 3 Bl. Com. 112 ; Com. Dig. h. t. ; Bac. Ab. h. t. ; Saund. Index, h. t.; Vin. Ab. h. t.
(b) Bull. N. P. 219.
(c) 2 Chit. Pr. 355.
(d) United States v. Peters, 3 Dall. 121.
(e) Act of September 24, 1789, s. 13.

office and duty, and which the superior court has previously determined, or at least supposes, to be consonant to right and justice.

The act so often cited gives this court the power to issue writs of *mandamus* in cases warranted by the principles and usages of .law, to any court or person appointed, holding office under the authority of the United States. The issuing of a *mandamus* to courts is the exercise of appellate jurisdiction, and therefore constitutionally vested in the supreme Court; but a *mandamus* directed to a public officer, belongs to original jurisdiction, and, by the constitution, the exercise of original jurisdiction by the supreme court is restricted to certain specified cases, which do not comprehend a *mandamus*. That part of the section which gives power to the supreme court to issue writs of *mandamus* to " persons holding office, under the authority of the United States," is not warranted by the constitution, and is void.(*a*)

§ 2.—Of the criminal jurisdiction of the supreme court.

2571. The criminal jurisdiction of the supreme court is derived from the constitution and the act so often cited,(*b*) which gives the supreme court exclusive jurisdiction of suits and proceedings against ambassadors, or other public ministers, or their domestics, as a court of law can have consistently with the law of nations. But it must be remembered that the act of April 30, 1790, ss. 25 and 26, declare void any writ or process whereby the person of any ambassador, or other public minister, their domestics or domestic servants, may be arrested or imprisoned.

(*a*) Marbury *v*. Madison, 1 Cranch, 175. See 3 Dall. 42 ; 9 Wheat. 529.
(*b*) Act of September 24, 1789, s. 13.

OF COURTS OF THE UNITED STATES.   95

No. 2572.   Book 4, tit. 4, div. 2, chap. 1, sec. 1, § 1.   No. 2575.

Division 2.—Of the local courts of the United States.

2572. The *local* courts of the United States have jurisdiction only over a limited territory, some larger and others smaller; they are circuit courts, district courts, and territorial courts.

CHAPTER I.—OF THE CIRCUIT COURTS.

2573. In treating of the circuit courts it will be convenient to consider, 1, their organization; 2, their jurisdiction.

SECTION 1.—OF THE ORGANIZATION OF CIRCUIT COURTS.

2574. This section will be divided into the following heads: 1, of the circuits; 2, of the judges; 3, of the officers of the courts; 4, the time and place of holding the courts; 5, of the removal of causes.

§ 1.—Of the circuit courts.

2575. The *circuit* courts are the principal inferior courts established by congress. There are nine circuit courts, which have jurisdiction respectively over their own circuits, as follows, to wit:

1. The first circuit is composed of the districts of New Hampshire, Massachusetts, Rhode Island and Maine.(*a*)

2. The second circuit is composed of the districts of Vermont, Connecticut, and Northern and Southern New York.(*b*)

3. The third circuit consists of the districts of New Jersey and Eastern and Western Pennsylvania.(*c*)

(*a*) Acts of April 29, 1802; March 26, 1812; March 30, 1820.
(*b*) Act of March 3, 1837.
(*c*) Ib.

96   OF REMEDIES.

No 2576   Book 4, tit. 4, div. 2, chap. 1, sec. 1, § 1.   No. 2577.

4. The fourth circuit includes the districts of Maryland, Delaware, and Virginia.(a)

5. The fifth circuit is composed of the districts of Alabama and Louisiana.(b)

6. The sixth circuit consists of the districts of North Carolina, South Carolina, and Georgia.(c)

7. The seventh circuit is composed of the districts of Ohio, Indiana, Illinois and Michigan.(d)

8. The eighth circuit includes the districts of Kentucky, East and West Tennessee, and Missouri.(e)

By a subsequent act,(f) it is enacted that the district court of the United States at Jackson, in the district of West Tennessee, shall in future be attached to and form a part of the eighth judicial district of the United States, with all the power and jurisdiction of the circuit court held at Nashville, in the middle district of Tennessee.

9. The ninth district is composed of the districts of Alabama, the Eastern district of Louisiana, the district of Mississippi and the district of Arkansas.(g)

2576. Owing to their remoteness from any justice of the supreme court, in several districts of the United States, there are no circuit courts held. But in these, the district court held there is authorized to act as a circuit court, except so far as relates to writs of error and appeals from judgments and decrees in such district court.

2577. By the act of congress,(h) it is provided, "That so much of any act or acts of congress as vests in the district courts of the United States for the districts of Indiana, Illinois, Missouri, Arkansas, the eastern district of Louisiana, the district of Mississippi, the northern district of New York, the western district of Virginia, and the western district of Pennsylvania,

---

(a) Act of Aug. 16, 1842.   (e) Act of March 3, 1837.
(b) Ib.   (f) Act of April 14, 1842, s. 1.
(c) Ib.   (g) Act of March 3, 1837.
(d) Act of March 3, 1837, s. 1. (h) Act of March 3, 1837, s. 3.

and the district of Alabama, or either of them, the power and jurisdiction of circuit courts, be, and the same is hereby repealed ; and there shall hereafter be circuit courts held for said districts by the chief or associate justices of the supreme court, assigned or allotted to the circuit to which such districts may respectively belong, and the district judges of such districts severally and respectively, either of whom shall constitute a quorum ; which circuit courts, and the judges thereof, shall have like powers, and exercise like jurisdiction as other circuit courts and the judges thereof; and the said district courts, and the judges thereof, shall have like powers, and exercise like jurisdiction, as the district courts, and the judges thereof in the other circuits. From all judgments and decrees, rendered in the district courts of the United States for the western district of Louisiana, writs of error and appeals shall lie to the circuit court in the other district in said state, in the same manner as from decrees and judgments rendered in the districts within which a circuit court is provided by this act.''

2578. In the District of Columbia, there is a circuit court established by particular acts of congress, composed of a chief justice and two associates.(a)

§ 2.—Of the judges of the circuit court.

2579. The justices of the supreme court are allotted among the circuits ; the judge of the supreme court allotted to a particular circuit, and the district judge of the district where the court is holden, compose the judges of the circuit court. The district judge may alone hold a circuit court, though no judge of the supreme court may be allotted to that circuit.(b)

(a) See Act of February 27, 1801 ; 7 Pet. 203 ; 12 Pet. 524 ; 3 Cranch, 159 ; 6 Cranch, 233 ; 8 Cranch, 251 ; 7 Wheat. 534.
(b) Pollard v. Dwight, 4 Cranch, 421.

The act of congress(*a*) provides, that on every appointment which shall thereafter be made of a chief justice, or associate justice, the chief justice and associate justices shall allot among themselves the aforesaid circuits as they shall think fit, and shall enter such allotment of record. And by a subsequent act,(*b*) it is directed that the allotment of the chief justice and the associate justices of the said supreme court to the several circuits shall be made as theretofore.

And, by a later act, the justices of the supreme court are required to allot the several districts among themselves. And in case no such allotment shall be made by them, at their sessions next succeeding such appointment, and also, after the appointment of any judge as aforesaid, and before any other allotment shall have been made, it shall and may be lawful for the president of the United States to make such allotment as he shall deem proper—which allotment, in either case, shall be binding until another allotment shall be made. And the circuit courts constituted by this act shall have all the power, authority and jurisdiction, within the several districts of their respective circuits, that before the 13th February, 1801, belonged to the circuit courts of the United States.

2580. The judges of the supreme court are not appointed as circuit court judges, or, in other words, have no distinct commission for that purpose; but practice and acquiescence under it, for many years, were held to afford an answer against this objection to their authority to act, when made in the year 1803, and to have fixed the construction of the judicial system. The court deemed the contemporary exposition to be of the most forcible nature, and considered the question at rest and not to be disturbed.(*c*)

(*a*) Act of April 29, 1802, s. 5.
(*b*) Act of March, 3, 1837, s. 4.
(*c*) Stuart *v.* Laird, 1 Cranch, 308.

2581. In case a vacancy exists by the death of the justice of the supreme court to whom the district was . allotted, the district judge may, under the act of congress, discharge the official duties of such deceased judge,(a) except that he cannot sit upon a writ of error from a decision in the district court.(b)

§ 3.—Of the officers of the circuit court.

2582. There are various officers attached to the circuit courts, the principal of whom are :

1. The *clerk*. This officer is appointed by the court, and in case of disagreement between the judges, the appointment shall be made by the presiding judge of the court.(c)   His duties are to issue writs, make and keep all the records of the court.

2. *Attorneys*, who have the usual powers of attorneys. They are admitted on motion, after having been admitted in other courts for a certain length of time, according to the rules of the respective courts. This being a court of law and equity, and it being an appellate tribunal, the persons appointed to conduct the business of suitors therein, are designated under the various appellations of attorneys, counsellors, advocates, solicitors and proctors.   The offices of *proctor* and *advocate* are derived from the civil and canon law, and are used in admiralty proceedings, as corresponding with attorney and counsellor in proceedings at law ; in equity proceedings they bear the names of *solicitor* and *counsellor*.

3. The *district attorney* is an officer appointed by the president, by and with the consent of senate. His duty is to prosecute, in such district for which he is appointed, all delinquents, for crimes and offences cognizable under the authority of the United States,

---

(a) Pollard v. Dwight, 4 Cranch, 428.   See Act of April 29, 1802, s. 5.
(b) United States v. Lancaster, 5 Wheat. 434.
(c) Act of February 28, 1839, s. 2.

100 OF REMEDIES.

No. 2583.   Book 4, tit. 4, div. 2, chap. 1, sec. 1, § 4, 5.   No. 2584.

and all civil actions, in which the United States shall be concerned, except in the supreme court, in the district in which that court shall be holden.(a)

4. The *marshal* of the district where the court sits, is the ministerial officer of the circuit court.

5. A *crier* and *tipstaves* are sometimes appointed, to make proclamations and keep order.

§ 4.—Of the time and place of holding circuit courts.

2583. By sundry acts of congress it is provided:

That a circuit court may be adjourned, from day to day, by one of its judges, or if none are present, by the marshal of the district, until a quorum be convened.(b)

That when it shall happen that no judge of the supreme court attends within four days after the time appointed by law, for the commencement of the session, a circuit court may be adjourned to the next stated term, by the judge of the district, or, in the case of his absence also, by the marshal of the district.(c)

That when only one of the judges directed to hold the circuit shall attend, such circuit court may be held by the judge so attending.(d)

§ 5.—Of the removal of causes in certain cases.

2584. To prevent the inconveniences which might happen in certain cases, the act of congress of March 2, 1809, imposes certain duties on the circuit judge, when the district judge is unable to hold a district court.

If the disability of the district judge terminates in

(a) Act of September 24, 1789, s. 35.
(b) Act of September 24, 1789, s. 6.
(c) Act of May 9, 1794.
(d) Act of April 29, 1802, s. 4.

OF COURTS OF THE UNITED STATES.

No. 2584.   Book 4, tit. 4, div. 2, chap. 1, sec. 1, § 5.   No. 2584.

his death, the circuit judge must remand the certified causes to the district court.(a)

By the act of March 3, 1821, s. 1, it is directed that in all suits and actions in any district court of the United States, in which it shall appear that the judge of such court is any ways concerned in interest, or has been of counsel for either party, or is so related to, or connected with either party, as to render it improper for him, in his opinion, to sit on the trial of such suit or action, it shall be the duty of such judge, on application of either party, to cause the fact to be entered on the records of the court; and, also, an order that an authenticated copy thereof, with all the proceedings in such suit or action, shall be forthwith certified to the next circuit court of the district; and if there be no circuit court in such district, to the next circuit court in the state; and if there be no circuit court in such state, to the most convenient circuit court in an adjacent state; which circuit court shall, upon such record being filed with the clerk thereof, take cognizance thereof, in the like manner as if such suit or action had been originally commenced in that court, and shall proceed to hear and determine the same accordingly; and the jurisdiction of such circuit court shall extend to all such cases so removed, as were cognizable in the district court from which the same was removed.

And by the act of February 28, 1839, s. 8, it is enacted, that in all suits and actions in any circuit court of the United States in which it shall appear that both the judges thereof or the judge thereof, who is solely competent by law to try the same, shall be any ways concerned in interest therein, or shall have been of counsel for either party, or is, or are so related to or connected with either party as to render it improper for him or them, in his or their opinion, to

---

(a) Ex parte United States, 1 Gall. 337.

sit in the trial of such suit or action, it shall be the duty of such judge or judges, on application of either party, to cause the fact to be entered on the records of the court; and also to make an order that an authenticated copy thereof, with all the proceedings in such suit or action, shall be forthwith certified to the most convenient circuit court in the next adjacent state, or in the next adjacent circuit; which circuit court shall, upon such record and order being filed with the clerk thereof, take cognizance thereof in the same manner as if such suit or action had been rightfully and originally commenced therein, and shall proceed to hear and determine the same accordingly, and the proper process for the due execution of the judgment or decree rendered therein, shall run into and may be executed in the district where such judgment or decree was rendered, and also, into the district from which such suit or action was removed.

SECTION 2.—OF THE JURISDICTION OF THE CIRCUIT COURTS.

2585. The circuit courts are courts of limited jurisdiction, and like all other courts where the jurisdiction is limited, the presumption of law is that a case is not within their jurisdiction, unless the contrary appears.(a) And in all cases the jurisdiction of the court must appear from the record, *per se*, strictly considered.(b) The usual way is to state the names of the parties thus: "A B, a citizen of the state of Ohio, against C D, a citizen of the state of Georgia."(c)

The jurisdiction of the circuit courts is either civil or criminal.

(a) Turner v. Bank of North America, 4 Dall. 11; Wood v. Mann, 1 Sumner, 580: Griswold v. Sedgwick, 1 Wend. 131; McCormick v. Sullivant, 10 Wheat. 192; Postmaster Gen. v. Stockton, 12 Pet. 584.

(b) Fisher v. Cockerell, 5 Pet. 248; Lessee of Reed v. Marsh, 13 Pet. 153.

(c) Wood v. Wagnon, 2 Cranch, 1.

§ 1.—Of the civil jurisdiction of the circuit court.

2586. The civil jurisdiction is either at law or in equity.

Art. 1.—Of the civil jurisdiction of circuit courts at law.

2587. This jurisdiction is exercised in four ways : 1, it is original ; 2, by appeal ; 3, by removal of causes from state courts ; 4, by mandamus.

1. *Of the original jurisdiction of the circuit courts at law.*

2588. The original jurisdiction of the circuit courts at law, may be considered, first, as to the matter in controversy; secondly, with regard to the parties litigant.

1° *The matter in controversy.*

2589. To give jurisdiction to the circuit court, the matter in dispute must exceed five hundred dollars.(*a*) The test as to the amount is not the result of the verdict, but the *amount claimed* in the declaration ; as, for example, in actions to recover damages for torts, the sum laid in the declaration is the criterion as to the matter in dispute.(*b*) So in an action of covenant, on an instrument under seal, containing a penalty less than five hundred dollars, the court has jurisdiction if the declaration demand more than that sum.(*c*)

In ejectment, the value of the land should appear in the declaration,(*d*) but though the jury do not find the value of the land in dispute, yet, if evidence be given on the trial, that the value exceeds five hundred dollars, it is sufficient to fix the jurisdiction ; or the court may ascertain its value by affidavits.(*e*)

When the matter in dispute arises out of a local injury, for which a local action must be brought, in

---

(*a*) Act of September 24, 1789, s. 11.
(*b*) Hulscamp *v.* Teel, 2 Dall. 356 ; Gordon *v.* Longest, 16 Pet. 97.
(*c*) Martin *v.* Taylor, 1 Wash. C. C. 1.
(*d*) Lessee of Lanning *v.* Dolph, 4 Wash. C. C. 624 ; Liter *v.* Green, 8 Cranch, 220.
(*e*) Den *v.* Wright, 1 Pet. C. C. 73.

order to give the circuit court jurisdiction, it must be brought in the district where the lands lie.(*a*)

2590. By various acts of congress,(*b*) jurisdiction is given to the circuit courts, in cases where actions are brought to recover damages for the violation of patent and copy rights, without fixing any amount as to limit, or as to the character of the parties.

2591. The circuit courts have jurisdiction, in cases arising under the patent laws. By the act of July 4, 1836, s. 17, it is enacted "that all actions, suits, controversies, and cases arising under any law of the United States, granting or confirming to inventors the exclusive right to their inventions or discoveries, shall be originally cognizable, as well in equity as at law, by the circuit courts of the United States, or any district court having the powers and jurisdiction of a circuit court; which courts shall have power, upon bill in equity filed by any party aggrieved, in any such case, to grant injunctions, according to the course and principles of courts of equity, to prevent the violation of the rights of any inventor as secured to him by any law of the United States, on such terms and conditions as said courts may deem reasonable : *Provided, however,* That from all judgments and decrees, from any such court rendered in the premises, a writ of error or appeal, as the case may require, shall lie to the supreme court of the United States, in the same manner and under the same circumstances as is now provided by law in other judgments and decrees of circuit courts, and in all other cases in which the court shall deem it reasonable to allow the same."

2592. In general, the circuit court has no original jurisdiction of suits for penalties and forfeitures, arising under the laws of the United States, nor in admiralty cases.

(*a*) 4 Hall's Law Journal, 78.
(*b*) Acts of April 17, 1800, s. 4; Feb. 15, 1819.

OF COURTS OF THE UNITED STATES. 105

No. 2593.　　　Book 4, tit. 4, div 2, chap. 1, sec. 2, § 1, art. 1.　　　No 2594.

2° Of the character of the parties.

2593. The cases in which suits may be maintained in the circuit courts, may be classed, as to the parties to them, as follows: 1, the United States; 2, suits between citizens of different states; 3, suits where an alien is a party; 4, when an assignee is plaintiff; 5, who may be defendant.

(1.) *When the United States are a party.*

2594. When the sum in controversy exceeds, besides costs, the sum of five hundred dollars, the United States may sue on all contracts in the circuit court;(*a*) but, in cases of penalties, the action must be in the district court, unless the law gives express jurisdiction to the circuit court.(*b*)

The act of March 3, 1815, abolishes the limitation of five hundred dollars in cases where the United States are plaintiffs, and s. 4, vests in the circuit courts jurisdiction concurrently with the district court, of all suits at common law where any officer of the United States sues under the authority of an act of congress; as where the postmaster general sues under an act of congress, for debts or balances due to the general post office.(*c*)

The circuit court has jurisdiction on a bill of equity, filed by the United States against the debtor of their debtor, they claiming a priority under the act of March 2, 1798, s. 65, though the law of the state, where the suit is brought, permits a creditor to proceed against the debtor of his debtor, by a peculiar process at law.(*d*)

No suit can be brought against the United States,

(*a*) Evans qui tam *v.* Ballen, 4 Dall. 342.
(*b*) 4 Dall. 342.
(*c*) Postmaster General *v.* Early, 12 Wheat. 146. See Dox *v.* The Postmaster General, 1 Pet. 318; Southwick *v.* The Postmaster General, 2 Pet. 447.
(*d*) United States *v.* Howland, 4 Wheat. 108.

106 OF REMEDIES.

No. 2595.   Book 4, tit 4, div 2, chap. 1, sec 2, § 1, art. 1.   No. 2595.

consequently the circuit courts have no jurisdiction in such cases.

(2.) Suits between citizens of different states.

2595. The judiciary act,(*a*) gives jurisdiction to the circuit court in suits of a civil nature, when the matter in dispute exceeds five hundred dollars in value, besides costs, between a citizen of a state where the suit is brought, and the citizen of another state; one of the parties must therefore be a citizen of the state where the suit is brought, for when neither of the parties is a citizen of such state, the court has no jurisdiction.(*b*)

The act requires that the parties shall be citizens, and it must appear on the record that they are such.(*c*) This citizenship, means a residence or domicil, in a particular state, by one who is a citizen of the United States. This must be, not merely a temporary, but a permanent domicil.(*d*) And when there are several plaintiffs or defendants, they must all be competent to sue and be sued in a circuit court, otherwise that court has no jurisdiction.(*e*)

To give the court jurisdiction in cases between citizens of the United States, the parties must be citizens of a state or states; the District of Columbia,(*f*) and the territories of the United States, not being considered as states for this purpose.(*g*)

(*a*) Act of September 24, 1789, s. 11.

(*b*) Shute *v.* Davis, Pet. C. C. 431 ; Wood *v.* Mann, 1 Sumn. 581; White *v.* Sumner, 1 Mason, 520; Kitchen *v.* Sullivan, 4 Wash. C. C. 84.

(*c*) Wood *v.* Wagnon, 2 Cranch, 1 ; 1 Cranch, 343 ; 4 Dall. 8 ; Paine, R. 594. An averment on the record that the parties are " of," or are " inhabitants " or " residents " of different states, is not sufficient. The record must allege that they are " citizens " of different states.

(*d*) Reed *v.* Bertrand, 4 Wash. C. C. 516 ; Cartlett *v.* Pacific Ins. Co. 1 Paine, 594 ; Rabauld *v.* D'Wolf, 1 Paine, 580 ; Knox *v.* Greenleaf, 4 Dall. 360.

(*e*) Strawbridge *v.* Curtis, 3 Cranch, 267. But see Shute *v.* Davis, Pet. C. C. 431.

(*f*) Hepburn *v.* Elzey, 2 Cranch, 448.

(*g*) New Orleans *v.* Winter, 1 Wheat. 91 ; Prescott's Lessee *v.* Fairfield, 1 Pet. 14.

OF COURTS OF THE UNITED STATES.   107

No. 2596.   Book 4, tit 4, div. 2, chap. 1, sec. 2, § 1, art. 1.   No. 2598.

(3.) Suits where an alien is a party.

2596. The eleventh section of the judiciary act,(*a*) vests jurisdiction in the circuit court over all suits of a civil nature, where an alien is a party; but these general words must be restricted by the provisions in the constitution, which give jurisdiction in controversies between a state, or the citizens of a state, and foreign states, their citizens or subjects; the statute cannot extend the jurisdiction beyond the limits of the constitution.(*b*)   The record must show that the party is an alien.(*c*)

When both parties are aliens the circuit court has no jurisdiction.(*d*)

An alien who holds lands under a special law of the state where he is resident, may maintain an action in relation to those lands, in the circuit court.

(4.) When an assignee is plaintiff.

2597. When the plaintiff sues on a right of action which has been assigned to him, to give the circuit court jurisdiction, the assignor of the contract must have been entitled to sue in the circuit court, if no assignment had been made; but to this general rule there is an exception in the case of bills of exchange,(*e*) the obvious policy of which is to prevent any thing which might impede their circulation.(*f*)

2598. As to the nature of the assignment, it has been held that where a note was payable to A B, or bearer, the bearer might sue in the circuit court, if properly qualified, without showing A B to be a fictitious person, or competent to have prosecuted the suit.(*g*)   Assignees by operation of law, as where an

(*a*) Act of September 24, 1789.
(*b*) Mossman *v.* Higginson, 4 Dall. 11.
(*c*) Turner *v.* Enrille, 4 Dall. 7; Micharlson *v.* Denison, 3 Day, 294.
(*d*) Montaret *v.* Murray, 4 Cranch, 46; 4 Dall. 420, note.
(*e*) Act of September 24, 1789, s. 11.
(*f*) Bullard *v.* Bell, 1 Mason, 251.
(*g*) Bank of Kentucky *v.* Wistar, 2 Pet. S. C. 318.

108 **OF REMEDIES.**

No. 2599.   Book 4, tit. 4, div. 2, chap. 1, sec. 2, § 1, art. 1.   No. 2600.

insolvent estate is vested in them by law, are embraced by the provision, as much as assignees in deed.(*a*)

2599. With regard to the nature of the claim assigned, the act is not confined to negotiable paper; equitable as well as legal assignments are included. The assignee of an open account is precluded, as much as the assignee of a deed.

It is said that this section of the act of congress has no application to the conveyance of lands from a citizen of one state to a citizen of another state. The grantee in such case may, in general, maintain his action in the circuit court, when otherwise properly qualified, to try the title to such lands.(*b*) But the sale must have been made *bonâ fide*, and not for the mere purpose of enabling the nominal purchaser to bring a suit; in case the sale is fictitious, the court will strike off the case from the record.(*c*)

(5.) *Who may be defendant.*

2600. The act(*d*) further provides that no person shall be arrested in one district, for trial in another, in any civil action before a circuit or district court. And no civil suit shall be brought, before either of the said courts, against an inhabitant of the United States, by original process, in any other district than that whereof he is an inhabitant, or in which he shall be found at the time of serving the writ.

A citizen of one state may be sued in another, under this act, if the process be served upon him in the latter ;(*e*) but, in such case, the plaintiff must be a citizen of the state where the suit is brought, or an alien.(*f*)

This clause respecting the not being served with

(*a*) Sere *v*. Pitot, 6 Cranch, 332.
(*b*) Briggs *v*. French, 2 Sumn. 252.
(*c*) Maxfield's Lessee *v*. Levy, 4 Dall. 330.
(*d*) Act of September 24, 1789, s. 11.
(*e*) McMicken *v*. Webb, 11 Pet. 25.
(*f*) Shute *v*. Davis, Pet. C. O. 431.

process out of the district in which the defendant resides, is the grant of a personal privilege, and not a
restriction of the jurisdiction of the court.   Being nothing but a privilege it may be waived, either expressly
or by implication, as by entering an appearance.(a)
But if the defendant appear and put in a plea, claiming
the benefit of the privilege, it is no waiver.(b)

2. Of the appellate jurisdiction of the circuit court.

2601. The appellate jurisdiction of the circuit court
may be exercised by means of, 1, writs of error;
2, appeals from the district court; 3, certiorari;
4, procedendo.

2602.—1. This court has jurisdiction to issue writs
of error to the district court, on judgments of that
court in civil causes, at common law ; but not in admiralty or maritime causes.(c)

The eleventh section of the judiciary act,(d) provides
that the circuit court shall have appellate jurisdiction
from the district courts, under the regulations and restrictions therein provided.

By the twenty-second section, final decrees and
judgments in civil actions in a district court, where
the matter in dispute exceeds the sum or value of fifty
dollars, exclusive of costs, may be re-examined, and
reversed or affirmed in a circuit court holden in the
same district, upon a writ of error, whereto shall be
annexed and returned therewith at the day and place
therein mentioned, an authenticated transcript of the
record and assignment of errors, and prayer for reversal, with a citation to the adverse party, signed by the
judge of such district court, or a justice of the supreme
court, the adverse party having at least twenty days'
notice.   But there shall be no reversal on such writ of

(a) Logan v. Patrick, 5 Cranch, 288.
(b) Harrison v. Rowan, Pet. C. C. 449.
(c) United States v. Wonson, 1 Gall. 5.
(d) Act of September 24, 1789.

110 OF REMEDIES.

No. 2603.   Book 4, tit. 4, div. 2, chap. 1, sec. 2, § 1, art. 1.   No. 2604.

error, for error in ruling any plea in abatement, other than a plea to the jurisdiction of the court, or for any error in fact. Writs of error shall not be brought but within five years after rendering or passing the judgment or decree complained of; or, in case the person entitled to such writ of error be an infant, *non compos mentis*, or imprisoned, then within five years, as aforesaid, exclusive of the time of such disability. And every justice or judge signing a citation or any writ of error as aforesaid, shall take good and sufficient security, that the plaintiff in error shall prosecute his writ to effect, and answer all damages and costs, if he fail to make his plea good.

The district judge cannot sit in the circuit court on a writ of error to the district court.(a)

2603.—2. Appeals from the district to the circuit court take place generally in civil causes of admiralty or maritime jurisdiction.

By the act of March 3, 1803, it is enacted, that from all final judgments or decrees in any of the district courts of the United States, an appeal, where the matter in dispute, exclusive of costs, shall exceed the sum or value of fifty dollars, shall be allowed to the district court next to be holden in the district where such final judgment or judgments, decree or decrees shall be rendered: and the circuit courts are thereby authorized and required, to hear and determine such appeals.

2604.—3. Although no act of congress authorizes the circuit court to issue a certiorari to the district court for the removal of a cause, yet if the cause be so removed, and instead of taking advantage of the irregularity in proper time and in a proper manner, the defendant makes the defence and pleads to issue, he thereby waives the objection, and the suit will be

---

(a) United States *v.* Lancaster, 5 Wheat. 434.

considered as an original one in the circuit court, made so by consent of parties.(a)

2605.—4. The circuit court may issue a writ of procedendo to the district court.

3. Of the removal of actions from the state courts.

2606. Actions may be removed from a state court into the circuit court, in two cases : 1, when the matter in dispute exceeds five hundred dollars, exclusive of costs; and 2, when parties claim title to land, under grants of different states.

2607.—1. The twelfth section of the judiciary act(b) provides in certain cases the right of removing a suit instituted in a state court to the circuit court of the district.   It is enacted by that law, that if a suit be commenced in any state court against an alien, or by a citizen of the state in which the suit is brought, against a citizen of another state, and the matter in dispute exceeds the aforesaid sum or value of five hundred dollars, exclusive of costs, to be made to appear to the satisfaction of the court, and the defendant shall, at the time of entering his appearance in such state court, file a petition for the removal of the cause for trial, into the next circuit court, to be held in the district where the suit is pending, and offer good and sufficient security for his entering in such court, on the first day of its session, copies of the said process against him, and also for his then appearing and entering special bail in the cause, if special bail was originally required therein, it shall then be the duty of the state court to accept the surety, and proceed no further in the cause.   And any bail that may have been originally taken shall be discharged.   And the said copies being entered as aforesaid in such court of the United States, the cause shall there proceed in the

---

(a) Patterson v. The United States, 2 Wheat. 221.
(b) Act of September 24, 1789, s. 12.

same manner as if it had been brought there by original process. And any attachment of the goods or estate of the defendant, by the original process, shall hold the goods or estate so attached, to answer the final judgment, in the same manner as by the laws of such state they would have been holden to answer final judgment, had it been rendered by the circuit court in which the suit commenced.

2608.—2. The constitution(a) extends the judicial power to controversies between citizens of the same state, claiming lands under grants of different states; and by a clause of the 12th section of the judiciary act, it is enacted, that if, in any action commenced in a state court, the title of land be concerned, and the parties are citizens of the same state, and the matter in dispute exceeds the sum or value of five hundred dollars, exclusive of costs, the sum or value being made to appear to the satisfaction of the court, either party, before the trial, shall state to the court, and make affidavit, if it require it, that he claims, and shall rely upon a right or title to the land, under grant from a state, other than that in which the suit is pending, and produce the original grant, or an exemplification of it, except where the loss of records shall put it out of his power, and shall move that the adverse party inform the court, whether he claims a right of title to the land under a grant from the state in which the suit is pending; the said adverse party shall give such information, otherwise not be allowed to plead such grant, or give it in evidence upon the trial; and if he informs that he does claim under any such grant, the party claiming under the grant first mentioned, may then, on motion, remove the cause for trial, to the next circuit court to be holden in such district. But if he is the defendant, he shall do it under the same regulations as in the before mentioned case of the

_____

(a) Art. 3, s. 2.

OF COURTS OF THE UNITED STATES. 113

No. 2609.   Book 4, tit 4, div 2, chap. 1, sec. 2, § 1, art 1   No. 2609.

removal of a cause into such court by an alien. And neither party removing the cause shall be allowed to plead, or give evidence of, any other title than that by him stated as aforesaid, as the ground of his claim.(a)

Application for removal must be made during the term at which the defendant enters his appearance.(b) If a state court agree to consider the petition to remove the cause as filed of the preceding term, yet if the circuit court see by the record that it was not filed till a subsequent term, they will not permit the cause to be docketed.(c) It will be in time, however, if the petition be filed at the time of putting in bail;(d) and a defendant in ejectment may file his petition when he is let in to defend.(e)

In chancery, when the defendant wishes to remove his suit, he must file his petition when he enters an appearance.(f)

4. Of the remedy by mandamus.

2609. The power of the circuit court to issue a mandamus, is confined exclusively to cases in which it may be necessary for the exercise of such a jurisdiction already existing; as, for example, if the court below refuse to proceed to judgment, then a mandamus in the nature of a procedendo may issue.(g) After a state court had refused to permit the removal of a cause on petition, the circuit court issued a mandamus to transfer the cause.

(a) See 9 Cranch, 292 ; 2 Wheat. R. 378.
(b) Gibson v. Johnson, Pet. C. C. 44 ; Eastin v. Rucker, 1 J. J. Marsh, 232.
(c) Pet. C. C. 44 ; Ward v. Arredondo, Paine, 410. Sed vide Gelston v. Johnson, 2 Pen. 625.
(d) Redmond v. Russell, 12 John. 153 ; Arjo v. Monteiro, 1 Caines, 248 ; Bird v. Murray, Colem. 58.
(e) Jackson v. Stiles, 4 John. 493.
(f) Livingston v. Gibbons, 4 John. Ch. 94.
(g) M'Intire v. Wood, 7 Cranch, 504 ; M'Clung v. Silliman, 6 Wheat. 598.

114 OF REMEDIES.

No. 2610.   Book 4, tit 4, div. 2, chap 1, sec. 2, § 1, art. 2.   No 2610.

Art. 2.—Of the equity jurisdiction of the circuit courts.

2610. Circuit courts are vested with equity jurisdiction in certain cases. The judiciary act of 1789, s. 11, gives original cognizance, concurrent with the courts of the several states, of all suits of a civil nature at common law or in *equity*, where the matter in dispute exceeds, exclusive of costs, the sum or value of five hundred dollars, between certain parties therein mentioned.

The act of April 15, 1819, s. 1, further extends the equitable powers of this court; it enacts " that the circuit court of the United States shall have original cognizance, as well in equity as at law, of all actions, suits, controversies, and cases arising under any law of the United States, granting or confirming to authors or inventors, the exclusive right to their respective writings, inventions, and discoveries; and upon any bill in equity filed by any party aggrieved, in such cases, shall have authority to grant injunctions according to the course and principles of courts of equity, to prevent the violation of the rights of any authors or inventors, secured to them by any laws of the United States, on such terms and conditions as the said courts may deem fit and reasonable : *Provided, however*, that from all judgments and decrees of any circuit courts rendered in the premises, a writ of error or appeal, as the case may require, shall lie to the supreme court of the United States, in the same manner and under the same circumstances, as is now provided by law, in other judgments and decrees of such circuit court."

And the act of August 23, 1842, s. 5, declares that the district courts as courts of admiralty, and the circuit courts as courts of equity, shall be deemed always open for the purpose of filing libels, bills, petitions, answers, pleas, and other pleadings, for issuing and returning mesne and final process and commissions,

and for making and directing all interlocutory mo-
tions, orders, rules, and other proceedings whatever,
preparatory to the hearing of all causes pending
therein upon their merits. And it shall be competent
for any judge of the court, upon reasonable notice to
the parties, in the clerk's office, or at chambers, and
in vacation as well as in term, to make and direct, and
award all such process, commissions and interlocutory
orders, rules, and other proceedings, whenever the
same are not grantable of course according to the rules
and practice of the court.

§ 2.—Of the criminal jurisdiction of the circuit courts.

2611. The judiciary act, section 11, gives the circuit courts exclusive cognizance of all crimes and
offences cognizable under the authority of the United
States, except where that act otherwise provides, or
the laws of the United States shall otherwise direct, and
concurrent jurisdiction with the district courts of the
crimes and offences cognizable therein. The jurisdiction of the circuit court in criminal cases is confined to
offences committed within the district for which those
courts respectively sit when they are committed on
land.

Although the national courts are to look to the common law in the absence of statutory provisions for the
rules to guide them in the exercise of their functions
in criminal as in civil cases, it is to the statutes of the
United States alone that they must have recourse to
determine what constitutes an offence against the
United States. The general government has no unwritten criminal code to which resort can be had as a
source of jurisdiction.(a)

(a) Ex parte Bollman, 4 Cranch, 75; United States v. Coolridge, 1 Wheat.
415; United States v. Bevans, 3 Wheat. 336; United States v. Hudson, 7
Cranch, 32.

CHAPTER II.—OF THE DISTRICT COURTS.

2612. In treating of district courts, the same division which was made in considering the circuit courts, will here be adopted, by taking a view of, 1, their organization ; 2, their jurisdiction. And in a third section will be examined the jurisdiction of special district courts.

SECTION 1.—OF THE ORGANIZATION OF THE DISTRICT COURTS.

2613. The United States are divided into districts, in each of which is a court called the district court, which is to consist of one judge, who is to reside in the district for which he is appointed, and to hold annually four sessions.(a) By subsequent acts of congress, the number of annual sessions in particular districts, is sometimes more, sometimes less ; and they are to be held at various places in the same district. There is also a district court in the District of Columbia.

2614. The judge of the district court appoints a clerk for said court, whose duties are to.issue writs and all other process, keep the records, and generally to perform the duties of a clerk of the court.(b)

By the third section of the act of March 2, 1809, it is enacted that in case the district judge in any district is unable to discharge his duties as by the said act is provided, the district clerk of such district shall be authorized and empowered, by leave or order of the circuit judge of the circuit in which such district is included, to take, during such disability of the district judge, all examinations and depositions of witnesses, and to make all necessary rules and orders, prepara- tory to the final hearing of all causes of admiralty and maritime jurisdiction.

2615. The marshal of the district is the ministerial

(a) Act of September 24, 1789.   (b) Act of September 24, 1789, s. 37.

officer who is to carry into execution the judgments, decrees and orders of said district court.

2616. The persons admitted to conduct the business of suitors in the district court, are designated by various appellations, of attorneys, counsellors, proctors, and advocates, in the same way that they are in the circuit courts.

2617. The district attorney is the officer who, on behalf of the United States, prosecutes all claims due to the United States, and for all offences committed in violation of the national laws.

SECTION 2.—OF THE JURISDICTION OF THE DISTRICT COURTS.

2618. The jurisdiction of the district courts is either civil or criminal.

§ 1.—Of the civil jurisdiction of the district courts.

2619. The civil jurisdiction of these courts extends, 1, to admiralty and maritime causes; 2, to cases of seizure on land under the laws of the United States, and in suits for penalties and forfeitures incurred under those laws; 3, to cases in which an alien sues for a tort, in violation of the laws of nations, or of a treaty of the United States; 4, to suits instituted by the United States; 5, to actions by and against consuls; 6, to certain cases in equity.

Art. 1. Of admiralty and maritime causes.

2620. The original admiralty and maritime jurisdiction of the district courts is exclusive, and is either ordinary or extraordinary.

1. *Of the ordinary jurisdiction in admiralty.*

2621. The ordinary jurisdiction in admiralty comprehends, 1, prize suits; 2, cases of salvage; 3, actions for torts; 4, actions on contracts, such as seamen's wages, pilotage, bottomry, ransom, materials, and the like.

1° Prize suits.

2622. The act of September 24, 1789, s. 9, vests in the district courts as full jurisdiction of all prize causes as the admiralty of England; and this jurisdiction is an ordinary inherent branch of the powers of the court of admiralty, whether considered as prize courts or instance courts.(*a*)

The act marks out not only the general jurisdiction of the district courts, but also that of the several courts in relation to each other, in case of seizure on the waters of the United States or elsewhere.

When the seizure is made in the waters of one district, the court of that district has exclusive jurisdiction, though the offence may have been committed out of that district.

When the seizure is made on the high seas, the jurisdiction is in the court of the district where the property is brought.

2° Cases of salvage.

2623. Under the constitution and laws, this court has exclusive original cognizance in cases of salvage; and, as a consequence, it has the power to determine to whom the residue of the property belongs, after deducting the salvage.(*b*)

3° Actions arising out of torts or injuries.

2624. By the delegation of jurisdiction to the dis-

(*a*) The English court of admiralty is divided into two distinct tribunals; the one having generally all jurisdiction of admiralty, except in prize cases, is called the *instance* court; the other, acting under a special commission, distinct from the commission given to judges of admiralty, to enable the judge, in time of war, to assume the jurisdiction of prizes, and called a *prize* court. Bro. Civ. & Adm. Law, ch. 4 and 5.

(*b*) M'Donough *v.* Dannery, 3 Dall. 183.

trict court in all admiralty and maritime causes, it has jurisdiction over all cases of torts or injuries committed upon the high seas, and in forts and harbors within the ebb and flow of the tide.(a) The following are examples; the district court, as a court of admiralty, may redress personal wrongs committed on a passenger, on the high seas, by the master of a vessel, whether those wrongs were by direct force or consequential injuries ;(b) and the owners as well as the captain of the vessel, are liable for an unlawful capture made by him.(c) A father, whose minor son has been tortiously abducted and seduced on a voyage on the high seas, may sue, in the admiralty, in the nature of an action *per quod*, etc., also for wages, earned by such son, in maritime service.(d) This court has also jurisdiction of petitory suits to reinstate the owners of vessels who have been displaced from their possession.(e)

4° *Of suits on contracts in the admiralty.*

2625. The fourth class of remedies in the admiralty, under its ordinary jurisdiction, is by suit on maritime contracts. This court has jurisdiction, concurrent with the courts of common law, over all maritime contracts, wheresoever the same may be made or executed, or whatsoever be the form of the contract.(f) But contracts regulated by the common law are excluded from the jurisdiction of the admiralty, by the seventh amendment of the constitution.(g)

(a) Martin v. Hunter's Lessee, 1 Wheat. 304 ; The Amiable Nancy, 3 Wheat. 546 ; De Lovio v. Boit, 2 Gall. 398 ; Plummer v. Webb, 4 Mason, 380.
(b) Chamberlain v. Chandler, 3 Mason, 242.
(c) Dean v. Angus, Bee, 369, 378.
(d) Plummer v. Webb, 4 Mason, 380.
(e) The Tilton, 5 Mason, 465.
(f) De Lovio v. Boit, 2 Gall. 398 ; Zane v. The President, 4 Wash. C. C. 453 ; The Mary, Paine, 671 ; Davis v. Brig, Gilp. 477.
(g) Bains v. The James, Baldw. 544.

120   OF REMEDIES.

No 2626.   Book 4, tit 4, div 2, chap 2, sec 2, § 1, art. 1.   No. 2626.

The maritime contracts over which the admiralty has jurisdiction are those which relate to the business, commerce, or navigation of the sea; such as charter parties, affreightments, marine loans and hypothecations, contracts for maritime service in building, repairing, supplying, and navigating ships; contracts and quasi contracts respecting averages, contributions, and jettisons; contracts relating to marine insurance; and those between part owners of ships. But unless a contract be essentially maritime, the jurisdiction does not attach.(a)

It is not indispensable that the services, on which suit is brought, should have been performed at sea, the jurisdiction of the admiralty attaches when the services are performed on a ship in port where the tide ebbs and flows.(b) Seamen employed on board of steamboats and lighters, engaged in trade or commerce on tide-water, are within the admiralty jurisdiction;(c) wages may, therefore, be recovered in the admiralty by the pilot, deck-hands, engineer and fireman on board of a steamboat;(d) but unless the service of those employed contribute in navigating the vessel, or to its preservation, they cannot sue for their wages in the admiralty; musicians on board of a vessel, who are hired and employed as such, cannot, therefore, enforce a payment of their wages by a suit *in rem* in the admiralty.(e)

2. *Of the extraordinary jurisdiction of the district court as a court of admiralty.*

2626. This jurisdiction is vested in the district court by various acts of congress: 1, in cases under the laws of imposts, navigation or trade of the United States;

(a) The Jefferson, 10 Wheat. 428 ; Thackarey v. The Farmer, Gilp. 529.
(b) 10 Wheat. 428 ; Peyroux v. Howard, 7 Pet. 324.
(c) Thackarey v. Farmer of Salem, Gilp. 532 ; Wilson v. The Steamboat Ohio, Gilp. 505.
(d) Gilp. 505.
(e) Turner v. Boat Superior, Gilp. 516.

OF COURTS OF THE UNITED STATES. 121

No 2627   Book 4, tit 4, div. 2, chap 2, sec. 2, § 1, art. 1   No 2628.

2, in cases of captures within the territorial limits of the United States.

1° *Of seizures under the impost and navigation laws.*

2627. It is enacted by the judiciary act, section ninth, that the district court shall have exclusive original cognizance of all civil causes of admiralty and maritime jurisdiction, including all seizures under laws of impost, navigation, or trade of the United States, when the seizures are made on waters which are navigable from the sea, by vessels of ten or more tons burden, within their respective districts, as well as upon the high seas; saving to suitors, in all cases, the right of a common law remedy, when the common law is competent to give it.

Cases of this kind are properly civil causes of admiralty and maritime jurisdiction, and cognizable in the admiralty; and the court is to decide them without the aid of a jury.

The process does not touch the person of the offender, the proceeding is in the nature of a libel *in rem.*(a)

It is the place of seizure, and not the committing of the offence, that gives jurisdiction to the court;(b) for, until there has been a seizure, the forum cannot be ascertained.(c)

2° *Of captures within the territorial limits of the United States.*

2628. The admiralty jurisdiction expressly vested in the district court, embraces also captures made within the jurisdictional limits of the United States. The court is authorized to take cognizance of complaints, by whomsoever instituted, in case of captures made within the waters of the United States, or within a marine league of the coasts and shores thereof.(d)

(a) United States *v.* La Vengeance, 3 Dall. 297 ; The Samuel, 1 Wheat. 9.
(b) U. S. *v.* Schooner Betsy and Charlotte, 4 Cranch, 443 ; Keene *v.* The United States, 5 Cranch, 304.
(c) The Brig Ann, 9 Cranch, 289.
(d) Act of April 20, 1818, s. 7 ; and see act of June 5, 1794.

122 OF REMEDIES.

No. 2629.   Book 4, tit. 4, div 2, chap 2, sec. 2, § 1, art. 2, 3.   No. 2630.

Art. 2.—Of jurisdiction in cases of seizures on land, and of forfeitures.

2629. The civil jurisdiction of the district court extends to seizures on land, under the laws of the United States, and in suits for penalties and forfeitures incurred under those laws. The act gives the court exclusive original cognizance of all seizures made on land, and such waters of the United States which are not navigable by vessels of ten or more tons burden, within their respective districts, and of all suits for penalties and forfeitures, as are incurred under the laws of the United States.(*a*)

In all cases of seizure made on land, the court sits as a court of common law, and its jurisdiction is entirely distinct from that exercised in cases of seizure on waters navigable by vessels of ten tons burden and upward.(*b*) Seizures of this kind are triable by jury; they are not cases of admiralty and maritime jurisdiction.(*c*)

Art. 3.—Of the jurisdiction of the court when an alien sues for a tort.

2630. The district court is also vested with jurisdiction, concurrent with the courts of the several states, or the circuit court, as the case may be, of all causes where an alien sues for a tort only, in violation of the law of nations, or of a treaty of the United States.(*d*) But, unless the case be in the admiralty, the suit of such alien must be against a citizen of a state; for, by the constitution, an alien's right to sue is restricted to that case.

(*a*) Act of September 24, 1789.
(*b*) 8 Wheat. 395.
(*c*) 4 Cranch, 443.
(*d*) Act of September 24, 1789, s. 9.

OF COURTS OF THE UNITED STATES. 123

No. 2631.   Book 4, tit. 4, div. 2, chap 2, sec 2, § 1, art. 4, 5.   No 2632.

Art. 4.—Of the jurisdiction of the court in suits by the United States.

2631. Jurisdiction is given to the district court to have cognizance, concurrent with the courts of the several states, and the circuit court, of all suits at common law, where the United States sue, and the matter in dispute amounts, exclusive of costs, to the sum or value of one hundred dollars.(*a*) And by a subsequent act,(*b*) cognizance is given to it, concurrent with the courts and magistrates of the several states, and the circuit courts of the United States, of all suits at common law, where the United States, or any officer thereof, under the authority of any act of congress, sue, although the debt, claim, or other matter in dispute shall not amount to one hundred dollars. These last words do not confine the jurisdiction given by this act to one hundred dollars, but prevent it from stopping at that sum; and, consequently, suits for sums over one hundred dollars are cognizable in the district, circuit and state courts, and before magistrates, in the cases here mentioned.

By virtue of this act, these tribunals have jurisdiction over suits brought by the postmaster general, for debts and balances due to the general post office.(*c*)

Art. 5.—Of jurisdiction by and against consuls.

2632. This court has jurisdiction by or against consuls and vice-consuls, exclusively of the courts of the several states, except for offences where other punishment than whipping not exceeding thirty stripes, a fine not exceeding one hundred dollars, or a term of imprisonment not exceeding six months, is inflicted. For offences above this description formerly the

(*a*) Act of September 24, 1789.
(*b*) Act of March 3, 1815, s. 4.
(*c*) 12 Wheat. 147; 2 Pet. 447.

124   OF REMEDIES.

No. 2633   Book 4, tit 4, div 2, chap 2, sec 2, § 1, art. 6   No. 2634.

circuit court only had jurisdiction in cases of consuls.(a) But by the act of August 23, 1842, the district courts have concurrent jurisdiction with the circuit courts, of all crimes and offences against the United States, the punishment of which is not capital. And by a late act(b) the punishment of whipping is abolished.

Art. 6.—Of the jurisdiction of the district courts in equity.

2633. By the first section of the act of February 13, 1807, the judges of the district courts of the United States shall have as full power to grant writs of injunction, to operate within their respective districts, as is now exercised by any of the judges of the supreme court of the United States, under the same rules, regulations, and restrictions, as are prescribed by the several acts of congress establishing the judiciary of the United States, any law to the contrary notwithstanding. *Provided*, that the same shall not, unless so ordered by the circuit court, continue longer than to the circuit next ensuing; nor shall an injunction be issued by a district judge in any case, where the party has had a reasonable time to apply to the circuit court for the writ.

2634. An injunction may be issued by the district judge under the act of March 3, 1820, §§ 4, 5, where proceedings have taken place by warrant and distress against a debtor to the United States or his sureties, subject by § 6, to appeal to the circuit court from the decision of such district judge in refusing or dissolving the injunction, if such appeal be allowed by a justice of the supreme court. On which, with an exception as to the necessity of an answer on the part of the United States, the proceedings are to be as in other cases.

(a) 5 S. & R. 545.
(b) Act of February, 28, 1839, s. 5.

Art. 7.—Of various points relating to jurisdiction of the district court.

2635.—1. The judiciary act vests authority in the judges of the district court to grant writs of *habeas corpus*, for the purpose of inquiry into the cause of commitment.

2636.—2. Other acts give them power to issue writs, take depositions, make rules, and the like. The acts of congress, already treated of, relating to the privilege of not being sued out of the district of which the defendant is an inhabitant, or in which he is found; restricting suits by assignees; and various other provisions, apply to the district court as well as to the circuit court.

2637.—3. By the ninth section of the judiciary act the trial of issues in fact in the district courts, in all causes, except causes of admiralty and maritime jurisdiction, shall be by jury.

§ 2.—Of the criminal jurisdiction of the district courts.

2638. By the act of August 23, 1842, s. 3, it is enacted, that the district courts of the United States shall have concurrent jurisdiction with the circuit courts, of all crimes and offences against the United States, the punishment of which is not capital.

SECTION 3.—OF THE JURISDICTION OF SPECIAL DISTRICT COURTS.

2639. There is a class of district courts of a peculiar description. These exercise the power of a circuit court, under the same regulations as they were formerly exercised by the district court of Kentucky, which was the first of the kind.

The act of September 24, 1789, s. 10, gives the district court of the Kentucky district, besides the usual jurisdiction of a district court, the jurisdiction of all causes, except of appeals and writs of error, there-inafter made cognizable in a circuit court, and writs of error and appeals were to lie from decisions therein to the supreme court, and under the same regulations. By the 12th section, authority was given to remove cases from a state court to such court, in the same manner as to a circuit court.

———

CHAPTER III.—OF THE TERRITORIAL COURTS.

2640. The courts of the organized territories of the United States, are established by the acts of congress establishing such territories. The courts thus esta-blished are generally the same in all the territories. In each of them there are,

1. A supreme court, composed of a chief justice and a number of associate justices, who have an appellate jurisdiction, and a general supervision of all the other courts in the territory. The court appoint their own clerk, and admit attorneys and counsellors to practice. The marshal of the territory executes the mandates of the court.

2. The territory is divided into districts, and in each district there is a court called the district court. A clerk is appointed by the court, and attorneys and counsellors are admitted. The marshal executes their process. The court in each district is held by one of the judges of the supreme court.

The district courts have the same jurisdiction in all cases arising under the constitution and laws of the United States, as is vested in the circuit and district courts of the United States. Writs of errors and appeals from the final decisions of the said courts, in all such cases may be made to the supreme court of the territory.

These courts exercise jurisdiction in all cases under the laws of the territorial legislature.

3. Besides these, there are probate courts, for proving last wills and granting letters of administration on the estates of persons deceased.

4. Jurisdiction is also given in certain cases to justices of the peace.

TITLE V.—OF THE COURTS IN THE SEVERAL STATES.

2641. Besides the courts of the United States, established by the national constitution, each state has an independent judiciary, with the exception of the power of removing certain cases from the state courts into the circuit courts of the United States, and the supervisionary jurisdiction of the supreme court of the United States in cases involving constitutional questions. The state courts are all established by their respective constitutions, with definite powers.

A review of the judicial system of each state, could only give an abstract of the several constitutions. This can best be studied by reading the constitutions themselves, which are accessible to every one.

TITLE VI.—OF ACTIONS IN GENERAL.

2642. Actions are sometimes divided into criminal and civil. A *criminal action* is a prosecution in a competent court of justice, in the name of the government, against one or more individuals, who are accused of having committed a crime. This does not belong to our subject.

2643. A *civil action* is one prosecuted for the recovery of a right or the redress of an injury. It

is a legal demand of one's right in a court of justice,
in the form prescribed by law; or it is a suit given by
law for the recovery of what is due.(a)   The term
action includes the whole course of legal proceedings
to obtain the redress for a civil injury.   Until judgment, the proceeding is properly called an action, but
not after, and therefore, a release of all actions, is
regularly no bar to an execution.(b)

The term *suit* is sometimes used instead of action.
Under the judiciary act of 1789, the word suit applies
to any proceeding in a court of justice, in which the
plaintiff pursues, in such court, the remedy which the
law affords him; in this sense an application for a
prohibition is, therefore, a suit.(c)

A distinction is sometimes made by applying the
term action to proceedings at law, and suit to those
in equity; thus we say an action at law and a suit in
equity.

Actions differ as they have for their object the
recovery of land, without damages, when they are
called *real actions;* when they are instituted to recover
some specific article of personal property, wrongfully
withheld from the plaintiff by the defendant, or a
compensation in money for an injury sustained, which
compensation is technically called *damages;* they are
then called *personal actions.*   When the object of the
action is the recovery of real estate and damages
for the illegal detention, they are denominated *mixed
actions.*

CHAPTER I.—OF REAL ACTIONS.

2644. *Real actions* are those brought for the specific

(a) Co. Litt. 285; 3 Bl. Com. 116.
(b) Co. Litt. 289, a.
(c) 2 Pet. 449. In its most extended sense, the word suit, includes not
only a civil action, but also a criminal prosecution, as an indictment, an
information, and a conviction before a magistrate. Ham. N. P. 270. See
Steph. on Pl. 427.

recovery of lands, tenements, or hereditaments.(a) They are either *droitural*, when the plaintiff, in these actions called the *demandant*, seeks to recover the property; or *possessory*, when he endeavors to recover the possession.(b)   Real actions are, 1, writs of right; 2, writs of entry; 3, writs ancestral.

By these actions, formerly, all disputes concerning real estates were decided, but now they are pretty generally laid aside in practice, on account of the great nicety required in their management, and the inconvenient length of their process; a much more expeditious method of trying titles, having been introduced by other actions, personal and mixed.

CHAPTER II.—OF PERSONAL ACTIONS.

2645. *Personal actions* are those brought for the specific recovery of goods and chattels, or for damages, or other redress for breach of contract, or other injuries of every description, the specific recovery of lands, tenements or hereditaments, only excepted.   Considered, 1, as to their *cause*, personal actions are *ex contractu*, or arising out of contracts, and *ex delicto*, or to redress some wrong or injury; 2, as to the *place* where they are to be tried, they are *local* or *transitory*; 3, as to the *object* pursued, they are *in personam* or *in rem*.

SECTION 1.—OF ACTIONS *ex contractu* AND *ex delicto*.

2646.—1. An action *ex contractu* is one which arises on a contract, and is brought for the recovery of damages, or of a thing which belongs to the plaintiff. These actions are account, assumpsit, covenant, debt, and detinue.   In Connecticut and Vermont there is an

(a) Steph. Pl. 3.   (b) Finch's Law, 257.

action used which is peculiar to those states, called an action of *book debt.*(*a*)

2647.—2. Personal actions in form *ex delicto*, which are principally for the redress of wrongs and injuries unconnected with contract, are case, trover, detinue, replevin and trespass. .

SECTION 2.—OF LOCAL AND TRANSITORY ACTIONS.

2648.—1. A *local* action is one in which the venue must still be laid in the county in which the cause of action actually arose. The present locality of action is founded, in some cases, on common law principles, and, in others, on positive enactments of statute law. Those which continue local by the common law, are—

1st. All actions in which the subject or thing to be recovered is in its nature local. Of this class are real actions, actions of waste, when brought on the statute of Gloucester, to recover with damages the place wasted, or the *locus in quo;* and actions of ejectment. All these are local, because they are brought to recover the seisin or possession of lands or tenements, which are local subjects.

2dly. Various actions, which do not seek the direct recovery of lands and tenements, are also local, by the common law; because they arise out of some local subject, or are in violation of some local right or interest. Within this class of cases are many'actions in which only pecuniary damages are recoverable; such are the common law action of waste, and trespass *quare clausum fregit;* and so are trespass on the case, for injuries affecting things real, as nuisances to houses or lands; disturbance of right of way; obstruction or

---

(*a*) In New York, Louisiana, California, and perhaps some other states, the forms of actions mentioned in the text have been abolished. The more simple division of actions on contracts and actions to redress injuries has been adopted.

diversion of water courses, and the like.(*a*) The action of replevin also, though it lies for damages only, and does not arise out of any violation of a local right, is nevertheless local.(*b*) The reason of its locality is the necessity of giving a local description of the taking complained of.(*c*)

2649.—2. The *transitory* are those personal actions which seek nothing more than the recovery of money or personal chattels, whether they sound in contract or in tort;(*d*) because actions of this kind are, in most instances, founded on the violation of rights which, in contemplation of law, have no locality. And it is true as a general position, that actions, *ex delicto*, in which a mere personalty is recoverable, are, by the common law, transitory; except when founded upon, or arising out of, some *local* subject.(*e*)

The venue in a transitory action may be laid in any county which the plaintiff may prefer.(*f*)

SECTION 3.—OF ACTIONS *in personam* AND ACTIONS *in rem*.

2650.—1. An action *in personam*, is one where the proceedings are *against the person*, in contradistinction to those which are against specific things or *in rem*.

2. An action *in rem* is one instituted *against the thing*, in contradistinction to personal actions, which are said to be *in personam*.

One of the most striking diversities between actions *in personam* and actions *in rem*, is, that the former follow the person liable; and the latter follow the thing which is their object, without reference to the person of the possessor.(*g*)

<hr>

(*a*) Gould on Pl. c. 3, § 105 ; 1 Chit. Pl. 271.
(*b*) 1 Saund. 347, note 1. But in Pennsylvania, replevin is a transitory action. Powell *v.* Smith, 2 Watts, 126.
(*c*) Gould on Pl. c. 3, § 111.
(*d*) Com. Dig. Actions, N 12.
(*e*) Gould on Pl. c. 3, § 112.
(*f*) Bac. Ab. Actions Local, etc. A (a).
(*g*) La Vengeance, 3 Dall. 297.

Courts of admiralty enforce the performance of a contract by seizing into their custody the very object of hypothecation; for, in these cases, the parties are not personally bound, and the proceedings are confined to the thing in specie.(*a*)

There are cases, however, when the remedy is either *in personam* or *in rem*, at the choice of the plaintiff. Seamen, for example, may proceed against the ship or cargo for their wages, and this is the most expeditious mode; or they may proceed against the master and owners.(*b*)

CHAPTER III.—OF MIXED ACTIONS.

2651. *Mixed actions* are such as appertain, in some degree, to both the former classes, and, therefore, are properly reducible to neither of them, being brought for the specific recovery of land, tenements or hereditaments, and for damages sustained for injury in respect to such property.(*c*)

Of this kind are ejectment and waste.

TITLE VII.—OF PARTIES TO ACTIONS.

2652. There are three constituent parts to every action, the *judex*, judicial power, or the court; the *actor*, or plaintiff, who complains of an injury done; the *reus*, or defendant, who is called upon to make satisfaction for it. Having examined the constitutions and powers of the court and the general nature of actions, it will be natural, now, to inquire into

---

(*a*) 2 Bro. Civ. and Adm. Law, 98.
(*b*) 4 Burr. 1944; 2 Bro. Civ. and Adm. Law, 396.
(*c*) Co. Litt. 284; Steph. Pl. 3; Com. Dig. Actions, D 4.

qualities or rights which persons have to bring actions, and who may defend them.

2653. Those persons who institute actions for the recovery of their rights, and those against whom they are instituted, are called *parties to actions;* the former are called *plaintiffs,* and the latter *defendants.* The term parties includes all persons who are directly interested in the subject matter in issue, who have a right to control the proceedings, make a defence or appeal from the judgment. Persons not having these rights are regarded as strangers to the cause.(*a*)

2654. It is evident that no one can recover in an action if he has no right; and no recovery can be had against one who is not bound by his obligation, or liable for a wrong. The party who institutes an action must therefore have a right, and he against whom it is instituted must be liable to the plaintiff. It is of the utmost importance, then, in bringing actions to have proper parties, for, however just and meritorious the cause of action may be, if a mistake has been made in the selection of wrong persons, either as plaintiffs or defendants, or by including too many or too few persons as parties, the plaintiff may in general be defeated.(*b*)

2655. Actions are naturally divided into those which arise, upon contracts, and those which do not, but accrue to the plaintiff from some wrong or injury committed by the defendant. This title will, therefore, be divided into two chapters, under which will be considered, 1, the parties to actions arising upon contracts; and, 2, the parties to actions arising upon injuries and wrongs committed by the defendant, unconnected with contracts.

(*a*) 20 How. St. Tr. 538, n.

(*b*) Morse *v.* Chase 4 Watts, 456: McIntosh *v,* Long, 1 Penn. 274; Conolly *v.* Cottle, 1 Breese, 286; Baker *v.* Jewell, 6 Mass. 460; Dob *v.* Halsey, 16 John. 34; Ehle *v.* Purdy, 6 Wend. 629.

CHAPTER I.—OF PARTIES TO ACTIONS ARISING EX CONTRACTU.

2656. The most important consideration in the selection of parties to actions arising on contracts, is to ascertain who has a right to bring them, and, this being known, who is liable on the contract, and against whom the right of the plaintiff is to be enforced. The subject is, therefore, divided into two parts, which will be separately considered: 1, of the plaintiff in actions *ex contractu;* and, 2, of the defendant in such actions.

SECTION 1.—OF THE PLAINTIFFS IN ACTIONS *ex contractu.*

2657. This section will be divided by considering separately, how and by whom an action ought to be brought: 1, between the original parties, when there is but one plaintiff; 2, when there are several plaintiffs; 3, when the plaintiff, if a woman, has been married since the making of the contract; 4, when one or more of the obligees, who had a joint interest, is dead; 5, when the sole obligee, or, if there are more than one, when all the obligees, are dead; 6, when the contract has been assigned voluntarily; 7, when the obligee has become bankrupt or insolvent; 8, when the plaintiff is a foreign government; 9, when the plaintiff is a corporation.

§ 1.—Between the contracting parties.

2658. In general, as civil actions are brought to repair some loss sustained, the party to whose use the fruits of the suit are to be appropriated, and whose interests have, in fact, been impaired, should complain. This is, perhaps, the case in actions *ex delicto,* but the rule is not universal with regard to breaches of contract. In making a choice of a party plaintiff, the suitor should be guided by considering, not whose losses are to be repaired, but with whom the agreement has been made, for he alone can enforce the performance, and complain when the contract has been broken. The suit must be brought in the name of the party in whom the *legal interest* in such contract is vested; for courts of law consider only legal rights, and courts of equity are guided by other rules, when a question about an equitable right arises, by which they supersede legal rules. Hence no action at law lies by the *cestui que trust* against the trustee, and the latter may set up the legal estate against the former;(*a*) for where there are two kinds of estates in different persons, the one equitable and the other legal, the person having the equitable estate must call in aid the legal estate, before he can recover in a court of law.(*b*) When, therefore, a bond is given to Peter in trust for Paul, the former must sue thereon, although the latter has an equity to use his name.(*c*) But when there is no trust, and the obligation is made with one agreeing to pay money to another, as when a promise, not under seal, was with A to pay B a sum of money, the latter may sustain an action.(*d*)

2659. It is a rule, that when a deed is *inter partes*, a stranger cannot sue upon a covenant therein, though for his benefit.(*e*) Every deed is in one sense *inter partes*, since none can be valid to which there are not proper. sides or parties; but this expression has a technical sense in which alone it is here used; it means an agreement professing in the outset, and before the stipulations are introduced, to be made between such

---

(*a*) In Pennsylvania, the cestui que trust may maintain ejectment.
(*b*) Doe d. Shewen *v.* Wroot, 5 East, 137.
(*c*) Offley *v.* Warde, 1 Lev. 235 ; Saunders *v.* Filley, 12 Pick. 554 ; Watson *v.* Cambridge, 15 Mass. 286 ; Weathers *v.* Ray, 4 Dana, 474.
(*d*) 1 Chit. Pl. 4 ; 3 B. & P. 149, n. a. ; Felton *v.* Dickinson, 10 Mass. 287 ; Cabot *v.* Hasgins, 3 Pick. 83. In New York, every action must be prosecuted in the name of the party in interest, except in the cases of an executor or administrator, a trustee of an express trust, or a person expressly authorized by statute, without joining with him the persons for whose benefit the suit is brought. Code of Procedure, §§ 91, 93.
(*e*) Co. Litt. 231.

and such persons. When the deed is not *inter partes*, he may sue whether it be indented or not.(*a*)

2660. When a man covenants with two or more persons, using words which *prima facie* import a joint covenant, but which nevertheless admit of being construed severally, there, if the interest and cause of action of each of the covenantees appears on the face of the deed to be several, the words will be taken disjunctively, and the covenant will be construed to be a several covenant with each, and each covenanter may bring an action for his several damages;(*b*) therefore, when a covenant though joint in its terms, was for the payment of an annuity to each of two persons, it was held that the interests of the covenantees were several, and that they should sue separately on the covenant.(*c*)

2661. When an action is brought on a simple contract, whether verbal or written, the plaintiff should be the person from whom the consideration actually moved.(*d*) And when there are several parties, and both the consideration and the beneficial interest are several, then the contract is several to each. Where, therefore, three gave a bond binding themselves, jointly and severally, to indemnify another, and two paid the damnification, it was held they could not join in suing the third for contribution.(*e*) But although the consi-

---

(*a*) 1 Chit. Pl. 4. Vide ante, n. 2005.

(*b*) Lane *v*. Drinkwater, 1 Cr. M. & R. 612.

(*c*) Withers *v*. Bircham, 3 B. & Co. 254.

(*d*) Crow *v*. Rogers, 1 Str. 592. See Archer *v*. Dunn, 2 W. & S. 237.

(*e*) Kelby *v*. Steel, 5 Esp. 194; Brand *v*. Boulcott, 3 B. & P. 235; Lombard *v*. Cobb, 2 Shepl. 222; Boggs *v*. Custin, 10 S. & R. 211; Graham *v*. Green, 4 Hayes, 188; Williams *v*. Alley, Cooke, 257; Vaughan *v*. Campbell, Mart. & Yerg. 63; Gould *v*. Gould, 6 Wend. 263; S. C. 8 Cowen, 168; Doremus *v*. Selden, 19 John. 213. In a case where the sureties paid the debt jointly by giving a joint note, they were allowed to join in an action against the principal. Appleton *v*. Bascom, 3 Met. 169; Chandler *v*. Brainard, 14 Pick. 285. In Ohio, by a statute, when a joint judgment is recovered against sureties, they must join in an action for reimbursement. Litter *v*. Horsey, 2 Ham. 209.

deration has moved separately from each, still if the legal interest is joint, the legal right is in all, and they must be joined as plaintiffs.(a)   In such case any one of the obligees, payees, or the assignee of one of them, may sue in the name of all, without their consent.(b)

When a note was made payable to A *or* B, it was held that A might maintain an action in his own name.(c)

2662. Tenants in common of land are in general ⌐ entitled to the rent, each for his share, so that each may make a separate distress or maintain a separate action.(d)   But where they have made a joint demise, unless the rent has been reserved to each for his share separately, they must join in an action for its recovery.(e)

2663. When the contract is entered into by an agent, the principal has, in general, alone the right to sue.(f)   But where an agent for the sale of goods contracts in his own name, and as a principal, the general rule is, that the action, on such contract, may be maintained, either in the name of the party by whom the contract was made, and who was, therefore, privy to it, or of the party on whose behalf and for whose benefit it was made; the former suing in respect of his privity, and the latter of his interest.

In such a case, the right of suit vested in the agent, is subject to the right of interference of the undisclosed principal; and if the defendant has acquired a right of set off against the agent, with whom he dealt without knowing the principal, he can claim that right

---

(a) 1 Roll. Ab. 31, pl. 9; Bac. Ab. B. 2, s. 1, Bouv. ed.
(b) Wright *v.* McLemore, 10 Yerg. 235.   See Gray *v.* Wilson, 1 Meigs, 394.
(c) 2 McLean, 139.
(d) Harrison *v.* Barnby, 5 T. R. 246: Com. Dig. Abatement, (E 10);
Martin *v.* Crompe, 1 Ld. Raymd. 340; Powis *v.* Smith, 5 B. & Ald. 851.
(e) Com. Dig. Abatement. (E 10).
(f) Scrimshire *v.* Alderton, Str. 1182.

against the principal, in the same way as if the agent had been the plaintiff on the record.(a)

When the contract by the agent is made by deed, and he is nominally a party to it, though in reality as agent for another, he alone can sue thereon.(b)

2664. The consignee of goods is considered as the owner of them, subject to the right of the vendor or consignor to stop them *in transitu*, and an action against a carrier for the loss of them must, in general, be brought in the name of the consignee, and not of the consignor,(c) except under special circumstances.(d)

2665. An infant may sue on a contract entered into with him, but he must sue either by guardian or *prochein ami*, who are to appear for him; a *prochein ami*, however, is not a party to the suit, but simply a person appointed by the court to look after the interests of the infant and to manage the case for him.(e)

2666. A person *non compos mentis* may maintain an action, which should be brought in his own name, and not in that of his committee.(f)

§ 2.—Of the number of plaintiffs who must join.

2667. When it has been ascertained who has the legal right to sue on a contract, the next question is to know whether others are not equally concerned with himself; for it is a rule that when the contract was made with several, whether it was under seal or by parol, if their legal interests were joint, they must all, if living, join in the action for the breach of the contract.(g)

(a) George v. Clagget, 7 T. R. 359; Carr v. Hinchliff, 4 B. & C. 547.
(b) See Shack v. Anthony, 1 M. & S. 573.
(c) Dawes v. Beck, 8 T. R. 330; Fragano v. Long, 4 B. & C. 219.
(d) Joseph v. Knox, 3 Camp, 320. See McIntyre v. Browne, 1 John. 221; Ludlow v. Bowne, 1 John. 1; Evans v. Nichols, 4 Scott, N. R. 43.
(e) Sinclair v. Sinclair, 13 M. & W. 640.
(f) Cooks v. Darson, Hob. 215; Thorn v. Coward, 2 Sid. 124.
(g) 1 Saund. 153, note 1; Yelv. 177, note (1); 8 S. & R. 308; 10 S. & R. 257; Anderson v. Martindale, 1 East, 497, 501; Thimblethorpe v. Hardesty, 7 Mod. 116.

All the partners of a firm must join as plaintiffs for the breach of a contract made with the partnership by third persons, because they are all jointly interested. And even where goods belonging to a firm, were sold by one of the partners in his own name, all must join in an action for the price of them.(*a*) In considering who are entitled to sue on such contract, reference must be had to the time when it was made, for subsequently admitted partners should not be joined, even though under an agreement to share in the profits and losses from a period antecedent to the contract.(*b*)

A nominal partner need not be joined in suing on a contract to which he was a stranger ;(*c*) but it is necessary to show distinctly that he had no interest either in the partnership or in the particular transaction.(*d*)

With regard to a dormant partner, he may be joined or not, at the election · of the ostensible partner,(*e*) when the purchaser or defendant dealt with the latter.(*f*)

Joint tenants being seised *per my et per tout*, and deriving by one and the same title, must sue jointly on their joint lease, and must join in debt and avowry for rent.(*g*)

Tenants in common may join or sever in an action on a contract relating to their estate, though they must sever in an avowry for rent.(*h*)

When a contract is made with several persons jointly and severally to them all, either all must join,

---

(*a*) Halliday *v.* Doggett, 6 Pick. 359.   But see contra, Glancy *v.* French, 1 Blackf. 353.

(*b*) Wilsford *v.* Wood, 1 Esp. 183.

(*c*) Kell *v.* Nainby. 10 B. & C. 20; Glossop *v.* Coleman, 1 Stark. 25.

(*d*) Tood *v.* Elworthy, 14 East, 210.

(*e*) Leveck *v.* Shaftoe, 2 Esp. 268 ; Wilkes *v.* Clark, 1 Dev. 178; Shropshire *v.* Shepperd, 3 Ala. 733.

(*f*) Lord *v.* Baldwin, 6 Pick. 348.

(*g*) Bac. Ab. Joint tenants, K ; Com. Dig. Abatement, (Eq.)

(*h*) Bac. Ab. Joint tenants, K ; Co. Litt. 180.

140   - OF REMEDIES.

No. 2668   Book 4, tit. 7, chap 1, sec 1, § 3, art. 1.   No. 2669.

or only one must sue; if, for example, the contract were to pay to A, B and C, three hundred dollars, or to each of them one hundred dollars, either of the payees might sue for his share of one hundred, but two of them could not bring a joint action to recover two hundred dollars.(a)   •

§ 3.—In case of a female obligee who marries.

2668. By the marriage, a woman comes so much under the power and control of her husband, that while the marriage subsists she can bring no suit without his consent, if for no other reason than that he is liable for the costs in case of failure. This will lead us to consider, 1, when the husband and wife must join; 2, when the husband may sue alone; 3, when the wife may sue alone; 4, when the husband and wife may join or not, at their election; 5, when the husband survives the wife; 6, when the wife survives the husband; 7, effect of the dissolution of the marriage, *lis pendens.*

Art. 1.—*When the husband and wife must join.*

2669. At common law the effect of marriage is to merge the separate existence of the wife, during coverture, into that of her husband, and to vest in him a right to the rents and profits of his wife's real estate, the interest in her chattels real, and the power of disposing of them, except by will; the right of reducing into possession her chattels real and her choses in action, and an absolute property in the rest of her personal estate in possession; and where property, real or personal, falls to the wife during the coverture, the husband acquires a similar right therein.

To have this effect the marriage must subsist *de jure;* proof of the existence of that relation will be inferred in all civil cases, save one, from it appearing to do so.

(a) Broom on Part. § 23.   See Southcote *v.* Hoare, 3 Taunt. 90.

To entitle himself to recover an action for criminal conversation, he must prove his marriage with the woman, by direct testimony.

The causes for which they must join, are those in which the wife claims in her own right, *in suo jure;* and where she claims in the right of others, *in alieno jure.*

1. *For causes in suo jure.*

2670. These causes arose either before or during the coverture.

1. In suing for causes which accrued to the wife in her own right *before* the coverture, she must be˘ invariably joined.(*a*)

2. For a cause of action arising *during* the coverture, where it accrued to her alone, and in her own right, she must be joined. And where a cause of action has arisen during the coverture, and it confers a right which will, when reduced to possession, belong jointly to the husband and wife, she must join in the suit for it; for example, when the wife is the *meritorious* cause of action, as if a bond or other contract under seal be made to her alone, or to her and her husband jointly, or in the case of her personal labor, if there is an express promise to her, or to her and her husband, she may be joined with her husband or he may sue alone.(*b*)   They must sue jointly on a breach of a covenant running with the land, of which they are joint assignees.(*c*)

2. *For causes in alieno jure.*

2671. These causes, as those mentioned under the last division, arise either before or during coverture.

1. For causes of action which arose *in alieno jure before* coverture, the wife must, in all cases, be joined.

(*a*) Morse *v.* Earle, 13 Wend. 271.
(*b*) Mitchinson *v.* Hawson, 7 T. R. 348.
(*c*) Middlemore *v.* Goodale, Cro. Car. 503.

2. When the cause of action has arisen *during* the coverture, she may be joined or not, according to circumstances. In general, when the wife is executrix or administratrix, as her interest is in *auter droit*, they must join in the actions; as, if a debtor to the estate has paid the debt to a third person, to pay to the wife, she must be joined in suing the receiver to recover it. But had it been paid under the husband's authority, he must have sued alone.(*a*)

Art. 2.—When the husband may sue alone.

2672. When a cause of action, in which the wife does not share, arises during the coverture, the husband must sue for it alone. In general, the wife cannot join in any action upon a contract made during coverture, as for work and labor, money lent, or goods sold by her during that time; and the husband may sue alone for the breach of contracts, in which, though in terms they have been made with the wife, as well as the husband, she does not share; as, of a promise by her debtor to pay the sum owing at a certain day, in consideration of forbearance of the husband.(*b*) And when the husband appointed an attorney to receive money due upon his wife's chose in action, and the attorney actually received the money, the husband alone must sue the attorney, and the wife cannot be joined in the action.(*c*)

Art. 3.—When the wife may sue alone.

2673. When the husband is *civiliter mortuus*, or has abandoned the country for so long a time that the law raises a presumption of his death, the wife may sue alone; but his absence, for only five years without

---

(*a*) Anon. 1 Salk. 282.
(*b*) Ankerstein *v.* Clark, 4 T. R. 616; Willis *v.* Nurse, 1 A. & E. 65, 72; Nurse *v.* Willis, 4 B. & Ad. 739.
(*c*) Hill *v.* Boyer, 17 Verm. 190.

being heard from, is not sufficient to enable the wife to sue alone.(a)

Art. 4.—When the husband and wife may join or not, at their election.

2674. When a cause of action, shared by husband and wife, has arisen during the coverture, if the right it confers, will, when reduced to possession, belong wholly to the husband, he may either sue for it by himself, or jointly with his wife. The husband may, therefore, sue by himself, or jointly with his wife, for the breach, during coverture, of simple agreements with his wife *dum sola;* for the breach of one given to her during coverture, and in which she is legally interested; for the breach of deeds, made with her before marriage or since; for arrears of rent, or breach of covenants, annexed to a reversion granted to both; or to a lease, by both, of wife's land.

In a case where an action by a woman for a breach of promise of marriage was compromised by the plaintiff's attorney, and he not knowing that she was then married to another person, and the defendant being also ignorant of such marriage, took a note payable to her in her maiden name, it was held the husband might alone maintain an action on the note, without joining his wife.(b)

Art. 5.—When the husband survives the wife.

2675. When the husband survives, he is entitled to the chattels real of the wife, by the right of survivorship, and also to all rents and profits accruing from her estate during the coverture; he is also entitled to all chattels given to the wife in her own right, during the coverture. To entitle himself to the choses in action of the wife, which have not been reduced to

(a) Tucker v. Scott, 2 Penn. 955.
(b) Templeton v. Crum, 5 Greenl. 417.

possession, the husband must, at common law, become the administrator of his wife, and recover them in that capacity.

Art. 6.—*When the wife survives the husband.*

2676. When the wife survives, she becomes entitled immediately to all her rights *in suo jure,* and *in alieno jure.*

1. She is entitled *in suo jure* to rights which accrued to her, 1, before the marriage, and which remain unsatisfied; and 2, since.

First, she is entitled to all chattels real which her husband had in her right, and which he did not dispose of in his lifetime, and to arrears of rent, which she was entitled to before the coverture, and which the husband did not reduce to possession.

Secondly, the wife will be entitled to all the rent accruing from a demise of her lands, made by herself and husband during the coverture, but she is not bound to confirm such lease. When she joins her husband in making a lease of her lands, the lease will be good during the coverture, but she may disaffirm such lease on again becoming *sui juris.* If, however, she once acknowledges that the lease was made with her free will, by confirming it expressly or by implication, as by receiving rent, due since the dissolution of the marriage, she cannot retract it. The wife is also entitled to a judgment, which was obtained in the joint names of her husband and herself, whether obtained for a debt due to the wife while sole, or upon a contract made with her during coverture, when she was the meritorious cause of action.(*a*)

2. As the husband had no actual interest in the property which the wife held *in alieno jure,* it follows

(*a*) Com. Dig. Baron & Feme, F 1; Bidgood *v.* Wray, 2 Bl. R. 1239.

that causes of action for such property, necessarily remain to her after his death.

Art. 7.—*Effect of marriage and its dissolution, lis pendens.*

2677.—1. When a suit is instituted by a single woman, or by her and others, and, while it is pending, she marries, the suit abates.(*a*)

2678.—2. When a suit is brought by husband and wife, in right of the wife, and, *lis pendens*, the husband dies, it will not abate, and the wife may proceed to judgment and execution, the death of the husband being suggested upon the record.

§ 4.—In the case of executors and administrators.

2679. In considering the persons who have the right to sue as executors or administrators, it will be requisite to examine, 1, the case of executors; and, 2, the case of administrators.

Art. 1.—*Of executors.*

2680. Executors are either rightful or wrongful.

1. *Of rightful executors.*

2681. It is evident that none but rightful executors can sue, for no man is allowed to take advantage of his own wrong. These rightful executors may be considered, 1, as to their kinds, or as absolute or conditional; 2, as to their numbers, or as sole or many; 3, as to the effect of their deaths.

1° *As to the kind of rightful executors.*

2682.—1. As to their kinds, executors are *absolute*, when appointed without any condition whatever by the will of the testator; these have the right to bring suits on all the mere personal contracts of the deceased, not running with the land, when he was the sole party

(*a*) 1 Chit. Pl. 437.

to the contract; and when he was one of several obligees, then the suit is to be brought by the surviving obligee, and in case of his death by the executor of the survivor, and the personal representatives of the partner who first died are not to be joined with him.(a)

2683.—2. A *conditional* or limited executor is one who is appointed for a limited time, or for a special purpose, as where he is appointed until the testator's son shall arrive at full age. He has similar rights, during the time in which he may serve, as an absolute executor, and a suit brought by him does not abate.(b)

2° As to the number of rightful executors.

2684.—1. When there is but *one* executor appointed, he has the whole management of the estate, and he brings suit in his own name as executor.

2685.—2. When there are *several* executors, they must all join in the action, because the whole as a unit represent the testator. But their non-joinder can only be taken advantage of in abatement, after oyer of the probate letters testamentary, by pleading that the executor therein named is alive and not joined in the action.(c)

3° As to the effect of their death.

2686. When there is a single executor, and he dies testate, at common law his executor continues the representative character, and so he is the executor of the first testator;(d) the appointment is considered not that of the last, but of the first testator, who, by creating the other his representative, impliedly gave him authority to continue that character in any one he should appoint by his own will. This principle has been changed in several states, and there, on the death

---

(a) 1 Chit. Pl. 22.
(b) Vide Taynton *v.* Hanway, 3 B. & P. 26.
(c) 1 Saund. 291, g.
(d) Plowd. 525.

of the first testator, administration *de bonis non, cum testamento annexo,* is granted.

If there are two executors, and they assent, on the death of one of them the whole representation remains with the other, and, at his death, the effect is the same as if he had been sole. And though the surviving executor may at first have refused, he may upon that event, take upon him the execution of the will.

2. *Of an executor de son tort.*

2687. An executor *de son tort* has no official character; being in the wrong, he can maintain no action, for this, among other reasons, that an executor must make *profert* of the probate and letters testamentary, and having none, he cannot do it. To constitute one as an executor *de son tort,* the interference must possess these three qualities:

1. It must be *unlawful;* for claiming or even taking goods under a claim of title, or doing mere acts of humanity, such as locking up the property, attending to the funeral, feeding cattle, without more, will not make a man an executor *de son tort.*

2. It must be by *acts of ownership as such,* as taking goods, cancelling a bond, and the like, but a mere trespass over land is insufficient.

3. It must be not only unlawful and an act of ownership, but it must be done *before* probate or administration granted, for otherwise the act would be a trespass or other injury to the rightful executor.

There is another kind of wrongful executor where probate is granted to a forged will; but, in this case, till it has been avoided by the proper tribunal, it is unimpeachable; and even when avoided, all transactions under it stand good.(*a*)

Art. 2.—*Of administrators.*

2688. Administration may be rightful or wrongful.

(*a*) Allen *v.* Dundas, 3 T. R. 125.

148 OF REMEDIES.

No. 2689   Book 4, tit. 7, chap 1, sec. 1, § 4, art. 2.   No. 2695.

1. *Of rightful administrators.*

2689. Their kinds are absolute or conditional. As to their numbers they may be one or many. At their death the administration is at an end or not.

1° *Of the kind of rightful administrators.*

2690.—1. As to their kinds, administrations are *absolute* and unlimited, or they are limited. An unlimited absolute administrator has the full power and authority to claim all the personal property of the intestate, and to bring suits for its recovery.

2691.—2. As to *conditional* or limited administrations, the rules which govern in cases of conditional executorship, generally apply to these cases.

2° *As to the number of rightful administrators.*

2692.—1. When *one* only has been appointed, he fully represents the intestate.

2693.—2. When there are *several,* they must all join in bringing suits; and if one of them dies, the action must be in the name of the survivor.

3° *Death of rightful administrators.*

2694. When such an administrator is *sole,* and he dies, administration *de bonis non,* must be granted to another. When one of *several* administrators dies, the administration vests in the survivors.

2. *Of wrongful administrators.*

2695. An administration is wrongful and voidable, when granted to an improper person; but until revoked, in such case, it is valid. It is void when a will is afterward proved, or when it is granted to the estate of a man who is alive. The acts of an administrator are wholly void, and he can, therefore, bring no action. There cannot be an administrator of his own wrong.

§ 5.—When one of several obligees is dead.

2696. When several persons have a *joint legal* interest in a contract, not running with the land, and they are all living, they must join in an action for the breach of it. When one of them is dead, then the survivors must sue, and the executor of the deceased cannot be joined with them; in such case the declaration, and indeed the writ, ought to show the fact of the death.

In the case of a joint contract, the executor of the deceased cannot sue, although the beneficial interest was in his testator.(*a*)   But when the interest of the obligees is *several*, the executor of the deceased may maintain an action for the share which was due or owing to his testator.   It has been holden that where a contract was made to three who had a joint interest, and two of them were paid their shares, the third might afterward sue alone for his proportion;(*b*) in such case the executor would, upon principle, have the right to sue for such share.   The reason why such suit can be maintained, is, that the parties have agreed to sever the contract, and make what was a joint, a several agreement.

§ 6.—When the cause of action has been assigned.

2697. When the contract is assignable at law, the assignee should sue in his own name.   In general a simple or merely personal contract, being a mere chose in action, cannot be assigned; but for the promotion of commerce, many such contracts may be so assigned, such as bills of exchange, promissory notes for the payment of money, and by statute, bonds for the payment of money, mortgages, bail bonds, and replevin

(*a*) Peters *v.* Davis, 7 Mass. 257.
(*b*) Garret *v.* Taylor, 1 Esp. N. P. 117; Baker *v.* Jewell, 6 Mass. 460; Austin *v.* Walsh, 2 Mass. 401; Beach *v.* Hotchkiss, 2 Conn. 697.

150 OF REMEDIES.

No. 2698.   Book 4, tit. 7, chap. 1, sec. 1, § 7, 8.   No. 2702.

bonds, so as to convey to the assignee the right to sue in his own name. And covenants running with the land pass with the tenure, though not made with assigns.

2698. Though not assignable at law, most choses in action are assignable in equity, and the assignee may sue on them in the name of the assignor, for his own use, without the consent of the assignor; but in these cases the defendant, in general, has a right to set off any just claim he had against the assignor at the time he first had notice of the assignment.

2699. For a breach of a covenant running with an estate in land, an assignee of such estate must be the plaintiff, for any breach committed *after* the assignment, and this without proving any attornment, but the assignee is not entitled to an action for any breach *before* the assignment.

2700. When the reversion has been assigned in several parts, or when it descends to several heirs, each is entitled to his proportion of the rent, and may maintain a separate action upon it.

§ 7.—In case of bankruptcy or insolvency.

2701. When a party to a contract becomes bankrupt, or is discharged under the insolvent laws, all his estate is assigned by operation of law, and vested in assignees. Unlike voluntary assignees of choses in actions not assignable at law, they in all cases are entitled to the legal right to sue on a contract made by the bankrupt or insolvents in their own names.

§ 8.—When a foreign government is entitled to sue.

2702. To entitle a *foreign government* to sue in its own name, it must have been recognized by the government of the United States.(a)

(a) 3 Wheat. 324; Story, Eq. Pl. § 55.

§ 9. When a corporation is entitled to sue.

2703. A corporation may sue in its corporate name on all contracts made on its behalf by its officers or agents;(a) and if a mistake has been made in its name in making the contract, it may sue in its true name,(b) and it can sue only in the name and style given to it by law.(c)

In general, a corporation chartered by the laws of one state can sue in the courts of another.(d)

A corporation aggregate not being in its corporate capacity a *citizen*, cannot sue in the courts of the United States a citizen of another state than the one in which it is located; but the court will look behind its corporate name, and if it be composed exclusively of the citizens of one state, it may sue a citizen of another state in those courts.(e)

Two corporations may join in an action to recover a joint claim, as where money was deposited in a bank to their joint names.(f) But although they may be tenants in common, if they can maintain each a separate action, they cannot join,(g)

SECTION 2.—OF DEFENDANTS IN ACTIONS *ex contractu.*

2704. This section will be divided as nearly as may be as the one which has immediately preceded it.

(a) Binney v. Plumley, 5 Verm. 500.
(b) Middleton v. McCormick, 2 Pen. 500; Hagerstown Turnpike v. Creeger, 5 H. & J. 122; Alloway's Creek v. String, 5 Halst. 323; Berks and Dauphin Co. v. Myers, 6 S. & R. 16.
(c) Porter v. Neckervis, 4 Rand. 359.
(d) Bank of Augusta v. Earle, 13 Pet. 519; Williamson v. Smoot, 7 Martin (Lo.) R. 31; Bank of Michigan v. Williams, 5 Wend. 478; Bac. Ab. Corporations, E 2, Bouv. ed.
(e) Hope Ins. Co. v. Boardman, 5 Cranch, 57; Bank of U. S. v. Deveaux, 5 Cranch, 61.
(f) Sharon Canal Co. v. Fulton Bank, 7 Wend. 412.
(g) Rehoboth and Seekonk v. Hunt, 1 Pick. 228.

152 OF REMEDIES.

No. 2705.   Book 4, tit. 7, chap. 1, sec. 2, § 1, art. 1.   No. 2706.

§ 1.—Between the original parties.

2705. At law, we have seen, a party cannot sue who has a mere equitable right; to entitle him to an action he must have a *legal right*. In order to sustain an action against a defendant, he must, therefore, be subject to a *legal liability*. A *cestui que trust* cannot, as such, sustain an action at law against his trustee, his remedy is in equity, unless otherwise provided for by the statutes of the states where the suit is brought; except, indeed, where the trustee has settled an account and the law raises, from that act, a promise to pay.(*a*) Under this present head our inquiries will be confined to the subject of liability *ex contractu*, and when only one person is liable. This liability will be considered with regard, 1, to simple contracts; 2, to contracts under seal; 3, to debts of record.

Art. 1.—*Of liability on simple contracts.*

2706.—1. The party upon an *express* contract, is he by whom it was concluded, and this, though the consideration inured to another's advantage, and the suit must in general be brought against him, whether it was made by him personally or by his agent.

The agent, when it clearly appears that he acted within the scope of his authority, and entered into the obligation or engagement in the name of his principal, is not liable on such contract. But where he concealed his principal, and acted in his own name, or where he entered into a personal obligation and engaged to fulfil the contract himself, as where he accepted a bill of exchange generally in his own name,(*b*) he is liable, unless in the case of a person acting in the capacity of agent for the government.(*c*)

(*a*) Bartlett *v.* Dimond, 14 Mees. & Wesb. 407.
(*b*) Thomas *v.* Bishop, Str. 955.
(*c*) Hodgson *v.* Dexter, 1 Cranch, 345.

OF PARTIES TO ACTIONS.   153

No. 2707.   Book 4, tit. 7, chap 1, sec. 2, § 1, art. 1.   No 2708.

An exception to this general rule is the case where the master of a ship, contracts for necessaries for his ship; he and his owners are both liable, if the necessaries were furnished abroad, or in this country, unless furnished on the credit of the owners; and he or his owners are liable upon a bill of lading, or for a loss of goods, unless the contract was made, not by the master, but the owners themselves.(a)

2707.—2. Upon *implied* contracts the party is equally liable as upon an express agreement.

In a policy of insurance, it is always understood, and, therefore, tacitly agreed, that the policy broker shall alone be liable to the underwriter for the premium, and that the assured shall pay it to the broker,(b) unless there has been some fraud or unfair dealing.

The consignor or shipper of goods is liable for the freight, and may, therefore, be sued for it, unless he stipulates to the contrary.(c)   But the consignee becomes liable for it, by accepting the goods,(d) for if he refuses the goods, he will not be liable unless upon his express contract, as if he ordered the shipment.(e) And so the indorsee of a bill of lading will also be liable by accepting the goods;(f) but this he must do as a principal, for in neither of these cases will the person who accepts the goods be liable, if he declares at the time of the acceptance that he acts as an agent.(g)

2708.—3. The *law* raises a contract, whenever any one obtains possession of another's property and unjustly detains it, whether he took it from the owner himself, or from a third person; and whether he knew at the time, that it belonged to another or not; as ₁

(a) Boson v. Sandford, Carth. 58.
(b) De Gaminde v. Pigou, 4 Taunt. 246.
(c) Moore v. Wilson, 1 T. R. 659.
(d) Cock v. Taylor, 2 Campb. 587; S. C. 13 East, 399.
(e) Christy v. Row, 1 Taunt. 300.
(f) 2 Campb. 587; 13 East, 399.
(g) 1 East, 507.

154   OF REMEDIES.

No. 2709   Book 4, tit. 7, chap. 1, sec. 2, § 2, art. 1   No. 2712.

where A took the goods of B, and sold them to C, B may sue A or C, at his choice, for goods sold.(a)

Art. '2·—Of liability on contracts under seal.

2709. The party to a deed, whether it be made by himself or his agent, is in general responsible as on a simple contract. But if the contract be made by an agent, and he covenants for the acts of another, though he describes himself as agent, he will be personally liable. As where he covenants in this form, "I A, agent and attorney in fact of B, do hereby covenant with C." For here the covenant is not that of B the principal, but of A, the agent or attorney.

Art. 3.—Of liability on debts of record.

2710. The defendant against whom a judgment has been recovered, must, if living, be sued thereon.

§ 2.—Of the number of defendants who must be joined.

2711. In the next place, let us inquire into the liability of several persons who have entered into a joint engagement.

Art. 1.—Of the joint liabilities on simple contracts.

2712.—1. When there are *several* obligors or contractors in a simple *express* contract, the rule is that all who in terms have *jointly* obliged themselves, are jointly liable, whether the form was a promising together, or after a promise by one, all binding themselves to observe it. Whenever the engagement is joint and several, the parties may all be sued jointly in one action, or each may be sued separately, but the plaintiff has not the choice of suing some, less than the whole, jointly; he must sue them separately, or sue all who are jointly bound and living.(b)

(a) Clarke v. Shee, Cowp. 197.
(b) 1 Saund. 153, note 1; Com. Dig. Obligation, G; Bac. Ab. Obligation D 4; Covenant D.

2713.—2. As instances of *implied* joint contract the following cases may be mentioned: where several persons, as a club, dine at a tavern, they are jointly chargeable with the entire reckoning, and not merely each for his share.(*a*) And where two employ an attorney to sue out a writ, there is an implied joint contract that they will pay him his fees.(*b*) But there may be an implied several contract, made by many, under certain circumstances.(*c*) On all implied contracts by a firm or partnership, all the partners must be sued.

Art. 2.—Of joint liabilities on contracts under seal.

2714. The rules in relation to express joint contracts are the same with independent contracts under seal. A man will not be held to be a party to a deed, whose name is introduced into it as a co-contractor, unless he sealed and delivered it, for the execution of it by his companion without authority, is not binding on him. A joint delivery does not make that a joint deed, which in its terms is several, nor vice versa.(*d*)

Art. 3.—Of joint liabilities on debts of record.

2715. When a judgment has been rendered, against two or more, the liability is always joint, and the original demand which is merged in it will make no difference, whether it was joint or not.(*e*) But a distinction must be observed between a judgment rendered on a right which becomes merged, and a judgment in *scire facias*, which is a mere award of execution. In the latter case the original right is not merged. Therefore, when a judgment in *scire facias*

(*a*) Forster *v.* Taylor, 3 Camph. 49. See Wathen *v.* Sandys, 2 Campb. 640.
(*b*) Ld. Raym. 127.
(*c*) Brown *v.* Doyle, 3 Campb. 51.
(*d*) 2 Roll. Ab. 148, 149.
(*e*) King *v.* Hoare, 13 Mees. & W. 506.

156   OF REMEDIES.

No. 2716.   Book 4, tit. 7, chap. 1, sec. 2, § 2, art. 4.   No. 2716.

has been given against two, bail on their recognizance, debt lies afterward against one only, since it is sued on the recognizance not the judgment.(a)

Art. 4.—Of the persons who cannot be joined on account of their liabilities.

2716. When, by the terms of the contract, the contractors are only severally bound, they cannot be joined in the same action, though the parties may stand in the same relative situations.(b) It must, therefore, appear upon the face of the proceedings in an action *ex contractu*, that their contract was joint, and the fact must be proved on the trial. If too many persons are joined, and the action cannot be supported as to some of them, it will fail as to the whole; when such defect appears upon the pleadings, the defendants may take advantage of it by demurrer, motion in arrest of judgment, or by writ of error; and when it does not appear, and the plaintiff cannot sustain his allegation by proof, he will be nonsuited upon the trial.

When one, of several defendants is not liable in point of law, as in the case of an infant or married woman, and he is included with those who are sued, the plaintiff will be nonsuited, because the contract at the time it was entered was not binding on them; but if one of the defendants, having been liable, becomes discharged by some after act, as by bankruptcy, the plaintiff may enter a *nolle prosequi* as to him. When the action is brought only against the persons who are responsible in point of law, and the defendants plead in abatement the non-joinder of such a person, as an infant or a feme covert, the plaintiff may reply the infancy or coverture.

(a) Williams v. Green, 8 Mod. 295 ; Gee v. Fane, 1 Lev. 225.
(b) Berkley v. Presgrave, 1 East, 226.

OF PARTIES TO ACTIONS. 157

No. 2717   Book 4, tit. 7, chap 1, sec. 2, § 3, art. 1, 2   No. 2719.

§ 3.—When a female obligor marries.

2717. By her marriage, the legal existence of a married woman is merged in that of her husband, so that she cannot defend any action brought against her on her contract, and when a suit is brought against her alone, she must plead her coverture. When she marries pending an action against her the suit does not abate, but goes on as if nothing had happened, for she shall not be able to defeat the plaintiff by her own act.

This head will be divided by considering, 1, when the husband and wife must be joined; 2, when the husband may be sued alone; 3, when the wife must be sued alone; 4, when the husband and wife may be joined or not at the election of the plaintiff; 5, who is to be sued in case of the death of the husband or wife.

Art. 1.—When the husband and wife must be joined.

2718. Where the wife entered into a several contract, *dum sola,* she and her husband must be joined in an action for a breach of it; and where she is a joint obligee with others, she and her husband must be joined in actions for the breach of such joint contract. As the wife can make no valid contract, during the coverture, without her husband's authority, it follows that she cannot be joined with her husband as a defendant in an action on such contract.

For causes *in alieno jure* where the wife alone represents the estate from which they are due, she must be joined as co-defendant.

Art. 2.—When the husband may be sued alone.

2719. When the wife cannot be considered either in person or property as creating the cause of action, as in the case of a mere personal contract during coverture, even when made exclusively for her benefit, the husband must be sued alone ; as when, in consequence of the misconduct of her husband, the wife is compelled to buy goods which are within the meaning of necessaries of life ; the husband is liable in those cases, although he may have given notice to the tradesmen not to trust her.

The term *necessaries* is not confined to the mere necessities of life, but includes such ornaments and superfluities of dress as are usually worn by women of the rank and appearance of the defendant's wife, or rather that which he allows her to assume.(a) But in case the wife is in fault, as if she goes away with an adulterer, the husband will not be liable.

Art. 3.—When the wife may be sued alone.

2720. When the husband is *civiliter mortuus*, the wife may be sued alone, upon her own contracts made *dum sola*, for otherwise the creditor would have no remedy.

Art. 4.—When the husband and wife may be joined at the election of the plaintiff.

2721. The husband and wife may be joined in a case where the contract was made by the wife before the coverture, although the husband may afterward, upon a new consideration, as forbearance, have agreed to pay the debt ; and he may be sued alone upon such new promise.(b) And when rent becomes due by the wife, on a lease made to her, or there is a breach of covenant during the coverture, the action may be against both, or the husband alone.(c)

(a) Waithman *v.* Wakefield, 1 Camp. 120.
(b) Drue *v.* Thorn, Alleyn, 73.
(c) Com. Dig. Baron & Feme, Y.

OF PARTIES TO ACTIONS. 159

No. 2722.   Book 4, tit 7, chap. 1, sec. 2, § 4, art. 1.   No. 2725.

Art. 5.—Who is to be sued on the death of the husband or wife.

2722.—1. The responsibility of the husband, for the wife's debts, continues only during the coverture, and, therefore, when the husband survives, he is not liable to be sued in that character, for any contract of the feme before coverture. But if judgment has once been obtained against the husband and wife jointly during coverture, the husband will be responsible on that, and he may be sued alone. He may be sued alone also for rent on a lease to the wife, incurred during the coverture.(a)

When the husband has neglected to collect her choses in action during the coverture, they belong to the administrator of the wife, and he may be sued for a debt by her before the marriage.(b)

2723.—2. When the wife survives, she may be sued upon all her unsatisfied contracts made before coverture. But although they may not have been paid, yet if they have been discharged by the bankruptcy and certificate of the husband, when they could have been proved under the commission, she will be discharged from all liability on account of such debts.(c)

§ 4.—In the case of executors and administrators.

2724. In examining the liabilities of executors and administrators, let us inquire, 1, who may be sued as such; 2, in what form; 3, for what causes.

Art. 1.—Who may be sued as executors or administrators.

2725. We have seen who may sue as executors and administrators, when they have claims as such against others. Those same persons may, in general, be sued upon the breach of contract of the deceased.

(a) 3 Mod. 189, n. k; Com. Dig. Baron & Feme, 2 B.
(b) Heard *v.* Stanford, 3 P. Wms. 409.
(c) Miles *v.* Williams, 1 P. Wms. 249.

160 OF REMEDIES.

No 2726   Book 4, tit 7, chap 1, sec. 2, § 4, art 2, 3.   No 2727.

Art. 2.—In what form they may be sued.

2726. All persons named as executors in the will may be sued jointly, whether they have all administered or not; or at the choice of the plaintiff those who have not interfered may be omitted. All who have administered must be sued jointly, but a mistake or omission in this respect can be objected to only by a plea in abatement. And if the testator has appointed several executors, some to administer one part of his estate, and others to manage another, although, with regard to each other, they are perfectly separate and independent, yet *quoad* creditors, they are to be considered but as one, and may all be jointly sued.(a) An executor *de son tort*, who became so before probate, may be sued jointly with the rightful executor, but not an administrator.

When there are several administrators, they must all be sued, or the defendant may plead in abatement.

Art. 3.—For what causes an executor may be sued.

2727. Executors and administrators may be sued on all simple contracts broken by him whom they represent, and they are bound to perform those unbroken, when they have assets, unless they are of an entirely personal nature, as where the deceased had undertaken to paint a picture, or teach an apprentice. But if the thing to be done may be accomplished by the executor, as well as by the testator, the executor is bound to fulfil the contract, if he has assets; as where the testator agreed to build a house by a certain day, and he died before the day, his executor must build it. In like manner, although the executor cannot teach an apprentice, yet if the master dies, the executor may procure some one to teach him; where the engagement was to teach him or cause him to be taught, it is the

(a) Cro. Car. 293.

duty of the executor to cause him to be taught, and to fulfil other covenants toward him, if he has assets.

2728. An executor is liable for breach of covenants annexed to an estate in one way, when the breach occurred before the estate passed to him, that is, in the lifetime of the testator, and in another, when it happened afterward.

1. In the first case the executor is liable for a breach of the covenant generally, to the extent of the assets in hands, applicable to such claim; because had the executor lived, his personal estate must have repaired it, and that is equally chargeable in the hands of his representative, who is, in law, the same person with himself.

2. When a term with covenants annexed to the land, passes to the executor, and he enters, he must perform them so far as the after profits of the land extend, for by law these are to be applied in fulfilling them, and not in the discharge of other demands against the testator, though of a higher nature. His liability is in general restricted to the assets he has in his hands, and, if sued as assignee, he may plead the actual state of the case.(a)   His peculiar liability depends upon his retaining possession, for when he assigns the term to another, he is liable only as having general assets, as if he had never entered.

§ 5.—When one of several obligors is dead.

2729. When the obligors were bound by a *joint contract*, and one of them dies, his executor or administrator is discharged at law from all liability, the survivor alone can be sued.(b)   And if the deceased

(a) Billinghurst v. Spearman, 1 Salk. 297; Remnant v. Bremridge, 8 Taunt. 191; 2 Moo. 94.
(b) Bac. Ab. Obligation, D 4; Vin. Ab. Obligation, P 20; Postan v. Stanway, 5 East, 261.   But in Pennsylvania it was held, that after the survivor was discharged as an insolvent, an action might be maintained against the executor of the deceased.

was a mere surety, his executors are not generally liable even in equity.(a)

If the contract were *several*, or joint and several, the executor of the deceased may be sued in a separate action, but he cannot be jointly sued with the survivor, because, if for no other reason, the executor is to be charged *de bonis testatoris* and the survivor *de bonis propriis*, and the judgment could not be so rendered.

§ 6.—When there has been a change of credit, and where the covenants run with the land.

2730. The action for the breach of a mere personal contract must be brought against the contracting party, and not the one to whom he has assigned his interest, because there exists no privity between such plaintiff and the assignee; as if one demise goods, and the lessee covenant for himself and his assigns to deliver the goods at the end of the term, and, before that time, assigns the goods to a third person, the assignee cannot be sued by the lessor for want of privity.

But when, by the agreement of the parties, there has been a change of credit, so as to transfer the liability from the original contracting party to another, or to only one of several obligors, then a separate action may be brought upon this new engagement.(b)

2731. When a covenant running with the land has been assigned, as, for example, where a lease, in which there is a covenant to pay rent, has been assigned by the lessee, the assignee is liable for all the rent which may thereafter accrue, while he retains the lease.(c) But his liability ceases when he assigns his interest, though even purposely to an insolvent person,(d) because he is liable only in respect of the estate.

(a) Weaver *v.* Shryock, 6 S. & R. 262. See 2 Whart. 362; 2 P. A. Browne, 31.

(b) In these cases there has been a species of novation, by which a new obligation is created. See Bouv. L. D. Novation.

(c) Bac. Ab. Covenant, E 3, 4.

(d) Bac. Ab. Covenant, E 4.

On an *express* covenant in a lease to pay rent, or to perform any other act, the covenantor, and his personal representatives having assets, are liable to an action of covenant during the lease, although they may have assigned their interest before any breach, because this is a personal covenant. And this liability remains, although the lessor or covenantee may have accepted rent from the assignee.(*a*)   But a distinction must be observed, when the covenant of the lessee is only *implied*, and the lessor has accepted rent of the assignee, his right of action against the lessee is gone.(*b*)   And an action of *debt* cannot be maintained against the lessee after assignment of the lease by him, and acceptance of rent from the lessee, even upon his express covenant, the proper action being *covenant*.(*c*)

§ 7.—When the defendant is a bankrupt.

2732. When the sole contracting party has been discharged as a bankrupt, and obtained his certificate, he is in general discharged from all debts due at the time of the bankruptcy, which could have been proved under the commission. But if the plaintiff can declare for a tort, the bankrupt is still liable.(*d*)   And a bankrupt's discharge, is not a bar to a proceeding *in rem*, to enforce a mechanic's lien.(*e*)

When there is a joint debt, and one of the debtors has been discharged as a bankrupt, the action may be brought against the solvent partner, though if commenced against both, upon a plea of the certificate in bar, the plaintiff may enter a *nolle prosequi* as to him, and proceed against the other.(*f*)

(*a*) 1 Saund. 241, note 5 ; Kunckle *v.* Wynick, 1 Dall. 305.
(*b*) 1 Saund. 241, b.
(*c*) 1 Saund. 241, n. 5.
(*d*) Parker *v.* Norton, 6 T. R. 695 ; Williamson *v.* Dickens, 5 Iredell, 259.   But see contra, Hatten *v.* Speyer, 1 John. 41 ; Forster *v.* Surtees, 12 East, 612.
(*e*) McCullough *v.* Caldwell, 5 Pike, 237.
(*f*) Noke *v.* Ingham, 1 Wils. 89.

§ 8.—When the defendant has been discharged as an insolvent.

2733. The insolvent discharged under the respective acts of the states, may still be sued. His person is liberated, but his property, present or future, is still liable for his debts.

§ 9.—When a corporation is a defendant.

2734. A corporation when liable to an action must be sued in its true name.(*a*)

It may be sued upon its express contracts, whether under seal or not, though formerly it required the solemnity of a seal to bind the corporation.(*b*) The ancient rule that a corporation can make a contract only by its corporate seal has been changed,(*c*) and now an action of assumpsit lies against a corporation aggregate, upon an express or implied promise.(*d*) The rule now appears to be the same in England. "If the corporation have helped themselves to another man's money," says a learned judge, "it would be absurd to say they must bind themselves under seal to return it."(*e*)

CHAPTER II.—OF PARTIES TO ACTIONS ARISING *EX DELICTO*.

2735. Having considered, in the preceding chapter, who ought to be made parties in actions *ex contractu*,

---

(*a*) Minot *v.* Curtis, 7 Mass. 441; Bank of Utica *v.* Smalley, 2 Cowen, 778; Porter *v.* Nockervis, 4 Rand. 359.

(*b*) 1 Bl. Com. 475; Bac. Ab. Corporations, D.

(*c*) Chestnut Hill Turnpike *v.* Rutter, 4 S. & R. 16; 12 Wheat. 64; 1 Cowen, 513; 6 S. & R. 16.

(*d*) Baptist Church *v.* Mulford, 3 Halst. 182; North Whitehall *v.* South Whitehall, 3 S. & R. 117; Canal Company *v.* Knapp, 9 Pet. 541; Fleckner *v.* U. S. Bank, 8 Wheat. 357; White *v.* Westport Man. Co. 1 Pick. 215; White *v.* Derby Fishing Co. 2 Conn. 260; Bac. Ab. Corporations, D, Bouv. ed.

(*e*) Per Lord Denman, C. J., Hall *v.* Mayor of Swansea, 5 Ad. & Ell. N. S. 547.

both plaintiffs and defendants, it now remains to inquire who ought to be made parties to actions *ex delicto*, or those which do not arise from any contract, but from some wrong or injury. These are either plaintiffs or defendants.

SECTION 1.—OF THE PLAINTIFF IN ACTIONS EX DELICTO.

2736. For the sake of perspicuity, a similar plan will be adopted as in the preceding chapter, by considering, 1, for what interest of the plaintiff an action may be maintained; 2, when that interest has been assigned; 3, the number of persons interested; 4, cases where the party injured is dead; 5, when one of several parties injured is dead; 6, when a married woman may be joined.

§ 1.—For what interest or right of the parties injured an action lies.

2737. Civil actions are brought to repair some loss sustained; the party to whose use the fruits of the suit are to be appropriated, and whose interests have been impaired, should therefore be made the plaintiffs. In general, the action must be in the name of the party whose *legal* right has been affected; and one having only an *equitable* interest, cannot in general sue in a court of common law, unless in cases where the action is against a wrong doer for an injury to the possession of the *cestui que trust*.(a) The numerous injuries which affect a man's interest, and for which the law gives an action, may be classed into, 1, those by positive misfeasance; 2, those which arise from a breach of public duty; 3, those which are the effect of omission of some private obligation; 4, those where the party injured may sue in form *ex contractu* or *ex delicto;* 5, those which are remedied by particular statutes.

(a) 2 Saund. 47, d.

Art. 1.—*Of actions for injuries by positive misfeasance.*

2738. These injuries or wrongs are, 1, to the person or personal rights; 2, to property; 3, to the relative rights.

1. *Injuries to the person and personal rights.*

2739. An injury to the absolute rights of a person may consist of an assault, a battery, menace, imprisonment, doing an injury by letting loose a dangerous animal, or erecting a nuisance and impairing one's health; by wrongs to his reputation, as by libel or slander, and by malicious prosecution. In all these cases but little difficulty attends the choice of suitors. The party who has received the injury must be made plaintiff, and he who has committed it, defendant.

2. *Of injuries to property.*

2740. The wrongs to property for which an action will lie, are trespass, obstructing incorporeal rights, deceit on sales, misrepresenting another's circumstances, slander of title, rescue, excessive or irregular distress, and impairing property bailed or on a lease. It is not always easy in these cases to say by whom the action should be brought. Examples may be found in the following cases:

1. When the right of a pew is disturbed, the proprietor, and not the parson or the trustees of the church, ought to be the plaintiff.(a)

2. When an injury is done to the possession, the party entitled to it must bring the action, but when it extends to the reversionary interest, the reversioner should be made plaintiff; for example, a man enters on land leased by A to B, and cuts down trees, rendering the property less valuable; A may bring an action for the injury he has sustained, and B may

(a) Frances *v.* Ley, Cro. Jac. 366.

OF PARTIES TO ACTIONS. 167

No. 2741.   Book 4, tit 7, chap. 2, sec 1, § 1, art 2.   No 2742.

institute an action of trespass for the wrong to his possession.(a)

3. When goods are sent to order by a carrier, the carrier, though not named by the vendee, receives them as his agent, and so the property is vested in the vendee on delivery to the carrier; and for any injury to the goods, while in the carrier's hands, the vendee must sue.(b)

4. The indorsement of a bill of lading, without consideration, does not transfer its contents; hence such an indorsement to an agent that he may receive the goods mentioned in it, does not entitle him to bring trover for them in his own name.(c)

3. *Of injuries to the relative rights.*

2741. When an injury has been committed to the relative rights, the superior may maintain an action for a wrong to the inferior, but not *vice versa;* for example, when one has committed a battery upon the wife, or had criminal connection with her, the husband may have an action against the wrong doer. But if an assault and battery be committed upon the husband, or a woman has had a criminal connection with him, the wife has no remedy. So a man may have an action for the seduction of his child or servant, and for violence or threats toward him, or for enticing him away; the child or servant, on the contrary, can have no action for any of these acts against the father or master.

Art. 2.—Of injuries by breach of public duty.

2742. Certain persons are required by their situation to perform a variety of acts toward others, for the breach or non-performance of which an action accrues

---

(a) Queen's College v. Hallett, 14 East, 439.
(b) Dutton v. Solomonson, 3 B. & P. 582.
(c) See Coxe v. Harden, 4 East, 241.

168 OF REMEDIES.

No 2743.　　　Book 4, tit. 7, chap. 2, sec. 1, § 1, art 3, 4.　　　No 2744.

to the party who is injured thereby. Such are false returns of writs, or neglect to execute them; unlawfully to permit a rescue or the escape of a prisoner; a sheriff taking insufficient pledges or none, when required by law to take them; the refusal by a common carrier to take a passenger when he has ability and the fee is properly tendered or paid; neglect or refusal to receive goods by such carrier, or injuring them after having received them; the refusal by an innkeeper to receive a guest when he has room; the unskilful treatment of diseases by surgeons; and the sale of unwholesome provisions by victuallers.

Art. 3.—Of injuries which arise from the omission of some private obligation.

2743. The person injured may maintain an action against one who commits waste, contrary to his duty, as tenant of the land; or neglects to repair a division fence, which he is bound to keep up; or for using his property in any way to the detriment or injury of his neighbor.

Art. 4.—Of injuries for which the plaintiff may sue in form ex contractu or ex delicto.

2744. There are some cases where the plaintiff may at his choice sue for a breach of contract, as to the form of action, but no further, as well *ex delicto* as *ex contractu;* thus for negligence in an attorney, case or assumpsit lies; and the same for a breach of warranty; or where a party having hired a horse for a particular journey, goes another, and does an injury to him, killing him, for example. In these cases the plaintiff cannot change the liability of the parties by merely adopting a different form of action; a single case will illustrate this rule. An infant hired a horse to go on a particular journey, and went another, and by unskilful treatment killed him; he was sued for the tort, but the plaintiff was not allowed to recover, because the cause of action arose out of a contract.(*a*) But an infant was held liable in trover, although the goods were delivered to him under a contract, and although they were not converted actually to his own use.(*b*)

Art. 5.—*Of actions given by statute.*

2745. In general, the party to whom an action is given, under a remedial statute, is marked out by its provisions, and he is usually the person injured, and, in that case, it is immaterial whether he has the legal or the equitable right to property on account of which the remedy is given.(*c*)

When an action is given by the statute to any one who will sue for the same, the party who brings the first suit has a right to maintain his action. In such case, when the penalty is to be recovered partly for the benefit of the informer, and partly for the use of the government, the suit instituted for its recovery is called an action *qui tam.*

§ 2.—When the interest of the party injured has been assigned.

2746. It will be remembered that rights of action arising *ex contractu,* cannot be assigned, except under special circumstances or in particular cases; the same rule holds as to actions arising *ex delicto,* whether the injury be to the person, personal or real property. But sometimes there is a transfer in fact, and, at other times, only in appearance, of the property relating to which the action arises; in these cases it is not always easy to make a proper choice of suitors.

When incorporeal real property is granted, the

(*a*) Penrose *v.* Curren, 3 Rawle, 351. See 25 Wend. 399; 3 Shepl. 233; Wilt *v.* Welsh, 6 Watts, 9.
(*b*) Vasse *v.* Smith, 6 Cranch, 226.
(*c*) Pritchit *v.* Waldron, 5 T. R. 14.

grantee's right and possessory title are coëval, both being conferred by the instrument of conveyance; any tort, therefore, committed after the grant, is an injury to the grantee, upon which he may have an action. But when the real property granted is corporeal, his possession is not united to his rights, until he has entered upon the land, either in fact or in contemplation of law. And if, between the time of the grant and of his taking possession, an injury is committed against the premises, the grantor, and not the grantee, will be the proper person to bring the suit, because bare possession is not title sufficient to redress a possessory injury.

The absolute owner of personal property, when entitled to the possession, is in law considered as if actually possessed, although in fact he may not be so, according to the maxim that absolute property in the personalty draws to it the possession;(a) and in such case he is the proper person to bring the action.

But to this general rule there is an exception, which is the case where goods are consigned to a factor.(b)

§ 3.—Of the number of plaintiffs for an injury.

2747. When an injury is committed against two or more persons, who have a joint legal interest in the property affected, they must, in general, join in the action, for when the damage to one is the same as to the other, they are jointly entitled to the damages which are to repair it, and this though the interest be several.(c) When only one loss has been sustained, only one satisfaction is due, and, as to this, the one has not a better claim than the other; of necessity, both must unite in claiming it.

(a) 2 Saund. 47, a, n. 1; Bac. Ab. Trover, C.
(b) Fowler v. Down, 1 B. & P. 44.
(c) Vide Jackson ex dem. Romun v. Sidney, 12 John. 185.

But where the inconvenience to one is distinct from that of the other, their claims for remuneration must be separate, because what affects the one is matter of indifferençe to the other. It is not the act complained of, but its *consequences*, and this ought to be kept constantly in mind in ehoosing plaintiffs.

Art. 1.—Of actions for injuries to several persons by positive misfeasance.

2748. Injuries of this kind are, 1, to the person and personal rights; 2, to property; and, 3, to the relative rights.

1. *Of injuries to the person and personal rights.*

2749. When two persons are beaten with the same stroke, the act by which they are injured is one, but as the consequences of the act, and not the act itself, must be redressed, the injury is several, and the two cannot bring a joint action, because one does not share in the suffering of the other. And so if two are slandered by the same speech, as "You, Peter and Paul, murdered John," or where several are unlawfully imprisoned by the same act, each must bring his separate action.

2. *Injuries to the joint property of several persons.*

2750. When several persons are possessed jointly of real or personal property as joint tenants, tenants in common, or bare occupants, they are jointly aggrieved by a trespass or other injury to it. Thus it was held that tenants in common(*a*) are jointly injured by disturbing an incorporeal hereditament annexed to their land, upon the same principle that they are so to thè land itself.(*b*) And, in the somewhat celebrated case of the Dippers at Tunbridge Wells,(*c*) it was

(*a*) Kielw. 55, Case n. 2.
(*b*) Hamon *v.* White, W. Jones. 142.
(*c*) Weller *v.* Baker, 2 Wils. 423.

172 OF REMEDIES.

No 2751   Book 4, tit 7, chap 2, sec. 1, § 3, art. 2.   No 2752.

held that persons who had separate rights, but were entitled to joint profits, might maintain a joint action against one who caused a damage to those profits.(a) When partners are slandered in their trade, the injury is joint, because the means of acquiring property is the object impaired, and in those means all the partners are concerned. If, in addition to the general, one of the partners has sustained special damages, he may bring a separate action.

3. Of injuries to the relative rights of several persons.

2751. When two or more persons stand in the same relation toward another, and one has an action against a third person for an injury to his relative rights, the rest may join with him in such action, as where a servant, who was jointly engaged to several masters, was beaten, and all the masters have suffered loss, they may join, because all share the damages occasioned. But if the servant was in their separate employment, the actions are several.(b)

Art. 2.—Of injuries arising from neglect of public duty.

2752. When an injury arises from the neglect of a public duty, as for permitting an escape, if the party escaped was a prisoner at the suit of several jointly, all are jointly aggrieved, since the damage is common to all. So where two church wardens sued a mandamus to an officer to swear them in, and, on his making a false return, joined in an action against him, the joinder was held right, though it was objected that the office of one, not being the office of the other, neither was the injury done to one done to the other. But the court held that the injury was joint, because the false return had rendered useless a writ sued at their joint expense.(c)

(a) See Coryton v. Lithebye, 2 Saund. 112.
(b) Ham. on Part. 46.
(c) Ward v. Brampston, 3 Lev. 362; S. C. 3 Salk. 202.

Art. 3.—Consequence of a non-joinder, or misjoinder of parties.

2753. When a party who ought to have been joined as plaintiff, is omitted in an action *ex delicto*, the objection can be taken only by plea in abatement, or by way of apportionment of the damages on the trial. In an action of this nature, the defendant cannot, as in actions *ex contractu*, give evidence of the non-joinder for the purpose of defeating the action.(*a*) And, if one of several part owners of a chattel, sue alone for a tort, and recover damages, this will be no bar to a suit by the other; for, in the first action, the defendant ought to have pleaded the non-joinder in abatement.(*b*)

When too many persons are joined as plaintiffs, and the objection appears on the record, it may be taken advantage of by demurrer, in arrest of judgment, or writ of error; if it do not appear on the record, the mistake may be a ground of non-suit on the trial, for the plaintiffs do not prove a right to what they claim, as some of them have no right at all.(*c*)

§ 4.—Cases where the injured party is dead.

2754. In case of contracts where the party who had a cause of action dies, his personal representatives have in general the right to sue and recover what was owing to him; but in the case of *torts*, when the action must be in form *ex delicto*, and the plea not guilty, the rule at common law was otherwise, it being a maxim that a personal action dies with the person: *actio personalis moritur cum persona.* But the meaning of this rule must be somewhat restricted. In a large and extended sense, all actions, except those for the recovery of real property, may be called *personal;* this is not the meaning of the maxim. It

(*a*) 1 Saund. 291, g.
(*b*) Sedgworth *v.* Overend, 7 T. R. 279.
(*c*) Co. Litt. 197, b.

174   OF REMEDIES.

No. 2755.   Book 4, tit 7, chap 2, sec 1, § 4, art. 1, 2.   No. 2756.

extends to all wrongs attended with actual force, whether they affect the person or property ; and to all injuries to the person only, without actual force.

Art. 1.—Of injuries to the person.

2755. When the wrong is altogether personal, as where the deceased has been injured by assault, battery, false imprisonment, libel, slander or otherwise, no action can be supported by his personal representatives. This rule appears to have been adopted for the purpose of preventing actions where the principal object would have been the gratification of revengeful feelings. Though a promise of marriage may be considered as a contract, yet it is so far personal that no action can be maintained by the executor of the promissee for a breach of it,(a) unless perhaps the testator sustained special damages.(b)

Art. 2.—Of injuries to personal property.

2756. Where the injury was done to personal property, and either the wrong doer or the party injured died, at common law there was no remedy by or against the personal representative, when the action must have been in form ex delicto, and the plea not guilty.(c) But if any contract can be implied, the executor of the injured party may bring a suit and recover damages ; as, if the wrong doer convert goods into money, an action of assumpsit may be brought against him by the executor.(d)

By statute of the English king 4 Edw. III., c. 7, an action is given to an executor for an injury done to the personal property of his testator in his lifetime ;

(a) Chamberlain v. Williamson, 2 M. & S. 408. See Latimore v. Simmons, 13 S. & R. 183 ; Stebbins v. Palmer, 1 Pick. 71.
(b) 13 S. & R. 185.
(c) Pitts v. Hale, 3 Mass. 321 ; Stetson v. Kempton, 13 Mass. 272 ; Wilbur v. Gilmore, 21 Pick. 200.
(d) Middleton v. Robinson, 1 Bay, 58.

and this right was extended to the executor of an executor, by statute of 25 Edw. III., c. 5; and by the 31 Edw. III., c. 11, administrators have the same remedy as executors. The principles of these statutes have been adopted by our courts as a part of the common law.

Art. 3.—Of injuries to real property.

2757. No personal representative can support an action arising *ex delicto* for any injury to real property, for the statutes just mentioned have been confined in their operation to injuries to personal property. An executor cannot, therefore, maintain an action of trespass *quare clausum fregit,(a)* nor merely for cutting down trees, or committing other waste in the lifetime of the testator.(*b*)

§ 5.—When one of several persons injured is dead.

2758. When several persons were jointly interested in the property injured, and one of them is dead, the action ought to be in the name of the survivor, and the executor of the deceased cannot be joined, nor can he sue separately.

If one of several plaintiffs, in an action in form *ex delicto*, dies pending the action, the suit does not abate, and the survivor may prosecute it to judgment.(*c*)

§ 6.—When a married woman may be joined.

2759. For an injury to the person or personal property of her husband, the wife cannot sue alone, nor can she join him, for she has no legal interest in either. She may join him, it is true, when they have been jointly maliciously prosecuted, but this is because she

---

(*a*) In Connecticut a contrary rule has been adopted. Griswold *v.* Brown, 1 Day, 180.

(*b*) Mason *v.* Dixon, W. Jones, 174.

(*c*) 2 Saund. 72, i.

176　　　　　　　　　OF REMEDIES.

No. 2760.　　　Book 4, tit. 7, chap 2, sec 1, § 6, art. 1, 2　　　No 2762.

herself had rights which were invaded; but in this case the husband, if he will, may sue alone.(*a*)

Art. 1.—*Injuries committed before coverture.*

2760. For injuries committed before marriage either to the person, personal or real property of the wife, when the cause of action would survive to the wife, she must join in the action.

For injuries committed before coverture, to the property of the wife, held by her *in alieno jure*, the wife must always be joined; as for a trespass to property held by the wife as executrix, when committed before marriage.

Art. 2.—*Injuries committed during coverture.*

2761.—1. When a wrong is committed against the person of the wife, during coverture, as by beating her person, or slandering her reputation, or by a malicious prosecution, she cannot sue alone, the suit must be by herself and her husband, for in that case the right to damages will survive to the wife. But when the injury to the wife deprives the husband for any time of her company or assistance, or if she be maliciously indicted, or imprisoned, and the husband is put to expense on those accounts, he may bring a separate action in his own name for these consequential injuries, which are, indeed, wrongs done to himself alone, and for this reason, he may, in the same action, proceed for a battery committed upon himself. And whenever, on account of an injury to the wife, he has sustained special damages, he may bring a separate action.

2762.—2. For an injury, during coverture, to the wife's *personal property* not reduced to possession, in fact or in law, by the husband, the husband and wife must join; and so in an action for disturbing a private office or employment filled by the wife alone.(*b*)

_____

(*a*) Com. Dig. Baron et Feme, X.
(*b*) Weller *v.* Baker, 2 Wils. 423.

When the wrong committed toward the wife's property had its inception before marriage, but was consummated after, the husband and wife may join, or the husband may sue alone; as, in case of trover before marriage and conversion afterward; or of rent due before marriage and a rescue afterward. For the same reason the wife must be joined in replevin for her goods taken while sole, though, it is said, in this case the husband may sue alone.

2763.—3. For the recovery of the *land* of the wife, and in a writ of waste to it, the husband and wife must join. But when the action is merely for the recovery of damages to the land during coverture, the husband may sue alone, or the wife may be joined.

Art. 3.—Of injuries against the wife in alieno jure.]

2764. When a feme covert sues *in autre droit*, as for example, as executrix, she and her husband must join.(*a*)

Art. 4.—By whom actions must be brought on the death of the husband or wife.

2765.—1. When the wife dies, and the husband survives, he may maintain an action for an injury to the land of the wife committed during the coverture.(*b*) But his remedy for injuries to her person does not survive.

2766.—2. When the husband dies, and the wife survives, any action for a tort committed to her, or to her personal or real property before marriage, or to her personal or real estate during the coverture, will survive to her.

SECTION 2.—OF DEFENDANTS IN ACTIONS *ex delicto*.

2767. This section will be divided, as nearly as may be, like the preceding.

(*a*) Off. Ex. 207; Buckley *v.* Collier, Salk. 114.
(*b*) Com. Dig. Baron & Feme, Z.

178   OF REMEDIES.

No. 2768.   Book 4, tit. 7, chap. 2, sec. 2, § 1, art 1.   No 2771.

§ 1.—Of liabilities between the original parties.

2768. In considering the injuries committed by a single individual, they may be classed into, 1, positive wrongs or common injuries; 2, those which arise from a breach of public duty; 3, those which are the effect of an omission of some private obligation; 4, those which are consequent upon a breach of contract.

Art: 1.—Of positive wrongs or common injuries by one person only.

2769. These wrongs are to the person or personal rights, and to property.

1. *Of injuries to the person and personal rights.*

2770. All natural persons, who have legal capacity to sue, are liable to be sued for tortious acts, unconnected with, or in disaffirmance of a contract; and, therefore, an infant may be sued like an adult for torts committed by him, as for slanders, assaults, batteries, trespasses, and the like. But a slave, who is not in general considered a person, but a thing, cannot be sued for a tort, as an action against him would be wholly fruitless, and though his master may, in some cases, be liable for the injury he has committed to property, he cannot be made responsible for his slander.

2771. The person doing the injury is the party liable, and whether he commits the wrong by his own hands or those of another, he is the one who does the injury, for he who acts by another acts himself: *qui facit per alium facit per se.* But there are some cases where it is not so easy to make a choice of parties: 1, when one man causes an injury to another at the instigation of a third person; 2, where the injury arises from executing an authority in law, whether the same be real or fictitious.

1. When without intention one man prejudices another by his wrongful act, at the suggestion of a

third, if he had the choice whether to interfere or not, he has no excuse; if, therefore, a servant by the command of his master, injures another man, the latter may maintain an action against him. But to render him thus responsible, he must be active in doing the mischief, and not be a mere instrument in the hands of another, for he cannot be said to commit an injury, if he had no knowledge of it. A servant who should carry a sealed libellous letter to a printer to be published, not knowing its contents, would not be guilty of the publication of the libel; and a servant who delivers to the sheriff an illegal writ, inclosed in a letter, not knowing its contents, is not answerable to him against whom it is executed.(a) But when the agent knew, or ought to have known, that he was forwarding the illegal affair, he is liable, though he may not have been the immediate actor in the matter; as, where an attorney at the request of his client issued an illegal writ, for example, an execution before he had a judgment.(b)

A master or principal is liable, in some cases, for the acts of his servant or agent, although he did not know any thing about them; he is answerable for their negligence or unskilfulness while acting in the course of his employ. But he is not answerable for the injury, if the servant at the time wilfully committed it on his own account; as if he wilfully drove his carriage against another. An exception to this rule is made on the ground of public policy, in relation to sheriffs, innkeepers, and common carriers, who are responsible for their agents.

When an injury has been committed by an animal, the owner will be responsible if he knew of the animal's evil propensity, and the injury has happened through his fault.(c)

(a) Coles v. Wright, 4 Taunt. 198.
(b) See Barker v. Braham, 3 Wils. 368.
(c) By the Roman law, when the master was sued for a wrong committed

180   OF REMEDIES.

No 2771.   Book 4, tit. 7, chap. 2, sec. 2, § 1, art. 1.   No. 2771.

2. When an injury arises from the execution of an authority in law, whether it be caused by executing, 1, a lawful writ in an unlawful manner; 2, an illegal writ; 3, from acting upon a groundless complaint; 4, receiving as an officer, a person as a prisoner who has been illegally taken; 5, and aiding a legal authority.

1st. An officer who executes a lawful writ in an unlawful way, though innocently, under the direction of his superior, will be liable for the injurious act; and if the plaintiff directed the manner of executing it, he will also be responsible.(a)

2d. The execution of the process of a court having jurisdiction of the parties and matter on which it is founded, may be justified by an officer, because although such process may be void, he is not allowed to judge of that, and may be punished for contempt if he do not execute it. But the plaintiff and his attorney are liable.(b)

3d. A justice of the peace who causes one to be arrested criminally, when he has jurisdiction, will be safe, if it does not appear that he acted knowingly in violation of law, as where he issued a warrant of arrest without a previous oath. But although his process may be illegal, it will justify the constable, who cannot inquire into its illegality, if the magistrate had jurisdiction.

4th. A jailer will be responsible for a false imprisonment and may be sued for it, if it appear upon the commitment that it is illegal.

5th. The sheriff may, in the execution of a lawful writ, call to his assistance the *posse comitatus;* that is, the aid of such citizens as may be requisite to enable

---

by his slave, or the owner for a trespass committed by his animal, he might abandon them to the person injured, and thereby save himself from further responsibility. Inst. 4, 9; Dig. 9, 1; Ib. 21, 1, 40. Similar provisions have been adopted in Louisiana. Art. 180, 181, 2301.

(a) See Menham v. Edmonson, 1 B. & P. 369.
(b) 3 Wils: 368.

him to execute such writ.(*a*) And in such case, although the sheriff may be acting without authority, yet it would seem that any person obeying his command, unless aware of that fact, will be protected.

2. *Of injuries committed against property.*

2772. An action lies against one who commits a trespass or any injury to personal property, or for appropriating it to the party's use, as in the case of trover and conversion. And, in all cases where he would be liable to an action, for a trespass committed by his agent or servant, to the person of another, he will be responsible for their acts, when committing an injury to the personal property of the plaintiff.

With respect to real property, a man may be sued for his misfeasance or malfeasance, as for obstructing ancient lights, neglect to repair fences, private ways, etc., when he is bound so to do. Such action may be against the occupier of the premises, and not the owner of the land, unless he covenanted to repair.(*b*)

Art. 2.—Of liabilities for a breach of public duty.

2773. When an injury arises in consequence of the neglect of a public duty, the person who filled the office in question is the party who is alone to be sued, for the duty was imposed upon him alone. But it is here to be observed, that a judicial officer while acting within his jurisdiction is not liable to any action for any apparent neglect of his duty, nor for any mistake he may commit in the execution of his office.

A ministerial officer, who is one acting by the authority of his superior, may be sued for the abuse of the authority given him; and he is generally responsible for the acts of his deputies.

(*a*) Vin. Ab. Sheriff, B.
b) Payne *v.* Rogers, 2 H. Bl. 350.

182 OF REMEDIES.

No 2774.   Book 4, tit 7, chap 2, sec 2, § 1, art. 3, 4.   No. 2775.

Art. 3.—Of liabilities arising from the neglect of a private obligation.

2774. When a party is required, by the situation in which he is placed, to perform certain things, and he neglects to do so, by which an injury accrues to the plaintiff, he may in general bring an action for the redress of the wrong. The following cases exemplify this rule :

1. When premises are wasted, the party liable is he who stood in the relation of tenant to the plaintiff at the time. If, therefore, Primus lease to Secundus, and Secundus demise to Tertius, who wastes the tenement, case in the nature of waste lies by Primus against Secundus, not against Tertius; because Primus' action being a breach of private duty connected with a tenure, and no tenure subsisting between Primus and Tertius, no duty is owing from one to the other. If, however, Tertius' misfeasance is commissive, and not permissive waste, Primus may sue him for injuring his reversionary estate, unless he has already sued or is suing Secundus.(a)

2. The occupant of a close, the owner of which is bound to maintain the fence which divides it from another, is liable to the neighboring landholder, for damages sustained in consequence of the fence going to decay, whatever agreement he may have made with a third person about repairing it.(b)

3. A person in possession of premises upon which a nuisance has been placed, is liable whether he raised it or not.(c)

Art. 4.—Of liabilities consequent upon a breach of contract.

2775. A common carrier and an innkeeper are insurers for the safety of the goods intrusted to them,

(a) Vide Berry v. Heard, Cro. Car. 242 ; Cudlop v. Rundall, 4 Mod. 9.
(b) Payne v. Rogers, 2 H. Bl. 349.
(c) Tenant v. Goldwin, 1 Salk. 360.

and are, therefore, liable for any neglect or misconduct, by which an injury accrues to them, and if they
employ persons to assist them, they are responsible
for their acts. A carrier, for example, must deliver
the goods to their address; if he forward them by a
porter, the latter is his agent, and he is liable for his
acts, unless there is an express or implied agreement,
that he may do so.(a)

§ 2.—When the interest has been assigned.

2776. It is a common principle of justice that no one
can be made answerable for an injury, unless it has
been committed by his express or implied command,
or by his own act. The assignee of an estate is not
liable, therefore, for a nuisance committed upon it
before he became the owner; but if he continue the
nuisance, he may be sued for such continuance. In
such case, however, there should be a request to
remove the nuisance.(b)

§ 3.—Of the number of persons liable for an injury.

2777. Joint liabilities may arise, 1, for common injuries; 2, for neglect of public duty; and, 3, for neglect
of private obligations.

Art. 1.—Of joint liabilities for common injuries.

2778.—1. When several persons join in an offence
or injury, they may generally be sued jointly, or any
number less than the whole may be sued, or each one
may be sued separately.(c) Each is liable for himself,
because the entire damages sustained were occasioned
by each, each sanctioning the acts of the others, so
that by suing one alone, he is not charged beyond his
just proportion. Any number less than the whole may

(a) Hyde v. The Trent and Mersey Nav. Company, 5 T. R. 396.
(b) Com. Dig. Nuisance, B.
(c) Williams v. Sheldon, 10 Wend. 654.

be sued, because each is answerable for his companion's acts. Thus a joint action may be brought against several for an assault and battery, or for composing and publishing a libel.(a)

But to this rule that for a joint injury a joint action may be brought, there is an exception, namely, that no joint action can be maintained for a joint slander; this exception seems to proceed upon the ground that each man's slander is his own, and it cannot by any means be considered that of another. Although this exception appears to be fully established, yet it is difficult to see the reason of it; when one of several trespassers gives the blow, he is considered as acting for the others, and, if they acted jointly, they may be jointly sued; why not consider the speaker, when acting in concert with others, as the actor for the whole in uttering the words? The blow is no more that of the person who did not give it, than the words are the words of him who only united with the other in an agreement that they should be spoken. In either case, upon principle, the maxim *qui facit per alium facit per se*, ought to have its force. Such, however, is not the law.

2779.—2. There is a distinction between mere personal actions for torts, and such as concern real property. If a tenant in common be sued for a tort, for any thing respecting the land held in common, he may plead the tenancy in common in abatement.(b)

Art. 2.—Of joint liabilities for neglect of public duty.

2780. When several officers join in their neglect of a public duty, or by doing an injurious act, for which they may be sued, they may be sued jointly or

---

(a) 2 Saund. 117, a; Bac. Ab. Actions in General, C; Harris v. Huntington, 2 Tyler, 129.

(b) Low v. Mumford, 14 John. 426; Sumner v. Tileston, 4 Pick. 309. See 10 Mass. 378.

severally.(*a*)   And if carriers act together as partners and injure a customer by neglecting their duty, as by losing his goods in their charge, they must be sued jointly.(*b*)

Art. 3.—Of the joint liabilities for the neglect of a private obligation.

2781. When the injury results from the neglect of a private obligation, as to repair a dividing fence, the rule, as far as respects strangers, seems to be, that all · occupying the land charged with the repair, whether as tenants or bare occupants, are liable jointly, each may be sued separately, or any number less than the whole may be made joint defendants, because a stranger cannot know the state of the property. So if a nuisance be upon the land, and the owner sells it, after which the nuisance is continued, the former owner and the purchaser may be jointly sued.(*c*)

§ 4.—Cases where the wrong doer is dead.

2782. We have seen that when the injured party dies, it is a general rule that no action can be maintained by his executors for the mere personal injury done to him, the maxim in such cases being *actio personalis moritur cum persona.* The same rule prevails when the wrong doer dies; in general no action lies against his personal representatives.

2783.—1. If the wrong doer dies before judgment, there is no remedy for any injury done to the person of the plaintiff; nor can an action be maintained against the executors of one who has broken his promise to marry.

2784.—2. For an injury committed by a testator to personal property, no action can in general be sustained against his executor; though if the testator

---

(*a*) Rich Sir Peter *v.* Pilkinton, Carth. 171.
(*b*) Buddle *v.* Wilson, 6 T. R. 369.
(*c*) Ham. on Partn. 88.

converted the property into money, assumpsit may be maintained against the executor; and if the property remains in specie in the hands of the latter, trover would lie against him, but not in his character of executor.

2785.—3. When the injury is against real property, no action will in general lie against the executor of the wrong doer; though if trees or other parts of the freehold be taken or converted into money, assumpsit will lie against the personal representatives; or if the trees remain in specie, trover may be maintained against him.(a)

2786.—4. When there are several wrong doers and one dies, the action may be brought against the survivor, or any number of them the plaintiff may select, or against one only.

§ 5.—When the wrong doer marries.

2787. The marriage of a woman changes her rights and liabilities so far, that she cannot alone enforce the former, nor can she alone be sued for the latter; in general her husband must be joined in actions by and against her.

2788. When she commits a tort before marriage, the action must be against the husband and wife jointly.(b) For torts committed by her during the coverture, as for slander, battery, and the like, the husband and wife must be joined; but they cannot be sued jointly for the slander uttered by both of them, because she cannot be made responsible for the slander uttered by her husband.

When the tort is joint, and she could be sued if she were a common person, then the action may be against them both jointly; as where the husband and wife committed an assault and battery, or in such case the

(a) Hambly v. Trott, Cowp. 373; 1 Saund. 216, a.
(b) Bac. Ab. Baron & Feme, L; Hank v. Harman, 5 Binn. 43.

husband may be sued alone.   Trover may be supported
against husband and wife for a conversion of goods
before marriage,(a) and for a conversion by husband
and wife, the husband may be sued alone.(b)

___

TITLE VIII.—OF THE PROCEEDINGS IN AN ACTION.

2789. We have seen that when a legal right has
been invaded, the plaintiff is entitled to his remedy,
for the redress of the injury, by an action; and having
ascertained who are the persons who must be made
both plaintiffs and defendants, our task now will be to
consider the proceedings which usually take place in
an action or suit at law.   In the discussion of this subject it will be necessary to inquire, 1, what is the proper form of the process ; 2, what is an appearance ;
3, into the pleadings ; 4, the declaration ; 5, the defence ; 6, the pleas ; 7, the replications ; 8, the rejoinder and subsequent pleadings ; 9, the demurrers ;
10, the nature of a case stated ; 11, the trial ; 12, the
arrest of judgment and new trial ; 13, the judgment ;
14, the proceedings in the nature of appeals ; 15, the
execution of the judgment.

___

CHAPTER I.—OF THE PROCESS.

SECTION 1.—OF THE GENERAL NATURE OF PROCESS.

2790. The writ or judicial means by which a defendant is brought in, or called upon to answer to the
complaint of the plantiff, is called *process*.   It is so
called, because it proceeds, or issues forth, in order to

___

(a) 2 Saund. 47, h, i.   (b) 2 Saund. 47, i.

bring the defendant into court, to answer the charge preferred against him.(a)

2791. According to the English law, the king is theoretically the fountain of all justice, and he is represented in chancery by the lord chancellor. Before the courts can have any jurisdiction, a writ must be issued out of chancery in the king's name, by which the defendant is commanded to satisfy the plaintiff, or else to appear in a court of law therein named, and answer for his default; this is called the *original* writ, and is required to give the law court jurisdiction of the case; it is a species of commission authorizing such a court to try the cause. All the writs which are issued *between* the return of the original, until judgment has been obtained, are called *mesne* writs; and all which issue afterward, are denominated *final* writs.

The original writ is issued under the great seal, and *tested*, that is, it concludes with an attesting clause in the name of the king himself, "witness ourself." All the other writs in the cause bear *teste* in the name of the chief justice; and these last writs are called *judicial* writs, by way of distinction from the *original* one obtained out of chancery.

In modern practice the original writ is frequently dispensed with by means of a fiction, and a proceeding by bill is substituted.(b)

2792. In the United States, the original writ, as in England, is generally dispensed with; the constitutions of the several states giving power to issue writs, so that with us what are called the mesne writs in England, are here *original* writs, and we have also *final* writs, into which two kinds all our writs are divided, there being no mesne or middle writs as in England.

The several constitutions of the states have provided the mode of issuing writs and process. They are generally issued in the name of "the commonwealth,"

(a) United States v. Noah, 1 Paine, R. 368.   (b) Steph. Pl. 54.

"the people," or "the state," as the constitution requires. These writs must be in writing or printing, signed by the clerk or prothonotary of the court; or in the name of, and attested by, the presiding judge; and sealed with the seal of the court.(*a*) They must be directed to the officer by whom they are to be served,(*b*) and should be dated,(*c*) and state the time when they are to be returned, which is called the *return day*.

2793. The usual mode of suing out a writ or process, is by filing a *præcipe* with the clerk or prothonotary. The *præcipe* is a brief written order, requiring that officer to issue a writ therein named, containing the names of the plaintiff and the defendant, and stating for what action. It is made by the attorney of the plaintiff in general, but it may be made by the plaintiff himself. On the receipt of the *præcipe*, the clerk or prothonotary makes out the writ, which is handed to the plaintiff.(*d*) This writ is delivered to the proper ministerial officer to be executed. When these writs issue out of the courts of the United States, they are directed to the marshal; when out of the state courts, to the sheriff.

2794. On the receipt of the writ, the ministerial officer is required to serve it according to its exigency, and make a return of it to the court, with a statement, indorsed upon it, setting forth what he has done; this statement is also called the *return*.

In the *service* of the writ, the sheriff or marshal has the right, when resisted, to call the *posse comitatus*, that is, the aid of such individuals as will enable him to execute it according to its exigency, and the commands of the law. But with respect to writs which issue, in

---

(*a*) The State *v.* Dozier, 2 Speers, 211.
(*b*) Wood *v.* Ross, 11 Mass. 271.
(*c*) Smith *v.* Winthrop, Minor, R. 378.
(*d*) This practice is not universal. In some of the states the writs are filled up by the attorney.

the first instance, to arrest in civil suits, the sheriff is not bound to take the *posse comitatus* to assist him in the execution of them; though he may, if he pleases, on forcible resistance to the execution of the process.(*a*) Before the sheriff uses any force, however, he ought to make a demand, for force ought to follow not precede the commands of the law.

2795. The *effect* of the sheriff's return is different when it regards himself, and when it affects others. It is conclusive against him, and he cannot gainsay it,(*b*) and when it is in his favor, as a return to a *fieri facias*, setting forth a valid excuse for not having sold goods, such as that they were destroyed by fire, or that the proceedings were stayed by a judge's orders, or the like, it is *primâ facie* evidence of the fact in his favor.(*c*) As between the parties to the suit, the return cannot be traversed, it being conclusive.(*d*) If false, the sheriff is liable to an action for making a false return.(*e*)

The sheriff is allowed to *amend his return* in certain cases, but never when manifest injustice will be done to either of the parties; and he may be compelled to make a sufficient return by attachment for contempt, when he neglects or refuses to make it, upon or after the return day.

SECTION 2.—OF THE DIFFERENT KINDS OF PROCESS.

2796. The usual processes to bring a party into court, so that judgment may be rendered against him, are, 1, the summons; 2, the capias; 3, an attachment.

(*a*) 2 Inst. 193; 3 Inst. 161.
(*b*) Hustick *v.* Allen, Coxe, 168; Murrell *v.* Smith, 3 Dana, 462; Blue *v.* Commonwealth, 2 J. J. Marsh, 26; Commonwealth *v.* Fuqua, 3 Litt. 41.
(*c*) Browning *v.* Harford, 7 Hill, N. Y. Rep. 120.
(*d*) Wilson *v.* Hurst, 1 Pet. C. C. Rep. 441; Diller *v.* Roberts, 13 S. & R. 60; Bott *v.* Burnell. 11 Mass. 163; Whitaker *v.* Sumner, 7 Pick. 551; Lawrence *v.* Pond, 17 Mass. 433.
(*e*) Stenson *v.* Snow, 1 Fairf. 263.

§ 1.—Of the summons.

2797. In *form*, the summons is a writ commanding the sheriff to summon, that is, notify the defendant, if within his jurisdiction, commonly called his bailiwick, to appear in court on a certain day, to answer the charge of the plaintiff.(*a*)   It may be issued at any time during term time, or in vacation, but it is usually tested, that is, dated as of a day during term, for it is presumed to have been issued by the immediate order of the court, as was probably the case in former times,(*b*) and it is made returnable on the first day of the next term, which, as has been observed, is the general *return day;* and the term to which the defendant is required to appear, is called the *appearance term.*

The act of notifying the defendant that a summons has been issued against him, is performed by reading the summons to him by the sheriff or his deputy, or by delivering him a copy of the writ; the former is called *personal* service of the writ, and the latter a *service by copy.*   This service may be made at any time after the writ comes into the hands of the sheriff, on or before the return day.   The sheriff is bound in this, as in every other case, to use due diligence in the execution of his writ; if he knows that the defendant is within his territorial jurisdiction, and he neglects to serve the writ, and returns that he could not find the defendant, he will be liable for all consequential damages.

After having served the summons, it is his duty to *return* it to the court whence it issued, with what he has done.   If the defendant has been served he returns it "served."   If, on the contrary, he has not been able

---

(*a*) 22 Vin. Ab. 42.

(*b*) Considerable diversity appears to exist as to the date of writs ; in some of the states they are tested, or dated on the day they issue, whether the same be in term or vacation.

to find him, his return is *non est inventus,* usually abbreviated " N. E. I.," that the defendant could not be found within his jurisdiction.

When the return of *non est inventus* has been made, the plaintiff may issue a second summons, returnable at another term, which is called an *alias* summons; if this should also be returned *non est inventus,* a third may be issued which is called a *pluries summons;* and if a fourth or fifth summons should be wanted, they are denominated respectively the fourth, *second pluries* summons, the fifth, *third pluries* summons, and so on numbering each future pluries in the order they are issued, until one has been served, and the proceedings go on as if the defendant had been summoned on the first writ.(*a*)

In some of the states, if, after summons has been issued, the defendant removes into another county in the same state, a writ may be issued directed to the sheriff of the county to which the defendant has removed, commanding him to summon the defendant to appear in the court whence the summons has been issued; this is called a *testatum* summons, differing from the common summons only in stating the fact of such removal.(*b*)

§ 2.—Of the capias.

2798. The *capias,* or more properly the *capias ad respondendum,* is a writ commanding the sheriff to take the body of the defendant, and have him before the court to answer the charge of the plaintiff. It is called a *capias ad respondendum,* or a writ of arrest to answer, to distinguish it from the *capias ad satisfaciendum,* commonly abbreviated *ca. sa.,* which is a writ of arrest to satisfy; this last is issued only after judgment, and is the most astringent writ of execution.

(*a*) 3 Bl. Com. 283.   (*b*) Walk. Intr. 516; 3 Bl. Com. 283.

The *capias ad respondendum* may be issued in term time, or in vacation, and, like a summons, it may be tested either during some day of the term, which is called the *teste day*, or at the time it is issued in vacation, as is provided for by the statute of the state. Let us now inquire, 1, against whom it may be issued; 2, for what causes; 3, how it is to be executed; 4, what is to be done after the arrest; 5, the return of the writ.

Art. 1.—Against whom a capias may issue.

2799. When a proper cause of action exists, a *capias* may be issued in general against all persons; but there are many cases where it would be injurious to the public interest that certain persons should be arrested in a civil action, and although, in our free country, we have abolished all personal privileges, yet where the public good requires it, privileges will be allowed, not indeed to the individual, but to the situation in which he is found. These privileges are either general and absolute, or limited and qualified.

1. Of absolute privileges.

2800. Those who are absolutely exempted from arrest, may be divided into the following classes:

1. Ambassadors, and their servants, when the debt or duty for which they are sued, has been contracted by the latter since they entered into the service of such ambassador.

2. Bankrupts, who have been finally discharged, for any debt which might have been proved by the creditor under the bankrupt proceedings.

3. Insolvent debtors, for any debt which was due or owing at the time of the insolvent's discharge.

4. Executors and administrators, when sued in their representative character.(a)

(a) But see Fitzsimons v. Salomon, 2 Binn. 440·

194 OF REMEDIES.

| No. 2801. | Book 4, tıt. 8, chap. 1, sec. 2, § 2, art 1. | No. 2801.

5. In some states women are exempt from arrest for any debt contracted by them.(a)

2. Of limited privileges.

2801. The classes of persons who are exempted from arrest in civil cases, for a limited time, are the following:

1. Members of congress. This privilege is not only that of the member, but also that of his constituents, and of the house of which he is a member; and every man is bound to know and take notice of this privilege.(b) The same privilege is extended to the members of the different state legislatures, in their own state. The time during which this privilege exists includes all the session of congress, or in case of the members of the state legislatures, during the session of their body, and a reasonable time for going to, and returning from the seat of government.(c)

2. Electors, under the constitution and laws of the United States, or of any state, are protected from arrest for any civil cause, while in the performance of their duty as such, and *eundo, mòrando, et redeundo*, that is, in going, staying at, or returning from an election.

3. Militia men, while in the performance of military duty, and sailors and soldiers in the service of the United States, or of the state, and *eundo, mòrando, et redeundo*.

4. All persons who, either necessarily or of right, are attending in any court or forum of justice, whether as judge, attorney, juror, party interested, or witness, and *eundo, mòrando, et redeundo*.

(a) In some of the states the defendant cannot be arrested for debt, unless there is strong presumption of fraud first established, for any contract the defendant may have entered into.
(b) Jeff. Man. § 3 ; Com. Dig. Parliament, D 17.
(c) Story, Const. §§ 856 to 862.

OF PROCEEDINGS IN AN ACTION. 195

No. 2802.   Book 4, tit. 8, chap. 1, sec. 2, § 2, art. 2, 3.   No 2803.

Art. 2.—For what causes a capias may issue.

2802. A capias can be issued only in cases where the plaintiff is *entitled to bail*, and cannot, as a summons, be issued of course, where the plaintiff has a cause of action. This is regulated by the local laws; in some of the states a defendant may be held to bail in all cases of debt, in others, he can be held to bail only where a *primâ facie* case of concealment of property is made to appear. Generally he may be arrested for his torts, either upon an affidavit of the cause of action being previously made, or upon its being made to appear after the arrest; in this latter case, the arrest is made at the risk of the plaintiff. And if a defendant be arrested, and upon an investigation it afterward appear, that the arrest has been improperly made, either the writ will be quashed, that is, annulled, or the defendant will be discharged on *common bail*, that is, by entering an appearance. This common bail is a formal entry of fictitious sureties in the proper office of the court. It is in the same form as special bail, but differs from it in this, that the sureties are fictitious persons, as John Doe and Richard Roe.(*a*)

Art. 3.—How a capias is to be executed.

2803. The service of this writ is made by arresting the defendant; by *arrest* is meant the detention of the defendant by the officer, who is required to execute the writ, so that he has the defendant in his power, and the latter submits to him. To constitute an arrest it is usual to seize, or touch, the person of the defendant, and that is certainly the safest mode to pursue,(*b*) yet it has been held that no manual touching of the body or force is requisite, when the defendant

(*a*) Steph. Pl. 56, 7; Grah. Pr. 155; Highm. on Bail, 13.
(*b*) 3 Bl. Com. 288; Huntingdon *v.* Blaisdell, 3 N. H. Rep. 318.

196 OF REMEDIES.

No 2804. Book 4, tıt 8, chap 1, sec. 2, § 2, art 4 No. 2805.

is within the power of the officer, and submits to his authority ;(a) as if the bailiff come into the room and tell the defendant he arrests him, and locks the door.(b) But an arrest cannot be made by words only.

Once in the power of the officer, if the defendant escape, he may be retaken, and for this purpose the officer is justified in breaking not only an inner, but an outer door. Before his arrest the officer cannot break an outer door in order to effect it ;(c) after his arrest and escape he may break such a door, not however until a demand has been made to open it ; for the law, ever anxious to preserve the peace, will permit no violence, unless it is impossible to avoid it. But this privilege of protecting the outer inlet from being broken in a civil case, is limited to the house of the defendant alone, and will not screen the house of another, where the defendant, with the owner's consent, flies for protection from a civil process.(d)

Art. 4.—Of proceedings after an arrest under the capias.

2804. When the defendant has been arrested and he is in custody, he must put in bail or be imprisoned. This leads us to consider the nature and kinds of bail.

1. *Of baıl below, or baıl to the sheriff.*

2805. We have seen that *common bail* consists in the formal entry on the record of fictitious names, in order to enter an appearance. The object of the arrest being to compel an appearance, the defendant is required, upon his arrest, either to go to prison, or to give a bail bond to the sheriff, conditioned that he

---

(a) Gold v. Bissell, 1 Wend. 215.
(b) Wıllıams v. Jones, Cas. T. Hard. 301 ; 2 New Rep. 211 ; Bull. N. P. 82 ; Strout v. Gooch, 8 Greenl. 127.
(c) Moore, 917, p. 668 ; Cooke's case, W. Jones, 429.
(d) Semayne's case, 5 Co. 93. See Still v. Wilson, Wright, 505.

will appear; this the sheriff is authorized, or indeed required, to take with sufficient sureties; this species of bail is called *bail below*, or bail to the sheriff. If the defendant do not appear according to the condition of the bond, the plaintiff is entitled to rule the sheriff to bring the body into court, or to take an assignment of the bail bond, and sue the defendant and his sureties upon that instrument.

On failure to give a sufficient bail bond, the sheriff may commit the defendant to prison.

2. *Of special bail, or bail above.*

2806. By *special bail* is understood a recognizance entered in the case, in which the defendant and his sureties become bound, in double the amount of the claim, with a condition that if the plaintiff shall reco-, ver in the suit, the defendant shall either pay the judgment and costs, or surrender himself to the sheriff, or that his sureties will do it for him. This is entering bail to the action, and is equivalent to an appearance. It is called special, because it particularly states what the sureties are bound to do, and it is called *bail above* to distinguish it from *bail below*, or bail to the sheriff.

After special bail has been entered, the plaintiff may object to their sufficiency, when the sureties are required to *justify*, that is, show that they are of pecuniary ability to pay the plaintiff's demand.

2807. The meaning of the word bail is to *deliver*, and the defendant is presumed to have been delivered into the custody of the sureties. If the sureties become dissatisfied, they may obtain a certificate from the clerk or prothonotary of the court, that they became bail for the defendant, which certificate, called a *bail piece*, when formally made under the seal of the court, is evidence of that fact, and authorizes the securities, also called the *bail*, to arrest the defendant, and commit him to prison, in discharge of their obligation or recognizance, and entitles them to have an *exoneratur*, or an entry made on the record that the defendant has been so surrendered, or committed to prison, which, when lawfully made, discharges them.

Art. 5.—Of the return of the capias.

, 2808. The return of the *capias* must be made according to the facts; if the writ has been served, the defendant has been arrested, the return is simply *cepi corpus;* if the defendant has been discharged on bail, *cepi corpus* and bail bond, or C. C. B. B. If the defendant could not be found, *non est inventus*, and if found, and he is sick, *cepi corpus et languidus,*(a) and if he has been rescued, the sheriff may return that fact.

§ 3.—Of the attachment.

2809. An *attachment*, as a civil proceeding, is a writ issued by a court of competent jurisdiction, commanding the sheriff, or other proper officer, to seize any property, credit, or right belonging to the defendant, in whose hands soever the same may be found, to satisfy the demand which the plaintiff has against him.

This writ always issues before judgment, and its object is to compel an appearance of the defendant; in this respect it differs from an execution, and it is unlike it in another respect, that the property attached cannot be sold without another process.

In some of the states, this process can be issued only against absconding debtors, or those who conceal themselves, so that a summons or capias cannot reach them ;(b) in others it is issued in the first instance, so

---

(a) See, for a form of this return, 3 Chitty, Gen. Pr. 249, n.
(b) In New York, by virtue of the new code of procedure, a summons may be issued against a non-resident, which is to be served by a publication in the public newspapers, and by mailing a copy of it, directed to the defendant's place of residence, when known. It issues only when it is made to appear that the defendant is a resident of the state or has property

that the property attached may respond to the exigency of the writ, and satisfy the judgment. When the property attached is a chose in action, a new party is introduced; the person who is indebted is called the *garnishee*, who is so denominated because he has notice of the attachment. From the time the garnishee has notice of the attachment, he is bound to keep the property in his hands to answer the plaintiff's claim, until the attachment is dissolved, or he is otherwise discharged.

2810. The attachments assume different forms according to the provisions of the laws of the different states. In Pennsylvania there are two kinds of attachments, namely, the *foreign*, which is a proceeding by a creditor against the property of his debtor, when the latter is out of the jurisdiction of the state, and is not an inhabitant of the same. The object of this process is in the first instance to compel an appearance by the debtor, though his property thus attached may be made eventually liable for the plaintiff's claim. This attachment is for the sole benefit of the plaintiff. The other form is the *domestic* attachment, which may be issued against any debtor, being an inhabitant of the commonwealth, when he has absconded from the place of his usual abode. Under this proceeding the goods attached are to be divided among the creditors of the defendant *pro rata*.

2811. By the Code of Practice of Louisiana, an attachment in the hands of third persons is declared to be a mandate which a creditor obtains from a competent officer, commanding the seizure of any property, credit or right, belonging to his debtor, in whatever hands they may be found, to satisfy the demand which he intends to bring against him. A creditor may

---

therein. The defendant may come in and take defence at any time before judgment; and if, after judgment, he satisfies the court he had no notice before judgment, he may make a defence at any time within one year after notice of the judgment, or within seven years after its rendition.

obtain such attachment of the property of his debtor in the following cases :

1. When such debtor is about leaving permanently the state, without there being a possibility, in the ordinary course of judicial proceedings, of obtaining any judgment against him, previous to his departure, or even when such debtor has already left the state never again to return.

2. When such debtor resides out of the state.

3. When he conceals himself to avoid being cited, and forced to answer to the suit intended to be brought against him.(a)

2812. By the local laws of some of the New England states, particularly of the states of Massachusetts, New Hampshire and Maine, personal property and real estate may be attached upon original process to respond to the exigency of the writ, and satisfy the judgment. In such case it is the common practice for the officer to bail the goods attached to some person, who is usually a friend to the debtor, upon an express or implied agreement on his part, to have them forthcoming on demand, or in time to respond to the judgment, when the execution thereon shall be issued.(b)

2813. In most of the states where the writ of attachment to compel an appearance is in use, the defendant may at any time before judgment *dissolve* the attachment, by entering special bail to the action; in which case the property attached is released from the operation of the writ, and the suit goes on as if a *capias* had been issued and special bail had been entered.

CHAPTER II.—OF THE APPEARANCE.

2814. The object of all the writs issued in commencing an action, is to compel the *appearance* of the

---

(a) Art. 239, 240. See Harris *v.* Dennie, 3 Pet. 292; Blanchard *v.* Cole, 8 L. R. 153.

(b) Story, Bailm. § 124.

defendant. At the same time the plaintiff also *appears*, and then the pleadings commence.

In former times in England, from which country we have derived so much of our law, the parties actually appeared in court in *term time*, on the return day of the writ, for all the pleadings and proceedings took place in court in term, and never in vacation. This appearance in court was either by the defendant himself, or by his attorney, but always in open court.

The parties being both in court personally, or represented by their attorneys, then made their several allegations before the judges, and the court received information as to the nature of the plaintiff's claim, and the defendant's defence, which was then called the *loquela*, and these allegations, on either side, have since acquired the denomination of *pleading* or *pleadings*.

In modern practice the *appearance* of the parties is no longer by actual presence in court, either by themselves or their attorneys; but still such an appearance is *supposed*, and exists in contemplation of law. When the defendant has not been arrested, an appearance is effected on the part of the defendant by making certain formal entries in the proper office of the court, expressing his appearance, as by the attorney's writing his name on the margin of the docket opposite that of the defendant. When the defendant has been arrested under a *capias*, the entry of special bail to the action is considered an appearance. No formality is requisite on the part of the plaintiff to express his appearance; upon the appearance of the defendant, as above described, both parties are considered as *in court*.

All persons may appear in person, and there are some classes who cannot appear by attorney, but must appear in person. These are persons who are not *sui juris*, and therefore have no capacity to appoint an attorney; as infants, who must appear personally or by guardian; married women, when sued alone, must appear in person, when sued with their husbands, the husband appoints the attorney for both; and idiots, who háving no capacity to appoint an attorney must appear in person, unless they have been placed under the care of a committee; in this last case, the committee may appear for the idiot.

When the defendant appears by attorney, there ought regularly, and there is always supposed to be, a *warrant* in writing executed by the defendant for that purpose.(*a*)

. The neglect to enter an appearance within four days after the return day, which time is called the *quarto die post*, will entitle the plaintiff to take a judgment for want of an appearance, unless the rules or the practice of the court have provided some other course.

CHAPTER III.—OF THE PLEADINGS.

SECTION 1.——GENERAL NATURE OF THE PLEADINGS.

2815. The parties being both in court, the next step to be taken is to plead. By *pleading* is meant the statement in a logical and legal form, of the facts, which constitute the plaintiff's cause of action, or the defendant's ground of defence; it is the formal ˙mode of alleging that on record, which would be the support, or the defence of the party in evidence. In a general sense, it is what either party to a suit at law alleges for himself in a court, with respect to the subject matter of the cause, and the mode in which it is carried on, including the demand which is made by the plaintiff; but in strictness it is no more than setting forth those facts or arguments which show the justice or legal sufficiency, of the plaintiff's demand,

---

(*a*) See, as to the necessity of having a retainer, ante, n. 2424.

and the defendant's defence, without including the statement of the demand itself, which is contained in the declaration or count.(a)

Formerly these pleadings were delivered orally, or in open court; but now they are drawn up in writing, and the attorneys of the opposite parties mutually deliver them to each other out of court, or file them in the proper office of the court.

The science of pleading was designed to render the facts of each party's case plain and intelligible, and to bring the matter in dispute between them to judgment.(b)   It is, as has been well observed, admirably calculated for analyzing a cause, and extracting, like the roots of an equation, the true points in dispute; and referring them with simplicity, to the court and jury.(c)

SECTION 2.—OF THE PARTS OF PLEADINGS.

2816. The parts of pleadings have been classified under two heads: 1, the *regular*, or those which occur in the ordinary course of an action; and 2, the *irregular*, or collateral, being those which are occasioned by mistakes in the pleadings on either side.

§ 1.—Of the regular pleadings.

2817. The regular pleadings are, 1, the *declaration* or count, which is a narrative of the plaintiff's cause of action; 2, the *plea*, which is an answer to the declaration, and states the ground of the defendant's defence; it is either to the jurisdiction of the court; or suspending the action, as in the case of a parol demurrer; or in abatement; or in bar to the action; or in replevin, an avowry and cognizance; 3, the *replication*, which is an answer to some matters alleged in

(a) Bac. Ab. Pleas and Pleading.
(b) Steph. Pl. 1.
(c) 1 Hale's Com. Law, 301, n.

the plea; and in case of an evasive plea, a *new assignment;* or in replevin, the *plea in bar,* to the avowry and cognizance; 4, the *rejoinder;* or in replevin, the replication to the plea in bar; 5, the *sur-rejoinder;* which, in replevin, is the rejoinder; 6, the *rebutter;* 7, the *sur-rebutter;* 8, pleas *puis darrein continuance,* when the matter of defence arises pending the suit.

§ 2.—Of the irregular pleadings.

2818. The irregular or collateral parts of pleading are, 1, the *demurrer* to any part of the pleadings above mentioned; 2, *demurrer to evidence* given at the trial; 3, *bills of exceptions;* 4, pleas in *scire facias;* and 5, pleas in error.*(a)*

***

CHAPTER IV.—OF THE DECLARATION.

2819. The parties being in court, the next step taken in the cause is to ascertain, by the pleadings of record, what is the cause of their dispute. The natural course is for the plaintiff to state the ground of his complaint; this is done by his declaration.

A *declaration,* anciently called a *tale,* and now known by the name of *narratio,* or usually abbreviated *narr.* or *count,* is a specification, in a methodical and legal form, of the circumstances which constitute the plaintiff's cause of action.*(b)* Though *declaration* be the general term, yet in real actions it is more properly called a *count.(c)* But this word *count* has still another meaning. It is derived from the French *conte,* which signifies a narrative or tale, and though used in the old books as synonymous with declaration, yet this

(*a*) Vin. Ab. Pleas and Pleadings, C.
(*b*) 1 Chit. Pl. 248 ; Bac. Ab. Pleas, B ; Com. Dig. Pleader, C 7 ; Steph. Pl. 36 ; Co. Litt. 17, a ; 3 Bl. Com. 293 ; Gould, Pl. c. 4, § 1.
(*c*) Steph. Pl. 36.

distinction must be now observed; when the plaintiff's complaint embraces only a single cause of action, and he makes only one statement of it, that statement is called, indifferently, a declaration or count, though the former is the more usual term; but when the suit embraces two or more causes of action (each of which of course requires a different statement,) or when the plaintiff makes two or more different statements of one and the same cause of action, each several statement is called a *count*, and all collectively a *declaration*.

The declaration, in an action at law, answers to the bill in chancery, the libel of the civilians, and the allegation of the ecclesiastical courts. It may be considered with regard, 1, to those general requisites or qualities which govern the whole declaration; 2, to its form, particular parts, and requisites.

SECTION 1.—OF THE GENERAL REQUISITES OF A DECLARATION.

2820. The general requisites of a declaration are, 1, that it must correspond with the writ; 2, that it state all the principal facts; 3, that it be certain and true.

§ 1.—The declaration must correspond with the writ.

2821. The first general requisite of a declaration is, that it must correspond with the process, 1st, as to the names of the parties to the action; 2dly, with regard to the number of parties; for if a writ is issued in the name of one plaintiff, and the declaration is in the names of several, it will be irregular ;(a) 3dly, when the plaintiff sues in one character, for example, as executor, he cannot declare generally, though if he merely styles himself executor, without stating that he *sues as* executor, he may do so, because in this last

---

(a) Rogers v. Jenkins, 1 Bos. & Pull. 383.

case, the demand is still the same ;(*a*) 4thly, as to the cause of action; for example, if the cause of action on the writ be debt, and in the declaration be assumpsit, or *vice versa*, the variation will be fatal, even after verdict.(*b*)

But, in general, the variance between the writ and declaration can be taken advantage of only by plea in abatement, or by special demurrer.(*c*)

§ 2.—Of the statement of all the essential facts.

2822. The second general requisite of the declaration is, that it shall contain a statement of all the facts necessary in point of law to sustain the action, and no more ;(*d*) for the plaintiff can recover only *secundum allegata et probata*, the allegation and the proof must be the same; he can, therefore, prove no material fact, which the declaration does not allege.

The declaration must show a title, or right of action, in the plaintiff, at the time of bringing the suit ; if it fail in this, it is insufficient to warrant a judgment in the plaintiff's favor ; for no subsequent allegation will entitle him to recover. He must recover upon the grounds on which he places his claim in the declaration, or not at all.(*e*)

If the declaration shows that the plaintiff had no cause of action, when the suit was commenced, as if he declare upon a promissory note which was not then due, he cannot recover ; for the plaintiff cannot recover for any matter accruing *after* the commencement of the suit, except *interest*, on demands carrying interest, that being recoverable up to the time of judgment, under the name of *damages*.

(*a*) 1 Bos. & Pull. 383, note b.
(*b*) Stamps *v.* Graves, 4 Hawkes, 102.
(*c*) Sargent *v.* Haynes, 2 Hill, S. C. 585; Haney *v.* Townsend, 1 McCord, 206 ; Young *v.* Grey, 1 McCord, 211.
(*d*) Co. Litt. 303, a.
(*e*) Bac. Ab. Pleas, etc., B 1.

Every thing connected with the *gist* of the action, or that without which it cannot be supported; all averments of any material facts; all conditions precedent, when the right of recovery depends upon them; and a request, when one is required, to support the action, must be stated in the declaration.

§ 3.—Of the certainty and truth required in a declaration.

2823. These circumstances must be stated with certainty and truth. The certainty necessary in a declaration, is to a certain intent in general, which should pervade the whole declaration, and is particularly required in setting forth the parties, the time, the place, and the subject matter.

2824.—1. It must be stated with certainty who are the *parties* to the cause, and therefore a declaration by or against " A B and Company," not being a corporation, is insufficient.(*a*)

2825.—2. In personal actions, the declaration must in general state a *time* when every material or traversable fact happened, and when a venue is required, time must also be mentioned.(*b*) But unless time constitute a material part of the contract declared upon, or where the date of a written contract or record is averred, or, in ejectment, in which the demise must be stated to have been made after the title of the lessor of the plaintiff, and his right of entry accrued, the precise time is not in general material. In these cases, therefore, the pleader may assign any time he pleases to any given fact, and prove another, for time is then not traversable.   This option is, however, subject to certain restrictions.

1. If the pleader does not wish to be held to prove strictly the time laid in his declaration, he should lay it under a *videlicit*.   The office of the videlicit is to

---

(*a*) Com. Dig. Pleader, c. 18.
(*b*) The King *v*. Holland, 5 T. R. 620 ; Steph. Pl. 311, 312.

show that the party does not mean to prove the precise time, or, in transitory action, the precise place; this is done by putting the words " to wit," or " that is to say;" for example, " And the said C D, afterward, to wit, on the   day of   1851," etc.

2. He should not lay a time intrinsically impossible, or inconsistent with the fact to which it relates; for a time so laid would in general be ground of demurrer; but when such a time is laid to a fact not traversable, though the statement of time be impossible or inconsistent, it will do no harm, upon the principle that *utile, per inutile non vitiatur.*

3. There are instances where time forms a material point in the merits of the cause; and in these cases, if a traverse be taken, the time laid is of the substance of the issue, and must be strictly proved, and its being laid under a videlicit makes no difference. In cases of usury, time is of material importance, because upon that depends whether it exists or not; thus where the declaration stated a usurious contract, made on the 21st day of December, 1774, for giving the day of payment of a certain sum to the 23d day of December, 1776, and the proof was that the contract was made the 23d day of December, 1774, giving the day of payment for two years, it was held that the verdict must be for the defendant.(*a*)

2826.—3. The third particular in which certainty in pleading is required, is that of *place*. The consideration of this subject will be postponed till we come to treat of the venue, when discussing the several parts of a declaration.

2827.—4. The next general particular which must be stated with certainty, is the *subject matter* of the suit, and it embraces all the material facts which constitute the cause of action. This comprehends, according to

(*a*) Carlise *v.* Trears, Cowp. 671; Gould, Pl. c. 3, § 66; Steph. Pl. 313.

the nature of the case, the *contract* declared upon, and the *breach* of it; or the *wrong* complained of, and its injurious consequences; or the *property* sought to be recovered, or in respect to which the alleged damages and injury have been done. But the requisite certainty relates only to the *manner* in which these particulars ought to be stated. When the facts necessary to be stated are known, they can be easily laid with certainty, which consists merely in alleging them so distinctly and explicitly as to exclude all ambiguity. It is not easy to say what degree of certainty is requisite in setting out the subject matter.(*a*) This will be more fully considered in the sequel.

SECTION 2.—OF THE FORM AND PARTS OF A DECLARATION.

2828. The several parts of a declaration are, 1, the title of the court and term; 2, the venue; 3, the commencement; 4, the statement of the cause of action; 5, the several counts; 6, the conclusion; 7, the profert and pledges.

§ 1.—Of the title of the court and the term.

2829. It must appear by the declaration in what court it has been filed; this is done by simply heading the declaration with the name of the court, as "In the Supreme Court for the Eastern District of Pennsylvania."

The pleadings, it will be remembered, were formerly *ore tenus;* and the title of the term, with reference to the ancient proceedings, is to be considered as a statement or memorandum of the time when the plaintiff comes into court, and alleges his cause of complaint; and as this could only be in term time, when the defendant was in court, consequently the declaration must be entitled in term.

(*a*) 1 Chit. Pl. 260, 261; Steph. Pl. 342.

§ 2.—Of the venue.

2830. The *venue* is the place from which the jury are *to come*, who are to try the issue.(*a*)   The statement of the venue follows in the margin, after the title of the declaration.

According to the former constitution of trial by jury, the particularity of place was rendered absolutely essential, in all issues which were to be decided by a jury; because the jury consisted of witnesses, or of persons who were in some measure cognizant of their own knowledge, of the matter in dispute; they were of course, generally to be summoned from the particular place, or neighborhood, where the fact happened;(*b*) and in order to know into what county the *venire facias*, or writ which commanded the sheriff to summon the jurors, should be directed, and to enable the sheriff to execute the writ, it was required that the issue, and, therefore, the pleadings out of which it arose, should show particularly what that place or neighborhood was.(*c*)   This place was called the *venue* or *visne*, from Vicinetum, or neighborhood, and the statement in the pleadings obtained the same name; and to allege a place, was said to *lay the venue*.   It was then the practice to summon the jurors from the immediate neighborhood where the facts to be tried arose, and, therefore, the venue was laid in the parish, town, or hamlet, as well as the county.   But when the jurors were taken from the body of the county, and they were no longer witnesses, it was sufficient to lay the venue in the county.

In the subsequent pleadings, the plea, the replication, and so forth, the venue must be laid to each affirmative traversable allegation, as in the declaration,

---

(*a*) Gould on Pl. c. 3, § 102; Steph. on Pl. 398; Arch. Civ. Pl. 86.
(*b*) Harg. Co. Litt. 125, a, n. (1).
(*c*) Fabrigas *v.* Mustyn, Cowp. 176, 7; 2 H. Bl. 161.

according to the principles already stated, until issue joined.

Another rule relating to the venue is, that it must be laid *truly*. Formerly the venue was of course laid where the facts arose, and it was for this reason that written contracts bore date at a certain place.(*a*) But when, in consequence of the changes in the constitution of juries, the reason ceased to operate, the courts began to distinguish between cases in which the truth of the venue was material, and those in which it was not so. A difference was now perceived between *local* and *transitory* actions, the nature of which has already been explained.(*b*)

In *local* actions the plaintiff must lay the *venue in the action truly;* in a *transitory* one, he may lay it in any county that he pleases.

§ 3.—Of the commencement of the declaration.

2831. The *commencement* of the declaration is that part which follows the venue in the margin, and precedes the circumstantial statement of the cause of action. It contains a statement, 1st, of the names of the parties to the suit, and, if they sue or are sued in another right, or in a political capacity, for example, as executors, assignees, and the like, the character or right in which they sue must be stated; 2dly, of the mode in which the defendant was brought into court, as, " C D was attached or summoned," as the case may be; 3dly, a brief recital of the form of action to be proceeded in. The following is the formula in assumpsit in such cases: " C D was summoned [or attached, when the defendant has been holden to bail,] to answer A B, of a plea of trespass on the case upon promises," etc.(*c*) Of course the form must vary with the different forms of actions.

(*a*) Gilb. Hist. C. P. 84.   (*c*) Steph. Pl. 47.
(*b*) Book 2. t. 6, c. 1, s. 2.

212 OF REMEDIES.

No. 2832.　　　Book 4, tit. 8, chap. 4, sec. 2, § 4, art. 1.　　　No. 2835.

§ 4.—Of the statement of the cause of action.

2832. Certainty in the statement of the cause of action is of the utmost importance; but this statement necessarily varies, according to the circumstances of each particular case, and the form of action. These will be briefly and separately considered.

Art. 1.—Of the statement of the cause of action in assumpsit.

2833. The statement of the cause of action in assumpsit is either special or general.

1. *Of special counts in assumpsit.*

2834. The rules to be observed in the structure of special counts, may be reduced to six, those which relate, 1, to the inducement; 2, to the consideration of the contract; 3, to the contract itself; 4, to the requisite averments; 5, to the breach; and, 6, to the damages.

1° *Of the inducement.*

2835. *Inducement* is the statement of matter, which is introductory to the principal subject of the declaration, and which is necessary to explain or elucidate it; such matter as is not introductory nor requisite to elucidate the substance or gist of the action, nor is collaterally applicable to it, is not inducement but *surplusage.* The inducement is in the nature of a preamble, and useful in making intelligible the statement of the facts in the declaration; for example, on a contract to pay money upon a consideration of forbearance, the declaration begins by stating the debt forborne, and the proceedings that were stayed.(a) The allegation in an inducement, when material, must

_____

(a) 1 Chit. Pl. 293; Steph. Pl. 257; Gould, Pl. c. 3, § 9; Lawes, Pl. 66, 67; Bac. Ab. Pleas, etc. I 2; 14 Vin. Ab. 405; 20 Vin. Ab. 345.

be proved; when immaterial, they may be rejected as surplusage.

2° Of the consideration.

2836. It is generally necessary to state upon what consideration the contract upon which the action is brought is founded, unless it be on a contract which is presumed by the law to be founded on a valuable consideration, as upon a bill of exchange or a promissory note; but in other simple contracts, the consideration must be stated, whatever may be the form of action. The consideration, as stated, must always correspond with the facts of the case, and be sufficient, in law, to support the promise as laid, and be coëxtensive with it.(*a*)

3° Of the statement of the contract.

2837. Next to the statement of the consideration, the contract itself is usually alleged, and this must be done by setting forth in some part of the declaration, either in the words in which it was made, or according to its *legal effect*, and if there be a variance, it will be fatal;(*b*) it must be stated or described as it operates or takes effect in law, although such statement or description should vary, literally, or in form, from the matter of fact to be shown in evidence. Where the contract is founded upon a legal liability, and implied, it is sufficient to state such liability, without alleging formally that the defendant promised, as in assumpsit on a bill of exchange.(*c*)   It is, however, more correct in all cases, to state that the defendant *undertook, super se assumpsit*, or words to that effect.

(*a*) Jones *v.* Ashburnham, 4 East, 464.   See ante, as to the nature of the consideration, n. 611.

(*b*) King *v.* Pippet, 1 T. R. 240;   Andrews *v.* Williams, 11 Conn. 326; Dorr *v.* Fenno, 12 Pick. 521; Churchill *v.* Merchants' Bank, 19 Pick. 532; Lent *v.* Padelford, 10 Mass. 230.

(*c*) Elsee *v.* Gatward, 5 T. R. 145.

2838. In stating the consideration, the whole of it must be mentioned, and it must be set forth in the declaration ;(a) but in stating the contract, it is sufficient merely to state the parts of the promise, the breach of which is complained of; and it is not requisite to state in the declaration other parts not qualifying or varying in any respect those the breach of which is complained of.(b)

When a contract is in the alternative, it must not be stated as an absolute contract, though the option may be in the party pleading.

On a contract in writing, the words of the contract must be pursued, when they are concise and intelligible, and when their effect is doubtful, that is the better course ; but the plaintiff is not required to set forth even the material parts in letters and words, the statement of the substance and legal effect will be sufficient.(c)

When there is a *variance* between the declaration and the proof, that is, a disagreement or difference between them, its effect will be fatal when the variance is in relation to something *material;* but when it relates merely to a matter of *form,* or an *immaterial matter,* it will not be so regarded.(d)

4° *Of averments.*

2839. By *averment* is meant a positive statement of facts, in opposition to argument or inference.(e)

2840. Lord Coke says, averments are twofold, namely, general and particular. 1. A *general* averment is that which is at the conclusion of an offer to make good, or prove, whole pleas containing new

---

(a) Brooke v. Lowrie, 1 N. & M. 342.
(b) Miles v. Sheward, 8 East, 7 ; Clarke v. Grey, 6 East, 567.
(c) Dorr v. Fenno, 12 Pick. 521 : Lent v. Padelford, 10 Mass. 230.
(d) Savage v. Smith, 2 Bl. Rep. 1104 ; 2 Saund. 206, a, n. 22 ; Ferguson v. Harwood, 7 Cranch. 408 ; Harrison v. Weaver, 2 Port. 542.
(e) Rex v. Horne, Cowp. 683, 684.

OF PROCEEDINGS IN AN ACTION. 215

No. 2841   Book 4, tit. 8, chap 4, sec 2, § 4, art. 1.   No. 2842.

affirmative matter, (but this sort of averment applies only to pleas, replication, and subsequent pleadings; for counts in avowries, which are in the nature of counts, need not be averred,) the form of such averments being *et hoc paratus est verificare.*

2841.—2. *Particular* averments are assurances of the truth of particular facts, as where the life of tenant, or tenant in tail, is averred; and in these, says Lord Coke, *et hoc*, etc., are not used. Again, in a particular averment, the party merely protests and avows the truth of the fact or facts averred; but in general averments he makes an offer to prove and make good by evidence what he asserts.

2842. Considered with regard to their effect, averments may be classed into material and immaterial averments. An averment is *material,* when it is of the gist of the action, when the action cannot be supported without it; an *immaterial* averment is the statement of unnecessary particulars, in connection with, and as descriptive of, what is material.(a) A distinction was formerly made between *immaterial* and *impertinent* averments; the former must, in many cases, have been proved, as in the following case: In an action brought on the statute of 8 Ann. c. 14, § 1, by a landlord against a sheriff, for taking in execution, and removing from the demised premises, the goods of the tenant, without leaving effects to satisfy a year's rent; the declaration stated the demise, which it described as reserving a certain annual rent, *"payable by four even and equal quarterly payments,"* etc. On the trial, a parol demise was proved; and it appeared there was no stipulation with regard to the time or times of paying the rent; and for this cause the plaintiff was nonsuited. Because, though it was confessedly unnecessary to state the time or times of payment in the declaration; though this statement was immaterial, as it was

(a) Gould on Pl. c. 3, § 185.

216   OF REMEDIES.

No. 2843.   Book 4, tit. 8, chap 4, sec. 2, § 4, art. 1.   No 2844.

indispensably requisite to allege a contract, reserving rent, and that had been stated as a whole contract, it must be proved.(a) An *impertinent* averment, was one which was irrelevant and foreign to the cause, and which might have been struck out as surplusage, as it need not have been proved.

In modern times, this distinction between immaterial and impertinent averments have been considered as untenable, and the two terms are treated as being synonymous. A more correct distinction has been made between material or impertinent averments and *unnecessary* averments. The former are those which need not be alleged, nor proved, if alleged; the latter consists of matter which need not be alleged; but being alleged, must be proved.(b)

2843. Averments must contain not only matter, but *form*. General averments are always in the same form. The most common form of making particular averments, is in express and direct words, for example: And the party *avers*, or *in fact saith*, or *although*, or *because*, or *with this that*, or *being*, etc. But they need not be in such words, for any words which necessarily imply the matter intended to be averred are sufficient.

2844. An averment is required when the obligation of the defendant to perform his contract depends on an event which would not otherwise appear from the declaration to have occurred; for without an averment of such an event, there would be no logical statement of the cause of action. In a special action of assumpsit, these averments usually relate to, 1, the performance, or the excuse for the non-performance of a condition precedent; 2, the defendant's notice of such performance; 3, the defendant's having been requested to perform his contract.

(a) Bristow v. Wright, Dougl. 665. See 1 Chit. Pl. 304; Gould on Pl. c. 3, § 186; Savage v. Smith, 2 W. Bl. R. 1101, 1104.
(b) Williamson v. Allison, 2 East, 446; Twiss v. Baldwin, 9 Conn. 292; Parton v. Holland, 17 John. 92; Vowles v. Miller, 3 Taunt. 137.

2845.—1. When the consideration of the defendant's contract was *executory*, or his performance was
to depend upon some act to be done or forborne by the
plaintiff, or on some other event, before the plaintiff
can be entitled to sue, he must have performed such
precedent condition, for on such performance his right
vests, unless he has a good cause for non-performance,
and he must, therefore, aver in his declaration that
such condition precedent, whether it were in the
affirmative or negative, or to be performed or observed
by him or by the defendant, or by any other person,
has actually been performed, or he must show some
excuse for the non-performance.   And when there
are *mutual conditions* to be performed *at the same time*,
the plaintiff must aver the performance or the readiness to perform his part of the contract.(*a*)

2846.—2. The rule as to notice appears to be this:
when the matter alleged in the pleading is considered
as lying more properly in the knowledge of the plaintiff than that of the defendant, then the declaration
ought to state that the defendant had notice of it; but
when the matter does not lie more properly in the
knowledge of the plaintiff than that of the defendant,
notice need not be averred.   Notice of the non-payment of a bill of exchange must be averred, because
that fact is more properly within the knowledge of the
plaintiff than of the defendant; but if the defendant
contracted to do a thing, on the performance of an act
by a stranger, notice need not be averred, for whether
the stranger has performed the act lies as much in the
defendant's as in the plaintiff's knowledge, and he
ought to take notice at his peril.(*b*)

2847.—3. A *request* must be stated in the declaration and proved upon trial, whenever it is essential
to the cause of action that the plaintiff should have

(*a*) As to what are mutual conditions, see ante, n. 618.
(*b*) 2 Saund. 62 a, n. 4; 1 Saund. 117, n. 2; Com. Dig. Pleader, C 75.

218 OF REMEDIES.

No 2848. | Book 4, tit. 8, chap 4, sec 2, § 4, art 1 | No 2848.

requested the defendant to perform his contract; as in an action for not delivering a horse, sold by defendant to the plaintiff, it is requisite to aver a special request before action brought, or there must be some allegation to dispense with it.(*a*)

There are two forms of pleading a request, the *special* and the *general*. The former must state by whom, and the time when, and the place where it was made; and when a request is essential to the support of the action, a special request must be stated, and it must be shown by and to whom the same was made, and the time and place of making it, so as to enable the court to judge whether the request were sufficient. The latter, commonly called the *licet sæpius requisitus*, or " although often requested so to do," without stating the time and place of request, though usually inserted in the breach to the money counts, is unnecessary, and the want of it will not vitiate the declaration.

5° Of the breach of the contract.

2848. That part of the declaration in which the violation of the defendant's contract is stated, is called the *breach;* this must in all cases be stated in the declaration, because it is the essential cause of action; when there has been no breach, there is no cause of action.

In assumpsit, it is usual to introduce the statement of the particular breach, with the allegation that the defendant, contriving and fraudulently intending, craftily and subtlely to deceive the plaintiff, neglected and refused to perform, or did perform the particular act, contrary to his previous stipulation or agreement. The breach must obviously be governed by the nature of the engagement; it ought to be assigned in the words of the contract, either negatively or affirmatively, or in words which are coëxtensive with its import and effect.(*b*)

(*a*) Bowdill *v.* Parsons, 10 East, 359.
(*b*) Com. Dig. Pleader, C 45 to 49 ; 2 Saund. 181, b. c.

OF PROCEEDINGS IN AN ACTION. 219

No 2849   Book 4, tit. 8, chap 4, sec. 2, § 4, art. 1.   No 2850.

When the contract is in the disjunctive, as on a promise to deliver a horse by a particular day, or pay a sum of money, the breach ought to be assigned that the defendant did not do the one nor the other.(a)

2849. The breach should *not vary* from the sense and substance of the contract, and be neither more limited, nor larger than the covenant; and care should be taken not unnecessarily to narrow it, for in this last case the plaintiff may be required to prove more than would have otherwise been required; for example, where a breach of covenant was assigned that the defendant had not used a farm in a husband-like manner, but on the contrary had committed *waste*, it was held, that the plaintiff could not give in evidence the defendant's using the farm in an unhusband-like manner, if such misconduct did not amount to waste, though if the latter part of the breach had been omitted, the evidence would have been admissible.

6° *Of the damages.*

2850. In personal and mixed actions, but not in penal actions, for obvious reasons, the declaration must allege, in conclusion, that the injury is to the damage of the plaintiff; and must specify the amount of damage.(b)

In personal actions there is a distinction between those which sound in damages and those that do not; but in either of these cases, it is equally the practice to lay damages. There is, however, this difference, that in the former case, damages are the main object of the suit, and are, therefore, always laid high enough to cover the whole demand; but in the latter, the liquidated debt, or the chattel demanded, being the main object, damages are claimed in respect to the detention only, of such debt or chattel; and are, therefore, laid in a small sum.

(a) Com. Dig. Pleader, C.
(b) Com. Dig. Pleader, C 84; 10 Rep. 116, b.

220 OF REMEDIES.

The plaintiff cannot recover greater damages than he has laid or claimed in his declaration.(a)

2. Of common counts.

2851. The *common counts* are certain general counts, not founded on any special contract, which are introduced in a declaration, for the purpose of preventing a defeat of a just right by the accidental variance of the evidence. These, in an action of assumpsit, are founded on express or implied promises to pay *money* in consideration of a *precedent debt*, and are, therefore, called *money counts;* they are of six descriptions: 1, the indebitatus assumpsit; 2, the quantum meruit; 3, the quantum valebant; 4, the account stated; 5, the breach of the common counts; 6, general observations on the money counts.

1° The indebitatus assumpsit.

2852. The *indebitatus assumpsit* is that species of action of assumpsit, in which the plaintiff alleges in his declaration, first a debt, and then a promise in consideration of the debt, that the defendant, being indebted, he promised the plaintiff to pay him. The promise so laid is generally an implied one only.(b)

2853. There is a striking conformity between the action of *indebitatus assumpsit* and the *pactum constitutæ pecuniæ* of the civil law. This latter was an agreement by which a debtor agreed to pay his creditor what was due to him; whence there arose a new obligation, which did not destroy the former, by which he was already bound, but which was accessory to it; and by this multiplicity of obligations the right of the creditor was strengthened.(c) The *pactum constitutæ*

(a) Com. Dig. Pleader, C 84 ; Vin. Ab. Damages, R. ; Tettce v. Prescott, 2 How. Mis. 686 ; Crabb v. Nashville Bank, 6 Yerg. 333 ; Maupin v. Tripplett, 5 Miss. 422 ; Hayton v. Hope, 3 Mis. 53.
(b) 1 Chit. Pl. 334 ; 3 Reeves, Hist. C. L. ; Yelv. 21, 70 ; Bac. Ab. Assumpsit, G.
(c) Poth. Ob. 457.

pecuniæ was a mere accessory obligation, and consisted in a promise to pay a subsisting debt, whether natural or civil, made in such a manner as not to extinguish the preceding obligation; it was introduced by the prætor to obviate some formal difficulties. The *indebitatus assumpsit* was invented to obviate a similar difficulty. To an action of debt, wager of law might have been opposed as a bar, but it could not to an action of *indebitatus assumpsit.(a)*

2° *The quantum meruit.*

2854. When a person employs another to do work for him, without any agreement as to his compensation, the law implies a promise, from the employer to the workman, that he will pay him for his services, *as much as he deserves* or merits. In such case the plaintiff may suggest in his declaration that the defendant promised to pay him as much as he reasonably deserved, and then he avers that his trouble was worth such a sum of money, which the defendant has omitted to pay. This is called an action on a *quantum meruit.(b)* When there is an express contract, for a stipulated amount and mode of compensation for services, the plaintiff cannot abandon the contract, and resort to an action for a *quantum meruit* on an implied *assumpsit.*

3° *The quantum valebant.*

2855. When goods are sold without specifying any price, the law implies a promise from the buyer to the seller that he will pay him for them *as much as they are worth.* The plaintiff in such case suggests in his declaration that he sold goods to the defendant, that he "promised to pay him as much as the goods were

(a) 4 Co. 91, 94. See 3 Wood. 168, 169, note c. ; 1 Vin. Ab. 270 ; Bro. Ab. Action sur le case, pl. 7, 69, 72 ; 6 Toull. Dr. Civ. Fr. n. 388, 396 ; Inst. 4, 6, 9 ; Dig. 13, 5 ; Code, 4, 18 ; Nov. 115, c. 6.
(b) 2 Bl. Com. 162, 163 ; 2 Phil. Ev. 82 ; 1 Vin. Ab. 346.

222   OF REMEDIES.

No. 2856.   Book 4, tit 8, chap. 4, sec. 2, § 4, art. 1.   No. 2857.

reasonably worth, and then avers that they were worth so much, that the defendant had notice thereof, and that he refused to pay for the same." This count differs from the *quantum meruit* in this. that the *quantum valebant* is confined to *goods;* in most other respects they are similar.

4° *The account stated.*

2856. An action of assumpsit upon an *account stated* may be maintained, when there has been a settlement of their accounts, between the parties, and a balance struck in favor of one of them. A count on an account stated, is almost invariably inserted in a declaration in *assumpsit* for the recovery of a pecuniary demand. It is in general advisable to insert such a count, unless the action is against persons who are incapable in law to state an account. It is not necessary to set out the subject matter of the original debt.(*a*)

The usual form of a declaration on an *account stated* alleges, that "the defendant on, etc., aforesaid, at etc., aforesaid, accounted with the plaintiff of and concerning divers sums of money, before then due by the defendant to the plaintiff, and then in arrear and unpaid, and that upon such accounting, the defendant was found to be in arrear to the plaintiff, in a certain named sum, and that being so found in arrear and indebted, the defendant, in consideration thereof, undertook and faithfully promised the plaintiff to pay him the same on request."

5° *Breach of the common counts.*

2857. A *breach* of the money counts must be stated in order to show the plaintiff's right to sue. Upon these counts the common breach is in general terms

(*a*) Milward *v.* Ingraham, 2 Mod. 44.

according to this formula: "yet the said defendant not regarding his said promises and undertakings, but contriving, and craftily and subtlely intending to deceive and defraud the said plaintiff in that respect, hath not (although often requested so to do,) as yet paid the said sums of money, or any part thereof, but has wholly neglected and refused, and still neglects and refuses so to do, to the damage of the plaintiff in the sum of   dollars, and therefore he brings his suit, etc." This breach necessarily varies in actions by and against partners, husband and wife, executors, etc.

These allegations of deceits, craftiness, subtlety and fraud, though usual, do not seem to be essential in such a breach.

6⁀ *General observations as to the money counts.*

2858.—1. Money lent may be recovered under the common count for *money lent*, charging that the defendant promised to pay the plaintiff for money lent. To recover, the plaintiff must prove that the defendant received the money, but it is not indispensable that it should have been originally lent; if, for example, the money had been advanced upon a special contract which had been abandoned and rescinded, and which cannot be enforced, the law raises an implied promise, from the person who holds the money, to pay it back · as money lent.

2859.—2. When one advances money for the use of another, with his consent or at his express request, although he be not benefited by the transaction,(*a*) the creditor may recover in an action of *assumpsit*, declaring for *money paid* for the defendant. But one cannot by a voluntary payment of another's debt, without his consent express or implied, make himself

(*a*) Hassinger *v.* Solms, 5 S. & R. 9; Addis on Contr. 226.

a creditor of that other.(*a*) *Assumpsit* for money paid will not lie where property, not money, has been paid or received ;(*b*) nor can money which has been paid to the defendant, either for a just, legal, or equitable claim, although it could not have been enforced at law, be recovered back as money paid. This rule appears to be the same in the civil law, for, according to that system, the payment to one of what is not due to him, *indebiti solutio,* if made through any mistake in fact, or even in law, entitles him who made the payment to an action against the receiver for repayment, *condictio indebiti.* This action does not lie, 1st, if the sum paid was due *ex equitate,* or by natural obligation ; 2dly, if he who made it knew that nothing was due, for *qui consulto dat quod non debebat, præsumitur donare.*(*c*)

The form of declaring is "for money paid by the plaintiff, for the use of the defendant, at his request."(*d*)

2860.—3. A count for *money had and received* is generally introduced in an action of *assumpsit* when money has been received by the defendant, which, *ex equo et bono,* ought to be paid over to the plaintiff. This count has been likened to a bill in equity, and it will be sustained whenever the defendant himself has actually received the money, for the use of the plaintiff, or which in equity and good conscience he ought to pay over to him. The thing received must either originally have been money, or that which the parties have agreed to treat as such, or which may fairly be inferred to be money.(*e*) The plaintiff may waive all

---

(*a*) Richardson *v.* McRay, 1 Const. R. 472 ; Ransalaer Glass Factory *v.* Reid, 5 Cowen, 603 ; Weakley *v.* Braham, 2 Stew. 500.

(*b*) Morrison *v.* Berkey, 7 S. & R. 246 ; 14 S. & R. 179. Sed vide Ainslie *v.* Wilson, 7 Cowen, 662 ; Pearson *v.* Parker, 3 N. H. Rep. 366 ; McLellan *v.* Crofton, 6 Greenl. 333.

(*c*) Dig. 12, 6 ; Code, 4, 5.

(*d*) Alexander *v.* Vane, 1 M. & W. 511.

(*e*) As to what shall be considered money, see Pickard *v.* Bankes, 13

OF PROCEEDINGS IN AN ACTION.   225

No. 2861.   Book 4, tit. 8, chap. 4, sec. 2, § 4, art. 2.   No. 2862.

tort, trespass and damages, and claim only money which the defendant has actually received. But this claim of the plaintiff is subject to any legal or equitable lien the defendant has upon it.(a) This count may be maintained where the money was *delivered* to the defendant *for a particular purpose*, to which he refused to apply it;(b) or where the defendant obtained the money from the plaintiff by *fraud* or false pretences ;(c) or where the money was obtained by *duress, extortion,* or *imposition;*(d) or upon an illegal contract, if the plaintiff was not *in pari delicto* with the defendant.(e)

Art. 2.—Of statement of the cause of action in debt.

2861. In the preceding article we have considered the requisites of a declaration with regard to the title of the court and term, the venue and the commencement, which apply generally to actions of debt as well as to actions of assumpsit. It will not be necessary now to reconsider these same matters.

1. *Form of the statement.*

2862. The debt demanded should be clearly described, and it ought to be the aggregate of all the sums to be due in the different counts. In general the declaration should be in the *debet* and *detinet;* that is, it ought to state that the defendant *owes* and unjustly *detains* the debt or thing in question. It is so brought between the original contracting parties. But to this rule there is one exception, the writ must be in the

East, 20 ; Lowndes *v.* Anderson, 13 East, 130 ; Mason *v.* Waite, 17 Mass. 560 ; Gilchrist *v.* Cunningham, 8 Wend. 311 ; Arms *v* Ashley, 4 Pick. 71 ; Floyd *v.* Day, 3 Mass. 405 ; Andrew *v.* Robinson, 3 Camp. 199.
    (a) Eddy *v.* Smith, 13 Wend. 488 ; Clift *v.* Stockdon, 4 Litt. 217.
    (b) De Barnales *v.* Fuller, 14 East, 590, n.
    (c) Bliss *v.* Thompson, 4 Mass. 488 ; Lyon *v.* Annable, 4 Conn. 350 ; Hasser *v.* Willis, 1 Salk. 28.
    (d) Morgan *v.* Palmer, 2 B. & C. 729.
    (e) 1 Steph. N. P. 335.

226   **OF REMEDIES.**

No. 2863   Book 4, tit. 8, chap 4, sec. 2, § 4, art. 2.   No. 2864.

detinet only, even between the original parties, when the action is instituted for the recovery of *goods* or *chattels*, as a horse, a ship, and the like; for it cannot be said a man owes a horse, or a ship, but only that he detains them.(*a*)

.The declaration should be in the *detinet* only when the defendant does not owe, but unjustly detains from the plaintiff the debt or thing for which the action is brought; this is the form of an action by an executor, because the debt or duty is not due to him, but it is unjustly detained from him ;(*b*) against an executor when he is personally responsible, the declaration should be in the *debet* and *detinet;*(*c*) when he is not personally liable, the declaration ought to be in the *detinet* only.

2863. Debt lies *for a sum certain,* whether it have been ascertained by the agreement of the contracting parties; or by judgment; or by statute, as, when this remedy is given for a penalty; or for the escape of a judgment debtor.

2864.—1. When the action is on a *simple contract,* the declaration must state the consideration of the agreement, precisely as in assumpsit; and it should state, either a legal liability or an express agreement, though not a promise to pay the debt. The formula is as follows: "For that the said defendant on, etc. was indebted to the plaintiff in   dollars, for [here state what the debt is for as in assumpsit] which moneys were to be paid to the plaintiff upon request; whereby and by reason of the non-payment thereof, an action hath accrued to the plaintiff to demand and have from the said defendant, the sums aforesaid, amounting in all to the sum of   dollars, yet the said defendant hath not paid the same," etc.

(*a*) 3 Bl. Com. 153, 154; Bac. Ab. Debt, F; 1 Lilly's Reg. 543.
(*b*) 1 Saund. 1.
(*c*) Bac. Ab. Debt, F.

OF PROCEEDINGS IN AN ACTION. 227

No. 2865   Book 4, tit. 8, chap. 4, sec 2, §4, art. 2.   No 2866.

2865.—2. When the action is founded on a *specialty*, the deed must in general be stated. No inducement or statement of the consideration is required, because the consideration is presumed. But when the plaintiff claims as assignee, as in the case of a reversion, he must show by way of inducement how his title to the action arose.

It must appear that the contract was under *seal*, but there are certain technical words which import a contract under seal, as *indenture, deed*, or *writing obligatory*.

2866. When the plaintiff declares on a deed, or the defendant pleads a deed, he must do it with a *profert in curiâ*, by declaring or pleading that he "brings here into court the said writing obligatory," or other deed. The object of this is to enable the court to inspect the instrument pleaded, the construction and legal effect of which is matter of law, and also to entitle the adverse party to oyer of it ;(a) but this must be understood with this restriction, that one who pleads a deed of any kind, *without making title under it*, is not bound to make a profert of it.(b)

To the above rule that he who declares on, or pleads a deed, and makes title under it, must make a profert of it, there are several exceptions.

1. A stranger to a deed, may in general plead it, and make title under it, without a profert.(c)

2. He who claims by operation of law, under a deed to another, may plead the deed without a profert.

3. When the deed is in the hands of the opposite party, or destroyed by him, a profert need not be made.

4. When it has been lost or destroyed by time or casualty, no profert is necessary.

(a) 10 Co. 92 ; 1 Chit. Pl. 414 ; 1 Archb. Pr. 194.
(b) Gould on Pl. c. 7, part 2, § 47.
(c) Com. Dig. Pleader, O 8.

228 OF REMEDIES.

No. 2867.   Book 4, tit. 8, chap. 4, sec. 2, § 4, art. 2.   No. 2868.

In all these cases, to excuse the want of a profert, the special facts which bring the case within the exception, should be alleged in the party's pleading.(a)

2867.—3. When the action is brought on a *record*, it is in general sufficient to follow the words of the record, as in the case of an action on a *recognizance of bail*, the declaration should follow the description in the entry of the recognizance, and should set forth in what court, and at whose suit, and for what sum, or cause, the defendant became bail.(b)

In declaring upon a *judgment*, it is sufficient to state "that heretofore, to wit, in such a term, in such a court, then holden at   , the plaintiff, by the consideration and judgment of that court, recovered against the defendant the sum of   dollars, which was adjudged by the said court to the plaintiff for his damages which he had sustained, as well by reason of the non-performance by the said defendant of certain promises and undertakings, made by him the said plaintiff, as for his costs and charges by him about his suit in that behalf expended."

When the judgment is in debt, the form of the declaration varies accordingly.

2868.—4. When an action of debt is brought on a *statute* at the suit of the party grieved, or by an informer, and the whole of the penalty is given to him, the commencement is the same as debt on a contract; but when the penalty is given to the government or to a body of men, as the guardians of the poor, the commencement, and other parts of the declaration, usually state that the plaintiff sues *qui tam*, etc.; that is, that he sues for himself *as well as* for the government, etc.(c) The offence or act charged must be

---

(a) Lawes on Pl. 96; 1 Saund. 9, a, note; Gould on Pl. c. 8, part 2; Steph. on Pl. 86, 88, 439, 441.
(b) Com. Dig. Pleader, 2 W 10.
(c) Esp. on Pen. Act, 5, 6; 1 Vin. Ab. 197; Com. Dig. Action on Statute, E; 1 Saund. 136, n. 1; 2 Saund. 374, n. 1.

stated to háve been committed or omitted by the defendant, and it must appear to have been within the provisions of the statute, and all the circumstances necessary to support the action must be alleged; for the conclusion *contra formam statuti* will not aid the omission.(*a*)

2. *Of the breach.*

2869. The breach in debt is nearly the same whether the action be in debt on a simple contract, specialty, record, or statute. The usual formula is, " Yet the said defendant, although often requested so to do, hath not as yet paid the said sum of   dollars above demanded, or any part thereof, to the plaintiff,(*b*) but hath hitherto wholly neglected and refused so to do; to the damage of the said plaintiff   dollars, and therefore he brings his suit," etc.

The damages in debt are merely nominal, and a small sum only is inserted, and when the action is by a common informer, who is not entitled to damages, none should be claimed.

Art. 3.—Of the statement of the cause of action in covenant.

2870. The action of covenant is brought on a deed. After stating the *commencement*, the declaration passes to the *inducement*, when that is required; but that is seldom the case, unless the action is by or against a person claiming or being sued in a derivative right, as at the suit of an heir or assignee. A *consideration* need not be stated, unless it is a condition precedent, or unless a conveyance operating under the statute of uses be pleaded. A *profert* of the deed or an excuse for the omission is required, as in debt on a specialty. No unnecessary matter should be stated in setting out

---

(*a*) 1 Saund. 135, note 3.

(*b*) When the action is *qui tam*, the form, instead of " to the plaintiff," should be " to the said commonwealth, and to the said —— who sues as aforesaid."

the contract. The *averment* by the plaintiff of a condition precedent must be made as in other cases; and the *breach* must be stated as already mentioned. The *conclusion* is mere matter of form, and if left out would not be fatal. The *damages*, being the principal object of the action, must be laid in a sum sufficiently high to cover the whole demand of the plaintiff.

Art. 4.—Of the statement of the cause of action in form ex delicto.

2871. When we come to discuss the different kinds of actions in form *ex delicto*, some of the rules relating to each, as to the form of the declaration, will be considered. This will enable us now to pass over this part of the subject, by examining only those rules connected with the *statement*, and which relate, 1, to the matter or thing affected; 2, the plaintiff's right to it; 3, the injury or wrong committed; and 4, the damages sustained.

1. Of the statement of the thing or matter affected.

2872. In describing the matter or thing affected, the pleader should use such terms in his declaration as are usually employed in law. The word *tenement*, we may remember, is any thing which may be holden, and it includes incorporeal as well as corporeal hereditaments; it is properly used in stating the premises in ejectment and trespass. The term *close* imports an interest in the soil, and not merely an inclosed field; and the word *way* is more technical than passage.

2873. When the declaration alleges any injury to goods and chattels, it is a general rule that their *quality*, *quantity*, and *value* or *price* be stated. For example, in an action of trespass for breaking the plaintiff's close, and taking away his fish, without showing the number or nature of the fish, the declaration was held to be defective.(*a*) With respect to

---

(*a*) 5 Co. 34, b. See 7 Taunt. 642.

OF PROCEEDINGS IN AN ACTION.   231

No. 2874.   Book 4, tit 8, chap 4, sec. 2, § 4, arf. 4.   No. 2874.

value, it should be specified in reference to the current coin of the United States; as "divers, to wit, two looking glasses, of great value, to wit, of the value of one hundred dollars, lawful money of the United States."(a)

But this rule is not so strictly construed but that sometimes it admits the specification of quality and quantity in a loose and general way. A declaration in trover for two *packs* of flax, and two *packs* of hemp, without setting out the weight and quantity of a pack, was held good after verdict;(b) and, upon the same principle, a declaration in trover for a *library* of books, without expressing what they were, has been allowed.(c)

The evidence to support a declaration as to quantity and value, need not exactly support the allegations contained in the declaration, and a variance between them is not fatal; for in these cases the plaintiff recovers according to his proof. But a verdict cannot, in general, be obtained for a larger quantity or value than is alleged.

The allegation with regard to quality, must in general be strictly proved as laid.

2. Of the statement of the plaintiff's right.

2874. The plaintiff's right or interest in the thing affected, ought to be clearly stated. It may arise from *some particular* duty of the defendant; or it *may be implied by law*, as the absolute rights of persons; or it may be a *general right* given by law; in these last two cases, it is unnecessary to state such a right in the declaration. In trespass to houses, it is in general sufficient to state the *possession* of the plaintiff.

When the right of the plaintiff consists in an obliga-

(a) In pleading. the term *value* is applied to inanimate things, *price* to animated beings. 2 Lilly's Ab. 629.

(b) 2 Saund. 74, b, n. (1.)

(c) A declaration in trespass, for breaking the plaintiff's close, and taking and cutting away his grain, grass, etc., is sufficient, without alleging the quantity and value of each article. Van Dyk v. Dodd, 1 Halst. 129.

tion on the part of the defendant to observe some particular duty, the declaration must state the nature of such duty. If the plaintiff's right arise from a breach of duty in respect of the defendant's particular character or situation, the particular situation of the defendant must be stated; as in an action against a common carrier, the declaration must state the particular situation of the defendant as such.

3. Of the statement of the injury.

2875. The declaration for injuries *ex delicto* varies according to the circumstances, whether the wrong has been committed with force and immediate, or whether it is consequential; and again, whether it arose from malfeasance, misfeasance, or non-feasance.

1. When the injury has been committed with force and is immediate, as in trespass, it is stated in the declaration without any inducement of the defendant's motive or intent, or the circumstances under which the injury was committed. In the statement of these injuries, the words *vi et armis* should be adopted; and the conclusion in trespass or other forcible injury is *against the peace* of the commonwealth.

2. In the declaration in an action on the case, when the injury is not immediate and with force, and the act or non-feasance complained of was not *primâ facie* actionable, not only the injury but the circumstances under which it was committed, ought to be stated; as, that the defendant, *well knowing* the mischievous propensity of his dog, permitted him to go at large.

The intent or motive of the defendant, in committing the act in question, is seldom necessary, but when it can be proved, it is advisable, in aggravation of the damages, to state the defendant's malicious intent; this is sufficiently done if it be substantially shown, in general terms, as *wrongfully intending;* and in action for a libel, it is usual to charge that the defendant

OF PROCEEDINGS IN AN ACTION.   233

No. 2876.   Book 4, tit. 8, chap. 4, sec. 2, § 4, art. 4.   No. 2876.

maliciously published it, but the word falsely is sufficient.

In actions of slander, it is usual, in order to show the meaning of the words used, to explain this meaning by means of an *innuendo*, as, "he, (meaning the plaintiff.") The use of the innuendo is only explanatory of some matter expressed; it serves to apply the slander to the precedent matter, but cannot add, enlarge, extend, or change the sense of the previous words, and the matter to which it alludes, must always appear from the antecedent parts of the declaration.(*a*)

The *time* when the injury was committed, is seldom material; and the *place* need be stated only in local actions, as in trespass to land, and in replevin. In transitory actions the injury may be charged to have been committed in the county where the action is brought.

4. *Of the statement of the damages in actions ex delicto.*

2876. In actions for torts, it is sometimes proper to state, in addition to the conclusion of the declaration *ad damnum,* etc., the damages resulting from the injury. These damages are either *general,* that is, such as the law implies; or *special,* or such as really took place, and which are not implied by law. When the act is injurious in itself, and the plaintiff has sustained both general and special damages, the latter are superadded to the former.

On the contrary, when the law does not necessarily imply that the plaintiff has sustained damages by the act complained of, the declaration should show the resulting damages with particularity; as when a master sues for beating his servant, the allegation *per quod servitium amisit* is material.

(*a*) Mix *v.* Woodward, 12 Conn. 262; Lindsey *v.* Smith, 7 John. 359; Bowdish *v.* Peckham, 1 Chip. 146; Caldwell *v.* Abbey, Hardin, 529; Watts *v.* Greenleaf, 2 Dev. 115. See Weir *v.* Hoss, 6 Ala. 881.

234 OF REMEDIES.

No. 2877.   Book 4, tit 8, chap 4, sec. 2, § 5, art 1.   No 2878.

A declaration in trespass concludes, generally, with an *alia enormia*, " and other wrongs to the said plaintiff then and there did, against the peace," etc. Under this allegation some matters may be given in evidence in aggravation of damages, though not specified in other parts of the declaration.(*a*) For a trespass in entering a house, the plaintiff may, therefore, give in evidence as aggravation, that the defendant debauched his daughter.(*b*)

The damages which the plaintiff claims must be the legal and natural consequences of the act of the defendant, for in considering a breach of a contract, an injury or a crime, the law looks to the immediate and not to any remote cause.(*c*) Therefore, in action for words, it is not sufficient special damages to allege and prove a mere wrongful act of a third person, induced by the slander ; as that a number of persons seized the plaintiff, in consequence of the slander, and beat him.

§ 5.—Of the several counts in one declaration.

2877. The next matter to be considered is, how far several counts may be joined, when the cause of action is the same.

Art. 1.—*Reasons for having several counts.*

2878. In every case the plaintiff has a right to insert in his declaration as many counts as he pleases ; but as each count purports, upon its face, to disclose a distinct right of action, unconnected with that stated in any other count, each one must, in itself, be single.

One object proposed in inserting two or more counts in one declaration, when there is, in fact, but one cause of action, is, in some cases, to guard against the danger

---

(*a*) Bull. N. P. 89 ; Bac. Ab. Trespass, I.
(*b*) Russell *v.* Corn, 6 Mod. 127.
(*c*) Bac. Max. Reg. 1 ; Bac. Ab. Damages, E.

of an insufficient statement of the cause, where a doubt exists as to the legal sufficiency of one or another of two different modes of declaring; but the more usual end of inserting more than one count in such case, is to accommodate the statement of the cause, as far as may be, to the possible state of the proof on trial; or to guard against the hazard of the proof's varying materially from the statement of the cause of action; so that if one of several counts be not adapted to the evidence, some of them may be so.(a)

Art. 2.—When several counts may be joined.

2879.—1. In *assumpsit* it is usual to put several counts in the same declaration; for example, on a suit upon a promissory note, a count is inserted on the note, and then the money counts follow, namely, a count for money lent, for money had and received, for money paid. And in a declaration on a contract to deliver goods sold, if the agreement was to deliver within a certain time, and at a particular place, the first count is adapted to such facts; the second to deliver on request; and the third within a reasonable time. It is frequently advisable to declare in different counts, the one on an executory, and the other on an executed consideration; the first to admit evidence of the defendant's agreement, at the time of making the contract, the other, of subsequent admissions or promises.

2880.—2. In *debt* on specialties and records, and in *covenants*, one count is in general sufficient, because the evidence does not vary from the statement in the declaration; and, in actions on a deed, a *profert* of the deed is requisite, or an excuse must be stated for not making it. But in debt on simple contract, legal

(a) Gould on Pl. c. 4, § 4; Steph. on Pl. 279; Doctr. Pl. 178; Dane's Ab. Index, h. t.

236   OF REMEDIES.

No. 2881.   Book 4, tit. 6, chap. 4, sec. 2, § 5, art. 3, 4.   No. 2883.

liabilities and penal statutes, it is frequently advisable to state the cause of action under several counts.

2881.—3. In actions for *torts*, it is also advisable to state the same cause of action under several counts in different ways, and in actions for slander, with innuendoes, so as to meet the probable evidence.

Art. 3.—*Of the form of the counts.*

2882. The first count should fully state a complete cause of action. In framing the subsequent counts for the same cause, care should be taken to avoid unnecessary repetition of the same matter; by a proper inducement in the first count, and concise reference in the subsequent, to such inducement, much unnecessary prolixity will be avoided.(*a*) The second and subsequent counts may commence with the words, "And whereas also," which are sufficiently positive.(*b*)

Art. 4.—*Of the effect of several counts.*

2883. If any one of the counts in a declaration be proved, although no evidence is given as to the others, the plaintiff is entitled to a verdict and judgment upon it, unless it be radically insufficient in law. And when more than one count is proved, the jury may assess entire or distinct damages on each. If distinct damages are assessed, judgment may be given upon either of the counts; but if the jury find entire damages' on all the counts, the judgment must be entire, in which case, if one of the counts be insufficient in law, the judgment may be arrested *in toto*, or a writ of error is sustainable.(*c*) When the defect is discovered

(*a*) Stiles *v.* Nokes, 7 East, 506.
(*b*) Hart *v.* Langfitt, 2 Ld. Raym. 842; Com. Dig. Pleader, C 33.
(*c*) Needham *v.* McAuley, 13 Verm. 68; Keirle *v.* Shriver, 11 Gill & John. 405; Walker *v.* Sargeant, 11 Verm. 327; Dryden *v.* Dryden, 9 Pick. 546; Stevenson *v.* Hayden, 2 Mass. 406; Barnes *v.* Hurd, 11 Mass. 50; State *v.* Bean, 19 Verm. 530.

before verdict, it is expedient to apply to the court for leave to strike out such defective count, or to amend, or to enter a *nolle prosequi* to such count; or at the trial to take a verdict only on the sufficient counts.(*a*)

§ 6.—Of the conclusion of the declaration.

2884. There are some actions where the object is to recover damages, and in others no damages can be recovered; a certain amount of damages should be laid or claimed, and the consequences of laying too little may sometimes embarrass the plaintiff; the damages should be laid according to a particular form; these will be severally considered.

Art. 1.—*In what case damages should be laid.*

2885. No damages should be laid in real actions. In personal and mixed actions, the declaration should conclude to the damage, *ad damnum :* but to this there are exceptions. In *scire facias* upon a record, which is an action merely to obtain an execution on an ascertained right of record, and in a penal action, at the suit of a common informer, no damages should be laid; in the latter case, the plaintiff's right to the penalty did not accrue until the bringing of the suit, and, therefore, he could have sustained no damage.

In assumpsit, covenant, case, replevin, and trespass, the object of the action is to recover damages. Although, in debt, that be not the principal object of the suit, still damages are recoverable.

Art. 2.—*Amount of damages to be claimed.*

2886. In those cases where the principal object of the action is to recover damages, the amount laid in the declaration should be sufficient to cover the real

(*a*) 1 Chit. Pl. 295.

demand; for, as we have seen,(a) the plaintiff cannot recover greater damages than he has declared for, and laid in the conclusion of his declaration; though when he left a blank for the damages, it was held good after verdict, as in that case the blank in the declaration was supplied by the writ.(b)

When the verdict is greater than the amount laid in the declaration, a *remittitur* should be entered for the surplus before judgment; that is, a formal entry should be made on the record, by which the plaintiff abates or remits the excess of damages found by the jury, beyond the sum laid in the declaration.(c)

In debt it is usual to lay the damages in such a sum as will cover the interest, because the damages are merely nominal, the object of the action being to recover a sum of money *eo nomine*, and in *numero*.(d)

Art. 3.—Of the form of the conclusion.

2887. The form of the conclusion is, " And therefore he brings his suit," etc. In ancient times, the plaintiff was required to establish the truth of his declaration in the first instance, before it was called into question by the pleadings, by the simultaneous production of his *secta*, that is, a number of persons as witnesses, to confirm his allegations.(e) The practice of thus producing a secta, gave rise to the very ancient formula almost invariably used at the conclusion of a declaration, as entered of record, " and thereupon he brings his suit," etc., *et inde producit sectam*, and though the actual production has, for many centuries, even in England, fallen into disuse, the formula still remains. The count, in a writ of right, never

---

(a) Ante, n. 2884.
(b) Proctor v. Crozier, 6 B. Mon. 268.
(c) 1 Saund. 285, n. 6; 4 Conn. 109.
(d) Rudder v. Price, 1 H. Bl. 550; Warner v. Theobald, Cowp. 588.
(e) Bracton, 214, a.

concluded with the ordinary production of suit; nor did the count in dower.(*a*)

§ 7.—Of the profert and pledges.

2888.—1. We have seen when a profert is necessary when the action is founded on a deed or record; a profert is also required in other cases, and it usually follows immediately after the conclusion to the damages. This occurs in cases brought by executors or administrators; in order to show their title to sue, they must make a profert of the letters testamentary or letters of administration, which are the foundation of their authority. In a *scire facias* the profert may be made in the middle or at the end of the declaration. The omission of a profert is now aided, unless the defendant demur specially for the defect.

2889.—2. It is usual to insert pledges to prosecute. Anciently it was necessary to find pledges or sureties to prosecute a suit, and the names of the pledges were added at the foot of the declaration; but in the course of time it became unnecessary to find such pledges; because the plaintiff was no longer liable to be amerced, *pro falsa clamora,* and the pledges were merely nominal persons, and now John Doe and Richard Roe are the universal pledges; but they may be omitted altogether,(*b*) or inserted at any time before judgment.(*c*) For although formerly they were of use to answer for the amercement of the plaintiff, in case he were nonsuited, barred of his action, or had a verdict or judgment against him, yet now they are not answerable. In case the plaintiff neglects to deliver or file his declaration within the time prescribed by law, or the rules of the court, or is guilty of other delays or defaults, he is adjudged *not to follow his suit,* or his

---

(*a*) 3 Bl. Com. 395; Gilb. C. P. 48; Steph. Pl. 427, 8; 1 Chit. Pl. 399.
(*b*) Arch. Civ. Pl. 171; Tidd's Pr. 455.
(*c*) Baker *v.* Phillips, 4 John. 190.

remedy as he ought to do, and thereupon a *non suit* or *non prosequitur* is entered; and he is said to be *non pros'd*. For suffering this *non pros*, the plaintiff was formerly liable to be amerced to the king for making a false complaint, and to pay costs to the defendant.(*a*)

CONCLUDING REMARKS.

2890. Having pointed out the general requisites, and the several parts of a declaration, it only remains to be observed, that many defects in it may be cured by the acts of the defendant. This is the case particularly with those which are merely formal and not substantial; these may be aided either by a plea or by a verdict for the plaintiff.(*b*) After verdict, when the issue joined absolutely, required on the trial, proof of the facts defectively or improperly stated, or omitted, and without which it cannot be presumed the judge would have directed the jury to give, or that the jury would have given the verdict, such defect, imperfection, or omission, is cured by the verdict at common law.

CHAPTER V.—OF THE DEFENCE, IMPARLANCE, AND OYER.

SECTION 1.—OF THE DEFENCE.

2891. The plaintiff having stated his claim in his declaration, his opponent is now bound to set up his defence. By *defence* is meant the denial of the truth or validity of the complaint, and not a justification. It is a general assertion that the plaintiff has no ground of action, which assertion is afterward extended and maintained in the plea.(*c*) It is somewhat similar to

---

(*a*) 3 Bl. Com. 295, 296.
(*b*) Com. Dig. Pleader, C 85, 87.
(*c*) 3 Bl. Com. 296; Co. Litt. 127.

the *contestatio litis* of the civil law; though the *contestatio litis* is rather the joinder of issue than a defence.(*a*)

Defence is of two descriptions; first, half defence, which is as follows, "*venit et defendit vim et injuriam, et dicit,*" etc.; or, second, full defence, "*venit et defendit vim et injuriam, et dicit,*" etc., (meaning "*quando et ubi curia consideravit,*" or, when and where it shall behoove him,) "*et damna et quicquid quod ipse defendere debet et dicit,*" etc.(*b*)   In strictness the words *quando*, etc., ought not to be added when only half defence is made, and after the words "*venit et defendit vim et injuriam,*" the subject matter of the plea should be immediately stated.(*c*)

It has now become the practice in all cases, whether full defence or half defence be intended, to state it as follows: "And the said A B, by C D his attorney, comes and defends the wrong, (or in trespass, force,) and injury, when, etc., and says," which will be considered only as half defence, where such defence should be made, and as full defence when the latter is necessary.(*d*)

If full defence were made expressly by the words, "when and where it shall behoove him," and "the damages and whatever else he ought to defend," the defendant would be precluded from pleading to the jurisdiction or in abatement, for by defending *when and where* it shall behoove him, the defendant acknowledges the jurisdiction of the court, and by defending the *damages*, he waives all objections to the person of the plaintiff.(*e*)

Although, formerly, defence was a matter of sub-

(*a*) See 2 Brown's Civ. and Adm. Law, 358, n. 21; Code of Pr. of Louisiana, art. 357; Code 3, 9, 1; Dig. 5, 1, 14, 1; Code 2, 59, 2.

(*b*) Co. Litt. 127, b; Bac. Ab. Pleas, D.

(*c*) Gilb. C. P. 188; 3 B. & P. 9, n. a.

(*d*) Wilkes *v.* Williams, 8 T. R. 633; Willis, 41; 2 Saund. 209 c.; 3 B. & P. 9.

(*e*) 2 Saund. 209 c; Bac. Ab. Pleas, D; 3 Bl. Com. 297, 298.

stance, it is now only matter of form, and the omission of it is aided by general demurrer.(a)

SECTION 2.—OF IMPARLANCE.

2892. Imparlance, from the French *parler*, to speak, or *licentia loquendi*, in its most general signification, means time given by the court to either party to answer the pleading of his opponent, as either to plead, reply, rejoin, etc., and it is said to be nothing but the continuance of the cause till a further day.(b) But the more common signification of the term is time to plead.(c)

Formerly the parties were allowed time to speak or confer together, so that they might endeavor to settle the matter in dispute. Now, time for pleading is allowed, in most cases, by general rules of practice, without any formal entry of an imparlance.

2893. Imparlances are of three kinds : 1, a common or general imparlance ; 2, a special imparlance ; 3, a general special imparlance.

1. A *general* imparlance is the entry of a general prayer and allowance of time to plead till the next term, without reserving to the defendant the benefit of any exception, so that after such general imparlance, the defendant cannot object to the jurisdiction of the court, nor plead any matter in abatement. This kind of imparlance is always from one term to another.

2. A *special* imparlance reserves to the defendant all exceptions to the writ, bill, or count ; and, after it, the defendant may plead in abatement, though not to the jurisdiction of the court, because, by praying an imparlance he admits its jurisdiction.

3. A *general special* imparlance contains a saving of all exceptions whatsoever, so that the defendant after

(a) Hole v. Burgoigne, 3 Salk. 271.
(b) Bac. Ab. Pleas, C.
(c) Lawes' Civ. Pl. 93, 94; 2 Saund. 1, n. 2.

this may plead, not only in abatement, but also plead a plea which affects the jurisdiction of the court, as a privilege. He cannot plead a tender, and that he always was ready to pay, because by craving time he admits he is not ready, and so falsifies his plea.(a) The last two kinds of imparlances are, it seems, sometimes from one day to another in the same term.

When, after an imparlance, the defendant pleads any thing which the imparlance waives or falsifies, the plaintiff may sign judgment as for want of a plea, or apply to the court to set it aside, or demur, or finally, specially reply the imparlance, by way of *estoppel;* that is, by showing in the replication that the defendant is precluded, by his own act, appearing upon the record, from availing himself of the matter alleged in his plea.(b)

SECTION 3.—OF OYER.

2894. When an action is founded on a deed, pleaded with a *profert in curiâ,* as before explained, the defendant is entitled, upon demanding it, to oyer of the instrument, the original meaning of which is to *hear* it read. Oyer, then, is a prayer or petition to the court, that the party may hear read to him the deed, stated in the pleadings of the opposite party, for such deed is by intendment of law in court, when pleaded with a profert. The origin of this sort of pleading, we are told, is, that in ancient times the generality of defendants were themselves incapable of reading.(c) By the modern practice, a compliance with the demand of oyer, is to furnish the attorney of the opposite party with a copy of the deed, or file it in the proper office.

Oyer is demandable in all actions, real, personal, and mixed.

(a) Tidd's Pr. 418, 419.
(b) Tidd's Pr. 419; 1 Chit. Pl. 420, 424; Bac. Ab. Pleas, C; Com. Dig. Pleader, D; 1 Sell, Pr. 265; Gould on Pl. c. 2, § 16, 20; Steph. Pl. 90.
(c) 3 Bl. Com. 299; Steph. Pl. 87.

Though formerly oyer was demandable of the writ, and of records, as well as of deeds, now it is not granted of a record or of the original writ, and can be had only in cases of *deeds, probates, letters of adminis-tration,* etc., of which profert is made on the other side. Oyer never was demandable of *private writings not under seal.*

When the party is not bound to plead the specialty or instrument with a profert, as in the case of a promissory note, and he pleads it with one, such profert is mere surplusage, and the court will not compel him to give oyer of it. And if profert be omitted, when it ought to have been made, the adversary cannot have oyer, but must demur.

Oyer is allowed to enable the party to plead with a full understanding of his case, and therefore he has a right to it whenever a profert is properly made; and the refusal of oyer in such case is error, though it is not error to grant oyer where it is not demandable of right. For the ordering of oyer is supposed to have been no prejudice to the party giving it; but the refusal of it is presumed to have been injurious to him who demanded it, as he is supposed to have been unable to plead advantageously without it.

CHAPTER VI.—OF PLEAS.

2895. A plea is the defendant's answer by matter of *fact*, to the plaintiff's declaration. It is distinguished from a demurrer, which opposes matter of *law* to the declaration.(a)

Pleas are divided into pleas *dilatory*, or those which delay the plaintiff's remedy, not by questioning the cause of action, but the propriety of the suit, or the

---

(a) Steph. Pl. 62.

mode in which the remedy is sought; or, *peremptory*, which deny the plaintiff's cause of action. Pleas were thus divided in imitation of the division of exceptions in the civil law. *Exceptiones aut perpetuæ sunt, aut temporales et dilatoriæ.*(a)

Subordinate to this, there is another division; they are either to the jurisdiction of the court; in suspension of the writ; in abatement of the writ; or in bar to the action. The first three belong to the dilatory class, the latter is of the peremptory kind.(b)

The most natural order of pleading, is that established by law, and which the defendant must pursue, to wit:

1. To the jurisdiction of the court.
2. To the disabilities of the parties.
3. To the count or declaration.
4. To the writ.

This appears to be the natural order of pleading, because each subsequent plea admits that there is no foundation for the former. But although this is the order generally adopted in the United States, yet it is not universal, for the want of jurisdiction may be taken advantage of, at any stage of the case.

These various kinds of pleas will be separately considered; and for that purpose this chapter will be divided into two parts, or classes.

CLASS I.—OF DILATORY PLEAS.

2896. Pleas which have obtained the name of dilatory pleas, are, 1, to the jurisdiction; 2, in suspension of the action; 3, in abatement; 4, to their form and effect; 5, replications and other proceedings to dilatory pleas.

SECTION 1.—OF PLEAS TO THE JURISDICTION.

2897. A *plea to the jurisdiction* is one which denies

(a) Dig. 44, 1, 3.
(b) Steph. Pl. 63; 1 Chitty's Pl. 425; Lawes' Pl. 36.

246 OF REMEDIES.

No. 2898.   Book 4, tit. 8, chap. 6, cl. 1, sec 1, § 1, art. 1.   No. 2899.

that the court has jurisdiction of the cause.(*a*) Such a plea, though in effect it abates the writ, yet it differs from a plea in abatement, principally in three points: 1, it must be pleaded in person; 2, only half defence must be made; 3, it should conclude *si curia cognoscere velit*, if the court will have further cognizance of the said plea.(*b*) A plea to the jurisdiction is not properly a plea in abatement, because the court do not abate the writ, nor give any judgment for costs, but merely dismiss the case.(*c*)

These pleas will be considered with regard to, 1, the cases in which they are allowed; 2, the mode of pleading them; 3, the time when they must be pleaded.

§ 1.—Cases in which pleas to the jurisdiction are allowed.

2898. Pleas to the jurisdiction may arise from various causes: 1, from the privilege of the defendant, by which he is exempted from liability to suits; 2, from the fact that the cause of action arose *out of the territorial jurisdiction of the court;* 3, from a want of power, in the court, to take cognizance of the *subject matter* of the suit.

Art. 1.—*Of the privilege of the defendant.*

2899. Some persons are privileged from suits of every kind; of course the courts have no jurisdiction in such cases, and the case must be dismissed upon the plea of privilege being established. Ambassadors cannot be sued, and the act of congress, besides punishing all persons who may have been active in procuring any writ against them, declares any writ or process sued out against any ambassador received by the President of the United States to be void;(*d*) and the

---

(*a*) Bac. Ab. Pleas, E 1, 2. Gould on Pl. c. 5, § 13; Steph. Pl. 63; 1 Chit. Pl. 427; Arch. Civ. Pl. 290.
(*b*) Steph. on Pl. 393.
(*c*) Bac Ab. Pleas, E 1.
(*d*) Act of April 30, 1790, s. 25. Vide ante, n. 2800.

consent of the defendant cannot give the court jurisdiction.(a)

Members of congress are also privileged from suits
while attending to their duties in congress, or going
to and returning from the same; this privilege is not
only their own, and that of their constituents, but also
of the house of which they are members.(b)

When the privilege is merely personal, it must be
asserted seasonably or it is waived.

Art. 2.—Of actions arising out of the jurisdiction of the court.

2900. Courts are divided into those of general, and
those of special or limited jurisdiction. The first have
cognizance of all *transitory* actions wherever the cause
may have accrued; because all actions of that kind in
general follow the person of the defendant. To the
latter, or courts whose jurisdiction extends only to
causes of action actually arising within certain local
limits, it is a good plea to the jurisdiction as well in
transitory as in *local* actions, that the cause of action
did not accrue within those limits. In these last cases,
however, it is not necessary to plead to the jurisdiction, for the exception may be taken advantage of
under the general issue.(c)

But even courts of general jurisdiction have no authority to try cases of a *local* nature arising in a foreign
jurisdiction, or in any place where the process of the
court cannot run ;(d) and the defendant may plead to
the jurisdiction. It seems, however, that where a local
action, not requiring a judgment *in rem*, as trespass
quare clausum fregit, for an injury to land lying in a
foreign country, is brought, even in a superior court,
exception may be taken to the jurisdiction, under the
general issue.(e)

(a) United States *v*. Benner, Baldw. 240.
(b) Jeff. Man. § 3; Story on Const. §§ 856 to 862. Vide ante, n. 2801.
(c) Bac. Ab. Pleas, E. 1.
(d) Bac. Ab. Pleas, E. 1.
(e) 10 Co. 68, 76 b.

248 OF REMEDIES.

No. 2901.　　　Book 4, tit. 8, chap. 6, cl. 1, sec. 1, § 2.　　　No. 2902.

Art. 3.—Of the want of jurisdiction of the subject matter.

2901. When the court has no cognizance over the subject matter of the suit, it is fatal to its jurisdiction, for it cannot under any circumstances undertake to try it, because it is not competent; as, if an action should be brought in the circuit court of the United States, to recover a less sum than five hundred dollars; or if a cause, exclusively of admiralty jurisdiction, should be brought in a court of common law. In these cases, it is not requisite to *plead* to the jurisdiction, for the court would dismiss the cause on motion; or even without motion, *ex officio;* for the whole proceeding would be *coram non judice*, and utterly void.

§ 2.—The mode of pleading to the jurisdiction.

2902. A difference must be observed between a plea to the jurisdiction in a court of *limited*, and one of *general* jurisdiction. In pleading in a court of the first class, it is only necessary to plead negatively, that is, to show by proper allegations that the court has no jurisdiction; in pleading in a court of general jurisdiction, on the contrary, it is requisite, both at law and in equity, not only to show that the court has not jurisdiction, but also to designate specially some other court which has it. But this rule does not apply when the court has no jurisdiction of the *subject matter*.

The plea to the jurisdiction must be signed by the defendant *in person;* for if it be signed by attorney, it is presumed he did so by *leave of court*, and the asking leave is tacitly admitting the jurisdiction. But such implied admission cannot aid the jurisdiction, except in cases in which the objection must be taken, if at all, by *plea* to the jurisdiction, and can be taken in no other way.(*a*)

(*a*) Bac. Ab. Pleas, E 2; Lawes on Pl. 91; Bac. Ab. Abatement, A.

It has already been observed that the plea must conclude "if the court will have further cognizance of the said plea."(a)

§ 3.—Of the time of pleading to the jurisdiction.

2903. The plea to the jurisdiction must be the first act of the defendant in court; it must therefore be before a *general* or even a *special* imparlance; for if, in a case of this kind, the defendant refers any other question than that of its jurisdiction, of which it must of necessity judge, it admits the jurisdiction, and having so admitted it he cannot afterward deny it.(b)

SECTION 2.—OF PLEAS IN SUSPENSION OF THE ACTION.

2904. A plea *in suspension of the action*, is one which shows some ground for not proceeding in the suit at the present period, and prays that the pleading may be stayed until that ground be removed. Of this class, which is very small even in England, is the *parol demurrer*, which, when an action of debt is brought against an infant heir, for a debt of the ancestor, or a real action against the infant, is a suggestion of the non-age of the infant, and a prayer that the proceedings may be stayed till he is of full age, when it is said the *parol demurs*.(c) This plea, it is believed, is unknown in this country.

SECTION 3.—OF PLEAS IN ABATEMENT.

2905. A plea *in abatement* of the writ, is one which shows some ground for abating or quashing the original writ, and makes a prayer to that effect. One of the cardinal rules relating to pleas in abatement is,

(a) Bac. Ab. Pleas, E 1.
(b) Co. Litt. 127, b.
(c) 3 Bl. Com. 300; Steph. Pl. 64. *Parol* signifies in French, *speech,* in Latin, *loquela,* which was the most ancient appellation of *pleading.* Steph. on Pl. 29.

that the plea must give the plaintiff a better writ; for unless the defendant can do this, the plaintiff could not be certain of bringing another suit correctly. Indeed, this is the criterion between a plea in abatement and a plea in bar.

The various grounds for which a writ may be abated relate either, 1, to the disability of the plaintiff; 2, to the disability of the defendant; 3, to the count or declaration; 4, to the writ.

§ 1.—Of the disability of the plaintiff.

2906. Pleas to the disability of the person do not strictly fall within the definition of pleas in abatement, for they do not pray "that the writ be quashed," but pray judgment "if the plaintiff ought to be answered." They are, however, classed among pleas in abatement.

Pleas *to the disability of the plaintiff* must relate to the time of commencing or continuing his suit, and either deny his existence, as that he or one of several plaintiffs at the commencement of the suit was a fictitious person, or dead ;(a) and when a sole plaintiff dies, pending the suit, his death may be pleaded in abatement; but by statute it is provided in several states, and perhaps in most of them, that his personal representatives shall be substituted; in case one of several plaintiffs dies, the action, in general, abates at common law, for by joining in the suit they assert a joint right of recovery, which, as such, is destroyed by the death of either of them; but this last rule is qualified to some extent, as to personal actions which admit of *summons and severance*, and in which an entire indivisible thing is to be recovered; for in such actions, after one of the plaintiffs has been summoned and severed, he ceases to be a party, and the other

---

(a) Com. Dig. Abatement, E 16, 17 ; Bac. Ab. Abatement, L.

OF PROCEEDINGS IN AN ACTION.   251

No. 2907.   Book 4, tit. 8, chap. 6, cl. 1, sec. 3, § 2.   No. 2907.

becomes the sole plaintiff, prosecuting for the whole amount, or matter in demand, and, therefore, if the severed plaintiff dies, pending the action, his death has no effect upon the suit.(a)

It may be pleaded that the plaintiff is an alien enemy, for such a person cannot maintain an action while he so remains. When the husband sues alone, in cases where his wife ought to be joined, the defendant may plead in abatement. When a woman marries pending a suit brought by her, she renders herself unable to proceed any further, and the writ must abate at common law; but, in some states, Connecticut and Massachusetts, for example, if a feme sole plaintiff marries, *pendente lite*, her husband is authorized by statute to appear, suggest the marriage upon the record, and then jointly with her proceed in the suit.

§ 2.—Of the disability of the defendant.

2907. Pleas in abatement to the person of the defendant are various, and relate to—

1. The *misnomer* of the defendant, and, when this takes place, the writ must abate. But the defendant must be careful in such case not to admit by his plea, or otherwise, on the record that he is sued by his right name, or in a name by which he is known; when, therefore, the defendant pleads, " And the *said* C D comes and defends," he admits he is the person sued; his plea should commence, " And A B, against whom the plaintiff has sued out his writ, by the name of C D," etc.

When there are several defendants they must all be

(a) Bac. Ab. Abatement, F. *Summons and severance* is a proceeding to separate one of several persons, who is a co-plaintiff, from the rest; this takes place when one of such persons neglects or refuses to appear. He may then be summoned to appear, etc., and if he refuses to join in prosecuting the suit, he is separated from it by a judgment of *severance*, or as it is technically called *ad sequendum solum*. See Bac. Ab. Summons and Severance, F; Bro. Sum. and Sev. ; Arch. Civ. Pl. 59 ; Bouv. L. D. h. t. ; Vin. Ab. h. t. ; Co. Litt. 139 ; Off. Ex. 96, 104.

252 OF REMEDIES.

No. 2908   Book 4, tit 8, chap. 6, cl. 1, sec. 3, § 3;   No. 2908.

named in full, describing each of them; and when sued as partners they cannot be sued by the name of the firm, as A B and Co.

2. The *coverture* of the defendant may be pleaded in abatement, when a *feme covert* is sued without her husband; and, as she is incapable of appointing an attorney, she must plead this matter in person.(*a*) But when the husband is *civiliter mortuus*, or is an alien enemy residing abroad, this matter may be replied, and she will be considered as a *feme sole*.(*b*) The marriage of a *feme sole* defendant does not abate the writ, it being unreasonable that the defendant, by her own act, should defeat the action of the plaintiff.

3. The *death* of a sole defendant, at common law, abated the suit; but that evil is remedied in some of the states by statutes which provide the substitution of personal representatives. And by the statute of 17 Car. II., c. 28, it is enacted that the death of either party, " between verdict and judgment, shall not be alleged for error, so as judgment shall be entered within two terms after such verdict."(*c*) By the statute 8 and 9 W. III., c. 2, §§ 6 and 7, it is enacted " that if there be two or more plaintiffs or defendants, and one of them should die, if the cause of such action should survive to the surviving plaintiff or plaintiffs, or against the surviving defendant or defendants, the writ or action shall not be thereby abated; but such death being suggested upon the record, the action shall proceed at the suit of the surviving plaintiff or plaintiffs, against the surviving defendant or defendants."   •

§ 3.—Of pleas in abatement to the count or declaration.

2908. There is no plea to the declaration alone, but

(*a*) 2 Saund. 209, c, n. 1.
(*b*) Com. Dig. Abatement, F 2; Gould on Pl. c. 5, § 86; 1 Chit. Pl. 438.
(*c*) Bac. Ab. Abatement, F.

in bar.(a) Formerly the defendant might demand oyer of the writ, and, then, the same being set forth, if there was any variance between the writ and the count, or between the record, specially mentioned in the count, the defendant might plead such variance or demur, move an arrest of judgment, or sustain a writ of error; but as oyer of the writ cannot be now demanded, such variance is no longer pleadable in abatement.(b)

§ 4.—Of pleas in abatement of the writ.

2909. Pleas *in abatement of the writ* have been greatly abridged, because oyer of the writ is no longer demandable, and it is only when an error is carried into the declaration that advantage can be taken of it. There are pleas in abatement of the writ, which do not require an examination of the writ itself. For example, if, in the declaration, one only of two joint contractors is named defendant, this is sufficient to show that the same non-joinder exists in the writ; for as the variance between the writ and the declaration is a fault, the defendant is entitled to assume that they agree with each other; and he may, consequently, without producing the writ, plead this non-joinder as certainly existing in this latter instrument. In all cases where no oyer is necessary, pleas in abatement of the writ may still be pleaded.

These pleas are, 1, to the writ; 2, to the action of the writ.

Art. 1.—Of pleas to the form of the writ.

2910. These pleas were formerly pleaded for mat- ters apparent *upon the face of the writ*, such as variance from the record, specialty, and the like; but as oyer

(a) 2 Saund. 209, d ; Johnson v. Altham, 10 Mod. 210.
(b) 1 Chit. Pl. 439.

254 OF REMEDIES.

No. 2911.   Book 4, tit. 8, chap. 6, cl. 1. sec. 4, § 1.   No, 2912.

can no longer be had, now pleas in abatement to the form of the writ are principally for matter *dehors*, existing at the time of suing out the writ, or arising afterward, such as misnomer of the plaintiff or defendant in the christian or surname.(*a*) Pleas to the form of the writ may also be pleaded, when persons suing or being sued as husband and wife, are not married; or one of the plaintiffs or defendants was a fictitious person, or dead at the time of suing the writ, or that other persons who are not sued ought to have been joined.(*b*)

Art. 2.—Of pleas in abatement to the action of the writ.

2911. A plea *to the action of the writ* is one which shows that the action is misconceived, or that it is in one form when it ought to be in another, as where case is brought where trespass is the proper remedy; or it may be pleaded to a second action for the same cause, pending the first. In penal actions, however, when two actions are brought for the same cause, the plea is in bar, because the party who first sues is entitled to the penalty.(*c*)

SECTION 4.—OF THE FORM, QUALITIES AND EFFECT OF DILATORY PLEAS.

§ 1.—Of the form.

2912. Care must be taken that pleas have their proper forms, for although it is a general rule that a mere prayer of judgment, without pointing out the appropriate judgment, is sufficient, because the facts. being shown to the court, it is bound to pronounce the proper judgment;(*d*) yet if the plea contain matter

---

(*a*) Com. Dig. Abatement, H 17.
(*b*) Com. Dig. Abatement E, H.
(*c*) Combe *v.* Pitt, 3 Burr. 1423.
(*d*) 1 Saund. 97, n. 1.

in *bar* of the action, and concludes in *abatement*, it is a plea in bar, and judgment shall be given upon it; for, if the plaintiff can have no cause of action, he can have no writ.(*a*)   But to discourage dilatory pleas, the courts have departed from this rule, in regard to the effect of the beginning and conclusion of such pleas.

A plea which contains matter only in *abatement*, concludes in *bar*, and it is found against the defendant, it is a plea in bar, and final judgment may be given, because, by praying judgment, if the plaintiff shall *maintain his action*, the defendant admits the writ to be good.(*b*)   And when a plea begins in *bar*, though it contains matter in *abatement*, and *concludes in abatement*,(*c*) it is a plea in bar, and final judgment may be given.

2913.—1. As to the *title of the term*, these pleas must in general be entitled of the term to which the action is brought, and before the defendant has done any thing to admit the jurisdiction of the court, or the right of the plaintiff to sue.

2914.—2. The *commencement* of these pleas may be considered, 1, as to the statement of the appearance; 2, the nature of the defence; 3, the prayer.

1. Pleas of misnomer should not admit that the defendant has been properly sued in his proper name, as, "And the *said* C D, sued by the name of E D." Here, by using the word *said*, he admits he is the same person.   The form should be, "And C D, sued by the name of E D."(*d*)

2. The nature of *defence* has already been stated.(*e*)

3. Pleas to the jurisdiction usually commence without any prayer of judgment, and conclude, "and this he, the said plaintiff, is ready to verify, wherefore he

---

(*a*) 2 Saund. 209, c.   (*d*) 2 Saund. 1, n. 2.
(*b*) 2 Saund. 209, d.   (*e*) Ante, n. 2891.
(*c*) 2 Saund. 209, c and d.

256　　　　　　　OF REMEDIES.

No. 2915.　　　Book 4, tit. 8, chap. 6, cl. 1, sec. 4, § 2.　　　No. 2916.

prays judgment, if the said court here will or ought to take cognizance of the said plea."(a)

A plea to the person of the plaintiff or defendant, in respect to the disability to sue or be sued, and not on account of misjoinder of one party, ought to conclude with a prayer, "if the plaintiff ought to be answered."

The plea in abatement of the writ, for matter apparent on the face of it, should begin and conclude by "praying judgment of the writ, and that the same be quashed." But where the plea is for matter dehors, as misnomer, the plea should conclude with that prayer.(b)

2915.—3. An affidavit of the truth of the facts stated in all dilatory pleas must accompany them.

§ 2.—Of the qualities and effect of dilatory pleas.

2916. A writ being *divisible*, may be abated in part, and remain good for the residue. The defendant may plead to part in abatement, and demur or plead in bar to the residue of the writ or declaration. When the matter contained in the plea goes to defeat only a part of the plaintiff's cause of action, the plea in abatement should be confined to that part, a plea to the whole would be defective.(c) But when the matter goes only in part in abatement of the writ, and concludes with a prayer that the whole may be abated, the court may abate so much of the writ as the matter pleaded applies to, if there be a plea to other parts of the declaration.(d)

Great accuracy is required in framing dilatory pleas; they must be certain to every intent, be pleaded without repugnancy, and must in general give the plaintiff

---

(a) 2 Saund. 209, d ; Bac. Ab. Abatement, P ; Com. Dig. Abatement, I, 12.
(b) 1 Saund. 318, n.
(c) Harries v. Jamieson, 5 T. R. 557.
(d) 2 Saund. 210, d.

a better writ, for this is the true criterion between a plea in abatement and a plea in bar. The commencement and conclusion of the plea should be correctly stated, otherwise the plaintiff may demur; where a plea concluded praying judgment *if*, instead of *of*, the plaintiff's bill was held bad on demurrer, though the words "and that the same may be quashed" were also added.

SECTION 5.—OF REPLICATIONS AND OTHER PROCEEDINGS
RELATING TO DILATORY PLEAS.

2917. After the defendant has pleaded a dilatory plea, the plaintiff may consider whether he can sustain his suit or not; if he cannot deny the truth of the matter alleged, and it is sufficient in law to quash the writ, he may enter a *cassetur breve;* that is, pray that the writ may be quashed, to the intent that he may sue out a better one, against the defendant.

Although the plaintiff cannot tacitly abandon part of his demand, or his proceedings against one of several defendants, without discontinuing the whole suit, yet in some cases he may, by entering an express agreement or acknowledgment on record, not further to prosecute his suit as to the whole or part only of the cause of action, or, if there be several causes of action(*a*) or defendants, as to some or one of them, and proceed as to the rest.(*b*) This acknowledgment or agreement is called a *nolle prosequi.*

In civil cases, a *nolle prosequi* is considered, not in the nature of a *retraxit*, as was formerly supposed, but only an agreement not to proceed against *some* of the defendants, or as to *part* of the suit.(*c*) A *nolle prosequi* is now held to be no bar to a future action, for the same cause, except in those cases where, from the

(*a*) 7 Wend. 301.
(*b*) 1 Pet. R. 80.
(*c*) 1 Saund. 207, note (2), and the authorities there cited.

nature of the action, judgment and execution against one, is a satisfaction of all the damages sustained by the plaintiff.(a)

If the plaintiff is satisfied he can never recover, he may enter a *retraxit*, or a withdrawal of his suit. It is called a *retraxit* from the fact that this was the principal word used when the proceedings were in Latin.

A *retraxit* differs from a *non-suit*, the former being the act of the plaintiff himself, for it cannot be entered even by an attorney;(b) while the latter takes place in consequence of the neglect of the plaintiff. A *retraxit* also differs from a *nolle prosequi;* the effect of a *retraxit* is a bar to all actions of a similar nature ;(c) a *nolle prosequi* is not a bar even in a criminal prosecution.

2918. If, after a full examination, the plaintiff declines to suffer a non-suit, enter a *nolle prosequi* or a *retraxit*, he may either demur, reply, sign judgment for want of a sufficient plea, or in some cases, he may amend either at common law or by virtue of a statute.

1. When the plea is untrue in fact, the plaintiff should *reply*, and the replication may begin without any allegation that the writ ought not to be quashed; it must not be as to a plea in bar, because that would be a discontinuance, but should conclude to the country. If an issue in fact be joined upon the replication, and found for the plaintiff, the jury should assess the damages, and the judgment is peremptory for the delay, that the plaintiff recover *quod recuperet*, and not that he answer over, *quod respondeat.(d)*

2. When the plaintiff *demurs*, he is not required to assign any special cause, though it is safest to demur

---

(a) Cooper v. Tiffin, 3 T. R. 511; Cooke v. Berry, 1 Wils. 98.
(b) 8 Co. 58 ; 3 Salk. 245.
(c) Bac. Ab. Non-suit, A.
(d) 1 Com. Dig. Abatement, I, 14, 15 ; Bac. Ab. Abatement, P ; 2 Saund. 210, n. 3.

OF PROCEEDINGS IN AN ACTION.

specially. In general, the judgment on the demurrer in favor of the *plaintiff*, to a plea in abatement, or to a replication to such plea, is only interlocutory, that the defendant answer over, *quod respondeat ouster.(a)* But when a plea contains matter which can be pleaded only in abatement, improperly commences or concludes in bar, the judgment on demurrer may be final.*(b)* It is a rule that when the judgment is *respondeat ouster*, no other plea in abatement will be allowed. When the judgment, on a plea in abatement, is for the *defendant*, it is that the writ or bill be quashed; or if a temporary disability or privilege be pleaded, that the plaintiff remain without day, until, etc.

3. A judgment may be *signed* by the plaintiff, as for want of a plea, in some cases where the plea is defective in substance; when the plea is defective in form the plaintiff should demur.*(c)*

4. When a misnomer has taken place, either of the plaintiff or defendant, and this is pleaded in abatement, the plaintiff may amend his declaration, and need not enter a *cassetur breve*. But when there is a non-joinder of one of several defendants, and this matter is pleaded, the plaintiff cannot amend, and must enter a *cassetur* before he commences a new action, or at least before the replication of *nul tiel record* to a plea in such new action of *autre action pendant.(d)*

CLASS II.—OF PLEAS IN BAR.

2919. When no dilatory plea has been offered, or if any, or all which the law allows, have been pleaded, and overruled as insufficient, the defendant may then plead to the action; for no judgment can be rendered against him, until he has been required to answer,

---

(a) 2 Saund. 210, n. 3.
(b) Bac. Ab. Abatement, P.
(c) Gray v. Sidneff, 3 Bos. & Pull. 395 ; Hixon v. Binns, 3 T. R. 185.
(d) Grah. Pr. 98 ; Bouv. L. D. Lis Pendens.

260 OF REMEDIES.

No. 2920.   Book 4, tit. 8, chap. 6, cl. 2, sec 1, § 1, 2.   No. 2921.

and has had an opportunity to contest, the merits or grounds of the suit; and these he is not bound to answer until he has exhausted or waived his right to interpose all dilatory exceptions. By pleading in bar to the action, the defendant waives all dilatory pleas of which he could have taken advantage before so pleading in bar; though he does not waive a right to plead to matters which may afterward accrue. By denying the cause of action itself, he tacitly admits the mode in which the remedy is pursued, to be correct.

Pleas in bar will be considered, 1, as to their nature; 2, as to their qualities; 3, their construction; 4, their form.

SECTION 1.—OF THE GENERAL NATURE AND KINDS OF PLEAS IN BAR.

§ 1.—Of their nature.

2920. A plea *in bar* to the action is one which shows some ground for defeating the action, and contains a prayer to that effect. Such a plea is unlike a dilatory plea, because it impugns the right of action altogether, instead of merely diverting the proceedings to another jurisdiction, or suspending them, or abating the particular writ; it is a conclusive answer to the action. Such a plea must, in general, deny all, or some essential part of the averments of facts in the declaration; or, admitting them to be true, allege new facts which obviate or repel their legal effect. In the first case, in the language of pleading, the defendant is said to *traverse* the matter of the declaration; in the latter to *confess and avoid it;* pleas of this kind, are, therefore, divided into pleas *by way of traverse,* and pleas *by way of confession and avoidance.*

§ 2.—Of kinds of pleas in bar.

2921. Pleas in bar are also classed into two other kinds: 1, the general issue; 2, a special plea in bar.

OF PROCEEDINGS IN AN ACTION.   261

No. 2922.   Book 4, tit. 8, chap. 6, cl. 2, sec. 1, § 2, art. 1.   No. 2922.

Art. 1.—*Of pleading the general issue.*

2922. The *general issue* denies in direct terms the whole declaration; as in personal actions, where the defendant pleads *nil debet*, that he owes the plaintiff nothing; or *non culpabilis*, that he is not guilty of the facts alleged in the whole declaration; or in real actions, where the defendent pleads *nul tort*, no wrong done; or *nul disseisin*, no disseisin committed. These pleas and the like are called general issues; by importing an absolute and general denial of all matters alleged in the declaration, they at once put them all in issue.

Formerly the general issue was seldom pleaded, except when the defendant meant wholly to deny the charge against him; for when he meant to avoid and justify the charge, it was usual for him to set forth the particular ground of his defence as a special plea, which appears to have been necessary, to apprise the court and the plaintiff of the particular nature and circumstances of the defendant's case, and was originally intended to keep the law and the facts distinct. And, even now, it is an invariable rule that every defence which cannot be specially pleaded, may be given in evidence at the trial upon the general issue, so that the defendant is in many cases obliged to plead the particular circumstances of his defence specially, and cannot give them in evidence on that general plea. But the science of special pleading having been frequently perverted to the purpose of chichane and delay, the courts have in some instances, and the legislature in others, permitted the general issue to be pleaded, and special matter to be given in evidence under it at the trial, which at once includes the facts, the equity, and the law of the case.(*a*)   In a writ of right the general issue is called the *mise.*

(*a*) 3 Bl. Com. 305, b; 2 Greenl. Ev. § 9.

As a general rule, the defendant is not allowed to plead specially such facts as amount to a total denial of the charge made against him, and may be given in evidence under the general issue, which, in such cases, must be pleaded.(a) But in many instances, where the defence consists of matter of law, the defendant may plead it specially, or give it in evidence under the general issue.

Art. 2.—Of special pleas in bar.

2923. *Special pleas in bar* are very various, according to the circumstances of the defendant's case; as in personal actions, the defendant may plead any special matter in denial, avoidance, discharge, excuse or justification of the matter alleged in the declaration, and which destroys the plaintiff's action; or he may plead any matter, which estops or precludes him from averring or insisting on any matter relied upon by the plaintiff in his declaration.

These special pleas either, 1, deny the facts stated in the declaration; 2, confess and avoid them; 3, are in discharge; 4, in excuse; 5, in justification; or 6, in estoppel.

1. *Of special pleas in denial of the facts stated in the declaration.*

2924. When a special plea denies the facts stated in the declaration, it is usually called a *special traverse*. All pleas in denial are generally traverses, for the meaning of this word is a denial; and, therefore, in pleading, to traverse is to deny, or controvert any thing which is alleged in the declaration, plea, replication, rejoinder, surrejoinder, or other pleading. But special traverses are not the only pleas which may properly be called special pleas in denial of the declaration; for the defendant may in his plea allege new

(a) 3 Bl. Com. 309.

OF PROCEEDINGS IN AN ACTION.   263

No. 2925.   Book 4, tit. 8, chap 6, cl. 2, sec. 1, § 2 art. 2.   No. 2926.

matter in contradiction to what is expressly stated in the declaration, or what is necessary to support it, though not expressly mentioned in it; as in an action on an arbitration bond, (that is, a bond given by a party to perform an award of arbitrators, to be made of some matter left to their arbitration,) if the plaintiff declares, as he may, upon the penal part of the bond merely, without setting forth the condition of it, the defendant, after craving oyer of the condition, may set it forth in his plea, and plead *nullum fecerunt arbitrium,* or that the arbitrators made no award.

2. *Of pleas in confession and avoidance.*

2925. These are pleas which confess the matters contained in the declaration, and avoid their effect by some new matter, which shows that the plaintiff is not entitled to maintain his action; as by admitting the contract declared upon, and showing that it is void or voidable on account of the want of ability of one of the parties to make it, as by coverture, or infancy, or the like; or by the mode in which the contract was executed, as by duress; or that it was contrary to law, as being against some statute which makes it void; for these circumstances are sufficient to defeat the plaintiff's claim.

3. *Of pleas in discharge.*

2926. Pleas in discharge are distinguished from those in avoidance; they are such as admit the demand, but instead of avoiding its payment or satisfaction, show that it has been discharged by some matter of fact or of law; as by having been already paid, or settled by the rendition of an award or judgment, or that the plaintiff has released the defendant; though he may not have given up his right, that he cannot recover because of the defendant's right of set off. So the defendant may avail himself of the discharge of the plaintiff's claim by matter of law, as alienage, or

264   OF REMEDIES.

No. 2927.   Book 4, tit 8, chap. 6, cl. 2, sec. 1, § 2, art. 2.   No. 2927.

the bankruptcy of the plaintiff; or his having been himself discharged from the contract by bankruptcy; or its being too late to sue him by reason of the statute of limitations.(*a*)

4. *Of pleas in excuse.*

2927. These also admit the demand or complaint stated in the declaration, and excuse the non-compliance with the plaintiff's claim, or the commission of the acts of which he complains, on account of the defendant's having done all in his power to satisfy the former, or not having been the culpable author of the latter. The following are examples of pleas in excuse:

1. A *tender and refusal.* Where the defendant tenders to the plaintiff what is due to him, and the plaintiff refuses to accept it, and afterward brings a suit for its recovery, the defendant in his plea may acknowledge the debt, and plead the tender, adding that he has always been and is still ready to pay it; this is called a plea of tender and *toujours et uncore prist,* and, on payment of the money into court, if the issue is found for him, the defendant will be exonerated from costs, and the plaintiff made justly liable for them.

2. *Self-defence.* When an action is brought for an assault and battery, the defendant may plead that the plaintiff assaulted him first, which obliged him to defend himself, and that if any harm happened to the plaintiff from such defence, the same was occasioned by his own assault first made upon the defendant. This is called a plea of *son assault demesne.* In like manner he may plead that the assault was committed in defence of those whom he had a right to defend on account of his relative position; as in defence of his wife, children, or servants.

3. The defendant may also plead that he has not

(*a*) Ham. N. P. 118, 119.

performed a contract, because he has been *prevented by
the plaintiff* from fulfilling his engagement.

4. In actions of trespass, he may plead that the injury occurred from *inevitable accident*, and without any
fault in him.

5. Of pleas in justification.

2928. Pleas in justification differ from pleas in excuse. In the latter the defendant relies upon the
plaintiff's conduct as his apology for his doing or not
doing the act in question; in pleas of justification, on
the contrary, the defendant professes purposely to have
done the acts of which the plaintiff complains, not on
account of his negligent or culpable conduct, but in
order to exercise that right which he insists in point
of law he might exercise, and in the exercise of which
he conceives himself not merely excused but justified.
The grounds of such justification seem to consist principally of matter of title or interest in or respecting
land, or matter of authority, mediately or immediately
derived from the plaintiff, or the general operation of
law from the particular circumstances of the case.

2929. In *form*, a plea of justification must show the
authority under which the defendant acted,(a) in order
that the court, who are alone the judges of the law,
may decide on its sufficiency, and also that the plaintiff
may know of its existence, and answer it if he can.
The defendant is therefore required to set forth the
instrument by which the authority was conferred, such
as a writ or the like, and also its direction, to show that
the defendant was authorized to execute it,(b) and out
of what court, and whence it emanated.(c) And a
justification under it, showing it has been returned,
must aver the fact with a *prout patet per recordum*, that
is, with an averment that such matter appears of

(a) Co. Litt. 283, a.
(b) Watkins v. West, Ld. Raym. 1530.
(c) Gray v. Hart, Salk. 517.

266   OF REMEDIES.

No. 2930.   Book 4, tit. 8, chap. 6, cl. 2, sec. 1, § 2, art. 2.   No. 2930.

record; which matter would be improper in a case where the defendant only alleged that the writ was sued out, because it is not a record until it is filed.(a)

6. Of pleas in estoppel.

2930. A plea in estoppel, is a preclusion in law, which prevents a man from alleging or denying a fact, in consequence of his own previous act, allegation or denial of a contrary tenor.(b)   Lord Coke says, "an estoppel is when a man is concluded by his own act or acceptance, to say the truth."(c)   And Blackstone(d) defines "an estoppel to be a special plea in bar, which happens when a man has done an act, or executed some deed, which estops or precludes him from averring any thing to the contrary."

A plea of this kind, like a plea in avoidance of the declaration, always advances new matter; but it differs from the latter in this, that instead of confessing or avoiding the plaintiff's allegations, it neither admits nor denies them, merely relying on the estoppel, and

(a) Brigstock v. Stanion, Ld. Raym. 108.   Mr. Hammond, in his excellent work on Nisi Prius, gives the reason why a *prout patet* is necessary. He says, "The defendant, we will suppose, concludes his pleading with a general verification, the effect of which is, that he will establish the allegations comprised in his plea, to the satisfaction of a *jury*.   This averment embraces every part of a plea, so that if it contains matter of record, the defendant has affirmed, that he will submit the question whether or not the record exists, to a jury : but this mode of proceeding is improper, inasmuch as that question must be decided by the court; therefore, he must single out the matter of record from the mass of the other allegations, and aver it with a *prout patet*, thereby affirming in effect that he will establish its existence by inspection of the court.   The same rule will be observed in all other pleadings ; and with regard to a count or declaration, the conclusion, ' and therefore he brings his suit,' is, in substance, that he brings his witnesses to prove the truth of its contents ; and as their testimony is not competent to establish a record, matters of that description must be averred here with a *prout patet*, the same as in other pleadings.   However, the omission of the averment in any case can only be objected to by demurring specially, because the opposite party may, notwithstanding, reply *nul tiel record*, and so is not inconvenienced by the omission."   Ham. N. P. 115.
(b) Steph. Pl. 239.
(c) Co. Litt. 352, a.
(d) 3 Com. 308.

after stating the previous act, allegation or denial of the opposite party, prays judgment if he shall be received or admitted to aver contrary to what he before did or said.

2931. An estoppel may arise either from *matter of record;* from the *deed* of the party; or from matter *in pays,* that is, matter of *fact.*

1. Any confession or admission made in pleading, in a court of record, whether it be express, or implied from pleading over without a traverse, will forever preclude the party from afterward contesting the same fact, in any subsequent suit with his adversary.(*a*) This is called an estoppel by *matter of record.*

2. As an instance of estoppel by *deed,* may be mentioned the case of a bond reciting a certain fact; the party executing that bond will be precluded from afterward denying, in any action brought upon that instrument, the fact so recited.

3. An example of an estoppel by matter *in pays,* occurs when one man has accepted rent of another; he will be estopped from afterward denying in any action with that person, that he was at the time of such acceptance, his tenant.(*b*)

2932. Every estoppel ought to be reciprocal, that is, to bind both parties; and this is the reason that regularly a stranger shall neither take advantage of nor be bound by an estoppel. But privies in blood, privies in estate, and privies in law, are bound by, and may take advantage of estoppels.

Art. 3.—Of special issues, sham and issuable pleas.

2933. There is a plea in bar, which does not strictly fall under either of these denominations, called a *special issue.* It differs from a *special plea in bar* in this: that the latter is, universally, a plea advancing *new matter,*

(*a*) Com. Dig. Estoppel, A 1.
(*b*) Com. Dig. Estoppel, A 3.

268   OF REMEDIES.

No. 2934   Book 4, tit. 8, chap 6, cl. 2, sec. 1, § 3.   No. 2935.

whereas the plea called the *special issue*, never advances such matter, but merely denies some material allegation, the denial of which is in effect a denial of the entire cause of action.

These several pleas are called, indifferently, *pleas to the action, pleas in bar,* or *pleas in chief.*

2934. Besides the general issue and special pleas, there is another kind known by the name of *sham pleas.* These are pleas known to be false, and are put in merely for the purpose of delay; as judgment recovered, that is, a plea that judgment has already been recovered for the same cause of action. These pleas are generally discouraged by the courts, and are treated as nullities.

An *issuable* plea is one which goes in chief to the merits, upon which the plaintiff may take issue and go to trial; or a demurrer for some defect in substance.

§ 3.—Of color in pleading.

2935. One of the principal rules relating to pleas by *confession and avoidance,* is, that they must give *color.* By color is meant an apparent or *primâ facie* right. The meaning of the rule that every plea in confession and avoidance, must give color, is, that it must admit an apparent right in the opposite party, and, therefore, rely on some new matter, by which that apparent right is defeated. An example will render this familiar. Suppose that an action is brought for the breach of a covenant, and the declaration fully states it; to this declaration the defendant pleads a release; the tendency of this plea is to admit an apparent right in the plaintiff, namely, that the defendant did, as alleged in the declaration, execute the deed on which the action is founded, and breach therein contained, and would, therefore, *primâ facie,* be chargeable with damages on that ground; but shows new matter, not before disclosed, by which that apparent right is done away, namely, that the plaintiff discharged him, by executing to him a release. But suppose again, that the plaintiff should reply that the release was obtained by duress; here he would admit that the defendant had, *primâ facie*, a good defence, namely, that the release was executed as alleged in the plea, and that, therefore, the defendant would be apparently discharged; but he relies on new matter, by which the effect of the plea is avoided, namely, that the release was obtained by duress. The plea, in this case, would *give color* to the declaration, and the replication to the plea.

But let it be supposed that the plaintiff had replied, that the release was executed by him, but to another person and not to the defendant; it is evident he would not admit the apparent validity of the release, and the replication would be informal as *wanting color*, because if the release were not to the defendant, there would not exist an apparent defence, requiring the allegation of new matter to avoid it, and the plaintiff might have traversed the plea by denying that the deed stated in the plea was his deed.

The color incident to all regular pleadings, in confession and avoidance, is called *implied* color, to distinguish it from another kind, which, though now unusual, is still sometimes inserted in the pleadings, and which is known by the name of *express* color. The term is usually applied to this latter kind. Color in this sense is defined to be a feigned matter, pleaded by the defendant in an action of trespass, from which a plaintiff seems to have a good cause of action, whereas he has in truth only an appearance or color of cause.(*a*)

Express color was used for the purpose of enabling a party to spread out his title upon the record; when the plea wanted implied color, then the pleader gave an express one by inserting a fictitious allegation of some colorable title in the plaintiff, which he at the

---

(*a*) Bac. Ab. Trespass, I, 4.

same time avoided by showing a better title in the defendant.(a)

2936. The qualities, which express color ought to have, are said to be—

1. It ought to be matter of title doubtful to a jury, as where the defendant pleads that the plaintiff claiming by a deed of feoffment, that is sufficient, for it is a doubt for men unlearned in the law, if land ought to pass by deed or by livery.

2. Color, as such, ought to have continuance, although it wants effect, as if a defendant give color, by color of a deed of demise to the plaintiff for the life of another, who, it appears, by the pleadings, was dead before the trespass; this is not sufficient, because the color does not continue; but the defendant may well deny the effect of it, namely, that the plaintiff claims by color of a deed of demise to him for life, whereas nothing passed by it; therefore there is a difference between the continuance of color and the effect of it.

3. The color ought to be such that if it were of effect, it would maintain the nature of the action, as in an action of assize, color of a freehold ought to be given.

4. Color ought to be given by the first conveyance, otherwise the conveyance before will be waived; and therefore where the defendant derived title to himself, by divers mesne conveyances, and gave color to the plaintiff by one who was last named in the conveyance, this was held insufficient; he should have given color by him who was first named in the conveyance.(b) In giving color under a feoffment, the word *charter* or *deed* must be used.(c)

SECTION 2.—OF THE QUALITIES OF PLEAS IN BAR.

2937. This section will be divided into eight heads:

(a) Steph. Pl. 225; Brown's Entr. 343, for a form of the plea.
(b) Allen's case, 2 Roll. Rep. 140. See, as to color, Leyfield's case, 10 Co. 91; Doct. Pl. tit. Color, 72; Bac. Ab. Pleas I, 8; Com. Dig. Pleader, 3 M 40; Steph. Pl. 220; Lawes on Pl. 126.
(c) 2 Roll. R. 140.

OF PROCEEDINGS IN AN ACTION. 271

No. 2938.   Book 4, tit. 8, chap. 6, cl. 2, sec 2, § 1, 2.   No. 2939.

1, of the adaptation of the plea to the nature of the action, and of its conformity to the count; 2, of what the plea must answer; 3, of what a plea in justification must confess; 4, of the singleness of the plea; 5, of the certainty of the plea; 6, of direct, positive and argumentative pleas; 7, of the capacity of the matter pleaded to be tried; 8, of the truth of the plea.

§ 1.—The plea must be adapted to the nature of the action, and conformable to the count.

2938. A plea in bar, it has already been stated, is an answer to the merits of the complaint, and always goes in denial of the alleged right of action. It must, therefore, be adapted to the nature of the action and comformable to the count. A plea which does not so conform, may be treated as a nullity; as where, to an action of assumpsit, the plea is *nil debet;* or *non assumpsit,* in debt.

The plea must not only be adapted to the nature of the action, but it should be conformable to the count; where, therefore, an assignee of a bankrupt declared that the defendant was indebted to the bankrupt, and promised the plaintiff as assignee to pay him, and the defendant pleaded that the cause of action did not accrue to the bankrupt within six years, this plea was held bad on demurrer, because the plea did not answer the promise in the declaration, and precluded the plaintiff from proving a promise to himself.(*a*)

§ 2.—What the plea must answer.

2939. Every plea must answer all it assumes in the introductory part to answer, and no more. When the plea begins only as an answer to part, the plaintiff cannot demur generally, his course is to take judgment by *nil dicit* for the part not answered.(*b*) But if the

(*a*) 2 Saund. 63, d.
(*b*) Lawes on Pl. 135, 136 ; Com. Dig. Pleader, E 1.

plea profess at its commencement to answer more than it afterward answers, the whole plea is bad, and the plaintiff may demur; as where in trespass the defendant assumes in the introductory part of his plea to justify the assault, battery and wounding; and afterward merely shows that by virtue of a writ he arrested the plaintiff, but shows no excuse for the wounding.(a) But if the part professed to be answered, which is not, is mere matter of aggravation, the plea need not justify that, and the answer of the matter, which is the gist of the action, will suffice.

§ 3.—A plea of justification must confess the facts pleaded.

2940. When the defendant undertakes to justify an act, he must necessarily admit the facts to be true. Every special plea of justification must, therefore, state circumstances which either excuse the facts complained of, or show them to be lawful.(b)

§ 4.—A plea must be single.

2941. Pleas are either single or double, that is, the defendant may rely upon a single ground, or plead several matters in his defence. At common law the defendant could only have pleaded one single matter to the whole declaration. This often abridged the justice of the defence, and caused perplexity and inartificial pleading; the party endeavoring to crowd as much reasoning as he could in his plea, however intricate, repugnant, or contradictory he might be by so doing. But when the declaration consisted of several parts, the defendant might have pleaded several matters to the different parts; as, not guilty to part of the declaration, and to another part a justification or a release; and when there were several defendants, each of them

(a) 1 Saund. 28, n. 1, 2, 3 ; 296 n. 1 ; Postmaster v. Reeder, 4 Wash. C. C. 678 ; Nevins v. Keeler, 6 John. 65 ; Van Ness v. Hamilton, 19 John. 349.
(b) Gibbon v. Pepper, Salk. 637 ; Scott v. Shepherd, 3 Wils. 411 ; 1 Saund. 13, 14, n. 3 ; 28, n. 1 ; Steph Pl. 219.

OF PROCEEDINGS IN AN ACTION.   273

No. 2942   Book 4, tit 8, chap. 6, cl. 2, sec 2, § 5.   No 2942.

might have pleaded a single matter to the whole, or several matters to different parts of the declaration. To remedy the inconveniences of the common law, the statute for the amendment of the law was enacted,(a) by virtue of which the defendant or tenant in any action or suit, or any plaintiff in replevin, in any court of record, may, with the leave of the said court, plead as many several matters thereto, as he shall think necessary for his defence.(b) But the statute does not appear to aid duplicity in the same plea.

When several pleas are pleaded, in virtue of the statute, in bar to one and the same thing or demand, each of them operates and is treated as if it were pleaded alone; each must stand or fall by itself;(c) no one of them can have the effect of dispensing with the proof of what is denied by another.

Duplicity must be objected to by special demurrer, and the particular duplicity must be particularly pointed out, and if the plaintiff do not demur he must reply to both material parts of the plea.

§ 5.—A plea in bar must be certain.

2942. By *certainty* in pleading is meant a clear and distinct statement of the facts, which constitute the cause of action, or ground of defence, so that they can be understood by the party who is to answer them, by the jury who are to ascertain the truth of the allegations, and by the court who are to give the judgment. Lord Coke states certainty to be of three sorts: 1, certainty to a common intent; 2, certainty to a certain intent in general; 3, certainty to a certain intent in every particular.(d)

(a) 4 Ann. c. 16, s. 4, 5.
(b) Chit. Pl. 512; 1 Saund. 337, a ; Bac. Ab. Pleas, K 1; Com. Dig. Pleader, E 2, 5; Id. C 41 ; Gould. on Pl. c. 8, part 1, § 18, 25.
(c) Grills v. Mannell, Willes, 380 ; Kirk v. Nowell, 1 T. R. 125 ; Rogers v. Old, 5 S. & R. 411.
(d) In the case of Dovaston v. Payne, 2 H. Bl. 530, Buller, J., said he remembered to have heard Mr. Justice Aston treat these distinctions as a

2943.—1. By certainty to a *common intent*, is to be understood that when the words are used which will bear a natural sense, and also an artificial one, or one to be made out by argument and inference, the natural sense shall prevail; it is simply a rule of construction, not of addition; common intent cannot add to a sentence words which were omitted.

2944.—2. Certainty to a *certain intent in general*, is a greater certainty than the last, and means what upon a fair and reasonable construction may be called certain, without recurring to possible facts which do not appear.(*a*)

2945.—3. Certainty *to a certain intent in every particular*, is that which precludes all argument, inference or presumption against the party pleading, and is that technical accuracy which is not liable to the most subtle and scrupulous objections, so that it is not merely a rule of construction but of addition; for when this certainty is requisite, the party must not only state the facts of the case in the most precise way, but add to them such as show that they are not to be controverted, and, as it were, anticipate the case of his adversary.(*b*)

§ 6.—A plea must be direct and positive, and not argumentative.

2946. A plea is a statement of facts, and not a statement of argument; it is therefore a rule that a plea should be direct and positive, and not by way of rehearsal, reasoning or argument; for although many matters may be alleged in a declaration by way of recital, or with a *quod cum*, that form must never be used in a plea. And if a plea be positive and direct,

jargon of words without meaning; they have, however, long been made, and cannot altogether be departed from.

(*a*) Spencer *v.* Southwick, 9 John. 317. See 1 Saund. 49, n. 1; The King *v.* Lyme Regis, 1 Dougl. 159.

(*b*) See Oystead *v.* Shed, 12 Mass. 506.

in the form of its language, yet if the substance be by way of argument, it is bad; as if an action be brought for not delivering up an indenture, by which it is stated that Titius granted a manor, it is no plea that Titius did not grant the manor; for it is no answer to the declaration except by way of argument. So in an action of trespass for taking and carrying away the plaintiff's goods, the defendant pleaded the plaintiff never had any goods; this appears to be an infallible argument that the plaintiff is not guilty, and yet is no plea.(a)

2947. It is a branch of this rule against argumentativeness that two affirmatives do not make a good issue,(b) because the traverse by the second affirmative is argumentative in its nature; as if it be alleged by the defendant, that a party died seised in fee, and the plaintiff allege that he died seised in tail, this is not a good issue, because the latter allegation amounts to a denial of the seisin in fee, but denies it by inference and argument only. This doctrine that two affirmatives do not make a good issue, is not taken so strictly, however, but that, in some cases, the issue will be good if there be a sufficient negative and affirmative in *effect*, though in the *form of words* there be a double affirmative; as if the defendant plead that he was born in France, and the plaintiff, that he was born in England, this is said to be a good issue.(c)

§ 7.—The matter pleaded must be capable of trial.

2948. Every plea should be pleaded so as to be capable of trial; it must, therefore, consist of matter of fact, the existence of which may be tried by a jury on the issue; or, if it contain matter of law, its sufficiency, as a defence, may be determined by the court

(a) Doct. Pl. 41 ; Dyer, 43.
(b) Com. Dig. Pleader, R 3 ; Co. Litt. 126, a.
(c) Tomlin v. Burlace, 1 Wils. 6. See Co. Litt. 126, a.

276 OF REMEDIES.

No. 2949.   Book 4, tit. 8, chap. 6, cl. 2, sec. 3, § 1.   No. 2951.

as on demurrer; or by the record itself, if it consist of matter of record; and if, in the same plea, matter of fact be so mixed with matter of law, that they cannot be separated, to be tried by the jury or the judge, the plea will be bad.(a)

§ 8.—The plea must be true.

2949. As the facts stated in the plea must be proved before the jury, when issue is taken upon them, it follows that, to be successful as a matter of defence, they must not only be true, but capable of proof; and if it appear judicially to the court, on the defendant's own showing, that he has pleaded a false plea, this is good cause of demurrer; as where an action of debt was brought upon a bond, conditioned for the performance of covenants contained in an indenture, and the defendant' pleaded with a profert that there were no covenants contained in the indenture, and, upon oyer by the plaintiff, it appeared that the deed did contain divers covenants on the part of the defendant, the plea was held insufficient.(b)

SECTION 3.—OF THE CONSTRUCTION OF PLEAS IN BAR.

2950. The general rules which prevail in the construction of pleas in bar are, 1, that they be most strongly construed against the defendant; 2, that a general plea, when bad in part, is bad for the whole; and, 3, that surplusage will not in general vitiate.

§ 1.—When a plea is construed against the pleader.

2951. The defendant is bound so to state his plea that it will be clearly understood, and as he is pre-

---

(a) The case of the Abbot of Strata Marcella, 9 Co. 25; Lawes on Pl. 138; Gould on Pl. c. 6, § 97; 1 Chit. Pl. 520.

(b) Smith v. Yeomans, 1 Saund. 316. See Coxe v. Higbee, 6 Halst. 695; Tucker v. Ladd, 4 Cow. 47; Brewster v. Bostwick, 6 Cowen, 34; Oakley v. Devoe, 12 Wend. 196; Henderson v. Reed, 1 Blackf. 347.

sumed to state it as favorably for himself as possible, when it has two intendments, it is construed against the pleader by adopting that which is most against his interest; as if, to an action on a bond, the defendant plead payment, it shall be intended to have been made after the day appointed for payment, if it do not aver to be otherwise; but this intendment does not obtain if inconsistent with some other part of the plea.

§ 2.—When a plea bad in part is bad for the whole.

2952. When a plea is entire, it is a unit; if bad in part, it is of course insufficient for the whole: as when there are several counts to a declaration, and the defendant pleads the act of limitation to the whole, and it is bad in part, the plea will be insufficient as to the residue.(a) So if several persons join in a plea, and it is bad as to one, it will not avail for the others.(b)

§ 3.—Of surplusage and repugnancy.

2953. Surplusage in pleading is a surperfluous and useless statement of matter, wholly foreign and impertinent to the cause. In general *surplusagium non nocet*, according to the maxim *utile per inutile non vitiatur;* therefore, if a man in his declaration, plea, etc., make mention of a thing which need not be stated, but the matter set forth is grammatically right, and perfectly sensible, no advantage can be taken on demurrer. In such case the unnecessary matter will be rejected by the court, and the pleadings will be considered as if it were struck out, or had never been inserted.

When, by an unnecessary allegation, the plaintiff shows he has no cause of action, or the defendant no defence, the opposite party may demur. But as the parties, both plaintiff and defendant, are bound to

---

(a) Webb v. Martin, 1 Lev. 48.   (b) 1 Saund. 28, n. 1.

state their cases formally, if the surplusage be not grammatically right, or it be absurd in sense, or so unintelligible that no sense can be given to it, the adversary may take advantage of the defect on special demurrer.(a)

If the party allege a material matter, with an unnecessary detail of circumstances, and the essential and non-essential parts of a statement are, in their nature, so as to be incapable of separation, the opposite party may include in his traverse the whole matter alleged; and as it is an established rule that the evidence must correspond with the allegations, it follows that the party who has pleaded such unnecessary matter will be required to prove it, and thus he is required to sustain an increased burden of proof, and incurs greater danger of failure at the trial. For example, if in justifying the taking of cattle damage feasant, in which case it is sufficient to allege that they were doing damage to his freehold, he should state a *seisin in fee*, which is traversed, he must prove a seisin in fee.(b)

2954. Repugnancy is where the material facts stated in a declaration, or other pleading, are inconsistent one with another. When the repugnancy relates to a *material* point, it may be taken advantage of by general demurrer; but when it is on some *immaterial* matter, it is a fault of form only, and no advantage can be taken of the defect but by special demurrer.

SECTION 4.—OF THE FORMS AND PARTS OF PLEAS.

2955. A plea may be considered under six principal divisions or parts. These refer to, 1, the title of the court; 2, the title of the term; 3, the names of the parties; 4, the commencement; 5, the body or substance of the plea; 6, the conclusion.

(a) Gilb. C. P. 132; Lawes on Pl. 64.
(b) Dyer, 365; Steph. Pl. 261; 2 Saund. 206, a, n. 22; 1 Smith's Lead. Cas. 328, note; 1 Greenl. Ev. § 51; 1 Chit. Pl. 524.

§ 1.—Of the title of the court.

2956. At the head of the plea, it is usual to state in what court it is pleaded; as "in the supreme court," or "in the court of common pleas."

§ 2.—Of the title of the term.

2957. Pleas to the jurisdiction or in abatement, must in general be entitled of the same term as the declaration; and though pleas in bar are also entitled of the same term, yet they may be entitled of the term of which they are pleaded; and, when the matter of defence has arisen since the first day of the term, the plea should be entitled specially of a subsequent day.

§ 3.—Of the names of the parties.

2958. The names of the parties in the margin are not indispensable to a plea; the surnames only are commonly inserted, and that of the defendant is the first stated, as "Roe ats. Doe." These usually correspond with the names in the declaration, or if the defendant plead by another name than that in the declaration, the difference should be shown in the margin, as "C D, sued by the name of E F, ats. A B."

§ 4.—Of the commencement of the plea.

2959. This part of the plea contains, 1, the name of the defendant; 2, the appearance; 3, the defence; 4, the actio non.

Art. 1.—Of the name of the defendant.

2960. When the defendant pleads a misnomer, care must be taken that he do not by his plea admit that he was sued |by his right name; as, "and the *said* John, sued by the name of James," for by using the word *said* he admits he is the person sued by the name of James. The plea should have commenced as follows: "and John, sued by the name of James."

280   OF REMEDIES.

No. 2961.   Book 4, tit. 8, chap. 6, cl. 2, sec. 4, § 4, art. 2, 3, 4.   No. 2963.

Art. 2.—*Of the statement of the appearance of the defendant.*

2961. After the names of the parties, the appearance and defence should be stated; *comes and defends,*
(*venit et defendit vim et injuriam*.) We have seen when
the defendant must appear in person, and when he may
appear by attorney;(*a*) this may be so stated in the
plea.

Art. 3.—*Of stating the defence.*

2962. The defence, it has already been stated, is
full defence or half defence, and its form has been
explained. Every plea in bar should begin with a defence; and when the plaintiff pleads only to part, and
confesses the residue, the defence should be confined
to the part intended to be pleaded to, and it ought not
to cover the whole charge in the declaration.(*b*)

Art. 4.—*Of the actio non.*

2963. After stating the appearance and defence, a
special plea in bar should begin with this allegation,
"that the said plaintiff ought not to have and maintain
his aforesaid action thereof against him," *actio non
debere habet.* This is technically termed the *actio
non*.(*c*) It always alludes to the time of the commencement of the action, and not to the time of the
plea.(*d*)

When the defendant admits that there was once a
good cause of action, which he avoids by matter of
discharge, *ex post facto*, he should say *actionem non;* but
when the matter of the plea shows that there never

(*a*) Ante, n. 2814.
(*b*) Com. Dig. Pleader, E 27.
(*c*) 1 Chit. Pl. 531: Steph. Pl. 394.
(*d*) It is reported in Dougl. 112, that Lord Mansfield said, *actionem non*
in every case goes to the time of pleading, and not to the commencement
of the action ; the doctrine has since been overruled. Evans *v.* Prosser, 3
T. R. 186 ; Le Bret *v.* Papillon, 4 East, 502.

was a good cause of action, the defendant should say, he ought not to be charged, or *onerari non debet*. When the matter of defence arose before the commencement of the action, *actio non*, etc., is in general the proper commencement; but no matter of defence arising after suit brought, can be pleaded generally, but ought to be pleaded in bar of the *further* maintenance of the suit; and if such matter arise after issue joined, it must be pleaded *puis darrein continuance;* and, if after trial, an *audita querela* is the only remedy.(*a*)

In pleading matters in estoppel, it is usual for the defendant, at the beginning of his plea, to say that the plaintiff ought not to be admitted to allege the fact or facts, on which he relies, and which he is precluded from asserting or proving, by reason of his having done some act inconsistent with them, instead of saying *actionem non*, or *onerari non*.(*b*)

§ 5.—Of the body or substance of the plea.

2964. This consists of, 1, the inducement; 2, the protestation; 3, the ground of defence; 4, *quæ est eadem;* 5, the traverse.

When examining the nature of a declaration, we considered the use and form of an *inducement;* and the qualities as to certainty of time, place, and other circumstances, have been the subject of our consideration in this chapter. The *protestando* and *traverse* will be postponed until the subject of replication comes to be discussed.

The *ground of defence*, or body of the plea, which states the substance of such defence, must necessarily depend upon the circumstances of each case; these should be stated with clearness, certainty, and by

---

(*a*) But it is now usual to grant relief on motion. See Bouv. L. D. Audita querela.
(*b*) Lawes on Pl. 140, 141.

appropriate words, a quality which, in pleading, is called *neatness.(a)*

When, in point of form, in trespass or other actions, the plea necessarily states the trespass to have been committed at some other time and place than that laid in the declaration, it is proper immediately preceding the conclusion of the plea, to allege that the supposed trespasses mentioned in the plea are the same as those of which the plaintiff has complained. This allegation is usually termed *quæ est eadem transgressio*, and in that case, the plea concludes with a traverse, of having been guilty at any other time or place, or the plaintiff may demur. The form is as follows : "which are the same assaulting, beating and ill-treating, the said John in the said declaration mentioned, and whereof the said John hath above thereof complained against the said James."(b)

§ 6.—The conclusion of the plea.

2965. A plea in bar should have a proper conclusion; this may be either to the country, or with a verification.

Art. 1.—Of conclusion to the country.

2966. When the plea of the defendant tenders an issue to be tried, the formula is called a *conclusion to the country.* The conclusion is in the following words, when the issue is tendered by the defendant : " And the said C D puts himself upon the country."(c) When it is tendered by the plaintiff the formula is as follows : " And this the said A B prays may be inquired of by the country." It is held, however, there is no mate-

---

(a) Lawes, Pl. 62.
(b) Vide 1 Saund. 208, n. 2 ; 2 Saund. 5 a, n. 3 ; Gould, Pl. c. 3, § 79 ; Arch. Civ. Pl. 219.
(c) That is, upon trial by jury of the country, of or concerning the matter which is put in issue.

rial difference between these two modes of expression.(a)
The plea should conclude to the country, when there is a complete issue between the parties; as where the general issue is pleaded, or where the defendant simply denies some of the material facts alleged in the declaration. When there is an affirmative on one side, and a negative on the other, or vice versâ, the conclusion should be to the country; and so it is though the affirmative and negative be not in express words, but only tantamount thereto.(b)

(a) 10 Mod. 166.
. (b) 2 Saund. 189; Co. Litt. 126, a : 1 Saund. 103; 1 Chit. Pl. 592. There is "much contradiction to be met with in the books, respecting the solution of the general question, when shall a pleading conclude to the country and when with a verification," says Mr. Hammond ; "it may not be unsuitable to bestow a few reflections on it, in this place, and examine, with some minuteness, the *principles* upon which the adoption of either form is founded.

"When a fact is asserted in an action, and the question whether it be true or false, submitted to the jury, their answer terminates the cause, in favor of the one party or the other; so that the whole merits of both the plaintiff's and defendant's case, are wound up in the truth or falsehood of the affirmation. Again: when a party concludes his pleading with a form of words, ' and of this he puts himself upon the country,' or, ' and this he prays may be inquired of by the country,' he puts the question to the jury, whether the fact asserted by his pleading, be or be not as he has affirmed it; whereas, if the conclusion is, ' and this he is ready to verify,' he in terms declares to his opponent, that he will prove his assertion, provided he is willing to stake the issue of the cause upon the single question, whether it be true or false; in the one case, he leaves his antagonist an option, in the other he does not. Now, whenever the one party may admit the truth of his adversary's affirmation, and disclose another fact that destroys the effect and conclusiveness which it would otherwise produce, it is obvious that the adversary cannot place the issue of the cause upon the single question of its truth or falsehood, and in such case, therefore, he cannot conclude his pleading to the country. Whilst, on the other hand, if no answer can be given to the affirmation; if it cannot be confessed and avoided; but if the merits of the cause *necessarily* rest upon and are involved in its truth or falsehood, such conclusion will be, under the limitations hereafter mentioned, the appropriate form.

. "To illustrate this: suppose the defendant pleads infancy to a declaration in assumpsit for money lent; if he has promised to pay the amount since he came of age, the plaintiff may reply the fact, and thereby cut down the defence. Now, if the plea is concluded to the country, the cause must be decided in favor of the one party or the other, as the defendant happens to have been an infant or an adult at the time the original contract was

284 OF REMEDIES.

No 2967   Book 4, tit 8, chap 6, cl. 2, sec 4, § 6, art. 2.   No 2967.

Art. 2.—*Of conclusion with a verification.*

2967. When *new matter* is introduced on either side, the plea must conclude with a verification or averment, in order that the other party may have an opportunity of answering it.(*a*)   The usual verification of a plea containing matter of fact, is in these words: " And this he is ready to verify," etc.(*b*)   In one instance, however, new matter need not conclude with a verification, and then the pleader may pray judgment without it; for example, when the matter pleaded is a negative.(*c*)   The reason of this is evident, a negative requires no proof, and it would, therefore, be impertinent and nugatory for the pleader, who pleads a negative matter, to declare his readiness to prove it. When the special plea contains a verification, it is usual for the defendant, at the conclusion, to pray

concluded, and the plaintiff is thereby prevented disclosing the fact, upon which the real merits of the case depend; hence the plea of infancy must conclude with a verification. But suppose, for the sake of argument, that a promise given by an infant to repay a loan is void; a plea of infancy to an action thereon, might, for any thing that has yet appeared, conclude to the jury, because the defence cannot, in any way, be gotten rid of; and as the conclusion subjects the plaintiff to no inconvenience, *he* has no ground of objection.   There is, however, a *formal* rule of pleading, that two negatives or two affirmatives cannot make an issue, but only an affirmative and a negative combined; because in the two former cases, the averment of the one party does not contradict that of the other in direct and positive terms, but only in an argumentative way: therefore, the plea of infancy in the case last supposed should conclude with a verification; not to give the plaintiff an opportunity of avoiding its effect, but that the issue between him and the defendant may, *for form's sake*, be taken by a direct traverse, hence comes the maxim, that all general issues must conclude to the country, because, in the first place, their effect cannot be avoided, and in the second, they directly negative the facts affirmed by the declaration.
   " Upon the whole, therefore, the rule, applicable alike to all cases, will be this: *where a pleading cannot be avoided, but the merits of the cause necessarily rest upon and are involved in the truth or falsehood of the facts therein disclosed, it will conclude to the country, provided it is a negative when the pleading which it answers is an affirmative, and an affirmative when the latter is a negative: if either of these essentials are wanting, the pleading will conclude with a verification.*" Ham. N. P. 97.
   (*a*) 1 Saund. 103, n. 1; Com. Dig. Pleader, E.
   (*b*) See Lawes, Pl. 144; 1 Chit. Pl. 537, 616; Willes, 5; 3 Bl. Com. 309.
   (*c*) Harvey *v.* Stokes, Willes, 5.

judgment if the plaintiff ought to have or maintain his action against the defendant, which is called the *demand* or *petition* of the plea. General issues, and such like pleas, are not concluded with prayer of judgment, but generally conclude by the defendant's putting himself upon the country. However, this rule is not without exception. When an action is founded on matter of record, in which case the general issue is *nul tiel record*, that there is no such record, the plea must not conclude to the country, like other general issues, but with an offer to verify the plea by the record, which, being matter of law, ought to be produced or proved not before the jury, but the judge.(*a*)

Every plea ought to conclude in the manner in which it is to be tried; for this reason, a plea to the writ, should conclude with reference to the writ; a common plea in bar, to the action; and in a plea of matter of estoppel, the defendant ought to conclude with relying upon the estoppel, *et sic de similibus.*(*b*)

CHAPTER VII.—OF REPLICATIONS.

2968. Having considered the nature, form, and qualities of pleas in bar, the next matter to be discussed is the nature, form, and qualities of replications. A *replication* is the plaintiff's answer to the defendant's plea.

SECTION 1.—OF THE GENERAL NATURE OF REPLICATIONS.

2969. When the defendant has pleaded and exhibited his defence, the plaintiff should consider whether it is, or is not, sufficient in law to defeat the action. If he believes that he cannot support his action, he should either obtain leave to discontinue, or he may

---

(*a*) Lawes, Pl. 148.   (*b*) Co. Litt. 303, b.

enter a *nolle prosequi* as to the whole or a part of the cause of action, unless there has been a demurrer for a misjoinder; if, on the contrary, he finds he can maintain his action, he must reply to the plea of the defendant.

The replication is in general governed by the plea. When the latter *concludes to the country*, the plaintiff must in general reply by adding a *similiter;* that is, he must also submit the matter to be tried by a jury, without adding any new matter to it, and must stand or fall by his declaration.(*a*) In such case he merely replies that as the defendant has put himself upon the country, he, the plaintiff, does so likewise, or the like. Hence this sort of replication is called the *similiter,* that having been the effective word when the proceedings were in Latin.(*b*)

When the defendant's plea *does not conclude to the country,* nor with a verification, as when the plaintiff declares on a judgment or other matter of record, and the defendant pleads *nul tiel record,* as that plea does not conclude to the country, though it contains a direct denial of the matter contained in the declaration, the plaintiff, in his replication, affirms the existence of the record, and concludes by praying an inspection of it, if it be a record remaining in the said court, in which the action is brought; or by giving a day to produce it, if it be a record of a different court.

When the plea of the defendant does not amount to *an issue,* or direct contradiction of the declaration, but is collateral to it, the plaintiff may plead again and reply to the defendant's plea, either by taking issue upon a special traverse taken in the plea; or by directly denying or traversing the plea; or by alleging

---

(*a*) In some states, as in Pennsylvania, the plaintiff may add new counts to his declaration, even on trial; but this is allowed by statute.

(*b*) 1 Chit. Pl. 549 ; Arch. Civ. Pl. 250.

some new matter in contradiction of the matter contained in it; or by confessing and avoiding it, by some new circumstance or distinction, consistent with the declaration; or by concluding the defendant from pleading the matter contained in the plea, by some matter of estoppel.

SECTION 2.—OF THE FORM OF THE REPLICATION.

2970. Having considered in the last section the general nature of a replication to a plea concluding to the country, and to a plea of *nul tiel record*, there remain now to be discussed the general rules with regard to the form of a replication.

§ 1.—Of the title of the court and of the term.

2971. It is usual to entitle a replication in the court and of the term of which it is pleaded, and the names of the parties are stated in the margin thus : " A B against C D." When new matter is stated in the replication, which occurred pending the suit, as the death of one of several plaintiffs or defendants between the plea and replication, it should be suggested, and a special imparlance may be stated in the replication.

§ 2.—Of the replication to a plea containing new matter.

2972. The replication to a plea containing new matter and a verification, may be considered with reference, 1, to the commencement; 2, to the body or substance of the replication ; 3, the conclusion.

Art. 1.—Of the commencement of the replication.

2973. The commencement of the replication, to a defendant's plea concluding with a verification, contains a general denial of the effect of the defendant's

plea, and begins with an allegation technically termed
the *precludi non*. It is usually in the following form:
" And the said A B, as to the plea of the said C D,
by him first above pleaded, says that he the said A B,
by reason of any thing by the said C D, in that plea
alleged, ought not to be barred from having and maintaining the aforesaid action thereof against the said
C D, because he says that," etc.

The rule that a plea in the commencement should
be confined to that part which it is intended to be
answered, equally applies to a replication. When the
body of the replication, therefore, contains an answer
only to a part of the plea, the commencement should
recite that part intended to be answered; for should the
commencement assume to answer the whole plea, and
the body contain an answer only to part, the whole
replication will be insufficient, and so *vice versâ.*(*a*)

Art. 2.—Of the body or substance of the replication.

2974. The body of the replication contains, 1, matter of estoppel; 2, a denial of the plea; 3, a confession and avoidance of the plea; or 4, a new
assignment.

1. Of replication by matter of estoppel.

2975. When the plaintiff can reply matter of estoppel, and such matter does not appear in the declaration
or any anterior pleading, the replication should set it
forth, and, for this purpose, care must be observed to
have the proper commencement and conclusion. If
the matter appear in the pleadings, the plaintiff may
demur to the plea.

2. Of the denial of the plea.

2976. The replication may directly deny or traverse the truth of the plea, either in whole or in part,

---

(*a*) 1 Saund. 28, n. 3, and 377, 378.

when it neither concludes the defendant by matter of
estoppel, nor confesses and avoids the plea.   The denial is either, 1, to the whole plea, or *de injuriâ*, etc.;
2, to part of the plea; and 3, to the effect of the plea,
and showing a particular breach.

1° *Denial of the whole plea, or* de injuriâ.

2977. When the action is founded on a contract,
and in replevin, the replication denies the facts, or one
of the facts, alleged in the plea in express words, a
replication *de injuriâ*, which will be explained directly,
till lately, could not be replied in such cases.

But in actions for torts, as trespass, or an action on
the case for slander, a replication, containing a general
denial of the whole plea, frequently occurs; it is called
a replication *de injuriâ suâ propriâ absque tali causâ*, or
de son tort demesne sans tiel cause.(a)   This replication
puts in issue, and compels the defendant to prove every
material allegation in his plea, and it is, therefore, frequently advantageous to the plaintiff to adopt it, when
by the rules of pleading it is allowed.   Though *de injuriâ* puts in issue the whole of the defence contained
in the plea,(b) yet this rule is subject to an exception,
that if the plea state some authority *in law*, which,
primâ facie, would be a justification of the acts complained of, the plaintiff will not be allowed, under *de
injuriâ*, to show an abuse of that authority, so as to
convert the defendant into a tort feasor *ab initio.*(c)

The import of this replication is to insist that the
defendant committed the act complained of, from a
motive and impulse altogether different from that insisted on in the plea.   For example, if the defendant
has justified a battery under a writ of capias, having
averred, as he must do, that the arrest was made by
virtue of the writ; the plaintiff may reply *de injuriâ*

(a) Crogate's case, 8 Co. 67.
(b) 5 B. & A. 420 ; Barnes v. Hunt, 11 East, 451 ; 10 Bing. 157.
(c) See Smith's Lead. Cas. 53 to 61.

suâ propriâ absque tali causâ, that the defendant did the act of his own wrong, without the cause by him alleged. This replication, then, has the effect of denying the alleged motive contained in the plea, and to insist that the defendant acted from another, which was unlawful, and not in consequence of the one insisted upon in the plea.(*a*)

The replication *de injuriâ* is allowed only when the plea consists merely of matter in *excuse* for a tort or injury committed.(*b*)　It can never be insisted on as giving a right.(*c*)

But in England, where the extent of the general issue has been confined in actions on contracts, and special pleas have become common in assumpsit, it has become desirable that the plaintiff, who has but one replication, should put in issue the several allegations which the special pleas were found to contain; for, unless he could do this, he would labor under the hardship of being frequently compelled to admit the greater part of an entirely false story.　It became important, therefore, to ascertain whether *de injuriâ* could be replied to cases of this description; and, after numerous cases, which were presented for adjudication, it was finally settled that *de injuriâ* may be replied in assumpsit, when the plea consists of matters of excuse.(*d*)

The form of the replication is, *"precludi non*, because he says that the said defendant at the same time when, etc., of his own wrong, and without the cause by him in his said second plea alleged, committed the said trespass in the introductory part of that plea, in manner and form as the said plaintiff hath above in his said declaration complained against the said defendant, and

---

(*a*) Steph. Pl. 186; Lawes, Pl. 151 ; 2 Chit. Pl. 523, 642; Ham. N. P. 120, 121 ; Arch. Civ. Pl. 264: Com. Dig. Pleader, F 19.
(*b*) See Ham. N. P. 120—126.
(*c*) Plumb *v.* McCrea, 12 John. 491.
(*d*) 3 C. M. & R. 65; 2 Bing. N. C. 579 ; 4 Dowl. 647.

OF PROCEEDINGS IN AN ACTION.   291

No. 2978.   Book 4, tit. 8, chap 7, sec. 2, § 2, art. 2.   No. 2981.

· this the said plaintiff prays may be inquired of by the country," etc.(*a*)

2° Of the denial of only part of the plea.

2978. In those cases where the plaintiff cannot reply *de injuriâ* to the whole plea, but must deny some particular fact or facts, he is obliged, 1, to ascertain what facts he ought to deny; and 2, the mode of denying them.

(1.) What facts ought to be traversed or denied.

2979. It is a general rule that a party may traverse or deny any *material* allegation in his opponent's pleadings, although it may have been unnecessary to have stated it precisely as laid; but when the allegation is not material it cannot be traversed.

(2.) Of the modes of special denial.

2980. The modes of traversing facts by the replication, are, 1, by the plaintiff protesting some fact or facts, denying the other, and concluding to the country; 2, by at once denying the particular fact intended to be put in issue, and concluding to the country; and 3, by formally traversing a particular fact, and concluding with a verification.

2981.—1. As the replication must be single, when the plea of the defendant, or indeed, when the pleading of either party contains several matters, and the opposite party is not at liberty to put the whole in issue, he may *protest* against one or more facts and *deny* the other; as if in assumpsit the defendant plead an accord and satisfaction, as that he delivered to the plaintiff, and the latter accepted, a pipe of wine in satisfaction of the promises stated in the declaration, the plaintiff may protest the delivery in satisfaction,

(*a*) 1 Chit. Pl. 585.

292 OF. REMEDIES.

No. 2981.   Book 4, tit 8, chap 7, sec. 2, § 2, art 2.   No 2981.

and reply that he did not accept the wine in satis. faction.(*a*)

A protestation, or, as it is called in pleading, a *pro. testando*, has been defined to be a saving to the party who takes it from being concluded by any matter alleged or objected against him, upon which he cannot join issue. It is only an exclusion of a conclusion, for it merely prevents the effects of such allegations in another action.(*b*)

Matter on which issue may be joined, whether it be the gist of the action, plea, replication or other plead. ing, cannot be taken by protestation;(*c*) although a man may take by protestation, matter that he cannot plead, as in an action for taking goods of the value of one hundred dollars, the defendant may make a protestation that they were not worth more than fifty dollars. It is obvious that a protestation repugnant to, or inconsistent with the gist of the plea, etc., cannot be of any benefit to the party making it.(*d*)

It is also idle and superfluous to make protestation of the same thing that is traversed by the plea, or of any matter of fact, which must depend upon another fact protested against; as that Peter made no will, and that he made no executor.(*e*)

Protestations are of two kinds:

1. When a man pleads any thing which he dares not directly affirm, or cannot plead without making his plea double; as, if conveying to himself, by his plea, a title to land, the defendant ought to plead divers descents from several persons, but he dares not affirm that they were all seised at the time of their death; or, although he could do so, it would make his

(*a*) Bac. Ab. Accord, C; Steph. Pl. 236.
(*b*) Plowd. 276, b; Finch's Law, 359, 366; Lawes, Pl. 141; 1 Chit. Pl. 590; Steph. 235.
(*c*) Plowd. 276, b.
(*d*) Bro. Ab. Prostestation, pl. 1, 5.
(*e*) Plowd. 276, b.

OF PROCEEDINGS IN AN ACTION.   293

No. 2982   Book 4, tit 8, chap 7, sec. 2, § 2, art. 2.   No. 2982.

plea double to allege two descents, when one descent would be a sufficient bar; then the defendant ought to plead and allege the matter by introducing the word "protesting;" thus protesting that such an one died seised, etc., and this the adverse party cannot traverse.

2. The other sort of protestation is, when a person is to answer two matters, and yet he can only plead to one of them, then in the beginning of his plea or replication, he may say "protesting," or "not acknowledging any such part of the matter to be true," and add, "but for his plea (or replication) in this behalf," etc.; and so take issue, or traverse, or plead to the other part of the matter; and by this he is not concluded by any of the rest of the matter, which he has by protestation so denied, but may afterward take issue upon it.(a)

The common way of making a protestando is in these words: "Because protesting that," etc., excluding such matters of the adversary's pleading as are intended to be excluded in the protestando, if it be matter of fact; or if it be against the legal sufficiency of his pleading, "Because protesting that the plea by him above pleaded in bar, or by way of reply, or rejoinder, as the case may be, is wholly insufficient in law."

No answer is necessary to a protestando, because it is never to be tried in the action in which it is made, but of such as is excluded from any manner of consideration in that action.(b)

2982.—2. A second kind of replication, is that which at once *denies the particular fact* intended to be put in issue, and concludes to the country, without any preamble and without any formal traverse. On

_____

(a) 2 Saund. 103 a, n. 1.   See 1 Chit. Pl. 534; Arch. Civ. Pl. 245; Com. Dig. Pleader, N; Vin. Ab. h. t.; Steph. Pl. 235.
(b) Lawes, Pl. 143.

294 OF REMEDIES.

No 2983.   Book 4, tit. 8, chap 7, sec 2, § 2, art. 2.   No. 2984.

account of its conciseness it is frequently adopted in practice.

2983.—3. When, in a replication or other pleading, it is necessary to show title in the plaintiff, or to introduce new matter inconsistent with that stated by the other party,(a) or when there are two affirmatives, which do not impliedly negative each other, or a confession and avoidance by argument only, a traverse is necessary, for otherwise the pleadings would run to infinite prolixity.(b)

2984. Before proceeding to the further discussion of this subject, it will be proper to inquire into the nature and use of a traverse. The word *traverse*, in pleading, signifies to deny or controvert any thing which is alleged in the declaration, plea, replication or other pleadings;(c) there is no real distinction between traverses and denials, they are substantially the same. However a traverse, in the strict technical meaning, and the more ordinary acceptation of the term, signifies a direct denial in formal words, "*without* this, that," etc.(d)

All issues are traverses, although all traverses cannot be said to be issues, and the difference is this; issues are where one or more facts are affirmed on one side, and directly and merely denied upon the other.

It is a general rule that when a traverse is *well tendered* on one side it *must be accepted* on the other, and hence it follows that there cannot be a traverse upon traverse, if the first traverse be material. But in cases where the first traverse is immaterial, there may be a traverse upon a traverse;(e) and when the plaintiff might be ousted of some right or liberty the law allows him, there may be a traverse upon a

(a) Com. Dig. Pleader, F 12, G 3.
(b) 1 Saund. 22, n. 2 ; Com. Dig. Pleader, G ; Bac. Ab. Pleadings, H.
(c) Lawes, Pl. 116, 117.
(d) Summary of Pleadings, 75 ; 1 Chit. Pl. 576, n. a.
(e) Gould on Pl. c. 7, § 43.

OF PROCEEDINGS IN AN ACTION.   295

No. 2985   Book 4, tit 8, chap 7, sec. 2, § 2, art. 2.   No. 2985.

traverse, although the first traverse include what is material.(a)

A traverse upon a traverse is one growing out of the same point, or subject matter, as is embraced in a preceding traverse on the other side; as where the defendant pleads title under a devise from Paul, alleging that he died seised *in fee;* the plaintiff replies that Paul died seised *in tail, absque hoc* that he died seised in fee, with a verification; the defendant cannot then rejoin that Paul died seised in fee, *absque hoc* that he died seised in tail; but must join 'the plaintiff's traverse, by re-affirming that Paul died seised in fee, as alleged in the plea, and conclude to the country; for both traverses would go to the *same point,* namely, whether or not Paul *died seised in fee,* the only material point in controversy, and to the determination of which the first traverse is precisely adapted.(b)

2985. Traverses may be divided into three kinds:

1. *General traverses.* A general traverse is one preceded by a general inducement, and denying, in general terms, all that is last before alleged on the opposite side, instead of pursuing the words of the allegations which it denies. Of this sort of traverse, the replication *de injuriâ,* in answer to a justification, is an example.(c)

2. Special pleas in denial of the declaration are usually called *special traverses.* A special technical traverse begins in most cases with the words *absque hoc,* (without this,) which words in pleading are a technical form of negation.(d)   It is a general rule

(a) Gould on Pl. c. 7, § 44; Com. Dig. Pleader, G 18; Bac. Ab. Pleas, H 4.
(b) Gould on Pl. c. 7, § 42; 1 Chit. Pl. 597.
(c) Bac. Ab. Pleas, H 1; Steph. Pl. 171.
(d) Lawes on Pl. 116 to 120.   These words, *" without this,"* are calculated to convey the most pointed denial, by putting, as it were, the matter denied out of the plea; but any other words which are equipollent or equivalent, and import an express denial or exclusion of the matter intended to be traversed, are sufficient.   A traverse, by the words *et non,* is therefore good; as if a party pleads that Peter was taken into custody by a warrant

that every matter which is the substance or gist of the plaintiff's action, or the defendant's defence, or is material to it, is traversable; but matters of inducement, and such as are not material to the action or defence, cannot be traversed. It is also a general rule that a special traverse must have a proper and sufficient inducement; for if there be no inducement to a special traverse, the issue will be a *negative pregnant*, by which term is meant such negative expression in pleading, as may imply or carry within it an affirmative. This is faulty, because the meaning of such form of expression is ambiguous; example, in trespass for entering the plaintiff's house, the defendant pleaded that the plaintiff's daughter had licensed him to do so, and that he entered by that license. The plaintiff replied that he did not enter by her license. This was considered a negative pregnant, and it was held that the plaintiff should have pleaded the entry by itself, or the license by itself, and not both together.(a)

It may be observed that this form of traverse may imply and carry within it, that the license was given, though the defendant did not enter by that license. It is therefore in the language of pleading said to be pregnant with the admission, namely, that a license was given; at the same time the license is not expressly admitted, and the effect therefore is, to leave it in doubt whether the plaintiff means to deny the license, or that the defendant entered by virtue of that license. It is this ambiguity which appears to constitute the fault.(b)

This rule against a negative pregnant appears, in modern times at least, to have received no very strict

returnable one day, *and not* by a warrant returnable another day, it is a good traverse of his having been taken on a warrant returnable on the latter day.

(a) Myn v. Cole, Cro. Jac. 87.

(b) Style's Pr. Reg. h. t.; Steph. Pl. 381 ; Gould on Pl. c. 6, § 29—37.

construction; for many cases have occurred in which, upon various grounds of distinction from the general rule, that form of expression has been considered free from objection.(a)

A traverse, commencing with the words "without this," is special, because, when it thus commences, the inducement and the negation are regularly both special; the former consisting of new matter, and the latter pursuing, in general, the words of the allegation traversed, or at least those of them which are material. For example, if the defendant pleads title to land in himself, by alleging that Peter devised the land to him, and then died seised in fee; and the plaintiff replies that Peter died seised in fee intestate, and alleges title in himself, as heir of Peter, *without this*, that Peter devised the land to the defendant; the traverse is special. Here the allegation of Peter's intestacy, etc., forms the special inducement; and the *absque hoc*, with what follows it, is a special denial of the alleged devise; that is, a denial of it in the terms of the allegation.

After traversing any allegation in the pleading of the adversary, it is usual to say, "in manner and form as he has in his declaration, plea, or replication, etc., in that behalf alleged," which is as much as to include in the traverse, not only the mere fact opposed to it, but that, in the *manner and form* in which it is stated by the other party; thus, in the case before mentioned, of traversing the party's title by devise, the defendant probably said, without this, that the ancestor devised *modo et forma*, etc., as the above form may have been concisely expressed, in the language of the old entries, when the proceedings were in Latin. These words, however, only put in issue the substantial statement of the manner of the fact traversed, and do not extend to the time, place, or other circumstances attending it,

---

(a) Com. Dig. Pleader, R 6; Steph. Pl. 383; Lawes, Pl. 114.

298   * OF REMEDIES.

No. 2986.   Book 4, tit 8, chap 7, sec. 2, § 2, art. 2.   No. 2986.

if they were not originally material and necessary to be proved as laid.(a)

A special traverse must not conclude to the country, but with a verification.

3. The third kind of traverse is called a *common traverse*. This kind differs from those commonly called traverses, principally in this, that it is preceded by no inducement, general or special; it is taken without an *absque hoc*, or any similar words, and is simply a direct denial of the adverse allegations, in common language, and always concludes to the country. It can be used only when an inducement is not requisite; that is, when the party traversing has no need to allege any new matter.(b) This traverse derives its name, it is presumed, from the fact that common language is used, and that it is more informal than the other traverses.

3° *Of denying the effect of the plea, and showing a particular breach.*

2986. It is frequently proper, in a replication, without confessing and avoiding the plea, to deny its effect, and show a particular breach of the contract declared upon; this occurs often in debt on bond, conditioned to perform covenants, and the like. When the defendant pleads matter in excuse, which admits of non-performance, it is sufficient if the plaintiff denies the plea, and he need not assign a breach in his replication; it must be remembered, however, that this rule does not apply to an action brought upon an award, which stands upon a particular ground. But in other cases when the defendant has pleaded performance, the replication must state the breach with particularity, and it should conclude with a verification, so that the defendant may have an opportunity of answering it.(c)

(a) Bac. Ab. Pleas, G 1; Lawes, Pl. 120. See Steph. Pl. 213; Gould on Pl. c. 6, § 22; Dane's Ab. Index, h. t.; Bac. Ab. Verdict, P.; Vin. Ab. h. t.; Bouv. L. D. h. t.
(b) 1 Saund. 103, b, n. 1.
(c) 1 Saund. 101; Com. Dig. Pleader, F 14, 15.

OF PROCEEDINGS IN AN ACTION. 299

No. 2987.   Book 4, tit. 8, chap. 7, sec. 2, § 2, art. 2.   No. 2988.

3. Of the confession and avoidance of the plea by the replication.

2987. The replication may, in the next place, admit either in words or in effect, the fact alleged in the plea, and avoid the effect of it by stating *new matter*. This replication is common in practice ; as where infancy is pleaded, the plaintiff may reply that the goods were for necessaries, or that the defendant, after he came of lawful age, ratified and confirmed the promise.

In form it is usual to admit the material facts alleged in the defendant's plea, in express terms, by stating after the words *precludi non*, "that although true it is, that the said demise was made to the said defendant, as in his said plea is alleged, yet for replication in this behalf the said plaintiff in fact saith that," etc. When the replication completely confesses and avoids the defendant's plea, it must not conclude with a traverse ; in such case there is no occasion to give color to the defendant in this replication; still, as it introduces new matter, it must conclude with a verification, so that the defendant may have an opportunity of answering it.(a)

4. Of a new assignment.

2988. When the plaintiff's declaration is conceived in general terms, or when, from the nature of the action, it is so framed as to be capable of covering several injuries, the defendant may not be sufficiently guided by the declaration to the true cause of complaint, and is, therefore, led to answer a different matter from that which the plaintiff had in view. For example, it may happen that the plaintiff has been twice assaulted by the defendant, and one of the assaults is justifiable, it being in self-defence, while the other may have been committed without legal excuse. Supposing the plaintiff to bring an action for the latter; from the generality of the statement in the declaration, the defendant is not informed to which of the two, assaults the plaintiff means to refer. The defendant may, therefore, suppose, or affect to suppose, that the first is the assault intended, and will plead *son assault demesne*. This plea the plaintiff cannot safely traverse, because an assault was committed by the defendant, under the circumstances of excuse here alleged; the defendant would have a right under issue joined upon such traverse, to prove the circumstances, and, to presume that such assault, and no other, was the cause of action. The plaintiff, therefore, in the supposed case, not being able safely to traverse, and having no ground either for demurrer, or for pleading in confession and avoidance, has no cause, but by a new pleading, to correct the mistake occasioned by the generality of the declaration, and to declare that he has brought his action, not for the *first*, but for the *second* injury or assault; and this is called a *new* or *novel assignment.(a)*

A new assignment is said to be in the nature of a new declaration;(b) it seems, however, more properly considered as a repetition of the declaration,(c) differing only in this, that it distinguishes the true ground of complaint, as being different from that which is covered by the plea. Being in the nature of a new or repeated declaration, it is consequently to be framed with as much certainty or specification of circumstances, as the declaration itself. In some cases, indeed, it should be even more particular.(d)

As the object of a new assignment is to correct a mistake occasioned by the generality of the declaration, it always occurs in answer to a plea, and is, therefore,

(a) See the form of a replication by way of *new assignment*, in Steph. Pl. 243.
(b) Bac. Ab. Trespass, I 4, 2; 1 Saund. 299, c.
(c) 1 Chit. Pl. 602.
(d) Steph. Pl. 245; Bac. Ab. Trespass, I 4.

OF PROCEEDINGS IN AN ACTION. 301

No. 2988.   Book 4, tit. 8, chap. 7, sec. 2, § 2, art. 2.   No. 2988.

in the nature of a replication. It is not used in any other part of the pleading.

A new assignment may be made in most actions, whether in form *ex contractu* or *ex delicto*, but it most frequently happens in trespass. In replevin, as the plaintiff must show the place with certainty where the taking was, it is said there can be no new assignment as to the place.(*a*)

Several new assignments may occur in the same series of pleading. Thus, in the example above mentioned, if it be supposed that *three* distinct assaults had been committed, two of which were justifiable, the defendant might plead as above to the declaration, and then by way of plea to the new assignment, he might again justify, in the same manner, another assault; upon which it would be necessary for the plaintiff to new assign a third; and this upon the first principle by which the first new assignment was required.(*b*)

As the new assignment introduces new matter, its conclusion must be with a verification, in order that the defendant may have an opportunity of answering it.

The new assignment is in the nature of a new declaration, and the defendant is required to plead to it, precisely as to a declaration; and as the plaintiff avers that the new assigned trespasses are other and different from those in the plea, he waives those which the defendant has justified, and it is not necessary to plead over again to the new assignment, any matter of justification, necessarily covered by the first plea.(*c*)

The plaintiff may reply precisely as to pleas to a declaration, and if the plea be such as to require a new assignment, the plaintiff should again new assign.(*d*)

(*a*) Corkley *v.* Pagrave, Freem. 238.
(*b*) 1 Chit. Pl. 614 ; 1 Saund. 299, c.
(*c*) Bac. Ab. Trespass, I 4, 2.
(*d*) 1 Saund. 299 c ; 9 Wentw. Pl. Index ; 2 Chit. Pl. 723.

Art. 3.—Of the conclusion of a replication.

2989. The general rules which relate to the conclusion of a replication are, that when it wholly denies the defendant's plea, consisting of matter of fact, it should conclude to the country. And when there is an affirmation on one side, and a negative denial on the other, the replication, as indeed all other pleading in such case, must conclude to the country, although the affirmative and negative be not in express words, but tantamount thereto. When new matter is alleged in a replication, it should conclude with an averment, in order to give the defendant an opportunity of answering it, and an appropriate prayer of judgment, for debt or damages only, according to the form of action.

SECTION 3.—OF THE QUALITIES OF A REPLICATION.

2990. Many of the rules which apply to the qualities of pleas, are alike applicable to the qualities of replications. A replication must, 1, answer so much of the plea as it professes to answer, and if it be bad in part, it is bad for the whole; 2, be conformable to, and not depart from the count; 3, be, like a plea, certain, direct and positive, and not argumentative, and that it also be triable; 4, be single.

§ 1.—The replication must answer the plea.

2991. To prevent a chasm or interruption in the pleadings, which in law is called a *discontinuance*, it is a rule that every pleading must answer the whole of what is adversely alleged.(*a*) A replication must, therefore, answer so much of the plea which it professes to answer, or it will be a discontinuance. It is a rule, also, that if an entire replication be bad in part, it is bad for the whole; as if to a plea of the statute of

(*a*) Com. Dig. E. 1, F 4; 1 Saund. 28, n. 3.

limitations to two counts of a declaration; the plaintiff should reply that the accounts were between the plaintiff and defendant as merchants; if this replication be bad as to one of the counts, it is bad as to the other; but this rule does not apply when the matter objected to is mere surplusage.(a)

' § 2.—The replication must not depart from the declaration.

2992. The replication must not depart from the declaration in any material matter; this rule equally affects rejoinders and subsequent pleadings. A *departure*, in pleading, takes place when a party quits or departs from the case or defence which he has first made, and has recourse to another.(b) The following will illustrate what is a departure in a replication: in assumpsit, the plaintiffs, as executors, declared on several promises alleged to have been *made to the testator*, in his lifetime; the defendant pleaded that she did not promise within six years, before the obtaining of the original writ of the plaintiffs; to this the plaintiffs replied, that within six years before they obtained the original writ, the letters testamentary were granted to them, whereby the action accrued *to them*, the said plaintiffs, within six years. This was held to be a departure, because in the declaration they had laid the promise to the *testator*, but, in the replication, alleged the right of action to accrue *to themselves as executors*.(c)

A departure in pleading is never allowed, for the record would, by such means, be spun out into endless prolixity; he who had departed from and relinquished his first plea, might resort to a second, third, fourth, or even a fortieth defence; pleading would, by such means, become infinite. He who had a bad cause

---

(a) Com. Dig. Pleader, F 25.
(b) Co. Litt. 304 a; 2 Saund. 84 a, n. 1; 1 Chit. Pl. 619; Steph. Pl. 405, 406.
(c) Hickman *v.* Walker, Willes, 27.

304 OF REMEDIES.

No. 2992.   Book 4, tit. 8, chap. 7, sec. 3, § 3, 4.   No. 2996.

would never be brought to issue, and he who had a good one would never obtain the end of his suit.(a)

Departures more frequently happen in rejoinders than in replications; they may take place in all pleadings subsequent to the plea.

2993. A distinction must be observed between a departure and those cases where matter is pleaded which maintains the previous pleadings; as, in trespass for taking a horse, if the defendant plead he took him for a *distress damage feasant*, the plaintiff may reply that the defendant afterward used the horse, which shows that he was a trespasser *ab initio*.(b)

2994. The only way to take advantage of a departure is by demurrer; and if, instead of demurring, the party plead over, and take issue upon the pleading containing the departure, and it is found against him, the verdict will not be disturbed on this account, if the matter pleaded by way of departure is a sufficient answer, in substance, to what is pleaded by the opposite party; that is, if it would have been sufficient if pleaded in the first instance.(c)

§ 3.—Of the certainty of the replication.

2995. Certainty in a replication, is as requisite as in a declaration or a plea, though certainty to a common intent is in general sufficient. When the replication is only to a part of the plea, the part alluded to must be pointed out with certainty.

§ 4.—The replication must be single.

2996. It is a rule, that the replication must not contain two answers to the same plea, or be *double*. It ought to be single, because the plaintiff ought not to

(a) Summary on Pl. 92; Bac. Ab. Pleas, L; Vin. Ab. Departure; 2 Saund. 84 a, n. 1.
(b) Com. Dig. Pleader, F 11.
(c) 1 Saund. 84; 1 Lilly's Ab. 444.

perplex the court with two matters, for ,if two issues were permitted to be joined upon two several traverses on the plaintiff's replication, and one should be found for the plaintiff, and the other for the defendant, the court would not know for whom to give judgment, the plaintiff or defendant. But a replication may frequently put in issue several facts, where they amount to only one connected proposition.(a)

When the plea is divisible in its nature, a replication may contain several distinct answers to its different parts; as where infancy is pleaded to a declaration consisting of several counts, the plaintiff may reply as to part of the demand, that it was for necessaries; to another part, that the defendant was of full age when the contract was made; and to another part, that he confirmed it after he came of age.(b)

CHAPTER VIII.—OF THE REJOINDER AND SUBSEQUENT PLEADINGS.

2997. This chapter will be divided into five sections: 1, of the rejoinder; 2, of surrejoinders, rebutters and surrebutters; 3, of issues; 4, of repleaders; 5, of pleas puis darrein continuance.

SECTION 1.—OF REJOINDERS.

2998. When the replication has been by way of traverse, it must have tendered an issue ;. or, if the plaintiff has demurred, an issue in law has been tendered, and, in either case, the result has been the joinder of issue, upon the same principles as above explained with respect to the plea, so that no further

---

(a) Humphrey v. Churchman, Rep. t. Hard. 289 ; Robinson v. Bailey, 1 Burr. 317 ; Lawes on Pl. 153.
(b) 1 Chit. Pl. 549, 550.

pleading on the part of the defendant is requisite, except to join in the issue. But when the replication is in confession and avoidance, the defendant may then, in his· turn, either demur, or by pleading, traverse, or confess, and avoid the replication; this answer of the defendant to the plaintiff's replication, is called a rejoinder.

The general requisites of a rejoinder are, that it be, 1, triable; 2, not double, but single; 3, certain; 4, direct and positive, and not argumentative; 5, not repugnant nor insensible; 6, conformable to, and not a departure from the plea. These rules have been sufficiently considered in treating of previous pleadings.

When the replication concludes with a verification, the rejoinder usually denies it, and concludes to the country, "and of this the said defendant puts himself upon the country," etc. But when he introduces new matter it must conclude with a verification, for the same reason that such a conclusion is required in a plea or verification, namely, that the plaintiff may have an opportunity of answering it. When the defendant denies several matters alleged in the replication, the rejoinder may conclude to the country, without putting the matters in issue severally and distinctly; for example, if to a plea of infancy the plaintiff has replied, that a part of the goods sold to the defendant were necessary clothing, and the residue necessary food, a general denial concluding to the country will be sufficient.(a)

SECTION 2.—OF SURREJOINDERS, REBUTTERS, AND SURREBUTTERS.

2999. The order and denominations of the alternate allegations of fact or pleadings, throughout the whole series, are as follows: *declaration, plea, replication,*

(a) Com. Dig. Pleader, H.

rejoinder, which have been considered; *surrejoinder*, *rebutter* and *surrebutter*. After surrebutter, the pleadings have no distinctive names, for beyond that stage they are seldom extended.

These last pleadings, surrejoinder, rebutter and surrebutter, are governed by the same rules as those to which the previous pleadings of the party adopting them is subject.

At any stage of these pleadings, when the party will not demur, the other course is to accept the tendered issue of fact, and also the mode of trial which the traverse proposes; and this is done in the case of trial by jury, by a set form of words, called a *joinder in issue*, or a *similiter*, by which the pleader recites that the opposite party "hath put himself upon the country," and then he avers that "he doth the like."(*a*)

SECTION 3.—OF ISSUES.

3000. It is of importance, before joining issue, to consider whether the issue tendered is such, that the parties may venture to go on to trial, so as to obtain the judgment of the court, and to avoid the necessity of a repleader, on account of the issue having been taken on an immaterial matter.

An *issue*, in pleading, is defined to be a single, certain and material point, arising out of the allegations or pleadings of the parties, by which some specific matter is affirmed on the one side, and denied on the other. This result being attained, the parties are said to be *at issue, ad exitum*, that is, at the *end* of their pleadings. The term issue, signifies also, in common parlance, the entry of the pleadings; but it is proper when only one plea has been pleaded, though to several counts, and issue is joined upon such plea. Issues may

(*a*) Steph. Pl. 76.

308   OF REMEDIES.

No. 3001.   Book 4, tit 8, chap 8, sec 3, § 1, art. 1, 2, 3.   No. 3004.

be considered with regard to, 1, their qualities; 2, their kinds; 3, the manner of procuring them.

§ 1.—Of the qualities of issues.

3001. Issues should, in general, be, 1, upon an affirmative and a negative; 2, single, and upon a certain point; 3, upon a material point.

Art. 1.—When an issue must be upon an affirmative and a negative.

3002. An issue should, in general, be upon an affirmative and a negative, and not upon two affirmatives; as, if the defendant plead that Peter is living, and the plaintiff reply that he is dead, it is more formal, though not indispensable, to deny that he is living; nor should the issue be on two negatives.(*a*)

Art. 2.—The issue must be on a single and certain point.

3003. It is a rule that the issue must be upon a single and certain point; but it is not necessary that such point should consist of a single fact; the issue should not be on a negative pregnant, which, we have seen, is a fault in pleading,(*b*) but it may be upon a disjunctive.(*c*)

Art. 3.—The issue must be upon a material point.

3004. The issue must be upon a material point, because, that is the only thing to be tried, for ,when the issue is immaterial, it cannot decide the question in dispute between the parties; as when a material allegation in the pleadings is not traversed, but an issue is taken on some other point, which, though

---

(*a*) Bac. Ab. Pleas, I 3; Com. Dig. Pleader, R 3; Martin *v.* Smith, 6 East, 557.
(*b*) Vide ante, n. 2985, and Com. Dig. Pleader, R 5, 6; Bac. Ab. Pleas, I 6.
(*c*) Com. Dig. Pleader, R. 7.

found by the verdict, will not determine the merits of the cause, and will leave the court at a loss for which of the parties to give judgment.(*a*) The following is an example : when in an action of assumpsit, against an administratrix, on promises of the intestate, she pleaded that *she,* instead of the intestate, did not promise ; after verdict a repleader was awarded.(*b*)

§ 2.—Of the kinds of issues.

3005. When considered as to their effect, issues are material and immaterial; when examined as to the mode by which they are to be tried, they are issues in law and issues in fact; when as to their regularity, they are formal and informal; and when as to the mode by which they are produced, they are actual or feigned.

Art. 1.—*Of material and immaterial issues.*

3006.—1. Issues are *material* when properly formed on some material point, which will decide the question in dispute between the parties; as, where the plaintiff declares in assumpsit on a promissory note, and the defendant pleads *non assumpsit,* on which issue is joined.

3007.—2. *Immaterial issues* are those which are predicated on some immaterial fact, which, though found by the verdict, will not determine the merits of the cause, and would leave the court at a loss how to give judgment : as where, to an action of debt on bond conditioned for the payment of *one hundred and fifty dollars* at a certain day, the defendant pleads the payment of *one hundred dollars,* according to the form of the condition, and the plaintiff, instead of demurring, tenders issue upon such payment, it is manifest that, whether the issue be found for the plaintiff or the

(*a*) 2 Saund. 319, n. 6 ; Com. Dig. Pleader, R 18.
(*b*) Anon. 2 Vent. 196.

defendant, it will remain equally uncertain whether the plaintiff is entitled or not to maintain his action; for in an action for the penalty of a bond conditioned to pay a certain sum, the only material question is whether the exact sum were paid or not, and a payment in part is a question beside the legal merits.(*a*)

Art. 2.—*Of issues in law and issues in fact.*

1. *Of issues in law.*

3008. An issue *in law* is one which admits all the facts, and rests simply on a question of law. It is said to consist of a single point, but by this it must not be understood that such issue involves, necessarily, only a single rule or principle of law, or that it brings into question the legal sufficiency of a single fact only. It is meant that such an issue reduces the whole controversy to the single question, whether the facts, confessed by the issue, are sufficient in law to maintain the action, or defence of the party who alleges them.

2. *Of an issue in fact.*

3009. An issue *in fact*, is one in which the parties disagree as to the existence of such facts, one affirming they exist, the other denying it. By the common law, every issue in fact, subject to some exceptions noticed below, must consist of a direct affirmative allegation on the one side, and a direct negative on the other.(*b*) But it has been holden that where the defendant pleaded that he was born in France, and the plaintiff replied that he was born in England, it was sufficient to form a good issue.(*c*) In this case it will be observed there were two *affirmatives*, and the ground upon which the issue was holden to be good is,

---

(*a*) Hobb. 113 ; 5 Taunt. 386.
(*b*) Co. Litt. 126, a ; Bac. Ab. Pleas, G 1.
(*c*) Tomlin *v.* Burlace, 1 Wils. 6 ; Tomlin *v.* Purlis, 2 Str. 1177.

OF PROCEEDINGS IN AN ACTION.   311

No. 3010.   Book 4, tit. 8, chap 8, sec. 3, § 2, art. 2.   No. 3010.

that the second affirmative is so contrary to the first, that the first cannot in any degree be true, if the last is not false.

The *exceptions* above mentioned to the rule that a direct affirmative and a direct negative are required, are the following:

1. The general issue upon a writ of right is formed by two affirmatives : the demandant, on the one side, avers that he has a greater right than the tenant; and, on the other side, the tenant claims to have a greater right than the demandant. This, which in personal actions is called an issue, is here called the *mise*.

2. In an action of dower, the count merely demands the third part of the acres of land, etc., as the dower of the demandant of the endowment of A B, heretofore the husband, etc., and the general issue is, that A B was not seised of such estate, etc., and that he could not endow the demandant thereof, etc.(*a*)   This mode of negation, instead of being direct, is merely argumentative, and argumentativeness is not generally allowed in pleading.

3010. Issues in fact are divided into general issues, special issues, and common issues.

1. The nature of the *general issue* was considered when discussing the several kinds of pleas in bar.(*b*) It is not requisite here to reëxamine the subject, but only to say that the general issue denies in direct terms the whole declaration.

2. The *special issue* is when the defendant takes issue upon any one substantial part of the declaration, and rests the weight of his case upon it ; he is said to take a special issue in contradistinction to the general issue, which denies and puts in issue the whole declaration.(*c*)

(*a*) 2 Saund. 329, 330.
(*b*) Ante, n, 2922.
(*c*) Com. Dig. Pleader, R 1, 2.

3. *Common issue* is the name given to that which is formed on the single plea of *non est factum*, when pleaded to an action of covenant broken. This is so called, because to an action of covenant broken there can properly be no general issue, since the plea *non est factum*, which denies the deed only, and not the breach, does not put the whole declaration in issue.(*a*)

Art. 3.—*Of formal and informal issues.*

3011.—1. A *formal issue* is one which is formed according to the rules required by law, in a proper and artificial manner.

3012.—2. An *informal issue* is one which arises when a material allegation is traversed in an improper or inartificial manner;(*b*) the defect of such an issue is cured by verdict.(*c*)

Art. 4.—*Of actual and feigned issues.*

3013.—1. An *actual issue* is one formed in an action brought in the regular manner, for the purpose of trying a question of right between the parties.

3014.—2. A *feigned issue* is one directed by a court, generally by a court exercising equitable powers, for the purpose of trying before a jury a matter in dispute between the parties. When in a court of equity any matter of fact is strongly contested, the court usually directs the matter to be tried by a jury.

But as no jury is summoned to attend this court, the fact is usually directed to be tried in a court of law upon a feigned issue; for this purpose an action is brought in which the plaintiff, by a fiction, declares that he laid a wager for a sum of money with the defendant, for example, that a certain paper is the last will and testament of Paul, then avers that it is his

(*a*) 1 Chit. Pl. 482; Lawes, Pl. 113.
(*b*) Bac. Ab. Pleas, G 2, N 5; 2 Saund. 319, a, n. 6.
(*c*) Stat. 32 H. VIII., c. 30.

will, and therefore demands the money; the defendant admits the wager, but avers that it is not the will of Paul, and thereupon that issue is joined which is directed out of chancery to be tried; and thus the verdict of the jurors at law, determines the fact in a court of equity.

These feigned issues are also frequently used in courts of law, by consent of parties, to determine some disputed rights, without the formality of pleading, and by this practice much time and expense are saved in the decision of a cause. But in all these cases the consent of the court must be previously obtained. To attempt the trial of a feigned issue, or fictitious action, on a pretended wager, where the parties have no rights, for the purpose of obtaining the opinion of the court on an abstract point of law, is a contempt of court, for which the parties and their attorneys may be punished.(a)

§ 3.—How issues are procured.

3015. To accelerate the pleadings of the parties, the courts have adopted certain general rules, by which the parties are required to put in their several pleadings within stated times, and in some states statutory provisions require them so to plead; on failure to plead as required, the court render judgment against the party in default. If, for example, the plaintiff fail to file his declaration, reply to the plea of his antagonist, etc., after being notified that a rule has been taken requiring him to file the declaration, replication, etc., then judgment of nonsuit is given against him. If the defendant, in like matter, upon a similar notice, neglect to plead, rejoin, etc., judgment is rendered against him for the plaintiff's claim, which judgment is, in general, only interlocutory.

(a) Henkin v. Guerss, 12 East, 248; Rep. t. Hard. 237. See Fletcher v. Peck, 6 Cranch, 147.

SECTION 4.—OF REPLEADERS AND JUDGMENTS NON OBSTANTE VEREDICTO.

3016.—1. When an immaterial issue has been formed, the court will order the parties to plead *de novo*, for the purpose of obtaining a better issue; this is called a *repleader*.

The motion for a repleader is made, when, on an examination of the record, the unsuccessful party conceives the issue joined was an immaterial issue, or such as is not proper to decide the action. In such cases, therefore, the court not knowing for whom to give judgment, will award a repleader.

When a repleader is granted the parties must begin to replead at the first fault. If the declaration, plea, and replication be all bad, the parties must begin *de novo;* if the declaration be good, and the plea and replication be both bad, the repleader must be as to both; but if the declaration and plea be both good, and the replication only be bad, the parties replead from the replication only.(*a*)

3017.—2. A judgment *non obstante veredicto*, is one rendered in favor of the plaintiff, without regard to the verdict obtained by the defendant. The difference between a repleader and a judgment *non obstante veredicto*, is this, that where a plea is good in form though not in fact, or, in other words, if it contain a defective title, or ground of defence, by which it is apparent to the court, upon the defendant's own showing, that in any way of putting it, he can have no merits, and the issue joined thereon be found for him, there, as the awarding of a repleader could not mend the case, the court, for the sake of the plaintiff, will at once give judgment *non obstante veredicto;* but when the defect is not so much in the title as in the manner of stating it,

---

(*a*) Vide Staples *v.* Haydon, 2 Salk. 579, for several rules as to repleaders. See Lawes, Pl. 175 ; Steph. Pl. 119.

and the issue joined thereon is immaterial, so that the court know not for whom to give judgment, whether for the plaintiff or defendant, there, for their own sakes, they will award a repleader; a judgment *non obstante veredicto* is always upon the *merits*, and never granted but in a clear case; a repleader is upon the *form* and manner of pleading.(*a*)

SECTION 5.—OF PLEAS PUIS DARREIN CONTINUANCE.

3018. A plea *puis darrein continuance*, or since the last continuance, is one which has arisen upon a fact which has happened since the last continuance of the cause, and after issue was joined. It is proper to consider, 1, in what cases such pleas are allowed; 2, the time when they must be pleaded; 3, their effects; 4, their form.

§ 1.—In what cases pleas puis darrein continuance are allowed.

3019. Pleas of this kind are in abatement or in bar, like other pleas.(*b*)   Though in general the defendant can regularly plead but once, after which, if there be an issue or demurrer, the cause is to be determined upon it, inasmuch as there can be but one verdict in the cause; yet if any new matter happens pending the writ, he may plead it notwithstanding a former plea, provided it be pleaded since the last continuance.

When the matter of defence has arisen since the commencement of the suit, and before issue joined, it cannot be pleaded in bar to the action *generally*, but must, when it has arisen before plea or continuance, be pleaded as to the *further* maintenance of the suit. When such matter has arisen after issue joined, *puis darrein continuance*.

(*a*) Com. Dig. Pleader, R 18 ; Bac. Ab. Pleas, M ; 18 Vin. Ab. 567; Arch. Civ. Pl. 358.
(*b*) Lawes, Pl. 173 ; Bro. Ab. Continuance, pl. 57 ; Bull. N. P. 310.

The usual matters pleaded *puis darrein continuance,* are matters in abatement, which have arisen since last continuance, as the marriage of a feme plaintiff; and this may be pleaded after a plea in bar, because ·the pleading of the latter waives only such matters in abatement as then existed; or they may be in bar, as a release, or the discharge of the defendant as a bankrupt.

§ 2.—When pleas puis darrein continuance must be pleaded.

3020. Formerly there were formal adjournments or continuances of the proceedings in a suit, for certain purposes, from one term to another, and, during the interval, the parties were, of course, out of court. When any matter arose which was a ground of defence, since the last continuance, the defendant was allowed to plead it, which allowance was an exception to the general rule that the defendant can plead but one plea of one kind or class. By the modern practice the parties are, from the day when by the ancient practice a continuance would be entered, supposed to be out of court, and the plaintiff is suspended until the day arrives to which, by the ancient practice, the continuance would extend; at that day the defendant is entitled, if any new matter of defence has arisen in the interval, to plead, according to the ancient practice *puis darrien continuance,* before the next continuance.

A plea *puis darrein continuance* may be pleaded after the jury are gone from the bar, but not after they have given their verdict.(*a*)

§ 3.—Effect of a plea puis darrein continuance.

3021. This plea is not a departure from, but is a *waiver of the first plea,* so that no advantage can afterward be taken of it; and to prevent the plaintiff being delayed *ad infinitum,* it is said there can be but one

(*a*) Lawes, Pl. 174.

plea *.puis darrein continuance;* for, if a second were allowed, there is no reason why a third, or any unlimited number, should not be permitted.(*a*)

§ 4.—Form of the plea puis darrein continuance.(*b*)

3022. A plea of this kind *must be certain,* for it is not sufficient to say that since the last continuance such a thing happened, but the day of the continuance must be shown, and also the time and place must be alleged where the matter of defence arose.(*c*)   When pleaded in abatement, the plea begins and concludes like those in abatement which are put in at first to the declaration.   A plea in bar, pleaded *puis darrien continuance,* begins by saying that the plaintiff ought not further to maintain his action against the defendant, and not that the former inquest should not be taken against him; because it is a substantive plea of itself, and comes in place of one previously pleaded; consequently it ought to be concluded with prayer of judgment, if the plaintiff ought further to maintain his action.   The plaintiff's replication should begin with saying that he, by reason of any thing alleged by the defendant in his plea, ought not to be barred from further maintaining it.   In other respects these pleas, and the pleadings upon them, are governed by the same rules of pleading as prevail in other cases, save that the facts stated in the plea must be verified on oath or affirmation of the defendant.

CHAPTER IX.—OF DEMURRERS.

3023. Demurrer, from the Latin *demorari,* or from the old French *demorrer,* to wait or stay, in pleading,

(*a*) Gilb. C. P. 105; Bro. Ab. Continuance, pl. 5, 41; Lawes, Pl. 174.
(*b*) See the form of a plea puis darrein continuance, Steph. Pl. 82.
(*c*) Lawes on Pl. 174; 1 Chit. Pl. 638.

imports, according to its etymology, that the party will *remain* and not proceed with the pleadings; because no sufficient statement has been made on the other side; but will wait the judgment of the court, whether he is bound to answer.

A demurrer may be taken by either party, at any stage of pleading before issue is joined. It may be for insufficiency, either in substance or in form; that is, it may be either on the ground that the case shown by the opposite party is essentially insufficient, or on the ground that it is stated in an inartificial manner, for the law requires in every plea, and all other pleadings, two things, the one that it be matter sufficient, the other that it be deduced and expressed according to the forms of law; and if either of these be wanting, it is cause of demurrer.

SECTION 1.—OF THE FORM OF DEMURRERS.

3024. Demurrers are, as in their nature, so in their forms, of two kinds; they are general or special.

§ 1.—Of general demurrers.

' 3025. A *general demurrer* is one which excepts to the sufficiency of some previous pleading in general terms, without showing specifically the nature of the objection; and such demurrer is sufficient, when the objection is on matter of substance.(*a*)

§ 2.—Of special demurrers.

3026. A *special demurrer* is one which excepts to the sufficiency of the pleadings on the opposite side, and shows specifically the nature of the objection and the particular ground of exception; " And the said C D, according to the form of the statute in such case

(*a*) 1 Chit. Pl. 639; Lawes, Pl. 167; Co. Litt. 72, a; Bac. Ab. Pleas, N 5; Steph. Pl. 61, where there is a form.

made and provided, states, and shows to the court
here, the following causes of demurrer to the said
declaration; that is to say, that no day or time is
alleged in the said declaration, at which the said causes
of action, or any of them, are supposed to have
accrued," etc.(a)

A special demurrer is necessary, when the objection
to the pleading turns on matter of form only; that is,
where notwithstanding such objections, enough appears
to entitle the opposite party to judgment, as far as relates to the merits of the cause. For by two statutes(b)
passed with a view to the discouragement of merely
formal objections, it is provided in nearly the same
terms, that the judges "shall give judgment according
to the very right of the cause and matter in law shall
appear unto them, without regarding any imperfection, omission, defect or want of form, except those
only which the party demurring shall specially and
particularly set down and express, together with his
demurrer, as the causes of the same."

Since the passages of these statutes, therefore, no
mere matter of form can be objected to on a general
demurrer; but the demurrer must be in the special
form, and the objection specially stated. On the
other hand, however, it may be observed, that on a
special demurrer, the party may, on the argument,
take advantage, not only of the particular faults which
his demurrer specifies, but also of all objections in substance, or regarding the very right of the cause, as the
statute expresses it, as do not require, within the
statute, to be particularly set down. It follows,
therefore, that unless the objection be clearly of the
substantial kind, it is the safer course, in all cases, to
demur specially. Yet where a general demurrer is
plainly sufficient, it is more usually adopted in

(a) See Steph. Pl. 62, for a form.
(b) 27 Eliz. c. 5, and 4 Ann. c. 16.

practice; because the effect of the special form being to apprise the opposite party more distinctly of the nature of the objection, it is attended with the inconvenience of enabling him to prepare to maintain his pleading by argument, or of leading him to apply earlier to amend. With respect to the degree of particularity with which, under the statutes, the special demurrer must assign the ground of objection, it may be observed, that it is not sufficient to object, in general terms, that the pleadings is "uncertain, defective and informal," or the like, but it is necessary to show in what respect it is uncertain, defective and informal.(a)

SECTION 2.—TO WHAT PLEADINGS THERE MAY BE A DEMURRER.

3027. The demurrer may be either to the whole or to a part of the declaration; and when there are several counts, or in covenants several breaches, some of which are sufficient and others are not, or one count is bad in part, the defendant should demur only to the latter; for if he were to demur to the whole declaration, some of which was good, the judgment must be given against him; and this rule applies with equal force to one count, part of which is sufficient and the residue is not, when the matters are divisible in their nature. But where there is a misjoinder either of parties or causes of action, the demurrer should be to the whole.(b)

SECTION 3.—OF THE EFFECT OF A DEMURRER.

3028. With respect to the effect of a demurrer, it is a rule that a demurrer admits all such matters of

---

(a) 1 Saund. 161, n. 1; Id. 337 b, n. 3; Steph. Pl. 159, 161; Mercer v. Watson, 1 Watts, 346.
(b) 2 Saund. 210, a.

fact as are sufficiently pleaded.(*a*) But although it admits the facts well pleaded, with a view to a determination of their legal sufficiency, it is strictly confined to˙this office, and cannot be used as an instrument of evidence on an issue in fact.(*b*) It is also a rule that a demurrer, when taken, must be accepted by the opposite party, for there can be no demurrer to a demurrer, because the first is sufficient, notwithstanding any inaccuracy in its form, to bring the record before the court for adjudication.

The party whose pleading is opposed by a demurrer, is bound formally to accept the issue in law which it tenders, by the formula called a *joinder in demurrer.*(*c*)

SECTION 4.—OF THE JUDGMENT ON A DEMURRER.

3029. In giving a judgment on a demurrer, the court will consider the whole record, and give judgment for the party, who, on the whole, is entitled to it.(*d*) For example, on a demurrer to the replication, if the court think the replication bad, but perceive a substantial error in the plea, they will give judgment, not for the defendant, but for the plaintiff, provided the declaration be good;(*e*) if the declaration in such case be also bad in substance, upon the same principle, the judgment will be given for the defendant; for, when judgment is to be given, whether the issue be in law or fact, and whether the cause have proceeded to an issue or not, the court is always to examine the whole record, and adjudge for the plaintiff or defendant, according to the legal right, as it may on the whole appear.

(*a*) Bac. Ab. Pleas, N 3; Com. Dig. Q 5; The Postmaster General *v*. Ustick, 4 Wash. C. C. 347.
(*b*) Pease *v*. Phelps, 10 Conn. 62.
(*c*) See form, Steph. Pl. 76.
(*d*) Com. Dig. Pleader, M 1, 2; Bac. Ab. Pleas, N 3; 1 Saund. 285, n. 5.
(*e*) Anon. 2 Wils. 150; Gelston *v*. Burr, 11 John. 482.

3030. This rule is, however, subject to the following exceptions :

1. If the plaintiff demur to a plea in abatement, and the court decide against the plea, they will give judgment of *respondeat ouster*, without regard to any defect in the declaration.(*a*)

2. The court will not look back into the record, to adjudge according to apparent right in the plaintiff, unless the plaintiff have himself put his action upon that ground.(*b*)

3. In examining the whole record, to adjudge according to the apparent right, the court will consider the right in matter of substance, and not in respect of mere form, such as should have been the subject of a special demurrer.(*c*)

CHAPTER X.—OF A CASE STATED.

3031. In connection with the pleadings, may be mentioned an anomalous kind of proceeding, which partakes something of an agreement, and also of pleadings. It is an agreement in writing, known as a *case stated*, between the plaintiff and defendant, that the facts in dispute between them, are as there agreed upon and mentioned. It must contain what are admitted facts, and not merely evidence of facts.(*d*)

The facts being thus ascertained, it is left to the court to decide for which party is the law. When there is no agreement to the contrary, the judgment of the court below is final, and no writ of error can be had upon it.(*e*) When it is desired to have the

---

(*a*) Balasyse *v.* Hester, Lutw. 1592; Hastrop *v.* Hastings, 1 Salk. 212; Carth. 172.
(*b*) Marsh *v.* Bultrel, 5 B. & Ald. 507, 511.
(*c*) Bac. Ab. Pleas, N 2.
(*d*) Deihl *v.* Ihrie, 3 Whart. 143.
(*e*) Dane's Ab. c, 137, a. 4, n. § 7.

judgment of the court in the last resort, it is usual to introduce a clause in the case, that it shall be considered in the nature of a special verdict. In that case, a writ of error lies upon the judgment which may be rendered upon it.

A writ of error will also lie to the judgment which may have been rendered upon such a case, when the parties have agreed to it, although it may not have been agreed to consider the case as a special verdict.(a)

The case, when thus stated, is put by either of the parties upon the *argument list*, which is a collection of all the cases where only questions of law are to be decided, and after it has been argued before the judges, they give their decision with their reasons for it, and judgment is entered for the plaintiff or defendant, as the law or right seems, in the opinion of the court, to be in favor of the one side or of the other.

CHAPTER XI.—OF THE TRIAL.

3032. By *trial* is meant the examination before a competent tribunal, according to the laws of the land, of the facts put in issue in a cause, for the purpose of determining such issue.(b)

The matters in this chapter will be discussed under the following heads: 1, of the nature and kinds of trials; 2, of calling the trial list; 3, of proceedings in the course of the trial.

SECTION 1.—OF THE NATURE AND KINDS OF TRIALS.

3033.· When the cause has been brought to an issue, as above stated, the next step is to bring it to trial, so

---

(a) Fuller *v.* Trévor, 8 S. & R. 529.
(b) Curtis *v.* Colston, 4 Mason, 232.

that a final judgment may be had upon it. If it be an issue in law, the trial is by the court. The case is then put on the argument list, and is decided by the judges alone, without the intervention of a jury; and the court also decides cases where the action is alleged to be founded upon a record, and the defendant has pleaded *nul tiel record*, that there is no such record; whether such record exist is a question of fact or not, but it is a matter of law whether, if it do exist, it is sufficient in point of law to maintain the action of the plaintiff, so that in truth, this is a question of law, rather than of fact. But when the issue arises on a question of fact, it is to be tried by the court and a jury. For this purpose, the cause is ordered upon the *trial list*, agreeably to the provisions of the local statutes and the rules of the different courts. This list is a collection of cases, which are at issue, in matters of fact, and which are to be submitted to a trial before a court and jury.

Formerly, there were several kinds of trials in England, some of which have been abandoned even in that country, and perhaps none of them were ever practised in this; these are, trial by *witnesses*, by *inspection*, by *certificate*, by *wager of battle*, and by *wager of law*.(a)

3034. The trial by jury, almost the only one for deciding issues in fact, has long received the unanimous panegyrics of the common lawyers as being the best safeguard of liberty, particularly in criminal cases; it is the greatest safety of a prisoner, when there is much excitement, either as to the person to be tried, or on account of the accusation which is brought against him.

In many instances, juries have been a bulwark of safety against the attacks of power.(b) Jurors have been represented as being "twelve invisible judges,

(a) See Bouv. L. D. Trial.
(b) Livingston, Rep. on a Penal Code, 13 ; 3 Story, Const. § 1773.

whom the eye of the corrupter cannot see, and the influence of the powerful cannot reach, for they are nowhere to be found, until the moment when the balance of justice being placed in their hands, they hear, weigh, determine, pronounce, and immediately disappear, and are lost in the crowd of their fellow citizens."(a) Too much reliance cannot be placed upon this institution in criminal cases, and particularly in those which assume somewhat of a political character.

But, although this high praise is justly deserved in criminal cases, this institution has been thought by some as not the best calculated to arrive at truth in civil actions. It cannot be denied, that many issues are presented for decision to juries who are entirely incompetent to comprehend them, and perhaps no judge or lawyer, of much experience, can be found who has not sometimes been shocked at the rendition of a verdict. This imperfection has been somewhat removed by the exercise, in certain cases, of the remedial power of granting a new trial.

Whatever its imperfections may be, the trial by jury seems to be firmly seated in the affections of the people, and will not probably be abandoned. By the constitution of the United States, it is secured and made to extend "to all suits at common law, where the value in controversy shall exceed twenty dollars;"(b) and most of the state constitutions contain provisions, that it shall remain as heretofore, and be inviolate.

The right to a trial by jury is confined to proceedings in courts of common law, where *legal rights*, as distinguished from *equitable*, are decided upon.

SECTION 2.—OF THE CALLING OF THE TRIAL LIST.

3035. The trial list, it has been observed, is a

_____

(a) Duponceau, Address at the opening of the Law Academy at Phila-delphia.
(b) Amend. art. 7.

collection of cases which are at issue and ready for trial. These are taken up in the order in which they are on the list, and, unless for a lawful cause shown to the court, they will be ordered for trial.

3036. The usual excuses alleged for not going on to trial, are:

1. Because the cause has been improperly put upon the list in violation of law, or the rules of the court, as if it be not at issue.

2. Because there has been some fraud or artifice used, to deprive the opposite party of some legal advantage to which he was entitled.

3. Because some material piece of evidence, or a material witness, cannot be had, after having used all lawful means to procure the same. In the case of an absent witness, it must be shown that his testimony is important, and that every effort has been used, by the party wanting his evidence, to secure it; for this purpose, a writ issued by the clerk or prothonotary of the court, under its express or implied authority, directed to the witness, commanding him to appear at the time and place of trial to testify, must be procured. It is called a *subpœna*. The party wanting the witness must have made an effort within the time prescribed by the rules of court, to serve it upon the witness; or if the party knew the witness was going away, he should have taken his deposition under a rule of court, or a commission after he had gone; if he has neglected to take these necessary steps, the absence of the witness will not avail him. The law requires, in all these cases, that the party should use due diligence, and his neglect ought not to delay his adversary.

4. Because a commission to take depositions has been issued and is outstanding.

5. Because the counsel employed by the party applying for a continuance, cannot attend on account of sickness, or other sufficient cause.

3037. The court in all these cases exercise a sound discretion, and will never force a party to a trial, who has used due diligence, and when by compelling him to trial, injustice may be done. When a sufficient cause is shown, which must always be under oath or affirmation, either of the party himself or of some other person, the cause will be continued till the next term, a continuance being necessary at each term, to keep the cause in court; but this continuance is seldom formally made, the causes being supposed to be continued without order of the court for that purpose.

If no lawful cause for a continuance be shown, but a temporary delay is required, the case may be put at the *foot of the list*, to be called again in its turn, or it may be left open, that is, in a condition to be taken up as soon as a short absence of counsel or a witness shall cease, or a temporary cause of delay has been removed.

When there is no cause for such delay, nor for a continuance till the next term, the case will be ordered for trial.

SECTION 3.—OF PROCEEDINGS IN THE COURSE OF THE TRIAL.

3038. These are, 1, the calling of the jury; 2, the opening of the case; 3, the evidence; 4, nonsuit; 5, signing bills of exceptions; 6, demurrer to evidence; 7, arguments of counsel; 8, charging the jury; 9, rendering a verdict.

§ 1.—Of the jury.

3039. By *jury* is understood a body of twelve men, selected according to law, for the purpose of deciding some controversy, or issue, on a matter of fact. The individuals of which the jury is composed, are called *jurors;* they are so denominated because they were formerly *sworn* to try the matters in issue. They still bear the same name, although many are now *affirmed*, instead of being sworn.

In civil cases, the jury never decide a question of law. They are merely to find the facts, and the court apply the law to them when so ascertained. The origin of juries is hid in the night of time. It is highly probable that this institution was not always what it is now. From the earliest times, even before regularly organized constitutions were established, when disputes arose, men must have been selected to decide them; these were generally the most ancient personages or the neighbors, the *equals* or *peers* of the contesting parties. These tribunals were common among the people of the north of Europe, who invaded the southern kingdoms and states of that portion of the globe. Being found convenient they were adopted by the nations invaded, and substituted in the place of the ancient tribunals in Germany, France, England and Italy. In most of these countries they disappeared by degrees, except in England. In that country trial by jury was established soon after the Norman conquest, and the institution was improved from time to time to what it is now. In the United States the mode of selecting juries, and the institution itself, have been greatly improved, so as to secure a fair and impartial body of men, from whom the twelve jurors, who are impanelled in any particular case, are to be chosen.(*a*)

(*a*) Morin claims the institution of trial by jury to be of French origin. He says, " En remontant à l'ordre judiciaire des Grecs et des Romains, ainsi qu'aux institutions des peuples du Nord, on y découvre des germes de cette juridiction, appliquées aux contestations civiles; mais de toutes les nations modernes, la France peut révendiquer l'honneur d'avoir, la première consacré le jugement d'un accusé par ses pairs (pares.) Cette institution, encore bien imparfaite, avait été transplantée en Angleterre lors de la conquête de ce pays par les Normands." Dictionnaire du Droit Criminel, voce, Jurés—Jury.

OF PROCEEDINGS IN AN ACTION.   329

No 3040   Book 4, tit. 8, chap. 11, sec. 3, § 1, art. 1, 2.   No. 3041.

The principal qualifications of jurors are,

1, That they be *sui juris;*

2, Of full age ;

3, Good and lawful men ; that is, not of an infamous character, for a man whose oath could not be received as a witness, cannot be a juror ;

4, Citizens of the United States ;

5, Residents of the district, county, or other territory, over which the court has jurisdiction.

Art. 1.—*Of the selection of the jury.*

3040. The jurors for the trial of civil cases, are selected by officers designated by the statutes of each state ; they are generally taken from among the electors for public officers, in such numbers as the laws require.

A writ called a *venire facias,* directed to the sheriff, commanding him to summon a certain number of jurors, is delivered to that officer in sufficient time to cause to be drawn the names of jurors, which are put into a box. By virtue of this writ he draws, with such officers as are authorized to act with him in this matter, the requisite number of jurors, summons them to attend court, at the time appointed for holding a term, and returns the venire to the court whence it issued, together with a list of the jurors summoned, which list is called the *array,* because the jurors summoned to attend court are *arrayed* or arranged on the *panel;* this latter word, signifying a schedule or roll, contains the names of the jurors summoned by virtue of the writ of *venire facias,* and annexed to that writ.(*a*)

Art. 2.—*Of the challenge of the jurors.*

3041. At this stage of the cause, after the *venire* has been returned, and before any juror has been

---

(*a*) See Co. Litt. 158, b.

330 OF REMEDIES.

No. 3042   Book 4, tit 8, chap. 11, sec 3, § 1, art. 2.   No. 3043.

selected to try the particular case, either party may object to the whole panel or array of jurors; this objection or exception thus made to the jurors is called a *challenge to the array.* The principal causes for making this challenge are, that there has been some fraud, or some illegal act, in drawing or returning the panel, for which the whole is vitiated. When the causes of the challenge are established by evidence to the satisfaction of the court, the whole *array* is set aside, and no trial can be had until another panel has been returned.

But when no motion has been made to set aside the array, and the party has not done some act by which he waived his right to insist upon such a course, as by objecting to a particular juror who may be called to try his case; then the clerk of the court draws from a box, where all the names of the jurors have been put in separate slips of paper, the names of twelve of them. Each party has a right to challenge two or such other number as may be authorized by the local statutes, without assigning any reason whatever, and as many of the others as he has a lawful reason for objecting to; this is called a *challenge to the polls.* Those challenges which may be made without assigning any reason, are called *peremptory challenges;* those made for some legal reason, are *challenges for cause.*

3042. A challenge to the polls is an objection made separately to each juryman, as he is about to be sworn. Challenges to the polls, like those to the array, are either principal or to the favor.

3043.—1. *Principal challenges* are made on various grounds:

1. *Propter defectum,* that is, on account of some personal objection, as alienage, infancy, old age, or the want of those qualifications required by the constitution or legislative enactments.

2. *Propter affectum,* because of some personal, or

actual partiality, in the juryman who is made the subject of the objection; on this ground a juror may be objected to, if he is related to the opposite party within the ninth degree, or is so connected by affinity; this is supposed to bias the juror's mind, and is a presumption of partiality.(a)   One who has expressed a wish as to the result of the trial,(b) or who has the smallest interest in the matter to be tried, may be challenged for this cause.

3. The third ground for challenging to the polls, is *propter delictum*, or the incompetency of the juror on the ground of infamy.

3044.—2. Challenges to the polls *for favor* may be made when, although the juror is not so evidently partial that his supposed bias will be sufficient to authorize a principal challenge, yet there are reasonable grounds to suppose that he will act under some undue influence and prejudice.   The causes for such challenges are manifestly very numerous, and depend on a variety of circumstances.   The fact to be ascertained is whether the juryman is altogether indifferent as he stands unsworn, because, even unconsciously to himself, he may be swayed to one side.   The line which separates the causes for principal challenges, and for challenges to the favor, is not distinctly marked.(c)

Art. 3.—Of the swearing of the jury.

3045. After the jurors have been selected, to the number of twelve, they are then to be sworn or affirmed.   This is done by the clerk or prothonotary of the court, or one of his deputies, administering an oath or affirmation to each juror.   The form of this oath or affirmation varies in different states, according

---

(a) Denn d. Hinchman *v.* Clark, Coxe, 446; McLellan *v.* Crofton, 6 Greenl. 307; 3 Day, 491.

(b) 4 Hargr. St. Tr. 748; Bac. Ab. Juries, E 5.

(c) Co. Litt. 147, 157, a; Bac. Ab. Juries, E 5; Bouv. L. D. Challenge.

to the provisions contained in the statute, but it is generally "to try the issue joined between the parties, and a true verdict give according to the evidence." This oath or affirmation, it must be observed, is one of those promissory obligations which is binding only on the conscience, the violation of which cannot be punished as perjury.

§ 2.—Of opening the case.

3046. The right of a party in opening the case, and the manner of making the opening, will be the subject of two articles.

Art. 1.—Of the right of opening.

3047. By opening a case is meant the act of beginning, or first addressing the jury, and stating the facts of the case. The right of opening is of great importance, because the party who begins will, if his opponent give any evidence, have the general reply, or last word to the jury, a privilege which powerful counsel can usually exercise with great advantage. The general rule is, that the party who alleges the *affirmative* of any proposition or *issue in fact*, should prove it, because a negative does not in general admit of the simple and direct proof, of which an affirmative is capable; and, therefore, the party who has to maintain or prove the only affirmative, or all the affirmatives, must begin to give the evidence, for, until that is done, the opposite party is not bound to answer; yet, cases may arise, where it is more easy to prove the negative; as if a defendant plead in abatement that another party *contracted jointly with him*, and that he ought to have been joined, and 'the plaintiff reply that the contract was *not so jointly made*, he might be able to prove the negative by producing and proving the defendant's separate undertaking to pay. It is an established rule that when the *onus probandi*, or burden of the proof of all the issues, is on the defendant, he is entitled to begin.(*a*)

But when there is one affirmative issue for the plaintiff to prove, and several other affirmative issues for the defendant to prove, then the plaintiff has the preference.(*b*)

Art. 2.—Of the manner of opening the case.

3048. In order to open his case to the court and jury understandingly, the counsel should, 1, be fully acquainted with the full extent of the plaintiff's claim, and the circumstances under which it is made, and of its justice and reasonableness; 2, know at least the outline of the evidence by which the case is to be supported; 3, be well acquainted with the legal grounds and authority in favor of the claim, or of the proposed evidence; and, 4, anticipate the expected defence, when that can be done, and be able to state the grounds on which it is futile, either in law or justice, and the reason why it ought to fail.

1. Of the statement of the plaintiff's claim.

3049. In making the statement of the plaintiff's claim, the counsel should state all the facts which the form of the declaration has embraced, because, if he omit some of them, besides the charge of unfairness to which such course might subject the counsel, it might mislead the judge, whose attention would not be par-

(*a*) In England there are some exceptions to this general rule, in actions for libel, slander, malicious prosecutions, and other actions for injuries to the person, in which cases the plaintiff has a right to begin and conclude, although there may be affirmative pleas. It is deemed but fair and reasonable that in such cases the plaintiff who brings an action, should be heard first to state his complaint. Carter *v.* Jones, 6 Car. & Payne, 64; S. C. 1 Moo. & Rob. 281. And in Arkansas, in an action on a penal bond, the plaintiff has a right to open and close, although affirmative pleas have been filed. Sullivan *v.* Rearden, 5 Pike, 140.

(*b*) Jackson *v.* Hesketh, 2 Stark, 521 ; Cotton *v.* James, 1 Moo. & Malk. 279.

334 OF REMEDIES.

No. 3050. • Book 4, tit. 8, chap. 11, sec 3, § 2, art. 2. 3051.

ticularly directed to such facts as had been omitted; but also it might subject the party to some inconvenience, as he would not be allowed to state a new claim or to prove it, with a view to obtain a verdict for more than he originally claimed.(a)

2. *Statement of the plaintiff's expected evidence.*

3050. In stating the evidence which he expects to give, the counsel ought to be very careful not to be too positive as to the proof which he will make, for although he may himself have examined the witnesses, perhaps on an examination in court there will be discrepancies between their statements to him, and an examination under the more impressive obligation of an oath in open court. A contrary course will render him liable to the observations of the opposite counsel, who will not fail to point out such discrepancies. When, however, a piece of evidence is positively certain, as where the same point will be supported by several respectable witnesses, or by a written document, the opening counsel ought to press such evidence upon the court and jury. In doing this the counsel will abstain from making any comments on the evidence, but merely state that he will produce it for the consideration of the jury.

3. *Statement of the points of law in the case.*

3051. In stating a point of law by anticipation, the counsel will have to observe a great deal of caution, for he may inadvertently suggest to the court, or to his opponent, an objection against his case, which did not occur to them, and he might betray a want of confidence in his case. But when the point must arise, the counsel may, by way of anticipation, induce the judge to take a favorable view of the point, and by a

---

(a) Patterson v. Zacheriah, 1 Stark. 72; Penson v. Lee, 2 B. & P. 332.

concise allusion, rather than by a regular argument, endeavor to satisfy the judge in favor of his client.

4. Of the anticipation of the expected defence.

3052. The counsel should anticipate the course of defence, which may probably be adopted by the opposite party; whether he will probably rely on some legal objection, either as to the law or the facts of the case; or whether, relying upon his speech to the jury, he will refrain from giving any evidence, and thereby entitle himself to the conclusion. The opening must therefore depend in a great measure on the circumstances of each case. If it is expected that the defendant will give no evidence, and rely upon some legal objection, it is advisable for the plaintiff's counsel to anticipate, argue against, and condemn all such objections, as being founded in neither law nor justice.

With regard to the facts, it is unnecessary to anticipate what will be proved by the other side, because these may be stated before giving the rebutting testimony.

§ 3.—Of the evidence.

PRELIMINARY OBSERVATIONS.

3053. The court and jury being in possession of the statement of the facts, and of the law of the plaintiff's case, supposing him to be entitled to the opening, the next step is to prove it, according to the rules established for ascertaining the truth of the facts, or by *evidence*. It is not within the compass of a work like the present, to enter into all the niceties and distinctions of the law of evidence, or what may be submitted to the jury in order to establish the truth; a mere synopsis of the law upon this subject will be attempted.

Various definitions have been given of evidence. It is that which makes clear or ascertains the very fact or point in issue;(*a*) or it is whatever is lawfully exhibited to a court and jury by which any matter of fact, the truth of which is submitted to investigation, is established or disproved.(*b*)

This word, and the words *proof*, *testimony* and *witness*, are sometimes used indifferently, or as synonymous; but they are very different, and will not be used in the same sense by any who are not guilty of negligence or carelessness. By *evidence* is meant what establishes the truth; *proof* is the effect of evidence; *testimony* is the statement of a witness made under oath or affirmation; and *witness* is a person who testifies or gives evidence of facts known to him. By the word *truth*, which is to be established by the evidence, is meant the actual state of things at the time spoken of.

By *competent evidence* is meant that which the law authorizes, and the very nature of the thing to be proved requires. *Credible evidence* is that which may be believed, and which has the appearance of being a statement of the truth; by *incredible evidence*, is meant what is lawfully produced as evidence, but which is not deserving of credit or belief; as, if a man were to swear he saw a horse flying, in this case he must be supposed to want to impose upon the court and jury, or that there was some delusion in his mind. *Satisfactory evidence* is what is sufficient to induce a belief that the thing is true, in other words, it is credible evidence. *Cumulative evidence* is that which goes to prove the same point which has been established by some other evidence; as if an attempt be made to prove a fact by the admission of the party, evidence of another verbal admission of the same fact is cumulative; but evidence of other circumstances, tending to establish

---

(*a*) 3 Bl. Com. 367.
(*b*) Bac. Ab. Evidence, *in pr.;* 1 Greenl. Ev. § 1; 1 Phil. Ev. 1; Wills on Cir. Ev. 2; 1 Stark. 8; 8 Toull. Dr. Civ. Fr. n. 2; Domat, 1. 3, t. 6, *in pr.*

the fact is not.(a)   *Direct evidence* is that which proves precisely the fact in question ; *indirect evidence* is that which does not prove the fact in question, but proves another, the certainty of which may lead to discover the truth of the one sought.   This induction may be necessary and infallible; for example, a question arises whether the defendant signed a certain paper, or performed a certain act, upon such a day, in Philadelphia; if it be strictly proved beyond a doubt that upon that day he was in England, the evidence, although indirect, will be conclusive.   But, on the other hand, the induction which arises from indirect proof may be only probable; and then only a stronger or weaker presumption will be the result.

3054. The object of all inquiry is truth, and the intention of the law is to adopt the best means of terminating disputes among the people, and to base their happiness on law and justice ; it seeks the best means of discovering the truth, and for this purpose it has established certain rules to guide the magistrate in its discovery.

With regard to things which pass or happen out of our observation, which can become the object of a legal inquiry, we can have no certain knowledge ; we have no conscious certainty of their existence, and we must therefore have recourse to other means in order to acquire any idea of them.   These means are the senses; the testimony of men, whether in writing or not; and analogy or induction, which are so useful in jurisprudence.

But all these means may deceive us, and often do so ; still, when they are directed by a right reason, although they do not bear the infallible mark or characteristic of truth, yet they often lead us to its discovery.   They sometimes produce convictions as strong as consciousness ; and for this reason this strong

(a) Parker *v.* Hardy, 24 Pick. 246.

persuasion has been called *moral evidence*, in opposition to demonstration, which has been denominated *mathematical evidence*.

However deceptive these means of ascertaining truth may be, we cannot do without them. They are indispensable in all the sciences, and particularly in civil life, and we must constantly have recourse to them. The certainty, or at least probability, of which they assure us, when well considered, are such that we cannot withhold our assent to them without imprudence, if not folly. And if these means, which nature has furnished us, sometimes fail, it is generally owing to the precipitation of our judgments.

Every thing that can be done to prevent these errors, has been provided by the law, by establishing rules which shall guide the magistrate called upon to decide upon the rights of his fellow citizens.

It is a general rule, applicable to all species of evidence, that the proof of facts derives its force from other known facts, from which we conclude that those which are unknown are true; either by drawing a consequence of a cause from its effect, or of an effect from its cause, or from the connection which one thing has with another. Thus, all the art of the human mind, all the prudence and experience of the judges, consists in drawing from a known fact a certain consequence, which makes known a doubtful fact.(*a*)

The subject of evidence will be divided into two branches: 1, under the first will be considered the nature, the object of evidence, the instruments by which truth is established, and the effect of evidence; 2, the manner of giving evidence will be discussed under the second.

FIRST DIVISION.

Of the nature, the object, the instruments and the effects of evidence.

3055. Evidence will be considered with reference,

(*a*) See 2 D'Augesseau, Plaidoyer 23ᵉ, p. 350, 351; ed. by Pardessus.

1, to its nature; 2, its object; 3, the instruments by which facts are established; and 4, its effect.

Art. 1.—Of the nature of evidence.

3056. Evidence, considered as to its nature, is, 1, primary; 2, secondary; 3, positive; 4, circumstantial or presumptive; 5, hearsay; 6, admitted; 7, confessed; 8, relevant and irrelevant.

1. Of primary evidence.

3057. Primary evidence is the best of which the case, in its nature, is susceptible; the term is opposed to secondary evidence, which supposes some other, or primary evidence behind.   The rule that the best evidence shall be required, does not demand the greatest amount of evidence which can possibly be given of any fact, its object is to exclude from the case any evidence which supposes better evidence in the possession of the party; for that better evidence may be withheld because it would prove facts differently from what the secondary would establish.   This rule then excludes only that evidence which indicates the existence of more original sources of information; but when there is no substitution of evidence, but simply a selection of weaker instead of stronger proof of the same nature, it is not required that the party should supply all the proof capable of being produced.   For example, when a written contract has been entered into, and the object is to prove what it was, it is requisite to produce the original writing, if it is to be obtained, and, in that case, no copy or inferior evidence will be received. But, being produced, its execution may be proved by only one or two attesting witnesses.

3058. To this general rule there are several exceptions :

1. As it refers to the *quality* rather than the *quantity* of the evidence, it is plain, as before observed, that the fullest proof every case admits of is not requi-

site ; if, therefore, there are several eye-witnesses to a fact, it may be sufficiently proved by one only.

2. It is not always requisite, when the matter to be proved has been reduced to writing, that the writing should be produced ; as if the narrative of a fact to be proved has been committed to writing, it may yet be proved by parol. A receipt for the payment of money, for example, will not exclude parol evidence of payment.(a) But this exception does not extend to those cases where the law requires the instruments should be in writing, such as records ; public documents; official examinations; deeds of conveyance of land; wills, other than nuncupative ; promises required to be in writing by the statute of frauds, and the like ; for in all these cases, the writing must be produced, if in the power of the party. And again, parol proof cannot be substituted for the written evidence of any contract which the parties have put in writing.(b) Nor can oral evidence be substituted for any writing, the existence of which is disputed, and which is material, either to the issue between the parties, or to the credit of witnesses, and is not a mere memorandum of some other fact.(c)

3. Another exception to the rule arises from considerations of public convenience ; for example, proof that an individual has acted notoriously as a public officer, is *primâ facie* evidence of his public character, without producing his commission or appointment.(d) But if the office is of a private nature, proof of the appointment of the agent must be made.(e)

(a) 4 Esp. R. 213. See 7 B. & C. 611 ; 1 Camp. 439 ; 3 B. & A. 566.
(b) Rex v. Holy Trinity, 7 B. & C. 611 ; Dennett v. Crocker, 8 Greenl. ·239 ; Spiers v. Wilson, 4 Cranch, 398.
(c) 1 Greenl. Ev. § 88 ; 1 Phil. Ev. 422 ; Vincent v. Cole, 1 M. & M. ·258.
(d) United States v. Reyburn, 6 Pet. 352 ; Milnor v. Tillotson, 7 Pet. ·100 ; Jacob v. U. S. 1 Brockenb. 520.
(e) Short v. Lee, 1 Jac. & Walk. 464.

2. Of secondary evidence.

3059. Secondary evidence is that species of proof which is admissible on the loss of primary evidence, and which becomes, by that event, the best evidence. The rule that secondary evidence shall not be given when the primary can be had, is grounded upon a reasonable suspicion that the substitution of inferior for better evidence arises from sinister motives, and an apprehension that the best evidence, if produced, would alter the case to the prejudice of the party. Besides, the secondary evidence is more liable to errors or mistakes than the primary; the copy of a written paper may be incorrect and differ from the original.

When primary evidence cannot be had, then secondary evidence will be admitted, because then it is the best. But before such evidence can be allowed, it must be clearly made to appear that the superior evidence is not to be had.(a)   The person who possesses it must be applied to, whether he be a stranger or the opposite party; in the case of a stranger, a *subpœna duces tecum* and an attachment, when proper, must be taken out and served; and, in the case of a party, notice to produce such primary evidence must be proved, before the secondary evidence will be admitted.(b)

When the original cannot be had, after due proof of its execution, the contents should be proved by a *counterpart*, if there be one, for that is the next best evidence; and, it seems, that no evidence of a mere copy is admissible, until proof has been given that the counterpart cannot be produced.(c)   If there be no counterpart, a copy may be proved by any witness

(a) See Ford v. Walsworth, 19 Wend. 334; Flinn v. McGonigle, 9 W. & S. 75 ; Woodsworth v. Barker, 1 Hill, 172 ; Harris v. Doe, 4 Blackf. 369 ; Doe v. McCaleb, 2 How. Mis. 756 : Bouldin v. Massie, 7 Wheat. 122.

(b) Pattôn v. Tybout, 7 S. & R. 116; Myer v. Barker, 6 Binn. 228; Drum v. Simpson, 6 Binn. 478 ; Reading R. R. v. Johnson, 7 W. & S. 317·

(c) King v. Castleton, 6 T. R. 236.

who knows that it is a copy, from having compared it with the original.(*a*)   If there be no copy, the party may produce an abstract, or give even parol evidence of a deed.(*b*)

But it has been decided that there are *no degrees in secondary evidence;* and when a party has laid a foundation for such evidence, he may prove the contents of a deed by parol, though it appear an attested copy is in existence.(*c*)

3060. This rule rejecting secondary evidence is subject to some exceptions, of which the following are the principal:

1. Records of a judicial court and public books or registers may be proved by an *examined copy;*(*d*) the reason of this is, that those books cannot be removed from place to place, because they might be wanted at two places at the same time; and because, being public, a fraud or error in the copy might be easily detected. But this exception does not extend to depositions, or affidavits, or an answer to a bill in chancery, when the party is indicted for perjury; nor perhaps in cases where the party denies his hand writing to a bond or recognizance, unless the copy has been made evidence by a special law.(*e*)

2. It is not in general necessary to prove the written appointment of public officers; proof of their acting as such, is, *primâ facie,* sufficient between third parties.

3. When the evidence is the result of voluminous facts, or of the inspection of many books and papers, the examination of which could not be conveniently made in court, the rule is so far relaxed, that secondary

---

(*a*) Bull. N. P. 254.
(*b*) King *v.* Metheringham, 6 T. R. 556; 10 Mod. 8.
(*c*) Brown *v.* Woodman, 6 Car. & P. 206; 8 Car. & P. 389.
(*d*) When the record has been lost or destroyed, its contents may be proved by secondary evidence.   Graham *v.* O'Fallow, 3 Mis. 507.
(*e*) See Rex *v.* Howard, 1 M. & Rob. 189; Bull N. P. 226; 1 Stark. Ev. 189; 1 Greenl. Ev. § 91.

OF PROCEEDINGS IN AN ACTION.   343

No. 3061.   Book 4, tit. 8, chap 11, sec. 3, § 3, div. 1, art. 1.   No. 3061.

evidence will be admitted ; as, if there be one invariable mode of drawing bills of exchange between the
parties, this may be proved by witnesses who know
the facts, without producing the bills.(a)

4. Inscriptions on walls, fixed tables, mural monu-
ments, gravestones, which cannot conveniently be
produced in court, may be proved by secondary
evidence.(b)

5. In the examination of a witness on his voir dire,
and in preliminary examinations of the same nature,
if the witness discloses the existence of a written instrument affecting his competency, he may also be
interrogated as to its contents ; the rule in this case is,
that if the objection arises on the voir dire, it may be
removed on the voir dire.(c)

3. Of positive evidence.

3061. Positive evidence is that which, if believed,
establishes the truth or falsehood of a fact in issue, and
does not arise from any presumption. Evidence is
direct and positive, when the very facts in dispute are
communicated by those who have the actual knowledge of them by means of their senses.(d)   In these
cases the *factum probandum* is attested by those who
speak from their own actual personal knowledge of its
existence, and the credit which we give it rests on our
faith in human testimony, sanctioned by experience.
We have only to fear that the witness wishes to
deceive, or that he has been deceived. When the
evidence is not direct and positive, there is danger
that we may not clearly perceive the connection
between the facts proved and the facts in controversy.

(a) 1 Greenl. Ev. § 93 ; 1 Phil. Ev. 433.
(b) Meyer v. Sefton, 2 Stark. R. 274.
(c) Phil. & Am. on Ev. 149 ; 1 Phil. Ev. 154 ; 1 Greenl. § 96.
(d) 1 Phil. Ev. 116 : 1 Stark. 19.

4. *Of circumstantial or presumptive evidence.*

3062. Circumstantial evidence is the proof of collateral facts, and differs from direct or positive proof in this, that it never proves directly the fact in question. A fact which is not positively known, is presumed or inferred from one or more other facts or circumstances which are known. Sometimes circumstances are so powerful that it is impossible to resist them, and then such circumstantial evidence is said to be *certain;* at other times such circumstantial evidence is not so conclusive, it is then said to be *uncertain,* or merely probable. Of the first kind is a case where a body is found dead, being that of a person of mature age, with a recent mortal wound, and the mark of a bloody *left* hand upon the *left* arm, the conclusion that he once lived, and that another person was present at, or about the time the wound was inflicted, may be considered certain; but whether the death was caused by suicide or murder, and whether the mark of the bloody hand was that of a murderer or of a friend who came to his relief, or to prevent the crime, is a conclusion which does not necessarily follow from facts proved. It is certain, too, that the bloody mark was not made by the deceased, because no man can make such a mark.(*a*) Another case of the certainty of circumstances, which renders the most positive testimony of a witness incredible, may be mentioned. A man is found dead, a witness swears he saw him shoot himself with a pistol which the deceased held in his hand; upon an examination the ball is extracted from the body, and found to be too large to enter into the pistol; in such case the witness ought not to be credited.(*b*)

3063. Presumptions are the consequences of a known fact, to make known the truth of an uncertain

(*a*) 14 How. St. Tr. 1324.
(*b*) Stark. Ev. 505. See Bouv. L. D. Circumstances, for a singular case where the circumstances contradicted the most positive testimony.

OF PROCEEDINGS IN AN ACTION.   345

No. 3064.   Book 4, tit 6, chap. 11, sec. 3, § 3, div. 1, art. 1.   No. 3064.

fact, the proof of which is sought.(a)   For example, if a question arise as to the right to an estate, between the possessor and a stranger, as to which is the owner, the law presumes that it belongs to the possessor, and he will be maintained in his possession until the other proves his right; for it is not common that a person should take possession without right, nor that the owner should allow himself to be deprived of his possession.

Presumptions, which are sometimes confounded with circumstantial evidence, are however different; circumstantial evidence is the *means* employed to come to the knowledge of one or more facts, in order to establish the existence of another; a presumption is an *inference* as to the existence of one fact, from the existence of some other fact, founded on a previous experience of their connection.(b)

To constitute such a presumption, a previous experience of the connection between the known and inferred facts is essential; this connection must be of such a nature, that as soon as the evidence of one is established, admitted, or assumed, the inference as to the existence of the other immediately arises, independently of any reasoning upon the subject.   Presumptions are either legal and artificial, or natural.

1° *Of legal presumption.*

3064. Presumptions of law consist of those rules, which in certain cases, either forbid or dispense with any further inquiry.   These presumptions derive their force either from the first principles of justice, the laws of nature, or the experience and conduct of human affairs, and the connection usually found to exist between certain things.   These presumptions are divided into two kinds, namely, *conclusive* or which

---

(a) 1 Domat, Lois Civiles, liv. 3, t. 6, s. 4, n. 1.
(b) 3 Stark. Ev. 1234; 1 Phil. Ev. 116; Gilb. Ev. 142; Poth. Ob. n. 840.

cannot be disputed, and *inconclusive* or which are disputable.(*a*)

3065.—1. *Conclusive*, imperative, or absolute presumptions of law, are rules determining the quantity of evidence requisite for the support of any particular averment, which is not permitted to be overcome by any proof that the case is otherwise.

Abstractedly considered, a presumption is the inference drawn of the resemblance between certain facts and probabilities, and reason would require that such presumption should yield to positive proof; and that if the means of demonstrating truth are at hand, it would be shutting our eyes, and becoming wilfully blind, to refuse to receive the light which would establish it against a presumption of law. If we reflect with attention, we will perceive that it would be neither reasonable nor possible, without opposing the very intent of the law, and going contrary to its wisdom, to admit evidence against presumptions which are its very foundation. This will be rendered manifest by an example: the incapacity of an infant to contract, is a rule founded on the general presumption that minors have not yet arrived at that age when the intellectual and moral faculties of man are entirely developed, and which produce that maturity of reason and that prudence, which are required to make a contract without temerity. That capacity, however, is not the same with every one. Temperament, climate, education, make it vary to infinity. Nature has not pointed out any certain signs; yet, without suffering greater inconvenience, the determination when each individual should be considered capable of entering into contracts, could not have been left open, as to each individual, so as to enable a jury to decide that question in every case. If such were the law, there would be required as many judgments as there are men.

(*a*) 1 Domat, Lois Civiles, liv. 3, t, 6, s. 4, n. 2.

OF PROCEEDINGS IN AN ACTION.   347

No. 3066.   Book 4, tit. 8, chap. 11, sec. 3, § 3, div. 1, art. 1.   No 3066.

The law has fixed the age, but it has not been fixed arbitrarily. After many observations, made during a long space of time, as to the period when the greater part of men acquire the faculties which they have at maturity, *ex eo quod plerumque fit*, the law has presumed that this age is twenty-one years; it has fixed this presumption as on a fact which was known, and which is generally true, before which time infants are not capable of making contracts against their interests. This is a general rule applying to all men.

Now could a plaintiff, who sued an infant, to enforce the performance of a contract he had made against his interest, ask to prove that the presumption of law which the infant invokes is not applicable to him, as he was, when the contract was made, a very shrewd young man, wanting only one day of being of full age, and that the presumption was contrary to truth? Certainly not, for that would be to make the provisions of the law subordinate to the decision of the court and jury, whose duty it is to observe and not judge the law. The rule is universal in its application. Leibnitz, for example, that universal genius, who at the age of twenty years had written an excellent work on the best mode of teaching and learning jurisprudence, and who, treading in the steps of Bacon, had dared to point out the *desiderata* of that science, that is, in what it was deficient, the great Leibnitz would not have been an exception to this legal presumption, although it might have been demonstrated that, as to him, it was evidently false, and that at twenty his reason was very superior to most people at thirty.

3066. Among the numerous cases where the presumption of law is conclusive, may be mentioned the following:

1. When the legislature has so declared; thus, by statute of limitations, when a debt has been created by simple contract, and it has not been distinctly

recognized or acknowledged within six years, as a subsisting obligation, no action can be maintained upon it, the law conclusively presumes it to have been paid.

2. The rules of the common law, established and declared through the medium of judicial tribunals, have equal validity. The uninterrupted enjoyment of an incorporeal hereditament, for a period beyond the memory of man, is a conclusive presumption of a prior grant of that which has been so enjoyed: if you permit me to have a right of way over your land, and I enjoy it, not only uninterruptedly, but exclusively, and adversely to your rights, for a sufficient length of time, this is a conclusive presumption of title in me.(a)

3. Conclusive presumptions are made in favor of judicial proceedings; thus the records of a court of justice are presumed to have been correctly made, and they are said to import absolute verity; *res judicata pro veritate accipitur*.(b) And those facts, without which a verdict could not have been found, will be presumed to have been proved, though they were not expressly and distinctly alleged upon the record, provided that it contains general terms to comprehend them by a fair intendment.(c)

4. It is conclusively presumed that a sane man intends to do what will be the probable consequences of his acts; the deliberate publication of slanderous words, which the publisher knows to be false, or he does not know to be true, raises a conclusive presumption of malice.(d)

5. Ancient deeds and wills, more than thirty years old, if unblemished and unaltered, are said to prove themselves; the subscribing witnesses are presumed

---

(a) Tyler *v.* Wilkinson, 4 Mason, 397 ; Hill *v.* Crosby, 2 Pick. 466 ; Strickler *v.* Todd, 10 S. & R. 63, 69 ; Best on Pres. 103, note (m).

(b) Dig. 50, 17, 207 ; Reed *v.* Jackson, 1 East, 355.

(c) Jackson *v.* Pesked, 1 M. & S. 234.

(d) Weckerly *v.* Geyer, 11 S. & R. 39 ; Fisher *v.* Clement, 10 B. & C. 472 ; Bowdell *v.* Osgood, 3 Pick. 379 ; Haire *v.* Wilson, 9 B. & Cr. 643.

to be dead.(*a*)   But, in the case of deeds, possession must have accompanied them.(*b*)

6. An estoppel is such presumption of law, that a party bound by it cannot disprove it.(*c*)

7. A conclusive presumption of legitimacy arises where a man and a woman are married and cohabit together, the children of the wife will be considered as legitimate, and proof of the mother's irregularities will not destroy the presumption: *pater is est quem nuptiæ demonstrant*.(*d*)   But this presumption may be rebutted by showing circumstances which render it impossible that the husband should be the father,(*e*) as impotency and the like.

8. It is a legal presumption that certain persons cannot commit certain crimes; in this class is an infant under the age of seven years, who cannot commit a larceny; a male infant under fourteen cannot commit a rape; a wife, while in the company of her husband, cannot commit a felony, it is presumed she acts by his coercion.

3067.—2. *Inconclusive* presumptions are those which may be overcome by opposing proof.   These, like the former, are the result of the general experience of mankind, that there is a connection between certain facts and things, the one being usually the companion or the effect of the other.   Of this class of presumptions, the following are a few of the numerous examples:

1. The law presumes that he who has possession of personal property is the owner of it; but possession of personal property, lately stolen, is *primâ facie* evidence of guilty possession, and if unexplained, is taken as conclusive.

(*a*) Tr. per Pais, 370; Winn *v*. Patterson, 9 Pet. 674; Bank of U. S. *v*. Dandridge, 12 Wheat. 70.
(*b*) Plowd. 6.
(*c*) 1 Greenl. Ev. § 22.
(*d*) 7 N. S. 553.
(*e*) Commonwealth *v*. Shepherd, 6 Binn. 283.

350 OF REMEDIES.

2. In like manner, possession of a bill of exchange
by the acceptor, of a promissory note by the maker,
will be a presumption that they have been paid; a
deed found in the possession of the grantee, having on
its face the appearance of a regular execution, will be
presumed to have been delivered by the grantor.

3. Every man is presumed innocent until the contrary is made to appear, and the rule is so strong that
when guilt cannot be established without proving a
negative, that must be done, though in general, the
burden of proof devolves upon the party who makes
an affirmative averment; for example, where the
plaintiff complained, that the defendant, who had
chartered his ship, had put on board articles highly
inflammable and dangerous, *without giving notice to the
master or others in charge of the ship,* whereby the vessel
was burnt; he was held bound to prove this negative
averment.(*a*)   In some cases, the presumption of innocence is sufficient to overthrow another presumption;
as, where, twelve months after her husband's death, a
woman married again, it was rightly presumed that
the husband was dead at the time of the wife's marriage, although the presumption of his death, in consequence of absence, does not arise till a much later
period.(*b*)

But there is an exception to the rule respecting the
presumption of innocence; when a libel has been sold
in a book store, by a servant in the ordinary course of
his employment, the bookseller, or master, will be
presumed to have authorized it, and it will be a guilty
publication in him, though an authority to commit a
breach of the law is not presumed.   This exception is
founded on public policy, lest irresponsible persons

(*a*) Williams *v.* E. Ind. Co., 3 East, 192; Bull. N. P. 298.   See Rex *v.*
Hawkins, 10 East, 211; Powell *v.* Milburn, 3 Wils. 355; Rodwell *v.*
Redge, 1 C. & P. 220.
(*b*) See Bouv. L. D. Death.

OF PROCEEDINGS IN AN ACTION.   351

No. 3067.   Book 4, tit 8, chap. 11, sec. 3, § 3, div. 1, art. 1.   No. 3067.

should be put forward, and the principal and real offender escape.

Another exception to the presumption of evidence, arises from the presumption of guilt, by the misconduct of the party, in his destroying evidence which he ought to produce, or to which the opposite party is entitled; as if a party should obtain papers from a witness, after the latter had been required to produce them under a *subpœna duces tecum*, and refuse to produce them.(a)   But a mere withholding of papers by a party, is not a presumption of guilt.(b)

4. A legal presumption of payment of a debt due by specialty arises, when it has been unclaimed, and without recognition for twenty years, in the absence of any explanatory evidence.   But this presumption does not, in general, attach until the completion of the twenty years,(c) but in some cases this presumption of payment has been made after eighteen years, but these cases are probably exceptions to the general rule.(d) This presumption is very easily rebutted, by showing that interest has been regularly paid,(e) that the obligor has admitted it had not been paid,(f) or other circumstances to rebut the presumption.

5. It is presumed that certain things continue as they are until the contrary appears.   When the existence of a person, personal relation, or a state of things is once established by proof, the law presumes that the person, relation, or state of things continues to exist as before, until the contrary is shown, or until a contrary presumption is raised, from the nature of the subject.   A party, once living, will not be presumed to be dead, until the presumption of death arises,

(a) Leeds v. Cook, 4 Esp. 256.
(b) Hanson v. Eustace, 2 How. U. S. Rep. 653.
(c) Oswald v. Leigh, 1 T. R. 270; Bouv. L. D. tit. Twenty Years.
(d) Rex v. Stephens, 1 Burr. 434; Clark v. Hopkins, 7 John. 556.
(e) Nixon v. Bynum, 1 Bailey, 148.
(f) 2 Harring, 124; Mat. on Pr. Ev. c. 19, 20; Best on Pres. part 1, c. 2, 3.

namely, when he has attained one hundred years,(a) or until he has been absent for seven years, without being heard from, when the presumption of life ceases, and the burden of proof is thrown on the other side.(b)

The relation of partnership, or other similar relations, are presumed to continue until a presumption arises of their dissolution.

Seisin once proved is supposed to continue until disseisin is shown.

The opinions of individuals are presumed to continue the same; and the state of mind, whether sane or insane, once established, is presumed to continue, until the contrary appears. In all these cases, he who asserts there has been a change, is bound to prove it.(c)

6. When a man makes a payment to another, it is presumed to be for a debt due to the receiver, and when he alleges the payment was made by error, he must prove it; for no man is deemed so imprudent as to pay a debt he does not owe. But if he to whom the money was paid denies having received it, and it is proved he did receive it, he will then be required to show that it was given in payment.(d)

2° *Of natural presumptions, or presumptions of fact.*

3068. Natural presumptions, or presumptions of fact, depend upon their own form and efficacy in generating belief or conviction on the mind, as derived from those connections which are pointed out by experience; they are independent of any artificial connections, and differ from mere presumptions of law in this essential respect, that the latter depend and are a branch of the particular system of jurisprudence to

(a) 9 Mart. Lo. R. 257.
(b) Hopewell v. De Pinna, 2 Campb. 113; Loring v. Steinman, 11 Metc. 204; Innis v. Campbell, 1 Rawle, 373.
(c) 1 Greenl. Ev. § 42.
(d) 1 Domat, Lois Civiles, liv. 3, t. 6, s. 4, n. 10.

which they belong; but mere natural presumptions are derived wholly by means of the common experience of mankind, without the aid or control of any particular rule of law, but simply from the course of nature and the habits of society. These presumptions fall within the exclusive province of the jury, who are to pass on the facts; in this they are aided by the advice and instructions of the court.

5. Of hearsay.

3069. Hearsay is that kind of knowledge which the witness states he has received or heard from others. It relates to that which is written as well as to what is spoken; it does not derive its value solely from the credit given to the witness himself, but rests, also, in part, on the veracity or competency of some other person. This kind of evidence is not competent to establish any specific fact, which from its nature is susceptible of proof by witnesses who speak of their own knowledge.(a)

Difficulties frequently arise in discriminating whether the evidence offered is *original* or *hearsay* evidence. What has been written or said by a third person is not necessarily hearsay evidence, when proved by a witness as having been so said or written. On the contrary, the very point in controversy is, not unfrequently, whether such things were written or spoken, and not whether they were true; and in other cases, such language or statements, whether written or spoken, may be the natural and inseparable concomitants of the principal fact in dispute. In such cases, it is obvious that the writings or words are not within the meaning of hearsay, but are original and independent facts, admissible in proof of the issue.(b)   When-

---

(a) Mima Queen v. Hepburn, 7 Cranch, 290.
(b) 1 Greenl. Ev. § 100.

ever the fact that such a communication was made, and not its truth or falsity, is the matter in controversy, the evidence to establish it will be considered as original. Upon this principle, evidence of general reputation, reputed ownership, public rumor, general notoriety, and the like, thöugh composed of the speech of a person not under oath, is original evidence and not hearsay; the subject of inquiry being the concurrence of many voices to the same fact.(a)

3070. There is a species of evidence which, although generally classed under the head of hearsay evidence, is original evidence; it is used not as a medium of proof to establish a distinct fact, but as being in itself a part of the transaction in question, when it is a part of the *res gestæ*, or the subject matter of inquiry, or things done. Upon an inquiry as to the state of mind, sentiments or dispositions of a person at any particular period, his declarations and conversations are admissible as part of the *res gestæ*.(b) So on an indictment for a rape, what the girl said so recently after the fact as to exclude the possibility of practising on her, has been held to be admissible evidence, as a part of the transaction.(c)

3071. Although generally classed as hearsay, yet if properly considered, the evidence usually given in cases of *pedigree* will be found to be original evidence. The question is the descent or parentage of an individual; and in order to ascertain the fact it is important to know how he was treated and acknowledged by those who were interested in him, or sustained toward

---

(a) See Bouv. L. D., Character and Notoriety; Foulkes *v.* Sellway, 3 Esp. 236.: Du Bost *v.* Beresford, 2 Campb. 512; Oliver *v.* Bartlett, 1 Brod. & Bing. 269.

(b) Barthelemy *v.* The People, 2 Hill, N. Y. Rep. 248. On the trial of Lord George Norton, for treason, the cry of the mob, who accompanied the prisoner on his enterprise, was received in evidence, as forming a part of the *res gestæ*, and showing the character of the principal fact. 21 How. St. Tr. 542.

(c) East, P. C. 414.

OF PROCEEDINGS IN AN ACTION. 355

No. 3072.   Book 4, tit. 8, chap. 11, sec. 3, § 3, div. 1, art. 1.   No. 3072.

him any relation of kindred or affinity. This may be shown by proving the declarations of deceased persons, who were related by blood or marriage to the person, and therefore interested in the succession in question; the declarations of all other persons are excluded.(a) General repute in the family, proved by a living member of it, is evidence of pedigree.(b)

Pedigree is the state of a family, as far as regards the relationship of the different members, their births, marriages and deaths, and the time when these events happened. These facts may be proved, not only by living witnesses, who heard of them from other members of the family, but also by the proof of written documents where the facts are stated. Thus an entry by a deceased parent, or other relative, made in a family Bible or missal, or any other book or document, or paper, stating the fact and date of the birth, marriage, or death of a child, or other relative, is considered as the declaration of such parent or relative, in a matter of pedigree.(c)

To the rule that hearsay evidence is inadmissible, there are some exceptions, which may be classified as follows: 1, those which relate to matters of public interest; 2, those relating to ancient possession; 3, declarations made by parties against their interest; 4, dying declarations; 5, the testimony of witnesses who become disqualified; 6, admissions; 7, confession; 8, relevant and irrelevant evidence.

1st Class of exceptions.—Matters of public interest.

3072. To this class may be referred all matters of a general or public interest.

(a) Whitelock v. Baker, 13 Ves. 514; Jewell v. Jewell, 1 How. U. S. R. 231; S. C. 17 Pet. 213; Cowen & Hill's note to 1 Phil. Ev. 240.
(b) Doe v. Griffin, 15 East, 293.
(c) 1 Phil. Ev. 186; 1 Stark. Ev. 55; The Berkley Peerage case, 4 Campb. 401; Watson v. Brewster, 1 Penn. St. R. 381; Douglass v. Sanderson, 2 Dall. 116.

By the term *public* is meant the whole body politic, or all the citizens of the state, and in this sense it is here to be taken; though sometimes it evidently means, when used in a restricted sense, only the inhabitants of a particular place; as when speaking of the people of New York, we say the public. When speaking of the *public* and *general* interest, the terms are frequently used synonymously, meaning a multitude of persons.(*a*) In regard to the admission of hearsay testimony, a distinction has been made between them. The term *public* is applied to all the citizens of the state; the term *general* signifies a less, though a large portion of the community.

All persons are presumed to be conversant in relation to public matters, on the same principle that every man is presumed to be conversant with his own affairs; and what is said by people generally about their common rights may be presumed to be true; evidence of common reputation is, therefore, received as regards public facts; as for example, a claim to a highway, on the ground that all have an interest in the truth, and the consequent probability that they are true.(*b*) But when the fact in question does not concern the members of the community, hearsay from such persons, wholly unconnected with the place and business, would be inadmissible.(*c*)

To be admitted, these declarations must relate to ancient rights, and they must have been made by persons supposed to be dead. They must also have been made before any controversy arose touching the matter to which they relate, or *ante litem motam*, for otherwise they might have been manufactured for the occasion. To avoid the mischiefs which would result

---

(*a*) Weeks *v.* Sparks, 1 M. & S. 690.
(*b*) 1 Stark. Ev. 195; 1 Greenl. Ev. § 128; Price *v.* Currell, 6 M. & W. 234.
(*c*) Crease *v.* Barrett, 1 C. M. & R. 929; Rogers *v.* Wood, 2 B. & Ad. 245; Weeks *v.* Sparks, 1 M. & S. 679.

from the admission of such after-made declarations, all *ex parte* declarations, even if made upon oath at a subsequent date to the beginning of the controversy, cannot be admitted.(*a*)

This reputation or hearsay, which is admitted on the ground of public interest, is evidence as well against a public right as in its favor.(*b*)

2d Class of exceptions.—Ancient possession.

3073. When the matters in controversy do not affect any public or general interest, hearsay evidence is not in general admissible; but an exception to this rule obtains in cases of ancient possession, for then ancient documents in support of it are good evidence.(*c*) But such documents must be known to be genuine, and there must be proof that they come from the proper custody; that some act has been done in reference to them, in order to assure their genuineness, and of claiming title under them.

Such ancient documents, purporting to be a part of the transactions to which they relate, and not a mere narrative of them, are receivable as evidence that those transactions actually occurred. An ancient deed, that is, one more than thirty years old, when it appears upon its face to be genuine, is evidence without express proof.(*d*)

3d Class of exceptions.—Declarations made against interest.

3074. Another exception to rejecting hearsay evidence is allowed in the case of declarations and entries, made in books by persons since deceased, and against the interest of the persons making them, at the time

(*a*) The Berkley Peerage case, 4 Campb. 401.
(*b*) Dfinkwater *v.* Porter, 7 C. & P. 181 ; Rex *v.* Sutton, 3 N. & P. 569.
(*c*) The proof of such documents, with actual possession, are evidence of what is called an *immemorial possession.* 9 Toull. n. 254.
(*d*) 1 Greenl. Ev. § 144, n. 1.

358   OF REMEDIES.

No 3075   Book 4, tit 8, chap. 11, sec. 3, § 3, div. 1, art. 1.   No 3075.

they were made. This evidence is received, because it is extremely improbable that it should be false, for men are not apt to say or do any thing against their interest, particularly as such declarations cannot be received in evidence during the lifetime of the declarant.(a)

4th Class of exceptions.—Dying declarations.

3075. When a man has received a wound, or other injury, which proves mortal, and he believes he must die, is in immediate danger of dying, and afterward does die in consequence of such injury, the statements which he makes as to the manner in which he received such injury, and by whom it was committed, are called his *dying declarations.* The solemnity of his situation, when every hope of this world is gone, and every inducement or motive to falsehood is silenced, when the mind is induced, by the considerations of a future life, to speak the truth, all these considerations together have been thought as equivalent to the party's oath in a court of justice.(b)

Though formerly it was contended that such dying declarations were receivable in all cases, both civil and criminal, yet the rule is firmly established, that they can be received only in cases of homicide, where the death of the deceased is the subject of the charge, and

---

(a) 1 Greenl. § 148.
(b) Rex v. Woodcock, 2 Leach's Cr. Cas. 556; Drummond's case, 1 Leach Cr. Cas. 378. The following lines, descriptive of the feelings and sentiments of such a man, have been put in the mouth of one who is about making dying declarations:

> Have I not hideous death before my view,
> Retaining but a quantity of life,
> Which bleeds away, even as a form of wax
> Resolveth from his figure 'gainst the fire ?
> What in the world should make me now deceive
> Since I must lose the use of all deceit ?
> Why then should I be false, since, it is true,
> That I must die here, and live hence by truth ?

OF PROCEEDINGS IN AN ACTION.   359

No. 3076   Book 4, tit. 8, chap. 11, sec 3, § 3, div. 1, art. 1.   No 3076.

the circumstances of the death are the subject of the dying declarations.(a)

5th Class of exceptions.—Testimony of witnesses subsequently dead, absent, or disqualified.

3076. When a witness has been examined on a former trial between the same parties, and the same point arises in issue in a second action, and the witness has since died, is absent, or has become disqualified, the testimony of such deceased witness may be proved; a witness will be allowed to prove what the first testified; but such testimony, of course, is not conclusive, for it is open to all objections to which it would be, if the first were present and testified to the same facts a second time.(b)

As to the things which must be proved, it may be remarked, that although formerly the rule was much more strict, yet now it is sufficient, if the witness is able to state the substance of what the first witness testified.(c)

When the witness has acquired an interest, since he gave his former testimony, in the subject matter about which he is called to testify, and his interest is on the side of the party calling him, he is not competent till he is released; nor can a subscribing witness be examined, if his interest was created by the party calling him.(d)

A witness cannot, by his act, by the subsequent voluntary creation of an interest, without the concurrence of the party, deprive him of the benefit of his testimony.(e) But this rule is subject to a qualification,

---

(a) Rex v. Mead, 2 B. & C. 605 ; Rex v. Hutchinson, 2 B. & C. 608, n. ; Wilson v. Boerem, 15 John. 286.

(b) Crary v. Sprague, 12 Wend. 41 ; Wright v. Tatham, 2 Ad. & Ell. 3.

(c) Cornell v. Green, 10 S. & R. 14, 16 ; Chess v. Chess, 17 S. & R. 409 ; Hill's notes to 1 Phil. Ev. 231 ; 1 Greenl. Ev. § 165.

(d) Hovell v. Stephenson, 5 Bing. 493 ; Bennet v. Robinson, 3 Stew. & P. 227 ; Schall v. Miller, 5 Whart. 156.

(e) 1 Stark. Ev. 118 ; Long v. Baillie, 4 S. & R. 222.

if the interest has been acquired for a fraudulent purpose, or to deprive the party of the testimony, or by
a wager, it will not disqualify him; on the contrary,
when it has been fairly acquired, either by contract or
by operation of law, it will be a bar.(a)

If the witness who has acquired a disqualifying interest, has previously made a deposition in the cause,
the deposition may be read in chancery, as if he were
since deceased; and it may also be read at law on the
trial of an issue out of chancery. Whether it can be
read in other trials at law, seems not certain.(b)

6. Of admissions.

3077. *Admissions* are declarations, which a party,
by himself, or those who act under his authority,
makes of the existence of certain facts. The term
admission is usually applied to civil transactions, and
to matters of fact, in criminal cases, where there is no
criminal intent; the term *confessions*, which is sometimes used as being synonymous, is generally considered as an admission of guilt. Though they are
different in these respects, and for that reason they
will be treated of separately, yet, in both cases the
rules of evidence are the same.

The admissibility and effect of evidence of this
description will be considered generally, first, with
respect to the nature, time, and manner of the admission; and, secondly, in relation to the parties to be
affected by it; thirdly, as to its effect.

1° Of the nature of the admission.

3078. To understand the nature of an admission, it
is necessary to know, 1, its form; 2, the time when it
was made.

(a) Forrester v. Pigou, 3 Campb. 380; Phelps v. Riley, 6 Conn. 266.
See Burgess v. Lane. 3 Greenl. 165.
(b) 1 Greenl. Ev. § 168; Gresley on Ev. 267.

3079.—1. The principal distinction of admissions as to their *form*, is, whether they are in writing, or not in writing.

Admissions in *writing* are releases, and other instruments, given by a party with a view to make them evidence of the facts therein contained; these, when pleaded, operate in general by way of estoppel, for the party is not only estopped from disputing the deed itself, but every fact which it recites.(*a*)

Judicial admissions are generally made in writing in court by the attorney of the party; they appear upon the record, as in the pleadings, and are generally conclusive upon the party, they being made for the purpose of being used as a substitute for the regular legal evidence of the fact on the trial, or in a case stated for the opinion of the court.

Verbal admissions are those which are made by speaking, and not reduced to writing. Such verbal admissions ought to be received with great caution, as they are subject to many misrepresentations and mistakes; and in all cases, the whole admission must be taken together.(*b*) When admitted, they are competent evidence only of those facts which may be established by parol evidence; they cannot be received to contradict documentary proof, or supply the place of existing evidence by matter of record.(*c*)

Implied admissions are those which are the consequences of the acts of the parties. When a party assumes a character, language, and course of conduct, he may be fairly presumed to admit the situation which is usual in such cases. When the existence of domestic, social or official relation is in issue, the *recognition* of such relation, by the person making it, is proof that such relation exists; as where a man assumed to act as a magistrate, this is an admission of his appoint-

(*a*) Stark. Ev. part 4, p 31; Com. Dig Estoppel, B 5; B. N. P. 298.
(*b*) Smith *v.* Blandy, Ry. & Me. 257.
(*c*) Scott *v.* Clare, 3 Campb. 236 ; 1 Bing. 73.

362 OF REMEDIES.

No. 3080.   Book 4, tit 8, chap. 11, sec. 3, § 3, div. 1, art. 1.   No. 3080.

ment or title to the office, so far as to render him liable
for misconduct or neglect in such office.(*a*) Admissions are implied from the *conduct* of a party; as, where
documents are suppressed, their contents are deemed
unfavorable to the party suppressing them;(*b*) making
out a bill in the name of an individual for goods sold,
is an admission they were sold to him.(*c*) Asking time
for the payment of a note or bill, is an admission of
the holder's title, and of the signature of the party
who asks the favor. Admissions may also be implied
from the *acquiescence* of the party; but to have the
effect of an admission, acquiescence must exhibit some
act of the mind, and amount to conduct in the party;
as, where an account has been presented, and it is not
objected to within a reasonable time, it will be presumed to be correct.(*d*) *Possession of documents*, or
constant access to them, may afford evidence that the
facts contained in them are true.(*e*) But the possession of an unanswered letter, is not, of itself, evidence
of acquiescence as to its contents.(*f*)

3080.—2. Having ascertained the form, the next
object of consideration will relate to the *time and circumstances of the admission.* Facts admitted in the
course of a treaty for the settlement of a controversy,
and offers or propositions of settlement between
litigating parties, expressly stated to be made without prejudice, are excluded on the ground of public
policy;(*g*) because if it were not for this salutary
rule, it would be impossible to negotiate a settlement
with any hope of success. And an offer to buy one's

(*a*) Rex *v.* Borrett, 6 C. & P. 124; Rex *v.* Gardner, 2 Camph. 513;
Trowbridge *v* Baker, 1 Cowen, 251.
(*b*) James *v.* Bion, 2 Sim. & Stu. 600, 606.
(*c*) Storr *v.* Scott, 6 C. & P. 241.
(*d*) Sherman *v.* Sherman, 2 Vern. 276; Willis *v.* Jernegan, 2 Atk. 252;
Freeland *v.* Heron, 7 Cranch, 147.
(*e*) Ragget *v.* Musgrave, 2 Car. & P. 556.
(*f*) Fairlie *v.* Benton, 3 C. & P. 103.
(*g*) Corry *v.* Bretton, 4 C. & P. 462; Healy *v.* Thatcher, 8 C. & P. 388;
Jardine *v.* Sheridan, 2 C. & K. 24.

peace by offering to pay a certain sum of money for a release, is not an admission of any obligation.(*a*)

When the admission has been obtained by duress, or imposition, or fraud, it cannot be received; but in civil cases admissions are receivable in evidence, provided the compulsion under which they have been given is legal, and the party has not been imposed upon.(*b*)

2° Who is bound by the admission.

3081. The effect of an admission will be different as it is intended to operate upon a single party; when it is made by one, and it is sought to make it apply to several; and when it is made by one person, and it is desired to be proved against another.

3082.—1. When there is but *one party* to be affected by the admission, the rule is very simple; he or some one authorized by him, must have made the admission. But the admissions of a party, who is not in fact interested, as where he sues for the use of another, are not allowed to disparage the title of his innocent vendee or assignee.(*c*)

3083.—2. When there are *several parties* to be affected, and the admission has been made by one of them only, as where there are several parties on the same side on a record, the admissions of one of them are not allowed to affect the others who happen to be joined with him, unless there is some joint interest, or privity in design, between them, although such admissions, in proper cases, may be received against him who made them.(*d*)   But when the parties have a joint interest, as in the case of partners, an admission made by one, is, in general, evidence against all.(*e*)

(*a*) Prussed *v.* Knowles, 4 How. Miss. 90.
(*b*) Collett *v.* Ld. Keith, 4 Esp. 212.
(*c*) Mandeville *v.* Welch, 5 Wheat. 277.
(*d*) Dan et al. *v.* Brown. 4 Cowen, 483.
(*e*) Purham *v.* Laynal, 8 Bing. 309.

364 OF REMEDIES.

No. 3084   Book 4, tıt. 8, chap 11, sec 3, § 3, dıv 1, art. 1   No 3084.

A mere community of interest, when the interest is not joint, is not sufficient, as in the case of executors, the admissions of one do not bind the other.(a)

3084.—3. Admissions made by *third persons, strangers to the suit*, are sometimes receivable in evidence. This happens when the issue is substantially upon the mutual rights of such persons at a particular time ; in this case the evidence is admitted in the same way as if it was between the parties themselves. Other instances when the admissions of third persons may be allowed, occur when the party has referred expressly to such third person for information, in regard to an uncertain matter in dispute; or to an interpreter, whose statements of what the party says are treated as identical with what the party says himself. The admissions of the wife bind the husband only when he has authorized them, and their relation alone is not sufficient. The admissions of an attorney of record, bind his client, in all matters relating to the progress and trial of the cause. As to the effect of admissions of the principal, as evidence against the surety, upon his collateral obligation, it may be remarked that to be binding they must be made during the transaction of the business for which the surety was bound, so as to become a part of the *res gestæ*. The admissions of a person are evidence against all who are privy to him in estate or by blood. Admissions made by the assignor of a personal contract or chattel will bind the assignee, when made while the assignor remained the sole proprietor, but when made after he had no longer any interest in the thing assigned, the right of the assignee, holding by a good title, is not to be cut down by the acknowledgment of the holder that he had no title.(b)

(a) Forsyth *v.* Ganson, 5 Wend. 558 ; Hammon *v.* Huntley, 4 Cowen, 493.
(b) Burrough *v.* White, 4 B. & C. 325 ; Woolway *v.* Rowe, 1 Ad. & Ell. 114.

OF PROCEEDINGS IN AN ACTION.   365

No. 3085.   Book 4, tit. 8, chap 11, sec. 3, § 3, div. 1, art. 1.   No. 3086.

7. *Of confessions.*

3085. The rules which govern confessions, in criminal cases, are, in general, the same as those which regulate admissions in civil cases. But it must be observed that no confession made by a third person or an agent can have any force against the accused, unless where several are acting together, and the acts of one are considered the acts of all; as in the cases of riot, conspiracy and the like; each is deemed as assenting or commanding what is done by any other in furtherance of the common object.(*a*) But when the crime has been completed, and the criminals no longer act together, the declarations of one of them then made, do not affect the others.

The evidence of admissions of guilt ought to be received with great caution, as instances of such confessions have been found to have been fatally incorrect. Confessions are direct confessions of guilt, or they are indirect confessions.

3086.—1. A *direct* deliberate confession of guilt, when voluntarily made, is considered as the best evidence that can be produced, and as such it is generally satisfactory. These confessions are either judicial or extra judicial.

1. A *judicial* confession is one made before a magistrate, or in court, in the due course of legal proceedings. When voluntarily made, without any illegal influence, they are deserving of credit. A preliminary examination, taken in writing, by a magistrate lawfully authorized, pursuant to a statute, or the plea of guilty, made in open court, to an indictment, are sufficient to found a conviction upon them.

2. *Extra judicial* confessions are those made by the accused, elsewhere than in court or before a magistrate,

(*a*) United States *v.* Gooding, 12 Wheat. 469 ; Commonwealth *v.* Eberle, 3 S. & R. 9; Wilbur *v.* Strickland, 1 Rawle, 458. Reitenback *v.* Reitenback, 1 Rawle, 362.

366   OF REMEDIES.

No 3087   Book 4, tit. 8, chap 11, sec. 3, § 3, div. 1, art. 1.   No. 3088.

whether such expressions be express or implied. All confessions must be *voluntary*, for if they have been made under any threat or promise, they are not to be relied upon. A confession forced from the mind by the flattery of hope, or the torture of fear, comes in such questionable shape, when it is to be considered as evidence of guilt, that no credit ought to be given to it.(*a*) What amounts to a threat or a promise is not easily defined.(*b*) A distinction must be observed with regard to a confession made after such promise or threat, when it is made before persons in authority and those not in authority: when it is made to the first, it is invalid; when to the last, upon an inducement held out by them, it is not so clear that they are invalid, and they may perhaps be treated as mixed questions of law and fact.(*c*)

3087.—2. *Indirect confessions* of guilt, are those which, in civil cases, are usually termed *implied* admissions.

8. *Relevant and irrelevant evidence.*

3088. In the discussion of the nature of evidence, our next inquiry will be to consider when it is relevant and when it is irrelevant. *Relevant* evidence is that which is applicable to the issue, and ought to be received; evidence is *irrelevant* when it is not so, and it ought to be excluded.

When facts are to be decided by the court without the aid of a jury, it is seldom useful to raise the question whether evidence is relevant or not, because before it is passed upon, it must be known, and it must be read or heard by the judge in order to decide upon its nature and quality. But in trials by

---

(*a*) Warrickshall's case, 1 Leach's Cr. Cas. 299; Knapp's case, 10 Pick. 489.

(*b*) 1 Greenl. Ev. § 219, 220, 221.

(*c*) 1 Greenl. Ev. § 223.

OF PROCEEDINGS IN AN ACTION.   367

No. 3089.   Book 4, tit. 8, chap. 11, sec. 3, § 3, div. 1, art. 2.   No. 3090.

jury, the presiding judge is required to determine all questions on the admissibility of evidence to the jury. When the admission depends on other questions of facts, such as whether the offered witness is interested, these preliminary questions of fact are, in the first instance, to be tried by the judge; and when the question is mixed, consisting of law and fact, so intimately blended as not to be easily susceptible of separate decision, it is then submitted to the jury.

Art. 2.—Of the object of evidence.

3089. The object of evidence is next to be considered. It is to ascertain the truth or falsehood of the allegations made by the parties in their pleadings. It has been discovered by experience that this is done most certainly by the adoption of the following rules, which are now binding as law : 1, the substance of the issue must be proved ; 2, the evidence must be confined to the issue ; 3, the affirmative of the issue must be proved.

1. *The substance of the issue must be proved.*

3090. It is a general rule, both in criminal and civil cases, that the evidence shall be confined to the point in issue; and that it is sufficient if the substance of the issue be proved.

As to the manner of supporting the issue, a distinction is made between allegations of matter of *substance,* and the allegation of matters of *essential description.* The former may be substantially proved, and that will be sufficient; but the latter must be proved with more strictness.(*a*)

When the allegations of *time,* place, quantity, quality and value are descriptive, they must be strictly proved, but when they are not descriptive of the

----

(*a*) Glassford on Ev. 309 ; 1 Greenl. Ev. § 56.

368   OF REMEDIES.

No 3091.   Book 4, tit 8, chap 11, sec. 3, § 3, div. 1, art. 2   No. 3091.

identity of the subject of the action, they are immaterial, and need not be proved strictly, as alleged: example, in trespass to the person, the material fact is the assault and battery; the time and place not being material, need not be proved as alleged; but in an action on a bill of exchange, the date alleged, being descriptive, must be proved.(a)

The party upon whom the burden of proof rests, is required to prove the substance of the issue ; a failure to prove it, must therefore be fatal, for he has not sustained his cause, and when there is a departure by proving a different agreement, then is that fault known as a *variance*, which in a general sense is a disagreement or a difference between two parts of the same legal proceeding, which ought to agree together, and, in the sense in which it is used, it is a disagreement between the allegation and the proof, in some matter which, in point of law, is essential to the charge or claim.   The following example will sufficiently point out the nature of such variance.   In an action where the plaintiff declared in covenant for not repairing, pursuant to a covenant in a lease, and stated the covenant, as a covenant " to repair when and as need should require," and issue was joined on a traverse of the deed alleged.   The plaintiff, at the trial, produced the deed in proof, and it appeared that the covenant was " *to* repair when and as need should require, *and at furthest after notice;*" the latter words having been omitted in the declaration.   This was held to be a variance, because the additional words were material, and qualified the effect of the contract.(b)   This, it will be observed, is a matter of substance ; when the variance is to matter of form, it is not regarded.

2. *The evidence must be confined to the issue.*

3091. As the parties come into court to settle a

(a) Glassf. on Ev. 309.
(b) Horsefall *v.* Tester, 7 Taunt. 385.   See 1 Greenl. Ev. § 66.

matter of difference between them, it is but just that they should confine the proofs to the matter in issue, for the party upon the other side does not come prepared to answer any thing else. But to this general rule, that evidence must be confined to the issue, there are several exceptions, among which are the following:

1. In general, evidence of collateral facts is not admissible; but when such fact is material to the issue joined between the parties, it may be given in evidence; as, for example, in order to prove that the acceptor of a bill knew the payee to be a fictitious person, or that the drawer had general authority from him to draw bills with the names of a fictitious payee, evidence may be given to show that he had accepted similar bills before they could, from their date, have arrived from the place of date.(a)

2. Although when special damage sustained by the plaintiff is not stated in the declaration, it is not one of the points in issue, and evidence of it cannot be received, yet, a damage which is the necessary result of the defendant's breach of contract, may be proved, notwithstanding it is not in the declaration.(b)

3. When evidence incidentally applies to another person or thing, not included in the transaction in question, and with regard to whom or to which it is inadmissible, yet if it bear upon the point in issue, it will be received.(c)

3. The affirmative of the issue must be proved.

3092. The general rule which governs in the production of evidence, is, that the obligation of proving any fact lies upon the party who substantially asserts the affirmative of the issue.

(a) Gibson v. Hunter, 2 H. Bl. 288.
(b) Ward v. Wood, 11 Price's R. 19.
(c) 1 Phil. Ev. 158 ; Willis v. Bernard, 8 Bing. 376.

370   OF REMEDIES.

No 3093   Book 4, tit 8, chap 11, sec 3, § 3, div. 1, art. 2.   No. 3093.

3093. To this rule there are some exceptions, among which are the following:

1. When a presumption of law arises in favor of the party who alleges the affirmative, the rule ceases to operate, and the negative must be proved; as when the issue is on the legitimacy of a child, it is incumbent on the party who alleges the illegitimacy to prove it, provided the parents have never been separated by divorce, and have lived in lawful wedlock ;(a) or where a person once living is alleged to be dead, and he not being so old that the presumption of his death would arise,(b) his death must be proved.

2. When the plaintiff grounds his right of action upon a negative allegation, and, where this negative is an essential element of his case; as where he sues for having been prosecuted maliciously, without probable cause, the plaintiff must show the want of probable cause by some affirmative proof, though the proposition be in negative terms.(c)

3. When the subject matter of a negative averment lies peculiarly within the knowledge of the opposite party, the averment is taken as true, unless disproved by that party.(d)

4. When the negative allegation involves a charge of criminal neglect of duty, whether official or otherwise ; or fraud; or the wrongful violation of actual lawful possession of property; the party making the allegation must prove it; for in these cases the law raises a presumption of innocence and quiet possession.

5. In equity, when a bill is filed praying that a contract may be annulled, on the ground that it was made with the defendant, who stood in a fiduciary relation

_____

(a) 2 Selw. N. P. 513 ; Morris v. Davies, 3 C. & P. 513.
(b) Wilson v. Hodges, 2 East, 313.
(c) Ulmer v. Leland, 2 Greenl. 134 ; Gibson v. Waterhouse, 4 Greenl. 226 ; 1 Camp. 199 ; 9 East,·361.
(d) Rex v. Turner, 5 M. & S. 206 ; Smith v. Jeffries, 9 Price, 257 ; Commonwealth v. Kemball, 7 Met. 304.

OF PROCEEDINGS IN AN ACTION. 371

No. 3094.   Book 4, tit. 8, chap 11. sec 3, § 3, div 1, art 3.   No. 3096.

to the plaintiff, the burden of proving its fairness is cast on the defendant.(a)

Art. 3.—Of the instruments by which facts are established.

3094. The instruments used in evidence are, 1, records and public documents; 2, private writings; 3, shop-books and other books; 4, witnesses.

1. *Of records and public documents.*

3095. In considering records and public documents, it will be proper to inquire into, 1, what they are; 2, the manner of proving them; 3, their effect; 4, the nature and proof of foreign laws and records.

1° *Of the nature of records and public documents.*

3096. Among the most certain instruments for ascertaining facts, may be mentioned records and public documents, made evidence by legislative enactment. A *record* is a written memorial, made by a public officer authorized by law to perform that function, and intended to serve as evidence of something written, said or done.(b) Records may be divided into those which relate to the proceedings of, 1, the legislature; 2, the courts; 3, other public documents.

(a) Cane v. Lord Allen. 2 Dow, 289; Gibson v. Jeyes, 6 Ves. 278; Montesquieu v. Sandys, 18 Ves. 313; Bellew v. Russell, 1 B. & Beat. 104.

(b) As to what is included in a record, see the following cases: The trial list is not a part of the record, Moore v. Kline, 1 Pennsyl. 129; nor is a bond for costs, Montgomery v. Carpenter, 5 Pike, 264; nor a writing sued on, Williams v. Duffey, 7 Humph. 255; Clark v. Gibson, 2 Pike, 109, unless made so by oyer or otherwise. See Pelham v. State Bank, 4 Pike, 202; nor is an affidavit made to support a part of the record which has been lost, Troy v. Reilly, 3 Scam. 119; S. C. 3 Scam. 259; nor are papers presented to a court, and acted upon merely as matters of evidence, Kirby v. Wood, 4 Shep. 81; nor the registry of a mechanic's lien, Davis v. Church, 1 W. & S. 240; nor is the state of demand, in the court for the trial of small causes, in New Jersey, Vandyke v. Bastedo, 3 Green, 224. See also Davidson v. Murphy, 13 Conn. 213; Hodges v. Ashurst, 2 Ala. 101; Davidson v. Slocum, 18 Pick. 464; officers of court, 7 How. Mis. 403; ex parte, Bishop, 4 Mis. 219; Lenox v. Pike, 2 Pike, 14; Updergraff v. Parry, 4 Penn. St. R. 291; McLendon v. Jones, 8 Ald. 298; United States v. Gamble, 10 Mis. 457; Child v. Risk, 1 Mor. 439.

372   OF REMEDIES.

No. 3097.   Book 4, tit. 8, chap 11, sec. 3, § 3, div. 1, art. 3.   No. 3099.

1. Of the legislative records.

3097. The constitutions of the Union and of the several states, and the legislative acts of the congress of the United States, and of the several states of the Union, are records of the highest kind; and the printed journals of congress have been so considered. These acts are general and public, or private, as we observed when treating of the nature of laws.

3098.—1. The courts will judicially *take notice* of the political constitution and form of government of their own country; and public statutes, which are supposed to exist in the memories of all, need no proof; but, for certainty of recollection, which, notwithstanding the presumption of law, no man can retain, constant reference is had to the records themselves, or to the copy of them contained in a book printed by public authority. Printed copies of public documents transmitted to congress by the President of the United States, and printed by the printer to congress, are evidence of such documents.(*a*)

3099.—2. Private statutes, resolutions, and other private acts, are to be proved according to the provisions of the common law, either *by means of a copy,* proved *on oath* to have been examined by the roll itself; or, by an exemplification under the great seal. But in several of the states the printed copy of the laws and resolves of the legislature, published by its authority, are held competent evidence; and it is sufficient *primâ facie,* that the book purports to have been so printed.(*b*) Sometimes a clause is introduced into a statute that it shall be taken notice of as if it were a public act; its mode of proof in that case, is the same as of a public statute.(*c*)

(*a*) Radcliff *v.* U. States Ins. Co. 7 John. 38; 1 Phil. Ev. 318.
(*b*) Biddis *v.* James, 6 Binn. 321; Young *v.* Bank of Alexandria, 4 Cranch, 388.
(*c*) Beaumont *v.* Mountain, 10 Bing. 404; Woodward *v.* Cotton, 1 C. M. & R. 44, 47.

OF PROCEEDINGS IN AN ACTION.   373

No. 3100.   Book 4, tit. 8, chap. 11, sec. 3, § 3, div. 1, art 3.   No. 3102.

(2.) Of judicial records.

3100. In considering the nature of verdicts and judgments of courts of record, they will be examined with reference, 1, to the parties to the suit; 2, to the matter directly in issue; 3, to a decision upon the merits.

1st. Of verdicts and judgments with reference to the parties to the suit.

3101. Those persons who institute actions for the recovery of their rights, and those against whom they are instituted, are the *parties* to the actions. The term parties, as has already been explained, includes all persons who are directly interested in the subject matter in issue, who have a right to make defence, control the proceedings, or appeal from the judgment. *Strangers* are persons who do not possess those rights.(*a*)

When a judgment has been rendered between the parties, they are bound by it; and to give full effect to the principle by which the parties are held bound by it, all persons who are represented by the parties, and claim under them, or are privy to them, are equally concluded by the same proceedings.

3102. By *privity* is meant the mutual or successive relationship to the rights of property; and privies are classified according to the manner of this relationship; they are privies *in estate,* as donor and donee, lessor and lessee, and joint tenants; privies *in blood,* as heir and ancestor, and coparceners; privies *in representation,* as testator and executor, administrator and intestate; privies *in law,* as where the law without privity of blood or estate casts lands upon another, as by escheat. But all these kinds of privity are reduced to three, namely, privity in estate, privity in blood, and privity in law. The reason why persons standing in this relation to the litigating party are bound by the

(*a*) Duchess of Kingston's case, 20 How. State Tr. 538, n.

374 OF REMEDIES.

No. 3103.   Book 4, tit. 8, chap. 11, sec. 3, § 3, div. 1, art. 3.   No. 3103.

proceedings to which he is a party, is, that they are identified with him in interest; and whenever this identity exists, all are alike concluded. Privies are therefore estopped from litigating that which is conclusive upon him with whom they are in privity.(a) The rule with regard to privies is, that its operation be mutual upon both parties; both litigants must be concluded, or the proceedings cannot be set up as conclusive for either.(b)

3103. There are several exceptions to the rule, which requires the identity of the parties, in order to make the record evidence. The principal are the following:

1. There is an exception to the rule in cases usually termed proceedings *in rem*, which includes not only judgments of condemnation of property as forfeited, or as prize in the admiralty, but also decisions of other courts directly upon the personal *status*, state or relations of the party, such as marriage, divorce, bastardy, settlement, and the like. Judgments of this kind are binding and conclusive, not only upon the parties actually litigating in the cause, but upon all others; because in most cases of this kind, every one who can be affected by such judgment has a right to appear and assert his own rights by becoming a party to the proceedings.(c)

2. Verdicts and judgments upon subjects of a *public nature*, such as customs and the like, are evidence between persons who are not parties to the proceedings; because in most, or all of such cases, evidence of reputation is admissible.(d)

3. When a judgment is to prove a *collateral fact*, it may be admitted, although the parties are not the

---

(a) Carver v. Jackson, 4 Peters, 85; Case v. Reeve, 14 John. 81.
(b) Wood v. Davis, 7 Cranch, 271; Davis v. Wood, 1 Wheat. 6; 1 Stark. Ev. 214.
(c) 1 Stark. Ev. 27, 28; 1 Greenl. Ev. § 525; 1 Phil. Ev. 328.
(d) 1 Phil. Ev. 327, 328.

OF PROCEEDINGS IN AN ACTION. 375

No. 3104.   Book 4, tit. 8, chap. 11, sec. 3, § 3 div. 1, art. 3.   No. 3104.

same. Of this there are numerous examples: thus, in order to prove the legal infamy of a witness, the record of his conviction may be shown; the record is evidence to let in proof of what was sworn to at the trial; or to show that a suit was determined, and the like. A further instance to illustrate the difference between the admissibility of a judgment as a fact, and as evidence of ulterior facts, may be mentioned the case where a judgment has been rendered against a sheriff, for the misconduct of his deputy, it is evidence against the latter of the fact that the sheriff has been compelled to pay the amount awarded, and for the cause alleged; but it is not evidence of the fact upon which it was founded, namely, the misconduct of the deputy, unless he was notified of the suit, and was required to defend it.(a)

4: A judgment may be used in favor of a stranger against one of the parties, to prove the existence of certain facts, or solemn declarations of judicial declarations of the party, contained in the record. But in such case, it is not conclusive, as establishing the fact, but it is to be considered as the deliberate admission of the party. Example, in the case of libel by a wife for a divorce on the ground of cruelty, the record of the conviction of the husband for an assault and battery upon her, founded upon his plea of guilty, is admissible to prove the judicial admission of the fact.(b)

2d. Of verdicts and judgments with reference to the matter directly in issue.

3104. A distinction must be remembered between a verdict and a judgment. A *verdict* is sometimes admissible in evidence, to prove the finding of some matter of reputation, or custom, or particular right. But, although in this case the verdict and not the judg-

(a) Tyler *v*. Ulmer, 12 Mass. 166. See Kip *v*. Bingham, 6 John. 158; 2 Pick. 304.
(b) Bradley *v*. Bradley, 2 Fairf. 367; Woodruff *v*. Woodruff, 2 Fairf. 475.

376 OF REMEDIES.

No. 3105.   Book 4, tit. 8, chap. 11, sec 3, § 3, div. 1, art. 3.   No. 3106.

ment is the material thing to be shown, yet unless a judgment has been rendered upon it, it is not admissible, because it may have been set aside, by granting a new trial, or the judgment upon it may have been arrested. As a judgment is not entered on a verdict upon an issue out of chancery, such a verdict may be given in evidence without a judgment.(a)

3105. To make a *judgment* conclusive upon the parties, it is required that it should have been rendered upon the matter directly in issue, and not on a thing incidentally brought in controversy during the trial. A record can be conclusive only on matters actually tried; on things material and traversable; for, if they were not so, they would not be brought into judgment. The general rule is clearly laid down, and may now be considered a rule of law, founded not less upon adjudged cases, than it is upon reason : first, that the judgment of a court of concurrent jurisdiction, directly upon the point, is, as a plea, a bar ; or, as evidence, conclusive between the same parties, upon the same matter, directly in question in another court. Secondly, that the judgment of a court of exclusive jurisdiction, directly upon the point, is, in like manner, conclusive upon the same matter, between the same parties, coming incidentally in question in another court for a different purpose.(b)

3d. Of verdicts and judgments in reference to a decision upon the merits. •

3106. To render such a judgment conclusive between the parties, the matter in issue must have been *decided upon the merits;* for if the plaintiff discontinue

---

(a) Bull. N. P. 234; Donaldson v. Jude, 2 Bibb. 60. See Delvan v. Worke, 3 Hawkes, 36; State v. Grayton. 3 Hawkes, 187; Murphey v. Guion's Ex'rs, 1 Car. Law Repos. 94; Ragan v. Kennedy, 1 Over. 94; Shaeffer v. Kreitzer, 6 Binn. 430; Felter v. Moliner, 2 John. 181.

(b) Per De Grey, C. J. in Duchess of Kingston's case, 20 How. St. Tr. 538; Harvey v. Richards, 2 Gallis. 299; Hidsham v. Dulleban, 4 Watts, 183, per Gibson, C. J.; Pearce v. Gray, 2 Y. and C. 322.

his action, or become nonsuit, or for any other cause there has been no judgment of the court upon the matter in issue, the proceedings are not conclusive. And if the declaration was so essentially defective that it would have been adjudged bad on demurrer, or if the trial went off for a technical defect, or because the debt was not due when the action was commenced, or because the court had not jurisdiction, or the plaintiff was temporarily disabled to sue, the judgment will be no bar to a future action.(a)

(3.) Of other public documents.

3107. These documents are very numerous, but the principle of their admission in evidence is generally the same; it is, that being made by public authority, by men appointed for the purpose, they are presumed to be true; and because they are located in particular places and cannot be removed without public inconvenience, certified copies, or examined copies, are allowed to be given in evidence; and in general the originals cannot be demanded. To this there is an exception; when the handwriting is required to be proved, as in the case of an indictment for perjury, in an answer in chancery, or of making depositions, or where a man has become bound of record to perform .an act, the original must be produced.

Among the documents which are made evidence, may be mentioned the journals of either branch of the legislature; official registers kept by authority of law, such as books of assessments of public taxes,(b) books of the post office, and customs, prison registers,(c) enrolment of deeds, the registers of births and mar-

---

(a) Sweigart v. Berk, 8 S. & R. 305; Wood v. Jackson, 8 Wend. 9; Hughes v. Blake, 1 Mason, 515; Lane v. Harrison, Munf. 573; Dixon v. Sinclair, 4 Verm. 354; N. Eng. Bank v. Lewis, 8 Pick. 113; Estill v. Taul, 2 Yerg. 467.

(b) Doe v. Seaton, 2 Ad. & Ell. 171; Doe v. Cartwright, 2 Ad. & Ell. 182; S. C. Ryan & Mo. 62; Rockendorff v. Taylor, 4 Pet. 349.

(c) State v. Thomas, 3 B. & P. 188; U. S. v. Johns, 4 Dall. 412.

378   OF REMEDIES.

No. 3107.   Book 4, tit. 8, chap. 11, sec 3, § 3, div 1, art 3   No 3107.

riages, made pursuant to the laws of any of the United States,(a) the registry of vessels at the custom-house,(b) the books which contain the official proceedings of corporations, and matters concerning their property, if the public in general are interested in it,(c) and the records of city councils and other municipal bodies.(d)

Wills are proved in the United States, before courts or jurisdictions specially established by the legislatures of the respective states, or by their constitutions. These are variously denominated probate courts, orphans' courts, registers' courts, etc. The usual mode of proving a will is, by calling the attesting witnesses, or where there are none, and the law allows it, other witnesses to prove the handwriting of the testator, and, when it is known, how he executed the paper purporting to be a will. This is generally done upon notice to the heir at law or other persons having an interest in the estate. At common law, the effect of this mode of probate is conclusive until reversed, as to personal property, but not as to real;(e) though in most of the states of the Union, the effect is the same on the real, that it is on the personal property. A court of common law will not take notice of a will, as a title to personal property, until it has thus been proved; and *letters testamentary*, which is a grant of authority by the officer appointed by law, to the executor named in the will, to execute the same.

Letters of administration are an instrument in writing under the seal of the court which takes the probate of wills, and a decree that such letters shall be and have

(a) Jackson v. King, 5 Cowen, 237 ; Richmond v. Patterson, 3 Ohio, 368 ; Sumner v. Sebeck, 3 Greenl. 223 ; Jacock v. Gilliam, 3 Murphey, 47 ; Milford v. Worcester, 7 Mass 48.
(b) U. S. v. Johns, 4 Dall. 412.
(c) Owings v. Speed, 5 Wheat. 420 ; Warriner v. Giles, 2 Str. 954, n. 1.
(d) Taylor v. Henry, 2 Pick. 401 ; Bishop v. Cone, 3 N. H. Rep. 513.
(e) See 2 Greenl. Ev. § 672 ; Bouv. L. D., tit. Letters Testamentary and of Administration.

been granted to certain persons is then entered in the book of records of the court. The letter of administration is in the nature of an exemplification of this record, and is received without other proof. It authorizes the grantee, called the administrator, to collect, manage, settle and administer the personal estate of the intestate; and, until repealed by lawful authority, the administrator is vested with all the power which the intestate had in the personal estate which he owned on the day of his death. Letters of administration are never granted, when the deceased left a will, except when the will is annexed to them.

2° *Of the manner of proving records and public documents.*

3108. Records are proved by the mere production of the record, without more, or by copy.

(1.) *Of the production of the record itself.*

3109. As a record is located in a particular place, and it cannot be removed, the *record itself* can be produced only when the cause is in the same court, whose record it is; or when it is subject to the proceedings of another court.

(2.) *Of proof of record by copy.*

3110. Copies of records are of three kinds: 1, exemplifications; 2, copies made by an authorized officer; 3, sworn copies.

3111.—1. An *exemplification* is a perfect copy of a record, so far as relates to the matter in question, and certified as to its correctness, first under the great seal, or secondly, under the seal of the particular court where the record remains.(a) The term exemplification, in its strict legal sense, ought to be understood as synonymous with *inspeximus,* and as importing something beyond the ordinary certified copy

(a) Bull. N. P. 227; 1 Gilb. Ev. by Lofft, 19; 3 Inst. 173; 1 Phil. Ev. 384, 385; 1 Greenl. Ev. § 501.

380 OF REMEDIES.

No. 3112.   Book 4, tit. 8, chap. 11, sec. 3, § 3, div. 1, art. 3.   No 3112.

under seal.(*a*) When produced it is usually admitted, even upon an issue of *nul tiel record*, as sufficient evidence.(*b*)

3112.—2. *Copies of a record* made by an authorized officer, *certified under the seal of the court*, are in general received as evidence. It is not in such case required to prove the seal, for the courts recognize without proof the seal of state, and the seals of the superior courts of justice, and of all courts established by public statutes. In this country the courts do not seem to make any distinction between an exemplification and a certified copy under seal. But the certificate must be of the whole record, and not of a mere extract ;(*c*) and when the certificate is, that it is a copy of the record, it will be presumed to be of the whole record.(*d*)

An *office copy* of a record is a copy authenticated by an officer intrusted for that purpose ; it is admitted in evidence upon the credit of the officer, without proof that it has been actually examined.(*e*) In the same court and in the same cause, an office copy is equivalent to the record, but in another court or in another cause, the copy must be proved ; unless in those cases where it is made the duty of the officer to furnish copies ; in this last case they are admitted in all courts under the same jurisdiction It may be stated generally, that in the United States an officer

(*a*) Page's case, 5 Co. 54.
(*b*) Vail *v.* Smith, 4 Cowen, 71; Pepoon *v.* Jenkins, 2 John. Cas. 118.
(*c*) Edmiston *v.* Schwartz, 13 S. & R. 135 ; Ingham *v.* Crary, 1 Pennsyl. 389. But see Rex *v.* Bellamy, Ry. & Mo. N. P. C. 174; Thompson *v.* Chauveau, 6 Mart. N. S. 458.
(*d*) Voris *v.* Smith, 13 S. & R. 334. In several of the states, the form of these certificates is regulated by statute. See Vance *v.* Reardon, 2 N. & McC. 299 ; Thompson *v* Chauveau, 6 Mart. N. S. 458; Commonwealth *v.* Phillips, 11 Pick. 28 ; Barry's Lessee *v.* Rhea, 1 Tenn. 345; Burton *v.* Pettibone, 5 Yerg. 443. A certificate that *it appears* to the officer that a judgment has been entered, etc., is insufficient. Wilcox *v.* Ray, 1 Hayw. 410. This form of certificate is technically called a *constat.* Co. Litt. 225 ; Page's case, 5 Co. 54. See McGuire *v.* Sayward, 9 Shep. 230.
(*e*) 2 Phil. Ev. 131; B. N. P. 229.

having legal custody of the public records, is, *ex officio*, competent to certify copies of their contents.

3113.—3. An *examined copy* is one made by a witness who has compared the copy with the original. This comparison may be made by the witness himself, or by the witness and another person reading and comparing the two; but it is not necessary that the persons examining should exchange the papers, and read them both ways.(*a*)   Proof by parol that such a copy was so made, and its production in court, accompanied with further evidence that the record from which the copy was taken was found in the proper place of deposit, or in the hands of the officer in whose custody the records are kept, is sufficient evidence of the record.

3114. When the *record is lost and it is ancient*, its existence and contents may sometimes be presumed; whether ancient or not, when it is proved to be lost, it may be supplied by secondary evidence.

3° *Of the effect of a record when proved.*

3115. When the record of a judgment has been established, in either of the modes above mentioned, it is conclusive between the parties and their privies, upon the same matter directly in question, in any other suit.   It is a general principle that such decision is binding and conclusive upon all other courts of concurrent power.   This principle pervades not only our own, but all other systems of jurisprudence, and has become a rule of universal law, founded on the soundest policy.   It is the maxim that when once a thing has been adjudged, it shall be considered thereafter forever settled.   *Res judicata*, say the *civilians*, *facit ex albo nigrum, ex nigro album, ex curvo rectum, ex recto curvum.*(*b*)

(*a*) Lynde *v.* Judd, 3 Day, 499; Hill *v.* Packard, 5 Wend. 387; Winn *v.* Patterson, 9 Pet. 663; Fyson *v.* Kemp, 6 Car. & Pay. 71.
(*b*) See Dig. 441, 2; 2 Kaimes, Eq. 367; 10 Toull. n. 65 et seq.

382 OF REMEDIES.

No. 3116.　Book 4, tit. 8, chap. 11, sec. 3, § 3, div. 1, art. 3.　No. 3116.

3116. In order to give to a judgment the force of the *res judicata*, there must be a concurrence of the four conditions following, namely:

1. Identity in the thing sued for.

2. Identity in the cause of action; for example, I have claimed a right of way over Blackacre, and a final judgment has been rendered against me, because I could not establish such a right of way: afterward I purchase Blackacre, and, as owner, I bring a suit for its recovery; the first decision shall not bar my claim, when I sue as owner of the land, and not for an easement over it, as I did in the first suit, which I claimed as a right appurtenant to my land Whiteacre.

3. Identity or privity of parties and of persons to the action; this is a consequence of the rule of natural justice; *ne inauditus condemnetur*, that no man shall be condemned unheard.

4. Identity of the quality in the persons for and against whom the claim is made'; for example, an action by Peter to recover a horse, and a final judgment against him, is no bar to an action by Peter, administrator of Paul, to recover the same horse.

The constitution of the United States, and the amendments to it, declare that no fact, once tried by a jury, shall be otherwise reëxaminable in any court of the United States, than according to the rules of the common law.(*a*)

Much discussion has taken place respecting the effect of a *former recovery* when different actions in tort have been brought, successively, in relation to the same chattel; for example, where an action of trespass is brought, and the defendant sets up a title to the chattel, and the issue is found for him; and the plaintiff afterward brings an action of trover for the same chattel, he is clearly barred, because the title to

---

(*a*) Parsons *v.* Bedford, 3 Pet. 433.

it was settled in the first action.(a) In the like manner, a judgment in trover for the defendant, upon the merits, is a bar to an action for money had and received, for money arising from the sale of the same goods.(b) But whether a judgment obtained by the plaintiff in trespass, without satisfaction, is bar to an action of trover for the same chattel, is a point upon which different opinions have been entertained.(c)

3117. Proof of public documents, not records, when properly made, has the effect of establishing the existence of such documents.

4° *Of the nature and proof of foreign laws, records, and other public documents.*

(1) *Of foreign laws.*

3118.' Courts do not take judicial notice of foreign laws, they must be proved as facts, and when such laws come in question, the party who seeks advantage of them is required to produce an authenticated copy, for it is presumed all civilized governments will allow their officers to give authentic copies of their laws when requested. Before the party can offer any inferior evidence, he must prove such request and refusal; on its being shown that such a refusal has been made, other evidence of the existence of the law may be given.

If an exemplification under the seal of the foreign state cannot be had, such laws must be verified by some high authority which the law respects not less than an oath, or by an oath or affirmation. Such a law may be proved to be a true copy by a witness who has compared and examined it with the original, or by a certificate of an officer properly authorized by

---

(a) Putt v. Roster, 2 Mod. 218; Putt v. Rawstern, 3 Mod. 1.
(b) Kitchen v. Campbell, 3 Wils. 304; S. C. 2 W. Bl. 827.
(c) 1 Greenl. Ev. § 533, and the cases cited in the note.

384 OF REMEDIES.

No. 3118.　　　Book 4, tit. 8, chap. 11, sec 3, § 3, div. 1, art. 3.　　　No. 3118.

law to give a copy, which certificate must itself be duly authenticated.(a)

When our government has promulgated a foreign law or ordinance of a public nature as authentic, this is held to be sufficient evidence of its existence.(b)

Foreign unwritten laws, usages and customs, must of necessity be proved by parol evidence. The usual course is to make such proof by the testimony of competent witnesses, instructed in the laws, customs and usages, under oath or affirmation;(c) this will be sufficient unless the law was a written one, and when it is alleged that it is so, such allegation must be proved by the person making it.(d)

The several states of the Union, in all matters not surrendered to the general government by the national constitution, are considered as *foreign to each other*, they being, each, sovereign and independent. Strictly, then, their laws and public documents, when wanted in another state, must be proved as foreign laws; and, accordingly, in some of them such proof has been required.(e) But in some other states their courts have relaxed the rule, and they, and the courts of the national government, have considered that the connection, intercourse, and constitutional ties, which bind the several states together, require some relaxation of the strictness of this rule, and they have accordingly held a printed volume, purporting on its face to contain the laws of a sister state, to be admissible as *primâ facie* evidence, to prove the statute laws of that state.(f)

The relations which reciprocally exist between the

(a) Church v. Hubbart, 2 Cranch, 237 ; Consequa v. Willings, 1 Pet. C. C. 225 ; Lincoln v. Battelle, 6 Wend. 182 ; Raynham v. Canton, 8 Pick. 296.
(b) Talbot v. Seaman, 1 Cranch, 37 ; Radcliffe v. U. S. Ins. Co. 7 John. 38.
(c) Church v. Hubbart, 2 Cranch, 237.
(d) Dougherty v. Snyder, 15 S. & R. 87 ; 2 L. R. 154.
(e) Brackett v. Norton, 4 Conn. 517 ; Hampstead v. Reed, 6 Conn. 480 ; Packard v. Hill, 2 Wend. 411.
(f) Biddis v. James, 6 Binn. 321.

OF PROCEEDINGS IN AN ACTION. 385

No. 3119.   Book 4, tit. 8, chap. 11, sec. 3, § 3, div. 1, art. 3.   No. 3119.

national go̍vernment on the one side, and the several states of the Union, compo̍sing the United States, on the other, are not considered as foreign, but as domestic. For this reason, the courts of the general government take judicial notice of all the public laws of the several states, whenever they are called upon to consider and apply them; and the courts of the respective states, in like manner, take judicial notice of all public acts of congress, including those which relate to the District of Columbia, exclusively, without any formal proof.(a) Those statutes which do not relate to the public, but are strictly private, must be proved in the usual way.(b)

(2.) Of foreign judgments and public documents.

3119. These judgments are of two classes: .
1. Judgments rendered by the courts of a foreign state or nation. A judgment rendered out of the United States or their territories, by a court *de jure*, or . even a court *de facto*,(c) in a matter within its jurisdiction, when the parties litigant have been notified, and have had an opportunity of being heard, either establishing a demand against the defendant, or discharging him from it, is binding and of full force.

The modes of authenticating such foreign judgments are, either by an exemplification of a copy under the great seal of a state; or by a copy proved to be a true copy, by a witness who has compared it with the original; or by a certificate of an officer, properly authorized by law to give a copy; in this last case the certificate itself must be duly authenticated.(d)

(a) Young v. Bank of Alexandria, 4 Cranch, 384; Owings v. Hall, 9 Pet. 607.
(b) Leland v. Wilkinson, 6 Pet. 317.
(c) Bank of North America v. McCall, 4 Binn. 371.
(d) Church v. Hubbart, 2 Cranch, 237; Sir Yeaton v. Fry, 5 Cranch, 335; Gardere v. Col. Ins. Co. 7 John. 514; Thompson v. Stewart, 3 Conn. 171.

386 OF REMEDIES.

No. 3119.   Book 4, tit 8, chap. 11, sec. 3, § 3, div. 1, art. 3.   No. 3119.

2. Judgments rendered in one of the United States, or of the territories of the Union.

Although the several states composing the United States, for many purposes cannot be considered in the light of foreign states to each other, yet they are so in all things not surrendered to the national government by the constitution ;(a) but still their mutual relations are rather those of domestic independence than of foreign alienation. The constitution has wisely provided that " full faith and credit shall be given, in each state, to the public acts, records, and judicial proceedings of every other state ; and that congress may, by general laws, prescribe the manner in which such acts, records, and proceedings shall be proved, and the effect thereof."(b)

By virtue of this constitutional authority, congress has passed several laws regulating the manner in which the laws of the states, records, and public documents shall be proved.

The first act passed upon this subject(c) enacts, " that the acts of the legislatures of the several states shall be authenticated by having the seal of their respective states affixed thereto : That the records and judicial proceedings of the courts of any state shall be proved or admitted, in any other court within the United States, by the attestation of the clerk, and the seal of the court annexed, if there be a seal, together with a certificate of the judge, chief justice, or presiding magistrate, as the case may be, that the said attestation is in due form. And the said records and judicial proceedings, authenticated as aforesaid, shall have such faith and credit given to them, in every court within the United States, as they have, by law or usage, in the courts of the state from whence the said records are, or shall be taken."

(a) Mills v. Durgee, 7 Cranch, 481 ; Hampton v. McConnell, 3 Wheat. 234.
(b) Const. U. S. art. 4, s. 1.
(c) Act of May 26, 1790.

OF PROCEEDINGS IN AN ACTION.   387

No 3119.   Book 4, tit. 8, chap. 11, sec. 3, § 3, div. 1, art. 3.   No. 3119.

As this act provided for only one kind of records,
and did not apply to the territories, it was found necessary to enact another,(a) which extends to "exemplifications of office books," and to the territories. It
enacts, "that, from and after the passage of this act,
all records and exemplifications of office books, which
are or may be kept in any public office of any state,
not appertaining to a court, shall be proved or admitted
in any other court or office in any other state, by the
attestation of the keeper of the said records or books,
and the seal of his office thereto annexed, if there be a
seal, together with a certificate of the presiding justice
of the court of the county or district, as the case may
be, in which such office is or may be kept; or of the
governor, the secretary of state, the chancellor or the
keeper of the great seal of the state, that the said attestation is in due form, and by the proper officer; and the
said certificate, if given by the presiding justice of a
court, shall be further authenticated by the clerk or
prothonotary of the said court, who shall certify, under
his hand and the seal of his office, that the said presiding justice is duly commissioned and qualified; or if
the said certificate be given by the governor, the secretary of state, the chancellor or keeper of the great
seal, it shall be under the great seal of the state in
which the said certificate is made. And the said
records and exemplifications, authenticated as aforesaid, shall have such faith and credit given to them
in every court and office within the United States, as
they have by law or usage in the courts or offices of
the state from whence the same are or shall be taken."
    "That all the provisions of this act, and the act to
which this is a supplement, shall apply, as well to the
public acts, records, office books, judicial proceedings,
courts, and offices of the respective territories of the
United States, and countries subject to the jurisdiction

_____

(a) Act of March 27, 1804,   2.

of the United States, as to the public acts, records, office books, judicial proceedings, courts and offices of the several states." Although no prudent practitioner will depart from the mode pointed out by the acts of congress, yet, it seems that this method óf authentication is not exclusive of any other, which the states mày deem proper to adopt.(a)

2. Of private writings.

3120. Private writings form a very numerous class; they are those which have been made between private individuals, and relating to their private affairs. Included in this class are deeds, bonds, bills, notes, letters of attorney, invoices, letters between the parties or their correspondence, and many others. As to their effects as evidence, they are governed by principles which apply to them all. They are to be considered as to their production, their proof, their effect.

1° The production of private writings.

3121. Such writings are, 1, in the hands of the party offering them; 2, in the hands of the opposite party; 3, in the hands of a stranger; or, 4, lost.

(a) Kean v. Rice, 12 S. & R. 203. As to the kind of cases to which these acts of congress extend, it has been observed that they "do not extend to judgments in *criminal* cases, so as to render a witness incompetent in one state, who has been convicted of an infamous crime in another. The judicial proceedings, referred to in these acts, are also generally understood to be the proceedings of courts of general jurisdiction, and not those which are merely of municipal authority; for it is required, that the copy of the record shall be certified by the clerk of the court, and that there shall also be a certificate of the judge, chief justice, or presiding magistrate, that the attestation of the clerk is in due form This, it is said, is founded on the supposition that the court, whose proceedings are to be thus authenticated, is so constituted as to admit of such officers; the law having wisely left the records of magistrates, who may be vested with limited judicial authority, varying in its objects and extent in every state, to be governed by the laws of the state, into which they may be introduced for the purpose of being carried into effect. Accordingly, it has been held, that the judgments of *justices of the peace* were not within the meaning of these constitutional and statutory provisions. But the proceedings of courts of chancery, and of probate, as well as of the courts of common law, may be proved in the .manner directed by the statute." 1 Greenl. Ev. § 505.

OF PROCEEDINGS IN AN ACTION.   389

No. 3122.   Book 4, tit. 8, chap. 11, sec. 3, § 3, div. 1, art. 3.   No 3124.

3122.—1. When a paper wanted as evidence, is in the *hands. of the party* who desires to use it, it is at once produced; and no secondary proof of its contents can be given until it has been proved to have been lost, if it be proved that it once existed.

3123.—2. When the instrument of writing is in the possession of the *adverse party*, and there is no duplicate, the courts of common law may make an order for the inspection of such writing; but this power is scantily used in the United States, unless given by statute. When, however, the action is *ex contractu*, and there is but one instrument between the parties, which is in the possession or power of the defendant, to which the plaintiff is an actual party or a party in interest, and of which he has been refused an inspection upon request, and the production of which is necessary to enable him to declare against the defendant, the court(a) may grant him a rule to produce the document, or give him a copy for that purpose.(b) And such order may also be obtained in some other special cases.(c) In all cases when an application for such a rule is asked, the party applying must make an affidavit of the circumstances on which his application is founded.

Another mode of compelling the production of such an instrument is by filing a bill in chancery; but this subject will be considered in another place.(d)

3124. The most usual course pursued when a writing is in the possession of the adverse party, is to give him or his attorney notice to produce the original. The object of this notice is to enable the party who

---

(a) It is said that such order cannot be granted by a judge at chambers. Willis *v.* Bailey, 19 John. 268.

(b) 3 Chit. Gen. Pr. 433; Wallis *v.* Murray, 4 Cowen, 399; Utica Bank *v.* Hilliard, 6 Cowen 62.

(c) Brush *v.* Gibbon, 3 Cowen, 18, n. (a)

(d) See, as to the rules in equity to compel the production of books, 1 Bald. 388; 1 Vern. 408, 425.

gives it to offer secondary evidence of the paper, should it not be produced under the notice.(a) This notice may be considered, 1, as to its form ; 2, by and to whom it should be given ; 3, when it should be served ; and, 4, its effects.

1. In general a notice to produce papers ought to be in writing, and state the title of the cause in which it is proposed to use the paper or instrument required;(b) it seems, however, it may be by parol.(c) It must describe with sufficient certainty the papers or instruments called for, and must not be too general and by that means uncertain.

2. The notice must be given by the party to the cause who desires to prove it, or by his attorney, to the opposite party or his attorney.(d)

3. It must be served a reasonable time before trial, so as to afford an opportunity to the party to search for and produce the instrument in question.(e) But when a paper is in court, a notice to produce it, given at the time of the trial, is sufficient.(f)

4. When a notice to produce an instrument or paper has been proved, and it is also proved that such instrument or paper was, at the time of the notice, in the hands of the party or his privy, the party who gave the notice should call for its production in court on the trial; the proper time for calling for it, is not until the party who requires it has entered upon his case. If upon such request he refuses or neglects to produce it, the party having given the notice, and made such proof, will be entitled to give secondary evidence of

---

(a) Reid v. Colcock, 1 N. & McC. 592.
(b) Graham v. Dyster, 2 Stark. R. 19.
(c) Smith v. Young, 1 Campb. 440 ; Contra, Cummings v. McKinney, 4 Scam. 57.
(d) 2 T. R. 203, n. ; Brown v. Littlefield, 7 Wend. 454; Lagow v. Patterson, 1 Blackf. 327.
(e) 1 M. & M. 96, 335, n.
(f) Anon. Anthon, N. R. 199 ; Board of Justices v. Fennimore, Coxe. 242.

OF PROCEEDINGS IN AN ACTION.   391

No. 3125.   Book 4, tit. 8, chap 11, sec. 3, ◊ 3, div. 1, art. 3.   No. 3125.

such paper or instrument thus withheld. The production of such papers, upon notice, does not make them evidence in the cause, unless the party calling for them inspects them, so as to become acquainted with their contents. In such cases, in England, the paper so examined becomes evidence for both parties; in the United States the rule is not uniform.(a)

3125. To this general rule, that notice must be given to the opposite party to produce papers, there are several exceptions:

1. When, from the nature of the proceedings, the party in possession of the instrument has notice that he is charged with the possession of it, as in the case of trover for a bond;(b) or when such writing is matter of defence, and the adverse party must have understood that it would necessarily come in question, notice to produce it will be dispensed with.(c)

2. When the party in possession has obtained the instrument by fraud, no notice is requisite to entitle the other party to give secondary evidence.(d)

3. When the instrument to be proved and that to be produced are duplicate originals; for then the original being in the hands of the other party, it is in his power to contradict the duplicate original, by producing the other if they vary.(e)

4. When the instrument to be proved is itself a notice, such as a notice to quit, or notice of the dishonor of a bill of exchange,(f) notice to produce the original is not necessary.

(a) Withers v. Gillespy, 7 S. & R. 14; Jordan v. Wilkins, 2 Wash. O. C. 482, 484, n.; Randall v. Ches. & Del. Canal Co. 1 Harring, 233; 1 Paine & Duer's Pr. 484. See the valuable notes to 1 Phil. Ev. 441, by Cowen & Hill, note 841.

(b) Hart v. Robinett, 5 Miss. 11; Hammond v. Hopping, 13 Wend. 505; Harden v. Kritsinger, 17 John. 393; McClean v. Hertzog, 6 S. & R. 154.

(c) Kellar v. Savage, 2 App. 199.

(d) Gray v. Kernahan, 2 Rep. Const. Ct. 65. See 7 Wend. 198; Davis v. Spooner, 3 Pick. 284.

(e) Jory v. Orchard, 2 B & P. 39.

(f) 1 Greenl. Ev. ◊ 561.

3126. It is enacted by the judiciary act of the United States, "that all the courts of the United States shall have power, in the trial of actions at law, on motion and due notice thereof being given, to require the parties to produce books or writings in their possession or power, which contain evidence pertinent to the issue, in cases and under circumstances where they might be compelled to produce the same by the ordinary rules of proceeding in chancery; and if a plaintiff shall fail to comply with such order to produce books or writings, it shall be lawful for the courts, respectively, on motion, to give the like judgment for the defendant, as in cases of nonsuit; and if the defendant fail to comply with such order to produce books or writings, it shall be lawful for the courts, respectively, on motion as aforesaid, to give judgment against him or her by default."

The proper course to pursue under this act, is to move the court for an order on the opposite party to produce such books or papers.

3127.—3. When the papers or writings wanted in evidence are in the hands of a third person, a different course must be adopted to procure their production. This is done by taking out a *subpœna duces tecum*, which is a writ commanding the witness to appear in court, at a time certain, and to bring with him the paper or instrument required. This writ, like the *subpœna ad testificandum*, when properly served on the witness, will be enforced by attachment against the person of the witness; and he may be punished as in other cases, for contempt.(a)

3128.—4. When a paper has béen lost, proof of the loss must be made by the party who had it in possession, before he can give secondary evidence of its

(a) The witness is bound to produce the paper, whether it be material or not. for of that the court alone is able to judge. Doe v. Kelly, 4 Dowl. 273. But see Rex v. Ld. John Russel, 7 Dowl. 693.

OF PROCEEDINGS IN AN ACTION. 393

No. 3129.   Book 4, tit. 8, chap. 11, sec. 3, § 3, div. 1, art. 3.   No. 3129.

contents. It is difficult to say what degree of diligence in the search is necessary, as each case depends upon its own circumstances; this is left to the wise discretion of the court, and not to the decision of the jury.(a).

2° Of the proof of private writings.

3129. The simple production of the instrument does not make it evidence. If it appears to have been altered, it is incumbent on the party offering it to explain this appearance, because unless it is accounted for it will cast a suspicion upon it which will render it an unfit instrument of evidence, until it has been removed. Where the alteration is noticed in the attestation clause, or in some other parts of the instrument, as having been made before its execution, it will be sufficient; or if it appears in the same handwriting and ink as the body of the instrument; or if it be against the interests of the party deriving title under it, as if a bond be altered from a greater to a less sum.(b) When nothing appears on the subject, it is not settled whether the alterations will be presumed to have been made *before* or *after* the execution of the instrument.(c)

When a material alteration has been made in the instrument by the party to be benefited by it, it will vitiate the deed; and even an immaterial alteration, if made fraudulently, will have the same effect. By *alteration* is meant an act done upon the instrument by which its meaning is changed.

The act of a mere stranger will not have this nullifying effect on the instrument, when done without the

(a) Page v. Page, 15 Pick. 368. See Short v. Unag, 3 W. & Serg. 45; Parks v. Dunklee, 3 W. & S. 291; Rex v. Morton, 4 M. & S. 48.

(b) Coulson v. Walton, 9 Pet. 789; Bailey v. Taylor, 11 Conn. 531.

(c) Gooch v. Bryant, 1 Shepl. 386; Pullen v. Hutchinson, 12 Shepl. 249; Bailey v. Taylor, 11 Conn. 531; Trowel v. Castle, 1 Keb. 22; Fitzgerald v. Fauconberg, Fitzg. 207; Morris v. Vanderen, 1 Dall. 67; Prevost v. Gratz, 1 Pet. C. C. R. 364; Bac. Ab. Evidence, F; Helfinger v. Shultz, 16 S. & R. 47; Jackson v. Osborn, 2 Wend. 555; M'Micken v. Beauchamp, 2 Lo. R. 290.

consent of the parties, for this is a mere act of *spoliation* or *mutilation* of the instrument, which does not change its legal operation, so long as the original remains legible, and, if it be a deed, any traces of the seal can be discovered. If by such spoliation the paper is totally destroyed, secondary evidence of its contents may be given.

(1.) *Of proof of the instrument when produced.*

3130. When the instrument is produced, freed from all suspicion, it must be proved by the subscribing witnesses, where there are any, or at least by one of them, if living and competent. A *subscribing witness*, sometimes called an *attesting witness*, is one who, upon being required by the parties to an instrument, signs his name to it to prove it, and for the purpose of identification. The witness must be desired by the parties to attest it, for unless this be done, he will not be an attesting witness, although he may have seen the parties execute it.(*a*) It is not, however, necessary that he should have seen the party write or subscribe his name; for if he is called immediately afterward, and the party acknowledges his signature to him, and requests him to attest it, this will be deemed part of the transaction, and therefore a sufficient attestation.(*b*) In general the attesting witness must prove its execution, and it is only when he cannot be procured, after every lawful effort has been made to secure his attendance, that evidence of his handwriting will be received.

3131. The principal exceptions to this rule, that the attesting witnesses to an instrument must be produced, are the following:

1. When the instrument is thirty years old, it is said

(*a*) McGraw *v.* Gentry, 3 Campb. 232.
(*b*) Hollenback *v.* Fleming, 6 Hill, N. Y. R. 303 ; Cusson *v.* Skinner, 11 M. & W. 168.

to prove itself, the witnesses being presumed to be dead, and other proof being supposed to be beyond reach of the party. In such case the instrument, to be free from suspicion, must come from the proper custody, or have been acted upon, or, in the case of a deed of land, have accompanied the possession so as to afford corroborative proof of its genuineness.(a)

2. It is not necessary to prove the instrument by the attesting witnesses, when it is produced by the adverse party, pursuant to notice, and he claims an abiding or permanent interest under it; because then the party producing it cannot call for proof, for by claiming an interest under it, he has admitted its execution.(b)

3. A third exception to the rule is allowed when the witnesses are incompetent at the time of their being offered, or, when owing to physical or legal obstacles, the party cannot adduce them: thus when the witness is dead or is presumed to be so;(c) or cannot be found after diligent inquiry;(d) or is out of the jurisdiction of the court;(e) or is insane;(f) or has been convicted of an infamous crime;(g) or has become the adverse party, or otherwise become interested, without the agency of the party requiring his testimony; or was incapacitated at the time of signing, unknown to the party, as where the witness was the wife of the obligor unknown to the obligee.(h)   If the witness has become blind, still he

---

(a) Plowd. 6, 7; Tr. per Pays, 370 ; 1 Greenl. Ev. §§ 21, 142, 570 ; 2 Poth. Obl. by Evans, 149 ; 1 Phil. Ev. 477 ; Cowen & Hill's Notes to 1 Phil. Ev. 477, note 904; Roscoe's Civ. Ev. 70 ; Matth. Tr. Ev. 271.

(b) Pearce v. Hooper, 3 Taunt. 60 ; 1 Phil. Ev. 483 ; Gardner v. Grove, 10 S. & R. 137.

(c) Mott v. Doughty, 1 John. Cas. 230; Dudley v. Sumner, 5 Mass. 463.

(d) Whittemore v. Brooks, 1 Greenl. 57.

(e) 5 Mass. 444 ; Cooke v. Woodrow, 5 Cranch, 13. ·

(f) Currie v. Child, 3 Campb. 283.

(g) Jones v. Mason, 2 Str. 283.

(h) Melius v. Brickell, 1 Hayw. 19.

must be called, because he is able to testify to the other parts of the *res gestæ* at the time of signing.(*a*)

4. When the recording acts make the record of a deed, or other instrument, of equal force of the original, it has been held that the original might be read in evidence, without proof of its formal execution;(*b*) but, without such statutory provision, the original must be produced and proved.(*c*)

5. Office bonds, or such as are required by law to be taken in trust for all persons concerned, in the name of some public functionary, from officers, guardians, executors and administrators, and such other persons who hold or are to get possession of money for others, and to be preserved in the public offices where they are registered for their protection. These bonds and their sufficiency, in general, require the approbation of some public officer before the party can enter into the duties of his appointment. It has been held in a solitary case that the execution of such bonds taken from the public repository, need not be proved, and that, to make them evidence, it is only requisite to prove the identity of the obligor with the party in the action.(*d*)

6. A sixth exception to the rule is the case of letters received in reply to others proved to have been sent to the party; as where a letter was addressed to the defendant at his place of residence, by an attorney, and sent by the post, to which the attorney received an answer purporting to be from the defendant; such letter thus received was admitted in evidence, without proof of his handwriting.(*e*)

(*a*) Cronk *v.* Frith, 9 C. & P. 197.
(*b*) Knox *v.* Silloway, 1 Fairf. 201.
(*c*) Brooks *v.* Marbury, 11 Wheat. 79. See Cowen & Hill's Notes to 1 Phil. Ev. 464, note 874, where the cases are collected.
(*d*) Kello *v.* Maget, 1 Dev. & Bat. 414. But see Biddis *v.* James, 6 Binn. 321.
(*e*) Overton *v.* Wilson, 2 Car. & Kit. 1.

7. The recital of one instrument in another, will frequently render the proof of its execution unnecessary.(*a*)

3132. When the instrument is produced, and the attesting witnesses cannot be found, the course then is to prove the handwriting of the witnesses, or, at least, of one of them; when this is done, it is in general sufficient to admit the instrument to be read, but this must be accompanied with proof of the identity of the party sued as the person who appears to have executed the instrument.(*b*) The paper has been allowed to be read, in some instances, by proving the handwriting of the person by whom it was executed, on proof of the identity of the person;(*c*) but it seems, in another case, such proof was not allowed, except where the party could not prove the handwriting of the witness.(*d*)

3133. When no one has seen the party execute the instrument, to establish it, recourse must be had to the proof of the party's handwriting. Every man's hand is different from the hands of others, and the characters which he forms in writing differ from similar characters formed by others; this is called his *handwriting*. The handwriting of a person is usually as distinguishable from others, as his face differs from those of other men; and when it is proved by a person who knows it, in general it may be relied upon; still, owing to the imperfection of men's judgments, mistakes may easily be made.

In all cases of this kind, where the witness did not see the party write the document, his knowledge must be derived from a *comparison of hands*. The testimony of the witness is the belief, which, upon comparing

---

(*a*) See Notes to 1 Phil. Ev. 89, by Cowen & Hill, note 168.
(*b*)Whitelock *v.* Musgrove, 1 C. & M. 511 ; Roden *v.* Ryde, 4 Ad. & Ell.
N. S. 626.
(*c*) Valentine *v.* Piper, 22 Pick. 90.
(*d*) Jackson *v.* Waldron, 11 Wend. 178.

398 OF REMEDIES.

No. 3134.　　Book 4, tit. 8, chap. 11, sec. 3, § 3, div. 1, art. 3.　　No. 3134.

the writing in question, with the recollection of the party's writing in his mind, derived from some previous knowledge, he entertains of their similitude. The witness declares his *belief* in regard to the writing in question; and he may be asked what are the reasons he has for such belief.

3134. There are several modes of acquiring this knowledge of the handwriting of another.

1. The first is from having seen him write. The proper mode of interrogating the witness is to ask if he knows the handwriting, and next what are the sources of his knowledge, whether he has seen him write, whether frequently or otherwise.(*a*) When he has seen him write frequently, more credit will be likely to be given to him by the jury, than if he had seen him write only once, and then only his name; still such evidence, although very light, may be sufficient;(*b*) and even a mark, which is so much more easily imitated, has been allowed to be proved by a person who had seen the party affix it to other writing upon several occasions.(*c*) This kind of evidence may be perfectly satisfactory, or it may leave the mind in great doubt; like probable evidence it admits of every possible degree, from the lowest presumption to the highest moral certainty.

2. Another mode of acquiring a knowledge of a party's handwriting is from having seen *letters*, or other documents, purporting to be his handwriting, and having afterward personally communicated with him respecting them; or acted upon them as genuine, with the consent or approbation of such party; or by such adoption of them by him in the ordinary transactions of life, as would induce a reasonable presumption that

(*a*) See Slaymaker *v.* Wilson, 1 Pennsyl. 216; Moody *v.* Rowell, 17 Pick. 490.

(*b*) Garrells *v.* Alexander, 4 Esp. 37; Lewis *v.* Sapio, 1 M. & Malk. 39. But see Powell *v.* Ford, 2 Stark. R. 164.

(*c*) George *v.* Surrey, 1 M. & Malk. 516.

they were genuine. Further evidence will of course be required to be given, *aliundè*, of the identity of the party, if the witness is not personally acquainted with him.

3. A third mode has been proposed, by first satisfying the witness by some evidence or information, other than the means above mentioned, that certain papers are genuine, and then desiring him to study them, and, having fixed an exemplar in his mind, he should give an opinion as to whether the paper in question was the party's handwriting. On this point the court were equally divided, and it seems very questionable whether such evidence ought to be received, because, if it be proper, documents irrelevant to the issue must be introduced.(*a*) Whether papers irrelevant to the record can be admitted, for the sole purpose of creating a standard of comparison of handwriting, does not appear to be settled.(*b*)

(2.) *Proof of the instrument when it is not produced.*

3135. We have already considered the nature of secondary evidence, and when it ought to be admitted. In case an original writing has been lost, or if in the

(*a*) Doe *v.* Sackermore, 5 Ad. & Ell. 703, 734.
(*b*) In a note to § 581, in the first volume of his excellent work on Evidence, Professor Greenleaf says, "In New York, Virginia and North Carolina, the English rule is adopted, and such testimony is rejected. Jackson *v.* Phillips, 9 Cowen, 94, 112; Titford *v.* Knott, 2 Johns. Cas. 210; Rowt *v.* Kile, 1 Leigh's R. 216; The State *v.* Allen, 1 Hawks, 6. In Massachusetts, Maine and Connecticut, it seems to have become the settled practice to admit any papers to the jury, whether relevant to the issue or not, for the purpose of comparison of the handwriting. Homer *v.* Wallis, 11 Mass. 309; Moody *v.* Rowell, 17 Pick. 490; Richardson *v.* Newcomb, 21 Pick. 315; Hammond's case, 2 Greenl. 33; Lyon *v.* Lyman, 9 Conn. 55. In New Hampshire and South Carolina, the admissibility of such papers has been limited to cases where other proof of handwriting is already in the cause, and for the purpose of turning the scale, in doubtful cases. Myers *v.* Toscan, 3 N. Hamp. 47; The State *v.* Carr, 5 N. Hamp. 367; Boman *v.* Plunkett, 3 McC. 518; Duncan *v.* Beard, 2 Nott & McC. 401. In Pennsylvania the admission has been limited to papers conceded to be genuine. McCorkle *v.* Binns, 5 Binn. 340; Lancaster *v.* Whitehill, 10 S. & R. 110.

possession of the opposite party, after notice, it has not been produced, in general secondary evidence of its existence will be received.

3° Of the effect of private writings when proved.

3136. When a private writing has been proved, it is to receive such a construction as its words will naturally bear. It must be presumed that when the parties reduced their agreement to writing, and used such terms as import a legal obligation, without any uncertainty as to the object or intent of such engagement, that they meant the whole contract should be there stated; and that no *colloquium* or *pourparlers* between the parties, and that no declarations or conversation at the time it was completed or before, which would contradict, add to, or alter the written agreement, should be proved, because they had been abandoned; and therefore, no evidence will be allowed for that purpose. But this rule, that a party is not allowed to give parol evidence to contradict, add to, or alter a written agreement, is confined to the exclusion of evidence of the language of the party, and not to the circumstances in which he was placed, nor to collateral facts.

The courts find but little difficulty in construing written contracts and other written documents, when they are expressed in clear and distinct terms, and in such case they will not admit parol evidence to contradict, alter or add to the written document; owing to ignorance or the imperfection of language, there are, however, too often, clauses in written contracts and wills that may bear several meanings. In these cases it is said there is *ambiguity*.(a)

3137. There are two sorts of ambiguities of words, *ambiguitas latens*, and *ambiguitas patens*.

(a) See, as to ambiguity, Bac. Max. 23 ; 1 Phil. Ev. 410 to 420 ; 3 Stark. Ev. 1021 ; Sugd. Ven. 113 ; Dig. 22, 1, 4 ; Dig. 45, 1, 8 ; Dig. 50, 17, 67.

1. The first occurs when the deed or instrument is sufficiently certain and free from ambiguity, but the ambiguity is produced by something extrinsic, or some collateral matter out of the instrument; for example, if a man devise his property to his cousin Peter, and he has two cousins of that name, in such case parol evidence will be received to explain the ambiguity. Here, it is to be observed, the ambiguity arises out of the paper itself, it is *latent* or concealed, and for this reason it may be explained by parol.

2. A *patent* ambiguity occurs when a clause in a deed, or other instrument, is so defectively expressed, that a court of law, which has to put a construction on the instrument, is unable to collect the intention of the party. In such case, evidence of his declarations cannot be admitted to explain his intention, and the clause will be void for uncertainty.(*a*)   But it is to be remembered that an instrument is not to be considered ambiguous, because an ignorant or uninformed person is unable to interpret it; and when words of art or science are used, the judge, in order to understand the writing, must know those terms.   It is for this reason, among others, that all the lights afforded by the collateral facts and circumstances, are allowed to shine upon the case, and that they may be proved by parol.(*b*)

But though the rule that no parol evidence can be given to contradict, add to, or alter a writing, be firmly established, yet it must be understood with this qualification, that such evidence may be adduced to show fraud or mistake;(*c*) and courts of equity constantly admit evidence to contradict or vary a writing, when it is founded on a mistake of material facts, and it would be unconscionable or unjust to enforce it against either party, according to its expressed terms.

(*a*) In Pennsylvania this doctrine is somewhat qualified.   Lessee of Dinkle *v.* Marshall, 3 Binn. 587.
(*b*) See 1 Greenl. § 298 ; Wigr. on Wills, p. 174, n. 200, 201.
(*c*) Doe *v.* Allen, 8 T. R. 147.

3138. The rule which forbids parol evidence to be given to contradict, add to, or alter a writing, applies only to agreements made *anterior to the writing.* New and distinct agreements upon a new consideration may be made to change such written contract, and, therefore, they may be proved without infringing the rule; as, where a man agreed in writing to build a house for another, and afterward, finding he would be a loser, he refused to go on, unless his employer would agree to give him a further sum, which he promised to do by parol, and he then went on. The builder was allowed to recover in assumpsit upon the last contract.(a)

3. *Of shop books, and other mercantile books.*

3139.—1. Though a *shop book,* which contains an account of the daily transactions of a merchant, or mechanic, or other person, of the sale of goods, or of work and labor done for him, is made by the party himself, without the concurrence of the party to be charged, yet when the entries have been properly made, in a proper book, at the right time, they are received in evidence to prove the sale and delivery of goods, and the performance of work and labor.

None but an *original entry,* so made, will be received in evidence. Let us now examine, 1, the requisites of such entry; 2, the manner of proving it; and, 3, its effect when proved.

1° *Of the requisites of an original entry.*

3140. To make a valid original entry, it must possess the following qualities:

1. It must be made in a *proper book.* In general, the books in which the first entries are made, belong-

---

(a) Munroe *v.* Perkins, 9 Pick. 298. See Lattimore *v.* Harsen, 14 John. 330.

OF PROCEEDINGS IN AN ACTION.   403

No 3140.   Book 4, tit. 8, chap. 11, sec 3, § 3, div. 1, art 3.   No. 3140.

ing to a merchant, tradesman or other person,(*a*) in which are charged goods sold and delivered, or work and labor done, are received in evidence, though made by the party himself, when such entries are proved by the suppletory oath of the person who made them, or in his unavoidable absence, by proof of his handwriting. This evidence, when the books are proved by the party himself, is received as part of the *res gestæ*, the entry being a contemporaneous act with the transaction.

To be received in evidence, the book must be a *book of original entries*, kept by the plaintiff himself, to register his affairs; and must have the appearánce of fairness, for upon being inspected by the court, if it do not appear to be a register of the daily business of the party, and to have been honestly made, it will be excluded. If it appear to have been fraudulently altered, in any material part, it will not be admitted, or, if so altered without fraud, such alteration must be explained.(*b*)   If the books appear to be fairly made, it is immaterial whether they are made in the form of a journal, day book, or ledger.(*c*)

There are many books which are not books of original entries, and consequently cannot be received in evidence, although entries charging persons with goods sold and delivered to them, or for work and labor performed at their request; a few of these will be enumerated. A book made by transcribing entries made on a slate by a journeyman, the transcript being made sometimes on the same evening, at other times

---

(*a*) In some states the books thus admitted in evidence, are restricted to those of shopkeepers, mechanics, and tradesmen ; those of other persons, such as planters, scriveners, schoolmasters, etc., not being allowed.   Geter *v.* Martin, 2 Bay, 173 ; Pelzer *v.* Cranston, 2 McCord, 328,; Boyd *v.* Ladson, 4 McCord, 76.

(*b*) Churchman *v.* Smith. 6 Whart. 106.

(*c*) Rodman *v.* Hoops, 1 Dall. 85 ; Thomas *v.* Dyott, 1 N & McC. 106 ; Cogswell *v.* Dolliver, 2 Mass. 217 ; Swing *v.* Sparks, 2 Halst. 59 ; Gale *v.* Norris, 2 McLean, 469.

404   OF REMEDIES.

No. 3140.   Book 4, tit 8, chap. 11, sec. 3, § 3, div. 1, art. 3.   No. 3140.

not until nearly two weeks after the work was done, was considered as not a book of original entries; and unconnected scraps of paper, containing entries of sales by an agent, on account of his principal, and appearing on their face to be irregularly kept, are not to be considered as a book of original entries.(*a*)

2. The entry must have been made in *proper time*, and in the course of business, and with an intention of making a charge for goods sold and work done; and they ought not to be made after the lapse of one day.(*b*) A charge made at the time when the goods were ordered and before delivery, in a book which was kept for the purpose, is not sufficient, although when the goods were delivered there was a mark made to indicate such delivery.(*c*)   There is one class of entries which derive all their force from the circumstance alone, that they were made by the party making them against their own interest, and it is immaterial, as to the time, when they were made; as where a man's clerk charges himself in the books of his employer with goods or money received by him on account of his wages.

3. An entry must be made in *an intelligible manner*, and not in figures or hieroglyphics, which are understood by the seller only ;(*d*) and it must not be made in a gross amount, but as goods are delivered or the work is done ; charges made in the gross of " one hundred days' work," or " for medicine and attendance," or " thirteen dollars for medicine and attendance on one of the general's daughters," were, therefore, rejected.(*e*) An entry of goods, without carrying out any price,

---

(*4*) Thompson *v.* McKelvey, 13 S. & R. 126.   See 2 Whart. 33 ; Prince *r.* Smith, 4 Mass. 455 ; Lynch *v.* Hugo, 1 Bay, 33 ; Wilson *v.* Wilson, 1 Halst. 94 ; Thompson *v.* McKelvey, 13 S & R. 126 ; Bell *v.* McLean, 3 Verm. 185.
(*b*) Waller *v.* Bollman, 8 Watts, 545.
(*c*) Rhoads *v.* Gaul, 4 Rawle, 404.
(*d*) 4 Rawle, 404.
(*e*) Lynch *v.* Petrie, 1 N. & McCord, 130 ; Hughes *v.* Hampton, 2 Const. Rep. 476.

OF PROCEEDINGS IN AN ACTION.   405

No. 3141   Book 4, tit. 8, chap. 11, sec. 3, § 3, div. 1, art. 3   No. 3141.

proves, at most, only a sale, and the jury cannot, without other evidence, fix any price.(a) The charges should be specific, and denote the particular work or service charged, as it arises daily, and the quantity, number, weight, or other distinct designation of the materials or articles sold or furnished, and the price or value should be attached to each item.(b)

4. The entry must be made *by a person having authority* to make it, for if made by a stranger it would not be evidence of any sale and delivery, or of work done,(c) and it must be made, when the party making it is authorized, with an intent to charge the person against whom it is made.(d)

2° *Of the proof of the original entry.*

3141. When the entries have been made by a clerk, or other authorized person, from the report of others, this kind of evidence is in the nature of hearsay; for when the clerk swears he made the entry at the time it bears date, he only establishes the fact that he made a record of what another told him, and that the book contains the statement of what was then told him. But when the entry was made by the person who sold and delivered the goods, or performed the work, whether as a principal or an agent, then the evidence assumes another character; it is a memorandum of a fact actually known to him, which he has not heard from others. Then, the entry acquires a value from this circumstance that it was contemporaneous with the principal fact done, forming a link in the chain of events, and being a part of the *res gestæ.* When the entry has been made by a clerk or other

(a) Hagaman v. Case, 1 South. 370.
(b) 2 Bailey, R. 449; 1 N. & McC. 130.
(c) Rhoads v. Gaul, 4 Rawle, 404.
(d) Waller v. Bollman, 8 Watts, 545. See Curran v. Crawford, 4 S. & R. 3, 5; Ingraham v. Bockjus, 9 S. & R. 285; Cook v. Ashmead, 2 Miles, R. 268.

406 OF REMEDIES.

No 3141.   Book 4, tit 8, chap 11, sec 3, § 3, div. 1, art. 3.   No. 3141.

authorized agent, the proof of such entry must be made by the clerk or agent himself, if he can be procured, but if he be *dead*,(*a*) or insane,(*b*) his handwriting may be proved by any one acquainted with it.(*c*) But the plaintiff is not competent, in such case, to prove the handwriting of his deceased clerk.(*d*) When the entry has been made by the plaintiff himself, he can in general prove the fact although he is a party on record, contrary to the general rule that an interested person cannot be examined as a witness. This rule has been adopted with some limitations in perhaps most of the states of the Union.(*e*) Though not in accordance with the ancient common law of England, this rule; which was adopted from the necessity of the case, as in the early settlement of America many persons could not keep clerks, is in conformity with other systems of jurisprudence.(*f*) When the

(*a*) His absence beyond the jurisdiction of the court, or beyond the reach of process, is not enough. Kenedy *v.* Fairman, 1 Hayw. 458; Whitfield *v.* Walk, 2 Hayw. 24; Wilbur *v.* Selden, 6 Cowen, 162. But in some cases the permanent absence of the clerk from the state, has been holden sufficient to let in proof of his handwriting. Elms *v.* Chevis, 2 McCord, 350: Tunno *v.* Rogers, 1 Bay, 480.

(*b*) Union Bank *v.* Knapp, 3 Pick. 96.

(*c*) Hay *v.* Kramer, 2 W. & Serg. 137.

(*d*) 1 Browne's R. App. liii.

(*e*) The practice of receiving such evidence is said by a learned judge to be "founded on a moral necessity. The whole commercial world," he says, "has in substance the same thing. The principles of it, I believe, were introduced into this country from Holland, by the first settlers of New England. Its origin doubtless was in commercial transactions, but its use became necessary, between man and man, in the common intercourse of life." Per Brainard, J., in Beach *v.* Mills, 5 Conn. 496. In some of the states, the rule has been established by a species of necessity and the decisions of the courts; in others, this kind of evidence is regulated by statutes, but their provisions vary very much in their details. See 1 Phil. Ev. 266, and note by Cowen & Hill, number 491; 1 Greenl. Ev. § 118, note 1.

(*f*) By the Roman law, a merchant's or tradesman's books of accounts, regularly and fairly kept, in the usual manner, were deemed presumptive evidence, and with the suppletory oath of the party, full proof of his claim. 1 Greenl. Ev. § 119. By the law of France, the books of merchants and tradesmen are required to be kept regularly, and written from day to day, without any blank, and seen and approved, (*paraphés et visés*,) at least once a year, by certain designated officers; when a merchant's or tradesman's books are so kept, and he is a man of probity, they are admitted as plaintiff, who made the entries, is dead, evidence of his handwriting will be received.(a)

In all cases the charge must be proved to be an original entry and not a mere transcript from another book, but when there is a mark, showing that the entry has been posted into another book, commonly called the ledger, that must also be produced.

3° Of the effect of an original entry when proved.

3142.—1. The book of original entries, when proved by the suppletory oath or affirmation of the person who made the entry, or by proof of his handwriting as above mentioned, is *primâ facie* evidence of the sale and delivery of goods or of work and labor done,(b) for the books and the suppletory oath are not conclusive; the testimony is still to be weighed by the jury, like any other in the cause, and the witness, who makes such suppletory oath, is subject to have his reputation for truth assailed equally with any other witness.(c) This is confined to personal property; a charge of a sale, or use, or occupation of real estate, would have no effect.(d) The goods may have been sold and delivered to the defendant himself, or to his agent, under an express or implied authority to buy them; and, therefore, necessary goods supplied to a man's wife or children are properly charged.

---

semi-proof, presumptive evidence, and with his suppletory oath, as full proof of his claim. Code de Com. art. 8 to 13. In Scotland, merchants' books, when properly kept, may be received in evidence with the " oath in supplement," as full proof; but a course of dealing, or other pregnant circumstances, must first be shown by proof *aliunde*. Tait on Ev. 273—277; 1 Bell's Com. 331, 5th ed. ; Glassford on Evidence, 550.

(a) McLellan *v.* Crofton, 6 Greenl. 307 ; Odell *v.* Culbert, 9 W. & S. 66 ; Bentley *v.* Hollandbach, Wright, R. 169 ; Prince *v.* Smith, 4 Mass. 455.

(b) 1 Swift's Ev. 84 ; Case *v.* Porter, 8 John. 211 ; Vosburg *v.* Thayer, 12 John. 261 ; Ducoign *v* Schreppel. 1 Yeates, 347 ; Wilmer *v.* Israel, 1 Brown, 257 ; Charlton *v.* Lecory, Mart. N. C. Rep. 26.

(c) Kitchen *v.* Tyron, 2 Murph. 314 ; Elder *v.* Warfield, 7 Har. & J. 391.

(d) Beach *v.* Mills, 5 Conn. 493. See Dunn *v.* Whitney, 1 Fairf. 9 ; Newton *v.* Higgins, 2 Verm. 366.

Although fully proved by the suppletory oath of the person who made the entry, such book is not evidence, in many cases, from the nature of the thing charged;(*a*) for example, a charge of money lent or cash paid; the time a vessel lay at plaintiff's wharf;(*b*) the delivery of goods to be sold on commission;(*c*) commissions on the sale of a vessel;(*d*) a delivery of goods under a special agreement;(*e*) delivery of goods to a third person; but where the delivery of goods to such a person is proved to have been made by order of the buyer, by competent evidence *aliunde*, the delivery itself may be proved by the books and suppletory oath of the plaintiff, in any case where the delivery to the defendant in person might be so proved.(*f*)

3143.—2. Many entries made in proper books, in the ordinary course of business, are admitted in evidence upon the ground that they are contemporaneous with the transaction they record. The *letter book* of a merchant, party in the cause, has been admitted as *primâ facie* evidence of the contents of a letter addressed by him to the other party, after notice to produce the original; for merchants usually keep such a book.(*g*) Contemporaneous entries, *made by third persons, in their own books*, in the ordinary course of business, the matter being within the peculiar knowledge of the party making the entry, and there being no apparent motive to pervert the fact, are generally received as original evidence; though the person who made them has no recollection of the fact at the time of

---

(*a*) In some states, as in Maine and Massachusetts, the amount is restricted to forty shillings, or other small sums. 1 Fairf. 9; Burns *v.* Fay, 14 Pick. 8.
(*b*) Wilmur *v.* Israel, 1 Browne, R. 257.
(*c*) Murphy *v.* Cress, 2 Whart. 33.
(*d*) Winson *v.* Dillaway, 4 Metc. 221.
(*e*) Nickle *v.* Baldwin, 4 Wats. & S. 290.
(*f*) Mitchel *v.* Belknap, 10 Shepl. 475.
(*g*) Pritt *v.* Fairclough, 3 Campb. 305; Hagedom *v.* Reid, 3 Campb. 377. See Sturge *v.* Buchanan, 2 P. & D. 573.

OF PROCEEDINGS IN AN ACTION.   409

No. 3144.   Book 4, tit. 8, chap. 11, sec. 3, § 3, div. 1, art. 3.   No. 3144.

testifying, provided he swears that he should not have made it, if it were not true.(a)

4. Of witnesses.

3144. The fourth class of instruments of evidence are witnesses.   A *witness* is one who, being sworn or affirmed according to law, deposes as to his knowledge of the facts in issue between the parties in a cause.

The testimony of witnesses can never have the effect of a demonstration, because it is not impossible, indeed, it frequently happens, that they are mistaken, or wish themselves to deceive.   There can, therefore, result no other certainty from their testimony than what arises from analogy.   When in the calm of the passions, we listen only to the voice of reason and the impulse of nature, we feel in ourselves a great repugnance to betray the truth, to the prejudice of another, and we have observed that honest, intelligent and disinterested persons, never combine to deceive others by a falsehood.   We conclude, then, by analogy, with a sort of moral certainty, that a fact attested by several witnesses, worthy of credit, is true.   This proof derives its whole force from a double presumption. We presume, in the first place, on the good sense of the witnesses that they have not been mistaken ; and, secondly, we presume on their probity that they wish not to deceive.   To be certain that they have not been deceived, and that they do not wish to mislead, we must ascertain, as far as possible, the nature and the quality of the facts proved; the quality and the person of the witness; and the testimony itself, by comparing it with the deposition of other witnesses, or with known facts.

This head will be divided into three subdivisions : 1, of the means used to obtain the attendance of wit-

_____

(a) Bunker *v.* Shed, 8 Met. 150.

410　　　　　　　　OF REMEDIES.

No. 3145　　　Book 4, tit. 8, chap. 11, sec 3, § 3, div 1, art. 3.　　　No. 3145.

nesses ; 2, of the character of the witness ; 3, of the number of witnesses required by law.

1° Of the means used to obtain the attendance of witnesses.

3145. Witnesses may be procured to attend and testify in a case, merely by being notified to attend, and if they attend in court they may be examined, although no process requiring their attendance has been taken out and served on them.(*a*) But the practice of relying upon witnesses without serving a *subpœna* upon them is very dangerous, because if they do not attend, their absence will be no legal cause for putting off the trial or continuing the cause.

The courts of common law have the inherent power to call for all legal proof required to establish the facts in issue between the parties ; and they, consequently, possess the authority to summon and compel the attendance of witnesses to come before them, and testify as to their knowledge respecting such facts.　The process usually employed for this purpose, is the writ of *subpœna ad testificandum.*　This writ is directed to the witness, commanding him to appear at court, to testify what he knows in the cause therein described, pending in the court out of which it issues, under a penalty mentioned in the writ.　When the witness is required to produce papers, to be read in evidence, a clause is inserted in the writ commanding him to bring them with him into court, and then the writ is called a *subpœna duces tecum.*(*b*)　In such case the paper should be particularly described, for a direction to produce all letters, papers and documents touching the matter in dispute, can hardly be relied upon.(*c*)

The writ of *subpœna* is sufficient to secure the attendance of the witness for one session or term of the

(*a*) De Benneville *v.* De Benneville, 1 Binn. 46 ; S. C. 3 Yeates, 558.
(*b*) 3 Chitty's Gen. Pr. 830, n. ; Amey *v.* Long, 9 East, 473.
(*c*) See Feance *v.* Lucy, Ry. & Mo. N. P. Cas. 341.

court; but if the cause be made a *remanet*,(a) that is, if it be postponed by adjournment to another term or session, the witness must be subpœnaed anew. With regard to the service of the *subpœna*, although regulated by statute and rules of courts in the several states, which vary materially in their details, yet it may be observed that it must be served long enough before the time appointed, so as to allow the witness a sufficient time conveniently to come from his residence to court;(b) and, in order to ground a motion for an attachment for the contempt of the witness for non-attendance, the *subpœna* must be served on the witness personally.

It is the general practice in the United States to pay witnesses for their attendance on the trial; this compensation is fixed by the local statutes, and, like all matters of this kind, varies in the different states of the Union. It is sufficient, in some states, to tender to the witness his fees for travel, from his home to the place of trial, and one day's attendance, in order to compel him to appear under the *subpœna;* and in others the tender must include, besides, his fees for returning; whether he is bound to attend from day to day, without being paid his fees, does not appear to be uniformly settled, but it seems he cannot be compelled to submit to an examination without such payment.(c)

3146. When the witness has been duly summoned, and his fees have been paid to him, or lawfully tendered, or the payment or tender have been waived, and he wilfully neglects to appear, he is guilty of a *contempt* of the process of the court, and may be punished by *attachment*, which is a writ in the name of

---

(a) Lee's Dict. of Pr. Trial, vii. ; 1 Sell. Pr. 434 ; 1 Phil. Ev. 4 ; 1 Greenl. Ev. § 309 ; 2 Tidd's Pr. 855 ; Bouv. L D. h. v.

(b) 1 Phil. Ev. 4.

(c) Paine & Duer's Pr. 497. In N. J. the witness is not bound to attend unless his fees are tendered at the time of service of the subpœna. Ogden v. Gibbons, 2 South. 518.

the People, the Commonwealth, the United States, or other denomination which represents the government, against the witness, directed to the sheriff or other officer, lawfully authorized to serve the same, commanding him to bring the witness before the court.(a) The witness is not deemed in contempt, until proof has been made that the *subpœna* was served on him, and that his absence has been with intent to disobey the *subpœna*, and that his fees were paid or tendered to him, or that he waived their payment. But even in such case, unless a palpable contempt be shown, a rule to show cause is granted in the first instance.(b) If the witness is in attendance in court by virtue of the *subpœna*, and he refuses to be sworn or affirmed, he is, of course, guilty of a *contempt of the court*, which is a wilful disregard of its authority, and he may be punished for it by fine or imprisonment, or both.

3147. But there are many circumstances which will excuse a witness for not attending, and which will cure this apparent contempt.

1. When the witness was imprisoned, whether lawfully or unlawfully, it is evident he could not attend, and upon this being shown he will be discharged from the attachment.

2. When the witness has become insane, or has been disabled by some accident from attending, he is not guilty of contempt.

3. When he is in the military or naval service of the United States, or of any state, and is not at liberty to attend without leave of his superior officer, and he cannot obtain the officer's permission, he is in no fault, and consequently not in contempt.

3148. In the case of a prisoner or a military man, who is wanted as a witness, the usual, and indeed the only proper process, to secure the attendance of such

(a) Grah. Pr. 555.
(b) Anon. Salk. 84; Concklin's Pract. 265.

OF PROCEEDINGS IN AN ACTION.   413

No 3149.   Book 4, tit. 8, chap. 11, sec 3, § 3, div 1, art 3.   No. 3149.

witness, is the writ of *habeas corpus ad testificandum;* this is a writ or process directed to the person having the witness in charge, commanding him to bring him before the court in order that he may testify.(a) This writ is grantable at discretion, on motion in open court, or by a judge at chambers, who has a general authority to issue writs of *habeas corpus.* In civil cases the application is made upon affidavit, stating the nature of the suit, and the materialty of the testimony, as the party is advised by counsel and verily believes, together with the fact of the restraint, and the circumstances which justify the issuing of the writ. When the witness is in lawful custody, the writ is served by leaving it with the person who detains the witness, and if he is unlawfully imprisoned, with the person who so holds him ; but if he is in the military or naval service, the writ is left with the officer immediately in command, to be served, obeyed, and returned like any other writ of *habeas corpus.*(b)

3149. In general the court which issues a *subpœna* cannot give it any force beyond its territorial jurisdiction ; but the courts of the United States sitting in any district, are authorized by statute to send *subpœnas* for witnesses into any other districts, provided that, in civil causes, the witness does not live at a greater distance than one hundred miles from the place of trial.(c)

A *subpœna* extends a protecting influence over the witness when it has been served upon him ; like a party attending court in a cause, he is protected from arrest, while going to the place of trial, while attending there for the purpose of giving evidence in the

---

(a) 3 Bl. Com. 130.
(b) 2 Phil. Ev. 374 ; 2 Tidd's Pr. 809 ; Concklin's Pr. 264 ; 1 Greenl. Ev. § 312.
(c) Statute 1793, c. 66, [22,] § 6 ; 1 Laws U. S. 312, Story's ed. In some of the states the courts are authorized to issue their *subpœnas* to persons any where in the state.

414 OF REMEDIES.

No. 3150.   Book 4, tit 8, chap. 11, sec 3, § 3, div. 1, art. 3.   No. 3150.

cause, and while returning home, *eundo mòrando et redeundo;* this protection also extends to a witness who comes, *bonâ fide,* to attend without being summoned.(*a*) The arrest of a witness, after he has been summoned, for the purpose of preventing him from attending court, is a contempt of court, and punishable as such. And it is a contempt to serve him even with a summons, if it be done in the immediate or constructive presence of the court upon which he is attending, and the service will be set aside.(*b*) But this freedom from arrest is a personal privilege, which, in general, a party can waive;(*c*) when, however, the privilege is not merely as a favor to the witness, but it is created by public policy, it cannot be waived; an ambassador, who has been arrested, does not waive his privilege by submitting to the arrest.(*d*)

3150. When the witness resides abroad out of the jurisdiction of the court, and refuses to attend, his testimony can be obtained in civil cases, by taking his *deposition* before a judge, or other magistrate, or a commissioner duly appointed by order of the court where the cause is pending; and when the commissioner is not a judge or magistrate, he should himself be first sworn or affirmed.

By a *deposition* is meant the testimony of a witness, reduced to writing, in due form of law, taken by virtue of a commission, or other lawful authority, of a competent tribunal. This mode of taking testimony in a foreign country, has always been common with courts of admiralty; now it is considered to be within

---

(*a*) Meekens *v.* Smith, 1 H. Bl. 636; Hurst's case, 4 Dall. 387; Norris *v.* Beach, 2 John. 294; Randall *v.* Gurney, 3 B. & Ald. 252. In New Jersey, the witness is not protected from arrest unless he is attending court under a subpœna. Rogers *v.* Bullock, 2 Penning. 516.
(*b*) Ex parte Edme, 9 S. & R. 147.
(*c*) Bours *v.* Tuckerman, 7 John. 538; Huntingdon *v.* Schultz, Harper, 452.
(*d*) United States *v.* Benner, Baldw. 240.

the inherent powers of all courts of justice. When the testimony of a witness who is in a foreign jurisdiction is required, the court in which the suit is pending may send to the court within whose jurisdiction the witness may be, a writ usually termed a *letter rogatory*, or a *commission sub mutua vicissitudinis obtentu, ac in juris subsidium*, so called from these words, which, when the proceedings were in Latin, it contained. The letter rogatory informs the court abroad of the pendency of the cause, and the name of the foreign witnesses, and the foreign court is requested to cause their depositions to be taken, in due course of law, for the furtherance of justice ; offering on the part of the tribunal making the request, to do the like for the other in a similar case. Interrogatories filed by the parties on each side, to which the answers of the witnesses are desired, usually accompany such letter. The commission is executed by the judge or commissioner who receives it, and the original answers, duly signed and sworn to by the deponent, and properly authenticated, covered by an envelope and sealed, are returned with the commission, to the court from which it issued.(*a*)

There are provisions which have existed in the statutes of the several states, from a very early period, to authorize the taking of depositions to be used in civil actions in the courts of law, in all cases where the personal attendance of the witness could not be had at the trial, by reason of sickness or other inability to attend ; and depositions are taken constantly of ancient, absent, and going witnesses.

3151. The testimony of witnesses may also ·be secured, in anticipation of a controversy, before any action is commenced ; this proceeding is generally authorized by the state laws, and these depositions of

(*a*) For forms and style of depositions, see Gresley, Eq. Ev. 77 ; 1 Greenl. Ev. § 320, n, 1.

416   * OF REMEDIES.

No. 3152.   Book 4, tit. 8, chap. 11, sec. 3, § 3, div. 1, art. 3.   No. 3152.

witnesses *in perpetuam rei memoriam* are taken whenever a person who cannot bring a suit anticipates that an action may be brought against him, and that there is danger he may lose the testimony of his witnesses, he thus perpetuates their testimony. Proceedings, in these cases, must be had before the courts or magistrates who are authorized, by the local statute, to act therein. Notice of the proceedings must be given to all persons known to have an interest in the matter to which the testimony is to relate; the names of the persons thus notified must be mentioned by the officer in the certificate or caption appended to the deposition; and the deposition must be filed among the records of the court *in perpetuam rei memoriam.* The effect of a deposition of this kind is, that its contents will be received in evidence, if the witness cannot be had on the trial; but it will affect only the parties who had an opportunity to cross-examine, and those in privity with them.

3152. By the judiciary act of the United States and its supplements,(a) depositions may be taken. Its provisions are as follows: when the testimony of any person shall be necessary in any civil cause depending in any district, in any court of the United States, who shall live at a greater distance from the place of trial than one hundred miles, or is bound on a voyage to sea, or is about to go out of the United States, or out of such district, and to a greater distance from the place of trial than as aforesaid, before the time of trial, or is ancient, or very infirm, the deposition of such person may be taken, de bene esse, before any justice or judge of any of the courts of the United States, or before any chancellor, justice, or judge of a supreme or superior court, mayor, or chief magistrate of a city, or judge of a county court or court of common pleas of any of the United States, not being of counsel or

(a) Act of September 24, 1789, s. 30, 1 Laws U. S. 64, Story's ed.

attorney to either of the parties, or interested in the event of the cause ; provided that a notification from the magistrate before whom the deposition is to be taken to the adverse party, to be present at the taking of the same, and to put interrogatories, if he think fit, be first made out and served on the adverse party, or his attorney, as either may be nearest, if either is within one hundred miles of the place of such caption, allowing time for their attendance after being notified, not less than at the rate of one day, Sundays exclusive, for every twenty miles travel.   And in causes of admiralty and maritime jurisdiction, or other causes of seizure, when a libel shall be filed, in which an adverse party is not named, and depositions of persons, circumstanced as aforesaid, shall be taken before a claim be put in, the like notification, as aforesaid, shall be given, to the person having the agency- or possession of the property libelled at the time of the capture or seizure of the same, if known to the libellant.   And every person deposing as aforesaid, shall be carefully examined and cautioned, and sworn or affirmed to testify *the whole truth*, and shall subscribe the testimony by him or her given, after the same shall be reduced to writing, which shall be done only by the magistrate taking the deposition, or by the deponent in his presence.   And the deposition so taken, shall be retained by such magistrate, until he deliver the same with his own hand into the court for which they are taken, or shall, together with a certificate of the reasons as aforesaid, of their being taken, and of the notice, if any given, to the adverse party, be by him, the said magistrate, sealed up and directed to such court, and remain under his seal until opened in court.   And any person may be compelled to appear and depose as aforesaid, in the same manner as to appear and testify in court.   And in the trial of any cause of admiralty or maritime jurisdiction in a district court, the decree in which may be appealed from, if either party shall suggest to and satisfy the court, that probably it will not be in his power to produce the witnesses, there testifying, before the circuit court, should an appeal be had, and shall move that their testimony shall be taken down in writing, it shall be so done by the clerk of the court. And if an appeal be had, such testimony may be used on the trial of the same, if it shall appear to the satisfaction of the court, which shall try the appeal, that the witnesses are then dead, or gone out of the United States, or to a greater distance than as aforesaid, from the place where the court is sitting; or that, by reason of age, sickness, bodily infirmity, or imprisonment, they are unable to travel or appear at court, but not otherwise. And unless the same shall be made to appear on the trial of any cause, with respect to witnesses whose depositions may have been taken therein, such depositions shall not be admitted or used in the cause. *Provided,* That nothing herein shall be construed to prevent any court of the United States from granting a dedimus potestatem, to take depositions according to common usage, when it may be necessary to prevent a failure or delay of justice; which power they shall severally possess; nor to extend to depositions taken in perpetuam rei memoriam, which, if they relate to matters that may be cognizable in any court of the United States, a circuit court, on application thereto made as a court of equity, may, according to the usages in chancery, direct to be taken.

And by another statute(a) authority is given to the clerk of any court of the United States within which a witness resides or where he is found, to issue a subpoena to compel the attendance of such witness, and a neglect of the witness to attend may be punished by

---

(a) Act of January 24, 1827, 3 Laws U. S. 2040, Story's ed.

the court whose clerk has issued the subpœna as for a contempt. And when papers are wanted by the parties litigant, the judge of the court within which they are, may issue a subpœna duces tecum, and enforce obedience by punishment as for a contempt.(*a*)

When the depositions have been thus taken, they may be used at the trial by either party, whether the witness was or was not cross-examined,(*b*) when it appears, to the satisfaction of the court, that the witness is then dead, or gone out of the United States, or is more than one hundred miles from the place of trial, or that by reason of age, sickness or bodily infirmity, or imprisonment, he is unable to appear in court to give his testimony.

2° Of the character of the witnesses.

3153. Having considered the means used to obtain the attendance of witnesses, let us next consider the character which they ought to bear, to entitle them to credit, and the nature of the testimony they give.

In default of written evidence, men must have recourse to *viva voce* or parol testimony, which is the statement of living witnesses as to the facts in dispute. In general, this kind of evidence is sufficient to establish all the facts necessary to support an issue, unless in those cases where the law has wisely provided that such testimony should be in writing. These last cases are provided for in the statutes for the prevention of frauds and perjuries.

It is true, there is no necessary connection between the truth of the facts to which a witness bears testimony, and the testimony itself. Who can affirm that a thing is true because it has been testified to be so by a witness? The witness may have been mistaken, or he

(*a*) For the form and style of depositions, see Greenl. Eq. Ev. 77.
(*b*) Dwight *v.* Linton, 3 Rob. Lewis, R. 57.

may desire to deceive. The testimony of men, then, may deceive us, and sometimes it does so. We are, nevertheless, obliged to have recourse to it, because we can know those things which pass, not within us, only from our senses, by the testimony of men, or by analogy; that is, by the induction which we make from a known fact, that another, which is unknown, is true.

When we are called upon to rely on the testimony of another in order to form a judgment as to certain facts, our belief is founded on a double presumption. We presume on the good sense and intelligence of the witnesses, that they have not been mistaken nor deceived; we presume on their probity, that they do not want to deceive us.

In order to confide in the testimony of men and to give credit to what they say, we must therefore ascertain:

1. That the witness has not been mistaken, and that he has not been deceived.

2. That he does not wish to deceive.

To be assured of this as much as possible, it is requisite to consider three things in relation to parol evidence: 1, the quality of the facts to be proved; 2, the quality and persons of the witnesses; 3, the testimony of itself, as compared with other known facts.

(1.) *Of the quality of the facts to be proved.*

3154. The facts to be proved are either possible or impossible, ordinary and probable, or extraordinary and improbable, recent or ancient; they may have passed or happened afar off or near us; they may be particular or public, permanent or transitory, clear and simple, or complicated; finally, they are almost always accompanied by circumstances which influence us more or less as to the judgment we are to adopt respecting them. All these things must be carefully examined in order to form a judgment of the merits of the testi-

OF PROCEEDINGS IN AN ACTION.   421

No 3155.   Book 4, tit. 8, chap. 11, sec. 3, § 3, div. 1, art. 3.   No. 3155.

mony, or of the degree of confidence to which it is entitled.

If the fact is impossible, the witness who would attest to it is not worthy of credit. Reason, and all the authors who have treated of the matter, teach us that the possibility of the fact attested, is the first, the most indispensable circumstance to induce us to have confidence in it. If, for example, a witness should swear he saw a man shoot himself by discharging in his head the contents of a pistol which he held in his hand, and that he thus killed himself; and upon an examination it should be found that the ball was so large that it could not enter into the barrel of the pistol; it is evident, in such case, that however respect- able the witness might be, however intelligent, and however positive, still he ought not to be believed;(a) or, if one should swear and testify that another has been guilty of the impossible crime of witchcraft.

When the facts are not of themselves impossible, there may still be an impossibility created by time and circumstances, at least they may show such an impossibility, that it would be absurd to give any confidence to a witness who would testify as to them.(b)

It is not necessary that facts should be impossible to destroy all confidence in the testimony of the witnesses; their improbability may be such as to render their belief impossible; but the degrees of probability are so difficult to ascertain, their shades so hard to find out, they vary in so many ways, and this difference is derived from so many causes, that it is impossible to give rules on this important point; even examples might give but an uncertain, a feeble, or perhaps a deceitful light.

3155. The time and the place where the facts have happened, may have much influence on the faith which

(a) 1 Stark. Ev. 505.
(b) See a striking example of this in Bouv. L. D. Circumstances.

ought to be given to the testimony of the witnesses. When the facts are recent, if they have happened where the witnesses are examined, or in its neighborhood, the testimony of the witnesses deserves more confidence; because they would feel a greater indisposition to disguise the truth, when they knew they could be contradicted by ocular witnesses, than they would be if they could not be so contradicted. This salutary influence diminishes in proportion to the length of time since the happening of the facts, and in the proportion of the distances when they took place. Besides the memory of men is the less to be relied upon, when the facts are of an ancient date. How then can we confide in it, when, in addition to this frailty or want of memory, the witness has an interest in disguising the truth?

3156. Whatever may be the facts in other respects, they are transitory or permanent. *Permanent facts* are those which continue to exist, and of which we may be assured at any time; as, where a man describes that a contract was made, or a murder committed in a particular room of a house, and that one of the contracting parties or the murderer entered by one of two doors on the south side of the room; here the fact that there are two southern doors is a permanent fact, whether the party entered by that door is a transitory fact. The facility with which the truth may be ascertained as to their testimony, makes the witnesses more cautious and circumspect, and induces others to place more reliance on what they say.

Transitory facts, on the contrary, which have existed but one instant, are to be credited with more caution, because not being capable of being tested by themselves, we must exclusively rely upon the report of others; the shorter their duration, the more liable has the witness been to be mistaken, and the more readily may he have been deceived.

3157. Facts happen either in public or in private.

When facts happen publicly, and can be testified to by many persons, the witness is more circumspect in giving his testimony, with all the circumstances attending it, because his testimony might be criticised by his neighbors. There must be strong motives indeed, to induce a man in such a situation to betray the truth. On the contrary, when the facts are represented as having happened in secret, or only before the witness, he is freed from all human restraint; he may with impunity, alter, disguise, or conceal the truth, without fear of contradiction.

(2.) *Of the quality and persons of the witnesses.*

3158. Let us next examine the precautions required to assure us, as far as possible, that the witness has neither been mistaken, nor desirous to deceive us; that he knows the truth, and does not wish to disguise it.

The most important consideration is doubtless to be certain he knows the facts; but the facts are not capable of demonstration, and are known only through the senses. It is then impossible to know a fact without having been present when it happened, and having seen it; for a man may be present without seeing what has happened; and in order to testify to it properly, he must have given attention to the circumstances, and fixed them in his memory. This is what is presumed of a witness who has been present at a transaction; for when he has merely heard of it from another, his testimony is mere hearsay, which, we have seen, is deserving of no weight, except in special cases.

No one will deny that the sense of hearing is infinitely more deceptive than that of sight; for, although there are facts which are more properly observed and known by hearing, as in cases of slander, seditious cries, and the like, yet it is very easy for the most honest witness, who is guided by the sense of hearing alone, to be mistaken in his judgment, as to the author of such slander. The experience of ages proves how little confidence ought to be placed in testimony of a fact, the knowledge of which is acquired alone by hearing.

It is certain that when a witness has acquired his knowledge of facts by more senses than one, he is entitled to more confidence than if he had acquired them by hearing alone. If, therefore, the witness has only heard the voice of the slanderer, without seeing him, he may easily be mistaken. The voice of a man, his accent, are liable to many alterations and variations, according to the passions which agitate him; according to his health, whether it is good or bad ; according to the circumstance of the fact that he was at a greater or less distance from the scene of action, and according to the nature of the obstacles which prevent us from seeing him whose voice we think we hear, it is very easy to be mistaken. But the testimony of such witness, acquires much force by other circumstances ; if, for example, after hearing the voice of one whom he takes to be Peter, he repairs to the place whence the sounds issued, and he there sees Peter, it is clear his testimony deserves much greater consideration.

Hearsay, we have seen, is not, in general, deserving of credit or confidence ; this seems to be the received opinion of civilians, canonists, and common lawyers, who in this respect perfectly agree with reason. The civilians divide witnesses into two classes. 1st. Those who depose of their own knowledge, *ex scientiâ*, who have acquired the knowledge of a fact by their own senses, by sight or hearing. This is the kind of testimony which the law requires. 2d. The second class of witnesses consists of those who depose upon the faith of others, *testes de credulitate*, who depose as to their belief, because they have heard the fact reported by others. They are generally unworthy of credit.

A witness is called to depose what he *knows*, not

what he *believes*.(*a*)   To know and to believe are very different things; belief is founded upon probable conjectures; knowledge is based upon that certainty which we acquire by our senses or by reason.   He who has neither seen nor heard the facts can only believe them, he cannot know them.

One of the surest means to induce a belief that the witness has a sufficient knowledge of the facts, is a detail of the circumstances; for little or no reliance can be placed on the bare assertion that such a fact is so.   This dryness in his deposition naturally induces a belief, that he has not given a sufficient attention to the facts, or that he wants memory, or that he desires to conceal some important circumstances.   A full detail of circumstances generally proves that the testimony is true, when they naturally agree with it, or that it is false, when they are not in unison with it.

The manner in which a witness deposes, inspires confidence or distrust; if his testimony is not conceived in affirmative terms, as where he says, *It may be, it seems to me, if I remember, if I am not mistaken,* and the like, he will not be credited as if he were firmly, and without any real or apparent prejudice, to state distinctly that the facts are in a particular way.(*b*) These dubitative formula, and all similar manner of speaking, which exclude certainty, weaken, and may even destroy the confidence which might otherwise be bestowed on the testimony of the witness who uses them.   Such testimony is not the less discredited because the witness says he *believes* the statement which he makes.   In general, it is not what he *believes*, but what he *knows* of his certain knowledge, which is asked of the witness.

(*a*) In some cases, a witness may give an opinion, or state his belief. Vide post. n. 3212.

(*b*) If the witness manifests any bias, his testimony will be suspected, though perhaps it may not be entirely rejected.   Newton *v.* Pope, 1 Cow. 109 ; Cook *v.* Miller, 6 Watts, 507.

He not only ought to know the facts about which he deposes, but he ought also to give the reasons of his knowledge: *Debet reddere rationem scientiæ suæ;* otherwise no reliance can be placed on his testimony. It is not sufficient that the witness gives a reason for what he says; that reason ought to have the appearance of truth. He must tell what he has seen, and not the consequences which he draws from them.

But it is not sufficient to be assured, as much as possible, of the knowledge of the witness, that he knows the facts and that he has not been mistaken; we must also be certain of his veracity, that is, that he does not wish to deceive, or betray the truth, nor conceal, or disguise it. It is in this particularly that uncertainty consists in parol evidence; and on this point, though in general they answer a good purpose, the precautions which reason points out, and the rules which the law has adopted, have still been found, in many cases, insufficient, and not very certain in their practical operation; so that in fact the most positive testimony is nothing but a probability.

Too much care cannot be taken to insure the veracity of the witnesses; hence the law requires that they shall testify under oath or affirmation to tell the truth, the whole truth, and nothing but the truth. For although the law requires of a witness who comes to testify in a court of justice that he shall tell the truth, and although his tacit promise to do so, be as obligatory upon him as if he made an express promise, yet his oath is not the less required. It considers it proper to recall to men their duties when they are called upon to perform them, and requires a person to promise to tell the truth at the moment he is about to be examined as a witness.

It seldom happens that men wish to deceive without some interest, some motive, or some moral defect; we, therefore, may well believe from analogy, that the witness will tell the truth, unless he is seduced from his duty by some sinister motive, or the want of some moral ability. To obviate this, the law has wisely excluded from examination all persons who are incompetent, though they may be credible. A distinction is made between *competency* and *credibility*. By the former is meant the legal ability of a witness to be heard as such in the trial of a cause; by the latter is understood one who is worthy of belief. Incompetent witnesses are persons, who, 1, want understanding; 2, have an interest in the matter in dispute; 3, cannot be admitted without violating the policy of the law; 4, have no religious belief; 5, have become infamous.

1st. Of the persons who want understanding.

3159. As the delivery of testimony is an act of the mind, it is clear that persons who want understanding cannot be examined as witnesses; a witness is to depose to facts he knows, and if he has no understanding he cannot know them. There are two classes of persons who want understanding.

3160.—1. *Infants.* A child is presumed incapable to be examined as a witness until he has attained his fourteenth year, and he cannot be examined as a witness until his capacity is shown, which may be by an examination in court. Doubtless many children under that age are capable of testifying in such a manner that reliance may be placed in their testimony, but still it will be received with caution.(*a*) When the witness is over fourteen, he may be sworn without a previous examination.(*b*)

3161.—2. *Idiots and lunatics.* It will be remembered that we defined idiocy to be a condition of mind in which the reflective powers are either entirely wanting, or are manifested to the least possible extent.

(*a*) 2 Tenn. R. 80.
(*b*) Den *v.* Vancleve, 2 South. 589, 652.

428 · OF REMEDIES.

No. 3162.   Book 4, tit. 8, chap. 11, sec. 3, § 3, div. 1, art. 3.   No 3163.

This state, it is evident, excludes the idea that an idiot understands what he has seen, or that he can convey such knowledge to others. He is *non compos mentis*, which is the generic name for all persons of unsound mind; it includes all species of madness, whether such madness arises from sickness, idiocy, lunacy or drunkenness. All persons *non compos mentis* are therefore incompetent as witnesses. And a person intoxicated is incapable of telling a straight story on which reliance can be placed, notwithstanding the maxim *in vino veritas.(a)*

2dly. Of persons who have an interest in the matter in issue.

3162. It seldom happens that a man desires to deceive when he is examined as a witness; we may, then, reason from analogy that a witness called to testify to facts in a court of justice, will tell the truth, unless he has an interest to betray it. But the same analogy which induces us to give a man credit for truth, when he has no interest, is a reason to believe he will not adhere to it, when his interest is against it. This judgment, founded on a simple analogy, has nothing in it on which we can rely as certain. Because a man who has an interest has falsified the truth, it is no reason that another should do the same thing; but in a doubtful case we must look at probabilities and presumptions; when the witness is in a condition which renders him suspected, we can have no reliance in him. When known motives raise reasonable suspicions against him, he is excluded.

3163. The interest which excludes a person from being a witness may be considered with regard to the *thing* or subject in dispute; the *quantity* of the interest; the *quality* of the interest; when the interest must *exist;* how an interested witness may be *rendered competent.*

(a) See Ray, Med. Jur. c. 22, § 300 to 311.

3164.—1. The bias or interest which excludes a person from being examined as a witness, must relate to the *thing* or subject in dispute. To be disqualified on this ground, the witness must gain or lose by the *event of the cause*, or the verdict must be lawful evidence *for or against him* in another suit, or the record must be an instrument of evidence for or against him;(*a*) but an interest in the *question* does not disqualify the witness.(*b*)

3165.—2. The *magnitude* of the interest is altogether immaterial; even a liability for the most trifling costs will create a sufficient disqualification.(*c*)

3166.—3. With regard to its *quality*, the interest must be *legal*, as contradistinguished from mere prejudice or bias, arising from relationship, friendship, or any of the numerous motives by which a witness may be supposed to be influenced.(*d*) It must also be a present, certain, vested interest, and not uncertain and contingent.(*e*) Whether a person who believes himself interested when he is not, is a competent witness, is a doubtful question.(*f*)

3167.—4. To disqualify a witness, the interest must *exist* at the time of the examination. The general rule seems to be that where a person is entitled to the

---

(*a*) Evans *v.* Eaton, 7 Wheat. 356 ; Evans *v.* Hettick, 7 Wheat. 453 ; Ness *v.* Van Swearingen, 7 S. & R. 192 ; Shirk *v.* Vanneman, 3 Yeates, 196 ; Gould *v.* James, 6 Cowen, 369 ; Henarie *v.* Maxwell, 5 Halst. 297 ; McGee *v.* Eastis, 5 Stew. & Port. 426 ; Wadham *v.* Turnpike Co., 10 Conn. 416 ; Page *v.* Weeks, 13 Mass. 199.

(*b*) Lewis *v.* Manley, 2 Yeates, 200 ; Ely *v.* Forward, 7 Mass. 25.

(*c*) Beach *v.* Swift, 2 Conn. 269: Scott *v.* McLellan, 2 Greenl. 199 ; Lowrey *v.* Summers, 7 Halst. 240

(*d*) Leach, 154 ; 2 Hawk. c. 46, s. 25.

(*e*) Ely *v.* Forward, 7 Mass. 25 ; Bean *v.* Bean, 12 Mass. 20 ; Lewis *v.* Manley, 2 Yeates, 200.

(*f*) The following cases are against the competency of the witness, namely: Plumb *v.* Whiting, 4 Mass. 518; Moore *v.* Hitchcock, 4 Wend. 292 ; Sentney *v.* Overton, 4 Bibb, 445 ; McVeaugh *v.* Goods, 4 Dall. 62. The cases in favor of competency are Long *v* Bailie, 4 S. & R. 222 ; Hanis *v.* Barkley, 4 Harper, 62 ; State *v.* Clark, 2 Tyler, 278 ; Fernsler *v.* Carlin, 3 S. & R. 130 ; Cassiday *v.* McKensie, 4 W. & S. 282.

testimony of another, the latter shall not be rendered incompetent to testify, where he has acquired such interest by the fraudulent act of the adverse party, for the purpose of preventing his testimony, or by any act of wantonness; but this would not prevent a witness in the regular course of trade from buying a claim or otherwise dealing, without fraud, and if then he became interested, he could not be examined, while he remained so.(a) If the witness had been examined, and his deposition was taken before he acquired the interest, his subsequent acquisition of it would not prevent the reading of his deposition in chancery, or on a trial at law, of an issue out of chancery.(b) It does not appear whether the rule applies with equal force with regard to reading, in trials at law, depositions of witnesses who afterward become interested.(c)

3168.—5. The *incompetency* arising from interest may be *removed* in various ways: first, by payment, for then the witness has no further interest;(d) secondly, the objection to incompetency may be removed by an extinguishment of that interest by a release, executed either by the witness when he would receive an advantage by his testimony, or by those who have a claim upon him, when his testimony would release him from his liability: and, in this case, he cannot refuse the release. Thirdly, although the witness may have an interest, if his interest is equally strong on the other side, he will be competent, for his interest is then said to be *balanced*. The witness is then reduced to a state

---

(a) Forrester v. Pigou, 3 Camp. 381 ; 1 Greenl. Ev. § 167, 168 ; Long v. Baillie, 4 S. & R. 222.

(b) Gresley on Ev. 267. See Gosse v. Tracy, 2 Vern. 698 ; Glyn v. Bank of England, 2 Ves. 42 ; Union Bank v. Knapp, 3 Pick. 108 ; 1 Smith's Ch. Pract. 344 ; Andrews v. Palmer, 1 V. & B. 21.

(c) Chess v. Chess, 17 S. & R. 412. See Wolfinger v. Fortman, 6 Penn. St. Rep. 294 ; Irwin v. Reed, 4 Yates, 512.

(d) Stark. Ev. part 4, p. 757.

of neutrality, by an equipoise of interest, and the objection to his testimony ceases.(*a*)

3169. In some instances the law admits the testimony of one interested, from the extreme necessity of the case; but these are exceptions to the general rule that interest renders a man incompetent. These exceptions are:

1. When a witness in a criminal case is entitled to a reward upon conviction of the offender. Although the witness may be entitled to a *reward* `from the government upon conviction of the offender; or to a restoration of the property stolen, as its owner; or to a portion of a fine, or penalty inflicted, still he is competent. This is allowed upon the ground of public policy, and to promote the public interest. The very statute which confers this benefit on the witness, who but for that statute, would have been a witness, virtually continues his competency.(*b*) When the reward is offered by a private person, the witness is still competent, on the ground that the public have an interest in his testimony, which cannot be taken away by the act of a private individual.(*c*)

2. When the witness would fall within the provisions of the rule, and would be excluded on the ground of interest, but he is made competent by statute. This frequently happens in relation to cases of petty convictions, when the informer is a competent witness by the provisions of the act inflicting the penalty.

3. Agents, carriers, factors, brokers, and other servants, when offered as witnesses, are competent, notwithstanding their interest, to prove the making of contracts, the receipt or payment of money, the receipt

---

(*a*) Cameron *v.* Paul, 6 Penn. St. R. 322; Ludlow *v.* The Union Insurance Company, 2 S. & R. 119.

(*b*) Gilb. Ev. 114; 1 Gilb. Ev. by Lloft, 245; Rex *v.* Williams, 9 B. & C. 549; 1 Phil. Ev. 92; United States *v.* Wilson, Bald. 78.

(*c*) 9 B. & C. 549.

or delivery of goods, and other acts within the scope of their employment;(*a*) and an agent can even prove his own authority, if it be by parol.(*b*)   But this privilege is confined to cases in the usual and ordinary course of business.

4. A witness may be competent, although interested, if his interest has been subsequently acquired by the fraudulent act of the opposite party.

3dly. Of persons who cannot be examined without violating the policy of
the law.

3170. It is against the policy of the law that persons holding certain relations with others should be examined as witnesses. These are, 1, husband and wife ; 2, party to a suit ; 3, attorneys ; 4, confessors ; 5, jurors ; 6, slaves ; 7, a party to a negotiable instrument.

3171.—1. *Husband and wife.* A party on the record is not a competent witness at common law; so neither is the husband or wife of the party competent to give evidence for or against the husband or wife.(*c*)   This rule is confined to this relation, no other is excluded ; a father and son, brothers and sisters, and the like, may be witnesses for each other, when not otherwise disqualified. The reason for excluding husband and wife from the witness box, and depriving them of the right to give evidence for or against each other, is founded partly on their identity of interest, and partly on a principle of public policy which deems it necessary to guard the security and confidence of private life, even at the risk of an occasional failure of justice. They cannot be witnesses for each other, because their interests are absolutely the same ; they are not witnesses against

---

(*a*) Barker *v.* Macrae, 3 Camp. 144 ; Scott *v.* Wells, 6 Watts & S. 357 ; Shepher *v.* Palmer, 6 Conn. 95 ; Hunter *v.* Leathley, 10 B. & C. 858.

(*b*) Lowber *v.* Shaw, 5 Mason, 242 ; McGunnagle *v.* Thornton, 10 S. & R. 251.

(*c*) Co. Litt. 6, b.

each other, because it is against the policy of marriage.(*a*)   This is the rule when either is a party in a civil suit or action ; but there is a distinction between these cases, and cases where neither is a party.

Where one of them, not being a party to the action, still is *interested in its result*, there is a distinction between giving evidence *for* or *against* each other.   It is an invariable rule that neither is a witness for the other, who is interested favorably in the result, and where the husband is disqualified by his interest, the wife is also incompetent.   On the other hand, where the interest of the husband, consisting in a civil liability, would not have protected him from examination, it seems that the wife must also answer, although the effect may be to subject her husband to an action. This case differs materially from those where the husband himself could not have been examined, either because he was a party or because he would criminate himself.(*b*)   The party to whom the testimony of the wife is essential, has a legal interest in her evidence ; and as he might insist on examining the husband, it would, it seems, be straining the rule too far to deprive him of the benefit of the wife's testimony.   In an action for goods sold and delivered, it has been held that a third person could prove that the credit was given not to the defendant, but to the husband of the witness.(*c*)

When neither of them is a party to the suit, nor interested in the general result, the husband or wife is, it seems, competent to prove any fact; for in *collateral proceedings*, when their interests are not immediately affected, they may testify, notwithstanding their evidence may tend to criminate or contradict the other,

(*a*) Co. Litt. 6, b ; Stein *v.* Bowman, 13 Pet. 223 ; Davis *v.* Dinwoody, 4 T. R. 678 ; Snyder *v.* Snyder, 6 Binn. 488 ; Corse *v.* Patterson, 6 Har. & John. 153.
(*b*) 1 Greenl. Ev. § 341.
(*c*) Williams *v.* Johnson, 1 Str. 504 ; B. N. P. 287.

434   OF REMEDIES.

No. 3172.   Book 4, tit. 8, chap. 11, sec. 3, § 3, div. 1, art 3.   No. 3173.

or may subject the other to a legal claim. The reason of this admission of evidence in such cases is, that the verdict in the action in which such witness testifies, cannot be used in an action against the other spouse; nor can such collateral proceedings, in a criminal case, affect the husband, although the testimony of the wife may criminate him, because such proceedings are *res inter alios acta.(a)*

3172. The rule that the husband and wife shall not be compelled to testify against each other, relates only to *lawful marriages*, or at least to such as are innocent in the eye of the law. A kept mistress is certainly not privileged, and she is a competent witness against the man by whom she is kept.(b) But cohabitation, and acknowledgment by each other as husband and wife, are in general conclusive between the parties, in all cases where the fact or incident of marriage, such as legitimacy or inheritance, are directly in controversy.(c)

As to the time when the relation of husband and wife commenced, it makes no difference; the principle of exclusion operates whenever the interests of either of them is directly concerned; and where a party married the witness of the other party, after she had been summoned to testify in court, she could not be examined.(d)

3173. When the relation has *ceased to exist*, the surviving husband or wife cannot be examined; when the representatives of the deceased spouse are parties to the suit, the survivor cannot be examined as a witness. The rule was established to secure domestic happiness, by sealing the mouths of the spouses in relation to con-

---

(a) Rex v. Bathwick, 2 B. & Adol. 639; Rex v. All Saints, 6 M. & S. 194; Henman v. Dickenson, 5 Bing. 183.
(b) Batthews v. Galindo, 4 Bing. 410.
(c) Campbell v. Twemlow, 1 Price, 81.
(d) Pedley v. Wellesley, 3 C. & P. 558.

OF PROCEEDINGS IN AN ACTION. 435

No. 3174.   Book 4, tit. 8, chap. 11, sec 3, § 3, div. 1, art. 3   No. 3174.

fidential communications between them.(a) But, as in the case of communications made to an attorney, when the wife derives the information from other sources, she is no longer protected, notwithstanding they related to transactions with her husband.(b)

3174. The rule that the husband and wife shall not be examined for or against each other, extends to criminal as well as to civil cases. But it is subject to various exceptions:

1. When her testimony is requisite to secure her from injuries from her husband, as when she would otherwise be exposed to personal injuries, without any remedy; indeed, whenever an injury is committed by husband and wife against each other, the injured party is admissible against the other,(c) on the ground of necessity.

2. On the same ground of necessity, a wife is admitted as a witness to testify to *secret facts*, which none but herself could know; as in the case of an appeal against an order of filiation, in the case of a married woman, she was held competent to prove her criminal connection with the defendant, though the husband was interested in the event,(d) but she cannot prove the non-access of her husband.(e)

3. In cases of high treason, the question does not appear to be well settled whether a wife is compellable or is competent to testify against her husband.(f)

4. The dying declarations of either are admissible,

(a) Stein v. Bowman, 13 Pet. 223; Monroe v. Twistleton, Peake's Ev. App. lxxxvii.; Aveson v. Kinnaird, 6 East, 192.

(b) Welles v. Tucker, 3 Binn. 366; Coffin v. Jones, 13 Pick. 445; Williams v. Baldwin, 7 Verm. 506.

(c) 1 East, P. C. 455; 2 Hawk. P. C. ch. 46, § 77; 2 Lewin, Cr. Cas. 287; 2 Yeates, 114.

(d) Commonwealth v. Shepherd, 6 Binn. 283; Rex v. Reading, Cas. temp. Hard. 79; Rex v. Luffe, 8 East, 193.

(e) Cope v. Cope, 1 M. & Rob. 260; Goodright v. Moss, Cowp. 594; Bouv. L. D. Access and Paternity.

(f) 2 Russ. on Crimes, 607; B. N. P. 286; 2 Stark. Ev. 404; 1 Greenl. Ev. § 345.

when the party is charged with the murder of the deceased.(a)

3175.—2. *Party to a suit.* A party to a suit cannot in general be examined as a witness. This rule had been established by reason and common sense, before it was sanctioned by the courts : *nullus idoneus testis in re suâ.(b)* It is subject to the following exceptions :

1. By the common law there are few instances in which the party's oath *in litem* will be admitted. This is allowed in those cases where the courts administer justice according to the course of the Roman law. The oath *in litem* is admitted in two classes of cases ; first, when it has been proved that the party against whom it is offered has been guilty of some fraud, or of some other tortious act of intermeddling with the complainant's goods, and no other evidence can be had of the amount of the damages ;(c) and secondly, when on grounds of public policy, it is essential to the purposes of justice. Example, under the first head, is the case of a bailiff, who, in the service of an execution, discovered a sum of money hidden in a wall, took it away and embezzled it, and greatly injured the goods of the defendant ; in an action brought against him by the person injured,

---

(a) Stoop's case, Addis. 381 ; People *v.* Green, 1 Denio, 614.
(b) Dig. 22, 5, 9.
(c) Tait on Ev. 280 ; 1 Greenl Ev. § 348. According to the Roman law, this oath was deferred by the judge to the plaintiff, in relation to the value of the thing which was the subject of the suit, whenever the defendant, contrary to the order of the judge, or by fraud, did not restore the thing sued for on the demand of the plaintiff, or fraudulently prevented its restoration. Thus it was a contravention of the order of the judge and the fraud of the party which gave rise to this oath. Dig. lib. 12, t. 3, 1. 3 et 5, § 4 ; Code lib. 5, t. 53. This oath was principally used in *bonâ fide* actions, as in the case of loan, called *commodatum,* deposit, the action for the restitution of dowry, the action by a pupil for the restitution of the things belonging to the pupilage, in arbitrary actions, real and personal. Dig. lib 6, t. 1, 1. 68 ; and lib. 12, t. 3, 1. 5. The plaintiff was allowed to estimate the thing in question, under his oath, at such price as he deemed right, subject, however, to some restrictions imposed upon him by the judge. Dig. 12, 3, 4. In case of theft, the oath of estimation was that the thing was worth a certain sum when stolen. Dig. 12, 3, 9.

the plaintiff was allowed to swear as to the damages he had sustained.(a) So, where a shipmaster received a trunk of goods on board of his vessel, and fraudulently broke it open and rifled it of its contents, on proof being made, aliundè, of the delivery of the trunk, the plaintiff was allowed to prove its contents ;(b) and, in imitation of the Roman law, a bailor, though plaintiff, was admitted as competent to prove the contents of a trunk, lost by the negligence of the bailee.(c) The grounds upon which this evidence is admitted are precisely the same as those of the Roman law, the fraud or wrong of the defendant and the necessity of the case.(d)

2. When the facts, from their nature, are likely to be known only to the party. Before he is admitted to testify as to them, a foundation must, however, be first laid for the party's oath, by proving the other facts of the case down to the time to which the party is to speak ; as when a written instrument of evidence is lost, it must first be proved, aliundè, that such instrument existed ; after which, if it was lost out of the custody of the party, his oath will be admitted to prove its loss and the circumstances attending it.(e) And in collateral matters which do not involve the matter in controversy, but which are auxiliary to the trial, and such matters as are addressed to the court on preliminary questions, as affidavits of the materiality of a witness, of diligent search being made for him or for a paper, of the death of a subscribing witness, and the like.

3. There is another class of cases in which, on

(a) Childrens v. Saxby, 1 Vern. 207.
(b) Herman v. Drinkwater, 1 Greenl. R. 27.
(c) Clark v. Spence, 10 Watts, 335 ; David v. Moore, 2 W. & S. 220. See Sneider v. Geiss, 1 Yeates. 34 ; Bingham v. Rogers, 6 W. & S. 495 ; E. Ind. Co. v. Evans, 1 Vern. 308.
(d) See the reasoning of Rogers, J., in Cook v. Spence, 10 Watts, 336, 337.
(e) Riggs v. Taylor, 9 Wheat. 486 ; Tayloe v. Riggs, 1 Pet. 591. Note 122 of Cowen and Hill's notes to 1 Phil. Ev. 69.

438 OF REMEDIES.

No 3175   Book 4, tit 8, chap 11, sec 3, § 3, div. 1, art. 3.   No. 3175.

grounds of public necessity or expediency, the oath *in litem* is allowed; as where a statute can receive no execution, unless a party who is interested be admitted as a witness.(*a*)

4. In equity, the answer of the defendant to a bill filed by the complainant, so far as it is strictly responsive to the bill, is evidence in his favor as well as against him.

5. When the situation of one of the parties has changed since the commencement of the suit, as where there were several persons in the same suit, and some of the defendants have been discharged by *nolle prosequi*, or changed by default, or by verdict. In *contracts*, when one of several defendants has suffered judgment by default, he may be examined by the plaintiff against the others.(*b*) And if the defence in such case goes merely to the personal discharge of the party pleading it, and not to that of the others, the plaintiff may enter a *nolle prosequi* as to him, and then, being no longer a party on record, he may be examined as a witness, if otherwise competent; as where one of the defendants pleads bankruptcy, and a *nolle prosequi* is entered.(*c*) When the action is founded on a *tort*, the liability of the defendants is joint, and 'as there is no contribution among wrong doers, witnesses are not to be excluded because the plaintiff has joined them with other defendants; and if the suit as to any of them is determined, he has no longer any interest in the event of the suit, and he is competent for the others, when his testimony cannot directly make for himself. When a witness has been joined with the others as defendant, for the purpose of excluding his testimony, the court will direct the jury to find a separate verdict in his favor, where there is no evidence in

---

(*a*) United States *v.* Murphey, 16 Pet. 203.
(*b*) Pipe *v.* Steel. 2 Ad. & El. 733, N. S.
(*c*) 1 Saund. 207, a.

OF PROCEEDINGS IN AN ACTION.   439

No. 3176.   Book 4, tit. 8, chap 11, sec. 3, § 3, div. 1, art. 3.   No. 3177.

the cause against him, for in that case he appears to
have been joined through the fraud and artifice of the
plaintiffs; and the acquittal in such case may take
place in the course of the cause, and before the other -
defendants have closed their defence.

3176.—3. *Attorneys.* To enable parties to actions
to consult legal advisers with safety, it is an established
rule that the confidential counsellor, solicitor or attorney of the party, cannot be compelled to disclose communications made to him as such, nor give up papers
delivered to him, nor letters sent to him, nor entries
he has made in that capacity. In order that a communication may be protected, it must have been made
to some *person* who possessed the character of counsel,
attorney, or solicitor, acting for the time being as the
legal adviser of the party; and this privilege extends
to all the necessary organs of communication between
the attorney and the client, and, for this reason, an
interpreter and an agent are considered as standing in
the situation of the attorney himself.(a)   The *purpose*
of the professional advice must be where the party
seeks aid upon the subject of his rights or liabilities.
There may have been no suit began or contemplated,
expected, or apprehended.(b)

3177. Some cases have been mentioned as exceptions to the rule that a legal adviser cannot disclose
what has been confidentially communicated to him;
but if they are properly considered, they will be found
not to come within the rule. The following are
examples of these cases:

1. When the attorney is himself a party to the
transaction, and especially if he were party to a fraud,

(a) Andrews *v.* Solomon, 1 Pet. C. C. 356 ; Jackson *v.* French, 3 Wend.
337 ; Parker *v.* Carter, 4 Munf. 273; Parkins *v.* Hawkshaw, 2 Stark. R.
239.   See a well written article in 17 Am. Jur. 304, where the author com-
bats, with much force, this received doctrine of the law.
(b) Greenough *v.* Gaskell, 1 M. & K. 102.

440   OF REMEDIES.

No. 3178.   Book 4, tit. 8, chap. 11, sec. 3, § 3, div. 1, art. 3.   No. 3179.

for, in that case, he would not acquire his knowledge professionally.

2. When the communication was made *before* the attorney was employed as such, or *after* his employment had ceased.(*a*)

3. Where, though consulted· as a friend, because he was an attorney, yet he refused to act as such, and was therefore consulted only as a friend.(*b*)

4. Where the matter communicated was not in its nature private, and could not be considered as a confidential disclosure; as where the defendant gave in- struction to his attorney what to plead.(*c*)

5. When the thing had no reference to the professional employment, though disclosed while the relation of attorney and client subsisted.(*d*)

6. When the attorney becomes an attesting witness, and thereby assumes another character for the occasion, then he is bound to give testimony as any other subscribing witness.(*e*)

3178.—4. *Confessors.* As a general rule, communications made by a person accused of crime, for the purpose of unburdening his conscience, made to a confessor, are not protected, and must be disclosed.(*f*)

3179.—5. *Medical persons.·* By the common law, those persons who have acquired knowledge of facts in families, in consequence of their being employed in their profession, are not protected from testifying; but in some states this protection is extended to them.(*g*)

(*a*) Cuts *v.* Pickering, 1 Ventr. 197 ; Vaillant *v.* Dodemead, 2 Atk. 524 ; Cobden *v.* Kendrick, 4 T. R. 431 ; Jackson *v.* McVay, 18 John. 330 ; Yor- dan *v.* Hess, 13 John. 494.

(*b*) Wilson *v.* Rastall, 4 T. R. 753 ; Hoffman *v.* Smith, 1 Caines, R. 157.

(*c*) Cormier *v.* Richard, 7 N. S. 179.

(*d*) Du Barre, etc., Peake's R. 97 ; Riggs *v.* Denniston, 3 John. Cases, 198.

(*e*) Mackensie *v.* Yeo, 2 Curt. Ecc. R. 866.

(*f*) In New York and Missouri, such communications are protected by statute. See Broad *v.* Pitt, 3 C. & P. 518 ; Joy on Conf. 49—58.

(*g*) Duchess of Kingston's,case, 11 Harg. St. Tr. 243 ; 20 Howell's St. Tr. 613 ; 3 C. & P. 518 ; Rex *v.* Gibbons, 1 C. & P. 97. By statute in New York and Missouri, " no person duly authorized to practice physic or

OF PROCEEDINGS IN AN ACTION. 441

No. 3180.   Book 4, tit. 8, chap. 11, sec. 3, § 3, div. 1, art. 3.   No. 3181.

3180.—6. *Jurors.*—1st. *Grand jurors* cannot be examined in usual cases, as to what they have learned in that capacity. This privilege does not extend beyond the votes given by them in any case ; the evidence delivered by the witnesses to them, and this is with a qualification mentioned below; and to the communications of the jurors with each other.(*a*) But they may be required to state whether a particular person testified before the grand jury.(*b*) The duration of the secrecy appears not to be definitely settled, but this injunction is to remain as long as the circumstances of each case and the public good require. In a case, for example, where a witness swears to a fact in open court, on the trial, directly in opposition to what he swore before the grand jury, there can be no doubt that the injunction of secrecy, as far as regards this evidence, would be at an end, and the grand juror might be sworn and examined as to what the witness testified in the grand jury room, in order that the witness might be prosecuted for perjury.(*c*)

2dly. *Traverse jurors* are excluded on the same ground of public policy, when offered to prove misbehavior in the jury in regard to the verdict.(*d*)

3181.—7. *Slaves.* It is said that a slave could not be a witness at common law, because of the unbounded

---

surgery, shall be allowed to disclose any information which he may have acquired in attending any patient in a professional character, and which information was necessary to enable him to prescribe for such patient as a physician, or to do any act for him as a surgeon:" This statute being passed for the benefit of the patient, he may waive its advantages. Johnson *v.* Johnson, 14 Wend. 637. See Hewit *v.* Prime, 21 Wend. 79, as to the extent of the protection, The French Code Pénal, art. 378, punishes medical persons who reveal secrets confided to them as such, except in cases where the law requires them to denounce criminals.

(*a*) Sykes *v.* Dunbar, 2 Selw. N. P. 815 ; Huidekoper *v.* Cotton, 3 Watts, 56.

(*b*) Freeman *v.* Arkell, 1 C. & P. 135, 137, n.(*c.*)

(*c*) 2 Russ. Cr. 616 ; Low's case, 4 Greenl. 439. But see contra Imlay *v.* Rogers, 2 Halst. 347 ; 1 Car. & Kirw. 519. Vide post, n. 3219.

(*d*) Vaise *v.* Dalaval, 1 T R. 11 ; Little *v.* Larrabee, 2 Greenl. 37, 41, note, and the cases there cited.

influence his master had over him.(a)   By statutory provisions in all our southern states, slaves are excluded; in some, all Indians; and even free negroes are incompetent, whenever the rights of a white man are involved.(b)

3182.—8. A party to a *negotiable instrument*, it has been held, is not allowed to give evidence to invalidate it, so as to show it to have been originally void; because no one who alleges his own turpitude ought to be heard: *Nemo, allegans suam turpitudinem, est audiendus*.(c) But this rule has been doubted, and the decisions in the several states of the Union are not uniform.(d)

(a) 4 Dall. 145, n. (1.) But see 1 St. Tr. 113; Macnally's Ev. 156.
(b) See 1 McCord, 43; 7 Monr. 91; 5 Litt. R. 171; 3 Har. & J. 97.
(c) This maxim does not invariably hold out to be true. A witness is competent to testify that his former oath was corruptly false. Rex v. Teal, 11 East, 309; Rands v. Thomas, 5 M. & S. 244.
(d) Professor Greenleaf, in his unrivalled treatise on the Law of Evidence, has collected most of the case in a note to § 385, in these words: "The rule, that the indorser of a negotiable security, negotiated before it was due, is not admissible as a witness to prove it originally void, when in the hands of an innocent indorsee, is sustained by the Supreme Court of the United States, in The Bank of the United States v. Dunn, 6 Peters, 51, 57, explained and confirmed in The Bank of the Metropolis v. Jones, 8 Peters, 12, and in the United States v. Leffler, 11 Peters, 86, 94, 95; Scott v. Lloyd, 12 Peters, 149; Taylor v. Luther, 2 Sumner, 235, per Story, J. It is also adopted in Massachusetts, Churchill v. Suter, 4 Mass. 156; Fox v. Whitney, 16 Mass. 118; Packard v. Richardson, 17 Mass. 122. See also the late case of Thayer v. Crossman, 1 Metcalf's R 416, in which the decisions are reviewed and the rule clearly stated and vindicated by Shaw, C. J. And in New Hampshire, Bryant v. Ritterbush, 2 N. Hamp. 212; Hadduck v. Wilmarth, 5 N. Hamp. 187. And in Maine, Deering v. Sawtell, 4 Greenl. 191; Chandler v. Morton, 5 Greenl. 374. And in Pennsylvania, O'Brien v. Davis, 6 Watts, 498; Harrisburg Bank v. Foster, 8 Watts, 304, 309. In Louisiana, the rule was stated and conceded by Porter, J., in Shamburg v. Commagere, 10 Martin, 18; and was again stated, but an opinion withheld, by Martin, J., in Cox v. Williams, 5 Martin, 139, N. S. In Vermont, the case of Jordaine v. Lashbrooke, was followed, in Nicols v. Holgate, 2 Aik. 138; but the decision is said to have been subsequently disapproved by all the judges, in Chandler v. Mason, 2 Verm. 198, and the rule in Walton v. Shelley approved. In Ohio, the indorser was admitted to prove facts *subsequent* to the indorsement; the court expressing no opinion upon the general rule, though it was relied upon by the opposing counsel. Stone v. Vance, 6 Ohio Rep. 246. In Mississippi, the witness was admitted for the same purpose; and the rule in Walton v. Shelly was approved. Drake v. Henly, Walker's R. 541. In Illinois, the indorser has

4thly. Of persons wanting religious principles.

3183. The next class of persons incompetent to testify consist of those, who, having no religious sentiment, cannot be bound by an oath, which we will presently see is an appeal to God, as the judge of the actions of men, and which necessarily presupposes his existence and power to reward him who avers the truth, or punish the hypocrite, who, under the pretence of telling the truth, states a falsehood.

3184. An *oath* is a declaration or promise made according to law, before a competent authority, to tell the truth; or it is the act of one, who, when lawfully required to tell the truth, takes God to witness that what he says is true. It is a religious act by which the party promises to man, and invokes God, not only to witness the truth and sincerity of his promise, but also to avenge his imposture or violated faith, or in other words to punish him for his perjury, if he shall be guilty of it.(*a*)   In an oath two things may be

been admitted, where, in taking the note, he acted as the agent of the indorsee, to whom he immediately transferred it, without any notice of the rule. Webster *v.* Vickers, 2 Scam. 295. But the rule of exclusion has been rejected, and the general doctrine of Jordaine *v.* Lashbrooke followed, in New York. Stafford *v.* Rice, 5 Cowen, 23 ; Bank of Utica *v.* Hillard, Ib. 153 ; Williams *v.* Walbridge, 3 Wend. 415. And in Virginia, Taylor *v.* Beck, 3 Randolph's R. 316. And in Connecticut, Townsend *v.* Bush, 1 Conn. 260. And in South Carolina, Knight *v.* Packard, 3 McCord, 71. And in Tennessee, Stump *v.* Napier, 2 Yerger, 35. In Maryland, it was rejected by three judges against two, in Ringgold *v.* Tyson, 3 H. & J. 172. It was also rejected in New Jersey, in Freeman *v.* Brittin, 2 Harrison, 192. And in North Carolina, Guy *v.* Hall, 3 Murphy, 151. And in Georgia, Slack *v.* Moss, Dudley, 161. And in Alabama, Todd *v.* Stafford, 1 Stew. 199 ; Griffing *v.* Harris, 9 Porter, 226. In Kentucky, in the case of Gorham *v.* Carrol, 3 Littel, 221, where the indorser was admitted as a witness, it is to be observed, that the note was indorsed without recourse to him, and thereby marked with suspicion ; and that the general rule was not considered. See further, 2 Stark. Evid. 179, note(A ;) 1 Phil. & Am. on Evid. p. 44 ; Cowen's note 78, and Suppt. ; Bayley on Bills, p. 586, note (b.) (Phillips and Sewall's Ed.) But each of these decisions against the rule in Walton *v.* Shelley, was made long before that rule was recognized, and adopted by the Supreme Court of the United States, except that in New Jersey, in which, however, the fact that the point had been settled in the highest national tribunal, does not appear to have been adverted to."
    (*a*) 1 Stark. Ev. 80; 1 Phil. Ev. 21; 1 Greenl. Ev. § 368; 10 Toull. n.

observed : 1, an invocation by which we take as witness the God of truth, who knows all things; and 2, the imprecation by which we ask him, as just and almighty, to avenge our perjury.(*a*)   This imprecation is either express or implied : "as you shall answer to God at the great- day," is in the express form; while it is implied in the usual formula, " so help you God."(*b*)

The oath is the means adopted by the most civilized nations to insure the engagement of the witness that he will tell the truth, and to confirm his testimony. It is an institution established as a precaution against the inconstancy or unfaithfulness of men, and to add, by the fear of divine punishment, to the other assurances which he from whom it is required cannot give, or which it would be unjust to ask of him.

The binding authority of an oath can exist only when the witness believes sincerely in a Supreme Being, who is "the rewarder of truth and avenger of falsehood."(*c*)   As to the *degree* of religious faith required, it is now settled that when the witness believes in a God who will reward or punish even in

---

343 ; Puff. book 4, c. 2, s. 4 ; Grot. book 2, c. 3, s. 1 ; Ruth. Inst.- book 1, c. 14, s. 1 ; Merl. Répert. Convention ; Dalloz, Dict. Serment; Dur. Dr. Tr. n. 592, 593.

(*a*) Omichund *v.* Baker, 1 Atk. 48 : Bentham, 1 Rat. of Jud. Ev. 366, has, in very forcible language. combatted the propriety of this part of an oath.   He says, " The supposition of its efficacy is absurd in principle.   It ascribes to man a power over his Maker; it places the Almighty in the station of a sheriff's officer ; it places him under the command of every justice of the peace.   It supposes him to stand engaged, no matter how, but absolutely engaged, to inflict on every individual, by whom the ceremony, after having been performed. has been profaned, a punishment, no matter what, which. but for the ceremony and the profanation, he would not have inflicted."   He condemns, as impious, the exercise or use of this power.   He further says, p. 371, note, " The power which leaves Omnipotence no alternative, is a power which any and every individual in the state, who is rash enough and foolish enough, may exercise at any time, and any number of times, at pleasure, on so simple a condition as that of getting a justice of the peace to join in the performance of the instantaneous ceremony."

(*b*) The form of the several kinds of oaths will be found in another place.

(*c*) 1 Atk. 48.

this world, he is competent.(a)   A want of this belief renders him incompetent. Every man is presumed to believe in God, and he who opposes a witness on the ground of his unbelief is bound to prove it. No man can be questioned as to his belief, and if he chooses not to disclose it, it cannot be inquired into; but when he divulges it, the fact that he has done so, may be proved like any other fact. A witness' belief may, therefore, be proved by showing his previous declarations and avowed opinions; and when he has avowed himself to be an infidel,(b) he may show a reform of his conduct, and change of his opinions since the declarations proved; when the declaration has been made for a considerable space of time, slight proof will suffice to show a change of opinion.(c)

5th. Of infamous persons.

3185. The fifth class of those who are incompetent as witnesses consists of *infamous persons.* By infamy is understood the state which is produced by the conviction of crime, and the loss of honor, which renders the infamous person incompetent as a witness. Infamy will be considered with regard to, 1, the crimes or punishments which incapacitate a witness; 2, the proof of the guilt; 3, the removal of the infamy; 4, its effect.

(*i.*) The crimes and punishments which are infamous.

3186. When a man is convicted of an offence which is inconsistent with the common principles of honesty and humanity, the law considers his oath as of no

---

(a) Ormichund v. Baker, Willes, 545 ; S. C. 1 Atk. 21 ; Wakefield v. Ross, 5 Mason, 18 ; 4 Phil. Ev. by Cowen & Hill, p. 1503.
(b) As to who is to be considered an infidel, see Bouv. L. D. h. t.
(c) Jackson ex dem. Tuttle v. Gridley, 18 John. 103 ; 5 Mason 16 ; Norton v. Ladd. 4 N. H Rep. 444 ; Easterday v. Kilburn, 1 Wright, 345 ; Attwood v. Wilton, 7 Conn. 66 : Curtis v. Strong, 4 Day, 51.

446 OF REMEDIES.

No. 3187.   Book 4, tit. 8, chap. 11, sec. 3, § 3, div. 1, art. 3   No 3187.

weight, and excludes his testimony, as of too doubtful and suspicious a nature, to be admitted in a court of justice, to deprive another of life, liberty or property.(*a*)   The crimes which render a person incompetent, when he has been lawfully convicted of them, are treason, felony, and all offences founded in fraud, which come within the notion of the *crimen falsi* of the Roman law,(*b*) as perjury, and subornation of perjury ;(*c*) suppression of testimony by bribery, or conspiracy to procure the absence of a witness;(*d*) conspiracy to accuse one of a crime, or to defraud him of his property ; forgery ;(*e*) barratry ;(*f*) piracy ;(*g*) swindling and cheating.(*h*)   It is the crime and not the punishment which renders the offender unworthy of credit.(*i*)

(*u*.) The proof of the guilt.

3187. Every man is presumed innocent until he is proved guilty.   In order to incapacitate the witness,

---

(*a*) Gilb. Ev. by Lofft, 256 ; Bull. N. P. 291; 1 Phil. Ev. 23.
(*b*) Leach, 496.   The extent of the *crimen falsi* is nowhere laid down with precision in the common law.   It includes all the offences mentioned in the text, and perhaps more. 1 Dods. R. 191.   In the Roman law, from which the term has been borrowed, it included every species of fraud and deceit.   Co. 9, 22 ; Dig. 48, 10 ; Hein. in Pand. pars vii. § 214–218 ; Merl. Répert. verbo Faux.   Toullier says, " Le faux, disent les criminalistes, s'entend de trois manières: dans le sens le plus étendu, c'est l'altération de la vérité, avec ou sans mauvaise intention ; il est à peu prés synonyme de mensonge ; dans un sens moins étendu, c'est l'altération de la vérité, accompagnée de dol, *mutatio veritatis cum dolo facta;* enfin, dans le sens étroit, ou plutôt légal du mot, quand il s'agit de savoir si le faux est un crime, le faux est l'altération frauduleuse de la vérité, dans les cas determinés, et punis par la loi."   Tom. 9, n. 188.   The common law has not used the term in this extensive sense when applying it to the qualification of witnesses, because convictions for many offences belonging to the *crimen falsi* of the Roman law, have not this effect.   Greenl. Ev. § 373.
(*c*) Co. Litt. 6 b.
(*d*) Bushell *v.* Barrett, Ry. & Mo. 434 : Clancey's case, Fortesc. 208.
(*e*) Rex *v.* Davis, 5 Mod. 74.
(*f*) Rex *v.* Ford, 2 Salk. 690.
(*g*) 2 Roll. Ab. 886.
(*h*) Fortesc. 209.
(*i*) 1 Phil. Ev. 25.   But if the statute declare a crime *infamous*, this will render the criminal incompetent to testify.   Phil. & Am. on Ev. 18; 1 Phil. Ev. 18 ; 1 Gilb. Ev. by Lofft, 256,

OF PROCEEDINGS IN AN ACTION. 447

No. 3188.   Book 4, tit. 8, chap 11. sec 3, § 3, div. 1, art. 3.   No. 3188.

he must have been legally found guilty before a court of competent jurisdiction, and a judgment must have been pronounced against him; the finding of a jury is insufficient, because it may be arrested or set aside. The judgment, and that only, can be received as the legal and conclusive evidence of the party's guilt, for the purpose of rendering him incompetent to testify.(a)

According to the foreign jurists, the judgment of an infamous crime, passed by a foreign tribunal, is sufficient to disqualify a witness, because, as they maintain, the state or condition of a person in the place of his domicil accompanies him every where.(b) But it has been held that a conviction and sentence for a felony in one of the United States, did not render the convict incompetent as a witness, in the courts of another state; though it might be shown to discredit him.(c)

(iii.) The removal of the disability.

3188. This may be done in two ways: first, by pardon; and, secondly, by a reversal of the judgment of conviction.

1. The effect of the *pardon* is to restore the witness to competency, when the disability is a consequence of the judgment according to the principles of the common law; but when the disability is annexed by the express words of a statute, a pardon will not have this curative effect.(d) The pardon must be proved by producing the charter under the great seal.

2. The party convicted will, of course, be restored to competency by the *reversal of the judgment;* and

(a) Rex v. Castel Carcinion, 8 East, 77; The People v. Whipple, 9 Cowen, 707.
(b) Story, Confl. § 620, and the authorities there cited; Fœlix, Traité de Droit Intern. privé, § 31; Merlin, Répert. verbo Loi, § 6, n. 6.
(c) Commonwealth v. Green, 17 Mass. 515; The State v. Candler, 3 Hawks, 393. But see State v. Ridgley, 2 Har. & McH. 120; Cole's lessee v. Cole, 1 Har. & John. 572.
(d) 2 Harg. Jur. Arg. 221, et seq.; 2 Russ. on Cr. 595; 11 Am. Jur. 360.

448 OF REMEDIES.

No. 3189.   Book 4, tit. 8, chap. 11, sec. 3, § 3, div. 1, art. 3.   No. 3190.

when the record of the conviction has been produced, the reversal must be shown by the production of the record of reversal.

(*iv.*) Effect of the conviction of an infamous crime.

3189. The disability thus created is different, as it operates upon the witness, or upon third persons.

1. Its effect *upon the witness* is not such as to deprive him of making an affidavit necessary for his exculpation or defence, for the law will not leave him entirely remediless; but he cannot be heard as a complainant.(*a*)

2. In regard to *third persons*, his testimony is universally excluded; and if he had attested any instrument previous to his conviction, his handwriting must be proved as if he were dead.(*b*)

3° *Of the number of witnesses.*

3190. As a general rule, one witness is sufficient to establish a fact, but to this there are exceptions, both in civil and criminal cases :

1. In cases of treason, though the crime was considered as sufficiently proved by one witness, yet owing perhaps to the duty of allegiance, which is due by every one to the government, which was considered as equal to the testimony of one witness, and probably to protect the accused from being too lightly convicted, in times of excitement, by the testimony of one witness, two witnesses became necessary by the provision of a statute,(*c*) the principles of which have been incorporated in the constitution of the United States, in these words: "No person shall be convicted of treason, unless on the testimony of two witnesses to the same overt act, or on confession in open court."(*d*)

_____

(*a*) Rex *v.* Gardiner, 2 Burr. 1117 ; Walker *v.* Kearney, 2 Str. 1148 ; 2 Salk. 461.
(*b*) Jones *v.* Mason, 2 Str. 833.
(*c*) 5 & 6 Ed. VI., c. 11, more distinctly enacted by stat. 7 W. III., c. 3, s. 2.
(*d*) Art. 3, § 3.

2. In order to prove the crime of perjury, formerly two witnesses were requisite, because otherwise there would be oath against oath, that of the prisoner on the one side, and of the witness on the other. In modern times this rule has been relaxed, but still there must be evidence besides the oath of the prosecutor or his witness, to balance the weight of that of the prisoner, and the presumption of his innocence; this may be shown by circumstances, which, if they are not tantamount to another witness, have the effect of destroying the oath of the prisoner, so as to let the testimony of the witness who has been examined against him have its full weight, without any contradiction.(a)

3. Upon the same principle that two witnesses, or one witness and sufficient circumstances to destroy the oath of the prisoner, are required in cases of perjury, two witnesses, or circumstances requisite to balance the oath of a respondent, are required to an answer in chancery, when the answer is positively, clearly, and precisely responsive to any matter stated in the bill. By calling on the defendant to answer an allegation which he makes, the plaintiff admits the answer to be evidence, and before he can be entitled to a decree, he must remove the effect of such answer, and prove the fact by another witness.(b)

4. To prove the usage of trade, of which all dealers in that particular line are bound to take notice, two witnesses are required.(c)

Art. 4.—Of the effects of evidence.

3191. In the examination of this subject, it will be necessary to inquire into the effect of, 1, foreign judgments; 2, foreign laws; 3, parol evidence.

1. Foreign judgments.

3192. When treating of records we discussed the

(a) Woodbeck v. Killer, 6 Cow. 118; Champney's Cas. 2 Lew. Cr. Cas. 258.
(b) Gresley on Ev. 4 ; 1 Greenl. Ev. § 260.
(c) Wood v. Hickok, 2 Wend. 501 ; Parrott v. Thacher, 9 Pick, 426.

effect of judgments rendered in foreign countries, and those of the courts of sister states of the Union; the subject was so fully examined, that a further consideration of it here will not be requisite.(a)

2. *Foreign laws.*

3193. The effect of foreign laws, when proved, is properly referable to the court; the object of proof of foreign laws, is to enable the court to instruct the jury what is, in point of law, the result of foreign laws, to be applied to matters in controversy before them. The court is, therefore, to decide what is the proper evidence of the laws of a foreign country; and when the evidence is given as to those laws, the court is to judge of their application to the matter in issue.(b)

3. *Parol evidence.*

3194. The effect of parol evidence is left wholly to the consideration of the jury in cases of jury trial, and of the court in other cases. When treating of the character of the witnesses,(c) we were necessarily led to the consideration of the facts and circumstances which were calculated to give effect to their testimony, or to detract from it.

3195. Having discussed the nature, the object, the instrument, and the effect of the evidence, which are the subject of the first branch of our inquiries respecting evidence, we will next consider the manner of giving evidence in court in the course of a trial before a jury, and thus carry on the proceedings in the cause until we shall have arrived at the end.

SECOND DIVISION.

Of the manner of giving evidence.

3196. The party entitled to begin, (which, to pre-

(a) See ante, n. 3119.   (b) Story, Confl. § 638.   (c) Ante, n, 3158.

OF PROCEEDINGS IN AN ACTION.   451

No 3197   Book 4, tit. 8, chap. 11, sec. 3, § 3, div. 2, art. 1.   No. 3198.

vent confusion, we will here suppose to be the plaintiff,) after having opened his case to the jury in the manner already pointed out, is now to proceed to give his evidence, which is called evidence *in chief.* This evidence should strictly follow and support the allegations and opening of the plaintiff, and it must be confined to such matters as the pleadings and opening warrant; for sometimes a departure from this rule will be highly inconvenient, if not fatal. Suppose, for example, that two assaults have been committed, one in January and the other in February, and the counsel open as to one assault only, and he proves his cause of action to have been an assault in January; he cannot abandon that, and afterward prove another, committed in February, unless the pleadings and openings extend to both ;(*a*) because, after proving even in part one cause of action, the plaintiff cannot abandon it and proceed to prove another.

3197. In laying the evidence before the jury, it is usual to adduce, first, formal proofs ; secondly, documentary evidence ; thirdly, examinations of witnesses under interrogatories; and fourthly, the parol evidence of living witnesses. But it is not possible to lay down any positive rule on the subject, as this course must vary according to circumstances. The order of proof is entirely within the wise discretion of counsel. It is a rule, that when a witness has once left the box, the party cannot recall him to any point he may have omitted, unless by leave of the judge, which is seldom refused.

Art. 1.—*Of the form of the oath and affirmation.*

3198 When the plaintiff calls a witness, before he can examine him, he must be sworn or affirmed. This

---

(*a*) Stante *v.* Pricket, 1 Camph. 473.

452   OF REMEDIES.

No. 3199   Book 4, tit. 8, chap. 11, sec. 3, § 3, div. 2, art. 1.   No 3199.

is done by the clerk of the court, or by some officer lawfully authorized for the purpose. The form of the oath is various, to suit the religious opinions of the several witnesses, and bind their consciences. 3199.—1. The most usual form of an oath is that upon the Gospel.(*a*) In this case the witness lays his right hand upon the Gospel, and the clerk then asks, or repeats, "You do swear that the evidence you will give in this case, wherein Peter is plaintiff and Paul defendant, you will tell the truth, the whole truth, and nothing but the truth, so help you God;" and the

---

(*a*) To trace the history of oaths would be instructive, and show the inefficiency of any system which has been adopted to keep men from betraying the truth. It is said that discord invented oaths. In the investigation of facts, it was found that some persons who related what they said they knew, had made false statements; to prevent a recurrence of this inconvenience, it was thought that men should make a promise to tell the truth; to make this more binding on their consciences, they were required to make such declaration in the presence of what they thought most dear; this was called an oath. The Persians, who were followed by the Greeks and Romans, swore by the sun; the Scythians by air and their scimitars; the Greeks and Romans also swore by their gods, especially *Fides* and *Fidius;* they also swore by their Genii; their women, by Juno; their laborers, by Ceres; Vestals, by Vesta, etc. In the Middle Age, oaths were taken upon the missal and the cross, with the hands placed upon the altar; upon the book and cross, at the door of the church; upon the ring or knocker of the church; coram altare, i. e. with one hand upon the altar, the other prepared for the oath; with the head inclined upon the altar; and this oath was considered as of great sanctity; the Gospels were touched upon the altar, and touched by the hand. *Inspectis Sacrosanctis,* i. e. in their sight, not touched like bishops and priests, who were not allowed to swear, *super sacra. Sub testamento Dei,* the Gospel being placed upon their heads. Upon the relics and tombs of the saints. which oath they sometimes required upon many relics which they touched. In the place called *Sanctum,* the cross being placed upon the head, a formula common to religious persons if accused of any crimes   The above oaths were called *Juramenta Corporalia,* because the Gospel, cross, or relics, being touched, they were made with the hand elevated or extended, that they might be distinguished from oaths which were made by an instrument, that is, by writing, for such oaths had equal validity. Many oaths were borrowed from the heathens, as oaths upon the head of a beast, or idols; upon arms, the usual oath of northern nations; upon bracelets; upon the arms, the hair, or the eyes of a mistress; by confirmation or joining hands; by laying hold of the hem of a garment; upon the sepulchre of a debtor. Jews swore by holding a chain fastened to the door of their synagogue. Matthew Paris says, that priests took oaths with their hand upon the bosom, and laymen by touching the book, as now. See Puff. lib. 4, c. 2; Fosbroke's Encycl. of Antiquities, verbo Oaths, vol. i. 432.

OF PROCEEDINGS IN AN ACTION. 453

No. 3200.   Book 4, tit. 8, chap 11, sec. 3, § 3 div 2, art. 1   No. 3201.

witness then gives his assent and kisses the book.
The beginning of this oath is made by the witness
taking hold of the book, after being required by the
officer so to do, and ends with the words "so help you
God." The form of this oath may be traced to the
Roman law,(a) and the kissing of the book is said to
be an imitation of the priests kissing the ritual, as a
sign of reverence, before reading it to the people.(b)

3200.—2. Another form is by the witness holding
up his right hand, while the officer repeats to him,
"You do swear by Almighty God, the Searcher of
hearts, that," etc., and adds, "and this as you shall
answer to God at the great Day;" to which the witness assents.

3201.—3. In another form of attestation, commonly
called an affirmation, the officer repeats, "You do
solemnly, sincerely, and truly declare and affirm,
that," etc., to this the witness assents. In the United
States, generally, all witnesses who declare themselves
conscientiously scrupulous against taking a corporal
oath, are permitted to make a solemn affirmation, and
this in all cases, as well criminal as civil.

(a) Nov. 8, c. 3 ; Nov. 74, c. 5 ; Nov. 124, c. 1.
(b) Rees, Clycl. h. v. In a book, entitled "The Oath a Divine Ordinance," by D. X. Junkin, A. M., of New Jersey, is given the following
account of the custom of kissing the book, when the witness is sworn. He
says, "It is, perhaps, not possible to determine when the custom of kissing
the book was first introduced. In Polydore Virgil's work 'De Rerum In-
ventoribus,' lib. 4, c. 12, he says—as we translate him—'Amongst us
(Christians) the apostles would swear—' God is my witness '—but far the
most usual mode of taking a solemn oath is by the Gospel (per Evangelium)
which the Emperor Justinian instituted : (as is made certain by his book
entitled 'Concerning the Most Holy Bishops.') Afterward it came into
use as at present, that he who swears the most solemn oath before the
magistrates, shall either touch with his hand, or shall kiss the book of the
Gospels, saying, 'so help me God and these holy Gospels '—because even
as the Gospels, the fountain of our religion, ought on no account to be violated, so a solemn oath should on no condition be broken.'" It would
seem that when this author wrote, in 1499, it was not customary to touch
the Gospel with the right hand, and also to kiss it—aut dextra manu tangat,
aut osculetur—either to touch or to kiss it. The ceremony had been in use
long before 1499—in usu venit. See Oughton's Ordo Juridicorum, tit.
lxxx ; Consett on Courts, part 3, sec. 3, § 3.

454 OF REMEDIES.

No 3202   Book 4, tit 8, chap 11, sec 3, § 3, div 2, art. 1.   No. 3202.

1. Of the objections to witness.

3202. When an objection to a witness is believed to exist, as where he is supposed to have an interest in the matter in issue, it is usual to make it known to the court, before he is sworn generally in the cause, which is termed being sworn *in chief,* and cause him to be sworn specially to make true answers, or on his *voir dire.* Formerly the rule was, that the objection must be made before the witness was sworn in chief, but now it may be made at any time during the trial. In a case of this kind where the witness is supposed to be interested, the party objecting to him may pursue one of two courses; first, examine him on his *voir dire* as to his interest; or, secondly, prove such interest by another witness.

Voir dire is a phrase in old French, which signifies to speak truly; when a witness is examined on his *voir dire,* he is sworn or affirmed in a particular way in this formula: " You do swear, (or solemnly, sincerely and truly declare and affirm,) that you will true answers make, touching the matter now before the court." The party objecting, having asked that the witness should be sworn on his *voir dire,* has made him his witness for that purpose, and he is bound by the answers of the witness. He has a right to begin the examination, and the other side may cross-examine him. When the answers of the witness disclose an interest, he is rejected, however insignificant such interest may be ; otherwise he is then sworn in chief, if he has not already been so.

But the objecting party may not be willing to trust the witness on his examination on his *voir dire,* and he may prove the interest either by another witness, or by some other legal testimony. He has not, however, the choice of both ; having examined the witness on his *voir dire,* he cannot contradict him by other

OF PROCEEDINGS IN AN ACTION.   455

No. 3203.   Book 4, tit. 8, chap. 11, sec. 3, § 3, div. 2, art 1.   No. 3203.

evidence.(a)   If the evidence offered *aliundè* to prove the interest has been rejected, as inadmissible, the party may then resort to the witness and examine him on his *voir dire*.(b)   If on his *voir dire* the witness says he does not know, or leaves it doubtful whether he is interested or not, his interest may be shown by other evidence.(c)

Whether the witness shall be admitted or not, is in every case determined by the court alone, that being its province, and the jury have nothing to do as to the competency of the evidence, they are merely to judge of its credibility.   When the question of interest is to be determined upon evidence *aliundè*, and it depends upon the decision of intricate questions of fact, the judge, in his discretion, may take the opinion of the jury upon them.(d)

2. Of the restoration of capacity of witness.

3203.   When the witness has been rejected on account of interest, he may be *restored* to his competency by a proper release.   When the interest or right is vested in the witness himself, he may divest himself of it by a release ; when it consists of a liability over to the party calling him, or to another person, it may be released by the person to whom he is liable.

(a) This is said not to be fully settled by the authorities.   Stebbins v. Sackett, 5 Conn. 258.   But the question of competency is a collateral question ; and the rule is, that when a witness is asked a question on a collateral point, his answer is final, and cannot be contradicted ; that is, it cannot be impeached by any collateral evidence.   Harris v. Tippett, 2 Campbell, 637 ; Philad. & Trenton Co. v. Stimpson, 14 Pet. 448 : Odiorne v. Winkley, 2 Gallis, 53 ; Harris v. Wilson, 7 Wend. 57.   When in the course of the trial it turns out in proof that the witness has an interest, his testimony may be stricken out.   Brockbank v. Anderson, 7 Man. & Gr. 295.

(b) Main v. Newson, Anth. Cas. 13.

(c) Shannon v. Commonwealth, 8 S. & R. 444 ; Galbraith v. Galbraith, 6 Watts, 112.

(d) Phil. & Am. Ev. 2, note (1).

456 OF REMEDIES.

No. 3204.   Book 4, tit. 8, chap. 11, sec. 3, § 3, div. 2, art. 1.   No. 3204.

As to the time of giving the release, it must at the latest moment be during the trial, before the testimony is closed, or it will be too late; if, however, the trial is not over, the court will permit the witness to be reëxamined, after he is released, and in that case, it may be sufficient to ask him if the testimony he has already given is true.(a)

The release must be given by a person having the right, or by one duly authorized in his behalf. When a person is authorized by another to act for him in relation to certain things, he must confine himself within his power; a release by a *prochein ami*, by an attorney of record, or by a guardian *ad litem*, is not sufficient for want of authority.(b) When there are several joint obligees or joint creditors, the release of one is in general sufficient.(c) A release by an infant not being absolutely void, cannot be objected to by a stranger.(d) It is not necessary that the release should be delivered to the releasee; it may be left in court for the use of the party,(e) or delivered to another person for him; he must, however, know that it was so delivered at the time he gives his testimony.(f)

But the witness may be rendered competent by a variety of other acts, which amount to a discharge of the obligation.(g)

3204. If the witness produced be liable to another objection, that of being infamous, the party who makes the allegation must prove it by the production of the record of his conviction. And if the disability have been removed, it must be established by the

---

(a) Wake v. Lock, 5 C. & P. 454; Doty v. Wilson, 14 John. 378; Tallman v. Dutcher, 7 Wend. 180.
(b) 4 Verm. 523; Fraser v. Marsh, 2 Stark. 41; Murray v. House, 11 John. 464.
(c) Co. Litt. 232, a.
(d) Walker v. Ferrin, 4 Verm. 523; Rogers v. Berry, 10 John. 132.
(e) Peaceable v. Keep, 1 Yeates, 576.
(f) Seymour v. Strong, 4 Hill, 225.
(g) 1 Greenl. Ev. § 430.

OF PROCEEDINGS IN AN ACTION.   457

No 3205   Book 4, tit 8, chap 11, sec. 3, § 3, div 2, art 2.   No. 3205.

production of the record of reversal; or if the witness have·been pardoned, by producing the pardon under the great seal.

After hearing all the testimony for and against the admission of a witness, the judge decides that he shall or shall not be heard; if his decision is in favor of the hearing, the opposite party has a right to a bill of exceptions, the nature of which will be fully explained hereafter;(a) if against his admission, then the party offering him may except. But from the decision of the judge there is no appeal in the course of the trial; the remedy is by a motion for a new trial, or by suing out a writ of error.

Art. 2.—Of the examination of witnesses for plaintiff.

3205. After all the objections to a. witness have been settled by the judge, and the witness is to be heard as a competent witness, he is first examined by the party producing him. This is called a *direct examination* or an *examination in chief*, to distinguish it from the examination of the opposite party, which is call a *cross-examination*.

It is proper here to remark, that on the application of either party, the judge may, for the purpose of promoting the ends of justice, in his discretion, make an order that the witnesses shall be examined out of the hearing of each other.(b)

The examinations are conducted orally in open court, under the regulation of the judge, and in presence of the parties, their counsel, and all other persons·who choose to attend court, unless they are witnesses and have been excluded. The counsel who has a right to the examination, is entitled to conduct it as

---

(a) Vide post, n. 3232.
(b) Rex v. Cook, 13 How. St. Tr. 348; 2 Phil. Ev. 395; 1 Greenl. Ev. § 342; The State v. Sparrow, 3 Murph. 487; 1 Phil. Ev. 268, and note by Cowen & Hill.

he pleases, if he does not violate the rules which have been established, and which will presently be discussed. In doing so he will be careful to abstain from a rude, overbearing manner, and pursue a dignified course toward the witness. Not unfrequently is a witness made an opponent by the manner in which he is questioned, and his feelings being once excited, he, perhaps unintentionally, supports the cause of the other side. Even where a witness is perverse and disposed to give a wrong coloring to the facts, a firm and dignified manner, on the part of counsel, will have a better effect toward the jury, in showing them the prevaricating character of the witness, than an overbearing and petulant mode of examination. Besides the witness will himself be subdued by such a prudent course on the part of the counsel, and become ashamed to show any partiality.

Although much must necessarily be left to the discretion of the judge in the examination of witnesses, on account of the difficulty of making stringent rules which shall govern in all cases, still, some general rules have been adopted to facilitate the examination, and to attain the ends of justice.

FIRST RULE.

3206. It may be safely stated, as a general rule, that no *impertinent* or *useless question* should be asked, because what does not belong to the case, if no other harm arise from it, wastes the time of the court and confuses the jury, by drawing their attention to other matter than that which they are impanelled to try.

SECOND RULE.

3207. As a general rule, the counsel who examines a witness in chief, has no right to ask a *leading question*, that is, such a question as puts into the witness' mouth the answer he is expected to give. In that case the examiner is said to *lead* the witness to the answer.

When the witnesses for either party are under examination in chief, the counsel on the other side ought
carefully to watch that no leading question be put,
and if there be even an inception of an irregular question, the answer to which might be prejudicial, he
should instantly interrupt the counsel, because by
waiting till the leading question has been stated, the
mischief may be complete, and when the question is
put in another form, the witness will answer it as it
was first stated.

3208. But this rule against leading questions, under
an examination in chief, is not without exceptions;
sometimes the ends of justice require that it should be
relaxed. Among such instances are the following:

1. When it evidently appears that the witness
wishes to conceal the truth, and to favor the opposite party.(a)

2. When, from the nature of the case, the mind of
the witness cannot be directed to the subject of inquiry,
without a particular specification of it, as where he is
called to contradict another as to the contents of a
particular letter which is lost, and cannot without
suggestion recollect the contents, the particular passage
may be suggested to him.(b)

3. When a witness is called to contradict another,
who stated that such and such expressions were used,
or such and such things were said, it is the usual practice to ask whether those particular expressions were
used, or those things were said, for the witness could
not probably answer, if the question were put to him
in the general form, by merely inquiring what was
said.(c)

In all cases it is much in the discretion of the court
whether leading questions shall be put, and they are

(a) 1 Stark. Ev. 149.
(b) Courteen v. Torese, 1 Campb. 43.   See 1 Greenl. Ev. § 435.
(c) 1 Stark. Ev. 152 ; 1 Greenl. Ev. § 435.

never forbidden when justice requires them. The permitting or refusing a leading question cannot be assigned for error.(a)

THIRD RULE.

3209. The witness must testify only to such facts as are, at the time, within his knowledge and recollection. He cannot therefore read a paper containing a statement of facts as his testimony, if he then has no recollection of those facts, because if the paper is proper to be submitted to the jury, they ought to have it as evidence, and not what the witness says. But the witness has, in all cases, a right to look at the paper to refresh and assist his memory, and may even be compelled to do so, if the writing is present in court.(b) The writing may have been made by himself or others, it may be an original or a copy, if it will assist the memory of the witness, he may use it; he must, however, speak not from what is written in the paper, but from his recollection.

3210. Professor Greenleaf has very properly classi-fied the cases in which writings are permitted to be used for this purpose.(c) These classes are:

1. When the writing is used only for the purpose of assisting the memory of the witness; in this case, the witness speaks of his own knowledge, and whether the paper is in court or not, is immaterial, except that if it be not produced, the other side may take advantage of that circumstance and press it upon the jury.

2. When the witness recollects having seen the paper before, and though he cannot on his examination say he has an independent recollection of the facts mentioned in it, yet he remembers that at the time he saw it, he knew the contents to be correct. In this case, the writing must be produced in court, in order

---

(a) Moody v. Rowell, 17 Pick. 498.
(b) Reed v. Boardman, 20 Pick. 441.
(c) 1 Greenl. Ev. § 437.

to enable the opposite party to cross-examine, and that the witness' memory shall be refreshed as to every part. 3. When the writing in question is not recognized by the witness, nor awakens in his memory any recollection of any thing contained in it; but, knowing it to be genuine, he is so convinced, on that ground, that he can positively swear to the fact; as where a paper is produced attested by the witness, and he says he has no recollection of the attestation, but he is certain that the signature to it is his own, and that he never subscribed his name as an attesting witness, without first having the paper acknowledged before him by the parties, this is a sufficient proof of the attestation of the deed.(a)

FOURTH RULE.

3211. Though the witness must depose to such facts only, as are within his knowledge, yet he is not required to give the *very words* used in a conversation, or to speak with such expressions of certainty as to exclude all doubt in his mind. When he has a strong impression of the fact, though it does not amount to absolute certainty, his testimony is admissible, and must be weighed by the jury.(b) And in some cases the *belief* of a witness will be received in evidence; thus, a witness may testify as to his belief of the identity of a person in question, or that the handwriting in question is or is not that of a certain person, provided he has had an opportunity of knowing the handwriting of such person; and if he testifies falsely as to his belief, as where he testifies that he believes the handwriting is that of Paul, when he knows it is that of Peter, he is guilty of perjury.(c)

(a) Maugham *v.* Hubbard, 8 B. B. & C. 16; Russell *v.* Coffin, 8 Pick. 143; 1 Phil. Ev. by Cowen & Hill, 475, note, 899.
(b) Clark *v.* Regelow, 4 Shepl. 246.
(c) Rex *v.* Pedley, Leach, Cr. cas. 365. See Thompson *v.* White, 4 S. & R. 137; 1 Stark. Ev. 41; 2 Pow. on Mortg. 555; 2 Hawk. c. 46, s. 167. As to the difference between *belief and knowledge*, see ante, n. 3158.

462 OF REMEDIES.

No. 3212.   Book 4, tit. 8, chap. 11, sec. 3, § 3, div. 2, art. 2.   3214.

FIFTH RULE.

3212. In general the *opinion* of the witness is not evidence, for he must speak of facts; but when matters of skill or judgment are involved, a person competent particularly to understand such matters may be asked his opinion, and it will be evidence. It is the constant practice to examine on questions of science, skill, and trade, or others of the same kind, persons of known experience, who, for this reason, are sometimes called *experts*. These testify, not only as to facts, but also give their opinions, which are properly received in evidence. It is for this reason the opinions of medical men are constantly admitted, as to the cause of disease, or of death, or the consequences of wounds, and as to the sane or insane state of a person's mind, as collected from a number of circumstances; but medical or other scientific men cannot give their opinions as to the merits of the cause, but only their opinions upon the facts proved.(*a*)

SIXTH RULE.

3213. A witness should not be asked, and if asked, he need not answer, any question which has a tendency to render him liable to any kind of punishment or to a *criminal charge;* or subject him to a forfeiture of his estate; or have a direct tendency to degrade his character.

3214.—1. It is exceedingly clear that a witness is not compellable to criminate himself, and whether he has answered the question in part, or not at all, he will be protected by the court; still he may answer if he chooses; and in such a case, the party who put the question will be bound by the answer, because the court cannot try such collateral facts, and the parties and the witness do not come prepared for its full inves-

(*a*) 1 Greenl. Ev. § 440; 1 Phil. Ev. 290; Wogan *v.* Small, 11 S. & R. 141.

tigation.(a)   But where the answer will only subject him to a civil liability, or pecuniary loss, or charge him with a debt, he is bound to answer.(b)   A party interested in the cause cannot be compelled to answer, though not named on the record.(c)

3215.—2. When the answer will subject the witness to a forfeiture of his estate, he will be protected, as he is when his answer will expose him to a criminal prosecution or penalty.

3216.—3. No man is bound to degrade his own character; he is, therefore, not bound to answer a question when the answer has a direct tendency to degrade his character. This rule applies only to those cases where the inquiry is not relevant to the nature of the issue, for if it be relevant, it must be answered, however strongly it may reflect on the character of the witness.(d)

SEVENTH RULE.

3217. A witness should not be asked, and he cannot be compelled, if asked, to disclose state secrets, or official communications between the heads of departments of state and their subordinate officers; or matter which is indecent or offensive to public morals, or injurious to the feelings and interests of third persons, the parties having, themselves, no interest except what they have themselves created.

3218.—1. *State secrets* are those things which are known only to some of the officers of the government, or of some branch of it. Those are matters which concern the administration of penal justice, or those which concern the administration of the government. The principle of public safety is the same in both cases,

(a) 1 Phil. Ev. 284.   See Rex v. Rudge, 2 Peake's N. P. Cas. 232.
(b) Baird v. Cochran, 4 S. & R. 397 ; Ness v. Van Swearingen, 7 S. & R. 192 ; Bull v. Loveland, 10 Pick. 9 ; Conover v. Bell, 6 Monroe, 157.
(c) Mauran v. Lamb, 7 Cowen, 174 ; Rex v. Woburn, 10 East, 395.
(d) 1 Phil. Ev. 279, and Cowen & Hill's Notes, note 521 ; 1 Greenl. Ev. 454, 455.

464 OF REMEDIES.

No. 3219.   Book 4, tit. 8, chap. 11, sec. 3, § 3, div. 2, art. 2   No. 3220.

and the rule of exclusion is applied no further than the attainment of that object requires; for example, in criminal trials, the names of the persons employed in the discovery of crime are not permitted to be disclosed, any further than is requisite to a fair trial of the question of the prisoner's innocence or guilt.(a)

3219.—2. For the same reason, the public good, communications *between the heads of departments of state and their subordinate officers*, are protected from disclosure; thus, communications between a provincial governor and his attorney general, on the state of the colony and the conduct of its officers;(b) the President of the United States and the governors of the different states, cannot be coerced to produce correspondence or official papers, or to disclose information communicated to them in their official capacity, when, in their opinion, the disclosure would be injurious to the public interest;(c) when such original evidence cannot be admitted, secondary evidence of the same facts will not be received.(d) It has already been stated that grand jurors cannot be examined, when their answers would be injurious to the public interest, as to what passed in the grand jury room.(e)

3220.—3. When the public good requires it, the mere indecency of disclosures does not suffice to exclude them; for this reason, on an indictment for a rape, or when the sex of a person claiming an estate tail comes in question, the inquiry as to it is allowed, and the witness may be compelled to testify. But when the evidence is not necessary for the administration of public justice, but the questions have been raised by the parties themselves, out of mere wanton-

---

(a) Rex v. Hardy, 24 St. Tr. 753, 811.
(b) Wyat v. Gore, Holt's N. P. Cas. 299; Cook v. Maxwell, 2 Stark. R. 183; Anderson v. Hamilton, 2 B. & B. 156, note.
(c) 1 Burr's Tr. 186, 187; Gray v. Pentland, 2 S. & R. 23.
(d) 2 S. & R. 23, 31; Yoter v. Sanoro, 8 Watts, 156.
(e) Vide ante, n. 3180.

ness or sport, or in disregard of the rights of others, such questions cannot be answered; as where the parties laid a wager as to the sex of an individual,(*a*) or whether an unmarried woman had a child.(*b*)

Art. 3.—Of the cross-examination.

3221. After the party who called a witness has closed his examination in chief, he is handed over to the counsel of the other side, to be cross-examined; but if he has simply been sworn, inadvertently, and not examined by the party who called him, the other party cannot examine him as if he had been so examined, but he may examine him as his own witness in chief.(*c*)

Every party has a right to cross-examine a witness produced and examined by his antagonist, in order to test whether the witness possesses the knowledge of the things he testifies; and if, upon examination, it is found that the witness had the means and ability to ascertain the facts about which he testified, then his memory, his motives, every thing, may be scrutinized by the cross-examination.

The object of the cross-examination is to sift the evidence, and try the credibility of the witness who has been called and given evidence in chief. It is one of the principal tests which the law has devised for the ascertainment of truth, and it is certainly one of the most efficacious. By this means the situation of the witness with regard to the parties and the subject of litigation, his interest, his motives, his inclinations and his prejudices, his means of obtaining a correct knowledge of the facts respecting which he testifies, the manner in which he used those means, his powers of discerning the facts in the first instance, and his

(*a*) Da Costa *v.* Jones, Cowp. 729.
(*b*) Ditchburn *v.* Goldsmith, 4 Camp. 152.
(*c*) 3 Chitty's Gen. Pr. 897.

capacity of retaining them and describing them, are fully investigated and ascertained. However artful he may be, the witness will seldom be able to elude the keen perception of an intelligent court and jury, unless, indeed, his story is founded on truth; when false, he will be liable to detection at every step.(a)

Under a cross-examination, the counsel may put any question at all relevant to the cause he may think fit, and in a manner however leading; but this is allowed because the witness is presumed to be favorable to the other side, and the rule already mentioned, as to the right of putting leading questions, under an examination in chief, equally extends to a witness under cross-examination; when it appears that the person is not a witness of the truth, but evidently endeavoring to conceal it from the counsel who is examining him, whether for or against the plaintiff, the most leading questions are permitted. But this right of putting leading questions appears to be somewhat qualified, for when a witness betrays an anxiety to serve the party against whom he was called and examined in chief, a direct leading question will not be permitted in cross-examination.(b)   This rests very much in the discretion of the judge, and the conduct and manner of the witness.

A witness cannot be asked under a cross-examination any thing as to a collateral fact, for the purpose of afterward impeaching his testimony by other witnesses who may contradict him. But with regard to any material fact in issue, a question may be asked of a witness for the purpose of contradicting him.

Much discretion is required in making a cross-examination; the witness will probably look upon the counsel for the party who cross-examines him with much distrust; the first effort of the counsel ought,

(a) Stark. Ev. 96; 1 Pil. Ev. 227; Fortes. R. Pref. 2, 4; Vaugh. 143; Bac. Ab. Evidence, E.
(b) 1 Stark. Ev. 162, n. (c)

OF PROCEEDINGS IN AN ACTION. 467

No. 3222.   Book 4, tit. 8, chap. 11, sec. 3, § 3, div. 2, art. 4.   No. 3223.

therefore, to be to gain his confidence, by acting toward him with perfect justice, and by appearing to consider him, as most witnesses are, disposed to tell the truth. It is only when he shows a perverse determination to conceal the truth, that a searching cross-examination ought to take place. There is great risk in the cross-examination, for if unfavorable evidence be elicited by such examination, it will be taken most strongly against the party so cross-examining.(a)

After the witness has been cross-examined, the party who examined him in chief has a right to reëxamine him to the same matter. He may ask all questions proper to draw forth an explanation of the sense and meaning of the expressions used by him on his cross-examination, when they are doubtful; and also the reasons why he used them. This evidence ought properly to be confined to the cross-examination, and it should not extend to any new matter.

Art. 4.—Of calling witnesses and giving evidence.

3222. The party may call as many witnesses as he pleases, and submit each one to an examination and cross-examination. If any one of his witnesses should turn out differently from what he expected, and instead of testifying for him, his evidence should be in favor of the other party, it is a disputed point whether he can be impeached by him; it seems but reasonable, however, that when a party has called a witness and given him credit, that he should not afterward be allowed to impeach the credit which he has given him. He may, however, establish by other witnesses the same point denied by a witness he had himself called.(b)

3223. When records are given in evidence they should be properly authenticated, and papers should

---

(a) See Wright v. Littler, Burr. 1244; 1 Bl. R. 346.
(b) Alexander v. Gibson, 2 Campb. 556; Ewer v. Ambrose, 3 B. & Cr. 746.

be proved by the subscribing witnesses, when there are any; and, when there are none, the handwriting of the parties should be proved. They should all be read, or it should be agreed that they be considered in evidence.

After all the evidence of the plaintiff has been given, the plaintiff closes his case.

3224. At this time, is to be considered whether the plaintiff has made out a case or not; if, in the opinion of the court, the plaintiff should not have proved a sufficient case to entitle him to a verdict, if the case were then submitted to the jury, and all his evidence admitted to be true, then it would be useless to proceed further in the case, as in point of law he cannot, by any possibility, recover, and therefore the plaintiff is nonsuited. If, on the other hand, the plaintiff has made a *primâ facie* case, then the court hears the testimony on the other side, which, in the case which has been supposed, would be for the defendant.

Art. 5.—Of the opening for defendant.

3225. In order to let the court and jury understand his case, the counsel for the defendant now opens his defence. The general course which he pursues is much like that adopted by the plaintiff in opening his case. He points out in what the case of the plaintiff is defective, if, in fact, it is not well founded; but, if well founded, he shows how the defendant has been discharged, either by the acts of the plaintiff, by acts of law, or on any other account; briefly stating all the facts and circumstances which have this effect, and the manner in which they will be proved.

Art. 6.—Of the examination of witnesses for defendant.

3226. The witnesses for the defendant are to be examined by him as those of the plaintiff were for him, and they are subject to the general rules of examination. The party calling a witness, when he examines him, is bound to examine him in chief, and is not allowed to pursue the examination in any other way. The witness is turned over to the plaintiff for cross-examination, and, after such cross-examination, the defendant may again examine him as to the cross-examination, or as to any fact which it may have elicited.

The defendant gives in all his evidence, verbal and documentary, as the plaintiff did to support his case, and having done so he closes.

Art. 7.—Of rebutting evidence.

3227. If the defendant has given testimony in his defence respecting any new matter, the plaintiff has a right to give new evidence, which is called *rebutting evidence*. This kind of evidence is allowed, to explain, repel, counteract, or disprove facts given in evidence on the other side;(a) it may be by proving facts directly opposite to those sworn to, or by circumstances, which are sufficient to rebut the most positive testimony.(b)

Art. 8.—Of impeaching witnesses.

3228. Every witness is liable to be impeached as to his character for truth. By *impeachment of a witness*, is meant an allegation, supported by proof, that a witness who has been examined, is unworthy of credit. Till impeached, every man's character is presumed to be good, and he who alleges it is not good, must, of course, be able to support his allegation by evidence. A witness' testimony may be impeached in three ways: 1, by disproving by other witnesses facts stated by him; 2, by general evidence of his want of character

(a) Scott v. Woodward, 2 McCord, 161.
(b) Nelson v. United States, Pet. C. C. R. 235.

470 OF REMEDIES.

No. 3229.   Book 4, tit. 8, chap. 11, sec. 3, § 3, div. 2, art. 8.   No. 3230.

for truth and veracity; and, 3, by showing his self-contradiction.

3229.—1. A witness' testimony may be impeached by *disproving the facts stated by him*, by the testimony of other witnesses; as, for example, if Titus, the witness, were to prove that the defendant had a conversation with the plaintiff, in the presence of Peter and Paul, and that both Peter and Paul made remarks to him at the time as to what then passed; and Peter and Paul should testify that they were not present at such conversation, and that they never remarked any thing to him upon the subject; it is clear, if they were worthy of credit, that Titus could not be believed.

3230.—2. Evidence may be given, generally, affecting a witness' credit as a man of veracity. It is his *character* which is attacked, not particular instances of his conduct. The examination of a witness, whose testimony attacks the general character of another, must be confined to his general reputation, and not be permitted to go into any particular facts. Every man of good reputation, is supposed capable at all times of supporting it by proof; but he cannot be expected to come into court to prove every part of his conduct during a long life, without any notice that it would be attacked.

The regular mode is, to inquire of the witness under examination, whether he knows the general character or reputation of the witness to be impeached, as to *truth and veracity;(a)* and if he knows it, what is his reputation. The additional question is put, whether

---

(a) A doubt has been raised, whether the inquiry ought to be confined to the witness' character for truth and veracity, or whether the question ought to be as to the general character of the witness impeached. In Kentucky, Hume *v.* Scott, 3 A. K. Marsh. 261; North Carolina, The State *v.* Boswell, 2 Dev. Law Rep. 209; in South Carolina, Anon. 1 Hill, So. Car. R. 251, the rule seems to be, that the inquiry extends to the whole character of the person impeached. The general rule, however, in the other states, is to inquire as to his character for truth and veracity.

OF PROCEEDINGS IN AN ACTION.   471

No 3231.   Book 4, tit. 8, chap. 11, sec 3, § 3, div. 2, art. 8.   No 3231.

the witness would believe him upon oath.(*a*) In answer to such evidence, the other party may cross-examine the impeaching witnesses, as to their modes of knowledge and the grounds of their opinions ; or he may attack their general character, and by fresh evidence support the character of his own witness.(*b*)

In order to *know* the character of another, and his general reputation, a man must be generally acquainted with those who know him, and the inquiry respecting him must be made where he is best known. A stranger going there making inquiry at the request of the party who impeaches the witness, is not such a person who knows the reputation.(*c*)

3231.—3. A third mode of impeaching a witness, is to show that he has made statements out of court, contrary to those made under oath on the trial. In these cases, however, this objection is confined to such matters as are *relevant to the issue;* for, in matters that are not so, his answer is conclusive, the court not having the power to try such immaterial statements, and the parties not coming there prepared for such a contest. Before the witness is contradicted, fairness and justice require that, in the case of verbal statements, he should first be asked as to the time, place and person involved in the supposed contradiction;

(*a*) The question, whether the witness under examination would believe the former witness, is frequently asked. This has been objected to for several reasons : first, that the witness, in giving his opinion, takes from the jury the right of forming an opinion for themselves; secondly, that it permits the introduction and indulgence of personal and party hostility in courts of justice. Phillips *v.* Kingfield, 1 Appl. R. 375, 379. But, besides, the fact whether the witness would or would not believe the one whom it is sought to impeach, must depend entirely on what he would say ; if he testified to a probable story or to a known fact, he must be believed ; and, if the most correct man testified to what is impossible, as that he saw a man shoot himself with a pistol which he held in his hand, and upon examination of the ball found in his body, it was too large to enter into the pistol, he ought not to be believed.

(*b*) 2 Phil. Ev. 432; 1 Stark. Ev. 182 ; 1 Greenl. Ev. § 461.

(*c*) Douglass *v.* Tousey, 2 Wend. 352; Boynton *v.* Kellog, 3 Mass. 192 ; Wike *v.* Lightener, 11 S. & R. 198 ; Kimmel *v.* Kimmel, 3 S. & R. 337.

because, if the question be put to him, generally, whether he said so and so, or whether he always told the same story, he may not recollect; and if his attention be called particularly to the time and place, when and where the conversation took place, and the person with whom he had it, he may remember the circumstances and explain it.(a)

A witness may also be contradicted by writings and facts. He may therefore be asked if he wrote a certain letter, but in this case, when the letter can be had, it ought to be handed to him, and he ought to be asked if he wrote it. If he acknowledges it, then the contents are evidence to contradict him, if the contents do in fact contradict what he has stated; if he denies it, then his handwriting may be proved by another witness, for the purpose of impeaching his credit.(b)

When evidence is given of contrary statements made by a witness, of a particular fact to impeach his veracity, his general character for truth is in some degree put in issue, and he may therefore support, by general evidence, that he is a man of strict integrity, and that he has a scrupulous regard for truth.(c)

Having now treated of the rules of evidence generally, and of their application in the trial of a cause, our next inquiries will lead us to the consideration of the several matters which occur in the course of a trial.

§ 4.—Of bills of exceptions.

3232. We have seen that when evidence is offered, either written or verbal, and there is any objection to its being received, the matter is referred to the court,

---

(a) The Queen's case, 2 Br. & Bing. 313 ; Angus v. Smith, 1 M. & Malk. 473 ; 1 Stark. Ev. 484 ; 1 Greenl. Ev. § 462, and the notes ; Notes to Phil. Ev. by Cowen & Hill, note 533 to 1 Phil. 308.
(b) Phil. & Am. on Ev. 932 ; The Queen's case, 2 Br. & Bing. 292.
(c) Phil. & Am. on Ev. 944.

and, after a full and fair examination, the judge's decision is in favor of its admission or against it. Frequently, indeed, almost always, the case turns upon the correctness of this judgment, for if the evidence is admitted, the verdict will probably be in favor of the party offering it, and if rejected, it will be against him. This is always the case when the evidence is of vital importance to the action. Such power, unless subject to revision, would, in the hands of a fallible, a corrupt, an ignorant or an arbitrary judge, be fraught with very dangerous consequences. Again, in his charge or directions to the jury, the judge is required to state to them the rules of law which are to guide them in making up their verdict, and they are bound to take the law to be as he states it to them; if, through ignorance or corruption, the judge should misstate the law, and the jury find their verdict accordingly, the party against whom this misstatement had been made would be without a remedy, if the law had not provided one to correct these evils. This is effected by a *bill of exceptions.*(a)

This bill of exceptions is the statement in writing of the objection made by a party in a cause, to the decision of the court on a point of law, which is clearly stated therein, and which, in confirmation of its accuracy, is signed and sealed by the judge or court who made the decision. The object of the bill of exceptions is to put the question of law on record, for the information of the court of error having cognizance of such cause.

The bill of exceptions is authorized by an English statute,(b) the principles of which have been adopted in all the states of the Union. It is thereby enacted that "when one impleaded before any of the justices, alleges an exception praying they will allow it, and if

(a) See Gibson v. Hunter, 2 H. Bl. 87; Bulkley v. Butler, 2 Barn. & Cr. 434; Appleton v. Sweetapple, 3 Dougl. 137.
(b) St. of Westm. 2, 13 Ed. I., c. 31.

474 OF REMEDIES.

No. 3233.   Book 4, tit. 8, chap. 11, sec. 3, § 4, art. 1.   No. 3233.

they will not, if he that alleges the exception writes the same, and requires that the justices will put their seals, the justices shall do so, and if one will not, another shall; and if, upon complaint made of the justice, the king cause the record to come before him, and the exception be not found in the roll, and the plaintiff show the written exception, with the seal of the justices thereto put, the justice shall be commanded to appear at a certain day, either to confess or deny his seal, and if he cannot deny his seal, they shall proceed to judgment according to the exception, as it ought to be allowed or disallowed." The statute extends to both plaintiff and defendant.

The object of a bill of exceptions is to put upon the record all the facts touching the decisions of the court respecting questions of law, which do not appear upon the record, and which arise in the course of the trial, so that when the case is afterward removed to an appellate court by a writ of error,(a) the bill of exceptions may be taken into consideration, and there finally decided, by which the decision of the court below will be affirmed or reversed.(b)

In the discussion of this subject, it will be proper to inquire into, 1, the cases in which a bill of exceptions may be had; 2, the time of making the exception; 3, when the bill must be signed; 4, the form of the bill; 5, its effect.

Art. 1.—*In what cases a bill of exceptions may be had.*

3233. In general, a bill of exceptions can be had only in a *civil* case.(c) When, in the course of trial of

_____

(a) The nature of this writ will be explained hereafter.
(b) See the whole course of proceeding on a bill of exceptions minutely stated in 3 Burr. 1692; Walton *v.* United States, 9 Wheaton, 651 ; 4 Peters, 102; and Brown *v.* Clark, 4 How. U. S. 4.
(c) At common law, exceptions do not lie in criminal cases. People *v.* Holbrook, 13 John. 90; United States *v.* Gibert, 2 Sumn. 19 ; Ex parte Barker, 7 Cowen, 143 ; and if sealed by the court below, will not be

OF PROCEEDINGS IN AN ACTION. 475

No. 3234   Book 4, tit. 8, chap 11, sec. 3, § 4, art. 2.   No. 3234.

a cause, the judge, either in his charge to the jury, or in deciding an interlocutory question, mistakes the law, or is supposed by the counsel on either side to have mistaken the law, the counsel against whom the decision is made may tender an exception to his opinion, and require him to seal a bill of exceptions;(*a*) and exception may be taken even when the judge refuses to charge the jury when required, as to a particular point of law,(*b*) but not when the judge neglects to do so, he not being required.(*c*) Nor will an exception lie to an opinion wholly abstract or out of the case, so as not to affect it, though such charge may be erroneous; and if a bill be signed in such case the court of error will not act upon it.(*d*) An exception does not lie where there is a right of appeal;(*e*) nor when the alleged error appears on the record;(*f*) nor to instructions on the facts;(*g*) nor for refusing to permit a witness to be reëxamined as to what he had testified, after a cause has been submitted to the jury, this being a matter of discretion in the court;(*h*) nor for exercising a mere discretionary power.(*i*)

Art. 2.—*When the exception must be made.*

3234. When evidence is ruled adversely to a party,

regarded in the court above. Middleton *v.* Commonwealth, 2 Watts, 285. Nor are exceptions to the proceedings of the sessions allowable in settlement cases. Newton *v.* Gloucester, 1 Halst. 405. But by statute they are allowed in criminal cases in several states. Commonwealth *v.* Hickerson, 2 Virg. Cas. 60 and note; Hooker *v.* State, 4 Ham. 348; 14 Pick. 370. In New York, by statute, exception may be taken in criminal cases, but they do not delay the execution of the judgment. Grah. Pr. 768, note.

(*a*) 3 Bl. Com. 372.
(*b*) Douglass *v.* McAllister, 3 Cranch, 300; Smith *v.* Carrington, 4 Cranch, 62; Fletcher *v.* Howard, 2 Aik. 115.
(*c*) Ex parte Baily, 479; Pennock *v.* Dialogue, 2 Pet. 15. '
(*d*) Clarke *v.* Dutcher, 9 Cowen, 674; Hughes *v.* Parker, 1 Port. 139; McDougal *v.* Fleming, 4 Ham. 79; Hamilton *v.* Russell, 1 Cranch, 318.
(*e*) Rathbone *v.* Rathbone, 4 Pick. 93; Piper *v.* Willard, 10 Pick. 34; 9 Mass. 228.
(*f*) Macker *v.* Thomas, 7 Wheat. 532.
(*g*) Brooke *v.* Young, 3 Rand, 106; Gilbert *v.* Woodbury, 9 Shepl. 246.
(*h*) Law *v.* Merrills, 6 Wend. 277.
(*i*) Clapp *v.* Balch, 3 Greenl. 219; Reynard *v.* Brecknell, 4 Pick. 302.

476 OF REMEDIES.

No. 3235. Book 4, tit. 8, chap. 11, sec. 3, § 4, art. 3. No. 3235.

it is usual to take an exception to the judge's opinion, and that is the proper time to do it; though it is unnecessary to stop the progress of the trial to allow time to prepare the bill of exceptions at the time, the judge merely makes a note that the exception has been taken, and the cause proceeds to the end; and, when more than one exception is taken, the same proceeding takes place. It not unfrequently happens that exceptions are taken on both sides, of course not to the same decision.(*a*)

Sometimes the exception is not to the decision on a point of evidence offered, but the opinion of the judge, either in general· to his charge to the jury, or to the answer which he has given on a point of law, submitted to him for his decision by the counsel. Exceptions of this kind must be made, according to some decisions, before the jury have withdrawn;(*b*) but, according to others, if the exception be made after the jury have returned into court with their verdict, but before it is delivered, it is in time.(*c*)

Art. 3.—When the bill must be signed.

3235. The bill of exceptions must be signed by the judge who tried the cause.(*d*) In general the bill must be signed at the term of the trial, and not at a subsequent term,(*e*) but the practice does not appear to be uniform.(*f*)

The bill ought to be signed upon notice of the time

(*a*) Liggett *v.* Bank of Pennsylvania, 7 S. & R. 219; Stewart *v.* Huntingdon Bank, 11 S. & R. 267; Pool *v.* Fleeger, 11 Pet. 185; Powers *v.* Wright, Minor. 66.

(*b*) Life and Fire *v.* Mechanics' Ins. Co. 7 Wend. 34.

(*c*) Jones *v.* Ins. Co. of N. A. 1 Binn. 38; 4 Dall. 249; Morris *v.* Buckley, 8 S. & R. 211; Lanuze *v.* Barker. 10 John. 312; Doe *v.* Kennedy, 5 Monr. 177; Dock *v.* Hart, 7 W. & S. 172.

(*d*) Law *v.* Johnson, 8 Cowen, 746.

(*e*) Sikes *v.* Random, 6 John. 279; Shipherd *v.* White, 3 Cowen, 32; Agnew *v.* Campbell, 3 Harr. N. J. Rep. 291; Pomroy *v.* Selmes, 8 Miss. 727; 1 Watts & Serg. 480.

(*f*) Nisbitt *v.* Dallam, 7 G. & John. 494.

and place, when and where it is to be done ;(*a*) this is required for the purpose of accuracy, for the signing of the bill by the judges is conclusive upon the parties.(*b*)

If the judge should refuse to sign the bill, according to the requirements of the statute, he may be compelled by a writ of *mandamus* issued against him by the superior court, commanding him to seal it, if the fact alleged be truly stated.   To this writ he must make a return ; if by his return he admits the facts to be truly stated, and he still refuses to sign the bill, he will be attached for contempt;(*c*) if, on the contrary, his return is that they are not truly stated, when in fact they are so, an action will lie against him for making a false return.(*d*)

Art. 4.—*Of the form of the bill of exceptions.*

3236. A bill of exceptions must be in a proper form, that is, it must truly state the case in which it was taken, the evidence offered and admitted or overruled, distinctly, or the point of law ruled about which the exception has been taken, and the decision of the court below.(*e*)   It must appear by the bill of exceptions that the court erred to the prejudice of the party excepting ;(*f*) that the error complained of was material,(*g*) and such error must be set forth distinctly.(*h*)

(*a*) 3 Cowen, 766 ; Bull. N. P. 316.
(*b*) Bingham *v.* Cabbot, 3 Dall. 38.
(*c*) Bristol *v.* Phillips, 3 Scam. 287.   In this case the judge refused to sign the bill of exceptions, and also to obey a *mandamus* from the supreme court, to sign the bill, and he was attached for contempt, whereupon he resigned his office.   A motion was then made, that the bill be taken and considered as true, and be allowed the same effect as though signed and sealed, the correctness of the bill not being denied.   This motion upon full consideration was granted.
(*d*) 3 Bl. Com. 372.
(*e*) A bill of exceptions must not be so framed as to refer the credit of the witnesses to the court above.   Carrington *v.* Bennett, 1 Leigh, 340 ; Ewing *v.* Ewing, 2 Leigh, 340.
(*f*) Holmes *v.* Gayle, 1 Ala. 517 ; Stone *v.* Stone, 1 Ala. 582.
(*g*) Stephens *v.* State, 14 Ohio, 386 ; Watson *v.* Brown, 14 Ohio, 473.
(*h*) Hare *v.* Harrington, Wright, 290.

It must be stated as made during the term at which the exception was taken, for in contemplation of law it is supposed the bill was signed when the exception was taken, though, as we have observed, it is in fact not signed until afterward.(a)　When the exception is taken, the party excepting is presumed in contemplation of law to *tender* to the judge a *bill of exceptions.* The bill should contain a certificate that the facts stated in it occurred on the trial, and it must be by the judge who tried the cause.(b)

Art. 5.—Of the effect of a bill of exceptions.

3237. The bill of exceptions, being part of the record, is evidence between the parties, as to the facts therein stated, and they cannot be disputed.(c)　When it states that certain facts appeared, it is to be taken that they were undisputed, or conceded by both parties.(d)　No notice can be taken of exceptions or objections not appearing on the bill.　And a bill signed by a judge who did not try the cause, or about a matter which is not the subject of such a bill, will not be regarded by the appellate court.

§ 5.—Of demurrer to evidence.

3238. After a party has given all the evidence he has in support of his cause, and the opposite party disputes its legal sufficiency, or its admissibility, in point of law, he may *demur to the evidence;* this may be by the party, plaintiff or defendant, but he must take the negative side of the issue. This is not unlike a demurrer in pleading. The demurrer in pleading is the taking of the facts pleaded from the consideration

(a) Patterson *v.* Phillips, 1 How. Miss. 572.
(b) Law *v.* Jackson, 8 Cowen, 746.
(c) Bingham *v.* Cabbot, 3 Dall. 38.
(d) Beach *v.* Packard, 10 Verm. 96.

of the jury, to be decided as a question of law, by the court. The demurrer to evidence is essentially a demurrer to the facts shown in evidence, the consideration of which, by this proceeding, is taken from the jury, and the whole matter in controversy is a question of law to be passed upon by the court.(a)

The principal rules regulating demurrers to evidence, are the following:

FIRST RULE.

3239. The party(b) demurring to evidence is required not only to confess the *existence* of the evidence offered, but admit the *fact* intended to be proved by it; a confession of the *truth* of the evidence, is not in all cases necessarily a confession of the fact intended to be proved by it. As a demurrer to evidence is intended to raise a question of law on the facts of the case, the facts must be admitted before such a question can arise. The demurrer, when properly tendered, *admits* the facts shown by the evidence, but denies their *sufficiency in law*, to maintain the issue in favor of the adverse party.(c)   Before the party demurring can require the opposite party to join in demurrer, he is required to make certain admissions, which will be considered in the discussion of these rules.

SECOND RULE.

3240. The *relevancy* of the evidence to the issue, is the only question which is raised by a demurrer to evidence, that is the sole question of law; whether

---

(a) Co. Litt. 72; Bac. Ab. Pleas, N 7.   But see Fowle v. Common Council, 11 Wheat. 320.   For a form of demurrer to evidence, see 4 Chit. Gen. Pr. 16.

(b) The demurrer to evidence can be taken only by the party who takes the *burden of the proof*, or *affirmative of the issue*, upon him.   A party holding the *negative* of the issue, cannot demur to evidence, after introducing repellant testimony, and compel his adversary to join in the demurrer Hart v. Colloway, 2 Bibb. 460.

(c) Coke Litt. 72.

what is given in evidence is, or is not sufficient to prove the point, is a question of fact, which must be admitted. Evidence is always relevant to the issue, which, *in any degree*, it conduces to prove; but then it must be relevant to the *whole* issue, for if it be so to *part* only, it is clear it could not warrant a finding of the issue, by the jury, in favor of the party exhibiting the evidence. The party demurring must be cautious, therefore, that the evidence if relevant at all, be not so to the whole issue.(*a*)

THIRD RULE.

3241. The demurrer must be to the *whole* of the evidence; because the whole of it may be sufficient to maintain the issue when a part would not; and therefore the defendant cannot demur to the plaintiff's evidence until he has gone through the whole.(*b*)

FOURTH RULE.

3242. A demurrer may be had to *any kind* of evidence, whether it is written or parol, direct or circumstantial. The manner of framing the demurrer, and of making the necessary admissions upon the record, is regulated by the nature of the evidence to which the demurrer applies.(*c*)

3243.—1. When all the evidence in support of the affirmative of the issue is *written*, there can be no doubt it may be demurred to; as where, on the general issue, the plaintiff exhibits a bond as evidence of the claim which is the subject of the suit, or a conveyance or record, as evidence of the title of the land demanded, for in such case there can be no variance in the statement of it.(*d*)

(*a*) Gibson *v.* Hunter, 2 H. Bl. 205. United States Bank *v.* Smith, 11 Wheat. 172; Gates *v.* Nobles, 1 Root, 344; Humphrey *v.* West, 3 Rand. 516.
(*b*) Proprietary *v.* Ralston, 1 Dall. 18.
(*c*) Gibson *v.* Hunter, 2 H. Bl. 206, 209.
(*d*) Bac. Ab. Pleas, N 7; Co. Litt. 72, a.

3244.—2. Formerly, it was supposed that no demurrer could be had to *parol* evidence, because no tenor can be predicated on it, and therefore, there was a danger of variance, in stating it upon the record. But in modern times, though it is said that a demurrer to evidence is considered an antiquated, unusual, and inconvenient practice,(*a*) it is not doubted that evidence of *any kind*, exhibited in support of the issue, may be demurred to, under the restrictions prescribed in the five rules following; so that if these conditions are complied with, by the party demurring, the opposite party must join in the demurrer, or waive the evidence.

1. When both parties *voluntarily join* in a demurrer to evidence, and the demurrer is properly framed, and with the necessary admissions stated upon record, the court must give judgment, although all the evidence exhibited in support of the issue may rest in parol.

2. When the *fact* itself is admitted on record, which it is the object of the evidence to prove; in such case the party exhibiting the evidence must join in the demurrer, or waive the evidence;(*b*) as if in trover against a bailee, the only evidence exhibited of a conversion is to prove the *mere negligence*, on the part of the defendant, in keeping the goods; the defendant, by admitting upon record the *fact* of negligence in keeping, may demur, and oblige the plaintiff to waive the evidence or to join in the demurrer. This confession the defendant might safely make, because, mere negligence never constitutes conversion in trover.

3. When parol evidence, exhibited in support of the issue, is certain and direct, that is, explicit, absolute, and without any qualification, the adverse party, by entering the evidence upon the record, together with

(*a*) The State *v.* Loper, 4 Shepl. 293.
(*b*) Brandon *v.* Huntsville Bank, 1 Stew. 320 ; Alexander *v.* Fitzpatrick, ·
4 Porter 405.

an admission that it is *true*, may demur, and compel the party exhibiting it to join in the demurrer, or waive the evidence; because in this case the admission of the evidence is the admission of the fact affirmed by it.(*a*)

4. When the evidence offered is not positive and determinate, the adverse party cannot demur to it, without stating it upon the record as certain and determinate, and admitting it in that form to be true.(*b*)

5. When the evidence is circumstantial, the party who demurs to it, must distinctly admit upon the record every fact, and every conclusion, in favor of the opposite party, which the evidence conduces to prove.(*c*)

3245. When the party, demurring to evidence of any kind, does not make the admissions required in the particular case upon the record, and, nevertheless, the opposite party joins in the demurrer, there is nothing on which the court can give a judgment on the demurrer; and, accordingly, in such case, the court must award a *venire de novo*, referring the facts to another jury for trial.

3246. On a demurrer to evidence, and joinder in demurrer, when both are properly framed, it is usual immediately to discharge the jury, as there is no question of fact to be tried by them; and if the plaintiff prevails on the demurrer, there may be a writ of inquiry of damages, which is to be executed afterward. Still, before they are dismissed, the jury may be re-

---

(*a*) Shields *v.* Arnold, 1 Blackf. 109; Burton *v.* Brashear, 3 A. K. Marsh, 276. But see Forbes *v.* Perrie, 1 Har. & John, 109.
(*b*) Gibson *v.* Hunter, 2 H. Bl. 207, 208.
(*c*) Feay *v.* Decamp, 15 S. & R. 227 ; Pawling *v.* United States, 4 Cranch, 219 ; United States *v.* Williams, Ware R. 175 ; Jacob *v.* United States, 1 Brock 520; United States Bank *v.* Smith, 11 Wheat. 320; Jackson *v.* United States, 5 Mason 425 ; Lowry *v.* Mountjoy, 6 Call, 65 ; Thornton *v.* Bank of Washington, 3 Pet. 40; Vaughan *v.* Eason, 4 Yeates, 54 ; Copeland *v.* New England Ins. Co. 22 Pick. 135 ; Clopton *v.* Morris, 6 Leigh, 278.

quired to assess the damages provisionally;(*a*) and, in such case, if the demurrer be determined in favor of the plaintiff, he will be entitled to judgment for the damages thus provisionally assessed.

In modern practice demurrers to evidence are rare, though they sometimes occur; the practice of taking a special verdict, the nature of which will be explained hereafter, is found more convenient.(*b*)

§ 6.—Of the arguments of counsel.

Art. 1.—General observations.

3247. In the course of a long trial, particularly when there are many points raised, and numerous witnesses examined, it is difficult, even with the best trained and disciplined minds, so to arrange the evidence which has been delivered that it shall apply with fairness to the pleadings on both sides; to sift what is not applicable, and reject it; what is collateral, and let it bear only a proper weight; to consider what is doubtful, and distinguish it from what is certain; what is worthy of credit from what is deserving of none; these, and many other points must be considered by the jury. It is the duty of counsel on both sides, so to arrange and explain all this, that the jury can fully understand the evidence, and the questions which, on their oaths, they are to decide; and the counsel should also state the questions of law which are involved in the case, submitting the law, however, to the direction of the court.

Counsel are sworn or affirmed to be true to the court and to the client, but they are not bound nor required by law to press the claims of a plaintiff, or the defence of a defendant, *per fas et nefas.* They are the ministers of justice, and she can never require that while

(*a*) 1 Lilly's Ab. 441 ; Fowler *v.* Macomb, 2 Root, 388 ; Hampton *v.* Windham, 2 Root, 199.
(*b*) Vide post, n. 3264.

484 . OF REMEDIES.

No. 3247.   Book 4, tit. 8, chap. 11, sec 3, § 6, art. 1.   No. 3247.

ministering at her altar they shall lend their powerful aid to promote iniquity.

To perform the obligations which counsel have undertaken, they must cultivate their talents, until, by assiduity, they produce a manly eloquence. To a certain extent eloquence is indispensable to the advocate, to enable him to represent, fully and fairly, the case of his client. This eloquence ought to be simple, vehement and pathetic, and entirely adapted for action and for the combat; it must not, therefore, be too much ornamented, too flowery, too brilliant, or too pompous, nor a mere parade to catch the approval of the bystanders.

He who undertakes the profession of an advocate, ought to sustain and establish it by reason, and all things calculated to adorn it, but mainly by a profound study of jurisprudence, and a thorough understanding of literature. A happy genius, whose speech is embellished by the graces produced by the belles-lettres, and an enlightened knowledge of the law, not only makes a just application of them, but, on proper occasions, touches the heart and elevates the understanding.

The shortest, and at the same time the most certain means of attaining this power, is to make a particular and constant study of the law, with a just discernment, which is to serve him as a rule and a guide.

It is said, perhaps truly, that eloquence is a natural gift, but probably all men possess it, though not in equal degrees. Nature makes men eloquent when roused by great interests and vehement passions. Whenever we are greatly excited we view things differently from other men. A man thus excited makes rapid comparisons, and employs similes, tropes, and metaphors; without observing it, he animates everything, and conveys to those who listen to him a kind of enthusiasm. As this gift of eloquence is given to all, it only requires cultivation to make it bear profitable

OF PROCEEDINGS IN AN ACTION.   485

No. 3247.   Book 4, tit. 8, chap. 11, sec. 3, § 6, art. 1.   No. 3247.

fruit. Much may be accomplished by this means; and a continued exercise, with a perfect knowledge of the case and of the law, will, to a great extent, supply any supposed natural deficiency.

Probity is the foundation of the advocate's eloquence; without this, he will find himself always suspected, and, not having the confidence of the judges and jury, the best reasons he advances will be looked upon with distrust, and fail to have the weight they deserve.

To his natural talents, his application and knowledge, must be joined great purity of language, elegance of style, a richness of brilliant and flowery expressions, a beautiful and noble elevation of thought and sentiment, and a guarded vivacity of imagination; the advocate must possess the art to paint objects so as to render them sensible and palpable, as it were, and with the aid of figures, introduced with skill, to animate his speech, sustain it, and give it a degree of elevation. He must remember that, without neglecting his exordium, which should be the object of his care, and calculated to gain the favorable attention of his hearers, he should in his peroration, or the end of his speech, throw the whole force of his reasoning, with dexterity and art, and end with some agreeable figure by which he takes leave of his audience, remembering, with Lord Bacon, that *melior est finis orationis quam principium.*(a)

Premising that the advocate possesses those natural and acquired advantages which have been mentioned, and a well earned character for honor and probity, still he must observe some rules which are indispensable; among which, may be mentioned the following:

1. The first is, to have perfect order and distinctness in all he says, and to commence by giving correct ideas of the affair in question; he should next explain

---

(a) De Augmentis Scientiarum, lib. 8, c. 2, par. 10.

all the circumstances, and afterward he must go directly to the point of law of the case.

2. The advocate should use skilfully and with energy the principal means which are calculated to influence his hearers, without passing over entirely in silence others which, in his opinion, may have less weight, as it is difficult to tell what reasons may convince the judges, some being satisfied by one, and others by another argument or motive.

3. There should always be a just proportion in the quality and length of the speech to the subject. It is ridiculous to use all the elegance of language, which ought to be employed in defending the life and honor of a prominent citizen, in a case concerning only a trifling pecuniary matter; and it is no less absurd to make as long a speech, where but a single question of fact or law is involved, as would be made when the case was extremely intricate and required much explanation.

4. The wise advocate ought to state the facts as they are, without any disguise whatever. A prudent lawyer will never attempt to make a speech to enlighten his auditors as to facts, without having previously examined them, and knowing all the reasons for and against the cause of his client; he will then be able to give full force to those in his favor, and destroy those of his adversary, without however violating the truth, or gratuitously wounding the reputation of the adverse party. The means he ought to employ, are drawn from principles of law and from reason. When he cites a decision, he ought to be careful to state it as it is; he ought not merely to show that such a decision has been made, but also the reason, and the principle upon which it has been so adjudged.

5. As the matters in the temple of justice ought always to be seriously discussed, and as they are always of importance to the parties, a wise advocate will abstain from all pleasantries and jests, too often

OF PROCEEDINGS IN AN ACTION.   487

No 3247.   Book 4, tit. 8, chap 11, sec. 3, § 6, art 1.   No 3247.

insipid, which, though they may excite a laugh, it is frequently at the expense of their author.

6. It is a rule, which cannot be too rigidly observed, that a speech should not be filled with useless circumlocutions, for they are injurious; they draw the attention from the real points of the case, and weaken the argument; and even when the advocate has a bad cause, the introduction of extraneous circumstances will have a tendency to prejudice wise judges against him, as it is easily shown that they could not have been introduced for a legitimate purpose.

7. But a perfect arrangement of thoughts and words is not sufficient to make an eloquent discourse; there is a beauty in the position of the body and the gesture, an agreeableness in the modulations of the voice, which, joined to a clear, firm and distinct pronunciation, are required to make an eloquent speech. In fact, the eloquence of gesture, of the face, and the proper modulation of the voice, are not less necessary than the words uttered by the speaker, and, not seldom, make as much impression as the words themselves. It must, however, be remembered, that to have any effect, these must be natural and without affectation; for, although an immovable orator, without grace, chills his auditors, yet he is not more defective than he who assumes a theatrical air, and, by his misplaced gestures and his affected manners, leaves upon the minds of his hearers nothing solid or convincing about his case, and only an unfavorable opinion as to himself. The first puts you to sleep; the last prevents you, by his speech, from thinking of what you came into court to hear.(a)

(a) The foregoing rules are condensed in the following lines:

" Be brief, be pointed; let your matter stand
Lucid in order, solid, and at hand;
Spend not your words on trifles, but condense;
Strike with the mass of thoughts, not drops of sense;
Press to the close with vigor once begun,
And leave, (how hard the task!) leave off when done;

488 OF REMEDIES.

No. 3248.   Book 4, tit 8, chap. 11, sec. 3, § 6, art. 2.   No. 3248.

Art. 2.—Of the speech of counsel for plaintiff.

3248. The counsel of the party who has the right to begin, which we suppose is the plaintiff, now argues his case to the jury. It is essential to the due administration of justice, that the counsel should be privileged and protected in the energetic discharge of his professional duty; that, when commenting with just severity, when the case requires it, upon the conduct of the parties or of witnesses, he may use strong epithets, however derogatory of the opponent or his attorney, or other agents employed in bringing or defending the action; for, if he were liable to an action for uttering such language, whether true or not, it would cramp, if not destroy the energy of counsel, which is considered so essential to society.(*a*) Respectable and sensible counsel, however, will always refrain from the indulgence of any unjust severity,

> Who draws a labor'd length of reasoning out,
> Puts straws in lines for winds to whirl about,
> Who draws a tedious tale of learning o'er,
> Counts but the sands on ocean's boundless shore,
> Victory in law is gain'd as battles fought,
> Not by the numbers, but the forces brought;
> What boots success in skirmish or in fray,
> If rout and ruin following, close the day?
> What worth a hundred posts maintain'd with skill,
> If these all held, the foe is victor still?
> He who would win his cause, with power must frame
> Points of support, and look with steady aim:
> Attack the weak, defend the strong with art,
> Strike but few blows, but strike them to the heart;
> All scatter'd fires but end in smoke and noise,
> The scorn of men, the idle play of boys;
> Keep, then, this first great precept ever near,
> Short be your speech, your matter strong and clear,
> Earnest your manner, warm and rich your style,
> Severe in taste, yet full of grace the while;
> So may you reach the loftiest heights of fame,
> And leave, when life is past, a deathless name."

(*a*) In Louisiana, it is enacted, "that no client or other person shall be held to be liable or responsible for any slanderous or libellous words uttered by his attorney at law, but attorneys at law shall be liable and responsible themselves, for any slanderous or libellous words by them uttered, any law to the contrary notwithstanding." Act of March 25, 1828, section 23.

both on their own personal account, and because brow-
beating a witness or other person, or abusing a party,
will injuriously affect their case, in the eyes of a respectable court and jury.

The counsel should, first, distinctly state the full
extent of the plaintiff's claim, and the circumstances
under which it is made; secondly, he should show how
it is supported by the evidence; thirdly, the legal
grounds, and authorities in favor of the claim.

3249.—1. The grounds on which it is founded, and
the statement of the claim, must be made out so clearly
that they shall make an impression on the minds of
the jury; for, unless these are distinctly shown, the
jurors will have an imperfect or confused idea of the
subject.

3250.—2. Too much care cannot be taken to classify
and arrange, in a natural order, all the facts which
have been detailed in evidence, and to show how they
bear on the case. In general, a few of the principal
facts are sufficient to maintain the issue on the part of
the plaintiff; these should be prominently set forth and
pressed upon the attention of the jury; others, which
are collateral, may be observed upon, but they must
be considered only as collateral; and those which have
inadvertently been introduced by the other side, which
have no relation to the true merits of the case, should
be exposed in their nakedness.

It will be the duty of counsel, too, at this stage of
the cause, to examine the character of the witnesses,
the manner in which they gave their evidence, and
other circumstances which are calculated to gain them
credence, or to deprive their testimony of any confidence.

When the defendant has given any evidence, it is
proper to examine his defence, and to show that it is
not supported by the facts, or that it is not warranted
by the pleadings, or that the evidence of the plaintiff

has effectually rebutted all such defence, or any other facts which the evidence warrants.

3251.—3. It is the duty of the counsel, also, to state all the points of law on which he intends to rely, and to refer to the authorities which support them. In some cases it is proper to read such authorities, and press them on the consideration of the court and jury.

Art. 3.—Of the speech for the defendant.

3252.—1. The speech of the defendant's counsel ought to show clearly what is the defence of the defendant, whether it acknowledges the cause of action of the plaintiff and shows some matter in discharge, or whether it denies that the plaintiff had any cause of action; the particulars of the defence should be distinctly stated, and all the circumstances attending it.

3253.—2. Next should be an examination of the evidence on both sides, and those facts which show that the plaintiff never had a cause of action, or, if he had one, that it had been discharged, should be pressed upon the consideration of the jury. The arguments of the counsel for the plaintiff, not well founded, should be attacked and exposed; and if any important fact has been omitted by him, in commenting upon the evidence, it should be pointed out to the jury.

3254.—3. The points of law made by the plaintiff should be examined, and, if found futile or not applicable to the case, should be explained, and authorities cited to show what is the law of the case.

Art. 4.—Of the reply of the plaintiff.

3255. In strictness, the reply of the plaintiff's counsel must be confined to such new matters and arguments as have been advanced by the counsel for the defendant. He cannot, therefore, again go into an examination of the whole case, and travel over the same ground which he formerly occupied. The prin-

OF PROCEEDINGS IN AN ACTION. 491

No 3256.   Book 4, tit. 8, chap 11, sec. 3, § 7, art. 1.   No 3256.

cipal business of the reply is to refute such unjust arguments as may have been pressed by the opposite counsel, and to show, when the truth will justify such course, that however plausible such arguments may be, they are not founded in law or in fact.

§ 7.—Of charging the jury, or the judge's summing up.

Art. 1.—*Of the form of the charge.*

3256. After the counsel on both sides have finished their addresses to the jury, the judge proceeds to *sum up*, as it is called, or *charge* the jury.

Before this is done, however, sometimes the counsel on both sides, or on one side only, present to the judge a statement of the *points* on which they request him to charge the jury. These points are brief statements of what the counsel conceive is the law of the case. In the course of his charge, the judge gives an answer to the several questions to which the points give rise.

In summing up, as in every other part of his conduct, impartiality is the first duty of a judge. He must not only be impartial, but he must pay a blind obedience to the law, whether it be good or bad. He is bound to declare what the law is, and not to make it: he is not an arbitrator, but an interpreter of the law.

When we consider that the jury in general are unlearned in the law, unaccustomed to examine cases with all their intricacies; that they may have been perplexed as well as enlightened by the speeches of the counsel, we will perceive that the accuracy of the summing up of the judge is of the utmost importance. To enable the jury to come to a just conclusion, it is incumbent on the judge correctly to state the law of the case, as well as the evidence, and the bearing of the latter. He may also direct the jury to find a verdict in a particular way, if they believe the evidence adduced by one of the parties, or the testimony on a particular point.

492 OF REMEDIES.

No. 3256   Book 4, tit 8, chap 11, sec 3, § 7, art 1.   No 3256.

The learned judge, in general, concisely states the ' precise issue between the parties. He explains the substance of the plaintiff's claims, and the grounds of defence. He then, to a certain extent, details the evidence which has been given in the cause, sometimes reading certain parts from his notes. It is usual for him to consider the evidence of the plaintiff in the first place, and whether he has given such proof of his claim as may warrant the jury to find a verdict in his favor, if the defendant had given no evidence; next he examines the evidence of the defendant, and points out where it affects the evidence of the plaintiff. In case the testimony given by the plaintiff can be reconciled with the apparent contradictory evidence of the defendant, he shows how that may be done; but when this is impossible, he leaves it to the jury to decide which is entitled to credit. In the course of this examination he comments occasionally on the nature of the evidence, and the circumstances which attach a credit to it, or which render it doubtful or incredible.

When any question of law happens to be mixed up with a question of fact, he states the rule of law according to which the jury are to decide, and informs them that as to the law they are bound to take it from the court; as to the facts, they are the sole judges, and must decide them upon the credibility of the evidence and witnesses; at the same time he may observe upon the manner and conduct of each, so as to assist the jury to come to a correct conclusion. A just judge will state what the law is, in clear, distinct, and unmistakable terms, without any attempt to qualify his opinion in any way. The jury are to be guided by his decision as to the law, and they and the parties have a right to have it clearly explained. He will leave the facts to the consideration of the jury, without any effort to take them from that body, who are alone lawfully authorized to pass upon them.

In case points of law have been submitted to him

OF PROCEEDINGS IN AN ACTION. 493

No. 3257.   Book 4, tit. 8, chap. 11, sec. 3, § 8, art. 1.   No 3258.

by the counsel on either side, he will decide them, and give clear and distinct answers to each, without any evasion, and direct the jury what is the law as to the points submitted to him.

He will also direct the jury as to the form of the verdict which they ought to find.

Art. 2.—Of exceptions to the charge.

3257. We have seen that exceptions have been taken in the course of the trial, whenever a cause for taking them arose; so an exception must be taken to the charge of the court as soon as it has been delivered. This is to be done in a respectful manner; for it is of the utmost importance to the parties, the counsel, and all others concerned, to support the dignity of the judge. If, by any inadvertence, the learned judge has omitted to state any material explanation of the law which it was his duty to explain, or neglected to answer any or all of the points submitted to him, these should be suggested; or, if he has misstated the evidence to the jury, an opportunity to set that matter right ought to be given to him, by calling his attention to it.

When an exception is taken to the charge of the court, the judge should state in the bill of exceptions the words used, without any attempt to qualify them in any way whatever. What he said to the jury has had its effect, and if any qualification is given to it, so that the court above have not the exact expression used, he may do great injustice to the party against whom a verdict has been found. A just, a noble, and impartial mind, will disdain to carry a point at the expense of justice.

§ 8.—Of the verdict.

Art. 1.—Of considering the verdict.

3258. After the judge has delivered his charge, the jury are required to consider their verdict. For this purpose, they have a right to withdraw from the bar or jury-box, and retire in charge of an officer, to a private room, there to deliberate on their verdict. They are not allowed to take with them any documents, without the leave of the court, for it is evident that, if the documents should be all on one side, as where depositions are taken to support the plaintiff's claim, and none upon the other, or his testimony has all been given *viva voce*, in open court, the parties would not stand upon equal ground.(*a*)

If, after having retired from the court, the jury cannot agree upon their verdict, and the court or judge is fully satisfied that they cannot agree, after having made many efforts to do so, the judge may, in his discretion *discharge* them from the further consideration of the case. In England this has the effect of putting the parties out of court, without any judgment, and of course each has to bear his own costs, and the plaintiff is allowed to bring a new suit for the same cause of action. If, in the new action, he should recover, he will not be entitled to the costs of the first.(*b*) In Indiana, when a jury in a civil cause was impanelled, heard a part of the evidence, and the jurors dispersed, by consent, and next day one of the jurors failed to appear, whereupon the jury was dismissed, and a new jury impanelled, the proceedings were held not to be erroneous.(*c*)

The jury may also be dismissed by *withdrawing a juror*, that is, requesting one of the jurors to leave the jury-box, by which means the proceedings in the suit are at an end, and each party must pay his own costs. This is usually done at the suggestion of the judge, when there are reasons why the case should not pro-

(*a*) See Wright *v.* Rogers, 2 Penning. 547.
(*b*) Vallance *v.* Evans, 3 Tyr. 865 ; Sealy *v.* Powis, 3 Dowl. 372 ; 1 Har. & Wal. 118 ; Everett *v.* Youells, 3 Barn & Ad. 349 ; Bonsor *v.* Clement, 6 Car. & Payne, 230.
(*c*) Harris *v.* Doe, 4 Blackf. 369.

OF PROCEEDINGS IN AN ACTION.   495

No 3259.   Book 4, tit. 8, chap. 11, sec 3, § 8, art 2   No. 3259.

ceed further. But the plaintiff may bring a new suit for the same cause of action.

Art. 2.—Of rendering the verdict.

3259. It may be remembered that the jurors were sworn "to try the issue joined between the parties, and a true verdict give according to the evidence." The *issue* is the question or matter in controversy between the parties, as appears upon the pleadings on record; and the term *evidence* means the proofs adduced by the parties before the jury in open court, consequently no verdict can be founded upon any other knowledge, and still less upon any hearsay information acquired by a juror out of court. If a juror has any knowledge of the facts, he ought to be examined like any other witness, in order to give the party against whom his knowledge would operate, an opportunity to contradict or explain what operates on the juror's mind.

The verdict should be in positive terms, one way or the other, and not in any doubtful mode of expression, but when it is a special verdict it may be in the alternative.

The law requires that the verdict shall be unanimous; the verdict of any number less than the whole twelve cannot be received, except by consent (*a*)

When the jury have agreed upon their verdict, they come into court, and after being placed in the jury-box, their names are called by the clerk of the court, to ascertain whether they are all present. The clerk then asks them, "Gentlemen of the jury, are you agreed upon your verdict?" Upon their assenting, he asks, "How say you, do you find for the plaintiff or the defendant?" The foreman of the jury then answers, either "We find for the plaintiff," if in an action of debt or assumpsit, so many dollars, debts or

---

(*a*) Campbell *v.* Wooldredge, Geo. Decis. part 2, p. 132.

damages, and costs; or if for the defendant, "We find for the defendant." The clerk then makes an entry of the finding, and, addressing the jury, says, "Gentlemen of the jury, hearken unto your verdict, as the court have recorded it, you say you find," and then repeats their finding, to which they all assent.

But after the jury have come in, at any time before the verdict has been delivered and *recorded*, either party has a right to ask that the jury shall be *polled*; that is, that each juror shall be asked separately what is his verdict.(a) If, upon being so polled, one should dissent from his fellows, the verdict cannot be received, because the jurors are not unanimous. In such case, or indeed in any other, when the jury are in doubt, they may ask additional instructions from the court as to the law, or they may recall any witness about whose testimony there is some disagreement among the jurors.(b) They retire again, and further deliberate upon their verdict, and the same form of receiving it is pursued, which was adopted in the first instance.

Art. 3.—Of the kinds of verdicts.

3260. A *verdict* is the *unanimous decision* made by a jury, and reported to the court, on the matters lawfully submitted to the jurors in the course of the trial of a cause.

In England, at common law, they have four kinds of verdicts in civil cases : 1, privy verdicts; 2, public verdicts; 3, general verdicts; and 4, special verdicts.

1. Of privy verdicts.

3261. A *privy verdict* is one delivered privily to a judge out of court. A verdict of this kind is delivered to the judge after the jury have agreed, for the convenience of the jury, who, after having given it, sepa-

---

(a) Johnson v. Howe, 2 Gilman, 342 ; Rigg v. Cook, 4 Gilm. 336.
(b) Blackley v. Sheldon, 7 John. 32.

rate. This verdict is of no force whatever until it is afterward delivered in open court. From its liability to abuse, this practice, it is believed, has seldom if ever obtained in the United States.(a) To relieve the jurors, after they have agreed, it is not unusual for the counsel to agree that the jury shall seal their verdict, and then separate. The *sealing of a verdict* is to put the verdict in writing, and put it in an envelop, which is sealed. When the court is again in session, the jury come in and give their verdict, in all respects as if it had not been sealed, and a juror may dissent from it, if, since the sealing, he has honestly changed his mind.(b)

2. Of public verdicts.

3262. A *public verdict* is one delivered in open court; this verdict, when received, has its full effect, and, unless set aside, is conclusive on the facts, and when a final judgment is rendered upon it, bars all future controversies in personal actions.

3. Of general verdicts.

3263. A *general verdict* is one by which the jury pronounce at the same time, in the terms of the issue, on the fact and the law, either in favor of the plaintiff or defendant.(c) The jury may find such a verdict whenever they deem it proper to do so, although the judge may direct them to find specially as to a particular fact, on which a legal question may be raised.(d) The verdict is general, when it finds the facts and the law, as, for instance, that a certain sale took place; it is special, when it finds certain facts,

---

(a) Goodwin v. Appleton, 9 Shepl. 453; Dornick v. Richenback, 10 S. & R. 84. See McMurray v. O'Neil, 1 Call, 246; Shamokin Coal Co. v. Milman, 3 Penn. St. R. 79.
(b) Sutliff v. Gilbert, 8 Ham. 405; Rigg v. Cook, Gilm. 336.
(c) Co. Litt. 228.
(d) Davizes v, Clark, 3 Ad. & Ell. 506.

498　　　　　OF REMEDIES.

No. 3264.　　　Book 4, tit. 8, chap. 11, sec. 3, § 8, art 3.　　　No. 3264.

leaving it to the court to decide whether those facts constitute a sale.(a)

When the verdict is general, and some of the counts in the plaintiff's declaration are bad, no judgment can be entered in favor of the plaintiff;(b) and if a judgment is entered by the court below, on the counts which are supposed to be good, the supreme court will reverse it on error.(c) But the rule, that when one of several counts is bad, no judgment can be entered on a general verdict, does not apply to the case of a general verdict in favor of the defendant when some of his pleas are bad.(d)

4. Of special verdicts.

3264. A *special verdict* is one by which the facts of the case are put on record, and the law is submitted to the judges. The jury have an option, instead of finding the affirmative or negative of the issue, as in a general verdict, to find all the facts disclosed by the evidence before them, and, after setting them forth, to conclude to the following effect: " that they are ignorant, in point of law, on which side they ought, upon those facts, to find the issue; that if, upon the whole matter, the court shall be of opinion that the issue is proved for the plaintiff, they find for the plaintiff accordingly, and assess the damages at　　　dollars; but if the court are of an opposite opinion, then they find for the defendant." This form of finding is called a *special* verdict.

A special verdict must find the facts, and not merely the evidence of facts; it is upon the facts the court must pass their judgment what the law is, and they are not required to draw any inference.(e) If it does

---

(a) Chidoteau's heirs v. Dominguez, 7 Mart. 521.
(b) Wilson v. Gray, 8 Watts, 37.
(c) Harker v. Orr, 8 Watts, 245.
(d) Wilson v. Gray, 8 Watts, 37.
(e) Lawrence v. Beaubion, 2 Bailey, 623; Brown v. Ralston, 4 Rand. 504; Bertrand v. Morrison, Breeze, 175; Henderson v. Allen, 1 H. & M. 235.

not find the material facts in detail, it is deficient,(*a*) and if defectively stated, it will not be aided by facts appearing elsewhere upon the record.(*b*)

3265. In practice the jury have nothing to do with the formal preparation of the special verdict; when it is agreed that a verdict of that kind shall be given, the jury merely declare their opinion as to any fact remaining in doubt, and then the verdict is adjusted without their further interference. It is settled, under the direction of the judge, by the counsel and attorneys on either side, according to the state of the facts as found by the jury, with respect to all particulars on which they have delivered an opinion, and with respect to other particulars, according to the state of the facts which, it is agreed, that they ought to find upon the evidence before them.

The special verdict, when its form is thus settled, is, together with the whole proceedings on the trial, then entered on record; and the question of law, arising on the facts found, is argued before the court in banc, and decided by that court, as in case of a demurrer. If either party be dissatisfied with their decision, he may afterward resort to a court of errors.(*c*)

3266. There is another mode of finding a special verdict; this is, when the jury find a verdict generally for the plaintiff, but subject, nevertheless, to the opinion of the judges or the court above, or a *special case* stated by the counsel on both sides, with regard to a matter of law.(*d*)

Art. 4.—*Of the requisites of a verdict.*

3267. A verdict must, 1, conform to the issue; 2, be certain.

(*a*) Hann *v.* Field, Litt. Sel. Cas. 376.
(*b*) Lee *v.* Campbell, 4 Porter, 198.
(*c*) Steph. Pl. 113; 3 Bl. Com. 377 ; Bac. Ab. Verdict, D, E; 1 Archb. Pr. 180.
(*d*) 3 Bl. Com. 378.

500   OF REMEDIES.

No. 3268.   Book 4, tit. 8, chap. 11, sec. 3, § 8, art. 4.   No. 3270.

1. Of the conformity of the verdict with the issue.

3268.—1. When there is but one issue, the verdict *must conform to it,* for that is the only thing to be tried and ascertained; and when it does not conform to it, no judgment can be rendered upon it, because the matter to be tried has not been found one way or the other;(a) and a verdict is equally bad if it find only a part of the issue.(b) The verdict must also negative all the pleas in the case, when found for the plaintiff.(c)

3269.—2. When there are several issues, the verdict must conform to them all; but though it is a general rule that the jury must answer all the issues, yet, when it appears that all the questions of the case are settled by the verdict, that will be sufficient, and the verdict will not be set aside, unless the omission to find the other issues prejudice the party complaining;(d) and where there is a finding on one issue in favor of the plaintiff, and no finding upon the others, the plaintiff may waive the other issues, or consent that a verdict as to them be entered against him.(e)

2. Of the certainty of the verdict.

3270. Another requisite of a verdict is *certainty,* for it is obvious that if there be no certainty in the verdict, the court cannot give judgment :(f) thus, upon a libel for the breach of the revenue laws, the verdict found for the libellants, '' the vessel, tackle, apparel, and cargo, *except that part of the cargo on which the duties have been paid,''* was held to be too uncertain to give a judgment upon it.(g) And in an action for

(a) Moody *v.* Keener, 7 Porter, 218. .
(b) Patterson *v.* United States, 2 Wheat. 221; Barnett *v.* Watson, 1 Wash. 272.
(c) Kilpatrick *v.* S. W. Rail Road Bank, 6 Humph. 45.
(d) White *v.* Bailey, 4 Conn. 272.
(e) Sutton *v.* Dana, 1 Met. 383.
(f) Stearn *v.* Barrett, 1 Mason, 153.
(g) Richards *v.* Tabb, 4 Call, 522.

freight and demurrage, a verdict in these words, " we find for the plaintiff, and are of opinion that the plaintiff has already received, out of the property of the defendant, payment in full for the amount of freight to which he is entitled," was set aside for uncertainty.(a) But a verdict will not be set aside for uncertainty, as to matters not essential to the gist of the action, if it find the material matter in issue, with sufficient certainty;(b) nor is mere surplusage sufficient to vitiate a verdict.(c)

Art. 5.—Of the amendment of verdicts.

3271. Until the verdict has been formally recorded and the jury have separated, they may *amend* their verdict; as where the jury, through a misconception of the effect of legal terms, returned a verdict, the very reverse of what they intended, the papers were again delivered to them, by direction of the presiding judge, before they had separated and left their seats, and the judge explained to them the meaning of those terms, and they corrected their verdict, it was holden that this proceeding was correct.(d)   But after the jury have been discharged and separated, they cannot be recalled to alter or amend their verdict.(e)

The proceedings on trial by jury at *nisi prius* or at *bar*, terminate with the verdict.

(a) Diehl v. Peters, 1 S. & R. 367.
(b) Pejepscot Proprietors v. Nichols. 1 Fairf. 256.
(c) Patterson v. United States, 2 Wheat. 221 ; Bacon v. Callender, 6 Mass. 303 ; Duane v. Simmons, 4 Yeates, 441.
(d) Ward v. Bailey, 10 Shepl. 316.   See The State v. Underwood, 2 Ala. 742.
(e) Sargeant v. The State, 11 Ohio, 472 ; Walters v. Junkins, 16 S. & R. 414.

CHAPTER XII.—OF THE PROCEEDINGS IN AN ACTION AFTER THE TRIAL AND BEFORE JUDGMENT.

3272. After the trial, the unsuccessful party may move the court, 1, to grant a new trial; or, 2, to arrest the judgment; or, 3, to give judgment *non obstante veredicto;* or, 4, to award a repleader; or, 5, to award a *venire facias de novo.*

SECTION 1.—OF A NEW TRIAL.

3273. A *new trial* is a reëxamination of an issue in fact, before a court and jury, which had been tried, at least once, before the same court and a jury; or it is "a reinvestigation of the facts and legal rights of the parties upon disputed facts," and either upon the same, or different, or additional evidence, before a new jury, and probably, but not necessarily, before a different judge.(*a*)   The origin and practice of granting new trials is concealed in the night of time; formerly they could be obtained only with the greatest difficulties, for it is a great principle of law, that the decision of a jury, upon an issue in fact, is in general irreversible and conclusive.(*b*)   But by the modern practice they are more liberally granted in furtherance of justice.   Still, it has been considered that the "important right of trial by jury requires that new trials should never be granted without solid and substantial reasons; otherwise the province of jurymen might be often transferred to the judges, and they, instead of the jury, would become the real triers of the facts.   A reasonable doubt merely, that justice has not been

(*a*) 4 Chit. Gen. Pr. 30.
(*b*) Formerly, the law provided one means of appeal from the verdict of a jury in certain cases by *writ of attaint;* upon this there was a kind of new trial, by twenty-four jurors.   This was applicable only in cases where the jury wilfully and knowingly gave a false verdict.   This kind of proceeding is abolished even in England, and perhaps was never adopted in the United States.

done, especially in cases where the value and importance of the cause is not great, appears to be too
slender for them."(a)

On the conclusion of a trial, it sometimes happens
that one of the parties is dissatisfied with the opinion
expressed in the course of the trial, by the judge who
tried the cause, and which produced the result against
him, whether it related to the effect or the admissibility of the evidence; or he may think the evidence
against him insufficient in law, when no adverse
opinion has been expressed by the judge, and yet he
may not have obtained a special verdict, or demurred
to the evidence, or tendered a bill of exceptions. He
is, in such case, at liberty to move the court in banc,
or a single judge, in some cases, during the time prescribed by the rules of court, to grant a new trial, on
the ground of the judge's having misdirected the jury,
or having admitted or refused evidence contrary to
law. He may apply for the same remedy, in other
cases, when justice does not appear to have been done
at the first trial; as where the verdict, though not
contrary to evidence, or on insufficient ground, in
point of law, is manifestly wrong in point of direction,
as contrary to the weight of evidence, and on that
ground disapproved of by the judge who tried the
cause; or the new trial may be moved for where new
evidence of a material fact has been discovered since
the trial, which the party did not know, and of course
could not produce before the jury; or when the losing
party has been taken by surprise, or in cases where
the damages given are excessive, or the jury have
misconducted themselves, or the parties attempted to
bias the jury unlawfully; in these and all other cases
where it appears that injustice has been done, or
might have happened, a new trial will be granted.

(a) Per Shippen, P. J., in Cowperthwaite v. Jones, 2 Dall. 56.

These reasons may be classed as follows: 1, matters which arose before or in the course of the trial; 2, the acts of the prevailing party; 3, the misconduct of the jury; 4, cases where the verdict is improper, because it is either against law, or against evidence; 5, the discovery of new evidence;. 6, because the losing party has been taken by surprise; 7, because the damages are excessive; 8, because the damages are inadequate; 9, because the witness has since been convicted of perjury.

§ 1.—For matters which arose before, or in the course of the trial.'

3274. These are, 1, want of notice; 2, the irregular impanelling of the jury; 3, the admission of illegal, or the rejection of legal evidence; 4, the misdirection of the judge.

Art. 1.—Of want of notice.

3275. The most obvious principles of justice require that a man should have a right to defend himself, when attacked; that he should be· allowed to explain his conduct when it is alleged he has violated the law, either by not fulfilling his legal engagements, or because he has committed a wrong, tort, or injury to another. Justice, therefore, requires that the defendant should have a sufficient notice of the time and place of trial; and the want of it, unless it has been waived by an appearance and making defence, will, in general, be sufficient to entitle the defendant to a new trial.(a) But the insufficiency of the notice must have been calculated reasonably to mislead the defendant.

Art. 2.—Of the irregular impanelling of the jury.

3276. The selection of a jury should be fairly made.

(a) Bull. N. P. 327 ; Attorney General *v.* Stevens & Prall, 3 Price, 72 ; 3 Dougl. 402 ; 1 Wend, 22. See Jamieson *v.* Pomeroy, 9 Penn. St. Rep. 230.

If there should be any fraud, by any of the officers to whom this service has been confided by law; as if a clerk in calling the names of the jurors, instead of calling the name of the person drawn, should substitute that of a friend of one of the parties in the cause; or, if no unfairness of this kind should occur, a person not qualified, as an infant or alien, should be put on the jury;(a) or if a person not regularly summoned and returned, should personate another, and serve on the jury;(b) or if a juror who was on a first trial is put on a second trial, and the fact is not known to the party until the second verdict is rendered;(c) all these are sufficient for granting a new trial.

Art. 3.—Of the admission of illegal and the rejection of legal evidence.

3277. When, in the hurry of a jury trial, the judge through inadvertence or mistake admits improper evidence, or rejects that which is legal, the court will, on a motion for a new trial, grant it, and set aside a verdict which has been obtained through this mistake, and the complaining party will not be sent to a court of error for redress. But a new trial will not be granted for the rejection of a witness on the supposed ground of incompetency, when another witness establishes the same fact, and it is not disputed on the other side.(d)

(a) Stainton v. Beadle, 4 T. R. 473.
(b) Norman v. Beaumont, Willes, 484; S. C. Barnes, 453. In Pennsylvania, by going on to trial the defect will be cured in both criminal and civil cases. But in Massachusetts, a new trial will not be granted because one of the jurors had not been drawn and returned according to law, if the objection be not made till after verdict; nor, in a capital case, because the juror belonged to another county. Armstead v. Hadley, 1 Pick. 38. A new trial will not be granted in Kentucky because a juror was an alien, though it was unknown to the party and his counsel till after verdict. Presbury v. The State, 9 Dana, 203; nor, in Tennessee, on the ground of the incompetency of the juror. Booby v. The State, 4 Yerg. 111. And if known at the time of trial, it is no valid objection in Missouri. Lisle v. The State, 6 Mis. 426.
(c) Herndon v. Bradshaw, 4 Bibb. 45; Craig v. Elliot, 4 Bibb. 272.
(d) 2 East, R. 451.

Art. 4.—Of the misdirection of the judge.

3278. A new trial will be granted for *any misdirection of the judge,* when such misdirection has caused, or is likely to cause injustice and an injury to the party against whom the verdict has been rendered ; for when no injustice has been done, and a new trial would be likely to produce the same result, it will not be granted. Such misdirection relates either to matter of law, or to matter of fact.

3279.—1. When the judge at the trial misdirects the jury on matter of *law,* material to the issue, whatever may be the nature of the case, the verdict will be set aside and a new trial granted, if such misdirection or instruction may have influenced their verdict,(*a*) But an erroneous opinion upon an abstract question of law, expressed by the judge in charging the jury, which is not involved in the decision of the case, is not a ground for reversing the judgment, or for granting a new trial;(*b*) nor will a new trial be granted for misdirection, where entire justice has been done.(*c*)

A new trial will be granted, if it appear that the charge of the presiding judge took from the jury a matter of fact in controversy between the parties ;(*d*) or where the opening and closing of the argument before the jury, which belonged to the defendant and was claimed by him, was assigned to the plaintiff.(*e*)

If the judge refuse or neglect to charge the jury, upon a material point, when requested by the counsel against whom a verdict has been rendered, if the verdict was so rendered for want of such instruction,

---

(*a*) Lane *v.* Crombie, 12 Pick. 177 ; Hoyt *v.* Dimon, 5 Day 479 ; Doe *v.* Paine, 4 Hawkes, 64 ; West *v.* Anderson, 9 Conn. 107.
(*b*) Reed *v.* McGrew, 5 Ham. 375 ; Jordan *v.* James, 5 Ham. 88.
(*c*) Johnson *v.* Blackman, 11 Conn. 342.
(*d*) United States *v.* Tillotson, 12 Wheat. 180.
(*e*) Davis *v.* Mason, 4 Pick. 156.

a new trial will be granted ;(a) but a new trial will not
be granted where the judge simply neglected to charge
the jury upon a point, when his attention was not
drawn to it.(b)

When the issue consists of a mixed question of law
and fact, and there is a conceded state of facts, the
rest is a question of law for the court ; and a misdirection in respect to such an issue will avoid the
verdict.(c)

3280.—2. Misdirection of *facts* will, in some cases,
be sufficient to vitiate the proceedings. If, for example,
the judge should undertake to dictate to the jury.(d)
When the judge delivers his opinion to the jury on a
matter of fact, it should be delivered as mere *opinion*
which they are at liberty to disregard, and not as instructions binding on them,(e)

It may be observed as a general rule, that a new
trial will not be granted on account of a misdirection,
either as to law or fact, when *injustice has not been done*,
and the verdict has not prejudiced the complaining
party.(f)

§ 2.—When a new trial will be granted in consequence of the
wrongful acts of the successful party.

3281. If the prevailing party, his agent, or attorney, has been guilty of any act of impropriety, by
which the jury have been induced to give a verdict
against the other party, this will be sufficient ground
for granting a new trial ; and in many cases evils arise

(a) Den v. Sinnickson, 4 Halst. 149 ; Coleman v. Roberts, 1 Mis. 97.
But the court may refuse to instruct upon a point upon which no evidence
was adduced.   Freeman v. Edmunds, 3 Hawke, 5.
(b) Alsop v. Swathel, 7 Conn. 500.
(c) Diover v. Gunton, 2 Wend. 596.
(d) See Hine v. Robbins, 8 Conn. 342.
(e) Trotter v. Saunders, 7 J. J. Marsh, 321 ; Dallam v. Handley, 2 A.
K. Marsh. 418 ; 12 John. 513.
(f) Mansfield v. Wheeler, 23 Wend. 79 ; Price v. Evans, 4 B. Munroe,
386 ; Selleck v. Turnpike Co., 13 Conn. 453.

and injury is sustained by the losing party, when it might be very difficult to prove the injury ; the courts, therefore, look with jealous eyes over such acts. Still, it is not easy to say what acts will be sufficient to authorize the court to grant a new trial. The following, of many examples, will suffice to show the nature of these wrongful acts ; as when a paper, not before submitted to the court, is surreptitiously handed to the jury, being material on the point in issue,(a) unless it appears that they have not looked into it.(b) So, if he have labored the jury, or used improper influence with them, or procured another to do so, to induce them to give a verdict in his favor, a new trial will be granted.(c) And even when handbills reflecting upon the plaintiff's character were distributed in court and shown to the jury on the day of trial, a verdict against him was set aside, upon application, and a new trial granted, although the defendant, by his affidavit, denied all knowledge of the handbills.(d) But if the other party is aware of such attempts, it is his duty to apply for their correction, and his neglect so to do, when in his power, will deprive him of the equity he had to claim a new trial ; he must be supposed to have acquiesced in them. When indirect measures have been resorted to, in order to prejudice the jury,(e) or tricks practised,(f) or unlawful attempts to suppress or stifle evidence, or thwart the proceedings, or to obtain an unconscionable advantage, or to mislead the court and jury, they will be defeated by granting a new trial.(g)

(a) Co. Litt. 227 b.
(b) Hakley v. Hastie, 3 John. 252.
(c) Knight v. Freeport, 13 Mass. 218 ; Blaine's Lessee v. Chambers, 1 S. & R. 169.
(d) Coster v. Merest, 3 Br. & Bing. 272.
(e) 3 Br. & Bing. 272.
(f) 11 Mod. 141.
(g) Grah. N. T. 56 ; 4 Chit. Gen. Pr. 59.

OF PROCEEDINGS IN AN ACTION.   509

No. 3282.   Book 4, tit. 8, chap. 12, sec. 1, § 3, 4.   No. 3283.

§ 3.—New trial granted on account of the conduct of the jurors.

3282. The jury are sworn well and truly to try the issue between the parties, and a true verdict give according to the evidence. Any misconduct in violation of their oaths, is a sufficient ground for granting a new trial; as where they found a verdict by a lottery;(a) but where each of the jurors set down a sum, in a case of *tort*, and the whole were added up together, and, to ascertain the average, the product was divided by twelve, for which amount the jury found their verdict, it was held there was nothing illegal in this mode of arriving at a verdict; because, in torts, and other cases where there is no ascertained demand, it can seldom happen that jurymen will, at once, agree upon a precise sum to be given in damages; there will necessarily arise a variety of opinions, and mutual concessions must be expected; a middle sum may, in many cases, be a good rule; and, though it is possible this mode may sometimes be abused by a designing juryman, fixing upon an extravagantly high or low sum, yet, unless such abuse appears, the fraudulent design will not be presumed.(b) It does not appear whether the jury agreed beforehand to be bound by the result, it seems they took this method simply to ascertain whether they could arrive at something like an agreement. Indeed, it would seem from what the presiding judge said, that this method was employed by the jury to "collect the sense of its members."(c)

§ 4.—New trial will be granted when the verdict is against law or the evidence.

3283.—1. When a verdict is found directly opposite

(a) Hale v. Cove, Str. 642; Mitchell v. Ehele, 10 Wend. 595.
(b) Cowperthwait v. Jones, 2 Dall. 56 ; Grinnell v. Phillips, 1 Mass. 542; Johnson v. Perry, 2 Humph. 569 ; Harvey v. Jones, 3 Humph. 157.   But in another case, where, beforehand, the jury agreed that the result, whatever it might be, should be the amount of their verdict, a new trial was granted.   Ellege v. Todd, 1 Humph. 43.
(c) 2 Dall. 55, 56.

to the direction or instruction of the judge on a matter
· of law, it must of necessity be set aside, or the jury,
and not the court, would determine the law, which
would be destroying the very constitution of a trial
by jury, that the judges are to decide the law, and the
jury ascertain the facts.* But a new trial will not be
granted, where, in the opinion of the court, substantial
justice has been done between the parties, although
the law arising from the evidence would have justified
a different result.(a)

3284.—2. A new trial will be granted, when injustice has been done, and the verdict is clearly against
evidence;(b) but not where justice has been done,
although the verdict be against the *weight of evidence*,
that is, that the proof on the side of the losing party,
in such case, is greater than that on the other.(c) A
verdict may be set aside, because it is against the
weight of the evidence, but in such cases the evidence
is not to be weighed in golden scales. In considering
such cases, the general rule is, that the verdict once
found shall stand; the setting aside is an exception,
and it ought to be an exception of rare and almost
singular occurrence.(d) This is especially the case
when two juries have determined the same way.(e)

(a) Smith v. Shultz, 1 Scam. 490. See Marr v. Johnson, 9 Yeager, 1.
(b) Corsies v. Little, 2 Green, 373 ; Brugh v. Shanks, 5 Leigh, 598 ; Yale
v. Yale, 13 Conn. 185; Wells v. Waterhouse, 9 Shepl. 131 ; Hudson v.
Williamson, 3 Brev. 342 ; Jenkins v. Whitehead, 1 Sm. & Mar. 157 ; Waite
v. White, 5 Pike, 640; Scott v. Brookway, 7 Mis. 61 ; Cassels v. The
State, 4 Yerg. 149; Wait v. McNeil, 7 Mass. 261 ; Zaleer v. Geiger, 2
Yeates, 522 ; Emmet v. Robinson, 2 Yeates, 514 : Lloyd v. Newell, 3 Halst.
296 ; United States v. Duval, Gilp. 356.
(c) Yarborough v. Abernathy, 1 Meigs, 483; Pettitt v. Pettitt, 4 Hump.
191 ; Todd v. Boone County, 8 Miss. 431 ; Bank v. King, 2 Green, 45;
Stanley v. Whipple, 2 McLean, 35; Harbour v. Reyburn, 7 Yerg. 432;
Kellogg v. Budlong, 7 How. Mis. 340.
(d) Hammond v. Wadhams, 5 Mass. 353.
(e) Coffin v. Newberryport Mar. Ins. Co., 9 Mass. 436 ; Fowler v. Etna
Ins. Co., 7 Wend. 270 ; Dorsey v. Dougherty, 1 A. K. Marsh. 182.

OF PROCEEDINGS IN AN ACTION.   511

No 3285.   Book 4, tit 8, chap 12, sec. 1, § 5, art. 1, 2   No 3287.

§ 5.—New trial will be granted when there has been newly discovered evidence.

3285. The nature of this evidence, and the fact of its
discovery, will be considered in two separate articles.

Art. 1.—Of the nature of newly discovered evidence.

3286. When evidence has been discovered since the
trial, which might have been produced before the jury,
it must be such, to entitle the party to a new trial, as
would have been *material,(a)* and not merely cumulative, and such as would have changed the verdict, if
produced, and which induces a belief that injustice has
been done.(*b*) It must appear that such newly discovered evidence is material to the issue, going to the
merits; and evidence merely to impeach the character
of a witness, is not of this nature;(*c*) and if the witness
who is now offered as newly discovered, was incompetent at the time of the trial, and has since become competent, this will not be considered as newly discovered
evidence.(*d*)

If matters might have been offered in evidence, but
were not, this is not the kind of newly discovered
evidence which is a ground for a new trial.(*e*)

It must be made to appear by competent affidavits,
that in truth the matters offered as new evidence, are,
in fact, material.(*f*)

Art. 2.—Of the discovery of the new evidence.

3287. The evidence must not only be material, but
it must have been discovered *since the trial,* and the

(*a*) Watts *v.* Howard, 7 Met. 478 ; Kirby *v.* Waterford, 14 Verm. 414.
(*b*) Mechanics' Fire Ins. Co. *v.* Nichols, 1 Harr. 410 ; Alsop *v.* Ins. Co.,
1 Sumn. 451 : Den *v.* Geiger. 4 Halst. 228 ; Pike *v.* Evans, 15 John. 210 ;
Gardner *v.* Mitchel, 6 Pick. 114 , Reed *v.* McGrew, 5 Ham. 375.
(*c*) McIntire *v.* Young, 6 Blackf. 496 ; Harbour *v.* Rayburn, 7 Yerg. 432.
(*d*) Sawyer *v.* Merrill, 10 Pick. 16.
(*e*) Reed *v.* Moore, 3 Iredell, 310.
(*f*) Hinds *v.* Terry, Walker, 80 ; Parker *v.* Hardy, 24 Pick. 246.

party must also have used due diligence, and every reasonable exertion in his power to procure it; for, if by using proper means he could have procured it, so as to produce it on trial, it will not be considered as new evidence, but its non-production will be attributed to his *laches* or neglect, from the effects of which a court will never relieve a party.

3288. New trials are now granted on the ground of newly discovered evidence, but with the following restrictions:

1. The testimony or evidence must have been dis. covered since the trial.

2. The party must have used due diligence to pro. cure it on the former trial.

3. It must be shown to be material to the issue.

4. It must go to the merits of the cause, and not merely impeach the character of a witness.

5. It must not be merely cumulative.(*a*)

§ 6.—A new trial will be granted when the party applying for it has been taken by surprise.

3289. By *surprise*, in practice, is understood that situation in which a party is placed, without any default of his own, which will be injurious to his interest.(*b*) The courts always do every thing in their power to relieve a party from the effects of a surprise, when he has been diligent in endeavoring to avoid it.(*c*)

(*a*) See, as to these several points, The People *v.* The Superior Court of New York, 10 Wend. 291 ; Rowley *v.* Kinney, 14 John. 186 ; Pike *v.* Evans, 15 John. 132 ; Guyott *v.* Butts, 4 Wend. 579 ; Moore *v.* Philadelphia Bank, 5 S. & R. 41 ; Bond *v.* Cutler, 7 Mass. 205 ; Evans *v.* Rogers, 2 N. & McC. 563 ; Stone *v.* Clifford, 5 Lou. R. 11 ; Nichols *v.* Alsop, 11 Lou. R. 409 ; Gravier's Curator *v.* Rapp, 12 Lou. R. 162 ; Drayton *v.* Thompson, 1 Bay, 263 ; Jones *v.* Lollikoffer, 2 Hawks, 492 ; Smith *v.* Shultz, 1 Scam. 491 ; Knox *v.* Work, 2 Binn, 582 ; Aubel *v.* Ealer, 2 Binn. 582, note ; Turnbull *v.* O'Hara, 4 Yeates, 446 ; Waln *v.* Wilkins, 4 Yeates, 461.

(*b*) Rawle *v.* Skipwith, 8 N. S. 407.

(*c*) 1 Clarke's R. 162.

A new trial will be granted to relieve a party'from the effects of a surprise ;(a) as, where a witness had been regularly subpœnaed by the defendant, and attended at the circuit, and was present shortly before the cause was called on, when he absented himself, without the knowledge or consent of the defendant or his attorney, and his absence was not discovered until after the jury were sworn. For want of this witness the defendant lost his cause. The court granted a new trial, because the party was taken by surprise, and because it appeared to the court that the witness, as well as all persons answerable over to the defendant, were insolvent.(b)   So, where an agreement was made between the attorneys that a suit should be dropped, and the case remained on the docket, and was brought to trial; the verdict was set aside on the ground of surprise.(c)   And where a deed had been in the hands of the attorney on the other side, and notice was given to him to produce it, which he did not do, and on the trial, first informed the attorney who had given him the notice, that before he received the notice, he had delivered the deed to another, a new trial was granted on the ground of surprise.(d)   Another instance of the grant of a new trial may be mentioned, where the party relied upon the same course being taken that had been adopted twice before; as, where documents had been read without objection on two former trials, and on the third they were excluded in consequence of an objection which had not been anticipated.(e)

To entitle a party to a new trial, the surprise must be such that he had no opportunity to move for a ·

(a) McFarland v. Clark, 9 Dana, 134.
(b) Ruggles v. Hall, 14 John. 112; Tilden v. Gardinier, 25 Wend. 663.
(c) Price v. McIlvaine, 3 Brev. 419.
(d) Jackson v. Warford, 7 Wend. 62.
(e) Helm v. Jones, 9 Dana, 26.

514   OF REMEDIES.

No. 3290.   Book 4, tit. 8, chap. 12, sec. 1, § 7, 8.   No. 3291.

continuance of the cause, and the record must show clearly that such was the fact.(a)

§ 7.—When a new trial will be granted for excessive damages.

3290. A new trial will be granted when the damages found by the jury against a defendant are unreasonably great and not warranted by law, or *excessive*. The damages are excessive, first, when they are greater than is demanded by the writ and declaration ;(b) and, secondly, when they are greater than is authorized by some fixed rules, and principles of law ; as, in cases of actions upon contracts, or for torts done to property, the value of which may be ascertained by evidence (c) But in actions for torts to the person or reputation of the plaintiff, the damages will not be considered excessive unless they are outrageous. In cases of this kind, where there is no certain measure of damages, the court will not substitute its own sense of what would have been the proper amount of the verdict, and therefore, will not set aside a verdict for excessive damages, unless there is reason to believe that the jury were actuated by passion, or by some undue influence perverting their judgment.(d)

§ 8.—When a new trial will be granted for inadequacy of damages.

3291. New trials are rarely granted on account of the inadequacy of damages given by the jury. When

---

(a) Thompson *v.* Porter, 4 Bibb. 70 ; Kirtley *v.* Kirtley, 1 J. J. Marsh 96.
(b) Hook *v.* Turnbull, 6 Call, 85 ; McIntire *v.* Clark, 7 Wend. 330.
(c) Coffin *v.* Coffin, 4 Mass. 41 ; Commonwealth *v.* Norfolk, 5 Mass. 435 ; Dodd *v.* Pierson, 6 Halst. 284.
(d) Jacobs *v.* Bangor, 4 Shep. 187. See Whipple *v.* Cumberland Man. Co. 2 Story, 661 ; Dodd *v.* Hamilton, 2 Tayl. 31 ; Allen *v.* Craig, 1 Green, 294, Boyers *v.* Pratt. 1 Humph. 90 ; Thompson *v.* French, 10 Yerg. 452 ; Sumnor *v.* Wilt, 4 S. & R. 27 ; Kèrn *v.* North 10 S. & R. 399 ; Coleman *r.* Southwick, 9 John. 45 ; Southwick *v.* Stevens, 10 John. 443 ; Bacon *v.* Brown, 4 Bibb, 91 ; Ogden *v.* Gibbons, 2 South. 518.

the damages can be appreciated, as where they are given upon a contract, or for an injury to real or personal estate, and they are so small that that fact raises a presumption that the jury have acted upon a mistake, and the judge who tried the cause is dissatisfied with the verdict, a new trial will be granted.(a) On the contrary, in actions for torts to the person or reputation, the smallness of damages is no ground for a new trial.(b)

§ 9.—A new trial will be granted on the conviction of a witness for perjury.

3292. Another cause for granting a new trial is, where a witness who testified is convicted of perjury; but the mere finding of a bill of indictment is not sufficient, though it may induce the court in some instances to stay the proceedings until the indictment has been tried.(c)

3293. These are the principal causes for granting a new trial; but without going further into detail, it may be stated that whenever injustice has been done, without the default of the losing party, and it is clearly manifest that such is the case, a new trial will be granted. The only object of granting a new trial is to prevent injustice.

SECTION 2.—OF ARREST OF JUDGMENT.

3294. By *arrest of judgment* is meant the refusal of the court having jurisdiction, to enter a judgment upon a verdict, a default, or a demurrer to evidence, for some cause apparent upon the record. The judgment

---

(a) Taunton Man. Co. v. Smith, 9 Pick. 11.
(b) Coyler v. Huff, 3 Bibb, 34 ; Shoemaker v. Livezely, 2 Browne, 286. In Virginia, a new trial is authorized by statute, in an action of slander, when the damages are too small. Rixey v. Ward, 3 Rand, 52.
(c) Beafield v. Petrie, 3 Dougl. 24 ; Petrie v. Millies, 3 Dougl. 27. See Harrison v. Harrison, 9 Price, 89.

of the court, which is a conclusion of law from the facts ascertained and spread out upon the record, must be collected from the *whole record;* the party who does *not,* from the whole record, appear entitled to judgment cannot have it, even though the verdict be found, or a default suffered, or a demûrrer to evidence determined in his favor; because, notwithstanding such verdict, default or demurrer, the whole record may disclose no right of action, or no legal defence in his favor. If in such case a verdict be found for the plaintiff, upon a declaration radically defective, or showing no cause of action, or for the defendant, on a plea in bar *totally void of substance,* judgment must regularly be arrested.

3295. Before further considering the causes for which a judgment may be arrested, it is proper to state that formerly judgments were constantly arrested for defects or faults merely formal, in the pleadings, or other parts of the record; but by the various English statutes of *amendments* and *jeofails,* which extend from the reign of Edward III. to that of Anne, and the principles of which have been generally adopted in this country, this evil has been remedied. Now no judgment can be arrested for a mere *formal* defect, nor for any *substantial* defect enumerated in, and specially cured by, some or other of these statutes.

In general, *substantial* defects are not cured by any of these statutory provisions; still some of them are cured by verdict or otherwise, upon common law principles, without the aid of any statute. The cases in which the common law has this healing effect will be the principal subject of our examinations under this head.

A judgment may be arrested for defects in the pleadings, and for defects in the verdict.

§ 1.—When judgment may be arrested for defects in the pleadings.

3296. It is an invariable rule that no defect in the

pleadings, which would not have been fatal to them on general demurrer, can ever be a sufficient cause for arresting a judgment;(a) because all such formal defects are aided, except upon special demurrer, assigning them for cause; and consequently, all formal defects, on either side, which would not have been fatal on general demurrer, are cured by the adverse party pleading over to issue, or by default, or, indeed, by omitting to demur specially.

But the rule is not universally true, è converso, that every defect in the pleadings, which would have been fatal on general demurrer, is a sufficient ground for arresting judgment, after a general verdict. If the pleading of the party, for whom such verdict has been found, is faulty, in omitting some particular fact or circumstance, without which he ought not to have judgment, but which is implied in, or inferable from, the finding of the facts, which are expressly alleged and found, the pleading is aided by the verdict; because the omission is supplied by the finding, and the court presumes that the fact or circumstance was proved to the jury.(b)

When a declaration or other pleading sets forth a good title or ground of action defectively, the imperfection will be cured by a verdict, because to entitle him to recover, all circumstances necessary in form and substance, to complete the title so imperfectly stated, must be proved at the trial, and it is but fair to presume that they were proved. But when no cause of action is stated, the omission is not cured by the verdict; because no right of recovery was necessary to be proved, or could be legally proved under such a declaration, there can therefore be no ground to presume that it was proved at the trial. This is the true

---

(a) 3 Bl. Com. 394.
(b) Lane v. Maine M. F. Ins. Co., 3 Fairf. 44; Kelton v. Bevine, Cooke, 90; Little v. Thompson, 2 Mis. 228.

distinction between such defects in a declaration as are, and such as are not, cured by the verdict for the plaintiff.(a) The same criterion extends, *mutatis mutandis*, to defects in the plea, or in any other parts of the pleadings.

In those cases where the facts are not implied in, or inferable from, those which are alleged and found, they cannot be presumed to have been proved to the jury. If the declaration is wholly defective in substance, as in the instance given by Blackstone of an action of slander for calling the plaintiff a *Jew*, a verdict will not entitle him to judgment; for the words charged, not being actionable, the finding of the jury cannot make them so. The defect in the declaration is not in the *statement* of the cause of action, but in the alleged *cause of action itself*. Nothing is implied or can be inferred from the finding, which can constitute a right of recovery.

A *default* does not cure any defects in the declaration, which would not have been aided on a general demurrer ;(b) because no fact can be presumed to have been proved, where there was no trial, and no proof exhibited. For this reason, the judgment will be arrested after a default, and it will have the same effect as a general demurrer to the declaration.

Upon the same principle which renders radical defects in a declaration incurable by verdict, all the other material defective pleadings on either side, will not be cured by the verdict. If, therefore, the plea

---

(a) See Rushton v. Aspinall, Dougl. 683 ; Read v. Chelmesford, 16 Pick. 128 ; Wheeler v. Train, 3 Pick. 255 ; Avery v. Tyringham, 3 Mass. 160 ; Moor v. Boswell, 5 Mass. 306 ; United States v. The Virgin, 1 Pet. C. C. 7 ; Farwell v. Smith, 2 Green, 133 ; Stilson v. Toby, 2 Mass. 591 ; Coleman v. Craysdale, 3 J. J. Marsh. 541 ; Dickerson v. Hays, 4 Blackf. 107 ; Stanley v. Whipple, 2 McLean, 35 ; Gaylord v. Payne, 4 Conn. 190 ; Spencer v. Overton, 1 Day, 183 ; Fuller v. Hampton, 5 Conn. 416 ; Hendricks v. Seely. 6 Conn. 176 ; Phelps v. Sill, 1 Day, 315 ; Russell v. Slade, 12 Conn. 455 ; Story v. Barrel, 2 Conn. 665 ; Schlosser v. Brown, 17 S. & R. 250.
(b) 1 Saund. 228, a, b, c, note (1).

discloses no legal defence, a verdict in favor of the defendant will not make the plea good; and, if the declaration is sufficient, a judgment may be arrested on the plaintiff's motion.(a)

A judgment may also be arrested for some radical defect in the *issue.* This is the case when the issue is immaterial, so that the court cannot discover, from the finding upon it, for which party judgment ought to be given.(b) Thus, if in an action against husband and wife, for a wrong committed by her alone, they plead that *they* are not guilty, and the verdict is for them, the judgment may be arrested,(c) because the verdict determines nothing from which the court can discover how judgment ought to be given, since the matter put in issue is not that which the declaration charges. The complaint is not that the *husband and wife* are guilty of the wrong, but only that the wife is so; and the verdict does not show, separately, whether she is or is not guilty, but only that *both* the defendants are not so.

§ 2.—When judgment may be arrested for defects in the verdict.

3297. Judgment may be arrested also for defects in the verdict.(d) This takes place when the verdict varies substantially from the issue; as where it varies from the issue by finding something foreign to it; in such case the court can give no judgment.(e)

A verdict is equally defective when it finds only a part of the matter in issue, omitting to find either way another *material* part; because it is the duty of the jury to find the whole issue, so that the court may give judgment upon all the material facts put in issue

---

(a) 3 Bl. Com. 395.
(b) Com. Dig. Pleader, R 18; 2 Saund. 319, a, b, (n. 6); Bac. Ab. Pleas, M 1.
(c) Coxe v. Cropwell, Cro. Jac. 5; Lawes' Pl. 170.
(d) Bac. Ab. Verdict, M.
(e) Bac. Ab. Verdict, O; Moody v. Keener, 7 Port. 218; Vines v. Brownrigg, 2 Dev. 537.

by the pleadings. A verdict finding the *whole substance* of the issue, is good, although it be silent as to what is immaterial, inasmuch as the latter can have no effect upon the merits of the controversy.(*a*)

A verdict which finds the whole issue, or the substance of it, is not vitiated by finding more; in this case the surplusage will be rejected: *utile per inutile non vitiatur.*(*b*)

When considering the nature of a general verdict, it was stated that where there were several counts in a declaration, some good and some bad, and the jury found a general verdict for the plaintiff, with entire damages, that is, without discriminating in the assessment of the damages between the different counts, the judgment may be arrested; for it is impossible for the court, judging, as it must, from the record alone, to discover on which count the damages were assessed, or what proportion of them may have been assessed on the one or the other.

In such cases, when entire damages are found for the plaintiff, and it appears, from the notes of the judge before whom the trial was had, that no part of the evidence exhibited to the jury applied to the bad counts, the verdict may be amended by order of the court, so as to apply to the good count only; and, after the amendment, the court will give judgment on the amended verdict, which will then find only on the good count, and on that count only.

The above rule, that judgment will be arrested when the verdict is general, and one of several counts is bad, applies only to *civil* cases; if, therefore, an indictment contains several counts, of which one is good and the others are defective, on a general verdict

---

(*a*) White *v.* Bailey, 14 Conn. 272. See Patterson *v.* United States, 2 Wheat. 221 ; Barnett *v.* Watson, 1 Wash. 272.

(*b*) Patterson *v.* United States, 2 Wheat. 221 ; Bacon *v.* Callender, 6 Mass. 303 ; Hunter *v.* Commonwealth, 2 S. & R. 298 ; Leineweaver *v.* Stoever, 17 S. & R. 297.

of guilty, the court will award the punishment on the good count only. Still, this rule is not inconsistent with the principle which prevails in civil cases; because, in criminal cases, no damages are assessed, nor is it the province of the jury to decide upon the punishment incurred by the offence, this being solely the duty of the court. It is in the power of the jury to find damages *separately* upon each of the counts, when some are good and others defective; when they do so, the court will arrest the judgment on the bad counts only, and give judgment for the plaintiff, for the damages assessed on those which are good.(*a*)

SECTION 3.—OF JUDGMENT NON OBSTANTE VEREDICTO.

3298. A judgment *non obstante veredicto*, or a judgment notwithstanding the verdict, is one rendered for the plaintiff, without regard to ·the verdict obtained by the defendant, the nature of which was considered when we were discussing the subject of pleading. This judgment is sometimes called a judgment *as upon confession*. In some cases it is expedient to take such judgment by the plaintiff, even though the verdict be in his own favor; for where the plea itself being substantially bad in law, and in confession and avoidance, involves a confession of the plaintiff's declaration, and shows that he was entitled to maintain his action, such judgment is, therefore, a judgment *as upon confession*, and safer than a judgment upon a verdict, which would be erroneous.(*b*)

SECTION 4.—OF A REPLEADER.

3299. A repleader is awarded when an immaterial issue has been formed, not proper to decide the action.

(*a*) Hancock *v.* Haywood, 3 T. R. 433, 435.
(*b*) Steph. Pl. 118. A defendant cannot move for a judgment *non obstante veredicto*. Smith *v.* Smith, 4 Wend. 468.

This was considered while we were treating of plead-ing, so as to require no further examination in this place.

SECTION 5.—OF A VENIRE FACIAS DE NOVO.

3300. A *venire facias de novo*, is a new writ awarded when, by reason of some irregularity or defect in the proceedings on the first venire, or the trial, the proper effect of that writ has been frustrated, or the verdict become void in law; as, for example, when the jury has been improperly chosen, or the verdict they have rendered is uncertain, ambiguous, or defective.(a) The object of the new writ is of course to obtain a new trial, and, accordingly, this proceeding is in substance the same with a motion for a new trial. When, however, the unsuccessful party objects to the verdict, in respect to some irregularity or error, in the practical course of the proceeding, rather than on the merits, the form of the application is a motion for a *venire de novo*, and not for a new trial; this is, however, seldom adopted, as by a motion for a new trial the same end is attained.

When the proceedings have been reversed on error, as will be hereafter explained, upon some irregularity or error committed by the court in the course of the proceedings, a *venire facias de novo* is awarded; but this writ is never granted when the cause of reversal is a defect in the plaintiff's right to recover.

❖

CHAPTER XIII.—OF THE JUDGMENT AND ITS INCIDENTS.

3301. Having examined all the preliminary pro-ceedings which can suspend a judgment, and disposed of them, if there is no legal obstacle, the next thing to be done is to pronounce judgment. In relation to

---

(a) Vide post, n. 3359.

the judgment, let us consider, 1, the form of judgments; 2, their kinds; 3, judgments for plaintiffs; 4, judgments for defendants; 5, judgments rendered before an issue is formed; 6, where judgments are to be given.

SECTION 1.—OF THE FORM OF JUDGMENTS.

3302. A *judgment* is the decision or sentence of the law, given by a court of justice or other competent tribunal, as the result of proceedings instituted therein, for the redress of an injury. The language of the judgment is not, therefore, that "it is decreed," or "resolved," by the court; but "it is considered," (*consideratum est per curiam*) that the plaintiff recover his debt, damages, possession, and the like, or that the defendant do go quit. This implies that the judgment is not so much the decision of the court, as the sentence of the law, pronounced and decreed by the court, after due deliberation and inquiry.

To be valid, a judicial judgment must be given by a competent judge or court, at a time and place appointed by law, and in the form it requires. A judgment would be null, if the judge had not jurisdiction of the matter; or, having such jurisdiction, he exercised it, when there was no court held, or out of his district; or if he rendered judgment before the cause was prepared for a hearing.

SECTION 2.—OF THE KINDS OF JUDGMENTS.(*a*)

3303. Considered as to the nature of the action, the plea, and the issue, judgments in civil cases are of four kinds, namely:

1. When the facts are admitted between the parties, but the law is disputed; as in case of judgment upon demurrer.

(*a*) For the kinds of judgments which are to be rendered in different actions, see book 4, tit. 9.

2. When the law is admitted, but the facts are disputed; as in case of judgment upon a verdict.

3. When both the law and the facts are admitted by confession, as by *cognovit actionem;* this is a written confession by the defendant, of the justice of the plaintiff's claim, subscribed but not sealed, and authorizing the plaintiff or his attorney to sign judgment and issue execution against the defendant, usually in a sum named. It is different from a *warrant of attorney,* which is an authority to confess judgment, given before the commencement of any action, and is under seal. The law and the facts may be confessed by the plaintiff as being against him, as in the case of a *nolle prosequi,* which is an entry on the record by which the plaintiff declares he will proceed no further.

4. By default of either party, in the course of legal proceedings, as in the case of *nihil dicit;* that is, when the defendant fails to put in a plea or answer to the plaintiff's declaration by the day assigned; or *non sum informatus,* when the defendant omits to plead or instruct his attorney so to do, after proper notice; or in cases of judgment by *non pros,* nonsuit, or as in the case of nonsuit, when the plaintiff fails to follow up his proceedings.

3304. When considered as to their effects, judgments are of two kinds, namely:

1. An *interlocutory* judgment is one given in the course of a cause before final judgment. When the action sounds in damages, and the issue is an issue in law, or when in fact, not tried by a jury, is decided in favor of the plaintiff, then the judgment is that the plaintiff ought to recover his damages without specifying their amount, for, as there has been no trial in the case by the jury, the amount of damages is not yet ascertained; the judgment is then said to be interlocutory. So, in like manner, a judgment rendered by *default* is a judgment of the same kind.

The judgment by default, is interlocutory in assumpsit, covenant, trespass, case and replevin, when the sole object of the action is damages; but in debt, damages not being the principal object of the action, upon a default, the plaintiff usually signs judgment in the first instance.

To ascertain damages, after an interlocutory judgment, a *writ of inquiry* is issued, in cases *sounding in damages*, according to the technical phrase,¶ that is, when the object of the action is to recover damages only, and not brought for the specific recovery of lands, goods, or sums of money.   This writ is directed to the sheriff of the county where the facts are alleged by the pleadings to have occurred, commanding him to inquire "by the oaths and affirmations of twelve lawful men of his county," into the amount of damages sustained by the plaintiff; and to return the inquisition, when made, to the court.

The finding of the sheriff and jury under such a proceeding, is called an *inquisition*, and upon the return of it, a final judgment may be rendered.

When the action is founded on a promissory note, bond, or any other contract in writing, by which the amount due may be easily computed, it is the practice, in some courts, to refer to the clerk or prothonotary the assessment of damages, and in such case no writ of inquiry is issued.

There is one species of interlocutory judgment which establishes nothing but the inadequacy of the defence set up; this is the judgment for the plaintiff on demurrer to a plea in abatement, by which it appears that the defendant has mistaken the law on a point which does not affect the merits of the case; and it being but reasonable that he should offer, if he can, a further defence, that judgment is, that he do answer over, in technical language, judgment of *respondeat ouster.(a)*

2. A *final* judgment is one which puts an end to

(a) Steph. Pl. 126 ; Bac. Ab. Pleas, N 4 ; 2 Arch. Pr. 3.

the suit. When the issue is one in *fact*, and it is tried by a jury, the jury at the time they try the issue assess the damages; then the judgment is final in the first instance, that is, that the plaintiff do recover the amount of the damages assessed. And when damages have been assessed by virtue of a writ of inquiry, after an interlocutory judgment, the judgment is final, that the plaintiff recover the amount of damages so assessed.(*a*)

When the issue is one of *law*, as in case of demurrer, the judgment rendered, is in the nature of the pleadings demurred to. Thus, the judgment on demurrer to a plea in abatement, if for the defendant, is that the writ be *quashed*, and if for the plaintiff, that defendant *answer over*, so that the judgment corresponds to that of the prayer of judgment in the demurrer.

For this reason, when a demurrer is joined on any of the pleadings in *chief*, as on the declaration, plea in bar, or other pleading, which goes to the action, the judgment is final;(*b*) if for the plaintiff, it is *quod recuperet;* if for the defendant, it is, that he go without day, *quod eat sine die.* The effect of a judgment on demurrer to any of the pleadings which go to the action for either party, is the same as it would have been on an issue in fact, joined upon the same pleadings and found in favor of the same party.(*c*) If the defendant demurs to the declaration, but concludes in abatement, (as by praying that the writ be quashed,) the plaintiff may join in the demurrer as in bar, by praying that his debt, or damages, be adjudged to him; and if his declaration be good, he shall have judgment *quod recuperet ;* because, by the demurrer, the declaration is confessed.(*d*) Such a judgment is also conclusive,

---

(*a*) Steph. Pl. 127, 128.
(*b*) In Mississippi, the judgment on a demurrer overruling a plea, should be *respondeat ouster;* if the judgment be final, it will be reversed. Randolph *v.* Singleton, 12 S. & M. 439.
(*c*) Bauer *v.* Roth, 4 Rawle, 83.
(*d*) Lawes on Pl. 172 ; Com. Dig. Pleader, Q 3.

by way of estoppel, as if it had been obtained on a verdict; and the facts thus established, can never afterward be contested between the same parties or their privies.

But when the action sounds in damages, as in covenant, case for a tort, trover, trespass, and the like, on demurrer, the judgment for the plaintiff is only interlocutory; and it is necessary, before final judgment, that the damages should be assessed by a jury.(a)

On the other hand, if, on demurrer to the declaration, to the plea in bar, or other pleading in chief, judgment is rendered for the defendant, it is final. The plaintiff can never afterward maintain against the same defendants, or those who were in privity with him, any similar or concurrent action for the same cause, that is, upon the same grounds as were disclosed in the first declaration; because the judgment, upon such a demurrer, determines the merits of the cause; and a final judgment, deciding the right in controversy, puts an end to the dispute.

But, to have this binding operation, the judgment on demurrer must have decided the *merits* of the action; for, if the plaintiff fails in his first action, from the omission of an essential allegation in his declaration, which allegation is supplied in the second, the judgment of the first will be no bar to the second, although both actions were brought to enforce the same right; because, in this case, as disclosed in the second declaration, the *merits* of the cause were not decided in the first.

And so if the declaration is adjudged ill on demurrer, because the action was misconceived, as where assumpsit is brought, where debt is the only remedy; or trespass, where the proper action is trover, the judgment on demurrer is no bar to a proper action, afterward brought for the same cause; for, in such case,

(a) Logan *v.* Jennings, 4 Rawle, 335.

the merits could not have been determined in the first action.

SECTION 3.—OF JUDGMENTS FOR THE PLAINTIFF.

3305. Much of the matter which might come under this head, has been already disposed of, while discussing the nature of interlocutory and final judgments. When the judgment is on a dilatory plea, it is *respondeat ouster*. When on an issue in *fact*, it differs according to the form of action; in account, it is *quod computet;* when in case, or when the action sounds in damages, it is, that the plaintiff do recover a certain sum of money for his damages, *quod recuperet;* in debt, that he recover his debt, and in general, nominal damages; when in detinue, that he recover the goods or the value thereof. These several judgments will be more fully considered when we come to treat of the several kinds of actions.

SECTION 4.—OF JUDGMENTS FOR DEFENDANT.

3306. When the judgment is for the defendant, if the issue, whether of fact or law, arise on a dilatory plea, the judgment is that the writ be quashed, *quod breve cassetur,* upon such pleas as are in abatement of the writ; that the pleading remain without day, until the objection be removed, upon such pleas as are in suspension only.

If the issue arises upon a declaration or peremptory plea, the judgment, in general, is that the plaintiff take nothing by his writ, and that the defendant go thereof without day, which is called a judgment of *nil capiat per breve.*

SECTION 5.—OF JUDGMENTS RENDERED BEFORE AN ISSUE IS FORMED.

3307. For the purpose of not interrupting the

course of proceedings of the action, judgments have hitherto been supposed to be awarded only upon the decision of an issue; but there are many cases where a judgment may be given before the formation of an issue, which will now demand our attention. These judgments, thus given before issue is joined, are given because of the fault or neglect of one of the parties, in failing to pursue his litigation; and this happens either with an intention of abandoning the claim or defence, or in consequence of a neglect to follow up within the period, which the practice of the court prescribes, the proceedings already commenced. When this occurs the adverse party becomes victor in the suit, as well as when an issue has been joined, and it is decided in his favor, by the entry of a judgment. These judgments are in favor of the plaintiff or of the defendant.

§ 1.—For the plaintiff.

3308. These judgments are of various kinds; if in a real action, the defendant holds out against the process of the court which has been issued against him, after it has been served, judgment is given for *default of appearance;*(a) and if, in actions real, personal or mixed, after appearance, he neither pleads nor demurs, when required by the rules of court; or if, after issue, he fails to maintain his pleadings till issue joined, by rejoinder, rebutter, etc., judgment will be given against him for want of a plea, which is called judgment by *nil dicit.*

Sometimes, instead of a plea, the defendant's attorney enters upon the record that he is not informed of any answer to be given to the action, judgment is then given against the defendant, and in this case is called a judgment by *non sum informatus*, this being the entry made upon the record.

(a) Booth, 19, 73 ; 2 Saund. 45.

Instead of a plea, when the defendant has no defence, he may choose to confess the action; or after pleading, he may, at any time before trial, both confess the action and withdraw his plea and other allegations; and the judgment against him, in these two cases, is called a judgment by *confession*, or by confession *relictâ verificatione*.

§ 2.—For the defendant.

3309. Judgment may also be rendered against the plaintiff before issue joined, in any class of actions for not declaring, replying, or surrejoining, etc., or for not entering the issue agreeably to the rules of court; judgments in these cases are *judgments of non pros.*(a)

The plaintiff may, if he chooses, at any stage of the action, after appearance and before judgment, declare that he "will not further prosecute his suit;" or, that he "withdraws his suit;" or, when a plea in abatement has been entered, he may pray that his writ "be quashed, that he may sue out a better one;" there is then given judgment against him, in the first case, of *nolle prosequi;* in the second, of *retraxit;* and in the last, of *cassetur breve.*

Another mode of rendering judgment for the defendant is to *nonsuit* the plaintiff. A judgment of nonsuit is given against a plaintiff when he is unable to prove his case, or when he neglects or refuses to proceed to trial of a cause after it has been put at issue, without determining such issue.

3310. A nonsuit is either voluntary or involuntary.

1. A *voluntary* nonsuit is an abandonment of his cause by a plaintiff, and an agreement that a judgment for costs be entered against him.

2. An *involuntary* nonsuit takes place when the plaintiff, on being called, when his case is before the

---

(a) From *non prosequitur.*

court for trial, neglects to appear, or when he has given no evidence upon which a jury could find a verdict; in such case no verdict is given, but judgment of nonsuit is rendered against the plaintiff.(a)

After issue has been joined, if the plaintiff neglects to bring such issue on to be tried in due time, as required by the course and practice of the court, in the particular case, judgment will be given against him for this default, and this is called a judgment as in *case of nonsuit.*

SECTION 6.—WHERE JUDGMENT OUGHT TO BE GIVEN.

3311. The judgment must be given by the judges of the court, and it was formerly pronounced in open court; but, although it is still supposed to be so, this practice has been so generally relaxed, that now, except in the case of an issue in law, there is no actual delivery of judgment in court or elsewhere. When the cause is in such a state that by the practice of the court the plaintiff or defendant is entitled to judgment, he obtains the signature or allowance of the proper officer of the court, expressing, generally, that judgment is given in his favor; and this is called *signing judgment.*

CHAPTER XIV.—OF PROCEEDINGS IN THE NATURE OF
APPEALS.

3312. The judgments obtained in the manner above described, however regular their form, may neverthe-

---

(a) The courts of the United States, 1 Pet. S. C. Rep. 469, 476 ; those of Pennsylvania, unless under special statutes, 1 S. & R. 360 ; 2 Binn. 234, 248 ; 4 Binn. 84 ; Massachusetts, 6 Pick. 117 ; Tennessee, 2 Overton, 57 ; 4 Yerg. 528 ; and Virginia, 1 Wash. R. 87, 219, cannot order a nonsuit against a plaintiff who has given evidence of his claim. In Alabama, unless authorized by statute, the court cannot order a nonsuit. Minor's R. 75 ; 3 Stew. 42. In South Carolina, 2 Bay, 126, 445 ; and Maine, 2 Greenl. 5 ; 3 Greenl. 97, a nonsuit may in general be ordered when the evidence is insufficient to support the action.

less be erroneous, or the plaintiff or successful party may have done some act which would render it unjust that they should be executed. The law has given a power either to the same court where the judgment was obtained, or to a superior court, to revise the proceedings. These modes of revision are principally four. They are, 1, by audita querela; 2, by writ of error; 3, by certiorari; 4, by false judgment.

SECTION 1.—OF THE REMEDY BY *audita querela.(a)*

3313. The object of issuing a writ of *audita querela*, is to be relieved from a judgment or execution, because of some injustice of the party who obtained it, which could not have been pleaded in bar to the action. It is a remedial process, which bears solely on the wrongful acts of the opposite party, and not upon the erroneous judgments or acts of the court. In its form, an *audita querela* is a regular suit in which the parties may plead, take issue on the merits, and, on a judgment upon such suit, a writ of error may be brought.(b) In this proceeding, 1, there must be proper parties; 2, the writ must be allowed; 3, there must be proper cases on which it lies; 4, there must be pleadings; 5, a judgment.

§ 1.—Of the parties.

3314. All parties aggrieved have a right to this writ, and the parties to the judgment and execution sought to be vacated, or their legal representatives,

---

(a) This writ is but little used, because in modern practice it is usual to grant the same relief on motion, which might be obtained by *audita querela*. Baker v. Judges of Ulster, 4 John. 191 ; Harper v. Kean, 11 S. & R. 290 ; Witherow v. Keller, 11 S. & R. 274.   In Virginia, Smock v. Dade, 5 Rand. 639.   In South Carolina, Longworth v. Screven, 2 Hill, 298 ; and Tennessee, Marsh v. Haywood, 6 Humph. 210, the remedy by *audita querela* is obsolete.   In Massachusetts and Vermont, it is regulated by statute ; Stanisford v. Barry, 1 Aik. 321 ; Lovejoy v. Webber, 10 Mass. 101 ; Brackett v. Winslow, 17 Mass. 153.

(b) Brooks v. Hunt, 17 John. 484.

must be made parties to such writ.(a) And where judgment against two is fraudulent as to one, both must join in bringing an *audita querela* to vacate it, notwithstanding one of the defendants was party to the fraud.(b) It lies also for bail when judgment is obtained against them by *scire facias* to answer the debt of their principal, and it happens afterward that the original judgment against the principal is reversed; for here the bail, after the judgment had against them, have no opportunity to plead this special matter, and they are therefore entitled to redress by *audita querela.(c)*

§ 2.—Of the allowance of the writ of *audita querela.*

3315. An *audita querela* is of common right and *ex debito justitiæ*, and need not be moved for,(d) but the *supersedeas* upon it must be moved for, and it will or will not be granted, according to the circumstances of the case.(e) The *audita querela* must issue out of the court where the record is.(f)

§ 3.—In what cases an *audita querela* lies.

3316. An *audita querela* is in the nature of an equitable suit, in which the equitable rights of the parties will be considered. It bears on the wrongful acts of the opposite party, and not on the erroneous judgments and acts of the court; it will not lie, therefore, where the cause of complaint is a proper subject for a writ of error,(g) although the remedy by error may have been taken away by statute.(h)

(a) Gleason v. Peck, 12 Verm. 56.
(b) Tittlemore v. Wainwright, 16 Verm. 173. See Melton v. Howard, 7 How. Mis. 103 ; Dane's Ab. c. 186, a. 1.
(c) Roll. Ab. 308.
(d) Nathan v. Giles, 5 Taunt. 558 ; 1 Marsh. 226.
(e) Waddington v. Vredenburg, 2 John. Cas. 227 ; Com Dig. Audita Querela, E 3 and 5.
(f) F. N. B. 105, B.
(g) Weeks v. Lawrence, 1 Verm. 433.
(h) Dodge v. Hubbell, 1 Verm. 491 ; Tuttle v. Burlington, Brayt. 27.

534

OF REMEDIES.

No. 3317.　　　　Book 4, tit. 8, chap. 14, sec 1, § 4, 5.　　　　No. 3318.

The party must have been injured, or be in danger of injury, in order to maintain this action.(a) It lies to relieve a defendant against whom a judgment has been recovered, and who is, therefore, in execution, or danger of execution, although he has a right to be discharged by matter which•has happened since the judgment; as, if the plaintiff has given the defendant a general release, or the latter has paid the debt to the former without obtaining satisfaction to be entered upon the record. It lies also where the matter of defence arose before judgment, and the defendant had no opportunity to plead it for want of notice, or, having notice, was deprived of the opportunity by the fraud or collusion of the other party.(b) In these, and the like cases, where the defendant is entitled to a discharge, and if he could have pleaded such matter, either at the beginning of the suit, or *puis darrein continuance*, the judgment would have been rendered on the other side, an *audita querela* lies to give him that relief to which in equity the complaining party is entitled.

§ 4.—Of the pleadings in an *audita querela*.

3317. In this writ, like a *scire facias*, the whole of the case is spread out; it is like a declaration, and it answers that purpose.(c) A declaration, however, may be filed, and then it should recite the whole record of the recovery, and show a sufficient *gravamen*, or cause of complaint.(d)

The proper plea to such an action is not guilty.(e)

§ 5.—Of the judgment.

3318. The judgment is for damages against the party who is guilty of the wrong, and to redress the

(a) Bryant v. Johnson, 11 Shep. 304.
(b) Johnson v. Harvey, 4 Mass. 485; Smock v. Dade, 5 Rand. 639; Wardell v. Eden, 2 John. Cas. 258.
(c) Dane's Ab. c. 186, a. 1, § 3.
(d) Com. Dig. Audita Querela, E 6; Dane's Ab. c. 186, a. 1, § 20.
(e) Little v. Good, 1 Aik. 363; Lovejoy v. Webber, 10 Mass. 103.

grievance of which the plaintiff complains.(a) On a verdict found for the complainant, the court cannot give a judgment for the defendant *non obstante vere-dicto,*(b) nor can there be a motion in arrest of judgment.(c)

SECTION 2.—OF THE REMEDY BY WRIT OF ERROR.

3319. When, in the course of the trial, an error has been committed as to a matter of *law,* which is not cured by the statutes of amendments and jeofails, nor by the common law, such error may be cured or removed by a writ of error, after a final judgment has been pronounced. In England, a writ of error, like an original writ, is sued out of chancery, directed to the judges of the court in which such judgment was given, and commanding them, in some cases, themselves to examine the record; in others, to send it to another court of appellate jurisdiction, to be examined, in order that some alleged error may be corrected. In this country, the constitutions of the several states vest in the supreme courts or courts of errors, of each state respectively, the supervisory power to revise the judgments of inferior courts. Writs of error issue out of such courts, directed to the inferior courts, commanding them to send the record into the supreme or superior court, to be there examined, and decided upon according to law and justice. The object of a writ of error is to reverse a wrongful judgment; it is brought by the party complaining of the judgment, whether he be plaintiff in the action or *plaintiff below,* or whether he be defendant in such action or *defendant below.* The party complaining of the alleged error is called *plaintiff in error,* and the opposite party *defendant in error.*

(a) 1 Aik. 363; 10 Mass. 103; Brackett v. Winslow, 17 Mass. 159; Dane's Ab. c. 186, a. 1, § 20.
(b) French v. Steele, 14 Verm. 579.
(c) See Nathan v. Giles, 5 Taunt. 558.

There are two kinds of writs of error: 1, the one, as has been intimated, by which the judges are authorized to correct any error of fact which ought not to have been committed, called a writ of error *coram nobis;* and 2, the writ of error which requires the inferior court to send the record into the superior court to be examined.

§ 1.—Of the writ of error coram nobis.

3320. In general there is no method of revising an error in the determination of *facts* but by a new trial, because the finding of the jury is conclusive; and although a matter should exist, which was not brought into issue; as, for example, if the defendant omitted to plead a release, which he might have pleaded, this is no error in the proceeding; it is only a mistake of the defendant. But there are some facts which affect the validity and regularity of the proceeding itself, and to remedy these errors the party in interest may sue out the writ of error coram nobis, so called, because the record and process upon which it is founded are stated in the writ to remain *"before us,"* that is, in the court in which the error remains, for this writ always lies in the same court where the record is. The death of one of the parties at the commencement of the suit; the appearance of an infant in a personal action, by an attorney, and not by guardian; the coverture of either party at the commencement of the suit, when her husband is not joined with her, are instances of this kind.(a)   Again, it has been decided that if the plaintiff in error die pending the writ, and the supreme court, notwithstanding, reverses the judgment, the defendant in error may bring error *coram nobis* there, upon this judgment of reversal, and assign the death of the plaintiff to the former writ, as error.(b)   Such

(a) 1 Saund. 101; 1 Arch. Pr. 212; Steph. on Pl. 140; Day v. Hamburgh, 1 Brown's Rep. 75; Hurst v. Fisher, 1 Watts & S. 441.
(b) Roll. Ab. 747.   See Beall v. Powell, 4 Geo. 525.

facts as these, whenever discovered and alleged, are errors in facts, and sufficient to reverse the judgment upon writ of error. To such cases the writ of error *coram nobis* applies, " because the error in fact is not the error of the judges, and reversing it is not reversing their own judgment." And for this reason, when the judgment is given on the verdict of a jury, finding the facts for the plaintiff in error, it is not that the former judgment be reversed, but that it be *recalled and revoked.*(a)

§ 2. Of writs of error.

3321. The second species is called simply a writ of error, and this is by far more common. Its object is to correct an error in law, committed in the proceedings, which is not amendable nor cured at common law, nor by any statute of amendment or jeofails.(b) In form, it is a suit between the same parties, sometimes reversed as to the one who complains and the other who defends, as when the defendant below becomes plaintiff in error; but, in fact, it is a question between the law and the judgment; it is not the original action between the parties which is judged, though the decision affects their rights only; it is the correctness or incorrectness of the judgment, and that alone, which is passed upon in a court of errors. It is the judgment which is to be judged.

A writ of error is in the nature of a suit or action, when it is to restore the party who obtains it to the possession of any thing which is withheld from him, not when its operation is entirely defensive, and it is considered as a new action. There must, therefore, be, 1, proper parties; 2, a proper writ; 3, bail given; 4, a return to the writ of error ; 5, an assignment of

(a) Fellows *v.* Griffin, 9 S. & M. 362.
(b) Gregg *v.* Bethea, 6 Porter, 9.

errors; 6, pleas in error; 7, an issue; 8 judgment in error.

Art. 1.—Of parties to proceedings in error.

3322. The parties to a writ are the plaintiffs in error, who may have been plaintiffs or defendants below; they may have been several, or there may have been only one; and there may be one or more defendants.

1. By whom.

3323. The writ of error to reverse a judgment, may be sued, 1, by a single person having the legal right; 2, by his privies; 3, by bail; 4, by remainder men and reversioners; 5, by vendee of land sold *pendente lite;* 6, in case of death; 7, in case of marriage; 8, in case of infancy; 9, by several persons.

1° *By a single person having the legal right.*

3324. A writ of error in a civil action, to reverse a judgment, should be brought by the person for or against whom it has been given, as the measure may originate with one or the other. As a general rule, no person can bring a writ of error who is not a party or privy to the record, or who is not prejudiced by it; and that he is such, must appear of record, and a want of such showing cannot be supplied by proof.(*a*)

2° *By privies.*

3325. Privies in blood, as the heir is to the ancestor; privies in representation, as the executor or administrator, to the testator or intestate; and privies

---

(*a*) Townsend *v.* Davis, 1 Kelly, 495. See Clayton *v.* Beedle, 1 Barb. 11; Hylton *v.* Brown, 1 Wash. C. C. Rep. 343 ; Steel *v.* Bridenbach, 7 W. & S. 150 ; Watson *v.* Willard, 9 Penn. St. R. 89. A writ of error will not be granted when not prayed for by the party himself, but by his friends, without his authority. Ex parte Dorr, 3 How. U. S. 103.

in estate, as the relation of donor and donee, lessor and lessee, may bring error when they are prejudiced by a judgment.(*a*) A terre tenant may, therefore, sue out a writ of error in his own name, without joining the legal parties.(*b*) And where there are several persons privy to a judgment, each having a distinct and several interest, each is distinctly entitled to a writ of error, and to maintain it by himself, and this notwithstanding a release by any other having like privity, in the same judgment, by a distinct title.(*c*)

3° *By bail.*

3326. Formerly, bail were allowed to bring a writ of error on a judgment against their principal;(*d*) but now, the rule is different.(*e*) The bail cannot reverse the judgment against their principal, nor the principal that against the bail, nor can they join in a writ of error.(*f*) The reason assigned for this is, that they are distinct judgments, which affect different persons.(*g*)

4° *By a remainder man or reversioner.*

3327. No writ of error lay at common law by the remainder man or reversioner, to reverse an erroneous judgment or recovery against the tenant in possession, until he became entitled to the land, except when he had been made a party to the record. But, by statute,(*h*) authority was given to the reversioner to sue in error, without waiting for that event; by equity this

(*a*) Bac. Ab. Error, B ; Porter *v.* Rummeny, 10 Mass. 64, 69.
(*b*) Finney *v.* Crawford, 2 Watts, 294.
(*c*) 10 Mass. 64 ; Shirley *v.* Lunenburg, 11 Mass. 379.
(*d*) Hooker *v.* Robinson, 1 Bulstr. 125.
(*e*) Atherton *v.* Hole, 1 Lev. 137.
(*f*) 1 Roll. Ab. 747.
(*g*) Inter Plaw & Richards, Palm. 567 ; Lancaster *v.* Keyleigh, Cro. Car. 300, 408, 574.
(*h*) 9 Rich. II. c. 3.

540 · OF REMEDIES.

No. 3328.   Book 4, tit. 8, chap. 14, sec. 2, § 2, art. 1.   No. 3330.

provision has been extended to a remainder man. When there are more remainders than one, the next in succession to the recoveree has alone a right to sue.(a)

5° *By a vendee of land sold* pendente lite.

3328. On a suit to recover land, if the tenant in possession sell it *pendente lite*, and he aliens it, the alienee cannot have error on the judgment afterward given, because he is not a party nor a privy to it; the vendor himself may have error after judgment, although at the time he had no interest, and if he shall be restored, the alienee may enter upon him.(b)

6° *Who may bring error in case of death.*

3329.—1. When there was but one party plaintiff or defendant, and judgment has been given against him, and then he dies, the writ of error to reverse it must be brought by his personal representative, provided it affects the personal fund, as in case of judgment for debt or damages. When it charges only the inheritance, with which the personal representative has nothing to do, as judgments in real actions, the writ of error is to be sued by the heir at law.(c) When the action is of a mixed nature, charging both the inheritance and the personal estate, as do judgments in mixed actions, the heir and executor may bring error jointly.

3330.—2. When a personal judgment has been rendered erroneously against two, and one dies, the survivor may bring error without joining the executor or administrator of the deceased; and in such case, the writ ought to aver the death of the party in order to account for the variance.(d)

(a) Anon. 5 Mod. 396.
(b) 1 Roll. Ab. 748; Bac. Ab. Error, B.
(c) F. N. B. 21 N.
(d) Brewer *v.* Turner, Str. 233.

OF PROCEEDINGS IN AN ACTION. 541

No. 3331.   Book 4, tit. 8, chap. 14, sec. 2, § 2, art. 1.   No. 3334.

3331. A writ of error abates by the death of one of the plaintiffs in error, before errors assigned.(*a*)

7° *Who may bring error in case of marriage.*

3332. If an erroneous judgment be recovered against a single woman, who afterward marries, the writ of error should be brought by herself and her husband jointly,(*b*) If such judgment is obtained against a married woman as a feme sole, the writ must be sued by the husband and wife jointly; and where, in such case, another person was sued jointly with the wife, and a joint judgment was rendered against them as joint trespassers, the other person ought to be joined in such writ of error, and the judgment being entire, if reversed, must be reversed as to both.(*c*)

8° *Who may bring error in case of infancy.*

3333. Until an infant has acquired a legal capacity, by arriving at full age, he cannot implead nor be impleaded, because he has no power to appoint an attorney; when he sues, he must therefore sue by his guardian or next friend. A writ of error sued out by him without any such protector is therefore irregular and will be quashed, unless his guardian or next friend be made a party to it ;(*d*) but when the infant sues in his own name, and there is a joinder in error, his disability will be considered as waived.(*e*)

9° *Who must bring a writ of error when several persons have an interest.*

3334. When the parties plaintiff in error are living, if there are several entitled to institute such proceedings, they should be joined, even though there are

(*a*) Boas *v.* Heister, 3 S. & R. 271.
(*b*) Haines *v.* Corlist, 4 Mass. 659.
(*c*) Whitmore *v.* Delano, 6 N. H. Rep. 543.
(*d*) Whitaker *v.* Patton, 1 Port. 9.
(*e*) McClay *v.* Norris, 4 Gilm. 370. See Moore *v.* McEwen, 5 S. & R. 373.

542 OF REMEDIES.

No. 3334   Book 4, tit. 8, chap. 14, sec 2, § 2, art. 1.   No 3334.

some not to be affected by the reversal of the judgment, and it is competent for one to join the others
without their consent;(a) for if there be a joint judgment against several, and a part of them only bring a
writ of error to reverse it, without alleging the death
of the others, the court will quash the writ on motion;(b) so also, when a writ of error was brought in
the name of A B " and others," without naming the
others, this was held to be a fatal defect.(c) If any
refuse to join in the suit, they may be summoned to
the court of errors, and there be severed, after which he
who· sued out the writ may go alone.(d) But when
the plaintiffs below are plaintiffs in error, they must all
join, because unless they can establish a joint right
they cannot recover; the rule in relation to severance
applies only to cases where the plaintiffs in error were
defendants below.(e)

The reason given why one of several parties against
whom a judgment has been rendered cannot bring a
separate writ of error, is, that a great inconvenience
would ensue, for by that means the plaintiff might be
delayed from having the benefit of his judgment,
though it should be affirmed once or oftener.

It is one of the cardinal principles of justice, that
every person who is to be directly affected in his
interest or rights by the judgment of a court of record,
is entitled to be named or described in the suit, to
have notice of it, and an opportunity of being heard,
and of defending his rights. If, therefore, a party to
a judgment in a real action die, those who, on his

(a) Jameson v. Colburn, 1 Stew· & Port. 253 ; Tombecbee Bank v. Freeman, Minor, 285 ; Fotteral v. Floyd, 6 S. & R. 315.
(b) Andrews v. Bosworth, 3 Mass. 223 ; Thomas v. Wyatt, 9 S. & M.
308 ; Miller v. Heard, 1 Eng. 73 ; Deneale v. Stumps' Executors, 8 Pet. 526.
(c) Beale v. Fox, 4 Geo. 403. See Borden v. State, 3 Eng. 399 ; Bowle's
Heirs v. Rouse, 3 Gilman, 408.
(d) 6 S. & R. 315 : Shirley v. Lunenburg, 11 Mass. 379 ; Bradshaw v.
Gallagher, 8 John. 558 ; Watson v. Whaley, 2 Bibb, 392.
(e) Gallaher v. Jackson, 1 S. & R. 492.

OF PROCEEDINGS IN AN ACTION. 543

No. 3335.   Book 4, tit. 8, chap 14, sec. 2, § 2, art. 1.   No. 3338.

decease, are entitled by descent or devise to the land or estate, have a privity by their interest, in the principal subject of the judgment, and must all be named in a writ of error to reverse it; and this whether they are tenants of the land or not; and if another than the heir or devisee be tenant of the land, it is the safest course to name him also.(*a*)

3335. If judgment be given against two executors, though only one appeared to the action, yet both must join in error to reverse the judgment. They must also so join when there is a general judgment against one, and a judgment of assets *quando* against the other.(*b*)

2. *Against whom.*

3336. The writ of error may be sued out, 1, against a single party when he is alone the party on record, or who has an interest; 2, against personal representatives, or the survivor in case of death; 3, against husband and wife in case of marriage; 4, against several parties, when they have obtained a judgment.

1° *When against a single person.*

3337. When the party who has obtained judgment, or is to be made defendant in error, has sued or been sued alone, of course he must, if living, be made the defendant in error without joining any other person with him, for it is a rule that a stranger cannot be a party to proceedings in error, either as plaintiff or defendant.(*c*)

2° *Who is to be made defendant in error, in case of death.*

3338.—1. When an erroneous judgment has been given for only one party, who dies, the writ must be

(*a*) Porter *v.* Rummeny, 10 Mass. 64; Satterfield *v.* Crow, 8 B. Monr. 553.
(*b*) Ham. on Parties, 269.
(*c*) Steel *v.* Bridenback, 7 Watts & Serg. 150.

544   OF REMEDIES.

No 3339.   Book 4, tit 8, chap. 14, sec. 2, § 2, art 1.   No 3341.

sued against his personal representative when the
action is personal; when it is real and the land has
descended, it must be against the heir, or where the
land has been aliened, either by the heir or the ancestor, against the heir, with a *scire facias* or notice to
the terre tenant; when the action is mixed, against
the heir (when the estate in question is an inheritance) and the personal representative, with a similar
scire facias to warn the terre tenant.

3339.—2. When there are several recoverers and
one dies, and the judgment is personal, the writ must
be sued against the survivor alone. If the action is
real or mixed, it must be against the heirs also, when
the estate is an inheritance, with a *scire facias*, when
requisite.(*a*)

3° *Who is to be made defendant in error in case of marriage.*

3340. A married woman cannot appear by attorney
in any suit, whether brought by or against her; if an
erroneous judgment be rendered in favor of a single
woman, and before a writ of error has been sued out
against her, she marries, her husband must be joined
in the writ; but if she marries after allowance of
the writ, the proceedings will be continued against her
alone, for she cannot by her act affect the rights of the
plaintiff in error.

4° *Who must be defendants in error when there are several persons in interest.*

3341. When there are several persons in whose favor
a judgment has been rendered, they must, if living,
all be made defendants to the proceedings in error,
even where the original suit was real, and one has
aliened his share of the land.(*b*)

(*a*) Bartholomew *v.* Belfield, 2 Bulstr. 244 ; Doe *v.* Jones, 2 M. & Selw.
472.
(*b*) F. N. B. 18 I.

Art. 2.—In what cases writs of error may issue, and the form of the writ.

3342.—A writ of error is grantable *ex debito justitiæ*, and not *ex merâ gratiâ*, in all cases of trials at common law, except treason and felony.(*a*)   This writ must be sued out within the time prescribed by the statute of limitations, in the state where the action was brought. The writ is issued out of the court as required by the constitution, and directed to the judges in whose court the record is which is to be removed, commanding them that if judgment be rendered, then the record and process, and all things touching the same, under their seals distinctly and openly they have before the justices of the court of errors, (naming it,) on the next return day, together with the writ itself; that the record and process being inspected, they may further cause to be done what of right and according to the laws and customs ought.   To this writ there must be an *allocatur*, that is, it must be allowed to be issued by one of the judges of the court out of which it issues, which in civil cases is a matter of course.(*b*)   The writ is then served upon the judges, or left in the office of their clerk or prothonotary, and in due time it is returned into the supreme court or other court of errors.

Art. 3.—Of bail in error.

3343. No bail in error was required at common law, so that the defendant, by suing out a writ of error, could delay the plaintiff, without giving any security for the prosecution of the writ, or for the payment of

---

(*a*) Skipwith *v.* Hill, 2 Mass. 35 ; Drowne *v.* Stimpson, 2 Mass. 441 ; Pembroke *v.* Abington, 2 Mass. 142.

(*b*) The want of an *allocatur* is not a good ground of objection after an appearance entered, and the argument has commenced. Eckert *v.* Wilson, 10 S. & R. 44. When a writ was issued without the allowance of the court, and a motion was made to quash it, an allowance, *nunc pro tunc*, was ordered, to bar the statute of limitations. Ferris *v.* Douglass, 20 Wend. 626. See Marsh *v.* The Commonwealth, 16 S. & R. 319.

the debt and costs, in case the judgment should be
affirmed, or the writ of error should be discontinued,
or the plaintiff in error should become nonsuit.(*a*) To
remedy this evil, the English courts put some restraints
upon the issuing of a writ of *supersedeas*, except when
there was a manifest or pregnant error. And by the
enactment of several statutes(*b*) this evil was completely
removed. It was thereby provided that no execution
shall be stayed or delayed, upon or by any writ of
error, or *supersedeas* thereupon to be issued, for the
reversing of any judgment in any action or bill of debt,
upon any single bond for debt, or upon any obligation,
with the condition for the payment of money only, or
upon any action or bill of debt for rent, or upon any
contract, sued in any of the courts of record," etc.,
"unless the person or persons in whose name or names
such writ of error shall be brought, with two sufficient
sureties, such as the court where the judgment was
given shall allow of, shall first be bound unto the party
for whom the judgment is given, by recognizance to
be acknowledged in the same court, in double the sum
adjudged to be recovered by the former judgment, to
prosecute the said writ of error with effect, as also to
satisfy and pay, if the said judgment be affirmed, or
the writ of error non-prossed, all and singular the
debts, damages and costs adjudged upon the former
judgment, and all costs and damages to be awarded for
the delaying of the execution."

The principles of these statutes have been reënacted
or adopted in perhaps all the states of the Union, in
some cases, with considerable modifications.

*Art. 4.—Of the return of the writ of error, and proceedings before
the assignment of errors.*

3344. The judges of the court below return the writ

(*a*) 2 Tidd, 1074.
(*b*) 3 Jac. I., c. 8; 3 Car. I., c. 4, s. 4.

of error with the record in the case, properly certified under their seal, to the supreme or superior court; and on the back of the writ of error is a statement made that they have done so, which is called the *return.*(*a*) In judgment of law, the record itself is removed to the court above from the court below, though, in fact, a transcript only is sent up.(*b*)

When the record, as returned by the justices of the court below, appears to be incomplete, the parties may suggest a diminution of the record, and pray a writ of *certiorari* to the justice, to certify the whole record.(*c*) After the record has thus been completed, it may. be amended, quashed, or abated.

3345.—1. At common law, great certainty was required in making the writ agree with the record, because no defects could be amended. But by a statute(*d*) which has been adopted in principle, in perhaps all the states, it is allowed to *amend* writs of error, as a matter of course, when there is any thing to amend by. But when the writ is returnable before judgment is given, this is a fault which cannot be amended.(*e*)

3346.—2. After the return of the transcript or record, the defendant in error may move to *quash* the writ for any fault not amendable by the above mentioned statute, or the practice of the courts under it; but a motion to quash, after a plea of *in nullo est erratum* is in general too late; if, however, injustice is likely to be done, the court will, of its own motion, quash it.(*f*) The writ may also be quashed for one judgment, and stand good as to the other; as upon a judgment in *scire facias* against bail, the defendant brought a writ of error *tam in reditione judicii quam adjudicatione*

(*a*) Tidd's Pr. 1088, 1092.
(*b*) Brown *v.* Clark, 3 John. 443.
(*c*) Tidd's Pr. 1109 ; Bassler *v.* Neisly, 1 S. & R. 472.
(*d*) 5 Geo. I., c. 13. See Finney *v.* Crawford, 2 Watts, 294.
(*e*) Arch. Pr. 214 ; 2 Dunl. Pr. 1142; Str. 807, 891.
(*f*) Downing *v.* Baldwin, 1 S. & R. 298.

executionis, the court quashed the writ,. as far as it related to the original judgment, because the bail had no right to bring error upon the judgment against his principal, and ruled it to stand good *quoad* the judgment against the bail on the *scire facias.*(*a*)   A writ of error will.also be quashed when final judgment has not been rendered in the court below.(*b*)

3347.—3. In personal actions at common law, when a sole plaintiff in error dies, or if one of several plaintiffs in error dies, before errors assigned, *the writ abates;* but the death after the assignment of errors, does not abate it.(*c*)   In some of the states, provisions are made by statute for the substitution of the executors or administrators of the plaintiff in error, when the cause of action survives. The death of the defendant in error does not abate the writ, and much less the death of one of several such defendants. The marriage of a woman, after she has sued out a writ of error, abates it; but the marriage of feme sole defendant in error, does not.(*d*)

The *effect* of abatement of a writ of error, is, that the plaintiffs, or their representatives, may sue out and prosecute a new writ; when it abates by the act or default of the party, the second writ is no *supersedeas.*(*e*) But when the case appears to require it, the court will order a *supersedeas* to stay the proceedings pending the second writ of error.(*f*)

Art. 5.—*Of the assignment of errors.*

3348. When the writ of error has not been quashed, nor abated, and the record has been certified, the

---

(*a*) Burr *v.* Attwood, Carth. 447.
(*b*) Spitter *v.* Ohio Wright, 106.
(*c*) Green *v.* Watkins, 6 Wheat. 260; Marshall *v.* Peck, 1 Dana, 609; Boas *v.* Heister, 3 S. & R. 271.
(*d*) Arch. br. 216.
(*e*) A'noi' 1 Ventr. 100; Sherrer *v.* Grier, 3 Whart. 14.
(*f*) Hardeman *v.* Anderson, 4 How. U. S. 640.

plaintiff in error should *assign,* that is, specify the errors of which he complains. If he fail to do so within the time prescribed by the rules and practice of the court, his writ may be non-prossed, because he did not follow up his complaint, as he was bound to do. Thus, where a case was brought up on a writ of error, but no assignment of errors was filed, and no appearance made for either party, the court ordered it to be struck from the docket.(*a*)

An assignment of errors is in the nature of a declaration. The assignment need not be very formal, its principal requisite is clearness and certainty. It is either of errors of *fact,* or errors of *law.*

3349.—1. Errors of *fact* may be assigned of such matters as do not appear upon the record, and of such facts, which, if true, prove the judgment to have been erroneous; as that the defendant below, being under age, appeared by attorney; that a feme plaintiff or defendant was under coverture at the time of commencing the action; or that the plaintiff or defendant died before verdict or interlocutory judgment. But nothing of which the party could have taken advantage in the court below, can be assigned for error in fact.(*b*) An assignment of errors in fact, should conclude with a verification.(*c*) In assigning the death of the defendant in error, the assignment ought not to conclude in the common way, but by praying a *scire facias ad audiendum errores* against the executor or administrator of the defendant in error.

3350.—2. Errors in *law* are common or special.

1. *Common errors* are, that the declaration is insufficient in law to maintain the action; and that the judgment was given for the plaintiff instead of the defendant, or *vice versa.*

(*a*) Smith *v.* Inferior Court, 4 Geo. 156. See Hunter *v.* Langmin, Minor, 99.

(*b*) Wetmore *v.* Plant, 5 Conn. 541.

(*c*) Sheepshanks *v.* Lucas, 1 Burr. 410.

550

OF REMEDIES.

No 3351   Book 4, tit 8, chap 14, sec. 2, § 2, art. 6.   No 3352.

2. *Special errors* are those which show particular defects in the record, and which render the judgment erroneous. Of these the plaintiff may assign as many as he pleases; but he can assign nothing for error which contradicts the record, or that was of advantage to the plaintiff in error, or that is aided by appearance, or which was not taken advantage of or excepted to in due time;(a) or to any matter of form which was not excepted to below, and which might have been amended there.(b)

Art. 6.—Of pleas in error.

3351. After the errors are assigned, the defendant in error is required to plead or demur. This he is bound to do within the time prescribed by law or the rules of the court, and a failure to do so will subject him to a reversal.

3352. Pleas in error are common and special.

1. The *common* plea, or *rejoinder*, as it is more frequently called, is *in nullo est erratum*, or that there is no error in the record or proceedings. This is in the nature of a demurrer, and at once refers the matter of law arising in the case to the judgment of the court.(c) This plea in general confesses all the facts pleaded, and where it was assigned for error that the defendant below, an infant, appeared by attorney, the plea *in nullo est erratum* was considered as confessing the fact.(d) But, if an error in fact be assigned that is not assignable, or be ill assigned, *in nullo est erratum* is no con-

---

(a) See Cook v. Conway, 3 Dana, 454; Cates v. Woolridge, 1 J. J. Marsh. 267; Osburn v. State, 7 Ham. part 1, p. 212 : Shirley v. Lunenburg, 11 Mass. 379 ; Hemmenway v. Hicks, 4 Pick. 497 ; Wetmore v. Plant, 5 Conn. 541; Hill v. West, 4 Yeates, 385 ; Collins v. Rush. 7 S. & R. 147 ; Brown v. Caldwell, 10 S. & R. 114 ; Milliken v. Barr, 7 Penn. St. R. 23 ; Murray v. Cooper, 6 S. & R. 126 ; Chase v. Hodges, 2 Penn. St. R. 48.

(b) In re Pennsylvania Hall, 5 Penn. St. R. 204.

(c) Hagget v. Commonwealth, 3 Met. 457.

(d) Moore v. McEwen, 5 S. & R. 373. See Goodwin v. Sanders, 9 Yerg. 91 ; Bliss v. Rice, 9 John. 159 ; Harvey v. Rickett, 15 John. 87.

fession of it, but shall be taken only for demurrer.(a) There cannot be an assignment of error in fact and error in law together,(b) for these are distinct things, and require different trials; and if, to such an assignment, the defendant in error pleads in nullo est erratum, this is a confession of the error in fact, and the judgment must be reversed; for he should have demurred for duplicity.(c) By pleading in nullo est erratum, the defendant in error admits the record to be perfect, the effect of his plea being, that, in its present state, the record is without error, so that after this plea the defendant in error cannot allege diminution or pray a certiorari.(d) But the court may, ex officio, award a certiorari, to prevent injustice.

2. Special pleas to an assignment of error contain matters in confession and avoidance, as a release of errors, the act of limitations and the like, to which the plaintiff in error may reply or demur, and proceed to trial or argument.

Art. 7.—Of the issue.

3353. On the issue being joined, if it be an issue in fact, according to the English practice, a record of nisi prius is made up, and the parties proceed to trial, as in common cases; and after verdict, the party for whom it is found, must move to put the cause in the paper for argument; and then, on producing the postea, the court will give judgment according to the finding. These cases, where an issue is formed on matter of fact, by pleadings in error, are extremely rare in this country.

(a) Tidd's Pr. 1117; Bac. Ab. Error, K 2.
(b) Where the assignment of errors contained errors in fact and errors in law, the court ordered the error in fact to be struck out, and reversed the judgment for the error in law.   Lewis v. Lawson, 1 Root, 262.
(c) Bac. Ab. Error, K 2; Moody v. Vreeland, 7 Wend. 55.
(d) Cheetham v. Tillotson, 4 John. 499.

552   OF REMEDIES.

No 3354.   Book 4, tit. 8, chap 14, sec. 2, § 2, art. 8.   No. 3354.

When an issue in *law* is formed, the case is put on the argument list, and it is argued before the judges of the court of errors, and by them decided, after hearing counsel on both sides. These cases require much consideration, as they often turn on very nice questions of law.

Before the court hear the argument, they require the plaintiff in error to furnish each of the judges with a *paper book*, which is a book or paper containing an abstract of all the facts and pleadings necessary to the full understanding of the case. This book should also state the points made by plaintiff in error, and also the cases or statutes to be cited in support of the positions of law taken by him.(*a*)

Art. 8.—*Of judgment in error.*

3354. Courts of error, in rendering their judgments, usually give the reasons or motives which induce them on one side or the other. The collection of reasons thus delivered by a judge for giving the judgment he is about to pronounce, is called his *opinion*. Such an opinion ought to be a perfect syllogism, the major of which should be the law ; the minor, the fact to be decided ; and the consequence, the judgment which declares that to be conformable or contrary to law.

The judgment in error, unless the court are equally divided in opinion, is to *affirm*, or to *recall*, or to *reverse* the former judgment; that the plaintiff be *barred* of his writ of error ;. or that there be a *venire facias de novo*.

The common judgment for the defendant in error, whether the errors assigned be in fact or in law, is,

(*a*) In Pennsylvania, the supreme court has adopted a convenient rule, that each party may furnish a paper book, stating the points made by such party, and also the authority by which they are supported, a copy of which must be furnished to the opposite party.

OF PROCEEDINGS IN AN ACTION.   553

No 3355.   Book 4, tit. 8, chap. 14, sec. 2, § 2, art. 8.   No 3355.

that the former judgment be *affirmed*. But a judgment may be good in part and erroneous in part; in that case the judgment below will be affirmed as to part, and reversed as to the other part; as where it was reversed for damages and affirmed for costs.(*a*) If the judgment below is not divisible, although good in part, and bad in part, it must be affirmed or reversed *in toto;* as where it is entered against two and it is erroneous as to one.(*b*)

On a demurrer to an assignment of errors, in fact or in law, for duplicity, the judgment, when for the defendant, is *quod affirmetur*. On a plea of release of errors, or the statute of limitations, found for the defendant, the judgment is that the plaintiff be *barred* of the writ of error.

When the judgment is for the plaintiff in error, for an error *in fact*, the judgment below is *recalled, revoked;* when for an error *in law*, it is *reversed, quod judicium reversetur*.

3355. In cases where there are several *dependent* judgments, and the principal one is reversed, the others cannot be supported; as if the plaintiff recover in debt upon a judgment; if the first be reversed, the second, which is founded upon it, will of course fall to the ground.(*c*)   But the reversal of the last judgment will not affect the first; as if judgment be given against executors in an action of debt, and, after, on a *scire facias*, judgment is given against them to have execution of their proper goods, and a writ of error be brought upon both judgments, if the first judgment be

---

(*a*) Cummings *v.* Pruden, 11 Mass. 206 ; Wales *v.* Fowler, Kirby, 236 ; Dixon *v.* Pierce, 1 Root, 138 ; Swearingen *v.* Pendleton, 4 S. & R. 396 ; Boaz *v.* Heister, 6 S. & R. 18 ; Barnett *v.* Barnett, 16 S. & R. 51.

(*b*) Boaz *v.* Heister, 6 S. & R. 18 ; Harman *v.* Brotherson, 1 Denis, 537 ; Davis *v.* Campbell, 1 Iredell, 482 ; Gaylord *v.* Payne, 4 Conn. 80.   By act of assembly in Pennsylvania, the court may in some cases reverse as to one of the defendants and affirm as to the other. Jamieson *v.* Pomeroy, 9 Penn. St. Rep. 230.

(*c*) Bac. Ab. Error, M 1 ; Roll. Ab. 777 ; 8 Co. 143.   See Hutchinson *v.* Commonwealth, 4 Met. 359.

554 OF REMEDIES.

No. 3356.　　Book 4, tit. 8, chap. 14, sec. 2, § 2, art. 8.　　No. 3358.

good and the last erroneous, the last judgment shall be reversed, and the first shall stand.(a)

3356. When the judgments are *independent* of each other, the reversal of one does not affect the other; as if, in an action of account, judgment be given *quod computet*, and afterward auditors are assigned, and upon the account, judgment is given also against the defendant with damages and costs, whereupon a writ of error is brought upon both judgments, the last one of which alone is found to be erroneous; in this case, the last judgment only shall be reversed, and not the first, which shall stand in full force, for these two are distinct and independent judgments.(b)

3357. A distinction is made in giving judgment by the court of error, when the judgment below is reversed, between those cases where the plaintiff below, is plaintiff in error, and where the defendant below, is plaintiff in error.

1. In the first case where the plaintiff below is plaintiff in error, and the judgment is reversed, the court above give such judgment as the court below ought to have given; for the writ of error is to revive the first cause of action, and to recover what ought to have been recovered in the first suit, in which the erroneous judgment was given.(c)

2. But if the judgment below be given against the defendant, and he bring a writ of error, upon which that judgment is reversed, the judgment shall be *quod judicium reversetur*, simply that the judgment be reversed; for the writ of error is brought only to be eased and discharged from that judgment.

3358. If the judgment of the court below has been given upon a case stated or a special verdict, and the court above reverse the judgment, the latter court

---

(a) Bac. Ab. Error, M 1.
(b) Williams v. White, Cro. Eliz. 806 ; S. C. Styl. 290.
(c) Garr v. Stokes, 1 Harr. 403 ; Swearingen v. Pendleton; 4 S. & R. 396.

OF PROCEEDINGS IN AN ACTION. 555

No. 3359.   Book 4, tit 8, chap. 14, sec. 2, § 2, art. 8.   No. 3361.

ought to give the judgment as it ought to have been given in the first place, whether the plaintiff or defendant below be the plaintiff in error.(a)

3359. When the judgment of the court below is reversed, a *venire de novo* will be granted in the following cases: first, because the jury were improperly chosen, or there was some irregularity in returning them; secondly, because the jury improperly conducted themselves; thirdly, because they gave *general* damages, upon a declaration containing several counts, one or more of which were defective; fourthly, because the verdict, whether general or special, is imperfect by reason of some ambiguity, or by finding less than the whole matter in issue, or by not assessing damages; or fifthly, because there has been some other defect or irregularity in the proceedings on the first venire, or the trial, by which the proper effect of that writ has been frustrated, or the verdict has become void in law. When this writ is granted, there must of course be a new trial.(b)

3360. Costs in error are generally given to the successful party, and the judgment is for the costs. But the regulations of the several states vary considerably upon this subject. In some cases, and under certain circumstances, in some of the states, no costs are allowed on reversal; in other cases, double costs are given.

3361. A part of the judgment of the court of errors, sometimes is a writ of *restitution*, when an erroneous judgment has been reversed. This writ is issued when property has been taken in execution, and the judgment has been reversed or set aside; this is to compel the plaintiff below, who has been paid the amount of his erroneous judgment, to restore to the opposite

(a) Stephens v. Cowan, 6 Watts, 513 ; Mosher v. Small, 5 Penn. St. Rep. 221. See Commonwealth v. Huffey, 6 Penn. St. Rep. 348.
(b) Miller v. Ralston, 1 S. & R. 309 ; Reed v. Collins, 5 S. & R. 351. Vide ante, n. 3300.

party the property which he has taken in execution, or, if such property has been sold, then to restore to him the price for which the same was sold.(a)

3362. After judgment in error has been thus given, the record remains in the court of errors. It is then required that it should be sent below, when it has been affirmed, to be executed; or if it has been reversed, and a *venire facias de novo* has been awarded, that the action may be tried again before such court. It is necessary for this purpose, that the record be *remitted* to the court below, and this is effected by means of a *remittitur*, which is an entry on the records of the court above, that the record of the case has been returned to the court whence it was removed. A certificate made by the clerk of the supreme or superior court to that effect is also called a *remittitur*. On the return of the record to the court from whence it was removed by writ of error, the case will be proceeded in by a *venire facias de novo*, by execution, or by *scire facias* against the bail in error, as the case may be, conformably to the judgment of the supreme court.

SECTION 3.—OF THE REMEDY BY CERTIORARI.

3363. A *certiorari* is a writ issued by a supreme or superior court having jurisdiction, directed to the judges or officers of an inferior court, commanding them to return the records of a cause depending before them in a particular case.(b)

In general, there are two ways by which a superior court, which has a supervisory power over all inferior jurisdictions, can correct the erroneous proceedings of inferior courts; the first is by writ of error, which is of right, in civil cases, *ex debito justitiæ*, and which lies

---

(a) Roll. Ab. 778; Bac. Ab. Execution, Q; 1 M. & S. 425; Boal's Appeal, 2 Rawle, 37; Bruere *v.* Britton, 1 Spencer, 168.
(b) Bac. Ab. Certiorari, A; 4 Vin. Ab. 330; Nels. Ab. h. t.

only *after judgment* rendered in the inferior court; the second is by *certiorari*, which is granted only at the discretion of the court, and generally lies at *any stage* of the proceedings in the court below. A question, which is not easily settled, frequently arises, which of these two remedies ought to be adopted in practice. It may, however, be laid down generally, that when the lower court proceeds *according to the course of the common law*, and the court above can give a right judgment, where the inferior court has given a wrong one, then a writ of error is the proper remedy. It is also equally clear, that when neither this course of proceeding can be had, nor such right judgment given, then the certiorari is the proper remedy.

The writ of *certiorari* is issued in two kinds of cases; in one species it accompanies a writ of error, and is issued for the purpose of compelling the production of the whole record, when a diminution has been suggested and shown. The other kind, which is the only one which shall occupy our attention under this section, does not accompany the writ of error, but lies in many cases where a writ of error cannot by law give a right judgment, when the lower court gives a wrong one, or in which the proceedings are not *according to the course of the common law*. In these cases, where the writ of error is not the proper remedy, the *certiorari* is the ground of the proceeding. It is first used to bring up the record and proceedings from the court below; when returned, the court above issues a notice to the party defendant or respondent, in the nature of a summons.(a) After this, the court above proceed to act, according to law and justice, in the decision of the case.

In the examination of this subject, we will consider, 1, the mode of obtaining a *certiorari*; 2, how the

(a) It has never been the practice in Pennsylvania to serve a copy of the writ of *certiorari* on the attorney on record, as in England ; nor is the writ, as is the case in the supreme court of the United States, accompanied with a citation to the party. Commonwealth *v.* McAllister, 1 Watts, 308.

558　　OF REMEDIES.

No. 3364.　　　Book 4, tit. 8, chap 14, sec. 3, § 1, 2.　　　No. 3365.

certiorari is to be returned; 3, how far a *certiorari* operates as a *supersedeas;* 4, when a *procedendo* will be ᵥordered.

§ 1.—Of the mode of obtaining a *certiorari*.

3364. The regular mode of obtaining a *certiorari* is, in general, by motion or petition, and the facts upon which it is granted must be established by the oath or affirmation of the applicant, unless such facts appear upon the record.(*a*). As a writ of *certiorari* is clearly not a writ *ex debito justitiæ*, because it lies to the court below in any stage of its proceedings, not always on the ground of an error in its judgment, but often merely for the purpose of examining its proceedings, in order to see that it has not exceeded its jurisdiction, or acted irregularly, on surmise of erroneous proceedings, the court above must exercise discretionary power in issuing this writ, not accompanying a writ of error, and must therefore not *allow* it to be issued, except when claimed by the government, and except in some cases where this writ, from long usage and for particular reasons, has become a matter of course. In general, security must be given to prosecute the writ of *certiorari* with effect.

§ 2.—How the *certiorari* is to be returned.

3365. The *certiorari* ought to be returned under the seal of the inferior court, or of the justices to whom it is directed; and if such court have no proper seal, it may be returned under any seal. It must be returned by the person to whom the writ is directed; but a return made by the clerk of the circuit court of the United States, to which a *certiorari* was directed, was held to be sufficient.(*b*)

(*a*) Finch *v.* McDowell, 7 Cowen, 538; Charlt. 279, 303; 8 Wend. 519.
(*b*) Stewart *v.* Ingle, 9 Wheat. 526. See 7 Cowen, 103; Ball *v.* Van Houten, 1 South. 32.

§ 3.—How far a *certiorari* operates as a *supersedeas.*

3366. After the cause has been removed by *certiorari*, there is no record in the court below, and, therefore, that court cannot proceed in the cause in any respect, and all its subsequent acts will be erroneous. If, before the delivery of the *certiorari* to the judges of the inferior courts, execution had been issued by the court, the judges to whom the *certiorari* was delivered ought immediately to have awarded a *supersedeas* to the sheriff, in order to have stopped the execution. The delivery of such *supersedeas* to the sheriff before he has commenced the execution of the writ, renders his subsequent acts wholly void; but if the execution was partially executed before the *supersedeas* was delivered to him, he may afterward go through with it.(*a*)

§ 4.—When a *procedendo* will be ordered.

3367. If the *certiorari* has been improperly issued, by a fraud upon the court, a false allegation, and the like, the courts above will issue a *procedendo* to the court, commissioners, or others below, to proceed in the cause or business. By this writ of *procedendo* the cause is remitted to the court whence the record came, and it commands the inferior court to *proceed* to the final hearing and determination of the same. It issues not only in the cases above mentioned, but also when it does not appear to the superior court that the suggestion upon which the cause has been removed, is sufficiently proved.

SECTION 4.—OF THE REMEDY BY WRIT OF FALSE JUDGMENT.

3368. In England there is an additional remedy by a writ which lies, when an erroneous judgment is

(*a*) Blanchard *v.* Myers, 9 John. 66: Patchin *v.* Mayor, etc. of Brooklyn, 13 Wend. 664; Kingsland *v.* Gould, 1 Halst. 161; Mairs *v.* Sparks, 2 South. 513; Gardiner *v.* Murray, 4 Yeates, 560.

given, in a court not of record, in which the suitors are judges.(*a*) Though this writ is perhaps never used in this country, it is proper, in a work like' the present, to take a brief view of it.

This writ may be sued out of chancery by any one against whom the judgment is given, his heir, executor, or administrator; or by any one who has sustained damages, though the other defendants do not join, as they ought to do, in error. If the writ be brought upon a judgment in the sheriff's court, it is in the nature of a *recordari;*(*b*) or, if upon a judgment in another court, it is in the nature of an *accedas ad curiam.*(*c*)

Upon the return of the writ, when the whole proceedings are certified, and not before, the plaintiff is required to assign errors. To compel a joinder in error, the plaintiff may have a *scire facias ad audiendum errores;* or he may serve a rule, as on a writ of error. And upon two *scire faciases ad audiendum errores* awarded, and *nihils* returned, or *scire feci* and default made, the judgment shall be reversed.

When the parties are once in court, the subsequent proceedings in false judgment are the same as in error.

CHAPTER XV.—OF EXECUTION.

3369. An execution has been called the life of the law, and the object of all the proceedings in an action is to obtain this writ. After a final judgment has been entered by the court, by which the plaintiff is adjudged entitled to a thing in the possession of the defendant, or to a sum of money which is to be paid by the latter to the former, unless the plaintiff's

(*a*) F. N. B. 18.
(*b*) See Bouv. L. D. Recordari facias loquelam.
(*c*) F. N. B. 18 ; Bouv. L. D. h. t.

adjudged right be suspended by proceedings in the nature of an appeal, or by his own agreement, he is entitled to sue an execution in order to obtain the fruit of his judgment.

By *execution* is meant the act of carrying into effect the final judgment of a court or other jurisdiction. The writ which authorizes the officer to carry into effect such judgment, and which is the object to be examined in this chapter, is also called an *execution*.

This chapter will be divided into five sections: 1, of the right to issue an execution; 2, of the form of execution; 3, of the time when an execution should be issued; 4, of the effect of an execution; 5, of the several kinds of executions.

SECTION 1.—OF THE RIGHT TO ISSUE AN EXECUTION.

3370. As a general rule the plaintiff, or party in whose favor a judgment has been rendered, may issue an execution, when his judgment is final, unless he has agreed to give a stay of execution, or the law authorizes the losing party to enter security, which has been done, for the purpose of staying such execution for a limited time; and when this has been done and the time has expired, the successful party may issue execution as a matter of course, subject at all times to the control of the court, and liable to be set aside, or modified, as the justice of the case may require.(*a*)

In some cases, however, execution cannot be taken out without leave of court; as, where in actions on a policy of insurance there is a verdict for the plaintiff against one of several underwriters, and the others have entered into a *consolidation rule,*(*b*) and agreed to

(*a*) See Commonwealth *v.* Magee, 8 Penn. St. Rep. 240 ; Irwin *v.* Shoemaker, 8 W. & S. 75 ; Harrison *v.* Soles, 6 Penn. St. Rep. 393.
(*b*) For the nature and history of this rule, see Bouv. L. D. h. t. ; 2 Marsh. on Ins. 701 ; Parke on Ins. xlix.; 3 Chit. Gen. Pr. 644 ; Graff *v.* Musser, 3 S. & R. 262, 265 ; Brown *v.* Scott, 1 Dall. 145 ; Merrihew *v.* Taylor, 1 Browne's R. Appx. lxvii.; Rumsey *v.* Wynkoop, 1 Yeates, 5 ; Towanda Bank *v.* Ballard, 7 Watts & Serg. 434.

be bound by it. When a verdict is taken *pro forma* at the trial, for a certain sum, subject to the award of an arbitrator, the sum. afterward awarded must be taken as if it had been originally found by the jury, and the plaintiff is entitled to enter up judgment for the amount, without first applying to the court for leave ;(*a*) but where a verdict is taken, and judgment entered up, for a less sum than is afterward found due by the award, the plaintiff cannot take out execution for the whole sum awarded, but only for the sum recovered by the judgment; for the residue he must proceed by attachment.(*b*)　On a writ of error *coram nobis*, it seems an execution taken out without leave of court is irregular.(*c*)

SECTION 2.—OF THE FORM OF EXECUTIONS.

3371. The execution is founded on the judgment, and must conform to it in every respect, as to the amount of the judgment and the parties,(*d*) unless some of the parties, when there are more than one, are dead, then the execution may recite the death and be issued in favor of or against the survivor.(*e*)　In Pennsylvania, upon the death of a plaintiff, after judgment, his executor may be substituted in his place,, and an execution reciting the fact, may be issued, without a *scire facias* to renew the judgment in favor of the executor;(*f*) and an execution issued by the executor, without a formal substitution, is voidable and not void; a party may, therefore, justify under it.(*g*)　In New Jersey such an execution will be

---

(*a*) 1 East, 401 ; but see Barnes, 58.
(*b*) Tidd's Pr. 910.
(*c*) Ribout *v.* Wheeler, Sayer's R. 166 ; Barnes, 201 ; 2 Bl. Rep. 1067.
(*d*) Commonwealth *v.* Fisher, 2 J. J. Marsh, 137 ; Washington *v.* Irving, Mart. & Yerg. 45 ; Palmer *v.* Palmer, 2 Conn. 462.
(*e*) Hamilton *v.* Lyman, 9 Mass. 14 ; Bowdoin *v.* Jordan, 9 Mass. 160.
(*f*) Darlington *v.* Speakman, 9 W. & S. 182.
(*g*) Day *v.* Sharp, 4 Whart. 339.

quashed.(a)   When the defendant dies after judgment, no execution can be had against his goods, without a *scire facias* against his representatives.(b)

Although the rule is firmly established that when the judgment is joint, the process to enforce its payment must also be joint, yet it is said to be more *technical* than *substantial*, and the court, out of which such process issues, will take care that it shall not be used so as to work injustice, and, for this reason, will protect a surety from an attempted disregard of a release to him by a creditor.(c)

SECTION 3.—OF THE TIME WHEN AN EXECUTION SHOULD BE
ISSUED.

3372. By statute of Westm. 2, an execution may be sued at any time within a year and a day after the judgment is signed, in cases where a *scire facias* is not required, or where execution is not stayed by writ of error, injunction, agreement, or the like; and when it is so stayed, within a year and a day after the removal of the bar. In several of the states, the time for issuing an execution has been extended beyond that time by statutory provisions.

If the writ of execution has been issued within the year, and it has been so executed as not to produce to the party the full benefits of his judgment, after it has been returned, he may have other writs of execution after the year, upon continuing the first writ down to them ;(d) the second, or other subsequent execution, may be of the same kind as the first, or of a different species; a *capias ad satisfaciendum* may, therefore, be issued after a *fieri facias*.(e)

The second execution of the same nature, issued on a judgment, is called an *alias*, and all future executions

(a) Harwood v. Murphy, 1 Green, 193. See Davis v. Helm, 3 Sm. & M. 17.
(b) Wilson v. Kirkland, Walker, 155 ; Hubart v. Williams, Walker, 175.
(c) Mortland v. Himes, 8 Penn. St. Rep. 265.
(d) Co. Litt. 290, b.
(e) Thorpe v. Fowler, 5 Cowen, 446.

ot which is called first pluries, the next, second pluries, etc.

SECTION 4.—OF THE EFFECT OF AN EXECUTION.

3373. An execution, issuëd by a court having competent jurisdiction, is a protection to the officer who is required and authorized to execute it, and whether it be regular or not, it is of no importance to him, except when the officer participates in the irregularity.(*a*) This salutary protection is wise, just, and necessary, because the officer has not the authority to impugn the authority of the court, and he cannot, therefore, inquire into the regularity of its proceedings. In this case, however, he must execute it according to its requirements, and he cannot, under color of authority, seize the goods of a stranger.(*b*)   He is protected only while obeying its requirements.

The rule, however, is very different when the court has no jurisdiction of the case, for then the officer is bound to pay no regard to its mandates. This reasonable responsibility the law casts upon him. If a court having jurisdiction in criminal cases only, should entertain an action of debt, give a judgment, and issue an execution, the sheriff could lawfully refuse to execute that process; and if he proceeded to execute it, he would be liable as a trespasser, together with the judges of the court, and the plaintiff, the whole of the proceedings being *coram non judice.*(*c*)

Though an irregular execution is a protection to the officer, when the court has jurisdiction, it is none to the parties who have sued it out; as if an execution be issued before a judgment has been entered.(*d*)

(*a*) Hart *v.* Dubois, 20 Wend. 236.
(*b*) See Green *v.* Morse, 5 Greenl. 291 ; Foss *v.* Stewart, 2 Shepl. 312.
(*c*) The case of the Marshalsea, 10 Rep. 76 ; Allen *v.* Greenlee, 2 Dev. 370.   But see The People *v.* Warren, 5 Hill, 440.
(*d*) See Baldwin *v.* Whittier, 4 Shep. 33.

OF PROCEEDINGS IN AN ACTION.   565

No 3474   Book 4, tit. 8, chap 15, sec. 5, § 1, 2, art. 1.   No 3377.

The vitality of an execution continues fron the time it reaches the sheriff, or other lawful officer's hands, until the day when it is returnable,(a) unless a *supersedeas* has been issued, and, from the moment it is known to the officer, the execution has lost all its protective virtue, and if the officer afterward proceed to execute the writ, he will be considered as a trespasser; but he will not be liable as such unless he actually knew of the existence of the *supersedeas*.

SECTION 5.—OF THE SEVERAL KINDS OF EXECUTIONS.

3374. Executions may be considered, 1, as to their end; 2, as to their object.

§ 1.—Executions considered as to their end.

3375. They are either final or not final.
1. An execution, which is used to make the money due on a judgment out of the property of a defendant, is called a *final* execution, because, when once executed, the object of the judgment has been obtained.
2. There is another kind which tends to an end, but is not absolutely final, as a *capias ad satisfaciendum*, by virtue of which the body of the defendant is taken, to the intent that the plaintiff shall be satisfied his debt, etc.; the imprisonment of the defendant not being absolute, but until he shall satisfy the same; this is called an execution *quousque*.

§ 2.—Of executions considered as to the objects they are to act upon.

3376. These may be divided into two classes: 1, those which are for the recovery of specific things; 2, those for the recovery of money.

Art. 1.—*Of executions to recover specific things.*

3377. The principal executions of this class, are

(a) Vail *v.* Lewis, 4 John. 450.

the *habere facias seisinam,* the *habere facias possessionem,* the *retorno habendo,* and the *distringas.*

3378.—1. The writ of *habere facias seisinam,* or writ of seisin, is an execution used in most real actions, by which the sheriff is directed that he cause the demandant to have seisin of the lands which he has recovered. This writ may be taken out at any time within a year and day after judgment. It is executed in nearly the same manner as a *habere facias possessionem,* and for this purpose the officer may break open the outer door of a house, to deliver seisin to the demandant.(*a*)

3379.—2. The *habere facias possessionem,* or writ of possession, is an execution, used principally, after a judgment in ejectment, in order to obtain the possession of the property recovered. The sheriff is commanded by this writ, that without delay he cause the plaintiff to have possession of the land in dispute, which is therein described; a *fieri facias* or a *capias ad satisfaciendum* for costs may be included in the writ; the duty of the sheriff, in the execution and return of that part of the writ, is the same as on a common *fieri facias* or *capias ad satisfaciendum.* In the execution of this writ, the sheriff is required to deliver a full and actual possession of the premises to the plaintiff. For this purpose he may break an outer or inner door if required, and should he be opposed by force and violence, he must raise the *posse comitatus.*(*b*)

3380.—3. The writ of *retorno habendo* is an execution in replevin, which recites that the defendant was summoned to appear to answer the plaintiff, in a plea whereof he took the cattle of the said plaintiff, specifying them, and that the said plaintiff afterward made default, wherefore it was then considered that the said plaintiff and his pledges of prosecuting should be in

---

(*a*) Com. Dig. Execution, E; Bac. Ab. h. t.; Wats. Office of Sheriff, 238; Bingh. on Ex. 115, 252.
(*b*) Wats. on Sheriff, 60, 215; Bac. Ab. Sheriff, N 3.

OF PROCEEDINGS IN AN ACTION.   567

No 3381.   Book 4, tit 8, chap 15, sec 5, § 2, art. 1.   No. 3381.

mercy, and that the said defendant should go without day, and that he should have return of the cattle aforesaid. It then commands the sheriff that he should cause to be returned the cattle aforesaid, to the said defendant, without delay, etc.(a) If the identical goods distrained are found in the hands of the tenant, undisposed of, and unincumbered, they may be taken by the sheriff upon the *retorno habendo;* if not, the sheriff may return an *elongata*, or, as it is called in law-French, *eloigné;* that is, that the goods have been removed out of the reach of the sheriff. When that return is made, the plaintiff may have a writ called a *capias in withernam*, by which the sheriff is commanded to take the defendant's own goods, which may be found in his bailiwick, and keep them safely, (not to deliver them to the plaintiff,) until such time as the defendant shall submit himself, and allow the distress to be taken. If the sheriff cannot execute the *withernam*, and is consequently obliged to return it *nihil*, there issues an *alias*, and then a *pluries withernam*, and if *nihil* be also returned to these, then follows a *capias* against the body of the defendant.(b)

3381.—4. The writ of *distringas* is used sometimes to enforce a compliance of what is required of a party, by a distress of his goods and chattels. In detinue, when judgment is rendered for the plaintiff, that "the said A B do recover against the said C D the goods and chattels aforesaid, or the sum of   dollars for the value of the same, if the said A B cannot have again his said goods and chattels, together with   dollars, his charges and costs;" then there issues a writ of *distringas* which recites the judgment; and then proceeds as follows: "And hereupon the said sheriff is commanded that he distrain the said C D by all his

---

(a) 2 Sell. Pr. 168 ; Bac. Ab. Replevin, E 5.
(b) See Woglam *v.* Cowperthwaite, 2 Dall. 68 ; Frey *v.* Leeper, 2 Dall. 131 ; Bradyll *v.* Ball, 1 Bro. C. C. 427 ; Ham. N. P. 454.

568   OF REMEDIES.

No. 3382   Book 4, tit 8, chap 15, sec. 5, § 2, art. 2.   No. 3384.

lands and chattels in his bailiwick, so that neither the said C D, nor any one by him, do lay hands on the same, until the said sheriff shall have another com. mand from our said court in that behalf, and that the said sheriff answer to our said court here for the issues of the same, so that the said-C D render to the said A B the goods and chattels aforesaid, or the said sum of dollars, for the value of the same; and in what manner the said sheriff shall have executed this the command of our said court, he is commanded to make appear," etc.

Art. 2.—*Of executions for the recovery of money.*

3382. The principal executions issued for the purpose of recovering money, are, 1, those which issue against the body of the unsuccessful party; and, 2, those which may be sued out against his goods, chattels and land.

1. *Of executions against the body.*

3383. The *capias ad satisfaciendum* and the attachment belong to this class.

3384.—1. A *capias ad satisfaciendum* is a writ issuing out of a court of competent jurisdiction, in a cause where judgment has been rendered, directed to a proper officer of the court, commanding him to take the defendant, and him safely keep, so that he may have his body in court on the return day, to satisfy, *ad satisfaciendum,* the plaintiff.(*a*)

In point of *form,* the *capias ad satisfaciendum* must pursue the judgment, be tested on a general teste day, unless otherwise provided for by statute, and it should be sealed with the seal of the court, and signed, like other writs, by its clerk or prothonotary. It must be for the same sum as that for which judgment was

(*a*) The use of this writ has been greatly restricted in most of the states of the Union; in some, as in Pennsylvania, it can be issued only for torts, and in cases of fraud or concealment of property in contracts.

given, unless a part of it has been since paid, or levied under a *fieri facias*, in which case it issues for the residue. If there are several defendants, it must issue against the whole of them.(*a*)   But there are many persons against whom it cannot be issued.   In all cases the reason why these persons are privileged, is the promotion of the public good, and not as a favor granted to particular persons.   These are ambassadors, and other public ministers and their servants; members of congress, and those of the state legislatures, are not liable to this process, *eundo, morando, et redeundo*, or going to, remaining, or returning from the places to which they were called by their public duties. Parties, their attorneys, and witnesses in court, in order to give them that freedom required to attend upon their respective obligations there, are also protected from the operation of this writ, *eundo, morando, et redeundo*.(*b*)   In Pennsylvania, it has been considered that a state of civilization should protect women from the operation of this writ, and an act has been passed forbidding their imprisonment for debts on their contracts, where there is no fraud.

This writ is *executed* by taking the defendant in custody, and keeping him in close confinement, generally within the public or county prison,(*c*) provided for such purposes, from which he is not to be discharged, except by due course of law ; for if the sheriff permit the prisoner to go at large, it will be an escape, for which he will, in general, become liable for the debt, although the prisoner voluntarily return and surrenders himself to prison before the return day.(*d*)   But

---

(*a*) Clark *v*. Clement, 6 T. R. 526.
(*b*) Broome *v*. Hurst, 4 Yeates, 124, n ; S. C. 4 Dall. 387 ; Parker *v*. Hotchkiss, 1 Wall. jr., 268.
(*c*) Jacobs *v*. Tolman, 8 Mass. 161.
(*d*) 13 John. 366 ; Dowdal *v*. Hamer, 2 Watts, 63 ; 8 John. 98 ; Shewell *v*. Fell, 3 Yeates, 17 ; S. C. 4 Yeates, 47 ; Wheeler *v*. Hambright, 9 S. & R. 390. A distinction is made as to the responsibility of the sheriff, between

this confinement has been rendered less rigorous than formerly, in many of the states, by allowing certain prison bounds, or jail limits; and in some states the defendant is discharged by giving security to the plaintiff that he will apply for the benefit of the acts for the relief of insolvent debtors. ⸱

The *effect* of the *capias ad satisfaciendum* is to confine the defendant in the custody of the sheriff, or in the county jail, or to such other place appointed by public authority to receive such prisoner.(*a*) The execution is considered, *quoad* him, as a satisfaction of the debt, during the confinement of the debtor, but if he die in jail, the plaintiff may have execution of his lands and goods, by virtue of the statute 21 Jac. I., c. ·24.(*b*) If the plaintiff consent to discharge the defendant, after he has been arrested under a *capias ad satisfaciendum*, though it be on terms which are not afterward complied with, or upon giving fresh security which afterward becomes ineffectual, the plaintiff cannot resort to the judgment again, or charge the defendant's person in execution; and the discharge of one of several joint debtors, extinguishes the judgment as to all the debtors, so that neither can afterward be taken, or held in execution.(*c*)

The usual *returns* to a writ of *capias ad satisfaciendum*,

cases where the action is in *debt*, and where an *action on the case* has been brought. In the former, if the jury find for the plaintiff, they must find for the whole debt and costs ; but in the latter, the jury may find such damages as they think proper. Duncan *v.* Klinefelter, 5 Watts, 141 ; 4 Yeates, 17, 47.

(*a*) Jacobs *v.* Tolman, 8 Mass. 161.

(*b*) Sharpe *v.* Speckenagle, 3 S. & R. 465 ; Cooper *v.* Bigalow, 1 Cowen, 56 ; Freeman *v.* Rushton, 4 Dall. 214.

_ (*c*) Ransom *v.* Keyes, 9 Cowen, 128 ; Yates *v.* Van Rensselaer, 5 John. 364 ; Masters *v.* Edwards, 1 Caines, 515 ; Bailey *v.* Kimbal, 1 Chip. 151 ; McLean *v.* Whiting, 8 John. 339. In South Carolina, the act of 1815 alters the common law, so that a plaintiff may discharge a defendant in custody under a *capias ad satisfaciendum*, for a time, with his consent, without impairing his rights, and he may retake him in execution. Eggart *v.* Barnestine, 3 McCord, 162. In Louisiana, when the parties agree to a temporary discharge, the defendant may be retaken. Abat *v.* Whitman, 7 N. S. 163 ; Martin *v.* Ashcroft, 8 N. S. 315.

are, that the sheriff has taken the defendant, whose body he has ready, commonly made in Latin *cepi corpus;* or that the defendant is not to be found in his bailiwick, *non est inventus.* On the latter return the plaintiff may sue out an *alias capias* into the same, or a *testatum* into a different county ; or, at his choice, he may have any other writ of execution suitable to the case, as, for example, a *fieri facias.*

In case of an *escape* or a *rescue,* though the sheriff be liable, because he ought to have taken the *posse comitatus,* still the plaintiff is not bound to look to the sheriff, because the latter may be insolvent ; the plaintiff may, therefore, sue out another execution, for the defendant will not be allowed to take advantage of his own wrong.

3385.—2. An *attachment* is a writ commanding the sheriff to arrest a particular person, who has been guilty of a contempt of court, and to bring the offender before the court. It issues whenever a party has been ordered by a rule of court to perform a certain act, and he has omitted to perform it ; as where he has been ruled to pay costs, or to perform an award. On the service of the attachment, the party is taken into custody and is confined in prison until he afterward obtains his discharge in due course of law.

2. Of executions against goods, chattels, and land.

3386. These writs of execution are, 1, the *fieri facias;* 2, the *venditioni exponas;* 3, the *levari facias;* 4, the *elegit.*

1° *Of the fieri facias.(a)*

3387. The most common of all writs of execution is the *fieri facias.* This writ is so called, because, when writs were in Latin, the words directed to the sheriff were, *quod fieri facias de bonis et catallis,* etc., that you

---

(a) For the history of this writ, see 2 Reeves' Hist. of the Law, 187 ; Bac. Ab. Execution, E 4.

cause to be made of the goods and chattels, etc.(a) The foundation of this writ is a judgment for debt or damages, and the party who has recovered such judgment is generally entitled to it, unless the plaintiff is delayed by a stay of execution, which the law allows in certain cases after the rendition of the judgment; or by his own agreement with the defendant; or by proceedings in error.

This subject will be examined with regard to, 1, the form of the writ; 2, its effect; 3, the manner of executing it; 4, what goods may be seized and sold under it; 5, the effect of seizure of personal property; 6, the seizure and sale of land under an execution; 7, the return.

(1.) *Of the form of the writ.*

3388. The writ of *fieri facias* is issued in the name of the government, and directed to the sheriff, (in the United States court to the marshal,) commanding him that of the goods and chattels (and where the lands are made liable for the payment of debts, of the lands and tenements) of the defendant, therein named, in his bailiwick, he cause to be levied as well a certain debt of   dollars, which the plaintiff, (naming him,) in the court of   (naming it,) recovered against him, as   dollars, like money, which to the said plaintiff were adjudged for his damages, which he had by the detention of the said debt, and that he, (the sheriff,) have the money before the judges of the said court, on a day certain, (being the return day therein mentioned,) to render to the said plaintiff his debt and damages aforesaid, whereof the said defendant is convict. It must be tested in the name of the officer, as directed by the constitution or laws: as "Witness, A B, chief justice, etc., the day of   anno Domini, one thousand

---

(a) Co. Litt. 290, b.

OF PROCEEDINGS IN AN ACTION.   573

No. 3389.   Book 4, tit. 8, chap. 15, sec. 5, § 2, art. 2.   No. 3389.

eight hundred and fifty one." It must be signed by the clerk or prothonotary of the court, and sealed with its seal.(*a*) The amount of the debt and costs must be indorsed on the writ.

The execution being founded on the judgment, must, of course, follow, and be warranted by it;(*b*) hence, when there is more than one plaintiff or defendant, it must be in the name of all the plaintiffs, against all the defendants, if living.

When it is against an executor or administrator, for a liability of the testator or intestate, it must conform to the judgment, and be only against the goods and chattels, or other property of the deceased, unless the defendant has made himself personally liable by his own false pleadings, or by waste, in which case the judgment is *de bonis testatoris si, et si non de bonis propriis*, and the *fieri facias* must conform to it.(*c*)

(2.) *Of the effect of the writ of fieri facias.*

3389. At common law, the writ bound the goods of the defendant, or party against whom it was issued, from the teste day; by which must be understood that the writ bound the property against the party himself, and all claiming by assignment from, or by representation under him,(*d*) so that a sale by the defendant, of his goods to a *bona fide* purchaser, did not protect them from the *fieri facias* tested before, although not issued or delivered to the sheriff till after the sale.(*e*) To remedy this manifest injustice, the statute of frauds(*f*) was passed, the principles of which have been adopted,

---

(*a*) An execution issued without a seal, from a court having and using a seal, is void, and of course all proceedings under it, are void also. Beal *v.* King, 6 Ham. 11 ; but, if it be sealed, although it is not signed by the clerk, it is valid.

(*b*) 2 Saund. 72, h, k ; Bingh. on Executions, 186.

(*c*) Bac. Ab. Execution, C 4 ; Swearingen *v.* Pendleton, 4 S. & R. 394 ; Todd *v.* Todd's Executors, 1 S. & R. 453; Com. Dig. Pleader, 2 D 15.

(*d*) Payne *v.* Drewe, 4 East, 538.

(*e*) Cro. Eliz. 174 ; Baskerville *v.* Brocket, Cro. Jac. 451.

(*f*) 29 Car. II., c. 3, s. 16.

574 OF REMEDIES.

No. 3389.　　　　Book 4, tit 8, chap. 15, sec. 5, § 2, art. 2.　　　　No. 3389.

in this respect, in perhaps all the states. It enacts "that no writ of *fieri facias*, or other writ of execution, shall bind the property of the goods of the party against whom such writ of execution is sued forth, but from the time such writ shall be delivered to the sheriff or under sheriff, or coroner, to be executed; and for the better manifestation of the said time, the sheriffs, their deputies or agents, shall, upon the receipt of any such writ, (without fee for doing the same,) indorse, upon the back thereof, the day of the month and year whereon he or they received the same."

When issued against a person who had died between the teste day and return day of the writ, it had, by relation back to the teste, the binding operation upon his personal property, that the executor was not entitled to it for the general payment of his debts.(a) . In the United States the statutes for the equal distribution of intestate's estates, have, perhaps, every where prevented this unjust preference.

Though the goods are bound from the time the execution comes into the sheriff's hands, the property in such goods is not *altered*, but continues in the defendant till execution executed.(b)

Another of its effects is the protection which it gives to the officer, while acting according to its exigencies. Being the delegated agent of the court, if the court had jurisdiction to issue the *fieri facias*, the sheriff or officer to whom it is directed, and who is bound to execute it, and all his deputies acting under it, are protected; but when the court has no jurisdiction, and the judges are themselves trespassers, the officer is subject to an action of trespass, as if he had no writ.(c)

(a) Den v. Hilman, 2 Halst. 180.
(b) Folsom v. Chesley, 2 N. H. Rep. 432; Churchill v. Warren, 2 N. H. Rep. 298; Bates v. Moore, 2 Bailey, 614.
(c) Barker's widow v. Braham, 3 Wilson, 376.

(3.) *Of the execution of the writ of* fieri facias.

3390. The sheriff has a right to enter into the premises of the defendant to search for his goods, if he can do so without breaking an outer door of the house,(*a*) nor can a window be broken for that purpose.(*b*) He may enter the house, if it be open, and being once lawfully entered, he may break open an inner door, or chest, without even a request to open them ; though, in general, it is more prudent to make such request, for the purpose of seizing the goods of the defendant. He may break an outer door of a barn,(*c*) or of a store, not connected with the dwelling house, and forming no part of the curtilage.(*d*) The sheriff is also authorized to enter the house of a stranger, for the purpose of executing his writ, provided the defendant's goods are there ; but his entry will be justifiable only on the event of the goods being there, for, if he should be mistaken in this respect, he will be a trespasser.(*e*) But, though authorized to enter a stranger's house, he cannot, of course, break open an outer door.

When the goods are found, the officer may seize them, and the taking of a part of them, in the name of the whole, is a good seizure of all.(*f*) The seizure is complete as soon as the goods are in the power of the officer,(*g*) and, although the sheriff may return that he levied on personal property, if it was not in his view, nor taken into custody, it is no levy as to subsequent judgment creditors.(*h*) Still, the indorsement on a *fieri facias* of levy on goods which the sheriff had

---

(*a*) Semayne's case, 5 Co. 92.
(*b*) Cooke's case, W. Jones, 429.
(*c*) 1 Sid. 186 ; S C. 1 Kib. 689.
(*d*) Hagerty *v.* Wilbee, 16 John. 287.
(*e*) Com. Dig. Execution, C 5.
(*f*) Lewis *v.* Smith, 2 S. & R. 142.
(*g*) Wood *r.* Vanarsdale, 3 Rawle, 401 ; Bullitt *v.* Winston, 1 Munf. 269 ; Lloyde *v.* Wykoff, 6 Halst. 218.
(*h*) Lowry *v.* Coulter, 9 Penn. St. Rep. 349.

576   OF REMEDIES.

No. 3391.   Book 4, tit. 8, chap 15, sec. 5, § 2, art 2.   No 3391.

levied upon by virtue of a former execution, will be considered a good levy under the second or last execution, because the goods so levied upon are considered as in his custody, and of course within his power.(a) To render the levy perfect, the articles seized should be designated in the execution, or in a schedule annexed,(b) and the sheriff should take possession within a reasonable time, in such a manner as to apprise every body of the fact of his having taken them in execution.(c) But if the defendant dispense with an actual seizure for his own benefit, the levy, as to him, will be valid.(d)

The *fieri facias* may be executed at any time before, and on the return day,(e) but not on Sunday, where it is forbidden by statute.

(4.) *What goods may be seized and sold under a* fieri facias.

3391.—1. In general, the sheriff may seize and sell all those articles which he can find, belonging to the plaintiff, and which are *choses in possession*, except such as are exempted by the common law, or by statute. The common law was very niggardly of these exceptions; it allowed only the necessary wearing apparel, and it was once holden that, if a defendant had two gowns, the sheriff might sell one of them ;(f) in modern times, with perhaps a prodigal liberality, a considerable amount of property, both real and personal, is exempted from executions by the statutes of several of the states. It is not the time nor the place here to consider whether such laws are most for the benefit or injury of the poor and honest man.

(a) Watmough v. Francis, 7 Penn St. Rep. 206.
(b) Barnes v. Billington, 1 Wash. C. C. 29.
(c) Wood v. Vanarsdale, 3 Rawle, 405 ; Lewis v. Smith, 2 S. & R. 142 ; 1 Whart. 116, 337 ; 1 Wash. C. C. 29.
(d) Troville v. Tilford, 6 Watts, 468.   See, as to what constitutes a sufficient levy, Burchard v Reese, 1 Whart. 377 ; Wood v. Vanarsdale, 3 Rawle, 401 ; McCormick v. Miller, 3 Penn. R. 230.
(e) Chase v. Gilman, 3 Shepl. 64 ; Devoe v. Elliott, 2 Caines, 243.
(f) Comb. 356.

OF PROCEEDINGS IN AN ACTION.   577

No 3391.   Book 4, tit. 8, chap 15, sec 5, § 2, art 2   No 3391.

When the defendant's goods are pawned, or demised or let for years, or they have been distrained, or in any other way are subject to a lien, in the hands of a third person, the sheriff can only seize and sell the right of the defendant in such goods, subject to the rights of such third person.

In general, *choses in action* cannot be taken in execution;(*a*) but in some of the states power is given to the sheriff under a peculiar process authorized by statute to attach the rights of the defendant to such *choses in action;* as where a debt is due by a third person to the defendant, the defendant's rights may be attached, and the third person is made a garnishee.

After having seized the defendant's goods, the sheriff should keep them in his possession till they are sold; for if they are left in the possession of the defendant, it will, in general, be considered a badge of fraud,(*b*) and another judgment and execution creditor may seize them, and the first levy will be invalid.(*c*) And if the first levy be made merely to keep off other creditors, this being against the policy of the law, it will not protect them from another execution;(*d*) and a direction to "stay proceedings," destroys the lien as it respects other creditors, and enables them to gain a preference.(*e*) Indeed, any act, which shows that the plaintiff has not a continuing mind to cause the writ to be executed, will, as between himself and third persons, or other creditors of the defendant, discharge

---

(*a*) Rhoads *v.* Magonigal, 3 Penn. St. R. 39.

(*b*) In Pennsylvania, it is not the practice to remove goods levied upon; and the lien of personal property is generally held to continue, though the goods are left in the hands of the defendant, unless fraud is proved. Swift *v.* Hartman, cited 2 Yeates, 435; Levy *v.* Wallis, 4 Dall. 167; Chandler *v.* Phillips, 4 Dall. 213. But see Cowden *v.* Brady, 8 S. & R. 510.

(*c*) Lewis *v.* Smith, 2 S. & R. 142.

(*d*) Corlies *v.* Stanbridge, 5 Rawle, 286.

(*e*) Hickman *v.* Caldwell, 4 Rawle, 280; Commonwealth *v.* Strembeck, 3 Rawle, 341.

578 OF REMEDIES.

No. 3392   Book 4, tit. 8, chap. 15, sec. 5, § 2, art. 2.   No 3393.

the property levied upon from his lien.(a) The lien will also be lost by taking a replevin bond.(b)

3392.—2. The next step to be taken by the sheriff is to advertise the goods levied upon for sale at public auction, for this is the only lawful way of disposing of them; he cannot keep them ᷉himself, and pay the plaintiff's debt, nor deliver them to the plaintiff in satisfaction of his execution; the plaintiff may, however, buy them as any other person, at their value.(c)

The sheriff must use a reasonable discretion in the sale of the goods; it seems that if a very inadequate price be offered for them, he should not sell them, but ought to return that they remain in his hands unsold for want of buyers, which is the proper return, when he has had no bid. The *fieri facias* being then out of his hands, he must wait until he shall be authorized to sell them by another writ, a *venditioni exponas*, the nature of which will hereafter be explained, and under this writ he will be obliged to sell at any price he can get.(d)

(5.) *Of the effect of seizure of personal property.*

3393. Although the seizure of personal property does not change or alter the title to it, and it remains in the defendant, as has already been observed, yet it has the effect of releasing the lands of the debtor, with regard to third persons. If, therefore, a judgment creditor who has the first lien on the lands of his debtor, issue an execution and levy on the personal property of the defendant, sufficient to satisfy his execution, he cannot afterward abandon that levy and claim to be. paid out of the proceeds of the land.(e)

(a) Howell v. Atkyn, 2 Rawle, 282; Weir v. Hale, 3 W. & S. 285; Mentz v. Hammon, 5 Whart. 150.
(b) Harrison v. Wilson, 2 A. K. Marsh. 547.
(c) Bac. Ab. Execution, C 4.
(d) Keightley v. Birch, 3 Campb. 521.
(e) Hunt v. Breading, 12 S. & R. 37; Taylor's Appeal, 1 Penn. St. R. 393; Duncan v. Harris, 17 S. & R. 436.

(6.) Of the seizure and sale of lands under execution.

3394. By the common law, lands were not liable to be sold for the payment of debts; it was against the policy of the feudal law to take the landed estates out of the hands of the aristocracy; and the same rule yet prevails in England. There the remedy given to a judgment creditor is a sequestration of the profits of the land by writ of *levari facias*, or the possession of one half of the land by writ of *elegit*, or. in certain cases, of the whole of it, by *extent*. In these cases the creditors hold the land until, out of the profits or rents, their claims are fully satisfied. Probably to protect British creditors a statute was passed by the British parliament(*a*) making lands and hereditaments, within the English colonies, chargeable with the debts, and subject to execution as personal estate. The practice of selling real estate under execution, having thus commenced, it has been firmly established by various acts of the state legislatures in most of the states of the Union, under certain checks and salutary regulations, to prevent abuse and unnecessary sacrifices.

One of the most prominent and prevalent of these regulations is to require the creditor to resort in the first instance to the personal estate, as the proper and primary fund, and to the real estate only after the personal property shall have been exhausted, and found insufficient to satisfy the claim.

Another restraint is to require that the estate shall be appraised, and if an inquest, to be held by the sheriff, shall be of opinion that the profits, rents and issues will be sufficient in a number of years; provided for by the statute, to pay all the liens upon it, then it shall not be sold, but it shall be delivered to the plaintiff, that out of the rents, issues, and profits, he may be paid the amount of his execution. This is the case

---

(*a*) 5 Geo. II., c. 7, A. D. 1732.

580 OF REMEDIES.

No. 3394   Book 4, tit. 8, chap. 15, sec. 5, § 2, art. 2.   No. 3394.

in Pennsylvania and Delaware, and the lands are extended by the writ of *liberari facias*, and possession is given to the creditor, as practiced upon the *elegit* in England; but if the lands are not *extended*, that is, if the rents, issues, and profits will not be sufficient in those states, to pay the liens or incumbrances in seven years, then they are *condemned*, and are to be sold without redemption. In other states, before a sale can take place, the lands must be valued, and, at the sale, must bring a certain proportion of such valuation; in some states, if the creditor will not take them at two-thirds of the appraised value, there is a delay upon giving additional security. In other states, a part of the defendant's land is absolutely protected from sale for the presumed benefit of himself and family. In Virginia, lands cannot be sold on execution; the English process of *elegit* and *extent* are there used.

As a further bar to the sale of landed estates, in some of the American commonwealths, a right of redemption is given to the defendant, provided it be exercised within a specified time.(a)

It is a rule in some states, that the lands of the defendant are bound by a judgment from the time of rendition, but this is far from being universal; in Louisiana, they bind from the time they are registered with the recorder of mortgages;(b) in Kentucky and Mississippi, lands are bound only from the time the execution reaches the sheriff's hand.(c)

The lien created by the judgment, continues only for a limited time, so as to operate against subsequent incumbrancers and *bona fide* purchasers, according to the statutes of the respective states.

(a) See Kent's Com. Lecture, 66. It has been deemed unnecessary to detail the various provisions of the statutes of the several states, not only because such details would be useless, as the reader must rely upon the statutes themselves, but because their provisions are subject to constant changes.

(b) Hana v. His Creditors, 13 Martin's R. 32.

(c) Bank U. S. v. Tyler, 4 Pet. 366; Million v. Riley, 1 Dana, 360.

Real estate held in reversion and remainder, is liable to be sold like an estate in possession, and an equity of redemption may likewise be the subject of a levy.

3395. The usual mode of making a levy, is to describe the land which has been seized under the execution by metes and bounds, as in a deed of conveyance ; as they cannot be sold, in some of the states, under the *fieri facias*, because an inquest must be held by the sheriff, to ascertain whether the land can, from its profits, rents, and issues, satisfy the debt within a certain time, the writ of *fieri facias* is returned to the court, with a levy and the proceedings of the inquest, and these things remain until the sheriff is authorized by a new writ, called a *venditioni exponas*, to sell the land levied upon.

Under this writ, or under the *fieri facias*, where lands may be sold without any other writ, the lands seized are advertised by the sheriff the time required by the local statutes, and they are sold at the time and place appointed, by public auction or outcry, to the highest and best bidder ; the writ is then returned to court, with a statement of what has been done, and the sale is subject to the approval of the court; or, for any material misdescription of the property, or any act of the sheriff, or of the inquest, not warranted by law, which may have been prejudicial to any of the parties, the plaintiff, defendant, or purchaser, it may be set aside ; and then a new sale is ordered by an *alias venditioni exponas*, which sale is also subject to this salutary supervision.

If the sale is affirmed, the sheriff then makes a deed to the purchaser, which conveys to him all the title which the defendant had in the land, and no more. To complete his title, the purchaser should procure the deed to be registered in the proper office.(*a*)

(*a*) In the New England states, with the exception of Rhode Island, the sheriff's official return of the proceeding under the execution, constitutes

(7.) Of the return of the writ of fieri facias.

3396. On the return day of the *fieri facias,* the sheriff ought to make his return of what he has done under the writ; and, should he neglect to do so, he may be called upon by rule to make such a return within a specified time, and if he do not then return it, or offer a lawful excuse for not so doing, the court will grant an attachment against him; but in some cases, where there is just cause for it, the court will enlarge the time within which he should make his return.

3397. The returns commonly made to a *fieri facias,* are the following:

1. When the sheriff has not found any goods belonging to the defendant, on which he could levy, he returns that fact in the common formula, *nulla bona.*

2. He returns *fieri feci,* when he caused to be made, out of the defendant's goods, the whole or a part of the money, which he has ready to be paid to the plaintiff.

3. That he has taken the goods of the defendant to a certain amount, which remain in his hands for want of buyers. In this case, he should be careful to specify what goods he has levied upon, for a general levy may render him responsible for the whole debt.

4. When he has levied upon land, he should so return and state what lands he has seized, by metes and bounds, so that when they are sold by him, he may make a definite deed for the same. He should also return what further proceedings, if any, have taken place since the levy.

3398. These several returns will be separately considered. 1. When the sheriff returns *nulla bona* to a

---

the title of the purchaser, as does the sheriff's return of the inquisition of the elegit in England, and no deed is executed, for the title rests upon matter of record. 4 Kent, Com. 434, 4th ed.

OF PROCEEDINGS IN AN ACTION.   583

No. 3399.   Book 4, tit. 8, chap. 15, sec. 5, § 2, art. 2.   No 3399.

fieri facias, that the defendant has no goods within his bailiwick, the plaintiff may sue out an *alias fieri facias*, and after that, when required, as if the same return be made to the *alias*, a pluries into the same county, or he may have a *testatum fieri facias* into a different county, suggesting that the defendant has goods there ; but the *testatum* cannot go into another state, because the laws under which it issues do not extend there. Instead of these, or any of these writs, the plaintiff may, on the return of *nulla bona* to a *fieri facias*, issue a *capias ad satisfaciendum*, where such writ is not forbidden by act of assembly.

2. When the sheriff returns *fieri feci*, he becomes liable to the plaintiff for the money he has made on the writ, and the plaintiff may compel him to pay it, either by a rule of court, or by action of debt founded on his return. If a part of the money be levied, and so the sheriff has returned, the plaintiff may have a *fieri facias*, or a *capias ad satisfaciendum*, for the residue; but in general the first execution must be returned, before a second can issue, because the second is founded on the return of the first, and usually it recites the first execution and the return.

2° *Of the* venditioni exponas.

3399. A *venditioni exponas* is a writ, as has already been intimated, by which the sheriff is commanded to sell goods and chattels, and in some cases, lands which he has taken in execution by virtue of a *fieri facias*, and which remain in his hands unsold.   The object of this writ, as it regards personal property, is to force the sheriff to sell when he has returned a levy unsold for want of buyers, and to bring him into contempt for not selling ;(*a*) he cannot, therefore, again return "not sold for want of buyers."(*b*)   Should he make

---

(*a*) Frisch *v.* Miller, 5 Penn. St. R. 310.
(*b*) Grah. Pr. 359 ; Com. Dig. Execution, C 8 ; 2 Saund. 47, 1 ; 2 Chit. Rep. 390 ; Cowp. 406.

584 OF REMEDIES.

No. 3400.   Book 4, tit. 8, chap. 15, sec. 5, § 2, art. 2.   No. 3401.

such a return, however, according to the English practice, an attachment will not be granted against him.(*a*) The proper way of próceeding, then, if the sheriff do not pay over the money, on or before the return of the *venditioni*, is to sue out a *distringas* against him, directed to the coroner; and if he do not sell the goods and pay over the money, before the return of that writ, he shall forfeit *issues*, that is, the goods and the profits of the lands of the defendant against whom the *distringas* has been issued, and which have been taken by virtue of such writ, to the amount of the debt.(*b*)

3° *Of the* levari facias.

3400. This writ is used for various purposes in England, against ecclesiastics, and, in certain cases, in favor of the crown. It is also used to recover a plaintiff's debt; it commands the sheriff to levy such debt on the lands and goods of the defendant, in virtue of which he may seize his goods, and receive the rents and profits of his lands, till satisfaction be made to the plaintiff.(*c*)

In Pennsylvania this writ is used to sell lands mortgaged, after a judgment has been obtained by the mortgagee, or his assignee, against the mortgagor, under a peculiar proceeding authorized by statute.

4° *Of the* elegit.

3401. The writ of *elegit* is but little used in the United States, because lands may be sold for the payment of debts. It is not entirely unknown in Virginia.(*d*)

(*a*) Leader *v.* Danvers, 1 B. & P. 358.
(*b*) 2 Saund. 47, n.
(*c*) 3 Bl. Com. 417 ; 11 Viner's Ab. 14.
(*d*) 4 Kent, Com. 434, 4th ed.

By the statute of Westm. 2, c. 18,(a) "where a debt is recovered or acknowledged in the king's court, or damages awarded, it shall be in the election of him that sueth to have a *fieri facias* to the sheriff, to levy the debt upon the lands and chattels of the debtor, or that the sheriff shall deliver to him all the chattels of the debtor, (saving his oxen and beasts of his plough,) and one half of the land, until the debt be levied upon a reasonable price or extent." From the election given to the plaintiff by this statute, and from the entry of the award of this execution on the roll, "quod elegit sibi executionem," etc., this writ derives its name.

On the receipt of this writ, the sheriff holds an inquest to ascertain the value of the lands and goods he has seized, and then they are delivered to the plaintiff, who retains them until the whole debt and damages have been paid and satisfied; during that time the plaintiff is called *tenant by elegit.*(b)

The writ of *elegit* must be returned. If lands have been extended under it, the inquisition must also be returned and filed, and when chattels have been appraised and delivered to the plaintiff, the sheriff should return on the writ that he delivered the goods at a reasonable price fixed by the jury.

Should the tenant by *elegit* hold over after his debt is fully satisfied, the defendant may recover his land from him, either by an action of ejectment, or by *scire facias ad computandum, et rehabendam terram*. This, however, is not the preferable remedy. It is a more general, and a more advisable mode, for the recovery of the lands from the tenant by elegit, to proceed by bill in equity. , If the lands are recovered back by an action at law, the plaintiff in that action will not be

---

(a) 13 Edw. I.
(b) Co. Litt. 289 ; Wats. on the Office of Sheriff, 206 ; Bac. Ab. Execution, C 2 ; 1 Archb. Pr. 272.

586 OF REMEDIES.

No. 3402.   Book 4, tit 8, chap 15, sec. 5, § 2, art. 2.   No. 3402.

entitled to any but the extended value, which is generally very low, and much below the real value. But in equity the tenant by *elegit* will be compelled to account, not for the extended value merely, but for the actual profits of the lands while in his possession.

✦

—

3402. Here end our investigations respecting an action. It will be recollected that it was considered who should be the parties to the action, by what means they should be brought into court, the statement of the plaintiff's claim in his declaration, the defence or plea, the replication, and other pleadings, until the parties came to an issue of law and of fact, and how such issues must be tried; the evidence and the proceedings in the course of the trial; the argument of counsel and the summing up of the judge; the verdict, judgment, and all the proceedings in the nature of appeals; and finally the execution and satisfaction of the plaintiff, when he was right, or his defeat and being obliged to pay the costs, when wrong. The whole is a beautiful, logical, and systematic arrangement; and, however it may sometimes be perverted, to promote injustice by chicanery and fraud, these being imperfections to which all human institutions are liable, it is still admirably calculated to attain substantial justice. It is true, that many technical rules might, by judicious hands, be pruned, and by that means additional vigor would be given to the institution; yet, with all its imperfections, the mode of attaining justice by an action at law, is one of the best contrivances that can be devised by so imperfect a being as man.

TITLE IX.—OF THE DIFFERENT FORMS OR KINDS
OF ACTIONS.

3403. Personal actions are most commonly divided
into two species: first, those which arise upon contracts; and secondly, those which are given for the
redress of wrongs, torts, or injuries. This title will,
therefore, be divided into four chapters; the first,
treating of actions arising *ex contractu;* the second, of
actions arising *ex delicto;* the third, of mixed actions;
and the fourth, of *scire facias.*

CHAPTER I.—OF ACTS ARISING EX CONTRACTU.

3404. These are, 1, account; 2, *assumpsit;* 3, covenant; 4, debt; 5, detinue; each of which will be considered in a separate section.

SECTION 1.—OF THE ACTION OF ACCOUNT.(*a*)

3405. The action of account, or more properly,
account render, is not common, because, in those states
where there is a court of chancery, the object is much
more readily obtained by a bill in equity; and because
the plaintiff has a more efficacious mode of proving
his claim, having, in addition to the usual proofs, the
responsive oath of the defendant; but still, its proceedings, and this form of remedy, are said in some cases
to be more efficacious and prompt than a suit in chancery. Courts of equity, however, have assumed jurisdiction in cases of account, concurrent with courts of
law, on the ground that they afford a more easy and
more complete remedy than courts of law.(*b*)

In considering the action of account, it will be
necessary to take a view of, 1, the parties; 2, the cause

(*a*) For the remedy in matters of account in equity, vide post, n. 3931.
(*b*) 13 Ves. 276.

for which it will lie; 3, the declaration; 4, the pleas and issue; 5, the evidence; 6, the judgment *quod computet;* 7, proceedings before auditors; 8, the final judgment; 9, the proceedings in error.

§ 1. Of parties in actions of account.

3406. It is a general rule that parties who have an interest in the case must all join and be joined, because it being founded on contract, no recovery can be had by any person except those who have the right, nor against any one, who, though liable, is so only with other persons. But it is not always easy to say whether all the parties who have a right, have such an interest as will entitle them to bring the action; as, where two persons are tenants in common of goods, and one bails them to a stranger to render him an account, he alone shall have the action. On the contrary, if both the tenants in common bail the goods, they must join in the action.(*a*)

So, on the other hand, all persons who are jointly liable must be made defendants, but care must be taken not to include as joint defendants persons who are not so jointly responsible; for example, where there are three or more partners, and one sues two of them in account, where each is responsible only for himself, the plaintiff must fail, because if he were to succeed he might make one of the defendants, who had received only his share of the partnership fund, liable for the acts of his co-defendant, unless there was a joint liability.(*b*)

At common law, account could be maintained only against a guardian in socage, a bailiff or receiver, or by one in favor of trade and commerce, naming himself merchant, against another naming him merchant,

---

(*a*) Bro. Accompt, pl. 32; Vin. Ab. Acc. E, pl. 14.
(*b*) Whelen *v.* Watmough, 15 S. & R. 153; McFadden *v.* Sallada, 6 Penn. St. R. 283.

and for the executors of a merchant; the reason
assigned for this is, that there was a privity, and the
law presumed them conusant of each other's disburse-
ments, receipts and acquittances.(a)

By statute, an action of account is given to executors,(b) to executors of executors,(c) to administrators,(d) and by another statute(e) actions may be
brought against the executors and administrators of
every guardian, bailiff or receiver, and by one joint
tenant, tenant in common, his executors and administrators, against the other as bailiff for receiving more
than his share, and against his executors and administrators.

Before the passage of this last statute, if one joint
tenant, or tenant in common, received all the profits,
the other could not maintain this action, unless he
actually had appointed him his bailiff or receiver.(f)

It has been held that joint partners in mercantile
adventures may have account render against each
other ;(g) but where two or more purchased a tract of
land together, under an agreement that it should be
resold and the profit divided, even if the transaction
had been a technical partnership, which is doubtful,
yet it was ruled that, as there was but one item to
settle between the parties, *assumpsit* might be maintained against him who had received the proceeds of
the re-sale; and it was not necessary to bring an action
of account render.(h)

Account render lies by the *cestui que trust* against

(a) Bac. Ab. Accompt, A.
(b) 13 Edw. I., c. 23.
(c) 25 Edw. III., st. 5, c. 5.
(d) 31 Edw. III., c. 11.
(e) 4 Ann, c. 16, s. 27.
(f) Co. Litt. 172 a, 186 a, and 200 b.; McAdam v. Orr, 4 W. & S. 550.
(g) Griffith v. Willing. 3 Binn. 317 ; Irvine v. Hanlin, 10 S. & R. 220 ;
Whelen v. Watmough, 15 S, & R. 153.
(h) Brubacker v. Robinson, 3 Penn. R. 295.

his trustee to enforce the payment of the trust fund;(a) by a landlord against his tenant, where, by the terms of the lease, the latter was to deliver an account to the former, for a proportion of the profits; for exam‧ ple, for the tolls of a mill;(b) by a client against his attorney at law, to obtain an account of moneys received by the defendant.(c)

A *bailiff* is one appointed by the owner of lands and other property, to collect the rents and profits of the same, and to make the best of them by his management, for the benefit of the owner; he is entitled to a reasonable compensation for his trouble and care, and may be made accountable by an action of account for the profits which he has made, or could have made by proper care. A *receiver* is one who receives money on account of another, for which he has agreed either expressly‧ or by implication to account for the same; at common law the receiver is allowed only such charges and expenses as are agreed upon by the parties.(d) The distinction between bailiffs and receivers, however proper in other cases, does not apply to partners in trade; for one partner, though charged as receiver, is entitled to every just allowance against the other.(e)

This action cannot be maintained against a minor as bailiff or receiver, because he is not able to make a binding contract; nor by an apprentice, as such, for, when acting in that capacity in the ordinary business of his master, he is only performing the business of his master as the master would have done;(f) but though he is not chargeable for the ordinary receipts of his master's trade, yet if he receive money not in

---

(a) Bredin v. Deven, 2 Watts, 95; Dennison v. Goehring. 7 Penn. St. R. 175.
(b) Long v. Fitzsimmons, 1 W. & S. 530.
(c) Bredin v. Kingland, 4 Watts, 420.
(d) 1 Dane's Ab. c. 8, § 4.
(e) 1 James v. Browne. 1 Dall. 340.
(f) 11 Coke 89, b. See Evans v. Birch, 3 Campb. 10.

such ordinary trade, he is liable as any other person; in that case, however, he must be charged as receiver or bailiff.(*a*) It does not lie against a disseisor or wrong doer, because there is no contract, express or implied, between such a person and the plaintiff; nor by one executor against the other, because the possession by one is possession by the other.

§ 2.—For what cause account render will lie.

3407. This action can be maintained only when there has been an express or implied contract between the parties, on which the action is founded,(*b*) and the amount due is uncertain and unliquidated. It is not requisite that the contract should be express, an implied contract is sufficient, and where the defendant has been guilty of a tort, when he has received the property or money of the plaintiff, he is liable to this action, if the plaintiff waives the tort.(*c*)

Whenever the account between the parties has been stated, and a balance found to be due, *assumpsit* is the proper remedy; but when the accountant was a bailiff, account is a concurrent remedy with *assumpsit* where there has been an express promise.(*d*)

He may in some cases have covenant or account, at his election; as, where one acknowledged by deed that he had received one thousand dollars from another to be adventured in trade in the West Indies, and promised to account; the remedy for the non-compliance of this agreement may be an action of covenant on the deed, or an action of account, at the election of the creditor.(*e*)

(*a*) 2 Inst. 379, 380.
(*b*) King of France *v.* Morris, cited 3 Yeates, 251. In Connecticut this action lies whenever a person has received money for the use of another; especially if it be received by a third, to be delivered over. Mumford *v.* Avery, Kirby, 163.
(*c*) Dane's Ab. c. 8, a. 2, § 10.
(*d*) Bac. Ab. Accompt, D.
(*e*) Bac. Ab. Accompt, D.

Account render is not a proper remedy to recover a thing *certain*, as if Peter deliver to Paul one hundred dollars to trade with, he shall not have an action of account for the one hundred dollars, but simply for the profits made out of it ;(*a*) nor to recover rent reserved on a lease ;(*b*) nor mesne profits ;(*c*) nor where one takes security, on the delivery of goods or money, for their return; for in such case the receiver cannot be said to be possessed of the goods or money, to render an account of the profits; besides when a person makes such a special contract his remedy is restricted to it.(*d*)

§ 3.—Of the declaration in account render.(*e*)

3408. Having seen who may bring an action of account render, and against whom it may be maintained, and for what causes it will lie, let us suppose the parties to be in court; the next step to be taken is the filing of a declaration by the plaintiff.

3409. The declaration is an amplification of the writ, with the addition of a formal commencement and conclusion, and showing, when against·a *receiver*, by whose hands the defendant received the money; for it is but reasonable that he should have this information, in order that he may meet the charge.(*f*) Though this rule may sometimes prove inconvenient to the plaintiff, because he may not know from whom the defendant received the money, yet the evil would be much greater to leave the defendant ignorant of what he was called upon to answer. To obviate the difficulty is simply to charge the defendant as *bailiff*,

---

(*a*) Bro. tit. Accompt, 35; but see Mumford *v.* Avery, Kirby, 163.
(*b*) Roll Ab. 116.
(*c*) Harker *v.* Whitaker, 5 Watts, 474.
(*d*) Dane's Ab. c. 8, a. 2, § 6.
(*e*) For forms of declarations in account render, see Read's Amer. Pleader's Assistant, 1 to 6; Im. Pr. 153; 1 Wentw. Pl.; 1 Mallory's Mod. Entries, tit. Account.
(*f*) Dane's Ab. c. 8, a. 1, § 4; Walker *v.* Holyday, 1 Com. 272. See Moore *v.* Wilson, 2 Chipm. 91; May *v.* Williams, 3 Verm. 239.

where the money he has received was from goods intrusted to him. A declaration, charging the defendant as bailiff and receiver, is proper when the defendant is such, in law and in fact, and has the property, without any interest in it himself. But the rule is different, in actions of account render, between tenants in common under the statutes of Anne, as well as in actions between partners; in such cases it is necessary to aver that the money was received for the common benefit of the plaintiff and defendant,(a) and that the defendant had received more than his share of the profits.(b)

3410. It is not necessary to be particular as to *time;* when the declaration charged that the defendant was receiver between 1658 and 1673, without any certain time, it was held sufficient; and a blank in the declaration, for the time during which the defendant acted as bailiff, is cured by a verdict.(c) It is not necessary that the *quantum* of money should be accurately stated; the object of the action is to ascertain it.

3411. The declaration should lay the damages as in other cases. But the rule, that the plaintiff shall not recover damages for more than he has declared for, is not applicable to account render; the plaintiff may, therefore, have a judgment for the arrearages for a greater amount than the damages laid in his declaration;(d) and when the plaintiff lays, in his declaration, the *value* of the chattels, and also damages, he obtains judgment, when entitled to it, for the value, and also for damages, distinguishing each.

(a) McFadden v. Sallada. 6 Penn. St. R. 283. See James v. Browne, 1 Dall. 339: Jourdan v. Wilkins, 2 Wash. C. C. 482; Co. Litt. 172, a; Wells v. Some, Cro. Cas. 240; Com. Dig. Accompt, E 2.
(b) Sturton v. Richardson, 13 M. & W. 17; Irvine v. Hanlin, 10 S. & R. 221.
(c) See Wright v. Guy, 10 S. & R. 227.
(d) Gratz v. Phillips, 5 Binn. 564.

§ 4.—Of pleas and issue in account render.

3412. In this action there is no general issue. The defendant may plead that he never was bailiff, or guardian, or receiver in fact;(a) but when sued as tenant in common, under the statute of Anne, if the declaration be properly framed, a plea that the de. fendant is not bailiff, nor receiver, would be insuffi. cient;(b) in such case, if the defendant means to deny the plaintiff's claim, he should traverse the tenancy in common. The defendant may also plead that he has fully accounted, either to the plaintiff or before auditors; or a release; arbitrament; bond given in satisfaction; or that the money was delivered to him for a specific purpose, which has been accomplished. But other matters which admit that the defendant was once liable, and might be made accountable, cannot in general be pleaded in bar to the action, but must be pleaded before the auditors;(c) to this rule, however, there are exceptions, for when the defendant admits he was once accountable, he may still plead a release, *plene computavit*, and the statute of limitations.

It is said that the defendant is not bound to plead at all in this action; he may admit upon record that he is willing to account, and, instead of a plea, he may come into court and say to the judges, "I am willing to account with the plaintiff, and pray that auditors may be assigned to take an account between me and the plaintiff;" and by such accounting, without resistance to the plaintiff's claim by pleading, will save the defendant from being mulcted in damages, for which

(a) The usual form is *ne unques bailiff*, etc. This may be pleaded together with *plene computavit*, and in this case the latter plea does not prevent the liability of the defendant to account. Whelen *v.* Watmough, 15 S. & R. 158.

(b) Wheeler *v.* Horne Willis, 208.

(c) Bac. Ab. Accompt, E; Com. Dig. Accompt, E 4, 5, 6; Godfrey *v.* Saunders, 3 Wils. 73.

he would have been liable if he had so unjustly resisted the plaintiff's claim.(a)

When a plea has been pleaded, and the issue is joined on this or any subsequent pleadings to which the parties may conduct the cause, the simple question to be decided is, whether the defendant ought to account or not. The cause is then placed on the trial list, and, in due time, comes to be tried by a jury.

§ 5.—Of the evidence in an action of account.

3413. It is a general rule, that the evidence must, in every case, support the plaintiff's allegations to entitle him to recover; for when the plaintiff makes a material allegation, he is required to support it by proof. In this action he must give evidence of privity, either of contract, express or implied, or by law. When the defendant is charged as guardian, bailiff or receiver, or tenant in common, or joint tenant, or partner, it must be proved that he acted in the specific character charged; for, if it be necessary to charge him in such character, it is also required to prove that he acted as such. We have seen that the measure of the liability of defendants is not the same; tenants in common and joint tenants being answerable for what they have actually received, without deducting costs and expenses for their trouble; and receivers being charged in the same manner, but allowed costs and expenses, in special cases, in favor of trade;(b) and guardians and bailiffs are generally held to account for what they might, with proper diligence, have received, deducting reasonable costs and expenses.(c)

(a) Gratz v. Phillips, 5 Binn. 568.
(b) This, as before observed, does not apply to the case of partners in trade. James v. Browne, 1 Dall. 340.
(c) Jourdan v. Wilkins, 2 Wash. C. C. 482; Irvine v. Hanlin, 10 S. & R. 221; Griffith v. Willing, 3 Binn. 317; Sargent v. Parsons, 12 Mass.
149.

The property or right in the money demanded, or goods bailed, must be precisely stated, and proved to be in the plaintiff, as laid, it being a material allegation; if, therefore, the declaration claims as for money of the plaintiff, and the evidence is of money belonging to the plaintiff and another as partners, the allegation in the declaration is not supported.(*a*)

When there are several defendants, they must be proved to be jointly and not severally liable, else one might be made answerable for the default of the other.(*b*)

As a special demand is not required to be made before action brought, it is not necessary to aver it in the declaration, nor to prove it on the trial.(*c*)

Under the plea of *plene computavit*, the defendant must show that he has accounted with the plaintiff, and that an ascertained balance had been agreed upon.(*d*) But, to this, there is an exception in those cases where the law presumes that there has been an account; as where the demand is against a servant for the proceeds of daily small sales, of which it is not the course to take written vouchers; in this case, it will be presumed that the defendant has accounted; but this presumption may be rebutted by the plaintiff proving that this course of dealing has not been adhered to, and that the defendant has not accounted.(*e*)

§ 6.—Of the judgment *quod computet.*

3414. When the jury find against the defendant, a judgment is rendered upon this verdict, that the defendant *do account, quod computet.*(*f*) This is but an

---

(*a*) 2 Wash. C. C. Rep. 482.
(*b*) Whelen *v.* Watmough, 15 S. & R. 158.
(*c*) Sturges *v.* Bush, 6 Day, 452.
(*d*) Baxter *v.* Hosier, 5 Bing. N. C. 288.
(*e*) Evans *v.* Birch, 3 Campb. 10.
(*f*) See the form of this judgment in Godfrey *v.* Saunders, 3 Wilson, 88.

OF DIFFERENT FORMS OF ACTIONS. 597

No. 3415.   Book 4, tit. 9, chap 1, sec. 1, § 7, art. 1, 2.   No. 3417.

interlocutory judgment, and its only effect, to compel the defendant to account before auditors to be appointed by the court. It does not conclude the defendant as to the dates, or sums mentioned in the declaration; it is the duty of the auditor to make proper charges, and to allow proper credits, without regard to the verdict.(a) A writ of error does not lie upon this judgment.(b)

If the jury return a verdict for the defendant, the judgment will of course be given for him, unless for some legal cause the verdict be set aside. In this case, when the defendant has pleaded in bar, and the bar is adjudged good, the plaintiff may have a writ of error; for this judgment is final till reversed.(c)

§ 7.—Of the proceedings before the auditors.

3415. Let us consider, 1, the appearance of the parties; 2, the hearing before auditors; 3, the report of the auditors; 4, the power of the court over auditors.

Art. 1.—*Of the appearance of the parties.*

3416. When the parties appear before the auditors, the case goes immediately to a hearing. Should the defendant neglect to appear before the auditors, upon proper notice, the course is, to obtain a certificate from them, stating such neglect or refusal, and, provided with this, the plaintiff may apply to the court for a *capias ad computandum.* By virtue of this writ, the defendant may be taken in custody, when he must put in bail to answer the condemnation.(d)

Art. 2.—*Of the hearing before the auditors.*

3417. The auditors sit as a court, having the power

(a) Newbold v. Sims, 2 S. & R. 317 ; James v. Browne, 1 Dall. 339 Sturges v. Bush, 5 Day, 452.
(b) Beitler v. Zeigler, 1 Penna. R. 135 ; 11 Co. 38.
(c) 1 Vin. Ab. Account, U, pl. 22.
(d) Keppele v. Keppele, 3 Yeates, 83, 84.

598 OF REMEDIES.

No. 3417.   Book 4, tit. 9, chap 1, sec. 1, § 7, art. 2.   No. 3417.

to hear all questions of law and fact which are presented to them;(a) and if the matters offered by the defendant in discharge of the plaintiff's demands, are disputed by the plaintiff, he may either demur or take issue before the auditors.(b)   As the proceedings before them are in the nature of a new action, the first thing to be done is to ascertain what facts are put in issue.   The plaintiff does not file a new declaration, but the defendant may plead new matter in discharge, which he could not have before pleaded.   In pleading before the auditors, the following rules are to be observed :

1. Whatever might have been pleaded in bar to the action, cannot be pleaded as a discharge before the auditors.(c)

2. Except in the case of a release or *plene computavit*, if the party is once chargeable and accountable, he cannot plead in bar, but must plead before auditors; these exceptions are because a release, and having fully accounted, are total extinctions of the right of action, of which the court is to judge; and even in these two cases, they must be pleaded specially, and cannot be given in evidence on *ne unques receivor*.

3. Nothing can be pleaded before auditors, which contradicts what has been formerly pleaded and found by the verdict, because, if this were allowed, there might be two contradictory verdicts, which would perplex the court, or two similar verdicts, which would be nugatory.(d)

If the matters offered by the defendant in discharge of the plaintiff's demands are disputed by the plaintiff, he may either demur or take issue before the auditors. When there are more points in dispute than one, there

---

(a) Parker *v.* Avery, Kirby, 353 ; Wood *v.* Barney, 2 Verm. 369.
(b) Crousillat *v.* McCall, 5 Binn. 438.
(c) Godfrey *v.* Saunders, 3 Wils. 113.
(d) Godfrey *v.* Saunders, 3 Wils. 314.

may be a demurrer or an issue on each, and they are to be certified by the auditors to the court, and then the matters of law are decided by the court, and the matters of fact by the jury. After this has been all finally settled, the result is returned to the auditors, who settle the account accordingly.(a)

If, on the trial of the issue, the plaintiff makes default, he shall be nonsuited; but he is not without remedy, for he may have a just claim, and the default may have been unavoidable. He may bring a *scire facias ad computandum*.(b)

In the examination of the case, the auditors are authorized to take all articles of account between the parties, incurred since the commencement of the suit, and the whole is to be brought down to the time when they make an end of the account.(c) But after a judgment *quod computet*, rendered against a receiver upon confession, if the auditors certify issues to be tried, the plaintiff upon trial of such issues, cannot give evidence of moneys received by the defendant during any other period than that described in the declaration, for the defendant confessed no more.(d)

Art. 3.—Of the report of the auditors.

3418. The very object of appointing auditors is to procure an account showing a balance in favor of one of the parties.(e) They are, therefore, required to make out an account showing the state of indebtedness on either side; but, if they file such an account, it is not objectionable. that they report that "the plaintiff has no legal demand at present against the defend-

---

(a) Crousillat *v.* McCall, 5 Binn. 433, 438.
(b) Wheaton's Selw. N. P. 5.
(c) Robinson *v.* Bland, 2 Burr. 1086 ; Couscher *v.* Tulam, 4 Wash. C. C. 442.
(d) Sweigart *v.* Lowmarter. 14 S. & R. 200.
(e) Finney *v.* Harbeson, 4 Yeates, 514.

ant."(a)   But a report stating simply that the defendant "has fully accounted," is bad.(b)

Art. 4.—Of the power of the court over auditors.

3419. The auditors are subject to the supervisory power of the court, who may correct abuses or any improper conduct of the auditors. If, therefore, either party has cause of complaint against the auditors, there is no mode of redress, but by complaint to the court; and when there is just cause of complaint, the court are bound to give redress; thus, if either party offer to join an issue, and the auditors refuse permission ; or if the auditors conduct themselves with any manner of impropriety, to the injury of either party, redress may be had by application to the court.(c)

§ 8.—Of final judgment.

3420. This is in favor of the plaintiff or of the defendant. In both cases it depends upon the report of the auditors ; for, when this is clear of fraud, and it has been made according to law, it is, like the verdict of a jury, the foundation on which the judgment rests.

Art. 1.—Of judgment for plaintiff.

3421. When the report certifies that the defendant has refused to account, judgment is entered that the plaintiff recover according to the value mentioned in his declaration, and there will be a similar result where he gives an imperfect account; in these cases the judgment is for the whole amount of the claim, and there is no occasion for a writ of inquiry to ascertain the value.(d)

If the report contain an account and a balance in

(a) Couscher v. Tulam, 4 Wash. C. C. 442.
(b) Spencer v. Usher. 2 Day, 116.
(c) Crousillat v. McCall, 5 Binn. 438.
(d) Cro. Eliz. 806.

favor of the plaintiff, the final judgment is, that the plaintiff recover against the defendant so much as the defendant is found in arrear.(*a*)

Art. 2.—Of judgment in favor of defendant.

3422. If the report of auditors be in favor of the defendant, it seems doubtful whether a judgment can be entered for him on the report.(*b*)   But he may bring an action of debt against the plaintiff for the sum in which he was found to be a creditor.(*c*)   ·

§ 9.—Proceedings in error on final judgment.

3423. It is a general rule that a writ of error lies on the final judgment of a court of law.   The final judgment in account render, may therefore be tested by proceedings in error.   If found erroneous, it may be reversed, but such reversal shall not affect the first judgment, if that be not incorrect.   And if the second judgment be reversed, a *capias ad computandum* may issue to compel the defendant to account again.(*d*)   But as the last judgment stands on the first, if such first judgment be reversed, the second must follow the same fate.(*e*)

SECTION 2.—OF THE ACTION OF ASSUMPSIT.

3424. The second kind of actions arising on contracts, is the action of *assumpsit*, in more common use than any other.   It may be defined to be an action for the recovery of damages for the non-performance

---

(*a*) Godfrey *v.* Saunders, 3 Wils. 94.   The late Chief Justice Tilghman, in the case Gratz *v.* Phillips, 5 Binn. 567, gives very sound reasons why the judgment in actions of account, may be for greater damages than are laid in the declaration.   His opinion well deserves a careful perusal.
(*b*) Crousillat *v.* McCall, 5 Binn. 433 ; McCall *v.* Crousillat, 3 S. & R. 7.
(*c*) 3 S. & R. 7.
(*d*) Cro. Eliz. 806, pl. 7.
(*e*) Vin. Ab. Account, pl. 22.

of a parol or simple contract; or, in other words, a contract not under seal, nor of record, a circumstance which distinguishes this remedy from others. It is so called from the word *assumpsit*, which, when the plead. ings were in Latin, was always inserted in the decla. ration as descriptive of the defendant's undertaking; within the meaning of the provisions of the statute of Westminster, it may be termed an action on the case, but now, when case simply is mentioned, it signi. fies an action for the redress of a tort, and is in form *ex delicto*.(*a*)

This section will be divided into five paragraphs : 1, upon what contracts assumpsit lies ; 2, of the declara. tion in assumpsit ; 3, of pleas in assumpsit ; 4, of the evidence in actions of assumpsit ; 5, of the judgment.

§ 1.—Upon what contract assumpsit lies.

3425. Assumpsit lies to recover damages for the breach of all parol or simple contracts, whether writ. ten or not written, for the payment of money or for the performance or omission of any other act.(*b*) Such contract may be *express* or *implied*, for the distinction

---

(*a*) See Ham. on N. P. 4 to 23 ; 1 Vin. Ab. 270 ; Bro. Ab. Action sur le case ; Com. Dig. Action upon the case upon assumpsit ; Bac. Ab. Assumpsit ; 3 Reeve's Hist. of the Law ; 1 Chit. Pl. 88 ; Browne on Actions, 318 ; Lawes on Pl. in Assumpsit.

(*b*) In the case of Meages *v.* Oyster, 4 Watts & Serg. 23, Chief Justice Gibson says, "*Assumpsit*, though in form an action on a promise, gives effect to the same principles that are administered through a bill in equity ; and its efficacy as a remedy has almost entirely withdrawn parol contracts from the jurisdiction of chancery." The action upon the case of *assumpsit* owed its origin to the inconveniences which followed the abuse of the wager of law ; for, in order to rid the demand of this matter of defence, the remedy by action upon the case was gradually extended, and, at last, made to embrace the various causes of complaint arising out of simple agreements. In the infancy of *assumpsit* no distinction was made between actions upon the case *ex contractu* and those *ex delicto*, both alike were comprised under the latter denomination, and the plea of not guilty was the general defence to each. Corbyn *v.* Brown, Cro. Eliz. 470. But now they are distinct forms of suit. Although the wager of law has been allowed in some of the states, Barnett *v.* Ihrie, 17 S. & R. 212, yet it is now abolished in perhaps all the states of the Union. Children *v.* Emory, 8 Wheat. 642.

between express and implied contracts, is not in the nature of the undertaking, but in the mode of proof.(a) A great mass of human transactions depend upon implied contracts, which are not written, but grow out of the acts of the parties; in these cases the parties are presumed to have made those stipulations, which, as honest, fair and just men, they ought to have made.(b) For the breach of these implied promises, an action of *assumpsit* may be maintained. It lies also in cases where it is impossible that there should have been a promise, but where the law imperatively and conclusively presumes a promise, from the existing relations between the parties, and raises the obligation to pay, so that when the relation is proved, the jury are bound to find the promise.(c) A few examples will illustrate this. A husband may be sued in assumpsit for the funeral expenses of his wife, he having been at the time of her death and burial in Europe, three thousand miles from the spot where she died; and executors are liable for the funeral expenses of the testator,

---

(a) *Assumpsit* cannot be maintained where there is no express contract and none can be implied; as where Peter and his wife lodged in the house of Paul, the brother of Peter, and both Peter and his wife assisted Paul in carrying on his business, Peter having brought an action for his services, and Paul having pleaded a set off for board and lodging; held, that neither could be charged for, unless the jury were satisfied that the parties came together on the terms that they were to pay and be paid; and if it were not so, no *ex post facto* charge could be made on either side. Davis *v.* Davis, 9 Car. & P. 87. See James *v.* O'Driscoll, 2 Bay, 101 ; Livingston *v.* Ackeston, 5 Cowen, 531; Griffith *v.* Potter, 14 Wend. 209 ; Urie *v.* Johnston, 3 Pennsyl. 212 ; and, in the case of parent and child, it has been held in Pennsylvania, that a child, living under his father's roof, as usual, was not entitled to wages from the father, unless he could prove a "clear, distinct and positive" contract, made *before* the services were rendered. Bash *v.* Bash, 9 Penn. St. Rep. 262 ; Defrance *v.* Austin, 9 Penn. St. Rep. 309 ; Swires *v.* Parsons, 5 W. & S. 358 ; Little *v.* Dawson, 4 Dall. 111 ; Candor's Appeal, 5 Watts & Serg. 513.

(b) Ogden *v.* Saunders, 12 Wheat. 341.

(c) This is very similar to the quasi-contracts of the civil law, the definition of which, according to the civil code of Louisiana, is "the lawful and purely voluntary acts of a man, from which there results any obligation whatever to a third person, and sometimes a reciprocal obligation between the parties." Art. 2272.

although they never gave orders upon the subject, and, owing to their absence, had no knowledge, at that time, either that the testator was dead or that they were executors.(*a*)

3426. Indeed, in some cases the law raises an obligation, as on an implied contract, where the defendant has expressly declared he would *not* be responsible; as where a husband wrongfully turns his wife out of doors, or a father wrongfully discards his children, and gives notice that he will not be responsible for any thing which may be furnished them, still the money may be recovered of him in an action of *assumpsit*, when necessaries, in the technical sense of the word, have been furnished them. But the law presumes a promise or implied contract, only when there has been no special agreement between the parties, still open and unrescinded, embracing the same, or some of the same subject matter of the implied contract.(*b*)

3427. Assumpsit does not lie where the plaintiff has a security of a *higher nature*, for in such case he must found his action upon it; and, therefore, assumpsit cannot in general be maintained where there is an express contract under seal,(*c*) but when the contract under seal has been partially altered and changed by a parol agreement, then *assumpsit* may be supported for its breach; though it will not lie upon a promise to pay a balance on an account stated, where the account is composed of items provided for by a contract under seal; yet, if, on the contrary, there are foreign items introduced into the account, and

---

(*a*) Jenkins *v.* Tucker, 1 H. Bl. 90.
(*b*) Kelly *v.* Foster, 2 Binn. 4; Felton *v.* Dickinson, 10 Mass. 287; Sheppard *v.* Palmer, 6 Conn. 100; Snow *v* Chapman, 2 Root, 99 : Speake *v.* Sheppard, 6 Har. & John. 81; Halloway *v.* Davis, Wright, 129; Arnold *v.* Paxton, 6 J. J. Marsh, 505; Stevens *v.* Cushing, 1 N. Hamp. 17; Algeo *v.* Algeo, 10 S. & R. 235.
(*c*) Baird *v.* Blagrove, 1 Wash. 170; Heard *v.* Wadham, 1 East, 630; Littler *v.* Holland, 3 T. R. 592.

included within the promise, then *assumpsit* may be supported.(*a*)

3428. When, for a *new consideration*, there has been a parol agreement to pay a debt, or perform a contract under seal, *assumpsit* is the proper remedy, whether the new promise be made by the debtor himself, or any other person; as, where the obligor promised the assignee of a bond, in consideration of forbearance, to pay him the amount due on the bond; for this is nothing but a parol contract between the obligor and the assignee, that he will do a certain thing for a valuable consideration, namely, pay him the money due on the bond.(*b*)   It is upon the same principle of a new contract, that *assumpsit* may be maintained upon an account stated between two partners, and a promise by the debtor to pay the other, although they were bound to each other, by writing under seal, to account.(*c*)

3429. *Assumpsit* does not lie upon a record; the proper remedy is an action of debt or *scire facias*, although there be a promise by the judgment debtor to pay it.(*d*)   *Assumpsit* will not lie on a judgment rendered in the courts of a sister state,(*e*) nor on a judgment of a justice of the peace.(*f*)

§ 2.—Of the declaration in *assumpsit*.

3430. There are two kinds of declarations in *assumpsit;* they may be on a *special* or a *general* assumpsit.   A declaration is *special*, when the plaintiff declares upon the original contract, setting out the

---

(*a*) Gibson *v.* Stewart, 7 Watts, 100.
(*b*) 1 Saund. 210, n. 1.   But without such new consideration, such a promise is void as a *nudum pactum.*   Codman *v.* Jenkins, 14 Mass. 99; Andrews *v.* Montgomery, 19 John. 162.
(*c*) Foster *v.* Allanson, 2 T. R. 483; Smith *v.* Barrow, 2 T. R. 478.
(*d*) Andrews *v.* Montgomery, 19 John. 162.   See Vail *v.* Mumford, 1 Root, 142.
(*e*) Garland *v.* Tucker, 1 Bibb, 361; McKim *v.* Odam, 3 Fairf. 94; 19 John. 162.   Sed vide Hubbell *v.* Coudry, 5 John. 132.
(*f*) Bain *v.* Hunt, 3 Hawks, 572; Ellsworth *v.* Barstow, 7 Watts, 314.

particular language, or its effect, whatever be the subject matter ; or when he declares upon a promissory
note, bill of exchange, policy of insurance, and the
like. It is *general*, when the plaintiff, instead of
setting out the particular language, or effect of the •
original contract, declares as for a debt, arising out of
the execution of the contract, where that constitutes
a debt; or upon the promise raised or implied by law
upon the execution of the contract, when no stipulated
amount is to be paid on its execution, in which case
the law implies that so much is to be paid as is reasonably due.

When, therefore, the plaintiff declares in assumpsit
upon the original contract, in either of the above
instances, the declaration is said to be in *special assumpsit*, because the original contract is specially
stated. But when, instead of declaring on the contract as it was originally made, or may be supposed to
have been made, the plaintiff declares upon the promises raised or implied by law, upon the execution of
such contract, the declaration is said to be in *general
assumpsit;* which is either *indebitatus assumpsit*, when
the plaintiff generally states that the defendant being
indebted to him in a certain specific sum, for what
was done under the contract, promised to pay that
sum to the plaintiff;(*a*) or upon a *quantum meruit* or

(*a*) There is a striking resemblance between the *pactum constitutæ pecunitæ*
of the civilians and our *indebitatus assumpsit.* This contract, in the civil
law, was an agreement by which a person appointed to his creditor a certain day or a certain time, at which he promised to pay; or it may be
defined, simply, an agreement by which a debtor promises his creditor to
pay him. By this pact an obligation arises which does not destroy the former contract by which the debtor was already bound, but which is accessory to it ; and by this multiplicity of obligations the right of the creditor
is strengthened. Poth. Ob. part 2, c. 6. s. 9. The *pactum constitutæ
pecuniæ* was a promise to pay a subsisting debt, whether natural or civil ;
made in such a manner as not to extinguish the preceding debt. It was introduced by the prætor to obviate formal difficulties. The action of *indebitatus assumpsit* is brought upon a promise for the payment of a debt, and
by such promise the right of action on the original is not extinguished nor
varied. It is not subject to the wager of law and other technical difficulties

quantum valebant, as they are called, stating generally that in consideration of what was done under the contract, the defendant promised to pay the plaintiff what he deserved, or what it was worth, and that he deserved, or it was worth so much.

3431. Whether the declaration shall be on the special contract, or whether it shall be general, depends upon the circumstances of each case. The cases will generally come within the following rules.

1. While the contract continues *executory,* the plaintiff must declare specially;(*a*) but when it has been *executed* on his part, and nothing remains but the payment of the price in money, by the defendant, which is nothing more than the law would imply against him, the plaintiff may declare generally, using the common counts, or he may declare upon the original contract, at his election.(*b*) If, by the special agreement, which was performed, the plaintiff was to be paid in specific articles, and not in money, the declaration must be special;(*c*) and if it was in money, and a term of credit was allowed, the action, though on the common counts, must not be brought until the term has expired.(*d*) When the plaintiff has been prevented from completing his contract,,by the defendant, the declaration must be special on the contract, because the whole has not been performed, and to enable him to bring general *assumpsit,* the plaintiff must have fully completed his agreement.(*e*)

---

to which the action was once liable.   4 Rep. 91 to 95; 1 Vin. Ab. 270; Bro. Ab. Action sur le case, pl. 7, 69, 72.   Vide ante, n. 2853.

(*a*) Kelly *v.* Foster, 2 Binn. 4; Arnold *v.* Paxton, 6 J. J. Marsh. 505; White *v.* Woodruff, 1 Root, 309; Russell *v.* South Britain Society, 9 Conn. 508.

(*b*) Perkins *v.* Hart, 11 Wheat. 237; Snyder *v.* Castor, 4 Yeates, 353; Miles *v.* Moody, 3 S. & R. 211; Gordon *v.* Martin, Fitzg. 303; Baker *v.* Corey, 10 Pick. 496; Pitkin *v.* Frink, 8 Met. 16.

(*c*) Cochran *v.* Tatum, 3 Monr. 305.

(*d*) Robson *v.* Godfrey, 1 Stark. 220.

(*e*) Algeo *v.* Algeo, 10 S. & R. 235; Donaldson *v.* Fuller, 3 S. & R. 505. Sed vide Perkins *v.* Hart, 11 Wheat. 237.

2. When a contract has been abandoned by mutual consent, after being partially performed, or is rescinded, or it becomes extinct, by some act on the part of the defendant, the plaintiff may resort to the common counts alone for remuneration for what he has done under the special agreement; but the fact of the defendant's hindering the plaintiff from completing his contract is not sufficient, for as we have just stated, in such case, the plaintiff must declare specially upon the agreement. The contract must be considered as at an end.(a)

3. When what was done by the plaintiff, was performed under a special agreement, but not in the stipulated time or manner, and yet it was beneficial to the defendant, and accepted by him, the plaintiff cannot recover upon the contract from which he has departed; his remedy is upon the common counts for the value of what the plaintiff has performed, and which has been of benefit to the defendant;(b) and if the contract has been fully completed and something additional has been done ; as, if a house be built upon a plan as per a written agreement, and additions are put to it, the declaration for a breach must be special, as far as the agreement goes, and general for the residue.(c)

The rules relating to the form of a declaration, on a special and on a general *assumpsit*, have been so fully considered, as to render any further remarks upon them in this place altogether unnecessary.

(a) Mead v. Degolyer, 16 Wend. 632 ; Linningdale v. Livingston, 10 John. 36; Raymond v. Bernard, 12 John. 274; Hollingshead v. Mactier, 13 Wend. 276.

(b) Streeter v. Hurlock, 1 Bingh. 34 ; Jewell v. Schrœppel, 4 Cowen, 564 ; Taft v. Montague, 14 Mass. 282 ; Hayward v. Leonard, 7 Pick. 181 ; Smith v. Proprietors, etc., 8 Pick. 178 ; Wadleigh v. Sutton, 6 N. Hamp. 15 ; Morford v. Ambrose, 3 J. J. Marsh. 690 ; Newman v. McGregor, 5 Ham. 351 ; Dubois v. Read, 1 Rep. Const. Ct. 472.

(c) Pepper v. Burland, Peake's Cas. 103; Dunn v. Body, 1 Stark. R. 175 , Robson v. Godfrey, 1 Stark. R. 220 ; Dubois v. Delaware and Hudson Canal Co. 1 Wend. 285 ; Wright v. Wright, 1 Litt. 181 ; McCormick v. Connolly, 2 Bay, 401.

§ 3.—Of pleas in *assumpsit*.

3432. The general issue is *non assumpsit*, that the defendant did not undertake or promise, as alleged by the plaintiff; under this issue the defendant may give most matters of defence in evidence. In consequence of its great convenience, it is generally pleaded.(*a*) But special matter may be pleaded in denial; or in confession and avoidance; or of special performance, or in excuse of performance; or in discharge of the *assumpsit*. The rules relating to these have been fully discussed.

§ 4.—Of the evidence in actions of *assumpsit*.

3433. As a contract, whether written or not written, express or implied, when not under seal, to be valid, must be made upon a sufficient consideration, and the declaration must state such consideration;(*b*) it follows, that before the, plaintiff can recover, he must *prove the consideration* for the alleged promise of the defendant; and this may be done by evidence of an express agreement as to the consideration, or, upon the common counts, it may be done by proof of the circumstances attending the transaction; and the privity between the plaintiff and defendant may be proved in the same way. This, of course, is required, for if the plaintiff is a stranger to the consideration, he cannot recover.

3434. The plaintiff will also be required to prove all the *material allegations* in the declaration, when the defendant pleads the general issue, for by such plea he traverses them all. He must also prove what

---

(*a*) Lawes, Pl. in Assumpsit, 520.
(*b*) When the declaration does not allege a consideration, it will be bad, even after verdict, and will be reversed on error. Hemmenway *v.* Hickes, 4 Pick. 497; Bruner *v.* Stout, Hardin. 225; Gains *v.* Kendrick, 2 Rep. Const. Ct. 339; Beverleys *v.* Holmes, 4 Munf. 95; Mosely *v.* Jones, 5 Munf. 23; Bailey *v.* Freeman, 4 John. 280; Wheelwright *v.* Moore, 1 Hall, 201; Benden *v.* Manning, 2 N. Hamp. 289; Connolly *v.* Cottle, 1 Breeze, 286. In Pennsylvania, however, it seems that a verdict has the healing power to cure this defect. Shaw *v.* Redmond, 11 S. & R. 27.

damages he has sustained by the breach of the contract; but he cannot recover more than the amount in the *ad damnum* laid in the declaration.(*a*)

3435. A *request* by the defendant must be alleged in the declaration and proved on the trial, in the actions upon the common counts. A past or executed consideration must be laid to have been done upon the request of the defendant, for otherwise it would not appear that the service, or what was done by the plaintiff, was not a voluntary courtesy;(*b*) and labor and service performed for one without his request or privity, however beneficial or meritorious, as in saving his property from fire, afford no ground of action;(*c*) and so, if the plaintiff put work upon the house of defendant without his consent,(*d*) or where a workman employed to do a particular job, adds extra work without consulting his employer,(*e*) he cannot recover, for no man can be compelled to become another's debtor. But if the person for whom the service has been rendered, knowing of the work, tacitly assent to it, it will be evidence from which a request may be inferred, and in this case, or where he promised to pay, he will be bound, and the action may be sustained.(*f*) But this implication of law will be avoided, by showing that the work was done on the credit of another person.(*g*)

A previous request may be inferred, as has already been mentioned, contrary to the fact; as where a husband wrongfully turns his wife out of doors, and she obtains credit for necessaries, the husband will be

---

(*a*) Steph. Pl. 318; Siltzell *v.* Michael, 3 W. & S. 333.

(*b*) Balcam *v.* Craggin, 5 Pick. 295; Parker *v.* Crane, 6 Wend. 647; Goldsby *v.* Robinson, 1 Blackf. 247. In Pennsylvania, a verdict cures this defect. Stoever *v.* Stoever, 9 S. & R. 434; Greeves *v.* McAllister, 2 Binn. 591.

(*c*) Bartholomew *v.* Jackson, 20 John. 28.

(*d*) Caldwell *v.* Eneas, 2 Rep. Const. Ct. 348.

(*e*) Hart *v.* Norton, 1 McCord, 22.

(*f*) James *v.* Bixley, 11 Mass. 37.

(*g*) Farmington Academy *v.* Allen, 14 Mass. 176.

liable, as if he had made a request.(a)   And when the defendant has been guilty of a trespass, as by taking the property of the plaintiff, and selling it, an action will lie for the money, the plaintiff waiving the tort, and a request need not be proved.(b)

3436. An entire stranger to the consideration, it is evident, has no right to recover; the plaintiff must therefore prove a *privity* between himself and the defendant. But in case of single contracts, if one person make a promise to another, for the benefit of a third person, the latter may maintain the action, and it seems also that it may be maintained by the other party.(c)

3437. To entitle the plaintiff to recover, it must appear that the contract is not *unlawful*. If the plaintiff, to establish his contract, must show such facts as make the contract unlawful, he cannot recover; but if he can establish his contract without showing such acts, he may recover; as, when a man lends money to another, to enable the borrower to lay a wager, with which the lender had no connection whatever; because the borrower might have applied it to any other use, if he had chosen.

If the contract is *executed* and the parties are in *pari delicto*, the law will not help either of them, and the plaintiff upon his own showing will be nonsuited. But in such case, if the contract is shown to be *wholly executory*, and not carried into effect, and money has been advanced by the plaintiff, he may recover it under the money counts. And where the parties are not in *pari delicto*, the innocent plaintiff may recover, in the same way, the money having been obtained from him by some wrong or unlawful advantage.

(a) Walker *v.* Simpson, 7 W. & S. 83; Robinson *v.* Gosnold, 6 Mod. 171; Van Walkinburg *v.* Watson, 13 John. 480.
(b) Hambly *v.* Trott, Cowp. 372.
(c) 1 Chit. Pl. 5.

3438. As to the proof of the money counts, we will pursue the same order in considering the evidence which relates to them, that was observed when speaking of the manner of declaring on them.

1. To prove *money lent*, the evidence must be that there was a loan by the defendant; the mere fact that the plaintiff delivered the money, or gave a bank check to the defendant, is not sufficient. It will be considered as *primâ facie* evidence of the payment, by the plaintiff, of his own debt antecedently due to the defendant.(*a*) The loan must have been essentially a loan of *money*, for a loan of *stock* would not be sufficient.(*b*)

2. The count for *money paid* is supported by evidence of actual payment, and of the defendant's prior request to make such payment, or his subsequent approval of the act. As to what shall be considered as money to entitle the plaintiff to recover, it seems that whatever has discharged the debt of the defendant, whether it be money, or goods, or land, is sufficient to support this count.(*c*)

But money may be paid not only to others for the defendant, but to the defendant himself, under a mistake or ignorance of facts, or under a misapprehension of the state of the contract under which he pays it; in this case it may be recovered back.(*d*) When the party paying the money was fully aware of all the facts, or had an opportunity of knowing them, but

---

(*a*) Cushing *v.* Gore, 15 Mass. 74; Cary *v.* Gerrish, 4 Esp. 9.

(*b*) Nightingal *v.* Devisme, 5 Burr. 2589; Morrison *v.* Berkey, 7 S. & R. 246. The following memoranda have been considered evidence sufficient of money lent: "Due A B eighty dollars on demand, B C." Hay *v.* Hyde, 1 Chipm. 214. "Lent R P $56." ' I say received by me, R P." Peniston *v.* Wall, 3 J. J. Marsh. 37.

(*c*) Ainslie *v.* Wilson, 7 Cowen, 662, 669; Bonney *v.* Seely, 2 Wend. 481.

(*d*) Wheadon *v.* Olds, 20 Wend. 174; Bank of Louisiana *v.* Ballard, 7 How. Miss. 371; Pearson *v.* Lord, 6 Mass. 84; Bond *v.* Hays, 12 Mass. 36.

was ignorant of the law, as where he paid a debt which was justly due, but about which he was mistaken in supposing it was not barred by the act of limitations, the money cannot be recovered back;(a) for when the defendant can with a good conscience receive the money, although he could not recover it by law, he shall not be compelled to pay it back.(b)

Proof that the money sued for was paid on an agreement which had been rescinded;(c) or under duress;(d) or on a judgment that is afterward reversed or vacated, will be sufficient to support this count.(e) But when restitution has been awarded, on the reversal of a judgment, assumpsit for money paid cannot be maintained, because the order of restitution is the only remedy.(f)

3. To support the count for *money had and received* the plaintiff must prove that the defendant has received or obtained possession of the money of the plaintiff, which, in equity and good conscience, he ought to pay over to the latter. The action lies only where money, or something which the parties have treated as money, has been received by the defendant. By this action, which has been considered as resembling a bill in equity, the plaintiff waives all torts, trespasses and damages, and claims only the money which the defendant has actually received. But, in equity, the plaintiff can recover only the balance,

---

(a) See Elliott v. Swartwout, 10 Pet. 137 ; Dickens v. Jones, 6 Yerg. 483 ; Bean v. Jones, 8 N. Hamp. 149.

(b) Morris v. Tarin, 1 Dall. 148 ; Bogart v. Nevins, 6 S. & R. 369 ; Irvine v. Hanlin, 10 S. & R. 219 ; Mann's Appeal, 1 Penn. St. R. 24 ; Hinkle v. Eichelberger, 2 Penn. St. R. 484.

(c) Gillet v. Maynard, 5 John. 85.

(d) Severance v. Kimball, 8 N. Hamp. 386.

(e) Duncan v. Kirkpatrick, 13 S. & R. 292 ; Clark v. Penney, 6 Cowen, 297 : Homer v. Barrett, 2 Root, 156 ; Sturgis v. Allis, 10 Wend. 354 ; Green v. Stone, 1 Har. & John. 405.

(f) 13 S. & R. 292.

after deducting all the legal and equitable claims of the defendant.(a)

It is not, however, necessary that the defendant should have actually received money; there are many things which, for this purpose, are treated as money. Therefore, where the defendant received bank notes, or promissory notes, or a note payable in specific articles, or credit on another's books, he may be considered as having received money.(b)

When money has been obtained by fraud, duress, extortion, imposition, or the taking of any unlawful advantage of the plaintiff, or where the plaintiff has paid the money to the defendant upon a forged instrument, and these facts are proved, the plaintiff may recover on the count for money had and received.

3439. When there are several plaintiffs, it must be proved that the contract was made with them all, because if all the promisees do not join, the plaintiff may be nonsuited; and if too many persons bring the suit, and some of them have no right, it is clear they cannot recover, and some failing, they must all be defeated.

3440. The plaintiff can recover only on the right which he has claimed to be entitled, by his declaration; if he sues in a particular capacity, as executor, assignee of a bankrupt, surviving partner, and the like, he must prove that he is invested with such a character.

3441. Though the plaintiff is thus required to show that all who sue are entitled to recover, yet, under the general issue, he is not required to prove that the

(a) Simpson v. Swan, 3 Campb. 291 : Mann's Appeal, 1 Penn. St. R. 24; Hinkle v. Eicherber, 2 Penn. St. R. 484; 9 Watts, 462 Irvine v. Henlon, 10 S. & R. 219; Tevis v. Brown, 3 J. J. Marsh. 175 ; Eddy v. Smith, 13 Wend. 488.

(b) Mason v. Waite, 17 Mass. 560: Ainslie v. Wilson, 7 Cowen, 662; Floyd v. Day, 3 Mass. 405 ; Willie v. Green, 2 N. Hamp. 333 ; Hinkley v. Fowle, 4 Shep. 285 ; Tutle v. Mayo, 7 John. 132 ; Grandall v. Bradley, 7 Wend. 311.

contract was made with all the defendants; because the non-joinder of defendants can, in general, be taken advantage of only by plea in abatement. But he must prove all the defendants whom he has sued on a joint contract, to be liable, or he will fail.(a)

§ 5.—Of the judgment in assumpsit.

3442. The judgment in *assumpsit* is either in favor of the plaintiff or defendant; when in favor of the plaintiff, it is that he recover a specified sum assessed by a jury, or on reference to the clerk or other officer of the court; when for the defendant, it is for costs.

SECTION 3.—OF THE ACTION OF COVENANT.

3443. In the next place we will treat of a third kind of action, arising *ex contractu*. This is the action of *covenant*, instituted for the recovery of *damages* for the breach of a *covenant*, or promise made in writing and *under seal;* for, by the common law, this action cannot be sustained on an instrument not sealed by the party, or his attorney duly authorized.(b)

It is proper here to point out a distinction between this action and the actions of *assumpsit* or debt. It is true, covenant is brought for the recovery of damages, like *assumpsit*, but the latter is not in general sustainable where the contract was originally under seal, or where a deed has been taken in satisfaction of a parol agreement; and though debt may be sustained upon

(a) Govitt v. Radnige, 3 East. 62, 70; Porter v. Harris, 1 Lev. 63; Max v. Roberts, 2 New Rep. 454; 1 Chit. Pl. 32.

(b) Gale v. Nixon, 6 Cowen, 445; Ludlum v. Wood, 1 Pen. 55; Tribble v. Oldham, 5 J. J. Marsh. 137; Bilderback v. Pouner, 2 Halst. 64. In Kentucky, by the statute of 1812, all writings thereafter executed without seal, stipulating for the payment of money or property, or for the performance of any other act, duty or duties, shall be placed upon the same footing with sealed writings containing the like stipulations, and to all intents and purposes, shall have the same force and effect, and the same species of action may be founded on them, as if sealed. Hanley v. Rankins, 4 Monr. 556; Hughes v. Parks, 4 Bibb, 60.

a simple contract, a specialty, a record, or a statute, yet it lies only for a sum of money *in numero*, and not where the damages are unliquidated and incapable of being reduced to a certainty, by an averment.

This, like the last section, will be divided into five paragraphs: 1, on what kind of claim or obligation this action may be sustained; 2, of the form of the declaration; 3, of the pleas and issue; 4, of the evidence; 5, of the judgment.

§ 1.—On what kind of claim or obligation this action may be sustained.

3444. It lies in all cases where there is a breach of a covenant, whether such covenant be contained in an indenture, or deed-poll, or any other writing under seal; whether it be express or implied by law from the terms of the deed; or for the performance of something *in futuro*, or that something has been done;(*a*) it may be not only for something which is past or something future, but also for something *in presenti*, as that the covenantor has a good title; and in this case, when he has not such title, the covenant is broken as soon as signed and delivered; as a general rule, however, covenant will not lie on a contract *in presenti*, as on a covenant to stand seised, or that a certain horse shall thenceforth be the property of another.(*b*)

Covenant is sometimes a concurrent remedy with debt, and in some cases it is a peculiar remedy.

It is *concurrent* with debt on a *direct* contract under seal, for the payment of a stipulated sum of money, either by way of penalty or otherwise;(*c*) it lies on a penal bond, but the breach assigned must be the non-payment of the penalty,(*d*) and not of the condition

(*a*) Com. Dig. Covenant, A.
(*b*) Sharrington *v.* Strotton, Plowd. 308.
(*c*) Bassett *v.* Jordan, 1 Stew. 352.
(*d*) United States *v.* Brown, Paine, 422.

of the bond, separated from the penal or obligatory part;(a) covenant is also a proper remedy for the breach of a contract under seal for the payment of a certain sum of money, to be discharged in good current bank notes.(b) It is the only remedy, when the liability is created by an agreement under seal; but when the law creates the liability, independently of the covenant, an action on the case may also be maintained.(c)

3545. Covenant is the *peculiar* remedy, where the obligation under seal is not direct but *collateral* merely, and where the damages are unliquidated, and debt will not lie; thus, where several covenantors bind themselves, or some one of them, to pay a certain sum of money, debt cannot be maintained against one of them only.(d) So where money is secured by an instrument under seal, to be paid by instalments, and they are not all due, no action but covenant will lie, unless there be a penalty, which becomes due on the payment of any one instalment, in which case debt will lie for the penalty.(e) And when part of an entire sum due on a sealed instrument is payable by instalments at fixed periods, and the residue in specific articles on demand, covenant will lie for the instalments, though there has been no legal demand of the specific articles.(f)

After a lessee has assigned his lease, and the lessor has accepted rent from the assignee, debt cannot be maintained against the *lessee* for any future rent; covenant is his only remedy.(g)

3446. Having considered the cases where covenant

(a) Huddle v. Worthington, 1 Ham. 423.
(b) Jackson v. Waddill, 1 Stew. 579 ; Scott v. Conover, 1 Hals. 222.
(c) Luckey v. Rowzee, 1 Marsh. 295.
(d) Harrison v. Matthews, 2 Dowl. N. S. 318.
(e) 2 Saund. 303, note b; Com. Dig. Action, F ; but if the sums payable at different times be independent sums, and not instalments of a larger sum. debt lies as well as covenant.
(f) Stevens v. Chamberlain, 1 Verm. 25.
(g) 1 Saund. 241.

may, and where it *must* be brought, let us now, on the other hand, examine those in which it *cannot* be maintained. In general it cannot be supported unless the contract is under *seal;* when it is by parol, the plaintiff must proceed by *assumpsit*, debt, or other suitable action. Covenant cannot be 'supported on a lease executed by the lessor only, though the lessee enters, and enjoys the possession ;(*a*) but it will lie, although the covenantee did not sign the indenture in which he is named as a party.(*b*) This action cannot be maintained by one partner against another, on the articles of partnership, though under seal, to compel the payment of the balance due to the partnership, from one of the partners, the proper remedy being an action of account or a bill in chancery.(*c*)

When the contract is under seal, and, afterward, it is varied in its terms, in a material part, by a verbal or parol agreement, such substituted contract must be the subject of an action of *assumpsit*, and not of covenant.(*d*) But a parol agreement by one party to a covenant to waive the performance of part of the agreement by the other party, is not such an alteration of the contract as will render necessary a change in the form of the action.(*e*)

§ 2.—Of the form of the declaration in covenant.

3447. The declaration must state that the *contract was under seal*, and it should not only state such a contract, but its delivery must also be alleged ;(*f*) and it should also make a profert of it, or show some excuse

---

(*a*) Trustees, etc. *v.* Spencer, 7 Hamm. part 2, 151.
(*b*) Lucke *v.* Lucke, Lutw. 305; Com. Dig. Covenant, A 1.
(*c*) Niven *v.* Spickerman, 12 John. 401.
(*d*) Vicary *v.* Moore, 2 Watts, 456 ; Heard *v.* Wadham, 1 East, 630; Littler *v.* Holland, 3 T. R. 590. See Ellmaker *v.* Franklin Fire Ins. Co., 6 W. & S. 443.
(*e*) McCombs *v.* McKennan, 2 Watts & Serg. 216.
(*f*) Perkins *v.* Reeds, 8 Miss. 33.

for the omission.(a)   It is not, in general, necessary
to state the consideration of the defendant's covenant,
for the seal is of itself evidence of consideration; but
when the performance of the consideration constituted
a condition precedent, then such performance must
be averred,(b) or the plaintiff must aver that he was
prevented by the other party.(c)

Only so much of the deed and covenant should be
set forth as is essential to the cause of action, and each
may be stated *according to its legal effect,* though it is
more usual to declare in the words of the deed; and
implied covenants may be set forth in the declaration
in the same manner as if they were expressed in the
instrument.(d)

The *breach* may be assigned in the negative words of
the covenant, where such general assignment amounts
to a breach; but enough must be placed upon the
record to show that the covenant has been broken,
and that the plaintiff has a cause of action.(e)   A
breach may also be assigned according to the substance, though not according to the letter of the covenant.(f)   It may be in the alternative, or there may
be several breaches in the same declaration, and, if
one be well assigned, the declaration cannot be held
ill on general demurrer.(g)

The action being brought to recover *damages* for the

(a) Read v. Brookman, 3 T. R. 151.
(b) Goodwin v. Lynn, 4 Wash. C. C. 714; Keatly v. McLaugherty, 4
Mis. 221; Knox v. Rinehart, 9 S. & R. 45; Harrison v. Taylor, 3 Marsh.
168; Gardiner v. Corson, 15 Mass. 503; West v. Emmons, 5 John. 179.
(c) Fannen v. Beauford, 1 Bay, 237; Clandennen v. Paulsel, 3 Mis. 230.
(d) Grannis v. Clark, 8 Cowen, 36; Barney v. Keith, 4 Wend. 502.   It
has been held in Pennsylvania, that where a mistake had been made in
drawing articles of covenant, the plaintiff might declare upon the articles as
they should have been drawn, according to the mutual agreement of the
parties, with proper averments, showing the mistake in the original. Gower
v. Sterner, 2 Whart. 75.
(e) Randel v. Chesapeake, etc. Co. 1 Harring, 151.
(f) Potter v. Bacon, 2 Wend. 583.
(g) Com. Dig. Pleader, 2 V, 2, 3; McCoy v. Hill, 2 Litt. 374.   See
Thome v. Haley, 1 Dana, 268.

non-performance or breach of a covenant under seal, they must be laid in the declaration, sufficiently high to cover the real amount.

§ 3.—Of the pleas and issue in action of covenant.

3448. Strictly speaking, there is no *general issue* in an action of covenant, for *non est factum* merely denies the deed, and only puts in issue the fact of its sealing and execution ;(*a*) and, when pleaded simply, it admits all material averments in the declaration.(*b*)

Of the special pleas, the following are the most common :

᠊ 1. *Non infringit conventionem* merely denies that the defendant has broken the covenants, but does not deny the deed ; it is not, therefore, the general issue ; still, it is a plea in bar.(*c*)   But when the breach is in the negative, then the plea of *non infringit conventionem* is bad, because both the breach and the plea being in the negative, there can be no issue.(*d*)

2. *Omnia performavit* is a good plea in bar, where all the covenants are in the affirmative.(*e*)

3. *Covenants performed* is pleaded in some states. In Pennsylvania, it admits the execution of the instrument, and supersedes the necessity of other proof, but it does not admit that the opposite party had performed his agreement.(*f*)   In Alabama, on the contrary, a plea of covenants performed does not admit the deed ; the plaintiff is required to prove his cause of action, as if no such plea had been filed.(*g*)   In Illinois, the

---

(*a*) In Ohio, under a statute, *non est factum* is a plea of the general issue in covenant, to which a notice of set off may be appended. Granger *v.* Granger, 6 Ham. 41.

(*b*) McNeish *v.* Stewart, 7 Cow. 474 ; Thomas *v.* Woods, 4 Cow. 173 ; Cooper *v.* Watson, 10 Wend. 202 ; Norman *v.* Wells, 17 Wend. 136.

(*c*) Phelps *v.* Sawyer, 1 Aik. 150 ; Bendor *v.* Fromberger, 4 Dall. 436 ; Roosevelt *v.* Fulton, 7 Cowen, 71.

(*d*) Bac. Ab. Covenant, L.

(*e*) Bailey *v.* Rogers, 1 Greenl. 189.

(*f*) Neave *v.* Jenkins, 2 Yeates, 107 ; Roth *v.* Miller, 15 S. & R. 105.

(*g*) Bryant *v.* Simpson, 3 Stew. 339.

plea of covenants performed, if not sustained, admits the plaintiff's right to recover only nominal damages.(a)

The defendant may plead any other matter specially, as infancy, a release, duress, gaming, and the like, which cannot be given in evidence unless pleaded; the defendant must answer all the breaches laid in the declaration, and if he pleads to the whole action a plea which is good as to one breach only, such plea is bad on demurrer.(b)

§ 4.—Of the evidence.

3449. As in this action there is no general issue, which traverses the whole declaration, the plaintiff is not required to prove the whole; that is, he is not required to prove what is admitted by the plea. The evidence is, therefore, confined to the particular issue raised by the special plea.

When the deed is not put in issue by the plea of *non est factum*, the defendant, at common law, admits so much of the deed as is spread upon the record; if other parts of the deed are required to support the plaintiff's case, he must prove them in the usual way.(c)   When the defendant has pleaded *non est factum*, the plaintiff must, of course, prove the allegations contained in his declaration, and prove the formal execution of the instrument on which he has declared. This is done by the production of the deed, and proving by the attesting witnesses, when they can be had, that it was signed, sealed and delivered by the obligor; and if any suspicion should arise from any alterations or erasures made in it, these must be removed before the deed can be read in evidence.(d)

(a) Reed v. Hobbs, 2 Scam. 297.
(b) Breckenbridge v. Lee, 3 Bibb, 330 ; Muldrow v. McCleland, 1 Litt. 5.
(c) Williams v. Sill, 2 Campb. 519.
(d) Whether interlineations and erasures in a deed were made before or after its execution, is a matter of fact for the jury ; and when the alteration is against the interest of the party claiming under it, the presumption

To prove the *signing and sealing*, it is not requisite that the witnesses should have seen either done by the covenantor; it is sufficient if he showed it to them, signed and sealed, and requested them to subscribe it as witnesses.(a) When there are several obligors or grantors, it is sufficient if there is but one piece of wax, with several impressions; or when there is but one seal, it is sufficient; for the covenantors or grantors following the first, will be presumed to have adopted his seal.(b)

Evidence must also be given of the *delivery* of the deed. This is done by showing that the grantor or obligor parted with the dominion over it, with an intent that it should pass to the grantee or obligee; it may be proved, like most facts *in pays*, by direct evidence, or by circumstances.(c) In general, if a deed be found in the hands of the grantee, it will be presumed to have been delivered;(d) on the contrary, if found in the hands of the grantor or obligor, no delivery will be presumed.(e)

The *registry* of a deed at the request of the grantor, for the use of the grantee, and the assent of the latter to the same, is evidence of *delivery*.(f) The act of recording a deed is not conclusive evidence of delivery,(g) and consequently it may be rebutted.(h)

Whether the deed was signed, sealed and delivered by the grantor or obligor, is a question of fact for the

---

is that it was made before or at the time of its execution. Heffelfinger *v.* Shutz, 16 S. & R. 44. See, as to the effect of alteration of instruments, Van Amringe *v.* Morton, 4 Whart. 382; Arrison *v.* Harmstead, 2 Penn. St. R. 191; Whithers *v.* Atkinson, 1 Watts, 236; Bac. Ab. Evidence, F.

(a) Munns *v.* Dupont, 3 Wash. C. C. 42.
(b) Bowman *v.* Robb, 6 Penn. St. R. 302. Vide 9 Am. Jur. 290, 297.
(c) 2 Greenl. Ev. § 297; Long *v.* Ramsay, 2 S. & R. 72; Brown *v.* Bank of Chambersburg, 3 Penn. St. Rep. 187.
(d) Dunn *v.* Games, 1 McLean, 321; Green *v.* Yarnall, 6 Mis. 326.
(e) Hatch *v.* Haskins, 5 Shep. 391.
(f) Hedge *v.* Drew, 12 Pick. 141.
(g) Maynard *v.* Maynard, 10 Mass. 456; Harrison *v.* Phillips' Academy, 12 Mass. 456.
(h) Gilbert *v.* North, Am. Ins. Co. 23 Wend. 43.

jury; under the issue of *non est factum*, therefore, the defendant may prove that the deed was delivered and still remains as an escrow;(*a*) or that it was void from the beginning; for example, that it is a forgery, or it was obtained by fraud, or executed while the defendant was insane, or intoxicated; or that it became void by subsequent acts, as by being materially altered, or cancelled, by tearing off the seal; or that the deed was delivered to a stranger for the use of the plaintiff, and that he refused it;(*b*) or that it was never delivered at all.(*c*)

3450. When covenants performed has been pleaded, the burden of proof lies on the defendant, for whenever the plea is in avoidance of the deed, the defendant has the *onus probandi*, cast upon him.(*d*) Under the plea of "covenants performed, with leave to give the special matter in evidence," the defendant may, in Pennsylvania, give evidence of any matter he might have pleaded, and which in law can protect him, and this without notice of special matter, unless called for.(*e*) But, under the plea of covenants performed, the defendant cannot avail himself of the difficulty of performing his covenants, in excuse.(*f*)

3451. The plaintiff must also *prove the breach* as laid in the declaration; and it is no excuse to the defendant that he has been unable to perform his covenant, if before the time of performance he disabled himself from so doing;(*g*) as where a brewer covenanted to deliver grains from his brew-house, and before the

(*a*) Wheelwright *v.* Wheelwright, 2 Mass. 447. See Blight *v.* Schenck, 10 Penn. St. R. 285; Union Bank *v.* Ridgely, 1 H. & G. 324.
(*b*) Read *v.* Robinson, 6 W. & S. 329.
(*c*) Roberts *v.* Jackson, 1 Wend. 478; Gardner *v.* Collins, 3 Mason, 90.
(*d*) He has therefore the right to open and close. Norris *v.* Ins. Co. of N. Amer. 3 Yeates. 84; Scott *v.* Hull, 8 Com. 296.
(*e*) Webster *v.* Warren, 2 Wash. C. C. 456; Rangler *v.* Morton, 4 Watts, 265; Bender *v.* Fromberger, 4 Dall. 439.
(*f*) Stone *v.* Dennis, 3 Port, 231.
(*g*) Heard *v.* Bowers, 23 Pick. 455; Hopkins *v.* Young, 11 Mass. 302.

time of delivery rendered them unfit for use by mixing
hops with them,(a) or where he covenanted to deliver
a horse and then poisoned him;(b) the covenant must
be proved to be substantially broken; if, for example,
the covenantor bind himself to keep the trees of an
orchard whole and undefaced, reasonable use and wear
only excepted, the cutting down of trees past bearing
was held to be no breach, because the preservation
of the trees for fruit was of the substance of the contract.(c)

3452. A few examples will be given to show what
is a sufficient breach of covenants. The covenants
which are thus broken are:

1. Covenants *against incumbrances.* Proof by any
competent evidence that incumbrances existed at the
time of signing the covenant, is evidence of a breach.(d)
As to what shall be considered an *incumbrance,* it has
been held a public highway passing over the land,(e)
a private right of way,(f) a lien by judgment,(g) or
any mortgage the covenantee was not bound to pay,(h)
a preëxisting right to take water from the land, are
each an incumbrance, and a breach of covenant against
incumbrances.(i)

2. Covenant of *seisin.* Evidence that the covenantor was not seised in fact, will be proof of a breach;
but if the covenantor was seised in fact, though by
wrong, it is sufficient to support his covenant.(j)

(a) Griffith v. Goodhand, Sir T. Raym. 464.
(b) Skin. 40; Bac. Ab. Covenant, H.
(c) 2 Stark. Ev. 148.
(d) Tuft v. Adams, 8 Pick. 547; Funk v. Voneida, 11 S. & R. 109; Bean
v. Mayo, 5 Greenl. 94; Bac. Ab. Covenant, H.
(e) Kellogg v. Ingersoll, 2 Mass. 97; Hubbard v. Norton, 10 Conn. 431;
Pritchard v. Atkinson, 3 N. H. Rep. 335.
(f) Harlow v. Thomas, 15 Pick. 68.
(g) Jenkins v. Hopkins, 8 Pick. 346.
(h) 11 S. & R. 109; 8 Pick. 547; Stewart v. Drake, 4 Halst. 139.
(i) See 2 Wheat. 45; 15 Verm. 683; 5 Conn. 497; 11 Gill & John. 472;
4 Ala. 21; 1 App. R. 313; Bac. Ab. Covenant, H.
(j) Marston v. Hobbs, 2 Mass. 433.

3. Covenant of *warranty*. Evidence of an actual ouster or eviction by one having a lawful title, is sufficient proof of the breach of this covenant; and it is not necessary that this should be with force. A judgment in ejectment, when the covenantor has had notice of the action, and was requested to defend it, is also evidence of the breach of this covenant.(*a*)   No tortious act of a stranger, by which the covenantee is put out of possession, will be a breach of the warranty.

4. Covenant for *quiet enjoyment*. To prove a breach of this covenant, it is in general necessary to show an actual ouster, by reason of some adverse right existing at the time of making the covenant, and not one subsequently acquired.(*b*)   Any tortious entry, by the covenantor himself, claiming title, will be a breach of this covenant.(*c*)

5. Covenant to *repair*. To prove the breach of this covenant, the plaintiff must show that the premises were essentially out of repair; and he will of course be confined to those matters expressly alleged as constituting the breach.

6. Covenant against *assigning a lease* and *underletting*. To constitute a breach of this covenant, the assignment of the lessee, or his under-letting, must be voluntary; for if the term be sold by a sheriff by virtue of an execution, or by assignees in bankruptcy, or by an executor, it is no breach of the covenant, unless the assignment is effected by the fraud of the lessee, as, where he confessed a fraudulent judgment, with the intent that the creditor should seize the term in execution. Proof must, therefore, be made that

(*a*) Hamilton *v.* Cutts, 4 Mass. 349; Collingwood *v.* Irwin, 3 Watts, 306. See Clark *v.* McAnulty, 3 S. & R. 364; Emerson *v.* Proprietors of Minot, 1 Mass. 464.

(*b*) Ellis *v.* Welch, 6 Mass. 246; Hurd *v.* Fletcher, 1 Dougl. 43; Evans *v.* Vaughan, 4 B. & C. 261.

(*c*) Sedgwick *v.* Hollenback, 7 John. 376; Seddon *v.* Senate, 13 East, 72. ¥

the defendant has voluntarily transferred the premises, or evidence of some unlawful act of the defendant by which the assignment has been effected.

When the *plaintiff sues as assignee of the covenantee*, he must allege and prove the conveyances, or the title by which he claims. When he claims as assignee of a covenant real, he must show himself grantee of the land, by a regular conveyance, from a person having the right and the legal capacity to convey, and that the breach has occurred since such conveyance.(*a*)

When the *defendant is sued as assignee of the original covenantor*, and the issue is on the assignment, the plaintiff may either prove an actual assignment, or give evidence of such facts from which it may be inferred; for example, possession of the premises leased, or payment of rent to the plaintiff. In his defence the defendant may show he holds as under tenant, and not as assignee; or that he is an assignee of only a part of the premises; or, if the state of pleadings admit it, he may show, that before the breach, he had assigned to another person; for after the assignee of the original covenantor has himself assigned to another, he is no longer liable for any breaches that may occur.

§ 5.—Of the judgment in covenant.

3453. When the judgment is for the plaintiff, it is that he recover a named sum for his damages, which he has sustained by reason of the breach or breaches of covenant, with full costs of suit.

The judgment for the defendant is, that he recover his costs by him in this behalf expended.

SECTION 4.—OF THE ACTION OF DEBT.

3454. The fourth kind of action arising *ex contractu*,

(*a*) Chase *v.* Weston, 12 N. H. Rep. 413 ; Roach *v.* Wadham, 6 East, 289 ; Milnes *v.* Branch, 5 M. & S. 411. See, as to what are covenants *real*, 2 Greenl. Ev. § 240.

OF DIFFERENT FORMS OF ACTIONS. 627

No 3455.   Book 4, tit 9, chap. 1, sec. 4, § 1.   No. 3456.

is the action of debt, so called because in legal consideration it is for the recovery of a debt *eo nomine* and *in numero;* and though damages are generally awarded for the detention of the debt, yet in most instances they are merely nominal, and are not, as in *assumpsit* and covenant, the principal object of the suit. The subject will be considered with reference to, 1, the kind of claim or obligation on which this action may be maintained; 2, the form of the declaration; 3, the plea; 4, the evidence; 5, the judgment.

§ 1.—Of the claim or obligation on which debt may be maintained.

3455. Debt lies for a *sum of money certain,* due by the defendant to the plaintiff; whether it have been rendered certain by contract between the parties, or by judgment, or by statute, as when a remedy is given for a penalty, or for the escape of a judgment debtor. Debts or obligations for which this action may be sustained at common law, may be classed under four general heads; 1, judgments obtained in a court of record on a suit; 2, specialties acknowledged to be entered of record as a recognizance; 3, specialties indented or not indented; 4, contracts without specialty, either express or implied.(*a*)

3456.—1. This action lies upon the *judgment* of a superior or inferior court of record, whether such judgment be rendered within the state, in a sister state, or a foreign country ;(*b*) but in such case the defendant must have had notice and an opportunity of defending himself.(*c*) In Alabama, it was held that debt might be maintained on a judgment, valid in the state where rendered, though not founded on personal service.(*d*)

(*a*) Respublica *v.* Lacaze, 2 Dall. 123 ; S. C. 1 Yeates, 70.
(*b*) McIntire *v.* Caruth, 1 Const. Rep. 457 ; Headly *v.* Roby, 6 Ham.
527 ; Carter *v.* Crews, 2 Porter, 81 ; Jordan *v.* Robinson, 3 Shep. 167.
(*c*) Darrach *v.* Wilson, 2 Miles, 116 ; Kilburn *v.* Woodworth, 5 John. 37.
(*d*) Hunt *v.* Mayfield, 2 Stew. 124.

At common law, debt was the only remedy, after a year and a day had elapsed after a judgment had been rendered, though a *scire facias* is now sustainable. Debt cannot be maintained after the judgment has been satisfied, either by an actual payment, or by construction of law; where, therefore, the defendant has been taken in execution on a judgment, and discharged by the plaintiff, no action can be supported on the judgment.(*a*)

In some of the states, debt may be maintained on the *decree* of a court of equity in another state, for the payment of money;(*b*) but in other states, the general doctrine is, that an action of debt cannot be sustained on a decree of a court of chancery.(*c*)

3457.—2. Debt lies also on a *specialty acknowledged to be entered of record;* as, upon a recognizance of bail, on a recognizance to the commonwealth, and on recognizance to a state in a criminal proceeding.(*d*)

3458.—3. Debt may be maintained on *specialties*, whether indented or not, or any contract under seal, to recover money due on the same; as, on single bonds, on charter parties, on policies of insurance under seal, and on bonds conditioned for the payment of money, or for the performance of any other act, by or against the parties to such specialties, and their personal representatives.(*e*)

3459.—4. Debt lies upon *contracts without specialty*, either express or implied; it is a more extensive remedy, for the recovery of money, than *assumpsit* or

---

(*a*) Vigers *v.* Aldrich, 4 Burr. 2482 ; Tanner *v.* Hague, 7 T. R. 420; Ponoher *v.* Holley, 3 Wend. 184.

(*b*) Evans *v.* Tatem, 9 S. & R. 252 ; McKim *v* Odom, 3 Fairf. 94 ; Williams *v.* Preston, 3 J. J. Marsh. 600 ; Drakely *v.* Rook, 2 Root, 138 ; Green *v.* Folley, 2 Stew. & Port. 441 ; Thrall *v.* Waller, 13 Verm. 231.

(*c*) Elliott *v.* Ray, 2 Blackf. 31 ; Van Buskirk *v.* Mulock, 3 Har. 184.

(*d*) State *v.* Folsom, 26 Maine, (13 Shepl.) 209 ; Commonwealth *v.* Green, 12 Mass. 1.

(*e*) Com. Dig. Dett, A 4.

covenant, for it lies to recover money due on legal liabilities, as for money lent, paid, had and received, or due on an account stated;(a) for work or labor, or for the price of goods, and a *quantum valebant* thereon;(b) or upon simple contracts, express or implied, whether verbal or written, whenever the demand for a sum is certain, or it is capable of being reduced to a certainty.(c)

3460.—5. This action is the *peculiar* remedy in some cases; as against a devisee of land for a breach of the covenant by the devisor.(d) It may also be sustained against a lessee for an apportionment of rent, where he has been evicted from a part of the premises by a third person; though, in such case, covenant may be maintained against the assignee of the lessee.(e)

3461.—6. On *statutes*, either at the suit of a common informer, or of the party grieved, debt is frequently the proper remedy. In some cases, it is given to the party by the express words of a statute, as for an escape out of execution.(f) When a penal statute expressly gives the whole or a part of the penalty to a common informer, and enables him to sue for the

---

(a) Com. Dig. Dett, A.

(b) Com. Dig. Dett, B; United States v. Colt. 1 Pet. C. C. 149.   •

(c) Bull. N. P. 167. When the obligation is to pay in something else than money, the decisions do not appear to be uniform, whether debt can or cannot be maintained. In Kentucky, debt does not lie on an obligation "for eighty dollars, to be discharged in bricks." Mattox v. Craig, 2 Bibb, 584. In Alabama, debt lies on a specialty for a sum certain, with privilege to the obligor to discharge the same "in cotton." Bradford v. Stewart, Minor, 44. It will lie on a note payable in "Louisiana funds," Hudspeth v Gray, 5 Pike, 157; or "in Philadelphia funds," January v. Henry, 2 Monr. 58; S. C. 3 Monr. 8; or "in North Carolina bank notes," Deberry v. Darnell, 5 Yerg. 451; or "in current bank notes," Young v. Scott, 5 Ala. 475; Wilson v. Hickson, 1 Blackf. 230; Osborn v. Fulton, 1 Blackf. 234; Scott v. Conover, 1 Halst. 222; Campbell v. Weister, 1 Litt. 30; Watson v. McNairy, 1 Bibb, 356. But see Wilburn v. Grier, 1 Engl. 255.

(d) Wilson v. Knubley, 7 East, 12.

(e) Stevenson v. Lambard, 2 East, 579.

(f) Porter v. Sayward, 7 Mass. 337.

same, debt may be sustained;(*a*) and he need not declare *qui tam* unless where a penalty is given for a contempt.(*b*)

3462.—7. Debt also lies in the *detinet* for goods, between the contracting parties; this action is instituted for the recovery of goods, as a horse, a ship, and the like; the writ must be in the *detinet*, for it cannot be said that a man owes a horse or a ship, but only that he detains them from the plaintiff.(*c*) This action differs from detinue, because it is not essential in this action, as in detinue, that the property in any specific goods should be vested in the plaintiff, at the time of the action brought;(*d*) and debts in the *debet* and *detinet* may be maintained on an instrument by which the defendant is bound to pay a sum of money lent, which might have been discharged, on or before the day of payment, in articles of merchandise.(*e*) The action must be in the *detinet*, when it is brought by or against an executor or administrator, for there is no duty owing by or to them; when they are plaintiffs, the debt is detained from them, when defendants, they detain, but do not owe the debt;(*f*) but it is said, where the heir is sued on a bond of the ancestor, by which he is bound, he should be charged in the *debet* and *detinet*.(*g*)

3463.—8. To maintain an action of debt, the demand must be for a sum certain, or for a pecuniary claim which may be readily reduced to a certainty. But it cannot be sustained on an agreement to pay money by instalment, before all the instalments are

(*a*) Com. Dig. Dett, E 1 and 2; Cato *v.* Gill, Coxe, 11; Crane *v.* ——, Coxe, 53.
(*b*) 2 Saund. 374, n. 1 and 2; 1 Saund. 136, n. 1.
(*c*) 3 Bl. Com. 153; 11 Vin. Ab. 321; Bac. Ab. Debt, F; 1 Lilly's Reg. 543; Dane's Ab. h. t.; Thompson *v.* Musser, 1 Dall. 458.
(*d*) Dy. 24, b.
(*e*) Young *v.* Hawkins, 4 Yerg. 171; Com. Dig. Dett, A 5; Bac. Ab. Debt, F. See Taylor *v.* Meek, 4 Blackf. 388.
(*f*) Bac. Ab. Debt, F.
(*g*) Waller *v.* Ellis, 2 Munf. 88.

due, unless when the debt is secured by a penalty ;(a)
if, however, there are separate debts due by the same
agreement, an action of debt will lie for the non-
payment of either of them ; and it also lies for the
annual interest of money payable on a bond, when the
principal is not due.(b)

§ 2.—Of the declaration in debt.

3464. The declaration is to be framed on different
principles, as it is on a simple contract, or on a specialty, or record.   When on a *simple contract*, it must
show the consideration on which the contract was
founded, precisely as in assumpsit ; and should state
either a legal liability, or an express agreement,(c)
though not a *promise* to pay the debt,(d) the words
agreed to pay should be used.(e)

When the action is founded on a *specialty* or *record*,
no consideration need be shown, unless the performance of the consideration constitutes a condition precedent, when the performance must be averred.(f)

When the action is founded on a *deed*, it must be
declared upon, except in the case of debt for rent.(g)
In debt for rent, due by indenture, the action is founded
on the fact of the occupation of the premises, and the
pernancy of the profits, the lease being alleged only by
way of inducement.

3465. The *breach*, or cause of action complained of,
must proceed only for the non-payment of money previously alleged to be payable ; and such breach is
nearly similar, whether the action in debt be on simple

(a) Fontaine v. Aresta, 2 McLean, 127 ; Rudder v. Price, 1 H. Bl. 554 ;
2 Saund. 303, n. 6.
(b) Sparks v. Garrigues, 1 Binn. 152.
(c) Tompkins v. Corwin, 9 Cowen, 255.
(d) Emery v. Fell, 2 T. R. 28, 30.
(e) Metcalf v. Robinson, 2 McLean, 363.
(f) Whitney v. Spencer, 4 Cowen, 39.
(g) Atty v. Parrish, 1 New R. 104.

contract, specialty, record or statute. It must be obviously governed by the nature of the stipulation. It ought to be assigned in the words of the contract either negatively or affirmatively, or words which are coëxtensive with its import and effect.(a) When the contract is in the disjunctive, as on a promise to deliver a horse on a particular day, or to pay a sum of money, the breach ought to be assigned that the defendant did not do the one nor the other.(b)　'

3466. *Damages* should also be laid in the declaration; as in this action they are merely nominal, and not, as in *assumpsit* or covenant, the principal object of the suit, they are generally laid in a small sum, as one hundred dollars; and in actions by a common informer, as he is not entitled to damages, none should be inserted.(c)

§ 3.—Of the pleas in debt.

3467. The general issue to debt on simple contract, or on statutes, or where the deed is only matter of inducement, is *nihil debet*;(d) in debt for rent by the lessor against the assignee of the lessee, this plea of *nihil debet* puts in issue the whole declaration.(e) *Nihil debet* is not a good plea to an action of debt founded on a specialty;(f) nor is such plea valid to an action of debt founded on a recognizance of bail;(g) nor on a judgment of a court of record, whose records import absolute verity;(h) nor on a foreign judgment;(i) nor to an action of debt on a decree of a

(a) Com. Dig. Pleader, C 45 to 49.
(b) 1 Sid. 440.
(c) Frederic v. Lookup, 4 Burr, 2021.
(d) 1 Stilson v. Toby, 2 Mass. 521; Burnham v. Webster, 5 Mass. 266; Bullis v. Giddens, 8 John. 82.
(e) Darthmouth College v. Clough, 8 N. H. Rep. 22.
(f) Boynton v. Reynolds, 3 Mis. 79.
(g) Bullis v. Giddens, 8 John. 82; Niblo v. Clark, 3 Wend. 24.
(h) Wheaton v. Fellows, 23 Wend. 375.
(i) Mills v. Duryee, 7 Cranch, 481; Cu.tis v. Gibbs, 1 Pen. 399; Chips v. Yancey, Breese, 2; Clark v. Day, 2 Leigh, 172; St. Albans v. Bush, 4

court of equity of a sister state; nor can *nul tiel record* be pleaded to such suit, because a decree of a court of chancery is not a record; and when the defendant means to deny the existence of such a decree, he must frame a plea to meet the averment of the decree in the declaration, and such plea must conclude to the country.(*a*)   .

To an action of debt founded on a record, the proper plea is *nul tiel record;* this denies the existence of the record, and, on its production, judgment is entered for plaintiff, or if it be not produced, for the defendant; for, in this case, the trial is by the court upon inspection.

The plea of *non est factum* is the proper plea to deny the existence of the contract when the action is founded on a specialty.(*b*)

In an action on a bond, containing a condition to pay on a certain day, the defendant may plead payment on the day, *solvit ad diem;* for, in effect, this is a plea of performance of the condition, and payment before a breach of the condition is a good discharge, without an acquittance.

When it is intended to take advantage of the legal presumption of payment of a specialty, after a lapse of twenty years, the defendant ought to plead *solvit post diem*, that he paid the debt after it became due. This is necessary, because if the plea be *solvit ad diem*, and it should appear that any interest was paid after the money became due, such subsequent payment would raise the strongest presumption that the debt was not paid on the day appointed. For the bond might be so old that the last payment was made more

Verm. 58; Larming *v.* Shute, 2 South, 778; Jacquette *v.* Hugunon, 2 McLean, 129. In Kentucky, on the contrary, it has been held that *nihil debet* may be pleaded to a foreign judgment. Williams *v.* Preston, 3 J. J. Marsh. 600.

(*a*) Evans *v.* Tatem, 9 S. & R. 252.
(*b*) Warren *v.* Consett, 2 Ld. Raym. 1500; Russell *v.* Hamilton, 2 Scam. 56.

than twenty years before, and the debt would be presumed to have been discharged since that time; still the plea would be falsified by proving that interest had been paid after the day appointed.(a)

Most other matters, which afford a defence to an action of debt, must be pleaded specially.

§ 4.—Of the evidence in an action of debt.

3468. As a general rule, when the defendant has pleaded *nihil debet* to an action of debt on a simple contract, or for an escape, or for a penalty given by statute, the plaintiff is required to prove every material fact alleged in his declaration, for this plea traverses the plaintiff's right to recover; and under it the defendant may give in evidence any matter tending to deny the existence of any debt, such as a release, satisfaction, delivery of goods, and the like, for the plea alleges that the defendant does not owe any thing to the plaintiff. But the statute of limitations cannot be given in evidence under the plea of *nihil debet;* it must be specially pleaded, in order that the plaintiff may reply such matters as may avoid the operation of the statute, or take the case out of its provisions. If, when the action is founded on a specialty, the defendant plead *nihil debet*, and the plaintiff instead of demurring take issue upon that plea, he will be obliged to prove the whole of his case, and admit the opposite party into a general defence.(b)

3469. Under a plea of *nul tiel record*, the only question at issue is the existence of the record;(c) but if the action be founded on a judgment rendered in another state, and the defendant has pleaded that he had no notice of the proceedings, he may show that fact, and in that case, the plaintiff may reply that the

---

(a) Moreland *v.* Bennett, 1 Str. 652; Bull. N. P. 174.
(b) Rawlins *v.* Danvers, 5 Esp. N. P. Cas. 39.
(c) Bennett *v.* Morley, 10 Ohio, 100.

defendant appeared and took defence, and this, if true, will be a complete answer to his plea.(a)

3470. The plea of *non est factum* only puts in issue the making of the deed; under this plea to an action on a bond, the defendant cannot give in evidence any thing arising under the condition of the bond.(b) When the action is brought against one obligor alone, who pleads *non est factum*, the plaintiff may maintain his action, although, on the production of the bond, there appears to be a joint obligor;(c) but if the action is against the obligor alone, as jointly and *severally* bound, the plaintiff cannot, under this plea, give in evidence a joint, and not a several bond of the defendant and the other person mentioned, though it agrees in date and amount with the bond described in the declaration,(d) for in this case the variance is fatal.(e)

3471. If the defendant rely on the lapse of time under the plea of *solvit ad diem*, or *solvit post diem*, and it appear that twenty years have elapsed since the money was due, unless a payment of interest, or part of the principal, after the plea of *solvit ad diem* as already explained, it will be a presumption of payment so as to entitle the defendant to a verdict; indeed a less period of time will have the same effect, if there are corroborating circumstances to raise such presumption.(f) But this presumption is very easily rebutted, by showing that interest has been regularly paid;(g) that the obligor has admitted the debt has not been paid,(h) or other circumstances to induce a belief that the money is still due; but the proof of

---

(a) Wright v. Weisinger, 5 Sm. & Marsh. 210.
(b) Rice v. Thompson, 2 Bailey, 339.
(c) Whelpdale's case, 5 Co. 119; Cabell v. Vaughan, 1 Saund. 291.
(d) The Postmaster General v. Ridgway, Gilp. 135.
(e) See Bean v. Parker, 17 Mass. 605; Rockefeller v. Hoysradt, 2 Hill, 616; Bayden v. Hastings, 17 Pick. 200.
(f) 2 Phil. Ev. 171; 2 Greenl. Ev. § 290; Bouv. L. D. tit. Twenty years.
(g) 1 Bailey, 148.
(h) 2 Harring. 124.

facts which show that the obligor was poor, and not likely to be able to pay the debt, is not sufficient.(a)

3472. As the law presumes every man innocent, until his guilt has been proved according to its requirements, in debt on a *penal statute* for a criminal omission of duty, whether official or otherwise, the plaintiff is required to prove his allegation, although negative in its character. But if the charge is, that the defendant did an act without being licensed, or authorized, the burden of proof lies on the defendant, because such matter lies particularly within his own knowledge.(b) The defendant in such action may, under the general issue, show any proviso in the penal statute, exempting him from the penalty; and he may avail himself of such proviso whether contained in that or any other statute.(c) Under this issue, he may also take advantage of any variance between the allegation and the proof on the part of the plaintiff; and where proof of a contract is essential in a penal action, the same proof is required as in an action on a contract.(d)

3473. When the plaintiff sues in debt *for an escape*, he must prove the judgment by a copy of the record; the delivery of the writ of execution to the officer; the arrest of the debtor; and the escape. The process may be proved by its production, or when it has been returned, by a certified or examined copy. The return to the writ is conclusive on the defendant, when made by him. When the process has not been returned, notice should be given to the defendant to produce it, and on his failure to do so, secondary evidence of it may be given.(e) The escape, if voluntary, may be

(a) 5 Verm. 236.
(b) 1 Greenl. Ev. § 79.
(c) Rex v. Inhabitants of St. George, 3 Campb. 222; 2 Greenl. Ev. § 285; 1 Phil. Ev. 318; 2 Phil. Ev. 165.
(d) Parrish v. Burwood, 5 Esp. 33; Everett v. Tindall, 5 Esp. 169; Partridge v. Coates, 1 Ry. & Mo. 153; S. C. 1 Car. & P. 534.
(e) 2 Phil. Ev. 377; 2 Greenl. Ev. § 288.

proved by the party escaping; the reason assigned for his admission is, that an escape is a thing of secrecy, a private transaction between the prisoner and the jailer; but on general principles, he appears to be competent, for he neither loses nor gains by the event of the immediate suit.(a)

3474. The plaintiff is of course required to prove the *breaches* assigned in his declaration.

§ 5.—Of the judgment in debt.

3475. The judgment in debt, when in favor of the plaintiff, is final at common law.(b)   It is in all cases that the plaintiff *recover his debt*, and, in general, nominal damages for the detention thereof; but when a judgment in debt is entered for a special sum, it will not be reversed because the word "debt" is omitted.(c)   When it appears that the judgment is not entered for a debt, but for damages, this is evidently an error, because it is for a thing which was not the object of the suit;(d) if, however, the judgment in debt be entered for an aggregate sum, equal to the debt and damages, the court will not set it aside upon that ground.(e)

In cases under the statute 8 and 9 W. III., c. 11, the judgment for the plaintiff is, that the plaintiff have execution for the damages sustained by the breach of a bond conditioned for the performance of covenants.

In general, judgment for the plaintiff is given for costs, except in some penal and other particular actions.

(a) 2 Phil. Ex. 398, 399; Hunter v. King, 4 B. & A. 210.
(b) 1 Chit. Pl. 108; Williams v. McFall, 2 S. & R. 280.   But it is said judgment in debt is not always final, for when it is for use and occupation, or for foreign money, or on a penal bond, an inquisition is necessary to ascertain the rent, or to fix the amount of damages at the impetration of the writ.   O'Neal v. O'Neal, 4 W. & S. 130.
(c) Tindall v. Tindall, 3 Har. 437.
(d) Guild v. Johnson, 1 Scam. 405; Heyl v. Stapp, 3 Scam. 95.
(e) Sandford v. Richardson, 1 Ala. 182.

When the judgment is for the defendant, it is that he recovers the costs.

SECTION 5.—OF THE ACTION OF DETINUE.

3476. The fifth form of action *ex contractu*, which will now be the subject of consideration, is that of detinue; it is but seldom used, having been superseded by other actions. Though this action is commonly classed among actions arising upon contract, because it is an action for the recovery of a personal chattel in specie, which has been delivered to the defendant, and is unlawfully detained by him; yet it might be classed with actions not arising on contracts, because it may be brought to recover a chattel, which the defendant has found, and unlawfully detains. This action may be considered with reference to, 1, the thing to be recovered; 2, the plaintiff's interest in it; 3, the injury; 4, the pleadings; 5, the evidence; 6, the judgment.

§ 1.—Of the things to be recovered in detinue.

3477. This action lies to recover specific chattels, known and distinguished from all others, and their identity must be ascertainable by some certain means; thus it lies for a particular horse or cow, or money in a bag, which may be identified; but it cannot be brought for a sum of money or corn, not identified, nor distinguishable from other corn, or money.(*a*) To entitle him to recover, the plaintiff must have a property in the chattel which is the object of the suit.

§ 2.—Of the plaintiff's interest in the thing to be recovered in detinue.

3478. An absolute or general property in the goods, and a right to immediate possession, will entitle a plaintiff to recover, although he never had the posses-

---

(*a*) 3 Bl. Com. 152.

sion.(a) But if the plaintiff have not the right to
immediate possession of the goods, and his interest be
in reversion, he cannot support detinue ;(b) the remainder man may, however, maintain detinue for goods
or slaves, after the decease of one having a life estate
in them, against the defendant, who held them in possession under a claim of title, without a demand.(c)
A person who has only a special property, as bailee,
and the like, may support this action, when he delivered the goods to the defendant, or they were taken
out of the custody of such bailee.(d)   It will lie also
in favor of trustees.(e)   As this action is to recover
the chattel sued for, it follows that the plaintiff must
be entitled to it, for if he have a right to only a part
of it, he cannot maintain this action.(f)

§ 3.—For what injury detinue will lie.

3479. The gist of this action is the wrongful detainer, and not the original unlawful taking.(g)   It
lies also against any person who has the actual
possession of the chattel, and who has acquired it by
lawful means, as either by bailment, delivery or finding;(h) and if the defendant had possession, but parted
with it before the suing out of the writ, he is still
liable,(i) although he has restored the possession to
the owner before the suit.(j)   Though it has been

(a) McDonnell v. Hall, 2 Bibb. 610; Haynes v. Crutchfield, 7 Ala. 189;
Berry v. Hale, 1 How, Miss. 315 ; Lynch v. Thomas, 3 Leigh, 682 ; 2 Saund.
47 a, n.
(b) Harper v. Gordon, 7 T. R. 9.
(c) Miles v. Allen, 6 Ired. 88.
(d) Bro. Ab. Detinue ; 2 Saund. 47, b, c, d ; Ramsay v. Bancroft, 2 Mis.
151 ; Boyle v. Townes, 9 Leigh, 158.
(e) Murphy v. Moore, 4 Ired. 118 ; Stoker v. Yerby, 11 Ala. 322.
(f) Bell v. Hogan, 1 Stew. 536 ; Miller v. Eatman, 11 Ala. 609.
(g) Charles v. Elliot, 4 Dev. & Bat. 468 ; Melton v. McDonald, 2 Mis. 45.
(h) 3 Bl Com. 152; Bac. Ab. Detinue, A ; Kettle v. Bromsall, Willes,
118.
(i) Pool v. Adkisson, 1 Dana, 110 ; Haley v. Rowan, 5 Yerg. 301 ; Ker-
shaw v. Baykin, 1 Brev. 301.
(j) Merritt v. Warmouth, 1 Hayw. 12 ; Merrit v. Merrit, Martin, 18.

the general opinion that detinue would not lie, where
there was a tortious taking, upon the fallacious ground
that, by the trespass, the title of the plaintiff was
divested,(a) it has been held that such taking does not
divest the title of the plaintiff, and that detinue lies
whether the property came into the possession of the
defendant rightfully or wrongfully;(b) in such case,
the plaintiff may waive the tortious taking, and maintain this action.(c)

Detinue cannot be supported against a person who
never had possession of the goods; as on a bailment to
a testator, where the executor never possessed the
goods, detinue will not lie against the latter;(d) nor
can it be maintained against a bailee, if, before the
demand, he lose them by accident.(e)

§ 4.—Of the pleadings in detinue.

3480.—1. As the identical goods are to be recovered
in specie, more certainty is requisite in the *declaration*,
in the description of the chattels, than in an action of
trover or replevin.(f) It is sufficient to declare in
detinue for a negro woman by name, without describing her complexion, her age, and the like; or for a
cow, without describing her color; or for a certain
number of knives and forks, without any particular
description;(g) and it is not necessary to state the
date of the deed.(h)

When the action is brought for several articles, the
value of each need not be stated separately in the
declaration, though the jury in their finding ought to
sever the value of each by their verdict.

(a) 1 Chit. Pl. 119.
(b) Pierce v. Hill, 9 Port. 151 ; Oakfield v. Bullitt, 1 Mis. 749.
(c) Owings v. Frier, 2 A. K. Marsh. 268.
(d) Isaack v. Clark, 2 Bulstr. 308.
(e) Bro. Detinue, pl. 1, 33, 40.
(f) 2 Saund. 74, a, b ; Co. Litt. 286.
(g) Haynes v. Crutchfield, 7 Ala. 189.
(h) Alcorn v. Westbrook, 1 Wils. 116.

In the case of a special bailment, it is proper to declare, at least in one count, on the bailment, and to lay a special request;(a) in other cases it is sufficient to declare upon the supposed finding, for this allegation is not traversable.(b)

The declaration must always contain an averment that the property belongs to the plaintiff.(c)

3481.—2. The *plea* of *non detinet* is the general issue. But special pleas may be pleaded; a defendant was allowed to plead, *puis darrein continuance,* the death of the slave, who was the object of the action;(d) and if goods were pawned to the defendant, he must plead this matter specially, that the goods were pawned to him for money remaining unpaid.

§ 5.—Of the evidence in detinue.

3482. To entitle himself to a verdict, the plaintiff must prove, 1, that he has a property in the goods;(e) 2, that the defendant had the possession of them; 3, that the goods were of some value; and 4, that they are the same claimed in point of identity.(f)

When the plaintiff seeks to recover damages for the detention previous to the suit, he must prove a demand before bringing his action;(g) but a demand is not necessary where the defendant had the possession, and claimed title to it before bringing suit.(h)

Under the general issue, the defendant may give in evidence a gift from the plaintiff, or any other evi-

---

(a) Kettle v. Bromsall, Willes, 120.
(b) Mills v. Graham, 1 New Rep. 140; Mortimer v. Brumfield, 3 Munf. 122; Irwin v. Wells, 1 Mis. 9; Anon. 2 Hayw. 136; Tunstal v. McClelland, 1 Bibb, 186; Cole v. Cole, 4 Bibb, 340: Jones v. Henry, 3 Litt. 46; Dunn v. Davis, 12 Ala. 135.
(c) Kent v. Armistead, 4 Mumf. 72; Price v. Israel, 3 Bibb, 516.
(d) Bethea v. McLennon, 1 Ired. 523.
(e) Barnley v. Lambert, 1 Wash. 308.
(f) 3 Bl. Com. 152; Felt v. Williams, 1 Scam. 206.
(g) Vaughn v. Wood, 5 Ala. 304; Brock v. Headen, 13 Ala. 370.
(h) Jones v. Green, 4 Dev. & Bat. 354.

dence which proves that the defendant does not detain the plaintiff's goods ;(*a*) and the statute of limitations need not be specially pleaded ; evidence to sustain the plea of the act of limitations, it seems, may be given under the plea of *non detinet*.(*b*)

§ 6.—Of the verdict and judgment in detinue.

3483.—1. The *verdict* and judgment in this action must be such, that a specific remedy may be had for the recovery of the goods detained, or a satisfaction in value for each parcel, in case they, or either of them, cannot be returned ; when, therefore, the action is for several chattels, the jury ought in their verdict to assess the value of each separately ;(*c*) but where there are two kinds of property, each composed of several individuals, each kind may be assessed in a gross sum; as where the action was for a cow and calf, and also for fourteen hogs, and the jury assessed the cow and calf at a gross sum, and the fourteen hogs at another, this was held not to be error.(*d*) If the jury neglect to find the value, the omission cannot be supplied by a writ of inquiry.(*e*)

3484.—2. The judgment is in the alternative that the plaintiff do recover the goods, or the value thereof, if he cannot have the goods themselves, and his damages for the detention, and full costs of suit.(*f*)

(*a*) Turner *v.* Allison, 3 Dana, 422; Smith *v.* Towne, 4 Munf. 191; Stratton *v.* Minnis, 2 Munf. 329 ; Dazier *v.* Joyce, 8 Port. 303; McCurry *v.* Hooper, 12 Ala. 823.   See Brown *v.* Brown, 13 Ala. 208.

(*b*) Morrow *v.* Hatfield, 6 Humph. 108 ; Elam *v.* Bass, 4 Munf. 301.

(*c*) Smith *v.* Wiggins, 3 Stew. 221 ; Cummings *v.* Tindall, 4 Stew. & Port. 357 ; Carraway *v.* Niece, Walker, 538 ; Haynes *v.* Crutchfield, 7 Ala. 189 ; Baker *v.* Beasly, 4 Yerg. 570 ; Buckner *v.* Higgin, 3 Monr. 59 ; Mulliken *v.* Greer, 5 Mis. 489 ; Thomas *v.* Tanner, 6 Monr. 52.

(*d*) Haynes *v.* Crutchfield, 7 Ala. 189.

(*e*) Cheney's case, 10 Co. 119 b.   See Bell *v.* Pharr. 7 Ala. 807.

(*f*) Brown *v.* Brown, 5 Ala. 508.

CHAPTER II.—OF ACTIONS ARISING EX DELICTO.

3485. Having fully considered the remedies which the law affords, in courts of law, on contracts, the next object of our inquiries will be the nature and kinds of actions which have been provided to redress wrongs and injuries, independent of contract. The actions which fall under this class are, 1, case; 2, trover; 3, replevin; 4, trespass.

SECTION 1.—OF THE ACTION ON THE CASE.

3486. An action on the case, or, more technically, an action of *trespass upon the case*, lies where a party sues for *damages*, for any wrong or cause of complaint, to which neither covenant nor trespass will apply.(a) In its most comprehensive signification, *case* includes *assumpsit* as well as an action in form *ex delicto;* but when simply mentioned, it is usually understood to mean an action in form *ex delicto*.

This action originated as follows: At the most remote periods of the English law, as far as we have any accounts, specific forms of action where used; these forms were compiled into a book styled *The Register of Writs, or Registrum Brevium*. In this book is to be found a form in which to express every injury remediable by writ of *trespass*, properly so called, and in which writ the words *vi et armis et contra pacem* were universally inserted. These *formulæ*, framed with wisdom and matured by experience, were considered as immutable unless by authority of parliament.(b) They were resorted to upon all occasions, and one or another was adopted suitable to the claim or demand of the plaintiff; the courts, with a jealous care, would not allow any alteration to be made in these forms.

(a) Steph. Pl. 15; Ham. N. P. 1; 3 Wooddes, 167; Griffin v. Farwell, 20 Verm. (5 Washb.) 151.
(b) Bract, lib. 5, c. 17, s. 2.

These writs, thus gathered together, were termed *brevia formata.* They where adapted to those causes of complaint that most frequently occurred.

In process of time, when other grievances arose, or existing evils, which till then had been overlooked or endured, became so intolerable as to require a remedy to reform them, the sufferers made application at the chancery for an original on which to ground their suit. The clerks not feeling themselves authorized to grant new writs, which indeed would have exceeded their authority, refused to grant them, and the legislature was required to interfere.

To remedy this evil, the twenty-fourth chapter of the statute of Westminster the second, was passed It provides that " whensoever from thenceforth in one case a writ shall be found in chancery, and in a like case falling under the same right, and requiring a like remedy, no precedent of a writ can be produced, the clerks in chancery shall agree in forming a new one, and if they cannot agree, it shall be adjourned to the next parliament, when a writ shall be framed by consent of the learned in the law, lest it should happen for the future, that the court of our lord the king, be deficient in doing justice to the suitors."

These provisions have been characterized as only declaratory of the common law, whose perfection could not endure the reproach that an evil should exist without a corresponding remedy. The very passage of the act, however, proves that just as the position may be in theory, in practice it was not then admitted.(*a*)

(*a*) Blackstone, the learned commentator of the English law, and the willing apologist of all its impeifections, in speaking of this statute, says, " So that the wise and equitable provision of the statute of Westm. 2, 13 Ed. I., c. 24, for framing new writs when wanted, is almost rendered useless by the very great perfection of the ancient forms. And, indeed, I know not whether it is a greater credit to our laws, to have such a provision contained in them, or not to have occasion, or at least very rarely, to use it." 3 Com. 184.

This action, then, originates in the power given by the statute of Westminister 2, to the clerks of chancery, to frame new writs in *consimili casu* with writs already known. Under this power they constructed many writs for different injuries, which were considered in *consimili casu* with, that is, to bear a strong analogy to *trespass*. The new writs invented for cases supposed to bear such analogy have accordingly received the appellation of writs of *trespass on the case*, (*brevia de transgressione super casum*,) as being founded on the particular circumstances of the case, thus requiring a remedy, and to distinguish them from the old writ of trespass; and the injuries themselves, which are the subject of such writs, are not called trespasses, but bear the general names of torts, wrongs or grievances.

Whether it was the intention of the framers of the statute of Westminister second, to give to new writs which might be framed under its provisions the same effect of the old writs, and they were to be placed on the same footing with the *brevia formata*, and like them serve as precedents in all future occasions; or whether they were to be revised, and cast anew into other moulds, which further experience might evince to be more convenient, is perhaps doubtful; certain it is that the latter doctrine prevailed.(*a*)

The writs of trespass on the case, though invented thus, *pro re nata*, in various forms, according to the nature of the different wrongs which respectively called them forth, began, nevertheless, to be viewed as constituting collectively, a new individual form of action; and this new genus took its place, by the name of *trespass on the case*, among the more ancient actions of debt, covenant, replevin, trespass, etc.

3487. The action of trespass on the case differs from the action of trespass *vi et armis*, and though the

(*a*) Littlet. R. 341.

distinction is somewhat subtle, still it is clear and well defined.(*a*) The criterion to distinguish the one from the other, is this: Trespass *vi et armis* lies for an injury committed *with force*, and by the *immediate* act of the defendant, directly applied, or *vis proxima*. The action of trespass on the case lies when the injury arises from *the remote consequences* of an act, and is not the effect of immediate force.

When the proximate cause of the injury is but a continuation of the original force, or *vis impressa*, the effect is immediate, and the appropriate remedy is an action of trespass *vi et armis;* but when the original force, or *vis impressa*, had ceased to act before the injury commenced, then there is no force, and the effect is mediate, and the proper remedy is trespass on the case. Thus, if the defendant threw a log in the street, and it fell on the plaintiff, and broke his arm, trespass would be the proper remedy; if, on the contrary, the plaintiff did not pass in the street till after night, and the log which had thus been thrown there still remained, and the plaintiff stumbled over it, and broke his arm, the remedy would be trespass on the case. In the first case the injury was committed with force, and by the immediate and direct act of the defendant; in the last, no force was used, and the injury was not immediate but consequential.(*b*)

The *intent* of the wrong doer is not material, and does not affect the form of the action; for example, the act of sending up a balloon is legal, yet, if in alighting, the areonaut should injure the plaintiff's

---

(*a*) The distinction between trespass and case has been abolished in some of the states. This is the case in Maine, Welch *v.* Whittemore, 25 Maine, R. (12 Shep.) 86.

(*b*) Legaux *v.* Feasor, 1 Yeates, 586 ; Cotteral *v.* Cummings, 6 S. & R. 348 ; Berry *v.* Hamil, 12 S. & R. 210 ; Spencer *v.* Campbell, 9 W. & S. 32 : Cole *v.* Fisher, 11 Mass. 137 ; Waldron *v.* Hopper, Coxe, 339 ; Carsten *v.* Murray, Harper, 113 ; Clay *v.* Sweet, 1 Marsh. 194 ; Winslow *v.* Beall, 6 Call, 44; Barnard *v.* Poor, 21 Pick. 378 ; Maull *v.* Wilson, 2 Harring. 443 ; Adams *v.* Hemmenway, 1 Mass. 145.

garden, trespass *vi et armis* would be the proper remedy.(*a*)

Having given this short account of the origin and nature of the action of trespass on the case, our next inquiry will be to ascertain, 1, in what cases this action lies; 2, the form and nature of the pleadings; 3, what evidence may be given by the parties; 4, the nature of the judgment.

§ 1.—When an action on the case lies.

3488. Such action may be maintained for injuries, 1, to the absolute rights of persons; 2, the relative rights of persons; 3, personal property; 4, real property; 5, on penal statutes.

Art. 1.—*When case is a remedy for injuries to the absolute rights of persons.*

3489.—1. Case may be maintained for any injury to the absolute rights of persons, when such injury is not direct, immediate and with force, but consequential; thus it lies to recover damages for an injury committed against the plaintiff individually for a nuisance, as in obstruction of a highway or public navigation;(*b*) for an injury done by a mischievous animal, when the owner had notice of his dangerous propensity.(*c*)

3490.—2. When the injury is committed under *color of process*, a distinction must be made between regular and irregular process. By regular process is meant that which is lawfully issued by a court or magistrate, having competent jurisdiction; irregular

---

(*a*) Guille *v.* Swan, 19 John. 381. See, as to intent, Keith *v.* Howard, 24 Pick. 292 ; Gates *v.* Neall, 23 Pick. 308 ; Gates *v.* Miles, 3 Conn. 64 ; Case *v.* Mark, 2 Ham. 169.

(*b*) Marriott *v.* Stanley, 1 Scott, N. R. 392 ; S. C. 1 M. & G. 568 ; Lancaster Canal Co. *v.* Parnaby, 3 P. & D. 162.

(*c*) Bull. N. P. 77 ; Domat, Lois Civ. liv. 2, t. 8, s. 2 ; Civ. Code of Lo. art. 2301 ; Jones *v.* Parry, 2 Esp. C. 482; Sarch *v.* Blackburn, 4 C. & P. 297 ; S. C. M. & M. 505 ; Smith *v.* Pelah, 2 Str. 1264.

648 OF REMEDIES.

No. 3491.   Book 4, tit. 9, chap. 2, sec. 1, § 1, art. 1.   No. 3491.

proceßs is that which has been unlawfully issued, and for which reason, it will be set aside by the court. When the process is *regular*, and the defendant has been damnified, as in the case of a malicious arrest, his remedy against the person who sued it out, and set it in motion, is by an action on the case, and not trespass;(a) but although the officer may be liable when a regular execution is unlawfully executed, the plaintiff is not liable, in an action on the case, for a tort committed by the sheriff in executing the writ, unless he joined in the unlawful act.(b) When it is *irregular and wholly void*, the proper remedy is by an action of trespass, not only against the plaintiff, but against the officer or court under whose authority it was issued; the officer who executed it will, however, be justified, if the court had jurisdiction.(c)

3491.—3. Case is the proper remedy for a vexatious suit, malicious prosecution, or wanton arrest, made by a prosecutor in a criminal proceeding, or a plaintiff in a civil suit, without probable cause, by a regular process or proceeding, which the facts did not warrant, as appears by the result.(d) The suit need not be altogether without foundation; if the part which is groundless has subjected the plaintiff to an inconvenience, to which he would not have been exposed had

---

(a) Swift v. Chamberlain, 3 Conn. 537; Shaw v. Reed, 16 Mass. 450; Shaver v. White, 6 Munf. 113; Kimball v. Molony, 3 N. Hamp. 376; Lovier v. Gilpin, 6 Dana, 321; Warfield v. Walter, 11 Gill & John. 80; Smith v. Story, 4 Humph. 169.

(b) Princeton Bank v. Gilson, 1 Spencer, 138.

(c) Kennedy v. Terrell, Hardin. 490; McCool v. McCluny, 8 Adol. & Ell. 449; 15 East, 615 note (c); Harper, 486; Vail v. Lewis, 4 John. 450; Cooper v. Halbert, 2 McMullan, 419.

(d) Winebiddle v. Porterfield, 9 Penn. St. R. 137. To support case for a malicious prosecution, there must be both malice and want of probable cause. Ray v. Law, 1 Pet. C. C. Rep. 210: McCullough v. Grishobber, 4 Watts & Serg. 201; Munns v. Dupont, 3 Wash. C. C. Rep. 31: Travis v. Smith, 1 Penn. St. Rep. 234; Weinberger v. Shelly, 6 Watts & Serg. 336; Cleek v. Haines, 2 Rand. 440. See Hays v. Younglove, 7 B. Monr. 545; Wilmarth v. Mountford, 4 Wash. C. C. Rep. 79; Kerr v. Workman, Addis. R. 270.

the valid cause of complaint alone been insisted on; for example, if the defendant has been arrested, and bail demanded for a larger amount than was due, if done for the purpose of vexation.(a)   But it must be remembered that no action lies merely for bringing a groundless civil suit, if unattended by the seizure of the person of the party, or of his property, for as to any expense he may be put to, this, in contemplation of law, has been fully compensated to him by the costs adjudged.(b)

3492.—4. This is the appropriate form of action, too, for injuries to the absolute rights of persons, when the right affected was *not tangible*, and consequently would not be affected by force, as reputation and health, the injuries to which are always remedied by action on the case, as libels and verbal slanders.

3493.—5. Case is not confined to injuries merely *ex delicto;* it is a concurrent remedy for many breaches of contract, not simply for the payment of money, whether the breach were nonfeasance, misfeasance, or malfeasance; thus, case lies against surgeons, physicians and apothecaries, for negligence or want of skill, and it is immaterial by whom the defendant was retained;(c) it lies also upon an express agreement for obstructing the plaintiff in the enjoyment of an easement, of which the defendant stipulated that the plaintiff should have the benefit.(d)   It is a proper remedy against bailees for neglect in the care of goods.(e)

3494.—6. It may be maintained against persons who by law are obliged to perform certain duties, and who refuse to fulfil them; as common carriers, who refuse

---

(a) Ray v. Law, 1 Pet. C. C. Rep. 210 ; Herman v. Brookerhoof, 8 Watts, 241.   See Sommer v. Wilt, 4 S. & R. 19.
(b) Murray v. Wilson, 1 Wils. 316 ; Sinclair v. Eldred, 4 Taunt. 7.
(c) Gladwell v. Steggall, 8 Scott, 60.   See 7 C. & P. 81.
(d) Mast v. Goodson, 3 Wils. 348.
(e) Govett v. Radnige, 3 East, 62, 70.

650   OF REMEDIES.

No. 3495   Book 4, tit 9, chap 2, sec 1, § 1, art. 2.   No 3495.

to take a passenger, having room; or an innkeeper, who refuses to receive a guest when he has sufficient accommodations, and the traveller tenders a reasonable reward for the accommodations required.(a) But the guest has no right to select a particular room in the inn, nor capriciously to ask *for unreasonable accommodations.(b)

Art. 2.—When case is a remedy for injuries to the relative rights of persons.

3495. For injuries to the relative rights, the action on the case is the appropriate remedy; when they are not with force, but consequential, this action lies. These rights exist in the husband for injuries done to the wife; the father, for wrongs to the child; the master, for torts committed against the apprentice; and for a guardian, for an offence or injury against his ward, but not *vice versâ*. The wife can maintain no action for an injury to the husband; or the child, the apprentice and the ward, for a wrong committed to the father, the master or the guardian respectively.

The husband may sustain an action on the case for criminal conversation with the wife, though trespass may also be maintained; case is the appropriate remedy for harboring a wife, an apprentice, or a ward.

A parent cannot maintain a suit, in the capacity of parent, for the seduction of his daughter; an action on the case(c) lies against the seducer, though not directly nor ostensibly for the seduction, but for the consequent inability of the daughter to perform those services for which she was accountable to her master, or

(a) Tell *v.* Knight, 8 M. & W. 269; Rex *v.* Jones, 7 C. & P. 213.
(b) 8 M. & W. 269.
(c) In Clough *v.* Tenney, it was held that case was the only remedy for a father, where the injury was done in the house of another. 5 Greenl. 446. When the offence has been committed in the plaintiff's house trespass lies, and the seduction is an aggravation. In Parker *v.* Elliott, 6 Munf. 587, it is said that for the seduction of a wife or daughter, case or trespass may be brought at the choice of the plaintiff. See 4 Hawks, 138, note; Gilmer, 33; Van Vactor *v.* McKillip, 7 Blackf. 578.

OF DIFFERENT FORMS OF ACTIONS. 651

No. 3496   Book 4, tit. 9, chap. 2, sec. 1, § 1, art. 3.   No. 3496.

to her parent, who, for this purpose, is obliged to assume that less endearing relation; and if it cannot be proved she filled that office, the action cannot be sustained.(a) It follows, therefore, that if the daughter was of full age, at the time of the seduction and impregnation, and the father was not entitled to her services, and actually she was not in his service, the father can maintain no action for the seduction. But if, at the time of the seduction and impregnation, the daughter was under the age of twenty-one years, though she was then living at another place, the father may maintain this action, provided he was then entitled to her services.(b) The gist of the action in these cases, is the loss of services, and the plaintiff sues *per quod servitium amisit*. As this action is for the recovery of damages, if none have been sustained, the action will not lie; where, therefore, the plaintiff has connived at the misconduct of the defendant with his daughter, no action lies.(c)

For a consequential injury done to his minor child, a parent may maintain case; as where the defendant compelled the minor to mount an unruly horse, in consequence of which his leg was broken, and the father was put to expense.(d) And for the abduction of a child an action on the case is the proper remedy, because, as in seduction, the parent here assumes the character of a master, and sues *per quod servitium amisit*.(e)

Art. 3.—Of the remedy for injuries to personal property.

3496. The remedy to redress injuries to personal property, not committed with force and not immediate, or where the plaintiff's right to such property is not

---

(a) South v. Denniston, 2 Watts, 474: Wilson v. Sproul, 3 Pennsyl. 49.
(b) Hornketh v. Barr, 3 S. & R. 36.
(c) Hollis v. Wells, 5 Penns. Law Journ. 30.
(d) Wilt v. Vickers, 8 Watts, 227. See Durden v. Barnett, 7 Ala. 169.
(e) Moritz v. Garnhart, 7 Watts, 303; Jones v. Tiver, 4 Litt. 25.

652 OF REMEDIES.

No. 3496.　　　Book 4, tit. 9, chap. 2, sec. 1, § 1, art. 3.　　　No. 3496.

in possession, but in reversion, is by an action on the case. The instances in which an action on the case can be maintained are very numerous; to go through them all would occupy much space, and it would be necessary to go into details not within the plan of this work. A few instances will be mentioned, which will give an idea of the whole.

1. This action lies for negligence in navigating ships;(a) but when both parties are guilty of negligence, and the mischief done was the result of the combined neglect of both parties, both are in *statu quo*, and neither can recover any compensation from the other.(b) The rule seems to be this, that although there may have been negligence on the part of the plaintiff, yet, unless he might, by the exercise of ordinary care, have avoided the consequences of the defendant's negligence, he is entitled to recover; if, by ordinary care, he might have avoided them, he is the author of his own wrong.(c)

2. When the act which has caused the injury is *immediate*, the party injured may elect to regard the negligence as the cause of the action, and declare in *case;* or to look upon the *act itself* as the injury, and declare in *trespass;*(d) as for negligence in driving carriages, or riding horses, or in conducting a railway train,(e) whereby the plaintiff or his property are injured. So

---

(a) Leame v. Bray, 3 East, 599 : Ogle v. Barnes, 8 T. R. 188; 1 P. & D. 103. See Parker v. Adams, 12 Met. 415 ; Gates v. Miles, 3 Conn. 64 ; Case v. Mark, 2 Ham. 169.

(b) Vernal v. Gardner, 3 Tyr. Rep. Exch. 85 ; Sills v. Brown, 9 Car. & P. 605 ; Monroe v. Leach, 7 Metc. 274 ; but, in such case, there is a remedy in the admiralty, where the damages will be apportioned. Hay v. Le Neve, 2 Shaw. 401, 405.

(c) Bridge v. G. J. Railway Co., 3 M. & W. 248. See Butterfield v. Forrester, 11 East, 60 ; Smith v. Dobson, 3 Scott, N. R. 336 ; S. C. 3 M. & G. 59 ; Raison v. Mitchell, 9 C. & P. 613 ; Turley v. Thomas, 8 C. & P. 103; Hawkins v. Cooper, 8 C. & P. 473.

(d) Blin v. Campbell, 14 John. 432; Dalton v. Favour, 3 N. Hamp. 465 ; McAllister v. Hammond, 6 Cowen, 342 ; Baldridge v. Allen, 2 Ired. 206 ; Chaflin v. Wilcox, 18 Verm. 605 ; Schuer v. Veeder, 7 Blackf. 342.

(e) Bridge v. G. J. Railway, 3 M. & W. 244.

OF DIFFERENT FORMS OF ACTIONS.   653

No. 3496.   Book 4, tit 9, chap 2, sec. 1, § 1, art. 3.   No. 3496.

it lies for negligence, by which sparks and igneous matter flew from the engine and destroyed by fire a stack of beans;(a) or for carelessly and negligently kindling a fire on the defendant's own land, whereby the property of the plaintiff, on the adjacent land, was burnt;(b) or by carelessly carrying fire, by which the plaintiff's stack-yard was destroyed; but not for accidental or wilful burning.(c)

3. Case will not lie for mere *nonfeasance*, where the undertaking was gratuitous only; but if the party promising have commenced upon his undertaking, case will lie for any *malfeasance* or neglect, in the performance of it.(d)   But where an officer is bound to perform a duty, as a sheriff, case will lie against him for nonfeasance.(e)

4. Case is the proper remedy for an injury caused by a *fraud* or *deceit*, which are done without force; as for making a fraudulent return by a sheriff to a writ of attachment, even when the writ is void;(f) to recover the price of a horse which had been paid for in counterfeit money;(g) for selling a blind horse for a sound price, though the purchaser examined the horse, if the blindness could not be discovered at first view;(h) for not informing a purchaser of lands of an outstanding incumbrance upon it;(i) for falsely representing the credit and circumstances of another, by reason of which credit is given to such a person, and a loss occurs; and in such case it is not necessary that there should have been an intent, on the part of the party

(a) Aldridge v. G. W. Railway, 1 Dowl. N. S. 247; S. C. Scott, N. R. 150.
(b) Harnard v. Poor, 21 Pick, 378.
(c) Maull v. Wilson, 2 Harr. 443.
(d) Hyde v. Moffit, 16 Verm. 271.
(e) Abbott v. Kimball, 19 Verm. 551.
(f) Humphrey v. Case, 8 Conn. 102.
(g) Lane v. Hogan, 5 Yerg. 290.
(h) Hughes v. Robinson, 1 Monr. 215. See McLane v. Fullerton, 4 Yeates, 522.
(i) Morgan v. Patrick, 7 Ala. 185; Ward v. Wiman, 17 Wend. 193.

654 OF REMEDIES.

No. 3496.   Book 4, tit. 9, chap. 1, sec. 1, § 1, art..3.   No. 3496.

making such representations, to defraud him to whom they were made;(a) and if there is a design to defraud the public generally, any one, suffering injury from it, may maintain this action;(b) for falsely representing to a buyer a metal to be copper, knowing it to be a composition, and an injury accrues to the purchaser.(c) Case lies against a justice of the peace, for concealing from a party the time when he gave judgment, so as to prevent an appeal;(d) and case is also the proper remedy against an officer for a breach of duty, whether intentional and malicious, or not.(e)   It lies against a sheriff for neglecting to arrest a defendant against whom he has a writ, when he has an opportunity; but in such case, the plaintiff must allege and prove special damages;(f) and this action lies when the sheriff arrests a person maliciously on a writ, after he knows that such a person is privileged.(g)

5. It lies for a *careless and wanton act by which a consequential damage is sustained;* as by the careless discharge of a gun, by which the owner or bailee is injured, if there was no intention, or reasonable ground of apprehension, on the part of the defendant, of causing the fright; when there is such intention, trespass is the proper remedy ;(h) so trespass is the lawful remedy for an injury sustained, in consequence of the defendant beating a drum in the highway, and the horse becoming frightened and running away.(i) Case, and not trespass, is the proper action by the owner of a vessel, against one who discharges a musket ball at

---

(a) Boyd v. Browne, 6 Penn. St. Rep. 310.
(b) Bartholomew v. Bentley, 15 Ohio, 659.
(c) Cornelius v. Molloy, 7 Penn. St. Rep. 293.   See Stiles v. White, 11 Met. 356 ; Oldham v. Bentley, 6 B. Monr. 428.
(d) Neighbor v. Trimmer, 1 Har. 58.
(e) Keith v. Howard, 24 Pick. 292 ; Gates v. Neal, 23 Pick. 308 ; Spear v. Cummings, 23 Pick. 224.
(f) Williams v. Mostyn, 7 Dowl. P. C. 38; S. C. 4 M. & W. 145.
(g) Boit v. Maguay, 7 (Eng.) Jurist, 127.
(h) Cole v. Fisher, 11 Mass. 137.
(i) Loubz v. Hafner, 1 Dev. 185.

OF DIFFERENT FORMS OF ACTIONS. 655

No. 3497   Book 4, tit 9, chap. 2, sec. 1, § 1, art. 3.   No. 3497.

the vessel, and wounds the master, by which the intended voyage is defeated, and the owner of the vessel is subjected to loss.(a)

6. When the injury is committed by an agent or servant, in the course of his employment, whether it be with force and immediate, or without force and consequential, the action against the principal or the master must be trespass on the case, when he is liable, unless it be done by his express command; and in that case, trespass will lie against both; and when there has been no command of the master or principal, trespass may be brought against the agent or servant, when the injury is committed with force.(b) So, if a defendant cause an injury with his dog, trespass is the remedy; if the dog cause the injury of his own accord, in the absence of his owner, and he is known to him to be vicious, the remedy is case.(c)

3497. This action is a *concurrent remedy* with *assumpsit* in many cases on breach of a verbal contract, either express or implied. It is concurrent with *assumpsit*, for the breach of a warranty,(d) though *assumpsit* is sometimes preferred, because a count for money had and received, may be joined to recover back the consideration. Case lies also against bailees for neglect, and cases of this kind are extremely numerous; against attorneys for any gross negligence or ignorance in their professional capacity.(e)

Case is the only remedy for an injury to reversionary personal property;(f) as for an injury done to the

---

(a) Adams v. Hemmensay, 1 Mass. 145.
(b) Barnes v. Hurd, 11 Mass. 57; Johnson v. Castleman, 2 Dana, 378; Campbell v. Phelps, 17 Mass. 246 ; Broughton v. Wallon, 8 Wend. 474.
(c) Dilts v. Kinney, 3 Green, 130.
(d) Stuart v. Wilkins, Dougl. 21 ; Williamson v. Allison, 2 East. 446. See Kiddell v. Burnard, 9 M. & W. 668; Levy v. Langridge, 4 M. & W. 337, in error.
(e) 1 Saund. 312, note 2.
(f) McGowan v. Chappen, 2 Murph. 61 ; Hilliard v. Dortch, 3 Hawks. 246.

656 OF REMEDIES.

No. 3498. Book 4, tit. 9, chap 2, sec 1, § 1, art. 4. No 3499.

plaintiff's cattle by the horse of the defendant ;(*a*) or where a slave has been hired out, the owner may sue a third party in case for an injury affecting his reversionary interest.(*b*) In these cases, trover and trespass will not lie, because, to support these actions, the plaintiff must prove that he was in possession,(*c*) or in case of trover that he had the right of possession.

Art. 4.—When case is a remedy for injuries to real property.

3498. These injuries are to real property corporeal, and to real property incorporeal.

1. *When case lies to remedy injuries to real property corporeal.*

3499. Injuries to real property corporeal, are either to the possession or to the reversion.

1. The injury to the *possession* takes place when the party in possession is injured by an act which is not the immediate cause of the loss, but arises from it, and is consequential ; as for placing a water spout near the plaintiff's land, so that the water, when it rained, ran upon it ; or for causing the water, which did not flow that way naturally, to run upon the plaintiff's land ;(*d*) or for digging so carelessly and negligently on his own ground, as to cause the neighbor's house to fall.(*e*)

This action lies for obstructing the light and air, when the plaintiff has the right, acquired by grant or prescription, by the erection of a building opposite to his window on the adjoining land.(*f*) It may be

(*a*) Wales *v.* Ford, 3 Halst. 267.
(*b*) Hawkins *v.* Phythian, 8 B. Mon. 515.
(*c*) Gordon *v.* Harper, 7 T. R. 9.
(*d*) 1 Chit Pl. 126, 141.
(*e*) Sheve *v.* Stokes, 8 B. Monr. 453. When the party wall has been built, and the adjoining owner is desirous of having a deeper foundation, he has a right to undermine such wall, using due care and diligence to prevent any injury to his neighbors ; and, having done so, he is not answerable for any consequential damages which may ensue. 17 John. 92 ; 12 Mass. 220 ; 2 N. Hamp. 534. See 1 Dall. 346 ; 5 S. & R. 1 ; Bouv. L. D. Party wall.
(*f*) 2 Chit. Pl. 378 ; Bouv. L. D. Ancient lights.

OF DIFFERENT FORMS OF ACTIONS. 657

No. 3500   Book 4, tit. 9, chap. 2. sec. 1, § 1, art. 4.   No. 3500.

brought by the tenant in possession, or by the person entitled by the immediate reversion, though the form of the declaration is not the same. It lies also for other nuisances to houses and lands, as for not repairing a privy near the plaintiff's house; for not emptying a cesspool or sewer ;(a) for obstructing the entrance to a house ;(b) for making noises and annoying the plaintiff in the occupation of his house,(c) by which the plaintiff has received an injury. For these and the like nuisances, and their consequent injuries, the party in possession may maintain an action on his possessory interest, and the reversioner on his reversionary rights.(d)

2. This action, in some cases, is *a concurrent remedy with covenant*, when an injury has been committed on real estate. The reversioner or remainder man, whether in fee, or merely for years, may support an action on the case, in the nature of waste, against either his tenant or a stranger, for commissive waste to his reversion ;(e) although there may be a covenant in a lease not to do waste.(f) The reason why the reversioner must bring case instead of trespass is, that he has not the possession, and that is required to maintain trespass.

2. *Case is the proper remedy for an injury to incorporeal real property.*

3500. For the reason just mentioned, that to support trespass, possession must be proved, that action cannot be supported against a defendant for an injury to an incorporeal right, and beside no injury can be committed with force against property which is not

(a) 1 Ld. Raym. 187, 1399, Stra. 634.
(b) Gov. & Co. of British Plate Manufacturers *v.* Meredith, 4 T. R. 794.
(c) 2 Bing. N. C. 134.
(d) Com. Dig. Nuisance, B.
(e) Saund. 252, d, note.
(f) Kinlyside *v.* Thornton, 2 Bl. Rep. 1111.

corporeal. The proper remedy to redress injuries against incorporeal property is an action on the case.(a) Thus it lies for obstructions made on a road, after the title of the plaintiff became vested,(b) or for using a private way, by one who had no right;(c) or for depriving the plaintiff of the use of a well on defendant's land, which he had a right to use ;(d) or for not repairing a private way, which defendant is bound to keep in repair.(e)

Art. 5.—Of the action on the case given by statute.

3501. When a statute gives an express remedy by action on the case, of course that is the proper form of action; sometimes, however, a statute prohibits an injury to an individual, or enacts that he shall recover a penalty or damages for such injury, without giving any particular form of remedy; this action may be supported in such cases.(f)

§ 2.—Of the pleadings in case.

3502.—1. The principal rules relating to a *declaration* in an action in form *ex delicto* have been considered in another place. It is only requisite here to observe that in an action on the case, the declaration ought not to state the injury to have been committed *vi et armis*,(g) nor conclude *contra pacem*, these being appropriate terms for an action of trespass. The form of the declaration depends much on the particular cir-

---

(a) Wetmore *v.* Robinson, 2 Conn. 529 ; Wilson *v.* Wilson, 2 Vern. 68 ; Marshall *v.* White, Harper, 122.
(b) Wright *v.* Freeman, 5 Harr. & John. 467.
(c) Lambert *v.* Hoke, 14 John. 383 ; Williams *v.* Esling, 4 Penn. St. Rep. 486.
(d) Shafer *v.* Smith, 7 Har. & John. 67.
(e) 2 Saund. 113, note 1 ; Id. 172, a, note 1.
(f) Com. Dig. Action upon Statute, A, F ; Id. Pleader, 2 S, 1 to 30.
(g) The words " with force and arms," will be rejected as surplusage, where the declaration shows that case is the proper action, and, in other respects, the declaration is in case, though the action may be denominated trespass. Marshall *v.* White, Harper, 122.

OF DIFFERENT FORMS OF ACTIONS. 659

No. 3503.   Book 4, tit. 9, chap. 2, sec. 1, § 3, art. 1.   No. 3506.

cumstances on which the action is founded. These must be clearly stated.(a)

3503.—2. The plea is usually the general issue of not guilty.

§ 3.—Of the evidence in case.

3504. This evidence is in favor of the plaintiff to support his case, or for the defendant, in order to maintain his defence.

Art. 1.—Of the evidence for the plaintiff.

3505.—1. The evidence of the plaintiff, in cases of this kind, must be sufficient to support the several averments in the declaration; but although the plaintiff must thus support his declaration, he is not required to prove any more of it than is necessary to constitute a good cause of action;(b) for example, although the declaration may charge malice and negligence on the defendant, in digging the foundation of his house below that of the plaintiff's, whereby the plaintiff suffered damages, yet proof of negligence alone will be sufficient to maintain his action.(c) And in an action against an innkeeper or a carrier, for the negligent keeping of goods in his care, whereby they were lost; proof of the loss will be considered as presumptive evidence of negligence on the part of such carrier or innkeeper, or their servants.(d)

3506.—2. In cases of *criminal conversation* with the

(a) Bridge Co v. Williams, 9 Dana, 403; Taylor v. Day, 16 Verm. 566; Gates v. Miles, 3 Conn. 64. When the plaintiff denominates his action case, and the averments in the declaration show a trepass, the declaration is bad on demurrer; and, even after verdict, judgment will be arrested, or, if given, a writ of error will lie. Barnes v. Hurd, 11 Mass. 57; Waldron v. Hopper, Coxe, 339; Case v. Mark, 2 Ham. 169; Taylor v. Rainbow, 2 H. & M. 423; Wickliffe v. Sanders, 6 Monr. 299; Vail v. Lewis, 4 John. 459; Warren v. Fisher, 1 Pen. 240; Hall v. Phillips, 1 Pen. 367: Horner v. Parker, 2 Pen. 648; Agry v. Young, 11 Mass. 229.

(b) Hutchinson v. Granger, 13 Verm. 386.
(c) Panton v. Holland, 17 John. 92.
(d) Story on Bailm. § 472, 529; 2 Greenl. Ev. § 219.

660 OF REMEDIES.

No. 3507.   Book 4, tit. 9, chap. 2, sec. 1, § 3, art. 1.   No. 3507.

plaintiff's wife, it is not necessary to prove the direct fact of adultery, although it is charged in the declaration; evidence of circumstances that lead to a fair inference as a necessary conclusion that the crime has taken place, is sufficient; but the circumstances which are to lead to this conclusion must be such as would induce the guarded discretion of a just man to the conclusion; for it must not lead a rash and intemperate judgment, moving upon appearances that are equally capable of two interpretations.(a) Evidence of general cohabitation will render the proof of particular facts unnecessary.(b)

To support an action against the defendant for adultery with the plaintiff's wife, the plaintiff must prove the existence of his marriage with the woman,(c) for general reputation is not sufficient; and also proof of acts of adultery, or of such circumstances which lead to that conclusion. This being proved, the plaintiff has made out a *primâ facie* case to entitle himself to damages. In order to aggravate the damages, he may, in this action, give evidence showing the state of happiness in which he and his wife lived previously to the act which is the subject of his complaint, and the relation or situation which the defendant bore toward him, and all the circumstances attendant upon the intercourse which existed between them; and, as part of the *res gestæ*, the conversations and letters of the wife; but these letters must have been written before any attempt at adulterous intercourse with the defendant; and this rule is established to prevent collusion between the husband and wife.(d)

3507.—3. To maintain an action for a *malicious prosecution*, the plaintiff must establish four points, namely:

(a) Loveden *v.* Loveden, 2 Hagg. Consist. R. 2, 3.
(b) Cadogan *v.* Cadogan, 2 Hagg. Cons. R. 4, note.
(c) Kibby *v.* Rucker, 1 Marsh. 391; Forney *v.* Hallacher, 8 S. & R. 159.
(d) Wilson *v.* Webster, 7 C. & P. 198.

1. That he has been *prosecuted by the defendant,* either criminally, or in a civil suit. It is immaterial that the plaintiff was prosecuted by an insufficient process, or before a court not having jurisdiction of the matter; because a bad indictment may serve all the purposes of malice, as well as a good one; and the injury to the party is the same where an irregular process issued, as if it had been regular, and before a court having jurisdiction. The fact of prosecution must be proved by a duly authenticated copy of the record and proceedings; and, in a criminal case, that the defendant was the prosecutor.

2. The plaintiff must show that the prosecution is *at an end.* This is generally proved by the record; but in some cases, it may be proved without producing the record. In the case of a civil suit, its termination may be shown by proof, a rule to discontinue on payment of costs, and that the costs were taxed and paid.(*a*) In a criminal *prosecution,* it must appear that the plaintiff was acquitted of the charge; either by a trial, or by being discharged by the court, without a trial.(*b*)

3. There must be a want of *probable cause;* for however malicious and unfounded the prosecution may have been, this action will not lie when there are apparent grounds of suspicion that the party has committed a crime or misdemeanor, and that the prosecution was undertaken from public motives;(*c*) or in a civil suit, if there is reason to infer that the party was actuated by an honest and reasonable conviction of the justice of his suit, although upon trial the defendant may in either case be acquitted. It is not necessary that the whole proceedings should be groundless; if part be so, the party will be liable; as where a plaintiff

---

(*a*) Bristow *v.* Haywood, 4 Campb. 213; French *v.* Kirk, 1 Esp. 80.
(*b*) Smith *v.* Shackelford, 1 N. & McC. 36; Goddard *v.* Smith, 1 Salk. 21.
(*c*) Ulmer *v.* Leland, 1 Greenl. 135.

662　　　　　　　　OF REMEDIES.

No 3508.　　　Book 4, tit. 9, chap. 2, sec. 1, § 3, art. 2.　　　No. 3509.

had a good cause of action for a small sum, and he demands bail for a sum four times as large, there the proceedings are malicious and without probable cause.(*a*)　Though the averment of want of probable cause is negative in its form and character, yet in general it must be proved by some affirmative evidence, unless the defendant by his pleadings dispenses with this proof.

4. The plaintiff must show he has sustained *damages*, and he may prove what losses he has sustained and to what indemnity he is entitled in consequence of the injurious acts of the defendant.(*b*)

3508. When there are several plaintiffs, they must prove a joint cause of action, such as a slander of both in their joint trade or employment, or an injury to their joint property, and the like, or they will be nonsuited.(*c*)

As in actions founded in tort, a recovery can be had against either, or a part only of the defendants, because all wrongs are several; it is not necessary to prove them all guilty, the plaintiff will recover against those whom he proves to have been guilty.(*d*)

Art. 2.—Of the evidence for the defendant.

3509.—1. Many matters may be given in evidence under the plea of the general issue, which will defeat the right of the plaintiff to recover. Under this plea the defendant may prove any facts which show that in equity and good conscience the plaintiff ought not to recover, and that he never had a good cause of action ;(*e*) or he may show matters *ex post facto*, which

---

(*a*) Reed *v.* Taylor, 4 Taunt, 616; Prince *v.* Thompson, 6 Pick. 193; Stone *v.* Crocker, 24 Pick. 81.
(*b*) Hadden *v.* Mills, 4 C. & P. 486; Thompson *v.* Mussey, 3 Greenl. 305; Sandback *v.* Thomas, 1 Stark. 306.
(*c*) 2 Saund. 116, a, note.
(*d*) Coryton *v.* Lithebye, 2 Saund. 115.
(*e*) Bird *v.* Randall, 3 Burr. 1353.

are his discharge; as a release, a former recovery, or satisfaction.(*a*) To this general rule of what may be given in evidence there are the following exceptions:

1. The *statute of limitations* must be specially pleaded; this is required in justice to the plaintiff, to enable him to rebut it, if he can.

2. A *justification* in slander, by alleging the truth of the words used, must be specially pleaded for the same reason, for unless this is done, all the plaintiff is required to do, is to prove the uttering of the words in the presence of persons who understood them.

3. The retaking a prisoner on fresh pursuit must also be specially pleaded.(*b*)

3510.—2. The plaintiff must prove that the relation of master and servant, or principal and agent, existed, when the act complained of was committed by the agent or servant of the defendant; this is frequently very difficult to prove, particularly when sub-contractors have been employed.(*c*)

3511.—3. The defendant, in an action for *criminal conversation* with the plaintiff's wife, may show in *bar* of the action that the husband and wife were divorced *à vinculo*, or that the plaintiff connived at the criminal intercourse, or suffered her to live openly and publicly as a prostitute,(*d*) or that he had voluntarily separated from his wife.(*e*) He may show in *mitigation of damages* the previous bad character and conduct of the wife for chastity; and these may be general or particular instances of unchastity. He may also prove that she made the first advances,(*f*) the husband's unlawful connections with other women,(*g*) his gross negligence

(*a*) Steph. Pl. 182, 183; Ham. N. P. 70, 71.
(*b*) 1 Chit. Pl. 433, 434.
(*c*) 1 Story on Ag. § 454 *a*, 2d ed.; Milligan *v.* Wedge, 12 Ad. & Ell. 737; Duncan *v.* Findlater, 6 Cl. & Fin. 894.
(*d*) Sanborn *v.* Neilson, 4 N. Hamp. 501.
(*e*) Fry *v.* Derstler, 2 Yeates, 278.
(*f*) Elsam *v.* Fawcett, 2 Esp. 562.
(*g*) Bromley *v.* Wallace, 4 Esp. 237.

with respect to the defendant, and any other acts which manifest a culpable indifference on the part of the husband.

By bringing this action, the husband puts the general character of the wife in issue ; but he cannot support it unless it is attacked ; she is, in this respect, like any other whose character is in issue.

3512.—4. When charged with a *malicious prosecution*, the defendant may disprove the charge of malice, or show the existence of probable cause for the prosecution.

§ 4.—Of the judgment in case.

3513.—1. The judgment for the plaintiff is, that he recover a sum of money, ascertained by a jury, for his damages sustained by the commission of the grievances complained of, and full costs of suit ; but when the judgment was entered for　　　dollars *debt* instead of *damages*, it was held to be valid.(*a*)

3514.—2. The judgment for the defendant is, that he recover his costs from the plaintiff.

SECTION 2.—OF THE ACTION OF TROVER.

3515. The action of trover and conversion owes its origin to the statute of Westminster the second ; it was formerly an action of trespass on the case, for the recovery of damages against a person who had found goods and refused to deliver them on demand to the owner, and converted them to his own use. It still belongs to the genus of actions on the case, but it has acquired a new and separate name, being the species known as *trover and conversion.*

Trover is a concurrent remedy with trespass, in general, when there has been a wrongful taking ; but the converse does not hold, for trover is frequently a proper remedy when trespass is not ; as for example,

(*a*) White *v.* McCall, Coxe, 93.

when goods are lent or delivered to another to keep, and he refuses to return them on demand, trespass cannot be maintained, because there was no unlawful taking, but trover may be.(a)   Again, in other cases, trespass may be proper, when trover cannot be sustained; as where a ferryman wrongfully put the horses of a passenger out of a boat, without farther intent concerning them, it may be a trespass, but it is not a conversion; for he did not interfere with the owner's dominion over the property, nor alter its condition. If he had made any farther disposition of them, inconsistent with the owner's right, it would have been a conversion.(b)   Whenever trespass *de bonis asportatis* lies, trover will lie.(c)   Trover lies also when there was no unlawful taking or entry, as in the case of finding; but to support trespass the taking or entry must have been unlawful.

Although, as in detinue, trover is brought in relation to a chattel, yet it differs from that action in this, that in detinue the suit is brought to recover the chattel itself, while in trover, it is instituted to recover damages for the loss sustained by the plaintiff in consequence of the conversion of the chattel by the defendant.(d)   Again, in detinue, at common law, the defendant was allowed to wage his law, which he could not do in trover, and this circumstance alone brought this action into more general use.

3516. The action of *trover and conversion*, or, as it is more simply called, the action of trover, is a remedy given by law to recover personal property wrongfully converted by another to his own use.   It is called trover from the French *trouver*, which signifies *to find*, but as it may be brought for any chattel converted by the

(a) Put v. Rawsterne, T. Raym. 472; Lechmere v. Toplady, 2 Vent. 170; 2 Saund. 47, k, l.
(b) Fouldes v. Willoughby, 8 M. & W. 540.
(c) Prescott v. Wright, 6 Mass. 20; Pierce v. Benjamin, 14 Pick. 356; Glenn v. Garrison, 2 Harr. 1.
(d) Norris v. Beckley, 2 Rep. Cons. Ct. 228.

defendant to his own use, in its form, trover is a mere fiction ; the form supposes the defendant might have come lawfully by the possession of the chattel, and, if he did not, yet by bringing this action the plaintiff waives the trespass; no damages are recovered for the act of taking, all must be for converting. This is the tort or *maleficium*, and to entitle the plaintiff to recover, two things are necessary: first, property in the plaintiff; secondly, a wrongful conversion by the defendant.(*a*) This subject will be considered with reference, 1, to the thing converted; 2, the plaintiff's right; 3, the nature of the injury; 4, the pleadings; 5, the evidence; and 6, the verdict and judgment.

§ 1.—The property affected.

3517. The property which is the subject of an action of trover must be a personal chattel,(*b*) but what is to be so considered is the question ; this action will lie for manure lying upon the ground and not incorporated with the soil,(*c*) and though the ordinary manure of a farm is a part of the freehold, yet the carrying it off to other premises is a severing, so that, for a subsequent sale by the wrong doer, trover will lie;(*d*) for after severance from the freehold, as in the case of trees,(*e*) if the property severed be taken away, or if coals in a pit be afterward thrown out, trover may be supported.(*f*)   Trover lies for title deeds,(*g*) for a

(*a*) Glaze *v.* McMillan, 7 Port. 279; Taylor *v.* Howell, 4 Blackf. 217; Hall *v.* Amos, 5 Monr. 89.
(*b*) Mather *v.* Trinity Church, 3 S. & R. 512, 513 ; Fleming *v.* Bevan, 2 Penn. St. Rep. 408.   To maintain trover, there must be either, 1, an unlawful taking of personal property from the owner, without his consent ; 2, an assumption of ownership of such property ; 3, an illegal use or abuse of it ; or 4, proof of demand and refusal.   Kennet *v.* Robinson, 2 J. J. Marsh. 84; Glaze *v.* McMillan, 7 Port. 279; St. John *v.* O'Connell, 9 Port. 466.
(*c*) Pinkham *v.* Gear, 3 N. Hamp. 484.
(*d*) Stone *v.* Proctor, 2 Chip. 116.
(*e*) See Sanderson *v.* Haverstick, 8 Penn. St. Rep. 294.
(*f*) Com. Dig. Biens, H. ; Bac. Ab. Trover, B.
(*g*) Weiser *v.* Seisinger, 2 Yeates, 537; Towle *v.* Lovet, 6 Mass. 394.

negotiable instrument, certificates of stock, a promissory note,(a) a note which has been paid, and left in the hands of the holder by mistake,(b) or bank notes, sealed in a letter,(c) or the copy of an account.(d) It may be supported for a copy of a record, which is private property, and may therefore be converted,(e) · though in general, it will not lie for a record, which is public property;(f) trover may be sustained for animals *feræ naturæ* reclaimed,(g) as wild geese which have strayed away, without regaining their natural liberty.(h) It is the proper remedy, in general, for the conversion of any sort of personal property, which is specific in its nature, and which can be described in the declaration; thus it will not lie for money had and received generally, because it is an attempt to convert an action of *assumpsit*, into an action of tort,(i) yet it lies for coin described as such, though not in a bag, or otherwise distinguishable from other coin, because the thing itself is not to be recovered in this action, but damages for the conversion.(j)

3518. But certain property cannot be recovered in trover, owing to its being in the custody of the law, as when it has been seized by virtue of some valid legal process,(k) nor when the title to the property

(a) Comparet v. Burr, 5 Blackf. 419; Todd v. Crookshanks, 3 John. 432; Kingman v. Pierce, 17 Mass. 247; Day v. Whitney, 1 Pick. 503; Jarvis v. Rogers, 15 Mass. 389; Sewall v. The Lancaster Bank, 17 S. & R. 285.
(b) Pierce v. Gilson, 9 Verm. 216. See Bisherer v. Swisher, 2 Penn. 748, contra.
(c) Moody v. Keener, 7 Port. 218.
(d) Fullam v. Cummings, 16 Verm. 697.
(e) Jones v. Winckworth, Hardr. 111.
(f) 1 Chit. Pl. 150. But, it seems, that an action of trover or replevin may be maintained in Massachusetts, for the recovery of parish records. Sawyer v. Baldwin, 11 Pick. 492; Stebbins v. Jennings, 10 Pick. 172.
(g) Hugh. Ab. Action upon the case of Trover and Conversion, pl. 3.
(h) Amory v. Flyn, 10 John. 102.
(i) Orton v. Butler, 5 B. & Ald. 652.
(j) Bac. Ab. Trover, D; Vin. Ab. Action of Trover, E. See Pettit v. Bouju, 1 Mis. 64.
(k) Jenner v. Joliffe, 9 John. 381; Pettigru v. Sanders, 2 Bailey, 549. Sed vide Hall v. Moore, Addis, 376.

can be settled only by a peculiar jurisdiction; as, for example, property taken on the high seas, and claimed as lawful prize, because in such cases, the courts of admiralty have exclusive jurisdiction.(a) Nor will it lie where the property bailed has been lost by the bailee, or stolen from him, or destroyed by accident, or from negligence; for such torts, case is the proper remedy.(b)

§ 2.—Of the plaintiff's right.

3519. To entitle the plaintiff to recover on this action, at the time of the conversion he must have had a property in the chattel, either general or special,(c) and also actual possession or right of immediate possession.(d) The rights of the plaintiff consist in having, 1, a general or absolute property; 2, a special property; 3, a bare possession; 4, a right to immediate and exclusive possession.

Art. 1.—Of general or absolute property.

3520. The person who has the absolute or general property of a personal chattel may support this action, although he has never had actual possession, because the general property in personal chattels creates a constructive possession; that is, the right to the chattel draws to it the possession.(e) Thus, when the general owner bailed the goods, as to a carrier,(f) or lent them to a party, the bailee has no special property or interest in them against the general owner; it follows, that the latter is entitled to immediate possession, and he may

(a) Cam. & N. 115, 143; Sonnaire v. Keating, 2 Gall. 325. But see Miller v. The Resolution, 2 Dall. 1.
(b) Hawkins v. Hoffman, 6 Hill, 586; Packard v. Getman, 4 Wend. 613; Johnson v. Stradder, 3 Mis. 359; Moses v. Norris, 4 N. Hamp. 304.
(c) Yoner v. Neidig, 1 Yeates, 19 Hastler v. Skull, 1 Tayl. 152.
(d) Mather v. Trinity Church, 3 S. & R. 312; Fleming v. Bevan, 2 Penn. St. R. 408.
(e) 2 Saund. 47, a, note 1; Bac. Ab. Trover, C.
(f) 2 Saund. 47, b.

OF DIFFERENT FORMS OF ACTIONS. 669

No 3521   Book 4, tit. 9, chap. 2, sec 2, § 2, art. 2   No 3521.

therefore maintain trover against a stranger.(a) Again, a remainder man, who never had possession of the chattel, may bring trover for plate pledged by the party who had the life interest in such plate, which by his death has become vested absolutely in the remainder man, even though the pawnee was not aware that the pawnor was a tenant for life.(b)

When the goods have been delivered on a void agreement, or the contract has been rescinded, the former owner may maintain trover against the other contracting party, because no property in the goods passes to the vendee or bailee ;(c) and so, when property is parted with by duress of imprisonment, or duress *per minas*, the transaction is void, and trover lies for the property without a demand.(d)

It is a general rule that a sale of stolen goods, made by the thief, does not pass any title to the vendee, but on account of public policy, the owner is not allowed, at common law, to bring a civil action for the recovery of his property, until after he has prosecuted the thief; and though his right is not destroyed, it is suspended ;(e) but if the goods be pawned to another, the pawnee acquires no title, and trover may be maintained against him. And if the goods have been sent to an auctioneer to sell, an action of trover may be maintained against him, although he sold them innocently, not knowing that they were stolen.(f)

Art. 2.—Of special property.

3521. A person having a special property in goods

(a) 2 Saund. 47, b.
(b) Hoare v. Parker, 2 T. R. 376.
(c) 2 Saund. 47, b, note (f).
(d) Foshay v. Ferguson, 5 Hill, 154.
(e) In some of the states the right is given to an owner by statute, to bring a civil action before he prosecutes the thief. Trover will lie, although the defendant may be acquitted of the felonious taking of the goods. Crosby v. Leng, 12 East, 409.
(f) Hoffman v. Carow, 22 Wend. 285.

or personal chattels, may bring trover against a stranger, who takes them out of his possession, as a borrower, a hirer, a factor, consignee, pawnee, or other bailee; or a sheriff, or trustee, or agister of cattle, or any other person responsible to his principal.(*a*) But a mere servant cannot support this action, because his possession is that of his master, and he has, therefore, no special property;(*b*) nor can a party who has a mere right of custody maintain this action; thus, parish officers cannot recover in trover from an ex-warden, the books kept by him while in office; the remedy is by *mandamus.*(*c*)

Though in general, a bailee, or other person having only a special property in the chattels, must have had *possession*, before he can maintain trover; yet, it seems, that one having only the *right of possession*, may support it; thus, it has been held, that the indorsee of a bill of lading, indorsed to him without value, and for the express purpose of stopping goods *in transitu*, may maintain trover against a wharfinger, who converted them.(*d*)

The rights of one who has a special property in the goods may be adverse to the general owner; as if the party having a special interest, deliver a chattel to the general owner for a particular purpose, he may, on the refusal of the owner to return it, the purpose being satisfied, maintain trover.(*e*)

Art. 3.—Of the bare right of possession.

3522. A man who has the bare possession alone, and loses it by the act of a wrong doer, is entitled to this action against the latter, because possession is

(*a*) 2 Saund. 47, b; Stirling *v.* Vaughan, 11 East, 626. Coleson *v.* Blanton, 3 Hayw. 152; Betts *v.* Mouser, Wright, 744.
(*b*) Bloss *v.* Holman, Owen, 52.
(*c*) Addison *v.* Round, 6 N. & M. 422.
(*d*) Waring *v.* Cox, 1 Campb. 369; 2 Saund. 47, d.
(*e*) 2 Taunt. 268.

primâ facie evidence of property; but such possession does not hold good against the true owner, because as soon as he appears the rights of the mere possessor cease. A finder of a chattel may maintain trover against a stranger, who wrongfully detains it from him.(*a*) And, for the same reason, a lessee, in the enjoyment under the lease, as against a wrong doer, may maintain trover against a stranger, without proving the title of the lessor, relying upon his own possession.(*b*)

Art. 4.—Of the right to immediate and exclusive possession.

3523.—1. Although the plaintiff may have a property in the thing which is the subject of the action, if he have not the right to *immediate* possession, he cannot maintain trover; for example, a reversioner cannot maintain this action, his remedy is by an action on the case. Upon the same principle, the purchaser of a chattel, although by the sale he acquires a right to it, yet he does not become entitled to the possession until he has paid the price, and until such time he cannot maintain trover. Nor can a *cestui que trust* maintain this action, while the legal right or title is in another.(*c*)

3524.—2. The plaintiff must have not only the right to *immediate* possession, but the *exclusive* right of possession to the chattels claimed. He must, therefore, have a right to the specific chattel for which he brings this action. If, therefore, a man buy goods undivided from the bulk, as one hundred bushels of wheat to be measured out of a heap of one thousand bushels, he cannot maintain this action for any specific wheat, because it cannot be told which was his until it has

---

(*a*) Amory *v.* Delamire, 1 Stra. 505; 2 Saund. 47, d; Clark *v.* Malory, 3 Harring. 68.
(*b*) Taylor *v.* Parry, 1 Scott, N. R. 576; S. C. 1 Man. & Gr. 604.
(*c*) Laspeyre *v.* McFarland, 2 Tayl. 187.

672   OF REMEDIES.

No. 3525.   Book 4, tit. 9, chap. 2, sec. 2, § 3, art. 1.   No. 3526.

been measured and set aside ;(a) or in the case of a manufactured article, if it be not specifically appropriated to the vendee, he has no such property as will maintain trover.(b)

For a similar reason a tenant in common, or joint tenant, cannot maintain trover against his co-tenant, while he remains in possession of the goods, though he denies the use of them to the other, because the possession of the one is the possession of the other.(c)

But if the thing in common be *destroyed*, or *sold* by one tenant in common, this will amount to a severance of the joint interest, and trover lies.

§ 3.—Of the nature of the injury.

3525. The injury called a *conversion*, consists in the sense it is used in relation to trover, either in the appropriation of the personal property in question to the party's own use and benefit, or in its destruction, or in exercising dominion over it, in exclusion of the rights of the owner or lawful possessor, or in withholding the possession from him, under a claim of title inconsistent with his own.(d)   The fact of conversion may be shown in three ways: by proof of, 1, the wrongful taking of the goods of another; 2, the wrongful assumption of the property in them, and the right of disposing of them; 3, the wrongful detention of them, after demand and refusal.

Art. 1.—*Of the wrongful taking.*

3526. The wrongful *taking* of the goods of another, who has the right of immediate possession, with intent

(a) 2 M. & S. 397; Zagury v. Furnell, 2 Camp. 240.
(b) Abington v. Lapscombe, 1 Gale & D. 230.
(c) White v. Osbourn, 21 Wend. 72; Hyde v. Stone, 7 Wend. 354; Herrin v. Heaton, 1 Shepl. 193; Weld v. Oliver, 21 Pick. 559; Newlin v. Colt, 6 Hill, 461; 2 Saund. 47, f and g; Fennings v. Grenville, 1 Taunt. 241; Heath v. Hubbard, 4 East, 121..
(d) Shipwick v. Blanchard, 6 T. R. 299, *arguendo;* Foulkes v. Willoughby, 8 M. & W. 540, 546, 551; Hutchinson v. Bobo, 1 Bailey, 546; Reid v. Colcock, 1 N. & McC. 592; Reynolds v. Schuler, 5 Cowen, 323.

to apply them to the use of the taker, or of some other person than the owner, or which has the effect of destroying or altering their nature, is a conversion.(a) But if there is no intent to interfere with the owner's dominion, or to change the condition of the property so taken, the trespass will not be considered a conversion; thus the mere turning horses out of a ferry-boat wrongfully is not a conversion of them.(b)   Drawing a portion of liquor out of a barrel, and filling it up with water, is a conversion of the whole, because it changes its nature.(c)

3527. The taking need not be actual; it is equally a conversion when it is *constructive;* as when a party assumes to dispose of, or exercise a dominion over personal property, to the exclusion and defiance of the plaintiff's right;(d) for example, the act of unlawfully levying upon and selling stills, without taking actual possession, will amount to a conversion on the part of a constable;(e) or the act of unlawfully distraining on the coals of the plaintiff, in the coal-house of another man, and selling them without removing them, will have the same effect;(f) and if a person find a raft of timber on a sand bar, in a navigable river, high and dry, and take possession of it, assume to dispose of it, hire a person to assist him in removing a part, and

---

(a) 2 Saund. 47, g; Thurston v. Blanchard, 22 Pick. 18; Durell v. Mosher, 8 John. 445; Harrington v. Payne, 15 John. 431 : Shipwick v. Blanchard, 6 T. R. 299, *arg.* ; Davis v. Waleb, 1 McCord, 213 ; Jones v. Duncan, 1 McCord 428; Farrington v. Paine, 15 John. 431; Woodbury v. Long, 8 Pick. 543.

(b) Foulkes v. Willoughby, 8 M. & W. 540 ; Plumer v. Brown, 8 Met. 578. According to these decisions, the ancient rule of law laid down in 1 Chit. Pl. 152; Bac. Ab. Trover, A ; 2 Wms. Saund. 47, note (o) ; and the works of other writers, that " whenever trespass for taking goods will lie, trover will also lie," cannot be supported.

(c) 1 Stra. 576; Dench v. Walker, 14 Mass. 500. See Young v. Mason, 8 Pick. 551.

(d) Bristol v. Burt, 7 John. 254; Murray v. Burling, 10 John. 172; Reynolds v. Shuler, 5 Cowen, 323.

(e) Burke v. Baxter, 3 Mis. 207.

(f) 5 Cowen, 323.

674   OF REMEDIES.

No. 3528.   Book 4, tit. 9, chap 2, sec. 2, § 3, art. 2.   No. 3529.

sell that person his interest in the remainder, reserving to himself the portion removed, it is a conversion of the whole.(*a*)

3528. There· are many cases where the taking of the property of another is justifiable or excusable, and then the act of taking alone will not be a conversion; as the throwing of goods into the sea by the master to save the ship.

Though the tortious act may have been a conversion, yet if, with a full knowledge of the circumstances, the owner of the property ratifies the act, or in any way becomes a party to the tort, he thereby abandons all right to bring an action of trover.(*b*)

Art. 2.—Of the wrongful assumption of the property.

3529. As in the case of wrongful taking, a *wrongful assumption of the property* and the right of disposing of the goods may be a conversion in itself, and render a demand and refusal unnecessary.(*c*)   Thus, if a mortgagor of personal property, or any one claiming under him, sell the entire property as owner, in exclusion of the rights of the mortgagee, such a sale is a conversion, and the mortgagee may maintain trover;(*d*) or where a carrier by mistake delivered goods to a wrong person, it was held that trover might be supported, though it would have been otherwise had they been lost by accident.(*e*)

The *misuse* of a personal thing delivered lawfully to the defendant, is a conversion which will enable the

(*a*) Gentry *v.* Madden, 3 Pike, 127.
(*b*) Hawes *v.* Parkman, 20 Pick. 90.
(*c*) Maguyer *v.* Hawthorn, 2 Harring. 71 ; Murray *v.* Burling, 10 John. 172 ; Liptrot *v.* Holmes, 1 Kelley, 381 ; Powell *v.* Olds, 9 Ala. 861 ; Ainsworth *v.* Partillo, 13 Ala. 460 ; Ripley *v.* Dolbier, 6 Shepl. 382.   See Jacoby *v.* Laussat, 6 S. & R. 305.
(*d*) White *v.* Phelps, 12 N. Hamp. 382.
(*e*) Youl *v.* Harbottle, Peake's Cas. 49.   See Bullard *v.* Young, 3 Stew. 46.

owner immediately to maintain trover ;(*a*) as where a hired slave was put to an employment to which the bailee had no right to put him, and he was lost, this was considered such a wrongful conversion by the bailee as rendered him liable to this action ;(*b*) and driving a hired horse a greater distance than is agreed, or in a different direction, will be considered a conversion.(*c*)   These decisions seem correct upon principle, because by misusing such property, the defendant assumes a right over it inconsistent with the general rights of the owner, and therefore converts the owner's property, to that extent at least.

In the case of *mixture* or *intermingling of goods*, a demand must be made and a refusal to deliver them, or the plaintiff must fail.   The reason assigned for this is, that *primâ facie* all the goods belong to the same person.(*d*)

But unless there has been some unlawful assumption of property, trover cannot in general be maintained for a mere nonfeasance ;(*e*) and, therefore, if a bailee by negligence, lose goods intrusted to him, the proper remedy is assumpsit or case.(*f*)

Art. 3.—Of the wrongful detention after demand.

3530.   Hitherto we have been considering those acts of the wrong doers which amount to a conversion of the property, without any demand being made of them, or any refusal on their part, to deliver it to its owner.   The *unlawful detention* of such property, after

---

(*a*) 6 Shepl. 382.
(*b*) Spencer *v.* Pilcher, 8 Leigh, 565.   See Horsely *v.* Branch, 1 Humph. 199.
. (*c*) Wheelock *v.* Wheelwright, 5 Mass. 104 ; Homer *v.* Thwing, 3 Pick. 492.   See Hart *v.* Skinner, 16 Verm. 138.
(*d*)   ond *v.* Ward, 7 Mass. 123, 127.   See Wengate *v.* Smith, 7 Shepl. 287. B
(*e*) McCombie *v.* Davies, 6 East, 540.
(*f*) 2 Saund. 47, c.

676 OF REMEDIES.

No. 3531.   Book 4, tit. 9, chap. 2, sec. 2, § 3, art. 3.   No. 3532.

a demand made by the owner or his agent, of the wrong doer to deliver such property, will be the subject of this article. In its examination it will be proper to inquire, 1, what is a wrongful detention; 2, what is a demand and refusal.

1. *What is a wrongful detention.*

3531. By a *wrongful detention* of goods is meant the act of a person who has the goods of another, whether his possession be' wrongful or otherwise, who holds them from the owner without lawful authority; such a wrongful detention of goods amounts to a conversion. Thus, where the possession is unlawful, as where the wrong doer has taken the goods of another unlawfully, and appropriated them to his own use, this is a wrongful detention; or, if the possession is legal, as where a party who had a particular right to the goods for a time, after the expiration of such time, refuses to return them upon proper demand to the owner, this is a wrongful detention, which is evidence of a conversion.(*a*) But before the holder or possessor of the goods can be put in the wrong, by making a demand of him to deliver them, care must be taken that his particular right has expired, or been extinguished; a demand of a horse from a hirer before the time for which he had been hired has expired, will not make him guilty of a conversion; and where the possessor has a lien upon the goods for a debt due to him, the amount must be paid or tendered to.him, before a demand and refusal will create a wrongful deten-tion.(*b*) When the possessor refuses to deliver the goods, not on account of his lien, but on other grounds, he is estopped from setting up his lien as a defence for a wrongful detention.

2. *Of the demand and refusal.*

3532. In general a *demand* is a request by an indi-

(*a*) Saund. 47, p.   (*b*) Jones *v.* Tarleton, 9 M. & W. 675.

vidual, having a right, to another to do a particular thing. Such demands may be express or implied. In cases where the taking of goods was lawful, in order to make their subsequent detention illegal, it is necessary to prove some assumption of right adverse to the owner's claim, before trover can be supported for their recovery. When the conversion is *direct*, as by an illegal taking, or a wrongful assumption of property, or a misuse of the chattel, we have seen the conversion is complete, without a demand; but to maintain trover for an *indirect* conversion, a demand is in general indispensable; because, the defendant being lawfully in possession of the goods, there is no conversion before he assumes a property in them; a refusal to deliver them to the owner, therefore, shows on his part, in fact an assumption of property in the goods, and is evidence of the prior conversion.(a)   The most usual way is to make an express demand, by a person having a lawful right so to do, upon the person who holds such goods, to deliver them to the owner; this is absolutely necessary when the chattels have not been illegally taken away, or there has not been a wrongful assumption of right to the goods, and in all cases it is advisable.   To render the defendant liable, there must be, 1, a demand in proper form; 2, it must be made by one lawfully authorized; 3, upon a person who has the goods in his possession; 4, there must be a refusal; 5, the demand and refusal must take place before the right of action accrues.

(1.) Of the form of the demand.

3533. When the demand is to be made, it ought to be in such form as will leave no reasonable doubt upon the mind of the person on whom it is made as to what is demanded. The demand may be verbal or in writing, and if it be made in both ways, and one is

---

(a) Wilton *v.* Girdlestone, 5 B. & A. 587 ; 2 Saund. 47 e.

678 OF REMEDIES.

No. 3534.   Book 4, tit. 9, chap. 2, sec. 2, § 3, art. 3.   No. 3534.

valid and the other defective, the demand will be sufficient.(a)   In order to secure sufficient evidence of the
demand, it is better to make it in writing; such an
instrument should give a formal notice of the owner's
right of property and possession, and make a formal
demand of delivery of such possession to the owner;
it should particularly describe the articles claimed,
for if there is a mistake in this respect, the plaintiff
may be defeated in his action; as where the plaintiff
demanded "fixtures" alone, and the goods sued for
were fixtures and also other goods, the demand was
held insufficient, except as to the fixtures.(b)   The
demand must also be an absolute demand, for one
which is qualified is insufficient; thus, where the owner
of a gun delivered it to Peter for a particular purpose,
and Peter wrongfully delivered it to Paul, from whom
it got into the defendant's possession, Peter gave notice
to the defendant that the gun was his, and added, "I
hereby demand the same of you, and require you to
deliver it up, *in the same plight it was when it was delivered to you.*" Defendant said, in answer, that the gun
had burst, and that he would rather pay ten times the
value than repair it; it was held that such demand
and refusal did not amount to a conversion.(c)

(2.) *By whom the demand should be made.*

3534. The demand may be made by the owner
himself, or by his agent duly authorized. As the
possessor is entitled to perfect security against another demand, he has a right to have sufficient evidence of the agent's authority when the demand is
made by him; and if, on the demand being made by
one who claims to act as agent, the party refuse, *bonâ
fide*, to deliver the property, on the ground that he is
not satisfied as to the agent's authority, the demand

(a) Smith v. Young, 1 Campb. 440.
(b) 3 D. & R. 255; Colegrave v. Dios Santos, 2 B. & C. 76.
(c) Rushworth v. Taylor, Q. B. 21 Law J. Rep. 80.

OF DIFFERENT FORMS OF ACTIONS. 679

No. 3535.   Book 4, tit. 9, chap. 2, sec. 2, § 3, art 3.   No 3535.

will be insufficient.(a) For this reason, as well as because a written demand can be better proved, it is better to make the demand in writing, and authorize the party in possession to deliver the goods to the agent.

As no one has a right to make a demand except the owner, or one authorized by him, it follows, that the demand must be made by or on behalf of the owner entitled to the goods, *at the time of the demand made;* if, therefore, the bailor sell the goods during the time of bailment, the purchaser, and not the bailor, is the party, after the sale, to demand the goods of the bailee, and, on refusal, to bring trover.(b)

When two persons are jointly entitled to the possession of the chattel, a demand of one is not sufficient without the authority of the other; as if two persons, jointly interested in the chattel, deposit it with the defendant, one cannot demand the possession of it alone; but unless the bailee receive them on the joint account, a demand by the party depositing it, is sufficient, notwithstanding any agreement between such person and another, unknown to the bailee, that the latter should hold them on joint account; and the reason appears to be, that the bailee was not answerable to such unknown person, under such circumstances.(c)

(3.) *Of whom a demand must be made.*

3535. The demand ought to be made, if possible, of the person who holds the goods in his own right, personally; but when that cannot be done, then a

---

(a) 2 B. & P. 464, note a. See West v. Tupper, 1 Bailey, 193 : Watt v. Potter, 2 Mason, 77 ; but where there is no request to see the authority, and the refusal to deliver the property turns upon other and distinct grounds, the demand will be good. 2 Mason, 77.. See Beckley v. Howard, 2 Brev. 94 ; Spence v. Mitchell, 9 Ala. 744.

(b) 4 Bingh. 106. See 5 M. & S. 105.

(c) May v. Harvey, 13 East, 197.

680 OF REMEDIES.

No. 3536.   Book 4, tit 9, chap. 2, sec 2, § 3, art 3.   No. 3536.

notice of the ownership of the goods, and a demand to deliver them, should be delivered at the party's house, in writing;(a) but it may be doubted whether this would be sufficient, unless followed by an absolute and general refusal to deliver up the goods; particularly where there is no obligation on the party to incur the trouble or expense of removing, or carrying, or sending the goods from his house to that of the claimant; as where he had found them.(b)

It is immaterial whether the person of whom the goods are demanded has them in his actual possession or not, if they are under his control, as if they are in the hands of his servants, and he has a controlling power over them, the demand will be sufficient; if, on the other hand, the demand is made of a servant, who refuses to deliver them, in consequence of the commands of his master, the conversion will be that of the latter; as where the agent of the state prison refused, by the direction and command of one of the inspectors, to deliver the goods to the plaintiff, the conversion was held to be that of the inspector, and trover might be maintained against him.(c)

(4.) *Of the refusal to deliver the goods on demand.*

3536. To be evidence of a conversion, the refusal must be *absolute* and unqualified; when the refusal to deliver property is absolute, unconditional and unqualified, it is equivalent to a conversion ;(d) but the qualifications and conditions must be reasonable, and founded in fact, or, at least, appear so at the time; for example, when a party bonâ fide claims a lien, or refuses to deliver them, not being satisfied, for just reasons, that the claimant is the owner, or has authority to

(a) Logan v. Houlditch, 1 Esp. 22.
(b) Gibbs v. Stead. 8 B & Cres. 528.
(c) Shotwell v. Few, 7 John. 302.
(d) Dent v. Chiles, 5 Stew. & Port. 383; 5 B. & A. 847.

receive them,(*a*) or the bailor asks time, for a just cause,(*b*) or the refusal may be considered only as the result of a reasonable hesitation, in a doubtful matter ;(*c*) in these cases it will, in general, be left to the jury to decide whether the qualifications or conditions of the refusal were reasonable.(*d*)   But a qualified refusal to deliver goods on the ground that the defendant had received a notice of a demand from a third party, is evidence of a conversion ; for the setting up the *jus tertii*, or keeping the goods to maintain the title of a third party, is to deprive the owner of his goods and denying his title, and, therefore, it is a conversion.(*e*)

3537. The refusal is generally express, but it may be *implied*. When it is the duty of the defendant to return the chattel to the rightful owner, as where he borrowed a horse from the plaintiff, and agreed to return him, a request in writing left at his house in the presence of one of his family, to return the horse, will be considered as a sufficient demand, and his neglect to return him, within a reasonable time thereafter, will be evidence of a refusal and of a conversion.(*f*)

The refusal should be made by a principal or by his authority ; a refusal by an *agent*, is not evidence of a conversion by the principal, unless the agent had a special authority to refuse,(*g*) or unless, from circumstances, it can be presumed such authority had been given, or the matter was within the scope of the agent's authority.(*h*)

3538. A refusal may be *justified* or *excused*, and then it will not be a conversion; as where the property has

(*a*) Mills *v.* Ball, 2 B. & P. 464 ; 5 Moore, 259 ; 2 M & W. 78.
(*b*) Dowd *v.* Wadsworth, 2 Dev. 130.
(*c*) Robinson *v.* Burleigh, 5 N. Hamp. 225.
(*d*) Vaughan *v.* Watt, 6 M. & W. 492 ; Dent *v.* Chiles, 5 Stew. & Port. 383.
(*e*) Atkinson *v.* Marshall, Exch. 21 L. J. R. 117 ; Gaunce *v.* Spanton, 7 M. & G. 903.
(*f*) Gow, 69 ; 7 C. & P. 339.
(*g*) Holt, 383.
(*h*) 2 Salk. 441 ; Catteral *v.* Kenyon, 2 G. & D. 545 ; 2 Saund. 47, g.

682   OF REMEDIES.

No. 3539   Book 4, tit. 9, chap 2, sec 2, § 3, art. 3.   No. 3539.

been attached by the creditor of the owner, before the demand, a refusal to deliver it would be justified;(a) but such an attachment, after a refusal, and a subsequent sale to pay the debt of the plaintiff, would be no justification, although it might be a mitigation of the damages, because, at the time of the refusal, the conversion was complete.(b)   The refusal may be excused where the party had it not in his power to deliver the property, as where a party said he would not deliver up the deed, because it was in the hands of his attorney, who had a lien upon it.(c)

3539. As to its *effects*, the refusal is presumptive evidence of a conversion, which may be· rebutted;(d) it may be shown that the goods were not in the power of the party,(e) or that they were delivered to the plaintiff or his agent before the demand and refusal; or that the defendant has a lien unsatisfied; or that the person who demanded, did not show any authority from the plaintiff when required; or, as in the case of a common carrier, that the goods were lost, and therefore there was no conversion;(f) or that the goods had been attached by lawful process, as the property of the plaintiff in the hands of the defendant.

When one *ground* for the refusal is given, the defendant can take advantage of no other; as, where the defendant·has a lien, which would be a sufficient ground, he refuses upon other grounds, he waives the lien, and, on the failure of the other grounds, he cannot resort to it.(g)

(a) 2 C. M. & R. 495.
(b) Irish v. Cloyer, 8 Verm. 33, 110.
(c) 1 Camp. 439.
(d) Thompson v. Rose, 16 Conn. 71; Lockwood v. Bull, 1 Cowen, 322; 2 Saund. 47, e.
(e) 1 Camp. 439.
(f) 2 Saund. 47, f.
(g) 1 Camp. 410, note; Clarke v. Chamberlain, 2 M. & W. 78; Wilson v. Anderton, 1 B. & Ad. 450; West v. Tupper, 1 Bailey, 193.

OF DIFFERENT FORMS OF ACTIONS.   683

No 3540.   Book 4, tit. 9, chap. 2, sec. 2, § 4, art. 1.   No 3542.

§ 4.—Of the pleadings in trover.

Art. 1.—Of the declaration.

3540. It will be proper to inquire, 1, what are the requisites of a declaration in trover; 2, what defects in it are cured by a verdict in favor of the plaintiff.

1. *Of the requisites of a declaration in trover.*

3541. These are, 1, the statement of the cause of action; 2, the proper averments; 3, the claim for damages.

3542.—1. The declaration should *state* that the plaintiff was lawfully possessed of certain goods and chattels, which he should describe as particularly as possible, avoiding repetition and unnecessary description of details, as of his own property, of a certain value, which should be mentioned, and that being so possessed, he, on a certain day, which should be specified, casually lost the said goods and chattels out of his possession; and that, afterward, on the day and year aforesaid, at the county aforesaid, they came to the possession of the defendant by finding.

The certainty in the description of *the thing lost* must be such as to identify it, but certainty to a common intent is all that is required ;(a) where the property was described as " a black mare, of the value of one hundred dollars ;"(b) or, that " the plaintiff being owner, and in possession, of a pair of oxen of the value of one hundred dollars, lost the same, and that the same were found by the defendant ;(c) or " old iron,"(d) or " fifty pieces or ends of deal boards ;(e) in

(a) Vanhauken *v.* Wickam, 2 South. 509 ; Taylor *v.* Morgan, 3 Watts, 333.
(b) Hedley *v.* Fullen, 1 Blackf. 51.
(c) Vanhauken *v.* Wickam, 2 South. 509.
(d) Talbot *v.* Spears, Willes, 70.
(e) Knight *v.* Baker, 11 Mod. 66 ; Haslegrave *v.* Thompson, Str. 810. The practice of annexing a schedule of the things lost to the declaration, has been disapproved of, as being improper. Kinder *v.* Shaw, 2 Mass. 398 ; Rider *v.* Robbins, 13 Mass. 284.

684 OF REMEDIES.

No 3542.   Book 4, tit. 9, chap 2, sec 2, § 4, art. 1.   No. 3542.

all these cases, the description was held to be sufficiently certain. But where the description is so general that the articles cannot be identified, it is bad for uncertainty; the following are examples: where the goods were described as "one hundred articles of furniture, and one hundred articles of wearing apparel," without further description;(a) or "two sheaves of corn," without stating the kind;(b) or of "some fish," without stating the quality or number of fish.(c) In these cases the description was deemed too loose and uncertain to identify the property, though in some of them the defects might be cured by verdict.

In the description of *promissory notes, bills of exchange, bonds,* and the like, they should be so stated that they may be readily identified; but the plaintiff is not required to state their dates or time of payment, because he has them not in his possession;(d) nor is he required to recite any part of the instrument.(e)

The *price* or *value* of the thing lost ought to be stated in the declaration; yet, if it should be omitted, it will not be fatal.(f) The defect can be reached only by special demurrer.(g)

A *time* should also be mentioned, but provided it is before action brought, it is immaterial.(h)

It is not necessary in trover to lay the *venue* at the

(a) Bac. Ab. Trover, F.
(b) Anon. Sty. 25.
(c) Playter's case, 5 Co. 34.
(d) Bank of New Brunswick v. Neillson, 3 Green, 337; Wilson v. Chambers, Cro. Jac. 262.
(e) Pierson v. Townsend, 2 Hill, 550.
(f) Pearpoint v. Henry, 2 Wash. 192. It is said, in an old authority, that if an action of trover be brought for a living chattel, it must be stated in the declaration to be of a certain *price;* and, if for a dead chattel, of a certain *value.* Wood v. Smith, Cro. Jac. 130; but elsewhere it is said there is no difference in these terms in a declaration. F. N. B. 88. Vide ante, n. 2873, note.
(g) Fry v. Baxter, 10 Mis. 302.
(h) Glenn v. Garrison, 2 Harr. 1; Tesmond v. Johnson, Cro. Jac. 428.

place where the conversion was, but some place should be alleged.(*a*)

The *finding* should be stated, but the omission of these words is not material after verdict; and the finding is not traversable;(*b*) and to state that the goods came to the possession of the defendant "by finding or otherwise," will not vitiate the declaration.(*c*)

3543.—2. The *averment* should be that the defendant, well knowing that the said goods and chattels were the property of the plaintiff, and of right to belong and appertain to him, but contriving, and fraudulently intending, craftily and subtlely to deceive and defraud the plaintiff in this behalf, has not yet delivered the said goods and chattels to the said plaintiff, although often requested so to do, but has hitherto refused and still refuses so to do ; and afterward, at a certain time mentioned, in the said county, converted and disposed of the said goods and chattels to his the defendant's own use.(*d*)   Thus, in an action styled an action of trespass, where the declaration charged "that the defendant took in his possession certain goods and chattels, the property of the plaintiff, that he refused, and still refuses, to deliver them to the plaintiff, though requested, and has converted them to his own use," is a sufficient averment, and sets out a case of trover.(*e*)   It must be averred that the plaintiff is entitled to possession.(*f*)

3544.—3. The declaration should lay the *damages*, in such sufficient sum, as to cover the value of the article, and such other injury as the plaintiff may have sustained.

(*a*) Bac. Ab. Trover, F 1.
(*b*) 1 Chit. Pl. 156.
(*c*) Peters *v.* Johnson, Minor, 100.
(*d*) Steph. Pl. 48.
(*e*) Glenn *v.* Garrison, 2 Harr. 1.
(*f*) Dearman *v.* Dearman, 5 Ala. 202.   See Davis *v.* Davis, 6 Blackf. 394.

2. *What defects in a declaration in trover are cured by verdict.*

3545. In general, all merely formal defects in a declaration are cured by verdict, when in favor of the plaintiff; these must be taken advantage of by special demurrer. It is for this reason, that although possession and the right of property should be in the plaintiff, it has been held that this defect was cured by the verdict for plaintiff;(*a*) and where a declaration, good in other respects, misstated the name of the defendant for that of the plaintiff, it was held that the mistake could be taken advantage of only by special demurrer; and, if there was a judgment by default, a special demurrer would not be allowed, except on the condition of pleading issuably.(*b*)

Art. 2.—*Of the plea in trover.*

3546. It is usual in trover to plead the general issue of *not guilty*, under which many matters in discharge may be given in evidence. But it is necessary to plead the statute of limitations and a release. The defendant may, however, plead specially any thing which admits the property in the plaintiff, and the conversion, but justifies the latter.(*c*) He may also plead a former recovery of damages given in an action of trespass for the same trespass or conversion.(*d*)

In general a plea amounting to the general issue in trover is bad; as a plea that the goods were sold pursuant to the order of the plaintiff;(*e*) or a plea alleging property in the plaintiff, and that the goods were taken as a distress for rent.(*f*)

(*a*) Good *v.* Harnish, 13 S. & R. 99.
(*b*) McLure *v.* Vernon, 2 Hill, S. C. Rep. 420.
(*c*) Hurst *v.* Cook, 19 Wend. 463 ; Coffin *v.* Anderson, 4 Blackf. 395.
(*d*) Sanders *v.* Egerton, 2 Brev. 45.
(*e*) Kennedy *v.* Strong, 10 John. 289.
(*f*) Briggs *v.* Brown, 3 Hill, 87.

OF DIFFERENT FORMS OF ACTIONS. 687

No. 3547.   Book 4, tit. 9, chap. 2, sec. 2, § 5, art 1.   No. 3548.

§ 5.—Of the evidence in trover.

Art. 1.—Of evidence for the plaintiff.

3547. Two principal points must be proved by the plaintiff, in order to sustain this action : 1, property in himself, and a right of possession at the time of the conversion ; 2, a conversion by the defendant of the thing sued for, before action brought.

1. *Of the proof of the plaintiff's property and right of possession.*

3548.—1. The plaintiff is required to show either a *general* and *absolute* or a *special property* in himself; the latter, when the party is entitled to possession, is sufficient to recover even against the owner himself.(*a*)

When the plaintiff claims title, under a *sale* made to him, he must show that the sale was completed before the conversion, and that he was entitled to possession; for if his right was liable to be defeated by stoppage *in transitu*, and the right of the seller was exercised, the buyer cannot recover the property sold, in an action of trover.

When an article is to be *manufactured*, as, for example, a ship, upon a special contract, and the price is to be paid in certain portions or instalments as the work progresses, the payment of the instalments, as they fall due, vests the property of the ship in the buyer;(*b*) but if the contract is general, without any express stipulations for advances, payments on account will not thus vest the property in the party who makes them.(*c*)

The possession, acquired *bonâ fide*, and for a valuable consideration, of a *bank note, bill of exchange* or *promissory note*, when indorsed in blank, or payable to the holder; or a government bond, payable to the

(*a*) Roberts *v.* Wyatt, 2 Taunt. 268 ; Spoor *v.* Holland, 8 Wend. 445.
(*b*) Woods *v.* Russell, 5 B. & Ald. 942, 946. See Johnson *v.* Hunt, 11 Wend. 137.
(*c*) See Mucklow *v.* Mangles, 1 Taunt. 318 ; Bishop *v.* Crawshay, 3 B. & C. 416 ; Goode *v.* Langley, 7 B. & C. 26.

holder, or other negotiable security, so payable or indorsed, is sufficient evidence of title, without showing any title in the person from whom he received it.(a)

The property sued for must of course be *identified*, for without this the plaintiff cannot show his title to it. Where the plaintiff declared for a bond, it was held he might call the obligor to prove its contents.(b)

3549.—2. After having proved his property to the chattel which is the subject of the action, the plaintiff must show his right to *present possession*, and that he had such a right *at the time of the conversion.* If the plaintiff has only a special property, he must, in general, give evidence of actual possession;(c) for possession, in trover, is *primâ fâcie* evidence of ownership;(d) and, when the defendant has color of title, the plaintiff must not only show possession in himself, but a title to the property.(e)   When the plaintiff has a general property in the goods, the law annexes the possession.(f)

2. *Of proof of a conversion.*

3550. The plaintiff must also show that there has been a *conversion* of the goods, by which he sustained an injury, for he cannot recover any damages if the chattel was of no value.(g)   What will amount to a conversion has already been sufficiently considered.

Art. 2.—Of evidence for the defendant.

3551. Under the general issue of not guilty, the defendant may, in general, show by any competent

---

(a) 2 Greenl. Ev. § 639; Story on Bills, § 415; Story on Prom. Notes, § 193—197; 2 Phil. Ev. 222.
(b) Smith v. Robertson, 4 Harr. & John. 30.
(c) Coxe v. Harden, 4 East, 211 ; Dennie v. Harris, 9 Pick. 361 ; Hotch-kiss v. McVickar, 12 John. 407 ; Sheldon v. Soper, 14 John. 352.
(d) Jones v. Sinclair, 2 N. Hamp. 319.
(e) Fightmaster v. Beasly, 7 J. J. Marsh. 410.
(f) 2 Saund. 47 a, note (I).
(g) Miller v. Reigne, 2 Hill, S. C. 592.

evidence, that the title of the goods was in himself, either absolutely as general owner, or joint owner with the plaintiff, or specially, as bailee ; or that he had a right to retain on account of his lien ;(a) or that he took the goods for a just cause, as for rent in arrear ;(b) or he may disprove the plaintiff's title by showing title in a stranger,(c) but he cannot set up the interest of such third person without showing a title of some kind in himself.(d)   He may prove facts, showing a license, or a subsequent ratification, or any other facts which support his special plea.

§ 6.—Of the verdict and judgment in trover.

Art. 1.—Of the verdict.

3552. The verdict is rendered for the damages which the plaintiff has sustained in consequence of the conversion of his goods by the defendant.   As a general rule, damages are allowed for the value of the property at the time of the conversion, with interest.(e)   But a difficulty arises to ascertain what is the property which has been converted; what was actually taken from the plaintiff, or what article improved by the work and industry of the defendant.   It is a general rule, that a wrong doer can never benefit by his own wrong, and as it would be extremely difficult to ascertain the value of the original property, without his labor, the whole shall be considered as the property of the plaintiff, and he will be entitled to damages accordingly ; as, where the defendant took logs of the plaintiff, and converted them into boards,

(a) Bull, N. P. 45 ; Skinner v. Upshaw, 2 Ld. Raym. 752.
(b) Wallace v. King, 1 H. Bl. 13 ; Kline v. Husted, 3 Caines, 275.
(c) Schermerhorn v. Van Volkenburgh, 11 John. 529 ; Rotan v. Fletcher, 15 John. 207.
(d) Duncan v. Spear, 11 Wend. 54.
(e) Matthews v. Menedger, 2 McLean, 145 ; Ewart v. Kerr, 2 McMullan, 141 ; Buford v. Fannen, 1 Bay, 273 ; McConnell v. Linton, 4 Watts, 357 ; Harger v. McMains, 4 Watts, 418.

690 OF REMEDIES.

No. 3553. Book 4, tit. 9, chap. 2, sec 2, § 6, art. 2. No. 3553.

the plaintiff may recover the value of the boards, and the verdict should be for that amount.(a) Where other losses, besides the value of the property, have been sustained, the plaintiff is entitled to recover damages for such injury, and the verdict should, therefore, include an amount sufficient to indemnify him; as, where the defendant converted a slave, the verdict should be for the value of the slave and for his labor.(b) The defendant cannot, however, recover damages for a greater injury than he has sustained; thus, where the plaintiff had a life estate in a slave, he can recover only the value of the life interest.(c)

When the subject is a *written security*, the verdict should be for the amount of the principal and the interest due upon it.(d)

The defendant may prove, in *mitigation of damages*, that the plaintiff has himself recovered the property, or it has been restored to him and accepted; the verdict should be for the actual injury occasioned by the conversion, including the expenses of recovery.(e) But if the taking was wrongful, and an action of trover for the recovery of the property be commenced, the defendant cannot, in mitigation of damages, tender the property so taken, to the plaintiff, and compel him to take it;(f) nor will such a tender avail the defendant, where the property has been essentially injured, after an action brought.(g)

Art. 2.—Of the judgment.

3553.—1. The judgment in trover, when the ver-

(a) Greenfield Bank v. Leavitt, 17 Pick. 3; Baker v. Wheeler, 8 Wend. 505. See Kid v. Mitchell, 1 N. & M. 334.
(b) Banks v. Hatton, 1 N. & McC. 221. See Jamson v. Hendricks, 2 Blackf. 94.
(c) Strong v. Strong, 6 Ala. 345.
(d) Roming v. Roming, 2 Rawle, 241; Mercer v. Jones, 3 Campb. 477.
(e) 17 Pick. 3; Yale v. Saunders, 16 Verm. 243; Hepburn v. Sewell, 5 H. & J. 212. See Pierce v. Benjamin, 14 Pick. 356, 361.
(f) Green v. Sperry, 16 Verm. 390.
(g) Hart v. Skinner, 16 Verm. 138.

dict is for the plaintiff, is, that he recover his damages and costs; its effect is to change the title of the property, so as to make it liable for the payment of the defendant's debts after satisfaction has been made;(a) and the defendant's title refers back to the time of the conversion.(b) The property is not changed by the default of the defendant, but by the recovery of the judgment against him, and the subsequent satisfaction.(c)

3554.—2. When the verdict is for the defendant, the judgment is, that he recover his costs.

(a) Rogers v. Moore, 1 Rice, 60 ; Chartram v. Smith, 1 Rice, 229 ; Robertson v. Montgomery, 1 Rice, 87 ; Osterhout v. Roberts, 8 Cowen, 43 ; Morris v. Berkley, 2 Rep. Const. Ct. 228 ; Hepburn v. Sewell, 5 Har. & John. 211.
(b) 5 Har. & John. 211.
(c) Carlisle v. Burley, 3 Greenl. 250.

INDEX.

INDEX. 719

J.

Jailer when liable for false imprisonment, 180.
Joinder of plaintiffs, husband and wife, 140.
  executors, 146.
  administrators, 147.
  obligees, 149.
  assignees, 149.
  defendants, on contracts, 154.
   husband and wife, 157.
   executors, 159.
   administrators, 159.
  parties to redress an injury, 171.
  in demurrer, what, 321.
  issue, what, 307.
  error, what, 550.
Joint injury, how redressed, 171.
  evidence required to prove a, 662.
  liability of wrong doers, 183.
  officers, 184.
  obligees, when to join in an action, 149.
  and several obligees, how to sue, 149.
  tenant of a chattel, right of, 22.
  tenants, how to distrain, 30.
   sue, 139.
Journals of the legislature, when evidence, 377.
Judex, or judicial power, what, 132.
Judgment for the plaintiff, when given, 529.
   by default, 529.
   nil dicit, 524, 529.
   non sum informatus, 524, 529.
   confession, 530.
   confession relictâ verificatione, 530.
   defendant, when given, 530.
  of non pros., 530.
  nolle prosequi, 530.
  cassetur breve, 530.

M.

R.

T.

V.

CPSIA information can be obtained
at www.ICGtesting.com
Printed in the USA
BVHW09s1002210918
528173BV00020B/817/P

9 781330 049495